MMPI CLINICAL AND RESEARCH TRENDS

MMPI CLINICAL AND RESEARCH TRENDS

edited by_____
Charles S. Newmark

PRAEGER

PRAEGER SPECIAL STUDIES • PRAEGER SCIENTIFIC

Library of Congress Cataloging in Publication Data

Main entry under title:

MMPI, clinical and research trends.

Includes bibliographies and index.
1. Minnesota multiphasic personality inventory.
I. Newmark, Charles S. [DNLM: 1. MMPI. WM145.3
M105]
BF698.8.M5M18   155.2'83   79-17777
ISBN 0-03-048926-1

Published in 1979 by Praeger Publishers
A Division of Holt, Rinehart and Winston/CBS, Inc.
383 Madison Avenue, New York, New York 10017 U.S.A.

9 038 987654321

Printed in the United States of America

to my Dad:
always loved, always needed and always there!

PREFACE

The purpose and scope of this volume focus on trends in research development and clinical applications of the MMPI. The volume attempts to update the use of the MMPI in a wide variety of settings while simultaneously discussing new and potential applications of this instrument.

The first chapter by James Webb and Kathleen McNamara presents an introduction to the configural interpretation of the MMPI based on various profile code types. The hypotheses are derived from various research and clinical sources, and the present content represents the authors' attempts to integrate these sources.

The next two chapters focus on the use of the MMPI in nonpsychiatric medical settings. James Mack (Chapter 2) provides a comprehensive review of the research concerning the personality adjustment of brain-damaged patients, emphasizing the use of the MMPI in the evaluation of brain-behavior relationships. In Chapter 3 Paolo Pancheri discusses numerous methodological difficulties encountered in psychosomatic research. This discussion is followed by the presentation of a series of studies investigating personality differences among patients suffering from a variety of medical illnesses.

The next three chapters discuss the personality characteristics of various psychopathological groups. Patricia Sutker and Robert Archer (Chapter 4) describe the addict groups, specifically opiate addicts, alcoholics, and abusers of other licit and illicit drugs. James Clopton (Chapter 5) then reviews the literature on the reliability of the MMPI in predicting suicide. In Chapter 6 Patricia Sutker and Albert Allain present a series of investigations that attempted to identify MMPI trait characteristics and/or type patterns, as well as other psychological variables, that might shed light on the nature or prediction of extreme violence with particular focus on women who murdered as compared with nonviolent female criminal offenders and male murderers.

Chapters 7 and 8 deal with outcome studies. Cathy Widom discusses the usefulness of MMPI profiles in the longitudinal prediction of adult social outcome, while Catherine Sanders analyzes the effects of personality correlates in relation with bereavement patterns.

The chapter by Charles Newmark and John Thibodeau (Chapter 9) deals with the empirical validity of the standard and abbreviated forms of the MMPI when compared with direct measures of psychopathology using an inpatient adolescent population. In Chapter 10 Harvey Skinner describes a model of psychopathology that may be used to integrate within a coherent, parsimonious framework the diverse studies that have used the MMPI clinical scales. Relating to Skinner's model, Joseph Kunce (Chapter 11) attempts to broaden the applicability of MMPI interpretation with his contention that elevated MMPI scores can be suggestive of adaptive behavioral styles as well as descriptive of maladaptive behaviors. In Chapter 12 Philip Erdberg discusses a unique systematic approach to providing feedback from the MMPI. A brief presentation of various automated MMPI systems is provided by Raymond Fowler in Chapter 13.

In Chapter 14 James Clopton reviews special MMPI scales in frequent use and then discusses the logic and methodology for empirically derived new scales. Thomas Faschingbauer (Chapter 15) then concludes with an innovative presentation of the future of the MMPI.

ACKNOWLEDGMENTS

The editor wishes to extend sincere appreciation to all of the contributors whose dedication and cooperation facilitated the smooth and orderly completion of this book. Appreciation also is extended to Carolyn C. Dingman, Tracey Hutchins, and Cornelia Curtis, who contributed significantly to the clerical tasks both in earlier drafts and in the final manuscript. I am indebted to the authors and publishers who have granted permission to reproduce their materials. These include the Ohio Psychology Publishing Company, Hemisphere Publishers, *Journal of Human Stress*, Scandanavian Medical Association, *Psychological Reports*, *Journal of Studies on Alcohol*, Williams & Wilkins Company, D. C. Heath and Company, Academic Press, and especially the American Psychological Association and the Psychological Corporation. Specific recognition is given as the materials appear in the book.

CONTENTS

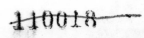

LIST OF TABLES

LIST OF FIGURES

1/CONFIGURAL INTERPRETATION OF THE MMPI

James T. Webb
Kathleen M. McNamara

INTRODUCTION

This chapter represents an attempt to provide, in concise form, interpretive hypotheses for various profile code types of the MMPI. Where possible, two-point, three-point, and (occasionally) four-point code interpretations are presented. These hypotheses are derived from various research and clinical sources, and the present content represents the authors' attempts to integrate these sources. The primary sources were Carson (1960), Carkhuff, Barnett, and Mc-Call (1965), Dahlstrom, Welsh, and Dahlstrom (1972), Drake and Oetting (1959), Fowler (1966), Gilberstadt and Duker (1965), Hovey and Lewis (1967), Lachar (1974), Marks and Seeman (1963), Swenson, Pearson, and Osborne (1973), Van de Riet and Wolking (1969), and Webb (1970). These are recommended to the reader as additional sources offering much more depth and detail.

This chapter assumes that the reader is familiar with the content, structure, and development of the MMPI as a psychometric instrument. Familiarity with the standard test manual is a minimal requirement. Persons seeking a more advanced knowledge of the test (and this should include all who plan to use it extensively in clinical work) are strongly urged to familiarize themselves with the material contained in two basic volumes by Dahlstrom, Welsh, and Dahlstrom (1972, 1975). Although the basic rationale is not complicated, the test's usefulness is greatly enhanced if the user has a detailed knowledge of its characteristics, including the item components of the various scales.

A general word of caution: The apparently routine and objective appearance of an MMPI profile tempts people to overlook other clinical data and to

This manuscript was originally published by the Ohio Psychology Publishing Company, Columbus, Ohio. Copyright 1978. Reprinted with permission.

adopt a rigid psychometric–sign–actuarial method of interpretation; indeed, the MMPI has enjoyed great esteem among some psychologists on the basis of its being particularly suited for such treatment. However, most clinicians who regularly use the MMPI in clinical practice see this as being, at best, a relatively barren procedure. At worst, it sometimes produces serious diagnostic errors in individual cases. The naive application of quantitative formulas for determining clinical decisions is especially hazardous for beginners in MMPI work. In all cases the patient's life situation must be considered in interpreting the profile. Likewise, the present chapter does not sufficiently incorporate modifications in interpretations resulting from age differences, intelligence levels, social or ethnic class, educational level, or marital status. In the future it is hoped these parameters will be incorporated to a greater extent.

Note: Most of the interpretations contained within refer to adult (age 18 or older), caucasian patients of 80 IQ or above, and/or education above seventh grade. When applied to persons different from this reference group, caution should be exercised. If the reader plans to use the MMPI with adolescents, refer to Marks, Seeman, and Haller (1974).

GENERAL APPROACH TO INTERPRETATION

In interpreting a test battery, one should begin with the patient's demographic characteristics (sex, age, education, social class, occupation) in combination with the clinician's knowledge of the base rate characteristics of the population being considered. Subsequently, and only in light of the above, can the patient's MMPI be interpreted in detail.

Step 1. Note the test-taking time (usually 60 to 75 minutes for an average IQ, mildly disturbed patient with education greater than 14). If shorter, suspect an invalid profile and/or an impulsive person. If longer than two hours, suspect major psychological deficit (for example, severe depression, thought disorders), unless the person has a below-average IQ and/or a reading ability less than seventh grade. Where reading ability is a problem, consideration should be given to using the tape-recorded method of administering the MMPI.

Step 2. Examine the answer sheet for erasures and hesitation pencil-point marks. Presence of these suggests the person took the test seriously and tends to contraindicate random marking.

Step 3. Plot the profile and examine the validity scales first. Steps 1 and 2, plus other data (for example, IQ score, educational or occupational attainment), may allow you to interpret profiles with highly elevated F scores and/or with major $F\text{-}K$ deviations from zero.

Step 4. Welsh-code the profile, and find in the Table of Contents the peak code, two-point, three-point code, and/or combined two-point code (for example, 21/12) that fits. The Welsh code uses the following symbols (*"'-/:#) to indicate elevations of scales in a shorthand fashion. Each symbol indicates an increment of 10 T score points beginning with the symbol # representing a T score of 30. Profiles thus may be represented briefly, but with reasonable accuracy, such as 9*8"627'13-45/0:#. Generally, the more elevated beyond T = 70 the two-point code, the more characteristic of the patient will be the description. With mild elevations (T = 60 to 65), descriptions generally can be interpreted only as tendencies.

Step 5. Examine the profile for such interpretable configurations as

Conversion V (scales 1 and 3 greater than scale 2 by 10 T points)
Paranoid valley (scales 6 and 8 greater than scale 7 by 10 T points)
High 4, low 5 or high 4, high 5
High 9, low 2, high *K*

Use these descriptions to add to or modify your interpretation from step 4.

Step 6. Examine the individual interpretations for each scale greater than T = 70 or less than T = 40 to aid in rounding out your interpretation made in step 5.

Step 7. Score Grayson's Critical Items and examine their "goodness of fit" with the profile interpretations and patients' clinical behaviors. If there is any doubt that the patients understood the items (or the MMPI generally) ask what they had in mind regarding several (or preferably all) of the Critical Items. Often this also provides a good lead-in to psychotherapy. Note: Persons who are older than age 30 or who have education beyond high school typically endorse many fewer Critical Items.

THE VALIDITY SCALES

The standard MMPI profile includes four scales to provide the clinician with a frame of reference for interpreting the clinical scales. However, in practice, each of these validity scales also has psychological correlates no less important clinically than those of the clinical scales, and their original function as validation devices has been all but overshadowed by their utility in providing clinical information.

The ? Scale

This is not a scale in the usual sense, but consists simply of the number of items that the individual omitted. No significance is attached to raw scores of 30 or below, but in those fairly rare cases in which the score exceeds 30 (and especially where it approaches 100 or more) it becomes essential to take into account its attenuating effect upon the clinical profile and to attempt to discover the source of the individual's "cannot say" propensity. If 100 or more items are unanswered (T above 70), the profile is invalid. If more than 60 items are left blank (T above 58), the validity is notably impaired. As the number of items omitted gets larger, the deviations of the other MMPI scales from T score = 50 typically are not as great as they otherwise would be, reducing the probability of obtaining a true picture of the person's unique personality characteristics.

If reading difficulties can be ruled out, moderate *?* elevation (T score 50 to 70) is generally indicative of obsessional indecision, often with elements of extreme intellectualization and not infrequently involving highly idiosyncratic interpretation of items. One familiar manifestation of this type of process is seen in the legalistic overcautiousness of some paranoid patients who, if permitted, may leave unanswered the majority of the items.

Individuals who are severely impaired psychiatrically often have markedly elevated *?* scores (T = 70+) simply on the basis of being unable to perform the decision-making task. A high score may also indicate a resistive, uncooperative patient. Note: Many patients with high *?* scores can be persuaded to respond in a definitive way to the neglected items, and it is a good idea to make the attempt routinely. Failing this, it is often instructive to score all neglected items in the significant direction and to compare the profile derived on this basis with the original, noting particularly any occurrences of incongruity that might result from a nonrandom selection of items left unanswered.

The *L* Scale ("Lie" Scale—15 Items, All Scored if Answered "False")

The *L* scale items were selected on the basis of face validity to identify persons who attempt to give an overly perfectionistic view of themselves. The items refer to attitudes and practices that typically have a very positive value culturally, but that are actually found—if they occur at all—only in most conscientious persons. Items example: "I do not always tell the truth" (scorable, *F*). A high (or very high) *L* score does not reduce the validty of the profile very much. *L* scale elevations correlate only moderately (.35) with scale *K*, and are independent of elevations on the clinical scales. *L* scale scores on the average increase slightly (2 to 5 T score points) in persons older than age 50.

A raw score of 4 (T = 50 to 60) or more suggests excessive rigidity or conscious deception, if it cannot be explained on the basis of occupation (for example, clergy) or naivete associated with a culturally limited background. The patient is trying to give socially approved answers concerning self-control and moral values, and is overly conforming and overly conventional. Often such persons are unaware of their behavioral impact on others.

In the general population, raw scores above 7 (T score above 60) occur with persons who have pathologically intense needs to present a good front combined with repression and conscious denial. These people emphasize moral issues, their own integrity, and scrupulousness. They are rigid, naively defensive, self-centered, and uncompromising. Their self-perception and lifestyle are unusually conventional. Nevertheless, they tend to be insecure, frustrated, repressive, deny or gloss over unfavorable traits in themselves, have little insight into their motives or behavior, and make poor psychotherapy candidates. (This does *not* hold if the high score is due to low intelligence, extreme naivete resulting from cultural deprivation, or very conscious deception. (High scores have been found to predict underachievement. The scale often does not detect deception in sophisticated individuals, and a high score in an individual of mature background may be associated with judgment deficiencies and should be further investigated in this light.

T scores above 70 are rare and indicate an introspective, excessively ruminative person with periodic anxiety and depression who has difficulty making friends quickly. High scorers have been described as tense, stereotyped, slow and unoriginal in their response to problems, lacking insight into their own motives and behavior, conventional, naive, passive, insecure, and unaware of their social stimulus value. Others tend to see this person as aloof and wary. Neurotic profiles (associated with poor stress tolerance) and lower SES status are common accompaniments. Rarely, high *L* scores are associated with sociopathic lying or manic clinical syndromes.

The *F* Scale
("Frequency" Scale—64 Items)

The *F* scale consists of 64 items that were answered in the same direction by 90 percent of the normal standardization group. Content varies widely. Item examples: "Everything tastes the same" (T); "I believe in law enforcement" (*F*). Mean *F* scale scores decrease with age from an average T score of 56 (for patients younger than 20) to a T score of 52 (for patients older than 40).

T scores above 80 suggest the following possibilities: error by the examiner in scoring the test; failure of the patient to understand the items; lack of co-operation, the patient having purposely responded in a random and haphazard fashion; distortion due to confusion, delusional thinking, or other psychotic processes; or distortion due to the wish to put oneself in a bad light or falsely to claim mental symptoms. (See below under *F-K* index.)

With a T score above 80 the examiner should entertain the hypothesis that the profile is invalid, and should attempt to check this out by considering the characteristics of the remainder of the profile and (with the booklet form) the patient's responses to repeated items, from the standpoint of intratest consistency. (See steps 1 and 2, General Approach.)

Elevations on *F* are highly correlated (approximately +.50) with elevations on scales 6 and 8 due to item overlap. If the clinical picture fits with 68/86 elevations, the profile may be interpreted, but with caution.

Occasionally, individuals who are intensely anxious and pleading for help may get *F* scores somewhat above 80 that are bona fide but do not represent psychotic distortions; in such cases the profile will be markedly elevated but interpretable. *F* appears to be positively correlated with severity of illness in a clinic population.

T scores between 65 and 80 indicate unusual or markedly unconventional thinking, and frequently appear in sullen, rebellious personalities of a schizoid, antisocial, or bohemian type. Young people struggling with identity problems and a need to define themselves by exhibiting nonconformity (the "beard and sandals" set) frequently score in this range on *F*. The profile in such cases is usually a valid one.

Individuals having moderately elevated *F* scores are likely to be described as moody, changeable, dissatisfied, opinionated, talkative, restless, unstable, and self-deprecating. Such an elevation reflects admitting to unusual problems and feelings, perhaps due to exaggeration or faking. (See *F-K* Index below.)

T scores between 55 and 65 suggest independence of thought. However, situational stress reactions, intact (but defensive) psychotics with *K* above a T of 55, acute neurotics, and character disorders typically score in this range, as do normal adolescents.

T scores less than 55 suggest that the person is sincere, calm, dependable, honest, simple, convenventional, moderate, and has narrow interests. Usually such persons are free of stress. Nevertheless, see *F-K* index, as some persons may try to deny or minimize problems.

The *K* Scale
(Correction Scale—30 Items)

The *K* scale items were selected due to their ability to identify false negative cases; 24 of the items are highly correlated with Edwards' Social Desirability factor. The scale is the product of efforts to devise empirically a scale to measure guardedness or defensiveness in text-taking attitude. In this sense *K* is a "suppressor variable." It measures approximately what *L* was intended to measure, but does so in a much more subtle and effective manner and is only moderately correlated with *L* scores. It is used as a correction factor for some of the clinical scales. Item example: "Often I can't understand why I have been cross or grouchy" (*F*). *K* also provides a measure of ego strength, reality contact, coping ability, and the intactness of emotional defenses. *K* scores are inversely related to elevations on scales 8, 7, and 0.

High *K* scorers (T above 65) are people who resist psychological evaluation and cannot tolerate any suggestion that they are insecure, that they have difficulties in social relations, or that they may not have their lives well ordered and controlled. They are intolerant and unaccepting of unconventional or nonconformist behavior in others. Markedly concerned about their own social stimulus value, they are nevertheless relatively insightless concerning their effect upon others. In a clinical situation they show much hesitance to be seen as patients and a great desire to ensure confidence and approval. They view emotional problems as weaknesses in others that they do not have. They see themselves as rational and normal.

Where none of the clinical scales is greater than T = 70, see the interpretation for "Normal Code with High *K*." Where scale 9 is elevated in addition to *K*, see the high 9, high *K* interpretation.

Moderate elevations on *K* (T of 50 to 65) are found in people described as independent, enterprising, ingenious, resourceful, sociable, reasonable, enthusiastic, and as having wide interests. Some elevation is seen as desirable prognostically (T = 50 to 65), as it indicates ego strength, reality contact, and adequate functioning of psychological defense mechanisms. Successfully treated patients appear to show some rise on *K* at the end of therapy. In this high average range, *K* suggests adaptiveness and the availability of ego resources.

High *K* generally contraindicates overt antisocial acting out, and is associated with low expectancy of delinquency in adolescents, especially females. Generally speaking, prognosis tends to be poor when *K* scores are extreme in either direction (that is, T above 65 or below 40).

A low *K* (T score below 45) suggests that the person's defenses are down, and that he or she is hurting emotionally. Emotional-behavioral controls are likely to be poor. This person is self-critical, has a poor self-concept, is blunt in dealings with others, and therefore typically has interpersonal difficulties. This is usually accompanied by caustic manners, suspicion of the motivations of others, and exaggeration of the ills of the world. Where 9 is the high point scale, see the high 9, low *K*, low 2 interpretation.

In terms of the *K* correction on other scales, be aware that the patient who gets an elevation on scale 8 by virtue of having a high *K* is not the same kind of person as the one who gets a high 8 by claiming or admitting 8-type problems and symptoms. The high *K* person is likely to be much less florid in the pathology presented clinically.

Note: Lower social class persons often obtain low *K* scores, not necessarily reflecting the above. Likewise, adolescents often score low on *K*, reflecting openness and self-criticism often in a search for identity involving a questioning of personal values.

The *F-K* Index

The *F-K* index (dissimulation index) is based on raw scores, not T scores. The ratio of *F* to *K* has been used as an indication of faking, good or bad, and somewhat more successfully in the latter case than in the former.

When *F* minus *K* is +11 or greater (fake bad), it suggests a conscious attempt to look bad (malinger); an exaggeration of problems, which could be a cry for help (representing acute turmoil) and/or overdramatization by a narcissistic, self-indulging, emotionally unstable person who expects immediate attention and pity; or an acutely psychotic person whose subjective perceptions are distorted, resulting in an endorsement of an unlikely set of very deviant items.

When F minus K is -11 or less, for example, -12, -13, and so on (fake good), it strongly suggests that the person is glossing over and minimizing problems in an attempt to "look good." The remainder of the profile should be interpreted with this response set in mind. It may be helpful to elevate mentally the profile scores above 50 by 5 to 10 T score points, while still maintaining the profile configuration.

F minus K index greater than -20 indicates that the patients are extremely defensive about revealing themselves psychologically. Because of this unwillingness to tolerate any suggestion of personal inadequacy, the test results are of doubtful validity. The pattern may be the result of conscious deception, extreme rigidity and naivete, or generalized negativism and refusal to cooperate. This tendency to present a distorted image is likely to generalize to the treatment situation and may be expected to interfere with the development of a therapeutic relationship.

THE CLINICAL SCALES

Scale 1
(*Hs*—33 Items)

Scale 1 items are of a fairly obvious nature mostly concerning bodily function and malfunction. This is a frequent high point in persons consulting a physician. The complaint items tend to be vague and nonspecific. While scale 1 rises slightly with physical disease, it is mainly a "character" scale and physically ill patients generally score higher on scale 2. Scale 1 is a gross index related to optimism-pessimism, and typically is moderately correlated with scales 2, 3, and 7.

High scores (T = 65) are pessimistic, immature, narcissistically egocentric, sour on life, stubborn, whiny, complaining, and generally handle their hostile feelings by making those around them miserable. When pressured, they may adapt a paranoid posture. Frequently they use somatic complaints to control others (see 13/31 code and Conversion V below). They tend to be cynical and defeatist, especially as regards others' efforts to help them. They are highly skilled in frustrating and infuriating physicians, and often they "shop" from doctor to doctor. They are often unambitious and lacking in drive. The symptoms usually reflect long-standing problems, not a reaction to immediate stress.

Typically, high 1 patients show little manifest anxiety and have a poor prognosis in psychotherapy. If anxiety is shown, a better prognosis in therapy is indicated. T scores over 65 indicate a hypochondriacal component even in patients who are physically ill.

Note: Scale 1 peaks are more frequent as age increases beyond 30. In college groups, peaks on scale 1 are rare. When scale 1 is greater than T = 85, suspect schizophrenia associated with somatic delusions (see 18/81 code). Schizophrenic patients may show such elevations on scale 1 early in their illness, before gross clinical signs are evident in their behavior or the test data. High scale 1 scores are associated with diagnoses of hypochondriasis neurasthenia, depression reaction, or hysteria.

Moderately low scale 1 (t = 40 to 50) persons are described as alert, capable and responsible, and as showing good judgment and common sense. Others may see this person as conscientious, though perhaps somewhat moralistic. Effectiveness in living is suggested by such a scale 1 score except when scale 2, 6, 7, 8, or 0 is high (T = 70+).

Very low scale 1 (T = 40 or less), particularly when scale 2, 6, 7, 8, or 0 is high (T = 70+), often reflects a disinterest in one's body to the point of not caring what happens and/or feelings of inferiority concerning physical appearance (see 278, low 1; high 0, low 1).

Note: Scale 1 is the lowest in the profile in 16 percent of male outpatients (third most frequent low point) and in 7 percent of female outpatients (fourth most frequent low point).

Relations with Other Scales

High 1, Low 4 Code (Males) and High 1, Low 5 Code (Females). This code is associated with home conflicts and unassertiveness in confronting problems. Such persons typically have difficulty expressing angry feelings, and instead tend to internalize them, often resulting in psychophysiological complaints. Pessimism, whining, and complaining are likely to be present.

12 Codes. (See also 21 codes.) These patients exhibit physical symptoms and complaints, with little demonstrable physical pathology. Frequent pain (particularly visceral), depression, irritability, fatigue, and somatic overconcern are characteristics, as are anxiety and physical tension. They repress and deny emotional problems, and manifest a somatization reaction with a general hypochondriacal picture. They lack insight and resist implications that symptoms are related to emotional causes or conflicts. Passive dependence and strong tendencies to turn their anger toward themselves rather than toward others are typical. Excessive drinking-alcoholism is not unusual in such persons and should be considered, particularly in psychiatric inpatient settings. They are unlikely to have feelings of depersonalization or suicidal impulses.

Medical patients with this pattern are difficult to treat because they appear to have learned to live with and to use their complaints. Although the patient may show a good response to short-term treatment, the symptoms are likely to return rapidly. This code is slightly more common in males, and is more frequent as age increases. Common three-point codes: 123/213, 127/217.

College men with 12/21 codes show tension, insomnia, and social discomfort, but do not show gross bodily manifestations. Typically they are unhappy, worried, introverted, and lack skills in dealing with the opposite sex.

College women appear depressed, worried, shy, insecure and self-conscious, lack skills dealing with the opposite sex, are indecisive, frequently seek reassurance, and often "freeze up" on examinations. Headaches are particularly common when scale 5 is low.

Diagnoses likely: hypochondriasis (two thirds of cases) and schizophrenia (one third of cases). The somatic overconcern group usually shows 123 or 127 code; the schizophrenia group typically are 128 codes (see below). Somatic concern of 12/21 patients usually centers around pain in the viscera, as opposed to 13/31 patients, who focus on difficulties in peripheral limbs or the central nervous system.

123 and 213 Codes. (See 1234 and 1237 codes; also see 213;231 codes.) These codes are found in persons who are typically nonpsychotic and free of confusion and bizarre thinking. Suicidal thoughts are unlikely, as are obsessions, compulsions, and self-deprecation. Instead, these patients show physical complaints, particularly regarding abdominal-visceral pain, weakness, and fatigue. Often these complaints are presented with some irritability, even though usually a passive dependence is evident. The patients' history typically shows chronic, long-standing hypochondriasis. Insight into their own behavior typically is absent, as is insight into cause and effect relations in behavior. Implications to the patients that their problems have an emotional basis will meet strong resistance.

With low point 4 this code particularly suggests passivity, lack of heterosexual drive, and sexual difficulties. With low point 9, it suggests a low energy level, a lack of vocational aggressiveness, and a strong tendency to "take to bed."

1234 Codes. (And probably 2134 codes.) Typically these people are alcoholics or heavy drinkers who are combative when drunk, and show hostility toward women, particularly when their strong dependency needs are frustrated. They show physical discomfort, particularly digestive difficulties (including ulcer, anorexia, nausea, and vomiting), along with tension, depression, hostility, and perhaps insomnia. Poor work and marital adjustment are likely. Mother dependency strivings appear to be in conflict with anger over felt rejection by the mother. Most typical diagnoses are passive-aggressive personality, anxiety reaction, and psychophysiological reaction.

1237 Codes. In addition to 123 profile characteristics (see 123 code interpretation), this group shows increased anxiety, fearfulness, inability to be assertive, feelings of inadequacy, and dependent interpersonal relationships, usually in addition to the psychophysiological ailments suggested by the 123 profile. Back and chest pains and epigastric complaints are particularly common in this group. These people are seen as weak, moody, fearful, highly inadequate, and unable to cope with everyday stress and responsibility. Chronic unemployment and alcohol-drug dependency may result. Such patients internalize anxiety and conflict. Males with this profile frequently marry a stronger woman, and in this relationship try to perpetuate the role of a weak, helpless child. Characteristic diagnosis: psychophysiological reaction with anxiety in a passive-dependent personality.

128 and 218 Codes. Often, these are younger patients having bizarre somatic complaints ranging over the entire trunk. These patients are usually psychotic or acutely prepsychotic, and have somatic delusions. In addition, they often complain of fatigue and weakness. Psychic distress is present, often along with strong feelings of alienation from society, even though there is strong underlying dependency.

129 and 219 Codes. Acute clinical distress, tensions, agitation, and restlessness are prominent, along with many physical complaints. Headaches and complaints such as spastic bowel are frequent. A neurological etiology must be considered, though it is at least as likely that the person is attempting to deny or mask depression or passivity-dependency in a hypomanic fashion.

13 and 31 Codes. (See Conversion V below.) High 1–3s and 3–1s typically are psychoneurotic and have symptoms involving eating, such as nausea or discomfort after eating or having eaten too much, and sometimes anorexia or hysterical vomiting. Their other major symptom is pain, which usually appears in the extremities (head, back, neck, arms, eyes, legs). Though such pain is less frequent in the viscera, when this occurs, it is usually high in the body cavity or in the extremities (in contrast to 12/21 code patients, who are more likely to complain about the lower body cavity). Other frequent symptoms include dizziness, weakness, fatigue, and numbness. Tension, anxiety, depression, and perplexity may be present (unless 2, 7, 8 are low and *K* is high; see 13/31, low 2, 7, 8 code).

For both sexes, 13/31 codes are more common in persons older than age 28. Common three-point codes for both sexes are 132/312 and 134/314.

In general, an accompanying elevation on 3 attenuates the overly pessimistic, complaining attitudes of the high 1 person, and where 3 is higher, the operation of denial and repression may even permit expressions of optimism.

Few of these patients are incapacitated by their symptoms, but they have a long history of insecurity, immaturity, and a tendency to develop symptoms under increasing stress. Long-standing needs for affection-attention are typical, along with demands for sympathy and a tendency toward overcontrol of needs and impulses. Egocentricity, immaturity, and repression are usually present. Most place little stress on the discomfort of their current emotional state, and they often object to psychological study, as they usually come because of a sore back, headache, or whatever somatic complaint they have and resent having their "minds" studied.

College women (5 percent of whom show this code) describe themselves as affectionate, partial, and thoughtful. Their peers, however, see them as selfish, self-centered, with frequent physical complaints, neurotic, dependent, high-strung, irritable, and emotional, with a strong orientation toward marriage.

College men often aggressively insist on knowing their test results and on being given definitive answers to their problems. They appear socially at ease, fluent, expressive, and confident. Typically, they do not return for professional help after the first or second session. They are self-centered, selfish, dependent,

and demanding. A primary complaint is that they do not get enough consideration from their families. They rationalize, blame others, and occasionally act out
(usually in passive-aggressive ways). They typically lack heterosexual drive.

Diagnostically, the overwhelming majority are neurotics with a very small
proportion of psychotics and almost no psychopaths. The modal diagnosis is
conversion hysteria or conversion reaction and psychophysiological reaction.
This code suggests a socially oriented, passive, dependent person utilizing soma-
tizations to achieve neurotic ends. Psychotherapy and reassurance about the
somatic aspects by a physician are indicated. The 13/31 code is more often
found in outpatients age 28 or older.

This is the second most common code type among both fathers and
mothers of child psychiatric patients. It is associated with mothers who are
extroverted, suggestible, protective of those close to them, and have many
strengths. This mother's code is associated with improvement in treatment for
both the mother and the child. Among fathers this profile is associated with a
strong need for acceptance, immature dependency, and the use of subtle strategies to gain affection rather than straightforward effort. The prognosis for the
child's treatment is not good when the father's code is 1-3 or 3-1.

Conversion V

Elevations on scales 1 and 3, with an intervening valley of 10 or more T
points at scale 2, form what has come to be called the "Conversion V." Persons
exhibiting this pattern are characterized by an extreme need to interpret their
problems in living in a way that is socially acceptable. They deny troubles or
inadequacies. Often they are sociable and extroverted, though social relations
are generally shallow and may have an exhibitionistic flavor. The anxiety-de-
pression ordinarily found in 13/31 persons is typically absent (except in 137 or
138 persons). They emphasize, but fail to show any real concern about, their
somatic symptoms. Many of them develop somatic displacements, which permits
a localization of the difficulty outside the personality; others develop psychological symptoms of a highly reasonable, socially acceptable type. In any case,
the real function of the symptoms is obscured by hysteroid operations. Secondary gains (interpersonal manipulations and/or avoiding responsibilities) through
illnesses are almost always present (along with a denial of social anxiety), and
may be to the point of selfishly and immaturely exploiting others.

"Normals" with Conversion Vs below 70 have been characterized as cheerful, outgoing, sociable people who tend to be optimistic and look on the bright
side of everything. Because of their repressive tendencies they frequently appear
flighty and immature. Under stress they often develop physical symptoms, but
ordinarily they appear exceedingly normal, responsible, helpful, and sympathetic.

Some persons interpret secondary Conversion V configurations (where
other scales are higher, but the V is still present). Though this may yield in-

formation about the person's potential mode of reacting under stress, caution should be shown in interpreting such a secondary Conversion V where scale 9 is the high point, as the likelihood exists that scale 2 is reduced because of the manic defenses being utilized.

13/31, High K, low 2, 7, and 8 Codes. Especially if *F*, 2, 7, and 8 are down, individuals are likely to be extremely defensive, presenting themselves as exceedingly "normal," responsible, helpful, and sympathetic. Such persons are very threatened by any suggestion of weakness or unconventionality in themselves. Often they are markedly organized around ideals of service and contribution to others at the level of overt behavior. They do not tolerate well the role of patient or the suggestion of emotional etiology of their problems because they see such problems as weaknesses.

132 and 312 Codes. (See also 13/31 code.) Patients with this pattern show 13/31 characteristics. In addition, they are particularly irritable, tense, feel weak and fatigued (particularly with low 9), are conforming, conventional, passive (particularly with low 4), and anxious to be liked by others (particularly with low 0).

134 and 314 Codes. Very likely in interviews to be argumentative, cocky, belligerent, snobbish, opinionated, and to have little insight as to why they alienate others. If they also fit a Conversion V pattern, their somatic complaints are likely to stem from anger, which is not openly expressed in a modulated fashion (though such anger will probably be clear to others because it is expressed in passive-aggressive ways). Conflicts over independence-anger versus dependence-nurturance are likely.

136 and 316 Codes. Often seen as rigid, stubborn, and oversensitive to the requests of others. If scale 3 is more than 10 T points higher than scale 6, overt paranoid features are unlikely. Nevertheless, these persons possess much anger that is not recognized or admitted. Persons are likely to rationalize any behavioral expressions of anger, and to have very little insight into their stimulus value. If scale 6 is less than 10 T points from scales 1 and 3, early paranoid schizophrenia must be suspected. Suspicious and competitive attitudes are present, but denied. They are often blandly repressive even in the face of ruthless power operations and overwhelming egocentricity. Prognosis is guarded.

137 Codes. Severe anxiety (often mixed with depression) and panic attacks are experienced, typically accompanied by cardiac complaints (such as tachycardia) or epigastric distress. The modal diagnosis is psychoneurotic anxiety reaction, though phobias about illness are also common. Poor vocational adjustment due to underachievement is likely. Often the patient is unrealistic about work and finances, and depends on a dominant spouse to take responsibility and to discipline the children. Such persons are rigid and adapt poorly to environmental changes. In psychotherapy these patients can be demanding and clinging, but are unable to accept aggressiveness in themselves or in others (particularly with low 4).

138/831/318 Codes. (See also 1832 codes.) These patients are typically agitated schizophrenics with numerous somatic complaints, religiosity, and religious delusions, though often they would be classified as chronic borderline. Occasionally, major conversion reactions and hypochondriacal concerns appear to prevent more florid schizophrenic patterns from occurring. In males, fears regarding homosexuality are common, even though "masculine" occupations are usually chosen. The modal diagnosis is paranoid schizophrenic reaction.

1382 Codes. In addition to the 138 interpretation, depression, heavy drinking, and suicidal preoccupation are very likely. Such patients are usually single or have poor marital adjustment. Typically they float from one job to another.

139 Codes. Chronic brain syndromes with trauma and personality disorder (or with a low scale 2 a conversion reaction) should be strongly considered with this code type. Occasionally this code reflects anxiety reactions. Numerous somatic complaints are present (for example, headaches, hearing and visual complaints, tremor, coordination difficulties), about which the patient is typically quite upset.

These patients have low frustration tolerance, are irritable, and show temper outbursts, often becoming combative or destructive. Interpersonal relations are stormy, and divorces are frequent. Often these patients have a history of being perfectionists and show little affection toward their family, though hostility is frequently shown directly (often physically), particularly following alcohol ingestion.

14/41 Codes. These patients often have a long history of socially unacceptable behavior and inadequacy in meeting the usual stresses and responsibilities of life. Frequently such individuals are able to maintain control over their impulses toward asocial behavior, but are likely to substitute a bitter, querulous, self-pitying style of life, and to become upset at rules, regulations, or demands of others. They may be expected to be self-centered, demanding, and preoccupied with physical complaints. Although they may show a good response to short-term, symptomatic treatment, they will probably be spasmodic in treatment and unlikely to persist long enough to make real gains. A drinking problem may exist. Common three-point codes: 143/413 and 142/412.

15/52 Codes. This is an uncommon code, particularly for females. In males this code suggests a passive life-coping style, along with a fussy, complaining, and cynical attitude. Somatic complaints are frequently the focus of such complaints. Such persons are usually of above-average IQ and middle class. Overt asocial acting out tends to be contraindicated.

In females this code must be interpreted differently depending on the patient's social class background. In urban, middle-class, relatively educated females, a 15/51 code suggests a pessimistic, immature, and complaining woman who nevertheless is interpersonally aggressive, competitive, and perhaps dominating, particularly in her relations with men. In rural, lower class, relatively uneducated females, the pessimism, immaturity, and complaining are present, but the aggressiveness may not be. Even so, such women typically have "masculine" interests and occupational expectancies (for example, tractor driving).

Note: In interpreting 15/51 codes for males or females, it is necessary to use the above interpretation, but then to examine the third highest scale in combination with scale 1 and scale 5 (that is, as though a two-point code). Common three-point codes for males: 153/513, 154/514, 152/512.

16/61 Codes. With elevations on scale 8 or scale 6 (T above 70), an elevation on scale 1 is often associated with somatic preoccupation and/or delusions, which suggests an acute psychotic episode against which the person is struggling. The somatic preoccupations and complaints represent a defense against psychotic mental processes (that is, an attempt to "hold oneself together" through bodily preoccupations). The somatic complaints typically are medically atypical or impossible. Persons with such profiles are typically hypersensitive to criticism, rigid, stubborn, grouchy, and overly quick to blame others. They resent requests that others make of them and feel put upon. Insight is poor.

16/61 codes are extremely rare for both sexes. Common three-point codes for males: 162/612, 164/614. Common three-point codes for females: 163/613, 168/618.

17/71 Codes. Such persons typically are chronically tense and anxious, with many tension-related somatic complaints. Obsessive overconcern with body complaints, along with intellectualization, is common. Though such persons often demand continued medical care, their behavior pattern is resistant to change. Underlying feelings of guilt, inferiority, and difficulties in being assertive are common. Diagnostically, most are neurotic. This code is twice as common in males. For both sexes, most common three-point codes are 172/712 and 173/713.

18/81 Codes. These patients often show a variety of vague and medically atypical physical complaints. Periods of confusion and disorientation are possible, and where these occur the possibility of a psychotic or prepsychotic condition should be considered. They are typically alienated interpersonally, as others see them as strange in thought and behavior. Some of these persons appear to be attempting to hold themselves together via somatic preoccupations-delusions to try to ward off a break with reality. Home life may have been severely disrupted by poor control over their hostility. This kind of patient shows little response to simple reassurance, and in treatment is unlikely to attain much insight into personality difficulties. Diagnostically, the possibility of an acute schizophrenic episode must be considered. Common three-point codes: 182/812, 183/813, 187/817.

19/91 Codes. (See 129 and 139 codes if scales 2 and 3 are very close to 9.) This is a rarely occurring code (approximately once every 200 patients), which may suggest central nervous system or endocrine dysfunction expressed in the form of a high energy level (perhaps agitation) combined with numerous somatic complaints.

Such persons are typically in acute distress, tense and restless, and show clear overconcern with body functions and possible disabilities, though this overconcern may be expressed in the form of verbal denial or attempts to conceal (or avoid confronting) physical dysfunctions. Where physical etiology has been ruled out, consideration should be given to the hypothesis that the patient is attempting to mask an underlying depression (particularly if scale 2 is below T = 45), and that the distress stems from strong dependency needs that the patient finds to be intolerable. Most common three-point codes: 193/913, 194/914.

10/01 Codes. An extremely rare (at least in outpatients) code, this occurs approximately once in 700 cases. Such persons are socially uncomfortable and withdrawn, and seen by others as aloof, passive, and unassertive. Numerous somatic complaints exist. In interpreting this code further, examine the third highest scale in combination with scale 1 and scale 0 (that is, as though a two-point code). When 10/01 code occurs with scale 8 as the third highest, schizoid withdrawal and social inadequacies, with chronic and numerous somatic complaints, are suggested. In 012/102 codes, depression is marked. Most common three-point code: 012/102.

Scale 2 (*D*)—60 Items)

Scale 2 items relate to matters such as worry, discouragement, self-esteem, and general outlook. Scale 2 is the most frequent peak in the profiles of psychiatric patients. It tends to be highly sensitive to current mood and mood changes, and its meaning tends to vary depending upon the characteristics of the remainder of the profile. In general, it is the best single, and a remarkably efficient, index of psychic distress, immediate satisfaction, comfort, and security; it tells something of how individuals evaluate themselves and their role in the world and of their optimism-pessimism. Note that average T scores on scale 2 rise with increasing age, though usually no more than 5 T score points.

Scales 7, 1, 8, and 0 are often elevated with 2. In general, these combinations with 2 suggest neurosis, almost never psychopathy, and only occasionally psychosis (particularly involutional depression). Scale 7 suggests an added anxiety dimension, scale 1 a somatic dimension, and scale 8 feelings of aloneness and alienation, as well as unusual thought patterns.

High 2 people are anxious and depressed, self-deprecating, silent and retiring, perhaps withdrawn, and are seen by others as aloof, timid, and more or less inhibited. They show a narrowing of interests, low frustration tolerance, poor morale; feel blue, discouraged, dejected, pessimistic about the future, useless; and show inability to concentrate and lack of self-confidence.

Moderate elevations indicate good therapeutic prognosis. Success with ECT is best when 2 is between 55 and 85, and when 2 is the highest scale.

Low 2 people (T = 40 to 50) generally are active, alert, cheerful and socially outgoing, and are likely to be seen by others as enthusiastic, self-seeking, and perhaps lacking in inhibitions and given to self-display. T scores below 40, however, often indicate a denial of depression in a cyclothymic, labile person. Low 2 scores are frequently found in younger persons. For male outpatients, scale 2 rarely occurs as the lowest scale in the profile (2 percent of the cases), and for female outpatients is the sixth most frequent low point (2 percent of the cases).

Peak 2

Where 2 is the only elevated scale, usually this will be a so-called reactive depression, even when the person may deny depressive feelings. With such denial, and particularly if scale 1 is low, attention should be given to a cautious evaluation of the suicidal risk. Whether or not denial is present, such persons are anxious and overly self-critical, often in an attempt to expiate guilt feelings by punishing themselves for their transgressions. They feel inadequate and express pessimism and a lack of self-confidence. Psychotherapy prognosis is generally good within a short time. Such patients often respond well to a directive-confrontive approach regarding why they are punishing themselves so harshly through their depression and self-criticism.

In college students, however, the peak 2 profiles are clinically less significant and more often reflect concern over situational problems (usually relations with opposite sex, studying, or vocational choice). Peak 2 college students typically resist efforts to go deeply into the origins of their problems, and instead try to get advice from a parent-surrogate.

When 0, 7, or 8 is elevated along with 2, the depression is intensified (see 20/02, 27/72, and 28/82 codes).

Peak 2, Low 9. Depression is likely to be moderate to severe, and physical concerns typically center around fatigue and loss of energy. Often such persons find it hard to arise in the morning, and postpone responsibilities due to feeling tired and unable to cope. Symptomatic treatment and firm reassurance typically bring good results, though one should strongly consider the directive-confrontive approach outlined above.

21 Codes. (See 12 codes; also 123, 213 if appropriate.) The interpretation is similar to that of the 12 codes, except that depression and tension-anxiety are more prominent features. The depression is usually of a restless, rather than apathetic, nature. As with the 12 codes, acting out is contraindicated (except for 1234/2134 code). In spite of the obvious distress, such persons are often poorly motivated for psychotherapy. This code occurs more frequently as age increases, and is more prevalent among males than females.

213 and 231 Codes. (See also 123 codes.) The interpretation is basically similar to that of the 21 code. These patients manifest depression and hypochondriacal concerns such as headaches, chest pain, or nausea and vomiting. They have an exaggerated need for affection, and typically feel they received little from their father. However, they show conflicts over emotional dependency, even though they often demand sympathy and get secondary gains from their symptoms.

23 Codes. (See also 32 code and 213/231 codes if appropriate.) Major characteristics are apathetic depression and overcontrol. They are "bottled up," feel filled with self-doubts, and feel helplessly unable to do things or even start them. Often (particularly with low 9) they feel weak, fatigued, and exhausted. Marked anxiety or episodes of anxiety are infrequent, and they have difficulty expressing their feelings. Typically their depression is of long standing, and response to psychotherapy is poor. They tolerate unhappiness and have accepted a low level of efficiency in their functioning. They lack insight, are resistant to psychological interpretations, and seldom seek help.

Diagnostically, about half are labeled psychotic and half psychoneurotic. Among psychotics they are labeled involutionals and psychotic depressives, manic-depressives, but rarely schizophrenic or paranoid and almost never manics or psychopathic. Among the psychoneurotics are many subtypes, with most being depressive reactions and a few conversion reactions. This code is more frequent in persons age 28 or older. Modal diagnosis: reactive depressions. Most common three-point codes: 231/321, 234/324, 237/327.

Males with 23 codes (particularly 234, 237, and 239) seem driven, serious, competitive, and industrious, but are also dependent and immature. Though they strive for increased responsibilities, they dread them also. It appears that what they really want is added recognition (which they often feel they are not receiving). Despite their conflicts these men are usually able to maintain adequate levels of working efficiency.

Women with 23 codes (particularly 23, low 5 or 23, low 9) show weakness and apathy, along with their prominent depression. Unhappiness is typically chronic and with a long history, and family and marital maladjustment is common (though divorce is not). In spite of their distress, they show little effort to seek help.

24 and 42 Codes. These patients have difficulty in maintaining controls over their impulses and conduct. After acting out in a socially unacceptable manner, they typically feel distress and guilt, though this concern may reflect situational difficulties (that is, being caught) rather than guilt from internalized conflict. Though the apparent conscience pangs may be severe (even out of proportion to the event), future acting out is quite likely to recur in a cyclic pattern. Heavy drinking, home and family problems, loss of social relations, and loss of employment very often accompany this pattern, often leading to alcoholism. Behaviors in such persons have a self-defeating or self-punitive tendency. Drug addiction and legal difficulties are common. Female patients may show crying episodes and a history of suicidal behavior. This is a frequent profile of unmarried mothers.

At the time of testing, this patient likely felt depressed, frustrated, dissatisfied, and restless. Pessimism about the future and distress about failures to achieve past goals are likely. Many show an inadequate and passive-dependent adjustment pattern. Their failure to achieve satisfaction in life results either in self-blame and depression or sometimes in projecting blame and having paranoid ideation.

Although these persons may express firm intentions to change their behavior, the pattern is persistent, and the long-range prognosis is not encouraging, although they may show rapid temporary improvement in a protected environment. Environmental modification, warm supports, and firm limits will probably be required, perhaps in addition to involvement of agencies that can have frequent contact with the patient. Modal diagnosis: personality disorder with depression and alcohol.

Note: 24/42 codes appear unrelated either to age or education, and most often have scale 7, 3, or 8 as the third highest scale; least often have scale 1 or 9 as the third highest.

243/423 Codes. In addition to the 24/42 interpretation, it is likely that the person is more intensely in conflict about maintaining control through repression and denial of anger. Anger is more likely to be expressed in passive-aggressive ways, or (if openly) in an unmodulated, angry overreaction. Such people may establish relationships with marginal, acting out persons, thereby vicariously satisfying their own antisocial tendencies. Immaturity, egocentricity, and lack of insight into their own stimulus value are also common.

247, 274, and 472 (Also 2743) Codes. Family or marital problems are suggested centering around angry feelings that the patient is unable to express and feels intensely guilty about. Feelings of social inadequacy, worry, and depression are often present. The presence of high 7 in this triad diminishes the likelihood of acting out behaviors, but increases the likelihood of ulcers. Excessive drinking may also occur. These patients are unlikely to be frank and open in discussing their problems, in spite of their discomfort. Additionally, they typically overreact to minor problems, and react to them as if they were emergencies. This code is highly associated with chronic, severe alcoholism, combined with anxiety, guilt, and feelings of inferiority. The history of these patients often shows an extremely close relationship with the mother (for males), and a father who was "hard-driving" and successful. Frequently these patients underachieve, as though afraid to try because of possible failure.

Males with this pattern are usually verbally hostile, dependent, and highly immature, particularly if scale 5 is also high. Marital discord is likely, and usually the wife is dominating and/or minimally involved in a short-term marriage.

Females (particularly with low 5) present themselves as weak, inferior, guilty, and submissive. They virtually invite others to dominate them in a patronizing and deprecating way. Such relationships often appear to be masochistic ways of atoning for guilt, usually concerning unexpressed and unacceptable anger.

Modal diagnoses: psychoneurotic depression, passive-aggressive personality. Therapy prognosis is often poor because of reluctance to endure the anxiety involved in treatment. Firm, directive, goal-oriented psychotherapy, perhaps including assertive training, appears indicated.

248 Codes. (284 and 482/842 codes are somewhat different.) Though depression, sullen anger, and family-marital problems are most likely present, such persons are less likely to engage in overt acting out than 24/42 code persons. Rather, they are more likely to withdraw into angry fantasy, feeling distrustful, alienated, and disaffiliated from others. Nevertheless they fear loss of control over their impulses and may be quite concerned over their unusual and disturbing thoughts. They are often seen by others as moody and unpredictable. Suicide attempts are relatively common. This is a common code among mothers of child psychiatry patients.

Diagnostically, schizoid personality and schizophrenic reaction must be considered, particularly if scales 4 and 8 are distinctly elevated and with T scores close to scale 2 (see 482/842/824 codes).

25/52 Codes. (See also 275/725 codes.) Males with this code are depressed, inner-directed, socially sensitive, and idealistic. At this time the person is relatively noncompetitive, perhaps to the point of passivity. Acting out against others is contraindicated (or reduced) and conflicts are likely to be handled ideationally and with a high degree of self-awareness, as well as a concern for social issues. Most often this code is associated with scale 7, 3, 4, or 0 as the third highest scale (rarely with scale 1). Further interpretations can be obtained by examining the third highest scale in combination with scale 2 as though it were a two-point code (for example, treat 257 as though 27 code).

Females very rarely score this code, and usually it is with scales 0, 3, 1, 6, or 8 as the third highest scale. Ahthough high 5 women usually are seen as aggressive, often dominating, such three-point codes (except for 256 and 258 codes) suggest that the ordinary high 5 interpretation does not hold. More likely in this code scale 5 is reflective of lower social class membership.

26/62 Codes. Characterize patients who are depressed, oversensitive to criticism, have a strong underlying hostility, and a long history of interpersonal difficulties and rejection. Paranoid trends are usually evident, and sensitivity, resentfulness, and aggressiveness and usually marked. Often these patients adopt a "chip on the shoulder" attitude in an attempt to reject others before they are rejected. Often such persons read malevolent meaning into neutral situations, and jump to conclusions on the basis of insufficient data.

When scale 6 is markedly elevated and/or other scales (particularly 4 and 8) are also above T = 70, the probability is increased that the patient is in the early phases of psychosis. Prognosis is typically guarded.

27/72 Codes. (See relevant three-point codes.) These codes are the most common in male psychiatric outpatients (8.6 percent) and fifth most common for female outpatients (6.4 percent). Self-devaluation, intropunitiveness, tension, and nervousness are characteristic of this group as a whole. Depression, anxiety, guilt, rigidity of attitudes, feelings of inadequacy, and sexual conflict are typical, along with loss of work efficiency, initiative, and self-confidence. Insomnia, excessive and nonproductive rumination, and suicidal ideation or attempts are typically found in 27/72 types, particularly when 8 is the next highest scale.

Some 27 elevation is considered desirable in candidates for psychotherapy, as this usually indicates internal distress with motivation for change, as well as some introspective bent. Extreme elevations, however, often mean that individuals are so agitated and worried that they cannot settle down to the business of psychotherapy, and other forms of therapeutic intervention become necessary.

Suicidal thoughts and tendencies are a real possibility with high 2-7 and 7-2, particularly with elevated 8 and low scale 1. In such cases careful evaluation of suicide potential is indicated. In cases of severe depression, electroshock therapy has been successful except when 2 and 8 exceed a T score of 84 or where more than four clinical scales exceed a T score of 80.

One half of a group of medical (as opposed to psychiatric) patients with high 2-7s were seriously depressed; the other half showed some symptoms of depression but mostly showed fatigue and exhaustion. They did not stress physical complaints, but mostly showed rigidity and excessive worry, particularly men. These patients were perfectionistic, unhappy with themselves, uncomfortable with others, were brooding, had a loss of self-confidence, and a marked loss of efficiency and initiative. Insomnia is common, along with feelings of sexual and social inadequacy. Men particularly seem highly motivated for personal achievement and recognition. These 2-7 patients do not respond well to psychotherapy, even though they usually improve spontaneously.

This code occurs more frequently in patients age 27 or older and in persons with education beyond high school.

Diagnostically, this code group is about equally divided between psychosis and neurosis. Differentiating neurosis from psychosis depends largely on the elevation of scales 8 and 6. If 8 is 10 or more T points below 7 and 6 is below T = 70, psychosis is extremely unlikely, and the most frequent diagnoses are anxiety reaction, obsessive-compulsive neurosis, and depressive reaction. If psychotic, the most common diagnosis is depression, usually manic depressive or involutional; schizophrenia is rare but does occur. Conversion reactions and psychopathy are contraindicated. However, some of these patients will commit antisocial acts on a neurotic basis. Most common three-point codes: 270/720, 278/728, 273/723, 271/721.

273 and 723 Codes. These persons are prone to accumulating stress through high strivings and high standards, which they often achieve. When stress and anxiety become intolerable, however, the individual is likely to present depressed, self-deprecating, clinging, dependent, docile, marked helplessly dependent interpersonal behavior with a tendency to inspire nurturant and helpful attitudes in others. Somatic correlates of anxiety are often present. The poignant helplessness of these persons not infrequently causes even experienced therapists to engage in nonfunctional protective maneuvers. Diagnostically, this type of problem is usually seen in the context of an anxiety or phobic reaction of relatively severe proportions.

275/725 Codes (Males): 27, Low 5 and 72, Low 5 (Females). Generally, they present themselves to others as passive, weak, inferior, guilty, and submissive (particularly if scale 4 is low). They are self-effacing, and invite and provoke others to be patronizingly superior, deprecating, impunitive, and seem to feel least discomfort in relationships when they are receiving such treatment. In the extreme they are frequently diagnosed as psychotics or depressive reactions, and in everyday life they are frequently described as "clown" personalities. Sometimes these people also score somewhat high on 4, suggesting anger that they feel guilt about and have difficulty expressing or accepting.

278/728 Codes. (Different from 287/827 codes.) Patients with this code are more likely to be neurotic than those with 287 or 827 code, though schizophrenia is still likely. Patients with 278 or 728 code show obsessive and depressive thinking, usually about their "failures," fears, and phobias. They feel hopeless, cannot concentrate on tasks, are shy and withdrawn, sensitive, indecisive, inhibited, lack social skills, and typically have recurring suicidal thoughts and insomnia. They are often meticulous, perfectionistic, and usually set unreasonably high standards for themselves, feeling intensely guilty when they fail to live up to these standards. Particular difficulty exists in making emotional commitments such as in establishing love relationships with the opposite sex, even though these patients often voice needs for this. Particularly with low scale 1, evaluate regarding suicide.

This code is uncommon in younger persons and in persons having less than a college education. Psychopathy is contraindicated. These patients frequently respond well to tranquilizers.

Males, with a low piont 4, suggest submissiveness, lack of heterosexual interests, and (if married) sexual inadequacy. Females, with a low point 5, suggest extreme anxiety, physical complaints, insecurity, and an almost masochistic need to atone for guilt over "bad" feelings. The atoning usually is through the self-punishment of depression, along with provoking others to anger.

28/82 Codes. (See relevant three-point codes.) Psychiatric patients with this code show withdrawal, depression, anxiety, alienation, and agitation. They are tense and jumpy, and complain of fatigue and weakness. Inefficiency and little need to achieve are typically observed. In college students, this code often reflects radicalism, particularly if 4 is also elevated (see 284 below).

They often show confusion and complain that they cannot think clearly or concentrate. Others see them as becoming inefficient in carrying out their activities. Often they fear losing control over their impulses. Suicidal thoughts and threats are quite likely, and hallucinations or delusions may be present. The premorbid personality of these patients is described as unsociable. Typically they avoid close interpersonal relations, keeping others at a distance, due to a fear of emotional involvement. Heterosexual problems are typical.

28/82 codes appear to be unrelated to education or to age. Diagnostically, a majority are psychotic, with most of these being psychotic depressions and some schizophrenics. A minority are neurotic and usually are diagnosed as mixed psychoneurosis but sometimes as depressive reaction. Hysteria and hypochondriasis rarely occur and psychopaths are almost never found in this code group. Psychotherapy prognosis in this group is poor, and chemotherapy may be indicated.

284 and 824 Codes. Schizoid or schizophrenia conditions are nearly always accompanied by some elevation on 2, 4, 8, and F. In addition to the 28/82 interpretation (above), anger and rebellion are strong components, usually being expressed in sullen, distrustful disaffiliation from others. Severe social and marital maladjustment is likely. Fears of loss of impulse control are typically great. Where acting out occurs, it is likely to be in strange or bizarre ways. Where 4 is distinctly elevated and with T scores close to 2 and 8, see codes 482/842.

287/827 Codes. Though this is a frequent code in outpatients (more so for males), persons with this code are more likely to be psychotic than 278 or 728 code. Prepsychosis or severe neurosis must be considered, however. Persons with 287/827 codes avoid close interpersonal relationships and are afraid of emotional involvement due to fears of becoming dependent. They are anxious, feel alienated from others, are distrustful of people in general, and may be unduly sensitive to criticism. These patients almost always have notable psychological deficits, usually in being unable to concentrate, confusion, episodes of dizziness, and reduced efficiency in carrying out duties and responsibilities. Anxiety, tension, and depression are prominent, usually along with insomnia, fearfulness, withdrawal, and complaints of memory loss and fatigue. Suicidal preoccupations and threats are likely, and must be considered if scale 1 is below $T = 45$. Conflicts over self-assertion and sexuality are often present. Labile and/or inappropriate affect may be present, along with possible hallucinations or other thought disturbances.

29/92 Codes. This code appears unrelated to age or education. Most commonly this code is associated with scale 4 or scale 3 as the third highest scale (for example, 294, 293). Patients with this code show psychic distress (in the form of anxiety and depression), combined with a high energy level. The high energy level reflects either a loss of control or an attempt at compensatory coping.

Three types of patients typically achieve such a code:

1. Patients for whom manic defenses are no longer effective, and an agitated depression results. Their manic defenses neither keep the environmental pressures from being overwhelming nor do they distract the patients from their gnawing depression. In some cases, however, the manic features may still be great enough to mask the depression from the patients themselves. Alcoholic histories are common in such cases.

2. Those with an agitated depression marked by overly expressive affect and openly narcissistic weeping and wailing with depressive rumination and self-absorption.

3. Encephalopathy where the patient is at least moderately aware of reduced functioning, shows perplexity, and feels mentally impotent but attempts to hide this from others. In such cases, the high 9 reflects an attempt at compensatory coping and denial of deficits. Often such patients will appear ritualistic, representing attempts to gain control over their life environment through excessive systematizing and structuring. Changes in daily patterns are particularly upsetting.

20/02 Code. This code is much more frequent in women than in men, and is more common in persons older than 27. In women, it is particularly associated with post-high school education. For both sexes, 20/02 codes most often have scale 7 or 4 as the third highest scale (for example, 207, 204).

The 20/02 code suggests a mild, but chronic and characterological, depression in a socially withdrawn and introverted person. The depression is often related to poor human relations and to perceived inadequacies in social skills. Such persons are inhibited, shy, and timid, particularly in interactions with the opposite sex. They are overinhibited and inept in social interaction. When scale 1 is the low point, the patient is likely to feel physically unattractive and inferior. Insomnia, guilt feelings, worry, and tension may be present. Common diagnoses are depressive reaction and occasionally schizoid personality.

Common among mothers of child psychiatry patients, these codes are associated with only moderate improvement of the child in treatment. Therapists see these mothers as in conflict about giving, keeping a rigid check on their own emotions to avoid loss of control, keeping people at a distance, especially sensitive to any demands and fearful of emotional involvement with others.

College students (particularly men) with this profile frequently seek counseling. They are unhappy, tense, worried, and complain of insomnia. They are introverted, socially insecure, and lack social skills, particularly with the opposite sex. Women with this profile (when scale 1 is the low point) typically have feelings of physical inferiority.

Scale 3 (*Hy*—60 Items)

Scale 3 consists of 60 items, most of which fall into two general types: rather specific somatic complaints and items that deny any emotional or interpersonal difficulty. In normals these two clusters show no tendency to occur together; in persons organized around hysteric operations they seem to be closely associated. Closer examination (Harris-Lingoes subscales) reveals five subclusters: denial of social anxiety, high need for affection, lassitude-malaise, somatic complaints, and inhibition of aggression.

High 3 people are typically conforming, immature, religious, extremely naive, and childishly self-centered in outlook. They are very demanding of affection and support, and endeavor to get these by indirect but obtrusively manipulating means. Often they are highly visible and active in social relations, but such relations are carried on at a superficial, immature level with little insight into how their behaviors are being interpreted by others. Some high 3 people act out sexually and aggressively in blatant fashion with convenient, and often incredible, inattention to what they are doing. They are, on the whole, blandly insightless people. Because they have strong needs to be liked, their initial response to treatment is apt to be enthusiastic. Their main defenses are repression and denial. Sooner or later, however, they become intolerant of the inevitable challenges to their defenses, frequently make impossible demands on the therapist, and become generally resistive, often whiningly complaining that they are being mistreated, that the therapist doesn't understand them.

The person with an elevated 3 is unlikely to be seen as psychotic, regardless of what shows on other scales (with the probable exception of 36/63 and 38/83 codes); the examiner should therefore be very wary about diagnosing psychosis when 3 is clearly elevated. Well-educated people tend to score higher than average, with a T score of 60 to 65.

Low 3. Little is known about low 3 people, but many of them seem to be socially isolated, tough minded, cynical, and generally misanthropic. When 3 is below T = 45 in an otherwise elevated profile, usually the person is exquisitely aware of distress and there is an absence of repression or denial.

Peak 3 (No Other Scale Above T = 70)

These persons present problems stemming from an unhappy home or marital situation, primarily a father who they describe as rejecting. Specific worries are difficulties with authority figures, scholastic failure, and lack of acceptance by their social group. Such patients are usually overconventional and have an overdetermined need to be accepted and liked. Commonly this is associated with reduced scores on *F* and 8, with *K* being at least moderately elevated. They gloss over and minimize any unusual or deviant behaviors, and emphasize their optimism and good relations with others. They have great difficulty with and are very uncomfortable in handling confrontive situations involving anger or self-assertiveness.

Males often show rebellion and hostility in covert ways. Females show somatic complaints, particularly dizziness, anxiety, tachycardia, palpitations, and headaches, particularly under stress. For both sexes acting out behavior or psychosis is unlikely, and response to advice and reassurance is usually quite good. Dynamic-interpretive therapy, however, is usually resented by these patients, though supportive counseling may lead to overdependency.

High 3, Low 5 (Women). (See low 5 interpretation.) In addition to the above peak 3 description, these women are particularly likely to have an ultrafeminine facade and to use "feminine wiles" to manipulate men. They are also likely to be seductive without knowing it. Sexual problems, lack of assertiveness, and an inability to express anger are common.

High 3, Low 0 (Women). Usually extroverted and aggressive and marriage-oriented with many social skills. Typically they lack insight and tend to be egocentric.

Peak 3, High K. Particularly when *F* and 8 are low, these people are constricted, overconventional, and have an extreme need to be accepted by others. They show an exaggerated striving to be liked and accepted. Characteristically, they maintain an unassailable optimism and emphasize harmony with others, if necessary at the expense of internal values and principles. They are likely to become extremely uncomfortable in, and therefore avoid, situations demanding angry response, independent decision, or the exercise of power. When such persons do show up in the clinic, which is infrequent, they are most resistant to considering that their difficulties may result from emotional conflict. It is also a remarkable fact that even in the face of catastrophic failure they often resolutely maintain that "things are going fine." Defeated feelings seem to be intolerable to these people.

31 Codes. (See 13 codes.)

32 Codes. (See also 23 codes.) 32/23 codes are more common for women than men, and more often obtained by persons older than 27. For males, 32/23 codes most often have scale 1, 8, or 9 as the third highest scale (for example, 321, 328, 329). For females, scale 1, 4, or 8 is most often the third highest (for example, 321, 324, 328).

Patients with this code show a variety of physical complaints, usually rather mild and rather clearly related to anxiety. Epigastric distress is the most frequent symptom, although headaches are also common. 32 code persons show more concern for their health and are somewhat less overtly depressed than 23 code persons. 32 code persons deny unacceptable impulses or ideas and feelings of social inadequacy. They are usually insightless, nonintrospective, and resistant to psychotherapy.

Females with 32 codes have a history of marital difficulties (though divorces are rare), frequently are sexually frigid and lacking desire for sexual relations with their husbands. They typically are depressed and complain about the infidelity or drinking of their husbands. This profile also frequently reflects menopausal difficulties. Women with this code frequently have episodes of palpitation, sweating, insomnia, fear, and abdominal pain. Typically (particularly with a low 5 and a high L) they complain of fatigue and exhaustion, yet may be quite conscientious in their work. They are extremely sensitive to criticism or rebuff. Commonly they feel inadequate and have significant self-doubt, but keep their emotions "bottled up" and are overcontrolled. They often tolerate chronic unhappiness.

Males usually are clearly in a state of anxiety (perhaps with depression), and show physical symptoms of dizziness, palpitation, inability to concentrate, and gastric distress (occasionally to the point of ulcers). Their concerns often center around business problems where they typically are both ambitious and conscientious, taking their responsibilities very seriously. These men are concerned about social conformity, deny unacceptable impulses or social insecurity, lack insight, and are resistant to psychodynamic formulations of their problems. They do, however, often profit from reassurance about their "physical" problems, and do not return for a second visit.

Modal diagnosis is neurotic depression, though psychosis must be considered where the profile is 326 or 328.

321 Code. These people show numerous hypochondriacal complaints such as constipation, diarrhea, genital pain, and hypertension. Women with this profile frequently have had hysterectomies. Men often show gastric distress and ulcers. Sexual marital problems are likely, as are conflicts about sex. Depression and worry related to feelings of inferiority, hopelessness, and perplexity are typical presenting symptoms. A high level of anxiety, often associated with insomnia and/or anorexia, usually accompanies.

These people are typically insightless concerning themselves or others, and often get themselves in uncomfortable interpersonal situations because of this. These people react to frustration by becoming intropunitively depressed, often in self-defeating ways. They are unable to express their emotions in well-modulated fashions, and consequently overreact often in ways that place them in a bad light.

The modal diagnoses are psychophysiologic reaction and depressive reaction. The prognosis for symptomatic relief is good, though their basic behavior patterns seem more resistive to psychotherapy due to lack of insight and resistance to psychological interpretations. Secondary gain often is associated with the symptoms. Schizophrenia or psychopathy is very unlikely with this code.

34/43 Codes. This is a common code among outpatients (second most frequent for females, seventh most frequent for males), but also is frequent in prison populations where it is the code most associated with incarceration for violent crimes. In males, 34/43 codes most often are associated with 2, 5, or 6 as the third highest scale (for example, 342, 345, 346). For females, scale 2, 6, or 8 is most often the third highest scale. Rarely is scale 0 the third highest scale for either sex.

34/43 code persons are angry, but markedly immature and egocentric, and have not developed appropriate ways of expressing their anger in modulated and timely fashion. Typically they discharge their anger in indirect, passive-aggressive ways. When aggressive actions toward others do occur, these persons deny hostile intent, and show a striking lack of insight. Apparently, some persons with this code repress, deny, and "bottle up" anger for long periods of time with no angry outlets, then explode in rage, committing crimes of serious assault or murder. Evaluation of emotional controls and of outlets for anger (even if passive-aggressive) should be made.

Persons with this code typically show marital disharmony, sexual maladjustment, sexual promiscuity, divorce, and alcoholism. Interpersonal relationships are usually tenuous, though many such persons establish enduring (though often turbulent) relationships with marginal, acting out individuals, thereby gratifying their own antisocial tendencies. If anger is expressed verbally by such people, it is likely to be rationalized and directed toward members of the immediate family.

Persons with this code wish to be dependent, but also wish to be independent (finding close relationships, expectancies of others, and rules very irritating). Often they vacillate angrily between being "called for too much" and "not being called for enough."

Women with this code particularly often have mild episodic psychosomatic complaints. Though the presenting physical complaints are typically numerous, almost none is acute in onset or incapacitating. Often these women have a superficial outlook on life and have overly perfectionistic attitudes toward themselves and others, with little ability to recognize shortcomings in themselves or their friends.

Although this code occurs more frequently in persons 27 or older (both males and females), college girls with 34 and 43 codes were described as impatient, but generally were similar to the general college population. They described themselves as having wide interests, loyal, conscientious, incoherent, talkative, energetic, reasonable, and frivolous.

The 34/43 codes are the most common codes among both mothers and fathers of child psychiatry patients. Their children tend to present as behavior disorders but a few are neurotic. Frequently these parents are subtly reinforcing the acting out behavior of their children as an indirect mode of expressing hostility toward their spouse. This seems particularly so when scale 9 is less than T = 70 and is 10 or more T score points lower than 4. These parents are excitable, resentful, demanding, and projecting, and one can expect a poor prognosis for their children in treatment.

Most frequently 34/43 patients are diagnosed as passive-aggressive personalities, though consideration should be given to the relative elevations of 3 and 4. If scale 3 is higher than scale 4, passive-aggressive personalities of the passive type are indicated. If scale 4 is higher, episodic acting out is likely to occur, followed by periods of inhibition and restraint, even up to one or two years. If both 3 and 4 are above T = 85, dissociative, amnesic, or fugue states may occur, involving acting out of sexual or aggressive impulses.

345/435/534 Codes (Males). These men are typically grossly immature and seen as sexually inadequate, frequently have fears of being homosexual, and may have engaged in exhibitionism or voyeurism. They appear to feel a need for different and more than usual sexual stimulation. When 3 is higher than 4, there is less likelihood that the feelings-desires have been acted upon, particularly if *K* is greater than T = 50.

345/436 Codes. (See also 36/63 codes.) Though outwardly appearing to be conforming, these people often have histories of episodic extreme acting out followed by long periods of inhibited and moderated behavior. Many establish enduring relationships with marginal, acting out individuals, thereby vicariously gratifying their own antisocial tendencies. Often such persons are hypersensitive to criticism, and are tense and anxious as a result of repressed anger toward members of the immediate family. This tension may be expressed in the form of gastrointestinal complaints and headaches. These people typically resent efforts to explain symptoms as psychogenic. Rationalization, denial, or even early termination of treatment are common.

35/53 Codes. (See 354 codes.) Though moderately common for male outpatients (approximately 2 percent of the cases), this code is uncommon for females. In males, 35/53 codes are associated with age greater than 28 and education beyond high school. Scale 4 or 6 is usually the third highest (for example, 345, 356) for males, whereas for females scale 4 or 1 is usually the third highest (for example, 354, 351).

In males, this code is frequently seen among fathers of child psychiatry patients. It is associated with the use of denial, repression, and passivity as a defense. Though appearing alert and interested, these fathers lack persistence and have a tendency to let things concerning their families take second place to their own narcissistic needs. These traits tend to be exaggerated when scale 9 is below a T score of 45. Physical complaints, such as headaches and exhaustion, are usually noted in such cases.

In females, interpretation is best accomplished by initially ignoring the elevated 5 so as to treat the three-point code (for example, 354) as though it were a two-point code (for example, 34). Subsequently, add the interpretation of scale 5.

36/63 Codes. On the surface these patients are hypersensitive to criticism, tense, anxious, and frequently have gastrointestinal symptoms or headaches. Closer inspection reveals deep (often unrecognized) feelings of hostility toward members of the subject's immediate family. Where the anger is recognized, it is well rationalized. These people resent psychogenic explanations of their difficulties, tending to rationalize, deny, or even terminate treatment early.

When 6 is higher than 3 by five or more T points, often the person is a hostile, egocentric individual who strives for social power and presitge even to the point of ruthless power manipulation. Typically they are rigid and defensively uncooperative. Some show marked paranoid features.

High 3s with a moderate elevation on 6 typically are blandly repressive of their own histility and aggressive impulses, denying any suspicious attitudes they have, and comfort themselves with what appears as a naive and rosy acceptance of things as they are. Somatic problems are more likely, while paranoid features or psychosis is not likely.

36/63 codes are more common among female patients than among males, and are more frequent in patients older than age 28. For females, scale 2 or 4 is most often highest (rarely scale 0 or 8). This code does not appear related to education level.

37/73 Codes. Relatively uncommon, this code is slightly more frequent in female patients than in male patients. For both sexes, scale 2, 4, or 1 is most frequently the third highest (for example, 372, 374, 371). Rarely is scale 0 or 9 the third highest. Clinically, these persons are characterized by tension, anxiety, and discomfort, perhaps to the point of insomnia. However, they show little insight and utilize repressive defenses. Often these persons display psychosomatic symptoms. Unresolved dependency yearnings and excessive self-criticism often underlie their anxieties.

38/83 Codes. This relatively uncommon code is slightly more frequent in female patients. For both sexes, scale 4, 1, 7, or 2 is most frequently the third highest scale (rarely scale 0).

These patients typically have major thought disturbances to the point of disorientation, difficulty in concentrating, and poor memory. Regression and autistic overideation are typically present, and thinking may even be delusional. Feelings of unreality and emotional inappropriateness are usually accompanied by complaints of blurred vision, dizziness, numbness, and headaches. Apathy and passive withdrawal are usually present. These people have an exaggerated need for affection, but are afraid of getting involved in dependent relationships. When they do make attempts to achieve affectionate responses from others, they typically act in immature, almost stereotyped ways. Major tranquilizers are typically indicated, and the prognosis is fair.

The most frequent diagnoses are schizophrenic reaction and dissociative reaction. Prognosis is fair in that over half of these patients show at least some improvement.

39 Codes. Complaints of this group show histories and presenting symptoms of episodic attack of acute distress, and attacks of anxiety, palpitations and tachycardia, or symptoms in the lower gastrointestinal tract. Occasionally their medical problems show a classic hysterical pattern, being both dramatic and medically atypical or impossible. Frequently these patients are described as verbally aggressive, have dependence-independence conflicts, and are particularly angry at a domineering mother. Their physical problems typically are not severe, and they respond readily to superficial psychotherapy, though episodes of acute distress may recur.

For both sexes, scale 4 is most often the third highest scale (for example, 394/934). Rarely is scale 0 the third highest.

30/03 Codes. This code is rare, particularly for males. In male outpatients, it occurs only once per 1,000 cases; in female outpatients, only once per 200 cases. In females, scale 1 or 2 is most often the third highest scale (for example, 012, 013).

Persons with 30/03 codes tend to be withdrawn in a passive and dependent fashion. They are unassertive socially, but appear to be relatively comfortable in this mode of adjustment. They repress uncomfortable feelings and avoid discomforting social situations. Reactions to stress often involve psychosomatic problems, and a Conversion V may be present in the profile (see 13/31 codes). Insight is often lacking. Typically, these persons are *not* psychotic or psychopathic.

Scale 4 (*Pd*—50 Items)

Items on this scale deal with general social maladjustment, absence of strongly pleasant experiences, and include complaints against family, feelings of having been victimized, boredom, and feelings of alienation from the group—of not being in on things.

High 4 (T above 70) people are characterized as angry, rebellious, disliking rules and regulations, and lacking identification with recognized conventions. Their revolt may be against family, or society, or both. Many high 4 persons exhibit an apparent inability to plan ahead, an inability to see themselves from another's viewpoint, and a reckless disregard of the consequences of their actions. Unpredictability, impulsiveness, and poor social judgment are features of their behavior. Whether they act out their anger behaviorally depends on whether scales 9 and/or 8 are elevated, and whether scale *K* is low. Heavy drinking and poor work and marital adjustment are common.

Social relationships are usually shallow, with the individual rarely developing strong loyalties of any kind. These people sometimes make a good first impression, but on longer acquaintance their unreliability, moodiness, and resentment become apparent. They may justify their disregard of convention on the basis of being "above" mere propriety, reflecting the high value many of them place on themselves. High 4 is associated with inability to profit from experience, including psychotherapy.

In estimating the amount of pathology reflected in a high 4 profile, age must be considered. High 4 profiles are "normal" for adolescents, who probably should be rebelling at least moderately. Beyond the age of 25, however, a high 4 profile should be considered unusual to a pathological degree. Elevation on 4 is a fairly stable feature in character disorders and the psychoses, reflecting a component of brooding resentment.

Moderate elevations on scale 4 (T = 60 to 70) are common among adolescents (ages 14 to 20), and appear to reflect their striving for independence from home. Extreme scores or unusual high-point combinations may still reflect pathology in this age group. In adolescent delinquents with 4 peaks, therapy appears to be less effective in producing changes than does increasing age.

Low scores on 4 (T below 50) tend to be passive, dependent, conventional, rigid, and overidentified with social status. Frequently they manifest very low levels of heterosexual aggressiveness, although they are affectionate and serious (see high 5, low 4). Often they seek reassurance in counseling concerning the attitudes of others toward them.

Peak 4

When scale 4 is the only scale above T = 70 (and to a lesser degree when scale 4 is 10 or more T points above all other scales), the interpretation of high 4 (see above) should be particularly considered. The likelihood of legal difficulties is high. Even when 4 is only moderately elevated a high 4, low 2 indicates an especially low probability of significant personality change occurring because the person feels little psychic distress. High 4, low 0 is particularly associated with aggressive behavior (though perhaps in a more socialized fashion) and with father conflicts. If *K* is elevated also, and if the patient is bright, the behaviors are likely to be well controlled, well covered, and engaged in only after forethought. "White-collar" difficulties with the law are more likely in such cases.

41/14 Codes. (See also 14/41 codes.) The patient likely will show a history of inadequacy in meeting the demands and restrictions imposed by society. These patients usually feel bitter about the restrictions they feel are placed on them, and tend to be complaining. Additional concern typically is expressed over physical symptoms, with emotional problems being denied. Persons with this pattern rarely seek psychotherapy voluntarily, and in psychotherapy are quite concerned about any demands made on them by the therapist. Rules and regulations are generally nettlesome to them.

For both sexes, scale 3 or 2 is most often the third highest scale (for example, 413, 412); scale 0 is almost never the third highest. If scale 2 or 3 is elevated quite closely to scales 4 and 1, it may be useful to examine 42/24 or 43/34 code interpretations.

413/431 Codes. In addition to the basic 41 and/or 43 code interpretations, family or marital problems are suggested, centering around feelings of hostility and aggression intermingled with feelings of social inadequacy. Excessive drinking, somatic complaints, and conflicts over dependence-independence are common.

42 Codes. (See 24/42 codes.)

43 Codes. (See 34/43 codes.)

45/54 Codes. Males with less than 14 years of education who score high on 4 and 5 often are narcissistic, bohemian types who leave little doubt as to their nonconformity. They are inner-directed and delight in defying and challenging convention. (Many overt homosexuals have this pattern and they usually are open about their sexual behavior. This is true only, however, when no other scales are significantly elevated.)

Males with college education or above are less likely to be blatantly nonconformist, but are more likely to engage in social causes or social movements that have an antiestablishment protest element. Often these men are quite self-aware and are able to communicate ideas clearly and effectively. For males, scale 3 or 0 is most often the third highest scale. Rarely is scale 1 or 0 the third highest.

Females with high 4 and 5 are rebelling against the feminine role, and their "masculine protest" generally becomes more clearly deviant as 4 becomes higher. In rural areas, the 45 profile for women often only indicates a nonfeminine, workoriented subculture. For females, scale 9 or 8 is most often the third highest (for example, 459 and 458), with scale 8 occurring more often in less educated women. In female profiles, it is often helpful to omit temporarily the elevated scale 5 and to interpret the three-point code (for example, 458) as though it were a two-point code (for example, 48).

For both males and females there often are underlying, but poorly recognized dependency longings against which the person is protesting, and about which he or she is in conflict.

435, 453, and 543 Codes. (See 354 codes.)

High 4, Low 5 Codes. (See low 5, high 4 codes.) In males, the low 5 reflects "hypermasculinity." This may be a genuine accompaniment of the elevated 4 and associated with less education and lower social class values. In a male with education above 14 years, however, it suggests a flamboyant protest and an attempt to present a hypermasculine facade in order to cover up underlying feelings of inadequacy and depression. These usually involve feelings of inadequacy in dealing with women, combined with attempts to "put women down" in order to bolster his own ego. In teenagers, this pattern is often associated with delinquency.

Women with this pattern are hostile-angry, but unable to express these feelings directly. Their anger is aimed particularly at men, and heterosexual problems are to be expected. Frequently such women passively-aggressively use sexual means to manipulate men. They frequently provoke others to anger and rage (particularly if scale 6 is also elevated), and then pity themselves because they have been mistreated.

46/64 Codes. This code is rare among adult "normals," though it is not uncommon among teenagers (ages 15 to 17). In outpatients it is three times more common for females than males, and suggests a less malignant picture for females. For both sexes, scale 2, 3, or 8 is most often the third highest scale. Rarely is scale 1 the third highest.

Patients with this code are angry, sullen, irritable, and suspicious, typically with histories of severe social maladjustment. They protect blame onto others, and typically do not show obsessive self-criticism or somatization. Often they are manipulative and rigidly argumentative (particularly with high L and K), and are often seen as obnoxious. They are oversensitive to criticism or to implied slights, and often jump to conclusions based on inadequate data. Drug usage, addiction, and alcoholism are common.

In men, the 46/64 code is often associated with psychotic, prepsychotic (particularly 468), or borderline (462, 463) conditions with paranoid features. When scale 4 is higher than scale 6, family and work difficulties are typical. When scale 6 is higher than scale 4, more blatantly paranoid features are observed. Though 64 men are more likely to control their anger, they may episodically show vicious outbursts to the surprise of those around them.

In women, the 46/64 code may be associated with psychosis or prepsychosis (468), but more often appears to be associated with passive-aggressive personalities who are angry at men, have problems accepting a feminine role, and who have dependence-independence conflicts (463). This pattern particularly occurs when scale 5 is below T = 40.

Diagnostically, neorotics, manics, and depressives rarely score 46/64 code. About one half are conduct disorders (including sociopaths and criminals of various kinds) and about one half are psychotic or prepsychotic (primarily paranoid schizophrenic).

462/642 Codes. People with this code typically are dramatically (perhaps histrionically), egocentrically in agitated psychic distress, and complain of anxiety, nervousness, and depression. Often this is a manipulative demand for sympathy and attention. Suicide threats are likely.

These people are mistrustful and skeptical of others (suspicious of their motivations) and particularly are resentful of (and have problems with) persons in authority. Often they passively-aggressively criticize, deride, or resist authority figures. When they get into trouble because of this, they project blame onto others and rationalize their difficulties. Impulse control may be lacking, and they may show a cyclic acting out pattern (see 24/42 code).

In conflict with their anger at authority, these persons have an exaggerated and self-centered need for affection and dependency (particularly if scale 3 is also elevated). It appears that much of their anger and criticism stems from a fear of becoming overly dependent upon (and thereby controlled by) others. Consequently, these people are often uncomfortable with others, and may show decreased interest and involvement in their work and families. Sexual and marital maladjustment is typically present.

Modal diagnoses: passive-aggressive personality; psychoneurosis, mixed type. Prognosis is fair to good for at least some improvement with psychotherapy.

463/643 Codes. These people typically have an inordinate demand for affection that they find difficult to satisfy. Usually their dependency needs are heterosexual, and are expressed in hostile, egocentrically demanding ways, even to the point of blatant manipulation and provocation. Usually, however, such demandingness is self-defeating, as their partners often soon become irritated and withdraw affection. Thus the elevated scale 6 reflects oversensitivity to criticism and rejection, chronic bitterness and resentment, as well as blaming others for their dissatisfaction. Insight is typically lacking. Marital maladjustment is likely.

In women this code is often associated with a low scale 5 (T below 40). In such cases passivity, clinging dependency, and physical complaints (such as menstrual irregularities and headaches) are often present.

Modal Diagnoses: psychoneurosis, mixed type; passive-aggressive personality. Prognosis: fair. Often these persons make excessive demands on the therapist, while at the same time being critical and deprecating of the treatment process.

468/648 Codes. This profile suggests a chronic and severe emotional disorder, most likely paranoid schizophrenia. These persons are suspicious, angry, and evasive. They ruminate angrily about real or imagined injustices done to them, and often have ideas of reference or delusions. Tangential or loose thought associations may be present. They are easily hurt by criticism, and tend to read malevolent meaning into neutral situations. Projection and rationalization are the main defense mechanisms. These patients typically deny their own anger (and other psychological problems), and instead attribute the anger to others. Elements of grandiosity are also often present, usually at least in the form of narcissism, egocentricity, and immature, demanding self-indulgence.

Poor sexual and marital adjustment is typical, with the patient blaming the partner. These patients often are impulsive and show poor judgment or insight. Suicide attempts are moderately frequent (and often serious) as are assault and drug usage-addiction. Acting out potential (that is, reduced impulse control) is greater when scale 8 elevation is close to that of 6 and 4; K is below T = 50; and/or when scales 9 and 2 are above T = 70.

Diagnostically, one half of the patients with this profile are psychotic (usually paranoid schizophrenic) and one half are personality disorders. Though therapeutic intervention with these patients is difficult (usually involving chemotherapy), over one half show at least small improvement.

47/74 Codes. (See 247/427/274 code types.) This code occurs in approximately 2.5 percent of the outpatient population, and is obtained equally by males and females. It is more common among younger patients (age less than 27). Most often scale 8 or 2 is the third highest scale.

Persons obtaining this code are typically broodingly and ruminatively resentful, particularly concerning home conflicts, which often involve feeling rejected by others and/or feeling overly restricted by others. These people find rules, regulations, and limits imposed by others quite irritating and anxiety-provoking. Though they typically are quite concerned with their own feelings and situation, they are markedly insensitive to the situations and feelings of others.

Behaviorally, these patients typically show a cyclical pattern. For a period they may act with little control or forethought while attempting to satisfy their desires. During this period they often trample unthinkingly on the feelings and wishes of others, often violating social and legal restrictions and engaging in excessive alcohol indulgence and sexual promiscuity. Following such a acting out spree, however, they show self-condemning guilt, remorse, and apparently deep regret, often to the point of excessive self-pity. Though their conscience pangs may be severe, even out of proportion to the actual behavior deviations, the behavioral controls (usually overcontrol) are temporary and further acting out episodes are to be expected.

These persons most often are diagnosed as neurotic or character disorder.

48/84 Codes. This code is the most frequent among female outpatients (8.7 percent), and the eighth most common among male outpatients (5.2 percent). For both sexes it is much more common in persons younger than age 27. Scale 7, 6, 2, or 9 is most often the third highest scale for both sexes.

In adolescents, this code is particularly common and often reflects a moderate to severe adolescent adjustment reaction characterized by feelings of alienation, identity problems, rebelliousness, and delinquency. Nevertheless, the possibility of a schizoid or prepsychotic process must be strongly considered.

Adults with this code almost always show severe problems, usually diagnosed as schizoid personality disorder or psychotic reaction. The latter diagnosis is particularly likely with a 486 or 846 profile, usually reflecting paranoid schizophrenia. A high likelihood of asocial acting out is associated with 48/84 codes (particularly 486/846, 482/842, and 489/849). Persons with 48/84 codes are unpredictable, emotionally distant from others, and are peculiar in thought and action, most often in the sexual area. Nonconformity, impulsiveness, and lack of empathy are typically present. Their educational and occupational histories are characterized by underachievement, uneven performance, and marginal adjustment. Poor social judgment and subtle communication problems are characteristic.

Historically, these people typically experienced intense family conflict. Many of these patients established an attitude of distrust toward the world quite early in life. As children, they learned to view others as hostile, rejecting, and dangerous. They also learned, however, that (in addition to withdrawal) they could protect themselves, and alleviate somewhat their painful anticipations of hurt and rejection, by striking out first in anger and rebellion. When this angry and rebellious attitude continues into adulthood, their social behavior continually causes alienation from others, which then leads to further feelings of rejection and hurt.

In some of these people, nomadism, social isolation, or even underworld membership is present. Crimes committed by persons with this profile (particularly when 6 and 9 are also elevated) are often senseless, poorly planned, or poorly carried out, and may include some of the most vicious and savage forms of sexual and homicidal attack.

Women with 48/84 profiles often have had out-of-wedlock pregnancies, and also have a history of forming relationships with men inferior to them who are "social losers." These women have low self-concepts and seem most comfortable with those who they feel are "no good." They fear emotional involvement and prefer to relate to others only sexually. Men with 48/84 profiles are more likely to act out in criminal fashion. Older males are likely to be sexual deviates. Often their acting out is self-defeating to the point of self-punishment. It is as though they often do things that seem to ensure that they will get caught.

Diagnostically, adult psychiatric patients are most often classified as schizoid personality disorder, prepsychotic, or psychotic reactions, mostly schizophrenic or paranoid.

48/84 with Low 2 and High F. Usually an aggressive, punitive person who likes to inspire anxiety and guilt in others. These people often drift into roles where such behavior is sanctioned, such as law enforcers, school disciplinarians, and some clergymen. Many of them are subsequently diagnosed clinically as psychopaths. The behaviors associated with this code range all the way from stern, punitive, and cold disapproval to clinical sadism. When these individuals find themselves in situations in which their guilt/fear-provoking operations are blocked, they are likely to feel unprotected, anxious, and uncomfortable. Many individuals diagnozed clinically as sociopaths exhibit this configuration.

482/842/824 Codes. In addition to the 48/84 descriptions above. these people are in acute psychic distress, showing depression, anxiety, nervousness, and irritability. Suicide attempts are relatively common. They are somewhat less likely to be diagnosed as schizophrenic as compared with 486/846 and 489/849 profile persons. Schizoid and depressive features, however, are apparent.

Often these patients are single. If married, marital discord is highly likely, often with sexual conflicts and difficulties. These patients are afraid of emotional involvement with others, and are oversensitive to anything that can be construed as an emotional demand on them. They are distrustful of others and question their motivations. Parodoxically, these patients often have exaggerated needs for affection and attention.

Clinically, these patients are emotionally labile, and have feelings of guilt, inferiority, and hopelessness.

486/846 Codes. (See 468/648 codes.)

487/847 Codes. In addition to the 48/84 characteristics, these persons show somewhat greater inclinations toward obsessive introspection and concern about their impulses and actions. Withdrawal and autistic thinking are somewhat more frequent. A clear anxiety and guilt component probably will be apparent. Where scale 2 is also elevated, it should be helpful to see 482/842 code interpretations.

489/849 Codes. The addition of an elevated 9 to the 48/84 code implies a greater likelihood of acting out along with reduced impulse control (particularly if K is below T = 45). Behavioral agitation is often present. Assaultiveness and combativeness must be considered.

49/94 Codes. This code is common among outpatients (5.8 percent of males, 6.4 percent of females), particularly patients age 26 or less. For males, scale 8, 5, or 3 is most often the third highest. For females, scale 8, 3, or 6 is most often the third highest.

This code is commonly obtained by character disorders and by adolescents (both normal and abnormal). This code is almost always associated with impulsiveness, arousal-seeking, self-indulgence, resentment of limits (rules or regulations), and some form of acting out behavior. Inordinate pleasure seeking and need for excitement are also characteristics. Legal, family, and employment difficulties occur frequently for these people. The farther beyond age 20 the person is, the more enduring is the pattern and the more maladjustment is indicated. Such people often repeatedly get into trouble with their environment, either legally or in ways that damage their family's reputation.

Persons with 49/94 codes tend to be overactive, impulsive, irresponsible, untrustworthy, and shallow and superficial in their relationships with others. They characteristically have easy morals, fluctuating ethical values, and readily circumvented consciences. A high percentage of these patients engage in extra-marital relationships and many have very poor marital adjustment. Empathy for others is lacking. To satisfy their own desires and ambitions, they may expend great amounts of energy and effort, but find it difficult to stick to duties or responsibilities imposed by others. In such situations they are typically hostile and manipulative, often covered over by rationalizations. In superficial contacts and social situations they often create favorable impressions because of their energy, talkativeness, and freedom from inhibiting anxieties and insecurities. However, their lack of judgment and self-control may lead them to excessive drinking and socially inappropriate behavior, resulting in alienating others.

Diagnostically, psychoneurosis can be virtually ruled out, and encephalopathy is rare. This code is frequent among 16 and 17-year-olds in the general population, and is typical of delinquent boys. Over one third of the boys with this code engage in some delinquent acts. In inpatient settings, over half of such persons (excluding adolescents) are diagnosed psychotic, primarily manic or schizophrenic (the latter particularly with 498/948 profiles). Of the remainder, many are psychopaths or character disorders (particularly with 493/943 codes).

Prognosis is generally quite poor for this group, with many terminating treatment early against professional advice. They seem to lack the ability to learn from past experiences and lack the ability to delay gratification of their desires, thus having difficulty in maintaining sustained effort. In relationship therapy, these patients are typically overactive, irritable, and hostile.

49/94 with Low 2. When scale 2 is below 50, emotional lability is often characteristic in a cyclothymic fashion. Aggressive behaviors often occur episodically in an impulsive fashion.

49/94 with Low 0. These people, though possessing the above 49/94 characteristics, typically have a well-socialized veneer and often are glib. Subtle manipulation of others is more likely than overt acting out in directly hostile ways.

492, 495, 497, and 490 Codes. Manifestly delinquent behavior is less likely with these codes than with 498, 496, and (to a slightly lesser degree) 493 and 491 codes.

493/943 Codes. These people are particularly insightless concerning their stimulus value and their anger. Additionally, their acting out is likely to be less frequent and more passive-aggressive. Some, however, may store up anger, which then may suddenly be unleashed in ragelike behavior, usually on a family member (see 34/43 codes).

495/945 Codes. (See 45/54 codes.) The additional elevation of scale 5 is associated with either a person who is blatantly and defiantly homosexual, or with a person who is well educated and whose impulsiveness and rebelliousness are more socialized and better controlled. Often these people involve themselves in social causes, particularly when scales 4 and 9 are only moderately elevated and when scale 7 is also at or above T = 70.

496/946 and 498/948 Codes. These codes should raise serious concern about destructive, assaultive, and even homicidal behavior. Recommendation for hospitalization is wise in such cases. This pattern has been observed often in persons exhibiting sudden violence in bizarre ways. Usually they strongly feel they have been wronged or slighted. Their judgment is poor as are typically their controls (particularly true if *K* is low).

40/04 Codes. A rather rare code, particularly for males. Scale 2, 6, or 8 is most often the third highest scale. Persons with 40/04 codes have substantial anger, but do not typically express it openly, and have difficulty being appropriately assertive. Rather they are likely to be sullen and to hold grudge feelings. Further interpretation depends on the three-point code or other configural analysis (for example, high 4, low 5). It is often helpful to omit scale 0 in the three-point code and interpret the remaining two-point code as modified by an elevated scale 0.

Scale 5 (*Mf*)—60 Items

Scale 5 items have to do with interests, vocational choices, aesthetic preference, and an activity-passivity dimension. The same scale is used for both sexes and is merely scored backward for females. It was originally intended to measure masculinity-feminity but is clearly not a pure measure of this dimension; it is, for example, strongly correlated with education and intelligence, and interpretive statements should take this correlation into account.

An elevation of scale 5 is never in itself sufficient reason to diagnose homosexuality, overt or latent. Moreover, homosexuals who wish to conceal their inversions appear able to do so with relative ease insofar as this scale is concerned.

High 5 males in general reflect sophistication and aesthetic interest. Clear deviations (for example, T greater than 75), where education is less than 14 or there is restricted cultural exposure, suggest nonidentification with the culturally prescribed masculine role. High scores tend to be relatively passive men (particularly if scale 4 is low); some are definitely effeminate in manner.

These men are seen as imaginative, introspective, and tend to have a wide range of interests. They appear to be idealistic, inner-directed persons who may be seen as quite socially perceptive and sensitive to interpersonal interactions. Their interest patterns are quite different from those of the average male. In persons with a broad educational and cultural background, this is to be expected, and may reflect such characteristics as self-awareness, concern with social issues, and an ability to communicate ideas clearly and effectively. In some men, however, the same interest pattern may reflect a rejection of masculinity accompanied by a relatively passive, effeminate, noncompetitive personality.

Low 5 males (T below 45) are easygoing, adventurous, perhaps somewhat coarse, and tend to show interests in mechanics, sports, and outdoor activities. They prefer action to contemplation, and lack insight into their own motives out of apparent disinterest. They are self-indulgent, independent, and often narcissistic.

Low 5, high 4 males (see high 4, low 5 code) strongly suggest an element of compulsive masculinity. The individual's efforts to appear flamboyantly masculine are overdone and inflexible, such as an exhibitionistic display of physical strength and endurance. These represent attempts to reassure himself of his masculinity, power, and control. Not surprisingly, if such people enter treatment they usually have very disturbing questions concerning their own indentity and maleness. In adolescents this pattern of low 5, high 4 is often manifested in delinquency.

High 5 females (T above 70) tend to be vigorous, aggressive, dominating, and competitive. They engage in activities and occupations (for example, mechanical, scientific) that are traditionally male. These women are typically confident, spontaneous but somewhat inhibited in those areas of living in which heterosexual implications are present. However, they become anxious in situations in which they are expected to adopt a feminine sexual role. In a known lesbian, a high 5 suggests a "butch," as opposed to a "femme." Some elevation on 5 is normal in girls aged 14 to 19, but rare after this age. Elevated 5 may also occur in women from atypical cultural backgrounds or the lower social class.

A high 5, high 4 profile is found in women who are rebelling against the traditional female role. Generally speaking, the high 5 woman's behavior becomes more clearly deviant with increasing elevation on 4.

Low 5 females (T below 45) are passive, submissive, modest, yielding, and demure—sometimes to the point of representing living caricatures of the feminine stereotype. They are typically concerned with presenting a neat, attractive, feminine appearance in their dress. Women who achieve extremely low T scores (below 40) are usually emotionally highly constricted. They assume burdens to an almost masochistic degree in a martyrlike fashion. Often they are, additionally, self-pitying and fault-finding in a "Jewish mother" way. They seem unable to tolerate pleasant experiences. Sexual dissatisfaction and frigidity are common, as are headaches. They often manipulate men via sex, guilt, or passiveness-aggressiveness.

Low 5, high 4 females are hostile, angry women. Most often they are particularly angry at men, and have a history of problems in heterosexual relationships. However, they are unable to express such feelings directly. Instead, they resort to various masochistic operations that provoke others to anger and rage, often then taking satisfaction in pitying themselves because they have been mistreated. There is often an accompanying elevation on 6, which reflects the degree to which the transfer of blame elements in this pattern becomes involved in a generalized paranoid posture. These women are often extremely adroit in eliciting rage, and this is likely to create special problems in therapeutic management.

51/15 Code. (See 15/51 code.)

52/25 Code. (See 25/52 code.)

527 and 5274 Codes (Male); 27, Low 5 and 274, Low 5 (Female) Codes. These people chronically present themselves to others as weak, inferior, guilty, and submissive. They are markedly self-effacing, shun any outward appearance of strength or pride, invite others to be patronizingly superior and deprecating, and appear to feel least uncomfortable when they are receiving such treatment. Ambivalence, immobility, and a sense of failure are characteristic. The clinical extreme of this form of behavior is the psychotic depressive reaction.

53/35 Codes. (See 35/53 codes.)

54 Codes for Males. (See 45/54 code types.)

56/65 Codes. Temporarily omit scale 5 and interpret the three-point code (for example, 564/654) as though a two-point code (for example, 46/64), subsequently adding the interpretation as an elevated scale 5.

57/75 Codes. Males with this pattern typically are highly inner-directed and introspective, and often are prone to depressive or anxious episodes. In persons of less than college education, this code is more likely to represent depression, anxiety, and obsessive rumination over self-inadequacies. Females with this code tend to be less overtly aggressive than would be expected just from a high 5 code. Heterosexual difficulties are somewhat more likely, often in the sense of intellectual competitiveness.

For both sexes the above interpretations should be modified and/or enhanced by considering the two-point code that results when scale 5 is omitted from the three-point code (for example, 572 should be interpreted as a 72 code).

58/85 Code. For both sexes, this code is best interpreted by temporarily omitting scale 5 and interpreting the three-point code (for example, 584/854) as a two-point code (for example, 48/84), subsequently adding the interpretation of an elevated scale 5.

59/95 Code. For males, the presence of the elevated scale 5 in this code reduces the likelihood of overt behavioral acting out, probably due to increased use of intellectualization type defenses. College students with a 59 low 0 pattern often have problems relating to a mother conflict.

For females, the elevated scale 5 probably increases the likelihood of overt aggressiveness, though whether such aggressiveness would be primarily verbal or behavioral depends on other factors. These women are likely to be irritable, competitive (particularly with men), and energetic. Initially, however, they are likely to be seen as confident, spontaneous, and uninhibited, though perhaps self-centered.

For both sexes further information is derivable by omitting scale 5 and examining the three-point code (for example, 594/954) as a two-point code (for example, 49/94).

50/05 Codes. Males with this code typically are particularly introverted, withdrawn, and anxious in their contacts with other people. They have many doubts about their adequacy, and have difficulty in being assertive. Often they reduce their overt anxiety by withdrawal and use of intellectualization in an attempt to remove emotional nuances. Difficulties and discomfort in heterosexual relations are common.

Females with this code typically are much less confident, spontaneous, vigorous, or aggressive than would ordinarily be expected from the high scale 5. Often these women have less education or are from lower or rural social background.

For both sexes further interpretation should be done by temporarily omitting scale 5 and examining the three-point code (for example, 507/570) as a two-point code (for example, 07/70).

Scale 6 (*Pa* –40 Items)

Scale 6 items tap such processes as sensitivity, being easily hurt, moral virtue, rationality, denial of suspiciousness, and complaints about others' shortcomings. This is one of the poorer MMPI scales from the viewpoint of performing its intended function of detecting paranoid thinking. Many clinically extreme paranoids show no elevation at all. However, persons with definite elevations on scale 6 almost always show hypersensitivity and have paranoid ideation, if not frank delusions. To a lesser extent, paranoid ideation occurs in persons with extremely low scores on scale 6 (T less than 40). The latter apparently are identified by virtue of being too cautious in what they say about themselves.

Scale 6 decreases slightly with increasing age, and is moderately correlated (approximately .45) with scales 8 and 4.

High 6 scorers (T above 80) virtually always indicate paranoid persons who are suspicious and brooding, harbor grudges, and usually feel in some way that they are not getting what is coming to them. In treatment, such persons are rigid and rationalistically argumentative. With a high 6, it is useful to examine the person's responses to individual scale items to differentiate general characterological paranoia from the presence of clearly delusional thinking.

Moderate elevation on 6 (T = 60 to 75) occurs in people with undue interpersonal sensitivity. This is often associated with a depressive reaction, and these people take too seriously the criticisms or remarks of others. Often they also feel pressed by their job or social obligations. These persons adopt an intropunitive role outwardly, but express hostility by arranging events where others are victimized (the "What did I do wrong?" syndrome).

Low 6 scores (T less than 40) tend to be stubborn, evasive, and wary, often feeling that dire consequences will follow upon their revealing themselves in any way. There may be, then, little essential difference between high and low scores on 6; this, of course, leaves unexplained why they differ in their responses to the items on this particular scale.

62/26 Codes. (See 26/62 codes.)

63/36 Codes. (See 36/63 codes.)

64/46 Codes. (See 46/64 codes, 462/642 codes, and 468/648 codes.)

65/56 Codes. (See 56/65 codes.)

67/76 Codes. This code is rather infrequent among outpatients for both sexes. Most often, scale 2 or 8 is the third highest scale in this code.

These patients are tense, anxious, and overly ruminative. They are hypersensitive, suspicious, and broodingly resentful. Though typically having severe underlying guilt, they project their problems onto others, often to the point of paranoid delusions. These persons brood about real or imagined wrongs, and typically have a history of disrupted interpersonal relationships that they have found quite dissatisfying (usually due to their misinterpretation). Diagnostically, these persons are often decompensating obsessive-compulsives. When scale 6 is higher than scale 7, blatant psychosis (most likely paranoid schizophrenia) is suggested.

68/86 Codes. This code is more commonly encountered in patients younger than age 26 and in persons with less than a high school education. Most often, scale 7 or 4 is the third highest scale with this code.

68/86 codes above T = 75 suggest paranoid schizophrenia unless clinically-behaviorally proved otherwise. Even when several other scales are more elevated than scales 6 and 8, the possibility of underlying paranoid schizophrenia must be considered when scales 6 and 8 are more than 10 T score points above scale 7 (called the "paranoid valley"). Note: When scales 6 and 8 are above T = 80, the *F* scale is often also elevated but does not necessarily represent an invalid profile.

These patients are usually acutely schizophrenic or preschizophrenic, typically with paranoid delusions. Depression, emotional inappropriateness, overideation, and fears or phobias often are present. These people spend much time in daydreams, are shy and anxious, and keep others at a distance. They show difficulty in concentrating, and their thinking is often autistic. The content of their thoughts is almost always unusual and unconventional. Suspicion, distrust, and grandiosity are typical. Behaviorally, these patients are often unpredictable.

These patients usually are single. Most have inner conflicts about sexuality. If married, the partner is likely to be emotionally deviant. Surprisingly, patients with this profile may show a history of reasonably adequate ability to work. though just prior to the onset of psychosis they were unable to function due to fatigue and inefficiency. In many cases no clear precipitating event is apparent.

Diagnostically, a majority are paranoid schizophrenic (particularly 684/864 profiles) or paranoid state. A minority reflect an organic brain syndrome or severely neurotic (particularly 687/867 codes).

69/96 Codes. This relatively uncommon code occurs most frequently among female patients. For both sexes, scale 4 or 8 is most often the third highest scale.

These patients are irritable, tense, jumpy, and often overreact to minor frustrations as though they were emergencies or were dangerous personal threats to them. Their symptoms include perplexity, difficulties in thinking and concentrating, and irritability, perhaps even to the point of violence. A manic, grandiose pattern is often evident.

These patients fear emotional involvement and keep others at a distance. They are highly oversensitive to criticism, either open or implied. They often have a pervasive suspiciousness and distrust, perhaps even ideas of reference (particularly if scale 8 is also elevated). In seeming contradiction, these patients often have an exaggerated need for affection. Family history may also reveal an overprotecting, affectionate mother who disciplined strictly, while the father was typically permissive.

Diagnostically, most often these persons are acutely psychotic, typically paranoid schizophrenic. Only occasionally are they diagnosed as neurotic.

694/964 Codes. These persons are likely to react to frustration with anger and violence. They have histories of social, family, and occupational disruptions, usually stemming from their hostility, poor judgment, and poor emotional control. Lack of insight is striking, and projection of blame onto others is typical. An assaultive, combative, or even homicidal potential must be carefully considered.

698/968 Codes. In addition to the above descriptions of 69/96 code persons, these patients are particularly likely to show mental perplexity and difficulties in thinking and concentrating. Tangential or loose associations are common, as are delusions and hallucinations. Paranoid suspiciousness, projection, and delusions are typical. Often these patients have severe inner conflicts about sexuality.

Almost all of these patients are diagnosed as schizophrenic, paranoid type.

60/06 Codes. This code is extremely rare for males and uncommon for females. For females, it is more common in patients older than 28, and most frequently is associated with scale 2 or 4 as the third highest scale. Though little is known about this two-point code, persons obtaining it appear to be shy, withdrawn, and socially uncomfortable. They are particularly sensitive to criticism, and tend to expect that others will not like or accept them. Typically, these people are highly conforming and exercise much self-control.

Scale 7 (*Pt*—48 Items)

Scale 7 items relate to anxiety symptoms, irrational fears, and self-devaluation, and is a general measure of anxiety, guilt, and ruminative self-doubt. High scorers tend to be obsessionally worried, tense, indecisive, and unable to concentrate. Low scorers are usually independent, relaxed, self-confident, and secure. Scale 7 correlates highly (approximately .80) with scale 8 and moderately (approximately .60) with scale 2. Scale 7 also correlates negatively to a moderate degree (approximately -.60) with *K*.

Individuals having marked elevations on this scale almost always exhibit extreme obsessionalism, but this must be differentiated from the so-called compulsive defense system. Many rigidly compulsive people show no elevation at all, presumably because their rigid organization wards off any feelings of insecurity, concern about their own worth, and so on, (that is, their obsessive-compulsive style works).

71/17 Codes. (See 17/71 codes.)

72/27 Codes. (See 27/72 codes.)

73/37 Codes. (See 37/73 codes.)

74/47 Codes. (See 47/74 codes.)

75/57 Codes. (See 57/75 codes.)

76/67 Codes. (See 67/76 codes.)

78/87 Codes. This code is a frequent one among psychiatric patients, particularly among males. For both sexes, it is more frequent among persons below age 27, and scale 2 or 4 is most often the third highest scale (see 278/728 and 478/748 codes).

Persons with 78/87 codes are evenly divided between psychotics and neurotics. When scale 8 is higher than scale 7, the likelihood of acute psychosis is greater. Patients with 78/87 codes show notable psychic distress characterized by anxiety, worry, and difficulties in concentrating or thinking efficiently. They are shy, socially uncomfortable, fearful, and lacking in confidence. Inferiority feelings and guilt feelings, particularly concerning sex, are likely. Typically, they feel inadequate in heterosexual relations, and poor sexual performance due to anxiety often occurs. Though typically conscientious, their fears and excessive worry typically lead them to have only mediocre or poor achievement. These persons may drink excessively in an attempt ro relax.

Insomnia and suicide attempts are common. When scale 8 is higher than 7, these suicide attempts are often bizarre, involving self-mutilation or punishment.

Modal Diagnosis: 782, depressive neurosis, obsessive-compulsive neurosis; 872, schizophrenic reaction; 784/874, schizophrenic reaction, schizoid personality disorder.

79/97 Codes. This relatively uncommon code is most often associated with scale 8 or 4 as the third highest scale.

Such patients are anxious often to the point of agitation. They are fearful, worry a great deal, and find it difficult to relax or to rid themselves of recurrent (almost constant) thinking about their fears. They tend to be self-centered and often immature, and many have periods of impulsive, inconsiderate behavior, which may cause difficulties in interpersonal relations.

Depression is usually present in patients with this code, particularly if scale 2 is also elevated (T above 70). Nevertheless, tension and agitated anxiety typically dominate the clinical picture, and the patient is likely to show symptoms such as backaches, muscle spasms, and insomnia.

70/07 Codes. This code is uncommon, particularly for male patients. Female patients most often show scale 2 or 8 as the third highest scale, while males typically have scale 5, 2, or 8 as the third highest.

Males with 70/07 codes are depressed, unhappy, tense, worry a great deal, have insomnia, and feel confused. They are generally introverted and shy, often to the point of being almost nonverbal. They are markedly indecisive, and have strong home life conflicts centering around their mothers and siblings. They lack social skills, particularly with the opposite sex. They typically lack a sense of accomplishment.

Females with this code show the same pattern as for men only if scale 5 is coded low. Otherwise, their problems are of less severe proportions centering around social insecurity, self-consciousness, lack of confidence, and difficulties in establishing relations with the opposite sex.

Scale 8 (*Sc*–78 Items)

Scale 8 items deal with social alienation, isolation, complaints of family alienation, bizarre feelings, influence of external agents, peculiar bodily dysfunctions, and general dissatisfaction. Scale 8 correlates highly with scale 7 (approximately .80) and moderately (approximately .55) with scales 4, *F*, and 2.

Caution: Do not interpret scale 8 too narrowly. It was developed on schizophrenic individuals and is valuable in the diagnosis of schizophrenic reactions. But a limited conception of this important scale will needlessly restrict its usefulness and, with extreme elevations, may promote an incorrect diagnosis of schizophrenia.

Note: The patients who are clinically most schizophrenic get T scores in the 80 to 90 range. Agitated neurotics, prepsychotics, and so-called pseudoneurotic schizophrenics score highest on 8.

High 8 persons almost always feel alienated, misunderstood, and not a part of the general social environment. They have fundamental and disturbing questions about their own identity, worth, and place in the world. They are confused about how one goes about the business of being a socialized human being. Many feel that they hopelessly lack something basic that is the key to successful relations with others.

Among high 8s are many painfully withdrawn people with little or no social relationships and who occupy themselves excessively with private autistic fantasy. A high score on 8 makes the prognosis for short-term psychotherapy relatively poor. Even with moderate elevations, there is usually some difficulty in thinking and communication. These people seem to be in contact and seem to be talking sense, but one is vaguely aware of not really understanding very well what it is they are saying. They appear habitually to avoid making direct, unequivocal statements.

Low 8 persons often are compliant and overly accepting of authority. They tend to have a very practical orientation, and usually are controlled and restrained, but friendly and adaptable.

89/98 Codes. This code occurs more frequently in patients younger than 27. Most often scale 4, 7, or 6 is the third highest scale.

These persons spend a great deal of time in fantasy and daydreams, are ruminative and overideational. They are fearful of, and avoid, close interpersonal relationships, and usually are suspicious and distrustful of others' motives. In interpersonal relations, such as therapeutic interviews, they often are highly distractable, jumping from topic to topic. This prevents others from getting to know them, but also hinders therapeutic focusing on any one issue long enough to come to grips with it. In the extreme, these persons may be disoriented, perplexed, negativistic, and suspicious. Delusions and hallucinations (particularly of a religious nature) are common, as are tension, agitation, and insomnia. They are particularly likely to disorganize under stress. These patients often show a history of high achievement aspirations but mediocre achievement. Educational and social difficulties are likely.

Diagnostically, the majority are psychotic, usually schizophrenic (particularly schizo-affective or excited catatonic). Encephalopathy must also be considered, particularly when scale 1 is also elevated beyond T = 70.

80/08 Codes. This code is three times more frequent for female patients than for males, even though it is rather uncommon for either sex. For both sexes, scale 7 or 2 is most often the third highest scale.

Persons with 80/08 codes are markedly withdrawn socially and avoid interpersonal relationships. They tend to be aloof, withdrawn, and anxious in their relationships with others, and feel alienated even from their own families. Much time is usually spent in personal fantasy. Typically, they also feel depressed, anxious, and misunderstood by others. They often feel confused about what is bothering them or what they want (or expect) from others. Insomnia may also be present. The amount of pathology indicated by this code appears somewhat greater for men than for women. Probable diagnosis: schizoid personality.

Scale 9 (*Ma*–46 Items)

Scale 9 items generally concern expansiveness, energy level, egotism, and irritability.

High scorers are energetic, expansive, generally outgoing, and uninhibited. They tend to become easily offended, however, and may be seen as tense and hyperactive. Many of these people have an unusual capacity for sustained activity and effort. T above 70 suggests maladaptive hyperactivity, grandiosity, verbosity, irritability, and insufficient inhibitory capacity. Often this is an attempt to stave off an impending depression (particularly if scale 2 is below T = 45). T scores in the range of 55 to 70 suggest a pleasant, outgoing temperament. Typically such persons are balanced, independent, and able to mobilize their resources effectively. They usually emphasize achievement as a means of gaining status and recognition.

Low scorers (T below 45) exhibit a low energy level, listlessness, apathy, and lack of drive; almost always they are lacking in self-confidence and a normal degree of optimism regarding the future. Typically, they find it very difficult to get out of bed in the morning. A very low score on 9 suggests serious depression even when scale 2 is not markedly elevated. It should be noted that low scale 9 scores increasingly occur as patients get older. A low 9 in a younger patient (age 35 or less) is very unusual and should receive extra attention.

91/19 Codes. (See 19/91 codes.)

92/29 Codes. (See 29/92 codes.)

93/39 Codes. (See 39/93 codes.)

94/49 Codes. (See 49/94 codes.)

95/59 Codes. (See 59/95 codes.)

96/69 Codes. (See 69/96 codes.)

97/79 codes. (See 79/97 codes.)

98/89 Codes. (See 89/98 codes.)

90/09 Codes. This code is rare, but is more common among female patients than among males. It does not appear to be associated with any particular scale as the third highest point, nor does it appear to be associated with age or education. Beyond this, little is known about this code. Perhaps the most likely interpretation is that the person, though basically shy and withdrawn, is attempting to ward off depression through use of manic defenses. Often it is helpful to ignore initially scale 0 in this instance and to examine the next two most elevated scales (for example, interpret 094 as though it were 94), and then use the elevated scale 0 to modify the interpretation, if necessary.

9-K Code. High 9, high *K* (T above 60), low 2 (T = 40 to 50) types are managerial, autocratic, power-oriented individuals whose compulsive energy and planful organization provoke a somewhat overwhelmed deference and submission in others. These people often make excellent administrators, possibly because ambiguity, uncertainty, and indecision are intolerable to them. They insist upon being informed and feel most uncomfortable in situations in which they are not. As might be expected, they do not as a rule respond productively to the typical psychotherapeutic situation.

High 9, low *K* (T below 45), low 2 (T = 40 to 50) types suggest competitive personalities. These individuals are insecure and organize their lives around competitive self-enhancement and tend to be extremely threatened whenever submissiveness or dependence is expected of them. They depend for their self-esteem on demonstrations of weakness in others and strength in themselves, and they exact a grudging, envious submission and respect from those with whom they interact. In women, one often sees an exhibitionistic emphasis on physical attractiveness, particularly if scale 5 is below T = 40. If such a person enters psychotherapy, the therapist may be treated to endless—and often quite fascinating—orgies of self-display, but the chances of a successful therapeutic outcome are poor.

Scale 0 (*Si*–70 Items)

This differs from the other nine scales in that the criteria do not involve a psychiatric syndrome. The items deal mainly with social participation, and this scale provides a quite useful index of behavior patterns and comfort in interpersonal relationships.

High scorers (T above 65) tend to be withdrawn, aloof, and anxious in contact with people. scores above 70 will, on rare occasions, identify a schizoid factor in well-controlled, socialized, prepsychotic personalities when this is missed by other scales. High scorers are typically quite aware of their social discomfort, and have feelings of personal inferiority. Elevated scores suggest a general absence of social supports for the person, an absence that should be considered in evaluating the clinical significance of other aspects of the profile.

Low scorers on 0 (T less than 45) are sociable, warm people who are active, assertive, and involved with groups. They are typically enthusiastic and outgoing. These characteristics, however, may cause others to see them as impulsive, immature, and as acting without sufficient forethought. Likewise, their competitiveness, persuasiveness, and social aggressiveness may cause others to see them as opportunistic and manipulative. Extremely low scores (T less than 35) suggest a flightiness and superficiality of relationships; these "hail-fellow-well-met" individuals have well-developed social techniques and very many social contacts, but they do not establish relationships of real intimacy.

Low scores on 0 (T below 50) typically reduce the pathology suggested by a patient's elevated scale scores. A low 0 indicates a social competence and adaptiveness, and suggests that the person may have found socially acceptable outlets for most pathological behavior.

01/10 Codes. (See 10/01 codes.)

02/20 Codes. (See 20/02 codes.)

03/30 Codes. (See 30/03 codes.)

04/40 Codes. (See 40/04 codes.)

05/50 Codes. (See 50/05 codes.)

06/60 Codes. (See 60/06 codes.)

07/70 Codes. (See 70/07 codes.)

08/80 Codes. (See 80/08 codes.)

09/90 Codes. (See 90/09 codes.)

Normal Code with Hi *K*

This configuration assumes that no clinical scale is above 70, that six or more clinical scales are below 60, that *F* is below 60, that *L* and *K* are greater than *F*, and that *K* is greater than *F* by 5 T score points.

When this configuration is obtained from a patient (particularly a psychiatric inpatient), it is often produced by one who is highly defensive about admitting psychological problems, because they are viewed as weaknesses. These patients avoid situations where their own performance will be inferior to that of others. Interestingly, however, they often are submissive and easily dominated by others, suggestible, and overly responsive to others' evaluations. They are also shy, anxious and inhibited, usually above average in intelligence, and with some college education. Further clinical interpretation can often be obtained by looking at the *F-K* index interpretation, as well as the interpretations of the *L* scores, *K* scores, and low-point scores.

REFERENCES

Carkhuff, R. R., L. Barnett, and J. N. McCall. 1965. *The Counselor's Handbook: Scale and Profile Interpretations of the MMPI*. Urbana, Ill.: R. W. Parkinson and Associates.

Carson, R. C. 1960. "An Introduction to MMPI Interpretation." Durham, N.C.: Duke University. Mimeographed.

Dahlstrom, W. G., G. S. Welsh, and L. E. Dahlstrom. 1975. *An MMPI Handbook. Vol. 2: Research Applications*. Minneapolis: University of Minnesota Press.

—— .1972. *An MMPI Handbook. Vol. 10: Clinical Interpretation*. Minneapolis: University of Minnesota Press.

Drake, L. E., and E. R. Oetting. 1959. *An MMPI Codebook for Counselors*. Minneapolis: University of Minnesota Press.

Fowler, R. D. 1966. *The MMPI Notebook: A Guide to the Clinical Use of the Automated MMPI*. Nutley, N.J.: Roche Psychiatric Service Institute.

Gilberstadt, H., and J. Duker. 1965. *A Handbook for Clinical and Actuarial MMPI Inpterpretation*. Philadelphia: Saunders.

Hovey, H. B., and E. G. Lewis. 1967. "Semiautomatic Interpretation of the MMPI." *Journal of Clinical Psychology* 23: 123–34.

Lachar, D. 1974. *The MMPI: Clinical Assessment and Automated Interpretation.* Los Angeles: Western Psychological Services.

Marks, P. A., and W. Seeman. 1963. *The Actuarial Description of Personality: An Atlas for Use with the MMPI.* Baltimore: Williams & Wilkins.

Marks, P. A., W. Seeman, and D. L. Haller. *The Actuarial Use of the MMPI with Adolescents and Adults.* Baltimore: Williams and Wilkins, 1974.

Swenson, W. M., J. S. Pearson, and D. Osborne. 1973. *An MMPI Source Book. Basic Item, Scale and Pattern Data on 50,000 Medical Patients.* Minneapolis: University of Minnesota Press.

Van de Riet, V. V., and W. D. Wolking. 1969. "Interpretive Hypotheses for the MMPI." Gainesville: University of Florida Medical Center. Mimeographed.

Webb, J. T. 1970. "The Relation of MMPI Two-Point Codes to Age, Sex and Education Level in a Representative Nationwide Sample of Psychiatric Outpatients." Paper presented at the Southeastern Psychological Association convention, Louisville, Ky., April 25.

2/ THE MMPI AND NEUROLOGICAL DYSFUNCTION

James L. Mack

The purpose of this chapter is to provide a comprehensive review of the research concerning the personality adjustment of brain-damaged subjects as measured by the MMPI. It is somewhat surprising, in view of the extensive literature that has accumulated on the MMPI, that no such review has yet been offered. Several short summaries have been presented within the contexts of personality adjustment and cerebral localization (Meier 1969), physiological bases of psychopathology (Reitan 1976), and the psychological effects of epilepsy (Hermann 1977). No one, however, has attempted to draw together the widely divergent approaches to the use of the MMPI in the study of patients with neurological dysfunction in order to give some focus to an increasing body of information. This chapter attempts to provide that focus, while compiling within one source the burden of the information thus far accumulated.

Perhaps the simplest and most straightforward introduction is to examine the MMPIs of a heterogeneous group of brain-damaged individuals to determine to what extent they tend to differ from the Minnesota standardization group. A great deal of information is available from early studies of MMPI responses by a wide variety of subjects. When the frequency of two-point code types of a group of 202 male and 206 female Minnesota neurological inpatients is compared with that of the Minnesota normal group, there is little correspondence; 13, 31, 12, 21, 23, 27, 28, 82, and 24 code types make up 47.3 percent of the male and 38.5 percent of the female neurological samples and only 11.4 percent and 16.5 percent of the male and female normal samples, respectively (Dahlstrom, Welsh, and Dahlstrom 1972, pp. 443–44). Results from several studies of brain-damaged subjects (Reitan 1955; Lezak and Glaudin 1969) have reported relatively high mean scores on the *Hs*, *D*, *Hy*, *Pt*, and *Sc* scales, findings consistent with the code types reported above. The applicability of the MMPI to brain-damaged patients, however, has been questioned. Krug (1967), using the Group Form of the test, found that brain-damaged subjects were inconsistent in responding to the 16 duplicated items. Yet the meaning of such "inconsistency," or even the best means of evaluating it, are far from clear (see discussion in Dahlstrom, Welsh, and Dahlstrom 1972, p. 141). Certainly the consistency of scale elevations across a wide variety of brain-damaged groups, which will become apparent as this review progresses, makes it difficult to argue that results are due to responding at the level of chance.

Perhaps a more serious issue has been raised by Lezak and Glaudin (1969), who suggested that the item content relevant to neurological problems is most frequent on the *Sc*, *Hs*, *D*, and *Hy* scales and that the typical interpretations given to such scales may not be entirely appropriate in a neurologically impaired group. While this objection has received relatively little attention in the literature, Baldwin (1952) eliminated 12 MMPI items judged by neurologists as most likely to be influenced by having multiple sclerosis and found little effect on reducing the high mean scores on the *Hs*, *D*, *Hy*, *Pt*, and *Sc* scales obtained by these patients. The application of an abbreviated MMPI, the Mini-Mult (Kincannon 1968), to a neurological population also has proved futile because individual patients do not appear to be accurately classified (Huisman 1974; Pantano and Schwartz 1978).

MMPI studies of patients with neurological dysfunction have broadly demonstrated two basic research strategies. In the first, the MMPI has been treated as an independent variable and evaluated as a predictor of diagnostic category. The second approach has consisted of treating the neurological status of the subject as the independent variable and using the MMPI to evaluate the effects of various neurological factors on personality adjustment.

THE MMPI AS INDEPENDENT VARIABLE: USING THE MMPI IN THE DIFFERENTIAL DIAGNOSIS OF BRAIN DAMAGE

Studies using the MMPI as an independent variable to predict the presence of brain damage have been of considerable interest and have generally been directed toward the use of the MMPI as a screening instrument in the identification of brain-damaged patients within a general medical setting or as a means of differentiating between neurological and psychiatric subjects who initially present with neurological complaints. Perhaps because of the findings described above indicating the extent to which neurological patients are likely to produce elevated clinical profiles, many studies have attempted to develop predictor scales to identify brain damage.

Hovey (1964) described a five-item scale that he found to discriminate between brain-damaged and nonbrain-damaged patients. Several studies have failed to cross-validate Hovey's findings in similar populations, however (Weingold, Dawson, and Kael 1965; Jortner 1965). Hovey (1965) has suggested that administering the scale prior to the diagnosis being established may be a critical factor in determining whether or not the scale classifies subjects with satisfactory accuracy. He subsequently replicated Jortner's study with more favorable results, reporting that 67 percent of patients were correctly diagnosed. Although only 36 percent of 39 patients with mixed types of brain damage were identified, nonbrain-damaged subjects and patients with multiple sclerosis were classified far more accurately (Hovey 1967). Parkinson's disease patients showed significantly higher scores on the scale than did matched nonbrain-damaged controls (Marsh 1972). Zimmerman (1965) found the scale to be effective in identifying severely impaired patients with long-standing traumatic head injuries and suggested that the scale may reflect the more permanent, residual effects of brain lesions. On the other hand, Black (1974) found the scale failed to identify a young group of patients with recent traumatic head injuries.

Several investigators have applied the scale in the differentiation of brain-damaged subjects from those who presented with neurological symptoms but were found to have psychiatric problems only (Maier and Abidin 1967; Dodge and Kolstoe 1971; Schwartz and Brown 1973) or from general psychiatric patients (Upper and Seeman 1968; Siskind 1976). While these authors occasionally found significant differences between the two types of patients (Upper and Seeman 1968; Siskind 1976), they were unanimous in reporting that the accuracy of classification was too low to be of use in the diagnosis of individual patients.

In general, the results suggest that Hovey's five-item scale produces low rates of false positives, as normals usually obtain low scores but many brain-damaged patients may be missed. Furthermore, there seems to be little justification for using the scale to distinguish brain-damaged patients who present with neurological symptoms from nonbrain-damaged patients with neurological symptoms.

Watson (1971) reviewed a number of studies of his own and others, and suggested that while ability tests have proved to be of limited value in discriminating brain-damaged patients from those with severe psychiatric problems such as schizophrenia, personality tests may be useful for such purposes. In a carefully cross-validated study he developed three MMPI scales, varying only in their length and in the extent to which particularly discriminating items were weighted, that significantly differentiated brain-damaged from schizophrenic males. Application of the scales to female subjects, however, afforded negative results.

Subsequent investigators have confirmed Watson's findings when his Sc-O (schizophrenia-organic) scales were administered to male patients with either brain damage or schizophrenia but not both (Neuringer, Dombrowski, and Goldstein 1975; Holland, Lowenfeld, and Wadsworth 1975). Among the three Sc-O scales, the long unweighted form has been found to provide the most accurate classification of subjects (Watson 1971; Neuringer, Dombrowski; and Goldstein 1975).

Watson was careful to emphasize that the scale seemed to reflect general psychopathology and was not designed to discriminate male schizophrenics who were brain damaged from those who were not. This admonition has proved justified in that two studies in which such a differentiation was attempted reported negative results (Holland, Lowenfeld, and Wadsworth 1975; Halperin et al. 1977). The belief that the scale identifies schizophrenics by their endorsement of psychopathological items was directly confirmed by a report that the standard *Sc* clinical scale differentiated schizophrenics from brain-damaged subjects as accurately as did the Sc-O scale (Ayers, Templer, and Ruff 1975).

Watson (1973) subsequently combined the scale with the Benton Visual Retention Test to develop a bivariate screening technique for discriminating brain-damaged patients from a wider range of psychiatric problems. He found that a regression equation that included both tests provided the highest accuracy in differentiating process schizophrenics from brain-damaged subjects, but the separation of the brain-damaged from reactive schizophrenics, affective psychotics, neurotics, character disorders, and alcoholics was best achieved by the Benton alone. These results have not been cross-validated, but have led Watson (1973) to suggest that ability-oriented tests may be more useful than the MMPI in distinguishing the effects of brain damage from less severe psychiatric difficulties, while the MMPI might best be used in the separation of severely disturbed psychiatric patients from the brain damaged.

Watson, prolific in his efforts to differentiate brain-damaged subjects from schizophrenics, also studied the use of several simple configural rules and reported the results of applying four signs to this discrimination problems. His fourth sign, an additive formula combining the raw scores of five clinical scales $(D + Mf + Sc - Pd - Ma)$ with a score of 40 or greater indicating schizophrenia, proved most accurate in several cross-validations, but, once again, the OSI (organic sign index) was useless with females (Watson and Thomas 1968). A failure of cross-validation was reported with young patients with recent traumatic head injuries (who had a mean profile code of 821'73496–50:); their mean OSI score was 42, within the schizophrenic range (Black 1974).

A further attempt to develop a simple configural sign for differentiating brain-damaged from general psychiatric patients was implemented by examining all possible additive and subtractive combinations of two clinical scales, using *K*-corrected T scores (Watson, Plemel, and Jacobs 1978). After several cross-validations, the *Hs* – *Pt* index showed the most promise. When *Hs* exceeded *Pt* by 10 or more T scores, it was likely that the patient was brain damaged; if *Pt* exceeded *Hs* by more than 15 T scores, the patient was quite likely to be schizophrenic. Differences within the +9 to –15 range were indeterminate. It should be noted that cross-validation was conducted with a number of psychiatric groups but only a single contrasted neurological group. The authors were careful to stipulate that as different neurological groups may produce different MMPI patterns, other MMPI signs may be necessary for their identification.

In basic MMPI sources two code types, 92 (Hathaway and Meehl 1951) and 139 (Gilberstadt and Duker 1965), have been associated with the diagnosis of brain damage, but independent attempts to validate these code types in the diagnosis of brain damage have proved fruitless (Schwartz 1969; Russell 1977).

Neither of these codes has been found to appear with sufficient frequency in either neurological or nonbrain-damaged populations to be of diagnostic utility.

Another configural key has been developed for the separation of brain-damaged and schizophrenic patients, based on sequential decision rules utilizing T scores on the three validity scales and *Sc* (Russell 1975). Cross-validation showed the key to be as accurate as the results of Watson and his associates. It appears that no difficulty was encountered with female subjects, although the data were not analyzed separately for each sex (Russell 1975). In a subsequent study Russell (1977) found the *Sc* T score alone, using a cutting score of 80 or greater, differentiated schizophrenics and brain-damaged patients as accurately as his key (Russell 1975). However, the accuracy of this simpler procedure was slightly reduced in a cross-validation sample. Russell (1977) reported the mean clinical profiles of his groups to be quite distinct, with the schizophrenics significantly higher than the brain damaged on the *F, D, Pd, Mf, Pa, Pt, Sc,* and *Si* scales and significantly lower on *K*.

The reports that schizophrenic profiles are likely to be considerably more pathological than those of brain-damaged nonschizophrenics and that special keys achieve their accuracy by simply measuring psychopathology raise serious questions about the need for the proliferation of special scales or signs to discriminate these two groups. In this context it is worth noting that Watson, Davis, and Gasser (1978), comparing the use of ability tests and personality tests to discriminate between brain-damaged and depressed patients, found that the MMPI *D* scale alone discriminated the groups more accurately than a number of ability tests, regardless of whether or not the groups were matched for estimated Full Scale IQ.

One final scale has been developed for the differentiation of brain-damaged and nonbrain-damaged patients, all of whom present with neurological complaints. This differentiation proved particularly difficult for Hovey's five-item scale (Maier and Abidin 1967). Shaw and Matthews (1965) studied two groups of extensively evaluated patients who had presented with neurological symptoms but half of whom were found to show no evidence of brain damage, although they were rather neurotic. The mean profile code of the brain-damaged subjects was '27316-, similar to the undifferentiated groups of brain-damaged subjects reported by Reitan (1955) and Lezak and Glaudin (1969). Yet the brain-damaged subjects were significantly lower than the nonbrain-damaged "pseudo-neurological" group on the *Hs* and *Hy* scales (Shaw and Matthews 1965).

A 17-item scale with a cut off of 7 or greater to rule out brain damage was developed through item analysis and then subjected to a rigorous cross-validation procedure. An additional group of 18 subjects with neurological complaints and an equivocal neurological history, who were eventually diagnosed as nonbrain damaged, was matched to a brain-damaged contrast group as before. The Ps-N (pseudo-neurological) scale correctly classified 67 percent of the nonbrain damaged and 78 percent of the brain-damaged subjects. Subsequently Shaw (1966) applied the Ps-N scale to the differentiation of pseudo-seizure patients and verified epileptics. Even though the pseudo-seizure patients were significantly lower than the pseudo-neurological patients on the *Hs* and *Hy* scales, as well as on the Ps-N scale, 11 of 15 were accurately classified, while only 1 of 15 epileptics was misclassified.

The Ps-N scale has also been reported to distinguish accurately early multiple sclerosis patients from conversion hysterics (Dodge and Kolstoe 1971) or from mixed psychiatric patients who presented with neurological symptoms but were not found to be brain damaged (Schwartz and Brown 1973). Inclusion of patients with both brain damage and emotional disturbance, however, seems to reduce the efficacy of the Ps-N scale to a considerable degree (Pantano and Schwartz 1978).

THE BRAIN AS INDEPENDENT VARIABLE: THE EFFECT OF TYPE OF BRAIN LESION ON PERSONALITY ADJUSTMENT

The issue of whether or not the MMPI may be useful in the differential diagnosis of brain damage is quite distinct from the utility of this test in the evaluation of the effects of differing types of neurological dysfunction. That a particular type of brain lesion may produce a high proportion of neurotic MMPI profiles may be unfortunate for the clinician attempting to identify a psychiatric basis for the patient's complaints, but it is of considerable interest to the neuropsychologist studying brain-behavior relationships. Interest has centered on the relationship of two neurological variables, type and locus of lesion, to emotional adjustment as measured by the MMPI. These questions may be of clinical significance, of course, and investigators have studied how MMPI results, regardless of whether or not characteristic of a particular type of lesion, may be of use in treatment or have explored the clinical significance of abnormal MMPIs within a particular neurologically impaired group.

Type of Lesion

Multiple sclerosis (MS) has been one of the more extensively studied neurological diseases in regard to personality adjustment. Several early studies reported MS patients as having *Hs, D,* and *Hy* scales elevated to a considerable extent above normal (Canter 1951; Baldwin 1952). Even when 12 items that seemed particularly relevant to the patients' symptoms were omitted, their profiles remained significantly elevated (Baldwin 1952). MS patients obtained significantly higher mean scores on the *Hs* and *Hy* scales than chronically ill non-neurological patients (Shontz 1955). When MS patients were compared to patients who presented with MS-like symptoms but were subsequently diagnosed as emotionally disturbed, however, neither MMPI mean scale scores nor Hovey's (1964) five-item scale significantly differentiated the two groups (Dodge and Kolstoe 1971). The Ps-N scale (Shaw and Matthews 1965), however, did significantly differentiate these groups (Dodge and Kolstoe 1971; Schwartz and Brown 1973).

More pertinent to the issue of brain-behavior relationships is the question of whether or not the MMPIs of MS patients are different from those of other brain-damaged subjects. In this context, it should be remembered that Hovey's five-item scale was able to distinguish normal from MS patients more accurately than from other brain-damaged subjects (Hovey 1967). The performances of MS and other brain-damaged patients both on more cognitive tests and the MMPI appear quite similar (Ross and Reitan 1955). While mean code types were much alike, Gilberstadt and Farkas (1961) found male veterans with MS showed significantly higher mean scores on the *D* and *Sc* scales than did a matched group of patients with traumatic head injuries. Using a sign approach involving the total number of scales with T scores in excess of 70 combined with T scores on *D*, Gilberstadt and Farkas (1961) devised a means of distinguishing the two groups, an approach that was partially confirmed by Matthews, Cleeland, and Hopper (1970). The latter study also found *Hs* to be significantly higher in MS patients, with *Hy* and *Pt* nonsignificantly higher.

The difficulties involved in assessing the emotional status of MS patients were made manifest in a study that compared two matched groups of such patients, one in which symptoms were in a state of exacerbation and the other in remission. Thirteen of 15 patients with exacerbated symptoms had MMPIs with two or more scales in excess of a T score of 70, while only 8 of 15 patients in remission showed as many elevations (Cleeland, Matthews, and Hopper 1970).

There is some evidence to suggest that the elevated scores found in MS patients are of clinical significance. When MS patients were categorized according to whether or not the *Hy* T score exceeded the *Pt* T score, the patients with significantly higher *Hy* scores were judged to be more disabled, both vocationally and generally, though not more emotionally impaired, than those with significantly higher *Pt* scores (Davis et al. 1971). Finally, Abramson and Tiege (1954) have reported 11 case studies in which MMPI results were found useful in developing treatment programs for the emotional problems of MS patients.

Two studies reported the MMPI results of patients with amyotrophic lateral sclerosis (ALS). Brown and Mueller (1970) found no specific profile associated with ALS, but nearly all of the patients had predominant elevations on *Hs, D,* and *Hy,* and only two of ten patients had no scales with T scores of 70 or greater. Such findings, of course, hardly serve to differentiate ALS patients from other brain-damaged patients or neurotics. Furthermore, when ALS patients were compared to scale score norms for a general medical population, the females were found to have slightly, but nonsignificantly, higher scores on the *Hs, D, Hy,* and *Sc* scales, while the men were not significantly different from the general medical group (Peters, Swenson, and Mulder 1978). One study of patients with myasthenia gravis reported results very similar to those seen in patients with MS or ALS, finding a mean group profile of 321'847– (Schwartz and Cahill 1970).

A study of patients with Huntington's chorea reported considerable evidence of emotional disturbance in both patients and their children, half of whom could be expected to develop the disease, but details of MMPI findings were not presented (Goodman et al. 1966). When Hungington's chorea patients were compared with a group of patients with mixed brain damage who were matched for age, education, and degree of cognitive impairment, there was no difference in terms of MMPI mean scale scores or the Goldberg index, a sign for discriminating psychotics from neurotics (Boll, Heaton, and Reitan 1974; Norton 1975).

An interesting study of patients in a nonpsychiatric, medical rehabilitation setting examined the MMPIs of three groups, patients with cerebrovascular disease, traumatic head injuries, and other types of central nervous system disorders, in three age ranges (Sand 1972). Not surprisingly, all groups showed mean scale scores elevated to a considerable degree above test norms, with *Hs, D, Hy, Pd,* and *Sc* the most deviant scales and *Mf* and *Si* the least. The first two groups' mean scores were not significantly different from one another, although the head trauma mean profile code showed the *Pd* scale as more prominent ('2438 compared to '2138), undoubtedly because the trauma patients were significantly younger. The remaining group of brain-damaged patients did show significantly higher scores than the other two groups on *D, Hy, Pt,* and *Sc* in comparison to the cerebrovascular patients and on *Hs, Hy, Pt,* and *Sc* in comparison to the head trauma patients. The most frequently occurring two-point code types in Sand's (1972) study were 31, 23, 21, 27, and 28, quite similar to the findings in a large group of mixed neurological patients (see Dahlstrom, Welsh; and Dahlstrom 1972, pp. 443–44).

Probably the most extensively studied neurological group has been seizure patients, particularly as both clinical reports and neurophysiological research have suggested that many of these patients may have lesions within the limbic system, thought to be a critical area for emotional responsiveness. Hermann (1977) has briefly reviewed some MMPI studies of seizure patients in the context of a broader review of the psychological effects of seizures. The earliest MMPI studies of seizure patients suggested they may be much like other brain-damaged patients, with elevations on the *Hs, D, Hy, Pt,* and *Sc* scales (Modlin 1947; Grayson 1951; Hovey, Kooi, and Thomas 1959).

While a special scale was developed for the identification of seizure patients, the Ep (epilepsy) scale (Richards 1952), subsequent attempts at cross-validation of this scale in separating seizure patients from either brain-damaged patients without seizures (Rosenman and Lucik 1970) or from nonbrain-damaged patients with pseudo-seizures (Shaw 1966) have proved fruitless. A later attempt at developing a similar scale also met with little success, although the investigators did report on 14 different MMPI signs that showed more promise than did a single scale on cross-validation, though still leaving considerable overlap between epileptics and neurotics (Hovey, Kooi, and Thomas 1959). The finding that a high number of neurotics are falsely identified as having seizures has made the 14 signs of little use in subsequent validation attempts (Jordan 1963).

In the studies of seizure patients reviewed above, no attempt was made to classify patients according to type of seizure, even though centrencephalic (grand mal and petit mal), temporal lobe (psychomotor), and other focal seizures may arise from anatomically distinguishable lesions. In an initial attempt to classify seizures more distinctly, Kløve and Doehring (1962) compared seizure patients with a specific etiology to those with seizures of unknown etiology, neurological patients without seizures, nonbrain-damaged patients with affective disturbance, and nonbrain-damaged medical patients and found no significant differences in either mean scale scores or high point scales. All groups tended to show elevations on the *Hs, D, Hy,* and *Sc* scales. Subsequent investigators have failed to discover any significant mean scale score or high-point differences in comparisons of temporal lobe epileptics with centrencephalics (Guerrant et al. 1962; Glass and Mattson 1973), with centrencephalics plus patients with non-temporal focal seizures (Small, Milstein, and Stevens 1962; Mignone, Donnelly, and Sadowsky 1970), and with major seizure and mixed seizure groups (Matthews and Kløve 1968).

When, however, temporal lobe seizure patients were separated according to their EEG findings into those with a unilateral focus, those with a bilateral focus consisting of a unilateral spike and a contralateral mirror focus, and those with bilateral independent spike foci, the last group showed significantly higher scores on the *D, Hy, Pd, Pa,* and *Pt* scales, as well as on Williams' (1952) Ca scale and the index of psychopathology (Ip), a combination of the *Pa* and *Sc* scales (Meier and French 1965a). It does not necessarily follow that the temporal lobe seizure patients with bilateral independent spike foci have a more disturbed personality adjustment as a direct result of the neuroanatomical locus of their lesions, even though these patients' seizures are of longest duration and least amenable to treatment. Their MMPI profiles may well reflect their response to the greater severity of their seizure problem. In a follow-up study to assess the effects of unilateral temporal lobectomy on the MMPI results of their original subjects, Meier and French (1965b) found the bilateral independent spike focus group showed more significant declines in mean scale scores on *Pa, Pt, Si,* Ca, and Ip than the other groups, even though the independent spike focus group showed the poorest response to surgery in terms of reduction of seizure frequency. Such a finding supports the notion that intrinsic pathophysiological variables may be contributing to the personality disturbance (Meier 1969).

Several studies have examined the relationship of various aspects of the seizures to MMPI scores. Aaronson (1959) found that seizure patients with auras of somatic symptoms obtained significantly higher mean scores on *Hs* than did other seizure patients. Graham (1958) has reported differences on the *Mf* and *Pt* scales to be associated with seizure frequency, and Hermann (1977) has reviewed an unpublished study showing that the interaction of siezure type, age of onset, and the length of time the patient has had seizures may all be important determinants of MMPI results. In contrast, studies of patients with temporal lobe seizures and other mixed types (Mignone, Donnelly, and Sadowsky 1970) and with major motor seizures (Matthews, Dikmen, and Harley 1977) have found no relationship between MMPI results and such factors.

Matthews, Dikmen, and Harley (1977) have noted a methodological problem in evaluating the effect of age of onset: many patients with early onset of seizures are too intellectually impaired to complete the MMPI. Therefore restricting early onset seizure patients to those who can complete the test results in a sample simultanenously being equated with late onset seizure patients in terms of cognitive abilities. When seizure patients who completed the MMPI were divided into those with relatively low or high IQ, the low IQ seizure patients obtained significantly higher mean scores on the *L, F,* and *Ma* scales than did high IQ seizure patients. Among brain-damaged patients without seizures, low IQ subjects also obtained significantly higher mean scale scores than did high IQ patients on the *F, Pd,* and *Sc* scales (Matthews, Dikmen, and Harley 1977), suggesting that MMPI results are influenced by cognitive impairment in seizure disorder as well as other types of brain damage, though not by age of onset, provided IQ is held constant. This conclusion is closely related to the suggestion of Reitan (1976) that MMPI results may be more affected by neuropsychological deficit than by neurological criteria such as type and locus of lesion.

A single study attempted to use the MMPI as a means of predicting the response of temporal lobe epileptics to temporal lobectomy in treatment of their seizures (Rausch, McCreary, and Crandall 1977). The authors found that those patients with relatively normal preoperative MMPIs showed a satisfactory social adjustment after surgery, but those patients with more abnormal preoperative MMPIs did not respond to surgery consistently as a group. Some improved in their social adjustment and some became worse (Rausch, McCreary, and Crandall 1977). The study was conducted with only ten patients, and details concerning either their MMPIs or neurological status are minimal. Therefore it is difficult to interpret these findings in light of Meier and French's (1965b) report that the preoperative group that was most disturbed, namely, the bilateral independent spike focus patients, showed the greatest postoperative changes on the MMPI. While further studies of the clinical correlates of MMPI findings among neurological patients are needed, they must be conducted in light of existing knowledge of the effects of brain lesions on the MMPI if they are to provide useful information.

Locus of Lesion

Studies concerned with the effect of locus of brain lesion on MMPI findings have examined subjects with lesions varying in terms of lobular, lateral, and cephalocaudal (front to back) dimensions. Lobular localization has been considered important in the clinical literature, particularly in reference to lesions occurring within the frontal or temporal lobes. Patients have been described as exhibiting two types of personality change after frontal lobe lesions, apathy and indifference and/or puerility and euphoria, while temporal lobe lesion patients have been considered to show a deepening of emotional responsiveness, including the internalizing and episodic discharge of anger and rage and the intensification of ethical-religious feelings (Blumer and Benson 1975).

Relatively few objective studies using MMPI findings of patients with lesions restricted to a particular lobe have been reported, however. Over two decades ago several studies of the effects of prefrontal leucotomies and lobotomies on the MMPI results of severely disturbed psychiatric patients were reported, with no conclusive findings. In a single case report, Andersen (1949) obtained serial MMPIs from a leucotomy patient and found that the D and Pt scales decreased significantly immediately after the operation but returned to preoperative levels within ten days. In larger groups of schizophrenics, Ruja (1951) found no significant changes on MMPI scales one month postlobotomy, while Vidor (1951) reported significant declines on the D and Pt scales following leucotomy. Regardless of the contradictory nature of the results, it is difficult to draw conclusions from ablations performed on patients with preexisting mental disturbance, as "therapeutic" changes in a severely disturbed patient might represent abnormal behavior in patients with no prior adjustment problems.

The transitory nature of the changes in the single case presented by Andersen (1949) gives occasion for an admonition regarding the time course of a neurological dysfunction and its consequent effect on MMPI results. That acutely occurring brain lesions produce far clearer psychological effects than chronic lesions has been amply demonstrated with regard to cognitive measures (for example, Fitzhugh, Fitzhugh, and Reitan 1962). Some of the differences between studies reviewed above (for example, Watson and Thomas 1968; Black 1974) may be due in part to the possibly greater effects of recently acquired lesions on personality adjustment. A related issue concerns the effect of the rate of lesion development on MMPI results. Green and Reitan (1975) have reported configural MMPI differences between tumor patients matched for lesion locus and size as a function of rate of growth, with more rapidly growing tumors producing more pronounced effects.

Thus the relationship between such factors as the time of lesion onset and the rate of lesion development should be considered in any examination of the results of brain lesions on personality adjustment. These factors have rarely been examined directly, except within the restricted example of seizure patients (for example, Mignone, Donnelly, and Sadowsky 1970; Matthews, Dikmen, and Harley 1977). Also, in the majority of studies covered in this review, the time course or rate of development of the brain lesions was not described.

Several authors have emphasized the influence of localization along the cephalocaudal dimension, contrasting the effects of frontal lesions with those of more posterior lesions, regardless of lobular locus. Andersen and Hanvik (1950) found that parietal lesion patients obtained significantly higher scores on F, D, and *Pt* and significantly lower scores on *K* than frontal lesion patients. This study was followed by the development of the P-F (parietal-frontal) scale to distinguish between focally brain-damaged patients as a function of lesion locus (Friedman 1950). Before this scale could be extensively applied, however, it was modified by the inclusion of a group of temporal lobe lesions within the posterior brain-damaged criterion group. Both temporal and parietal lesion patients showed mean profiles with prominent elevations on the *D* and *Pt* scales, while the frontals showed a relatively flat mean profile, with a mild peak on the *Sc* scale (Williams 1952). Contrasting the anterior and posterior lesion groups, Williams (1952) then developed a predictor scale, Ca (caudality), for determining the locus of brain lesion along the cephalocaudal dimension with patients who were known to have focal lesions.

Meier and French (1964) found the Ca scale to identify correctly more than 75 percent of their temporal lobe seizure patients prior to temporal lobectomy. However, while operative Ca scores no longer distinguished the temporal lobe patients, such scores remained an accurate means of identifying a nonoperated control group of temporal lobe seizure patients on retesting. Meier has argued (Meier and French 1964; Meier 1969) that the decrease in Ca scores following lobectomy suggests a direct relationship between the presence of an actively discharging epileptogenic focus and the presence of those personality features that make up the Ca scale. In other words, Meier (1969) is inclined to support the notion that the personality features characteristic of temporal lobe seizure patients are a direct consequence of their neurological impairment.

While the findings of Williams (1952) and, in part, those of Meier and French (1964) suggest that cephalocaudal, if not lobular, localization may affect MMPI results, Vogel (1962), with rather small groups of patients, obtained no MMPI differences as a result of lobular locus of lesion. Dikmen and Reitan (1974a), with a somewhat larger group of patients, though still smaller than those of Williams (1952), found no MMPI differences between anterior and posterior lesion subjects. Obviously, more data from a wider variety of neurological settings will be required to resolve this controversy.

Should localization along the cephalocaudal dimension prove to be a significant influence on MMPI measures of personality adjustment, some problems in the interpretation of these data remain. Meier (1969) has examined the problems inherent in these findings in some detail, and the following points are based largely on his comments. The findings of Williams (1952), who essentially included all of the cases of Andersen and Hanvik (1950) and Friedman (1950) in his sample, are not really consistent with the clinical reports of the personality adjustment of patients with frontal lobe lesions (Blumer and Benson 1975), but are more compatible with the positive report of MMPI changes following prefrontal leucotomy (Vidor 1951). The frontal lobe lesion patients of Williams (1952) show a relatively flat mean profile, with no findings that would suggest either the apathy or euphoria described in clinical accounts of the behavior of some of these patients (Blumer and Benson 1975). Of course, Williams does not present individual profiles, so it is possible that his mean MMPI results may result from combining two very different types of reactions to frontal lobe lesions. This post hoc explanation is quite speculative, however, and clearly requires objective validation. This possibility dramatically emphasizes the difficulty inherent in the clinical interpretation of results presented in the form of grouped data, a point that will be discussed in the last section of this chapter.

A second issue deals with the implications of high mean scores on the *D* and *Pt* scales reported for patients with posterior lesions (Williams 1952). Posterior lesions typically produce a host of sensorimotor symptoms that are quite apparent to most patients and in marked contrast with the minimally apparent effects of lesions of the frontal lobes, the area classically described as "silent." Thus the heightened elevations on scales reflecting anxiety and dysphoria may only represent a secondary emotional reaction to perceived changes in sensorimotor function rather than a direct consequence of neurological impairment. These findings also do not consider the clinical reports of the presence of gross denial of illness in some patients with chiefly right posterior brain lesions (Weinstein and Kahn 1955), findings that have not been evaluated through MMPI studies.

Finally, as Meier (1969) has aptly noted, the division along the cephalocaudal dimension between the frontal and temporal lobes, assigning the latter to the posterior aspect of the brain, is inconsistent with our knowledge of the complex role of the limbic system in the production of emotional responses. Differences between anterior and posterior temporal lobe lesions, for example, could well be as significant for personality adjustment as for language processing. Furthermore, thalamic lesions have been reported to produce changes in emotional responsiveness (see discussion in Riklan and Levita 1969), and a single MMPI study found a significant decrease on the *Ma* scale following stereotaxic thalamic surgery (Jurko, Andy, and Giruintano 1974). Clearly, no simple explanation will suffice to account for the reportedly wide variety of changes noted to follow brain lesions varying along the cephalocaudal dimension.

In Meier's (1969) review of clinical and experimental studies of the relationship of cerebral localization and personality adjustment (only 9 of the 56 studies actually concerned MMPIs of neurological patients), little support was found for the role of hemispheric laterality of lesion as a factor influencing adjustment. Since 1969 the picture has changed. Much of the recent concern with hemispheric asymmetries stems from clinical reports describing the association of left hemisphere lesions with catastrophic reactions and depression (Gainotti 1972) and right hemisphere lesions with indifference (Gainotti 1972) and denial (Bear and Fedio 1977). Experimental studies have suggested that patients with right hemisphere lesions may have more difficulty than left lesion patients in comprehending (Heilman, Scholes, and Watson 1975) or even discriminating changes in (Tucker, Watson, and Heilman 1977) the emotional tone of speech. An extensive literature concerning hemispheric asymmetries in the processing of emotion in normals has suddenly blossomed. Not surprisingly, MMPI researchers have increasingly examined the influence of laterality of lesion on adjustment.

Several studies have reported no significant differences between patients with right or left unilateral hemispheric lesions in terms of MMPI mean scale scores (Vogel 1962; Meier and French 1965a; Mignone, Donnelly, and Sadowsky 1970; Dikmen and Reitan 1974a). In contrast, Black (1975) found that while both groups had relatively high mean MMPI profiles, the right lesion patients were significantly lower than the left lesion patients on the *F, D, Pa, Sc,* and *Si* scales. With a somewhat older group, more comparable to the subjects of Dikmen and Reitan (1974a), Gasparrini, Satz, and Heilman (1978) found significant right-left differences that were comparable to those of Black (1975), though fewer in number. Patients with right hemisphere lesions had significantly lower scores on the *D* scale, although their mean *D* scale score of 54.5 was within normal limits. Both groups obtained significantly higher mean profiles than normals, but while 7 of the 16 left hemisphere lesion patients had at least two scales greater than T of 70, none of 8 right lesion patients showed such a degree of abnormality. The mean code type of the left hemisphere patients was '287932-, not strikingly different from that of other brain-damaged groups reviewed above, but the mean code type of the rights seems unusual, '94386- (Gasparrini, Satz, and Heilman 1978). Of particular importance is the finding that the groups did not differ on several cognitive and motor tests (aphasics had been excluded from the left lesion group). Thus the differences in MMPI results did not appear attributable to differences in degree of psychological impairment.

Attempts have been made to explain MMPI differences between patient groups on the basis of degree or type of cognitive impairment rather than on type or locus of lesion. Doehring and Reitan (1960) compared the MMPI results of aphasic and nonaphasic brain-damaged patients but found no significant differences; both groups had relatively elevated scale scores. In an essentially similar study, however, Dikmen and Reitan (1976b) found aphasics to show significantly higher scores on the *Pd* and *Sc* scales. The group differences on these two scales in the earlier study (Doehring and Reitan 1960), while large, were too variable to demonstrate a significant difference, so the two studies should not be considered in conflict. It is hardly surprising to find that 12 of the 15 aphasics in the later study had left hemisphere lesions, and thus the high *Pd* and *Sc* scores may be consistent with the clinical observations of previous investigators (Gainotti 1972). But Dikmen and Reitan (1974b) caution that the high scores on *Pd* and *Sc* may not have the same clinical implications that they would have for non-brain-damaged patients. The study of Matthews, Dikmen, and Harley (1977) also provides some support for the notion that degree of psychological deficit may influence MMPI results.

Louks, Calsyn, and Lindsay (1976) more directly assessed the role of psychological deficit in producing MMPI changes. From a large group of brain-damaged patients they used the Halstead-Reitan neuropsychological battery to classify patients as either "left" or "right" lesioned, without regard for neurological information. While they did not report any analysis of mean scale scores, and thus their results cannot be compared to the studies reviewed above, they found that the Goldberg Psychotic-Neurotic index classified their subjects with considerable accuracy. Twelve of 15 "left" lesioned and 10 of 15 "right" lesioned patients obtained scores in the psychotic and neurotic range, respectively. This means of classifying individual subjects allows direct comparison to the results of Gainotti (1972) and is consistent with the presence of more catastrophic reactions occurring in the "left hemisphere" patients. It is not so clear, however, that the neurotic scores obtained by most of the "right hemisphere" patients necessarily correspond to the indifference described by Gainotti (1972), as a patient may obtain a neurotic score on the Goldberg index by scoring high on *Hy* (consistent) and *Pt* (inconsistent), while high scores on *L* would reduce the chance of a neurotic classification.

In contrast with the findings of Louks, Calsyn, and Lindsay (1976), Stevens, Milstein, and Goldstein (1972) used a procedure that reversed the roles of the cognitive tests and the MMPI. They compared the performance of high and low scorers on each MMPI scale on a number of cognitive tests and found no significant relationships between the personality and ability measures. This approach, of course, prevented the use of configural aspects of MMPI profiles and thus may have obscured relevant MMPI variance.

Additional considerations concerning the influence of lesion laterality on MMPI results have been raised by the work of Lansdell and his associates in their studies of patients undergoing temporal lobectomies for the treatment of seizures. Rather than report mean T scores, they utilized the Taulbee-Sisson (T-S) count, a method of classifying subjects as neurotic or schizophrenic based on 16 two-scale comparisons, with a high, or neurotic, score reflecting relatively high scores on the *Hs, D, Hy,* and *Pt* scales. Initially, Lansdell and Urbach (1965) found no differences in postoperative T-S counts as a function of laterality of lesion. However, among the right temporal lobe patients, the greater the extent of brain tissue removed, the lower, or more schizophrenic, the T-S score. This relationship was true only for male patients. Subsequently, Lansdell (1968) found that high, or neurotic, preoperative T-S scores, again only in men, were associated with large right temporal removals, that is, patients with neurotic scores were likely to have more extensive right temporal lobe disease, requiring more extensive ablations of epileptogenic tissue.

While Lansdell's work suggested some relationship between emotional adjustment and right temporal lobe disease, the meaning of the T-S scores within this population required further study. Lansdell and Polcari (1968) then trained an experienced interviewer in the meaning of the T-S count by having him study a range of T-S scores on patients with whom he was familiar. The rater then was required to rate blindly the T-S scores of another group of temporal lobe patients with whom he also was familiar. The ratings correlated significantly ($r = .41$) with the actual T-S scores but with no other MMPI scale except *Pd* ($r = -.32$). The rater characterized low T-S scores as tending to have weak egos and problems in relationships, high scorers seemed to focus on their illness and its disrupting effects on their social functioning, while midrange scorers seemed normal and socially appropriate.

The findings of Lansdell and his associates illustrate three important points. First, clinical approaches to the evaluation of the meaning of MMPI profile configurations may well yield results suggesting the clinical significance of the MMPI in neurological patients, even though the classificatory significance (for example, neurotic versus schizophrenic) may not be appropriate. While a cautious attitude regarding the clinical utilization of MMPI results in neurological patients (see Reitan 1976) is appropriate, one should not be too eager to dismiss even simple sign approaches as conveying no useful information. Second, it can be very difficult to assess the meaning of relationships between brain lesions and personality adjustment when the premorbid (preoperative in the case of Lansdell and Urbach 1965) personality adjustment of the patient is not considered. Caution is required before one ascribes a change in personality to the effect of brain damage without a knowledge of the subject's prior adjustment. Furthermore, it is possible that effects of brain lesions may be obscured in those patients whose premorbid adjustments were moved in the direction of normality by their lesion. Finally, the finding that the relationship between the extent of neurological dysfunction within a single hemisphere and personality adjustment was specific to men may explain previously reported discrepancies between studies concerning the effects of lesion laterality. It has become increasingly apparent that men and women have differences in their degree of cerebral lateralization of cognitive abilities (McGlone 1978), yet few MMPI studies of the effects of laterality of brain lesion have analyzed results with regard to sex differences.

SUMMARY AND CONCLUSIONS

While many methodological problems and theoretical questions remain to be studied, it seems to this reviewer that the MMPI has proved to be a useful instrument in the evaluation of the personality adjustment of patients with neurological dysfunction. Perhaps the most problematic use of the test is as a means of differential diagnosis. Nearly all of the studies tend to indicate that neurological patients are likely to show more abnormal MMPIs than appropriately matched normal controls but less abnormal MMPIs than patients with severe psychiatric problems. On the other hand, brain-damaged patients generally tend to have elevations on the *Hs, D, Hy,* and, to a lesser extent, *Pt* and *Sc* scales, elevations that tend to make them very difficult to distinguish from either neurotics or patients with nonneurological chronic illness. Results have suggested that the MMPI may be used to separate the brain-damaged patient from severe psychotics using any number of special scales, signs, or keys, but one may question the value of such procedures because the *Sc* scale used alone may be as effective a discriminator. Furthermore, it is not clear how well this discrimination problem actually reflects clinical needs. It may be that the differentiation of nonschizophrenic brain-damaged patients from nonbrain-damaged schizophrenics is as easily assessed during an initial interview or even on the basis of presenting complaints as with the MMPI or any other psychological test. No study has established the effectiveness of the MMPI in discriminating schizophrenics who are brain damaged from those who are not. One may respond that this latter question may have no relevance to patient treatment, but psychological referrals continue to raise the question.

The results of research on the question of differentiating neurotics from brain-damaged patients have been most informative. It seems clear that neither mean T scores nor profile configurations have been useful in this regard, except perhaps when the neurotics are depressed (Watson, Davis, and Gasser 1978). The Ps-N scale (Shaw and Matthews 1965), however, has proven to be a fairly accurate means of distinguishing between neurotics and neurologically impaired subjects when both present with "neurological" symptoms. Nevertheless, more cross-validation studies in a wide variety of clinical settings are needed. The Ps-N scale, for example, may not be useful when patients have both neurological and emotional problems (Pantano and Schwartz 1978).

The most important clinical question concerning the use of the MMPI with neurological patients has been raised by several investigators (for example, Lezak and Glaudin 1969; Reitan 1976). To what extent can we safely extend the clinical implications of profile configurations derived from the study of patients with psychiatric problems to a neurological population? The few studies that have directly considered this issue would lead us to believe that the MMPI, interpreted in the usual fashion, does provide relevant and valid information regarding personality adjustment that can be used in the diagnosis and treatment of the neurologically impaired, but this issue has not been actively studied. In particular, more information is needed regarding the behavioral correlates of various profile types within neurological settings. Because of the predominance of elevations on the *Hs, D, Hy, Pt,* and *Sc* scales, it may be that more refined profile types reflecting behavioral homogeneity within the neurological setting will need to be identified before the utility of the MMPI in this regard can be fully determined. There would appear to be little justification for the proliferation of special research scales for differential diagnosis, when the need for an examination of the clinical meaning of information we now possess is so great.

The question of the clinical implications of MMPI results in neurological patients certainly relates to the second major focus of the present review, the relationship of brain lesions to personality adjustment. There has been little basis to support the conclusion that different types of neurological illnesses, such as multiple sclerosis, Huntington's chorea, epilepsy, and cerebrovascular disease, produce discriminably different personality adjustments. Locus of lesion, however, has proved a more fruitful subject, although the results reviewed allow no firm conclusions. While early investigations emphasized the role of the cephalocaudal dimension as a determinant of the emotional effects of brain damage, more recent work has suggested that the laterality of brain lesions may play an important part. Several studies have argued that neurological variables in general are probably less important than psychological deficit in influencing personality adjustment (see Reitan, 1976, for a review), but others have reported clear difference in MMPI results as a function of laterality of lesion when the hemispherically damaged subjects showed no differences in cognitive abilities (Gasparrini, Satz, and Heilman 1978). Furthermore, the MMPI studies suggesting that right hemisphere patients are inclined to show significantly lower scores of the *D* scale than left lesion patients are consistent with clinical observations of the behavior of patients with unilateral hemispheric lesions (for example, Gainotti 1972).

The influence of cognitive deficits in producing personality maladjustment is related to the question of whether or not the emotional effects of brain lesions are a direct consequence of neurological damage or simply a secondary emotional reaction to perceived sensorimotor changes (Meier 1969). This issue is crucial, both in terms of the treatment needs of brain-damaged patients and in terms of our understanding of brain-behavior relationships; yet it is a difficult question to answer. Those who have advocated a direct neurological effect have used evidence that is inferential and indirect, but it is difficult to conceive of a direct means of distinguishing between these two interpretations of the emotional effects of brain damage.

It appears that the role of degree and type of cognitive deficit in the production of MMPI abnormalities (Dikmen and Reitan 1974b), as well as the role of sex (Lansdell and Urbach 1965), must be considered along with laterality and lobular (or at least cephalocaudal) localization of lesion in subsequent studies. Of course, there is an inherent problem in attempting to evaluate the effects of locus of lesion, sex, and degree and type of cognitive deficit simultaneously. Such studies will require a large number of subjects. It will not be surprising if we continue to see a number of studies that simply are not able to evaluate a number of variables sufficiently to yield clearly interpretable results. It is quite likely that cooperative studies, conducted simultaneously in several settings, may be necessary.

Two further qualifications must be made with regard to the design of MMPI studies of neurological patients. It is apparent that any study of patients with a neurological disease that produces cognitive impairment to a degree sufficient to make the MMPI impossible to administer in some cases will minimize whatever aspect of emotional difficulties occurs as a consequence of the cognitive impairment. The range of cognitive impairment will have been automatically curtailed by the exclusion of subjects too impaired to complete the MMPI (Matthews, Cleeland, and Hopper 1970). Unfortunately, this criticism is justified for most objective measures of personality functioning other than observer behavior rating scales.

The second difficulty confronting anyone who attempts to evaluate the effects of neurological dysfunction on personality, measured by the MMPI or any other procedure, is that it is almost impossible to reach firm conclusions regarding the effects of a neurological problem on personality adjustment without some knowledge of the patient's premorbid adjustment. In clinical work it is not unusual to be asked to evaluate a patient's change in personality following brain damage, only to find the patient behaving much as always, though perhaps with less successful inhibition of existing defenses. The anxious person may have become more anxious, the repressed individual, more repressed, and the somatically preoccupied may have more florid complaints. The way in which a patient responds to neurological dysfunction is as likely to be affected by premorbid personality as by the type or extent of brain lesion or cognitive deficit. While this admonition scarcely seems revolutionary, it should be noted that few studies among those reviewed for this chapter even mention this difficulty.

One final concern must be raised in regard to a large number of the studies of the MMPI of neurological patients. Results are typically presented in the form of mean profiles of clinical scales in order to demonstrate group differences. Unfortunately, a number of investigators interpret the mean profile of a group as if it were the profile of an individual patient, when, in fact, no patient within that group may actually have a profile configuration similar to that of the group mean. This totally unjustifiable approach to the evaluation of personality madadjustment in a group of individuals has been criticized (Butcher and Tellegen 1978), yet it is all too common. Such a procedure often leads investigators to minimize the degree of maladjustment in the group as a whole, because mean T scores that are significantly higher than test norms are likely to be below the elevation required to be significant in the interpretation of an individual profile. Even more important, however, is the likelihood that individuals within a group may be showing a considerable degree of maladjustment of differing types, such that the actual picture of their individual responses to the effects of brain damage is totally obscured.

The MMPI, properly analyzed and interpreted, appears to be a useful instrument for the evaluation of brain-behavior relationships, but many questions remain to be answered. Future studies will need to be more comprehensive in their scope, more cognizant of the multiplicity of variables that need to be considered, and more clinical in their evaluation of the results of individual patients.

REFERENCES

Aaronson, B. S. 1959. "Hypochondriasis and Somatic Seizure Auras." *Journal of Clinical Psychology* 15: 450–51.

Abramson, H. A., and E. Tiege. 1954. "Minnesota Test as a Guide to Therapy in Multiple Sclerosis." *Annals of the New York Academy of Science* 58: 648–55.

Andersen, A. L. 1949. "Personality Changes Following Prefontal Lobotomy in a Case of Severe Psychoneruosos." *Journal of Consulting Psychology* 13: 105–07.

——, and L. J. Hanvik. 1950. "The Psychometric Localization of Brain Lesions: The Differential Effect of Frontal and Parietal Lesions on MMPI Profiles." *Journal of Clinical Psychology* 6: 177–80.

Ayers, J., D. I. Templer, and C. F. Ruff. 1975. "The MMPI in the Differential Diagnosis of Organicity vs. Schizophrenia: Empirical Findings and a Somewhat Different Perspective." *Journal of Clinical Psychology* 31: 685–86.

Baldwin, M. V. 1952. "Clinico-experimental Investigation into the Psychologic Aspects of Multiple Sclerosis." *Journal of Nervous and Mental Disease* 115: 229–342.

Bear, D. M., and P. Fedio. 1977. "Quantitative Analysis of Interictal Behavior in Temporal Lobe Epilepsy." *Archives of Neurology* 34: 454–67.

Black. F. W. 1975. "Unilateral Brain Lesions and MMPI Performance: A Preliminary Study." *Perceptual and Motor Skills* 40: 87–93.

——. 1974. "Use of the MMPI with Patients with Recent War-Related Head Injuries." *Journal of Clinical Psychology* 30: 571–73.

Blumer, D., and D. F. Benson. 1975. "Personality Changes with Frontal and Temporal Lobe Lesions." In *Psychiatric Aspects of Neurologic Disease*, edited by D. F. Benson and D. blumer, pp. 151–70.

Boll, T. J., R. Heaton, and R. M. Reitan. 1974. "Neuropsychological and Emotional Correlates of Huntington's Chorea." *Journal of Nervous and Mental Disease* 158: 61–69.

Brown, W. A., and P. S. Mueller. 1970. "Psychological Function in Individuals with Amyotrophic Lateral Sclerosis (ALS)." *Psychosomatic Medicine* 32: 141–52.

Butcher, J. N., and A. Tellegen. 1978. "Common Methodological Problems in MMPI Research." *Journal of Consulting and Clinical Psychology* 46: 620–28.

Canter, A. H. 1951. "MMPI Profiles in Multiple Sclerosis." *Journal of Consulting Psychology* 15: 253–56.

Cleeland, C. S., C. G. Matthews, and C. L. Hopper. 1970. "MMPI Profiles in Exacerbation and Remission of Multiple Sclerosis." *Psychological Reports* 27: 373–74.

Dahlstrom, W. G., G. S. Welsh, and L. E. Dahlstrom. 1972. *An MMPI Handbook*. Vol. 1. Minneapolis: University of Minnesota Press.

Davis, L. J., D. Osborne, P. J. Siemens, and J. R. Brown. 1971. "MMPI Correlates with Disability in Multiple Sclerosis." *Psychological Reports* 28: 700–02.

Dikmen, S., and R. M. Reitan. 1974a. "MMPI Correlates of Localized Cerebral Lesions. *Perceptual and Motor Skills* 39: 831–40.

——. 1974b. "Minnesota Multiphasic Personality Inventory Correlates of Dysphasic Language Disturbances." *Journal of Abnormal Psychology* 83: 675–79.

Dodge, G. R., and R. H. Kolstoe. 1971. "The MMPI in Differentiating Early Multiple Sclerosis and Conversion Hysteria." *Psychological Reports* 29: 155–59.

Doehring, D. G., and R. M. Reitan. 1960. "MMPI Performance of Aphasic and Non-Aphasic Brain Damaged Patients." *Journal of Clinical Psychology* 16: 307–09.

Fitzhugh, K. B., L. C. Fitzhugh, and R. M. Reitan. 1962. "Wechsler-Bellevue Comparisons in Groups with Chronic and Current Lateralized and Diffuse Brain Lesions." *Journal of Consulting Psychology* 26: 306–10.

Friedman, S. H. 1950. "Psychometric Effects of Frontal and Parietal Lobe Brain Damage." Ph.D. dissertation, University of Minnesota.

Gainotti, G. 1972. "Emotional Behavior and Hemispheric Side of the Lesion." *Cortex* 8: 41–55.

Gasparrini, W., P. Satz, and K. M. Heilman. 1978. "Hemispheric Asymmetries of Affective Processing as Determined by the MMPI." *Journal of Neurology, Neurosurgery and Psychiatry* 41: 470–73.

Gilberstadt, H., and J. Duker. 1965. *A Handbook for Clinical and Actuarial MMPI Interpretation*. Philadelphia: Saunders.

Gilberstadt, H., and E. Farkas. 1961. "Another Look at MMPI Profile Types in Multiple Sclerosis." *Journal of Consulting Psychology* 25 : 440–44.

Glass, D. H., and R. H. Mattson. 1973. "Psychopathology and Emotional Precipitation of Seizures in Temporal Lobe and Non-Temporal Lobe Epileptics." *Proceedings of the 81st Annual Convention of the American Psychological Association* 8: 425–26.

Goodman, R. M., C. L. Holt, L. Terango, G. T. Perrine, and P. L. Roberts. 1966. "Huntington's Chorea: A Multi-Disciplinary Study of Affected Parents and First Generation Offspring." *Archives of Neurology* 15: 345–55.

Grahma, L. R. 1958. "Personality Factors and Epileptic Seizures."*Journal of Clinical Psychology* 14: 187–88.

Grayson, H. M. 1951. *A Psychological Admissions Testing Program and Manual.* Los Angeles: Veterans·Administration Centers, Neuropsychiatric Center.

Green, T. K., and R. M. Reitan. 1975. "Effect of the Rate of Lesion Development on Behavioral Adaptations in Intracranial Neoplasms." *Neuroscience Abstracts*, no. 1068. p. 692. Bethesda, Md.: Society for Neuroscience.

Guerrant, J., W. Anderson, A. Fischer, M. Weinstein, R. M. Jaros, and A. Deskins. 1962. *Personality in Epilepsy*. Springfield, Ill.: Charles C. Thomas.

Halperin, K. M., C. Neuringer, P. S. Cavies, and G. Goldstein. 1977. "Validation of the Schizophrenia-Organicity Scale with Brain-Damaged and Non-Brain-Damaged Schizophrenics." *Journal of Consulting and Clinical Psychology* 45: 949–50.

Hathaway, S. R., and P. E. Meehl. 1951. *An Atlas for the Clinical Use of the MMPI*. Minneapolis: University of Minnesota Press.

Heilman, K. M., R. Scholes, and R. T. Watson. 1975. "Auditory Affective Agnosis." *Journal of Neurology, Neurosurgery, and Psychiatry* 38: 69–72.

Hermann, B. P. 1977. *Psychological Effects of Epilepsy: A Review*. MS. 1430. Washington, D.C. American Psychological Association.

Holland, T. R., J. Lowenfeld, and H. M. Wadsworth. 1975. "MMPI Indices in the Discrimination of Brain Damaged and Schizophrenic Groups. *Journal of Consulting and Clinical Psychology* 43: 426.

Hovey, H. B. 1967. "MMPI Testing for Multiple Sclerosis." *Psychological Reports* 21: 599–600.

——. 1965. "Reply to Weingold, Dawson, and Kael." *Psychological Reports* 16: 1122.

——. 1964. "Brain Lesions and Five MMPI Items." *Journal of Consulting Psychology* 28: 78–79.

——, K. A. Kooi, and M. H. Thomas. 1959. "MMPI Profiles of Epileptics." *Journal of Consulting Psychology* 23: 155–59.

Huisman, R. E. 1974. "Correspondence Between Mini-Mult and Standard MMPI Scale Scores in Patients with Neurological Disease." *Journal of Consulting and Clinical Psychology* 42: 149.

Jordan, E. J. 1963. "MMPI Porfiles of Epileptics: A Further Evaluation." *Journal of Consulting Psychology* 27: 267–69.

Jortner, S. 1965. "A Test of Hovey's MMPI Scale for CNS Disorder." *Journal of Clinical Psychology* 21: 285.

Jurko, M. F., O. J. Andy, and L. P. Giurintano. 1974. "Changes in the MMPI as a Function of Thalamotomy." *Journal of Clinical Psychology* 30: 569–70.

Kincannon, J. C. 1968. "Prediction of the Standard MMPI Scale Scores from 71 Items: The Mini-Mult." *Journal of Consulting and Clinical Psychology* 32: 319–25.

Kløve, H., and D. G. Doehring. 1962. "MMPI in Epileptic Groups with Differential Etiology." *Journal of Clinical Psychology* 18: 149–53.

Krug, R. S. 1967. "MMPI Response Inconsistency of Brain Damaged Individuals." *Journal of Clinical Psychology* 23: 366.

Lansdell, H. 1968. "Effect of Extent of Temporal Lobe Surgery and Neuropathology on the MMPI." *Journal of Clinical Psychology* 24: 406–12.

——, and A. R. Polcari. 1968. "The Meaning of the Taulbee-Sisson Configurational Score on the MMPI with Neurosurgical Patients." *Journal of Clinical Psychology* 24: 216–19.

——, and N. Urbach. 1965. "Sex Differences in Personality Measures Related to Size and Side of Temporal Lobe Ablations." *Proceedings of the 73rd Annual Convention of the American Psychological Association*, pp. 113–14.

Lezak, M. D., and V. Glaudin. 1969. "Differential Effects of Physical Illness on MMPI Profiles." *Newsletter for Research in Psychology* 11: 27–28.

Louks, J., D. Calsyn, and F. Lindsay. 1976. "Personality Dysfunction and Lateralized Deficits in Cerebral Functions as Measured by the MMPI and Reitan-Halstead Battery." *Perceptual and Motor Skills* 43: 655–59.

McGlone, J. 1978. "Sex Differences in Functional Brain Asymmetry." *Cortex* 14: 122–28.

Maier, L. R., and R. R. Abidin. 1967. "Validation Attempt of Hovey's Five-Item MMPI Index for CNS Disorders." *Journal of Consulting Psychology* 31: 542.

Marsh, G. G. 1972. "Parkinsonian Patients' Scores on Hovey's MMPI Scale for CNS Disorder." *Journal of Clinical Psychology* 28: 529–30.

Matthews, C. G., C. S. Cleeland, and C. Hopper, 1970. "Neuropsychological Patterns in Multiple Sclerosis." *Diseases of the Nervous System* 31: 161–70.

Matthews, C. G., S. Dikmen, and J. P. Harley. 1977. "Age of Onset and Psychometric Correlates of MMPI Profiles in Major Motor Epilepsy." *Diseases of the Nervous System* 38: 173–76.

Matthews, C. G., and H. Kløve. 1968. "MMPI Performances in Major Motor, Psychomotor and Mixed Seizure Classifications of Known and Unknown Etiology." *Epilepsia* 9: 43–53.

Meier, M. J. 1969. "The Regional Localization Hypothesis and Personality Changes Associated with Focal Cerebral Lesions and Ablations. In *MMPI: Research Developments and Clinical Applications*, edited by J. N. Butcher, pp. 243–62. New York: McGraw-Hill.

——, and L. A. French. 1965a. "Some Personality Correlates of Unilateral and Bilateral EEG Abnormalities in Psychomotor Epileptics." *Journal of Clinical Psychology* 21: 3–9.

——. 1965b. "Changes in MMPI Scale Scores and an Index of Psychopathology Following Unilateral Temporal Lobectomy for Epilepsy." *Epilepsia* 6: 263–73.

——. 1964. "Caudality Scale Changes Following Unilateral Temporal Lobectomy. *Journal of Clinical Psychology* 20: 464–67.

Mignone, R. J., E. F. Donnelly, and D. Sadowsky. 1970. "Psychological and Neurological Comparisons of Psychomotor and Non-Psychomotor Epileptic Patients." *Epilepsia* 11: 345–59.

Modlin, H. C. 1947. "A Study of the MMPI in Clinical Practice with Notes on the Cornell Index." *American Journal of Psychiatry* 103: 758–69.

Neuringer, C., P. S. Dombrowski, and G. Goldstein. 1975. "Cross-Validation of an MMPI Scale of Differential Diagnosis of Brain Damage from Schizophrenia." *Journal of Clinical Psychology* 31: 268–71.

Norton, J. C. 1975. "Patterns of Neuropsychological Test Performance in Huntington's Disease." *Journal of Nervous and Mental Disease* 161: 276–79.

Pantano, L. T., and M. L. Schwartz. 1978. "Differentiation of Neurologic and Pseudo-Neurologic Patients with Combined MMPI Mini-Mult and Pseudo-Neurologic Scale." *Journal of Clinical Psychology* 34: 56–60.

Peters, P. K., W. M. Swenson, and D. W. Mulder. 1978. "Is There a Characteristic Personality Profile in Amyotrophic Lateral Sclerosis?" *Archives of Neurology* 35: 321–22.

Rausch, R., C. McCreary, and P. H. Crandall. 1977. "Psychosocial Functioning Following Successful Surgical Relief from Seizures. Evidence of Prediction from Preoperative Personality Characteristics." *Journal of Psychosomatic Research* 21: 141–46.

Reitan, R. M. 1976. "Neurological and Physiological Bases of Psychopathology. In *Annual Review of Psychology*, edited by M. R. Rosenzweig and L. W. Porter, vol. 27, pp. 189–216. Palo Alto, Calif.: Annual Reviews.

———. 1955. "Affective Disturbances in Brain Damaged Patients." *Archives of Neurology and Psychiatry* 73: 530–32.

Richards, T. W. 1952. "Personality of the Convulsive Patient in the Military Service." *Psychological Monographs* 66, no. 346.

Riklan, M., and E. Levita. 1969. *Subcortical Correlates of Human Behavior.* Baltimore: Williams & Wilkins.

Rosenman, M. F., and T. W. Lucik. 1970. "A Failure to Replicate an Epilepsy Scale of the MMPI." *Journal of Clinical Psychology* 26: 372.

Ross, A. T., and R. M. Reitan. 1955. "Intellectual and Affective Functions in Multiple Sclerosis." *Archives of Neurology and Psychiatry* 73: 663–77.

Ruja, D. H. 1951. "Personality Changes Following Prefrontal Lobotomy in Twenty-five Schizophrenic Patients." *American Psychologist* 6: 499.

Russell, E. W. 1977. "MMPI Profiles of Brain Damaged and Schizophrenic Subjects." *Journal of Clinical Psychology* 33: 190–93.

———. 1975. "Validation of a Brain Damage vs. Schizophrenia MMPI Key." *Journal of Clinical Psychology* 31: 659–61.

Sand, P. 1972. "MMPI Profile Characteristics in Testable Brain Damaged Patients Within Several Age/Diagnostic Categories." *Rehabilitation Psychology* 19: 146–52.

Schwartz, M. S. 1969. "'Organicity' and the MMPI 1–3–9 and 2–9 Codes." *Proceedings of the 77th Annual Convention of the American Psychological Association* 4: 519–20.

———, and J. R. Brown. 1973. "MMPI Differentiation of Multiple Sclerosis Versus Pseudo-Neurologic Patients." *Journal of Clinical Psychology* 29: 471–74.

Schwartz, M. L., and R. Cahill. 1970. "Personality Assessment in Myasthenia Gravis with the MMPI." *Perceptual and Motor Skills* 31: 766.

Shaw, D. 1966. "Differential MMPI Performance in Pseudo-Seizure, Epileptic, and Pseudoneurologic Groups." *Journal of Clinical Psychology* 22: 271–75.

———, and C. G. Matthews. 1965. "Differential MMPI Performance of Brain Damaged vs. Pseudo-Neurologic Groups." *Journal of Clinical Psychology* 21: 405–08.

Shontz, F. C. 1955. "MMPI Responses of Patients with Multiple Sclerosis." *Journal of Consulting Psychology* 19: 74.

Siskind, G. 1976. "Hovey's 5-Item MMPI Scale and Psychiatric Patients." *Journal of Consulting Psychology* 19: 74.

Siskind, G. 1976. "Hovey's 5-Item MMPI Scale and Psychiatric Patients." *Journal of Clinical Psychology* 32: 50.

Small, J. G., V. Milstein, and J. R. Stevens. 1962. "Are Psychomotor Epileptics Different?" *Archives of Neurology* 7: 187–94.

Stevens, J. R., V. Milstein, and S. Goldstein. 1972. "Psychometric Test Performance in Relation to the Psychopathology of Epilepsy." *Archives of General Psychiatry* 26: 532–38.

Tucker, D. M., R. T. Watson, and K. M. Keilman. 1977. "Discrimination and Evocation of Affectively Intoned Speech in Patients with Right Parietal Disease." *Neurology* 27: 947–50.

Upper, D., and W. Seeman. 1968. "Brain Damage, Schizophrenia, and Five MMPI Items." *Journal of Clinical Psychology* 24: 444.

Vidor, M. 1951. "Personality Changes Following Prefrontal Leucotomy as Reflected by the Minnesota Multiphasic Personality Inventory and the Results of Psychometric Testing." *Journal of Mental Science (British Journal of Psychiatry)* 97: 159–73.

Vogel, W. 1962. "Some Effects of Brain Lesions on MMPI Profiles." *Journal of Consulting Psychology* 26: 412–15.

Watson, C. G. 1973. "A Simple Bivariate Screening Technique to Separate NP Hospital Organics from Other Psychiatric Groups." *Journal of Clinical Psychology* 29: 448–50.

———. 1971. "An MMPI Scale to Separate Brain-Damaged from Schizophrenic Men." *Journal of Consulting and Clinical Psychology* 36: 121–25.

——, W. E. Davis, and B. Gasser. 1978. "The Separation of Organics from Depressives with Ability- and Personality-Based Tests." *Journal of Clinical Psychology* 34: 393–97.

Watson, C. G., D. Plemel, and L. Jacobs. 1978. "An MMPI Sign to Separate Organic from Functional Psychiatric Patients." *Journal of Clinical Psychology* 34: 398–400.

Watson, C., and R. Thomas. 1968. "MMPI Profiles of Brain Damaged and Schizophrenic Patients." *Perceptual and Motor Skills* 27: 567–73.

Weingold, H. P., J. G. Dawson, and H. C. Kael. 1965. "Further Examination of Hovey's 'Index' for Identification of Brain Lesions: Validation Study." *Psychological Reports* 16: 1098.

Weinstein, E. A., and R. L. Kahn. *Denial of Illness*. Springfield, Ill.: Charles C. Thomas.

Williams, H. L. 1952. "The Development of a Caudality Scale for the MMPI." *Journal of Clinical Psychology* 8: 293–97.

Zimmerman, I. L. 1965. "Residual Effects of Brain Damage and Five MMPI Items." *Journal of Consulting Psychology* 29: 394.

3/ THE MMPI IN PSYCHOSOMATICS: METHODOLOGICAL ISSUES

Paolo Pancheri

The term "psychosomatic" has been used in many different and often conflicting ways. Sometimes it has been used to denote hysterical symptoms (paralysis, pain, anesthesia) occurring in the absence of any physiological dysfunction or anatomical lesion. When used as a synonym for psychophysiological disorders, it refers to any somatic symptom linked to anxiety and emotional problems, but lacking a demonstrated organic basis. These disorders include some types of headaches, muscular aches due to tension, some functional tachycardias, and some digestive system disorders. At other times, the term describes a rather precise group of somatic illnesses in which anxiety or emotional factors play an important etiopathogenic role. Bronchial asthma, ulcerative colitis, some dermatoses, and rheumatoid arthritis are examples of this group. Today, the term "psychosomatic" tends to be associated with the study of the relationship between environmental stimuli, emotions, and personality variables, on one hand, and onset of somatic illnesses, on the other. Thus "psychosomatics" should include neither the study of psychophysiological disorders associated with anxiety nor the investigation of conversion hysteria. It should be emphasized, however, that no clear and definitive boundary exists between the "classical" psychosomatic illnesses and a bona fide somatic disease, because personality structure and emotional determinants can play a more or less important role in any disease.

Predisposition to disease actually depends on two general factors: the potency of the pathogenic agent and the biological resistance of the person. Pathogenic agents of low intensity therefore can cause illness in conditions of weakened biological defenses. The resistance or predisposition of the biological terrain to disease partly depends on the emotional reactivity of the person and on his or her emotional state during any particular period of time. Studies on stress have shown that when environmental and psychological stressors elicit emotional arousal, a complex physiological reaction ensues. (Frankenhaeuser

1975; Levi 1972; Mason 1975a, 1976b). Prolonged or especially intense or frequent emotional reactions to stressful situations can lead to permanent modifications of the biological terrain (illness precursors) through the activation of the immunitary, endocrine, and autonomic nervous systems. At this stage, a precipitating factor may result in a manifest disease.

The intensity of the emotional reaction is determined by the relevance and potency of the stimulus and by the individual's personality structure; and the particular characteristics of the psychobiological response (emotion) are in turn conditioned by genetic factors, imprinting, learning, and biological changes over time. In this way, a complex network of psychobiological interactions is created in which personality structure plays a relevant and sometimes determinant role in disease. Because of the important effects of emotional factors on the biological substrate, it is conceivable that they may be involved to a greater or lesser degree in every somatic illness, and should be considered together with the other particular covariables at work. In this framework, psychosomatics can be defined as the study of the relationship between stimuli, personality, emotions, and alterations of the biological substrate leading to illness.

THEORETICAL CONSIDERATIONS

An important and as yet unresolved problem in psychosomatics regards the elaboration of interpretive models to account for psychosomatic phenomena. It is the interpretive model that determines the methodology to be used and therefore the selection of instruments to assess personality and emotional variables. One of the most striking characteristics of contemporary psychosomatic research is the paucity of theoretical models to interpret the large amount of empirical data collected. Earlier theories about psychosomatic disorders were heavily influenced by Freud and psychoanalytically oriented researchers, and until recently the psychoanalytic interpretation proposed by Franz Alexander (1950) in his basic works has been the most widely accepted explanation of these disorders.

In recent times, Bahnson (1964, 1969) has presented a more empirically oriented, but still psychoanalytically based, conceptualization of psychosomatic disorders. He attempted to answer one of the most elusive questions in psychosomatic medicine: Why does a similar situation of conflict and anxiety in some cases lead to a neurotic or psychotic disorder and in other cases to a psychosomatic illness? Bahnson understood that intensity of emotional conflict alone could not account for the whole range of clinical problems. Therefore he introduced a second determinant variable, the type and intensity of the defense mechanisms commonly seen in different disorders. In his model the combination of intense conflictual drive and denial and repression can lead to a psychosomatic or somatic disorder, while intense conflict associated with projection and displacement may result in a psychiatric disturbance. Bahnson's model overemphasizes the so-called intrapsychic process at the cost of understanding the importance of social interactions as sources of internal conflict. It also is unable to explain the relationship between psychic process and biological mediation, which is the second elusive question in psychosomatic medicine.

A few years later, Levi (1972, 1974) proposed a model focusing on interactions between the person and his or her environment. In his model the principal role is ascribed to the psychosocial stimuli, that is, those stimuli arising from interpersonal relationships that generate psychological and biological reactions. This "psychobiological program" is activated by the psychosocial stimuli and produces more or less persistent physiological modifications eventually leading to disease. Other interacting variables can retard or accelerate this process. Undoubtedly, Levi's model has the merit of emphasizing social relationships and of focusing attention on the physiological aspects of the emotions, but it neglects the issue of intrapsychic stimuli and the question of psychiatric versus somatic disorder.

When combined, neither Bahnson's intrapsychic model nor Levi's psychosocial model adequately accounts for the variety of psychological disturbances, nor does either clarify why in some cases the "somatic pathway" and in other cases the "behavioral pathway" predominates the expression of emotional conflict. This problem has been recently discussed by Pancheri and Benaissa (1978), who have proposed an interpretive model derived from clinical and psychophysiological observations. The model considers the question of somatic versus behavioral pathways of emotional expression and suggests the possibility of a balance between biological and behavioral correlates. In the view of this model, intense and prolonged or frequent emotional arousal can lead either to a psychosomatic or psychiatric disorder, depending on whether the person's style of emotional reaction favors prevalently somatic or behavioral channels. The choice of one or the other pathway, then, is a function of the person's characteristic reaction style. This style may be in part genetically determined and in part learned as a consequence of life experiences (Figure 3.1).

The need for an adequate model in psychosomatics transcends the issue of theoretical interest. It is the model that guides the choice of experimental design, the selection of samples, the interpretation of results, and naturally the construction of assessment and measurement instruments. Psychosomatic research, therefore, needs a model that not only can explain psychosomatic phenomena but also is coherent and logically compatible with the instruments used to validate it. It is in this perspective that the study of the usefulness and limits of the MMPI in psychosomatic research should be seen.

The MMPI is empirically derived and not based on any a priori theoretical constructs. It is not compatible with psychodynamic models, such as Bahnson's, because the test items and scales have been derived from patients diagnosed in standard nosological terms, and psychiatric nosology is notoriously insignificant for the testing of psychoanalytic theory. In fact, the psychological dimensions relevant to psychoanalysis are not explorable with the MMPI, despite the at-

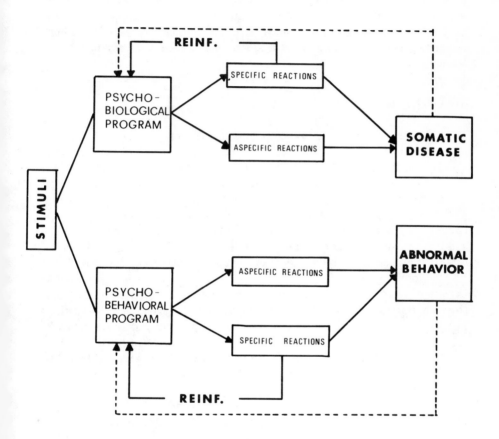

FIGURE 3.1: Interpretive model of the interrelationships among stimuli, styles of emotional reaction, and onset of illness. From P. Pancheri and C. Benaissa, "Stress and Psychosomatic Illness," in *Stress and Anxiety*, ed. C. D. Spielberger and I. G. Sarason, vol. 5, 1978. Copyright 1978, Washington, D.C., Hemisphere Publishers. Reprinted by permission.

tempts by many authors. The MMPI is more compatible with psychosocial models, such as Levi's, but has wider possibilities of application, because in Levi's model personality characteristics are secondary to psychosocial stimuli and psychobiological reactions. A psychometric personality assessment instrument such as the MMPI seems to find its maximum internal coherence and applicability in the context of a model centered on a hypothesized dichotomy between physiological and behavioral expression of emotional conflict. Here the task of the MMPI is to reveal sensitively the presence of psychiatric pathology or subclinical emotional disturbances that can then be confronted with corresponding evidence of physiological arousal independently of any theoretical assumption.

METHODOLOGICAL CONSIDERATIONS

Because the emotions and their physiological correlates play a relevant role in the genesis of somatic dysfunctions and diseases, assessment of the emotional state and of the progress of the patient can provide pertinent information about the determinants of the disorder and the present factors influencing its development. The problem of assessing the emotional state by means of a psychometric personality inventory is, nevertheless, a methodologically complex issue in psychosomatic research. Actual personality structure at the moment of clinical and psychometric evaluation is in fact the result of premorbid personality characteristics interacting with the patient's reaction to his or her present illness.

In ordinary clinical conditions it is difficult to distinguish personality characteristics predating the illness that might have contributed to its onset from those traits reactive to the actual situation of distress and subjective suffering. The situation is further complicated by the possibility that the patient's emotional reaction may negatively feed into psychophysiological channels, thus affecting the course of the illness. If this happens, it is no longer possible to distinguish those variables contributing to onset of illness from those influencing its course.

A large part of the psychosomatic research conducted in the past using objective personality assessment instruments is methodologically weak, because the experimental design did not provide for the separation of causal and reactive personality traits and characteristics. A patient with a physical illness is subjected to numerous and potent stressors capable of producing intense and complex emotional reactions. Subjective suffering, pain, hospitalization, separation from family and social relationships, and worry about health and life itself are all factors acting upon and modifying premorbid personality. Moreover, in many cases the biological alterations caused by the illness act directly on the mesencephalic and cortical structures implicated in emotional control, modifying emotional reactivity.

Any personality assessment of psychosomatic patients should thus consider the actual emotional state both as a function of premorbid personality and as a reaction to the present stressful situation. It is clear that these two aspects are interdependent in that the present reaction to illness depends on the premorbid personality structure, and both in turn influence the onset and course of the illness.

One of the most frequent objectives of psychosomatic research has been the identification of those personality typologies associated with various somatic and psychosomatic diseases. To this end, the MMPI has been widely used, but with rather poor results. The personality profiles identified for various diseases generally seem to reflect the degree of suffering of the patient and the reaction to the illness rather than a specific typology. Studies of bronchial asthma have shown aspecific neurotic profiles with various combinations of code types from scales *Hs, D,* and *Hy* (Heiskell, Rhodes, and Thayer 1959; Jones et al. 1976; Resh 1970). Similar results were also found for cases of gastrointestinal diseases, and particularly for gastroduodenal ulcer (Ely and Johnson 1966; Lewinsohn 1956) and ulcerative colitis (Fullerton, Kollar, and Caldwell 1962; Reda et al. 1968). The configurations of the neurotic triad in the average profiles of these groups reflect varying degrees of anxiety, depression, and worry about health. In some cases, significant differences were found between groups affected by various intestinal diseases (Lourens 1973; West 1970), but the data are confounded because the groups compared had different objective and subjective symptoms, different durations of the disease, and some of the patients came from different backgrounds. The mean profiles of the rheumatoid arthritis groups are likewise unintepretable because the control groups were composed either of normal subjects (who were not suffering the same distressing conditions of pain and illness) or of subjects with pathologies different from those of the experimental groups (Moos and Solomon 1965; Nalven and O'Brien 1968; Wyatt 1970).

Within the group of so-called classical psychosomatic illnesses, infarct and coronary diseases have been the elective field of application for the MMPI, both in prospective and retrospective studies (Bakker and Levenson 1967; Brozek, Keys, and Blackburn 1966; Bruhn, Chandler and Wolf 1969; Ibrahim et al. 1966; Lebovits et al. 1967; Mordkoff and Rand 1968; Ostfeld, Lebovits, and Shekelle 1964). Once again, the mean profiles from coronary disease patients are very similar to those of other types of patients with serious pathologies. In all these groups, the data revealed by the MMPI are too general and aspecific to have predictive value for a particular typology. A recent unpublished study by the Psychiatric Clinic of Rome University compared mean profiles of four groups of hospitalized patients afflicted with different somatic diseases (Figure 3.2). Although the resulting code types and configurations were slightly different, these differences did not reach statistical significance.

In conclusion, research aimed at isolating specific personality patterns associated with particular diseases has proven disappointing despite the efforts expended. The identification of specific premorbid patterns requires very precise experimental design and control, which cannot easily be achieved in a clinical context.

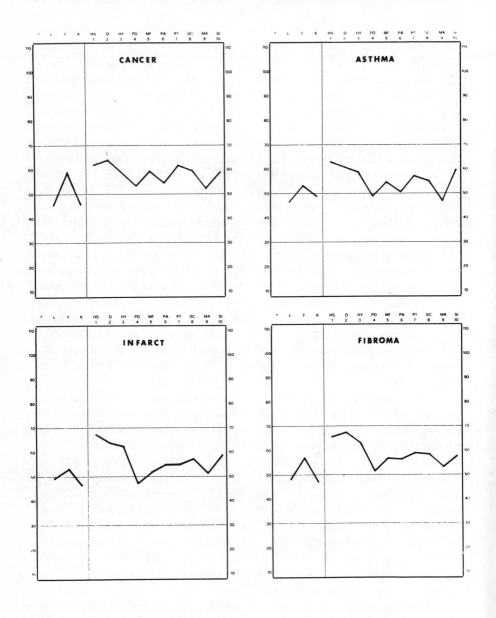

FIGURE 3.2: Mean MMPI profiles of four groups of medical patients in the same hospital. *Source*: Constructed by the author.

Despite the complex problems involved, both retrospective and prospective studies have been done to clarify the role of personality in the genesis of illness. While retrospective studies invariably suffer from the confounding of pre- and postmorbid personality traits, prospective studies, if adequately designed, lend themselves well to the investigation of this problem (Jenkins 1971; Ostfeld, Lebouits, and Shekells 1964). However, this type of research is technically very difficult to execute because it requires an extensive evaluation of a large normal population sample and an extremely prolonged follow-up period. Apart from the time and technical handicaps involved, it should be noted that personality changes may have occurred since the time of first assessment, thereby reducing the importance of the initial personality configuration as a pathogenic factor in illness. All factors considered, such studies are best conducted on selected samples of normal subjects at high risk for psychosomatic disorders in conditions where the necessary follow-up period is limited and when all other interacting variables can be controlled.

In the clinical setting where evaluation is done on patients already affected with somatic illnesses of unequal duration, information about premorbid personality can still be obtained through a careful selection of control groups. One possibility is to select healthy subjects at high risk for the disease in question. This method has been used to investigate personality correlates of coronary pathology (Ibrahim et al. 1966; Shekelle, Ostfeld, and Lebovits 1970), but has not yet been applied to other areas. A second approach would compare subjects displaying an asymptomatic form of a particular disease with persons actively suffering from the same disease (Solomon and Moos 1965). Another type of experimental design uses controls matched with the experimental subjects on subjective symptomatology, personal suffering, and duration of illness, but who differ in the disease diagnosed (Ermini et al. 1978).

In designs of this type, one of the principal difficulties is the selection of controls who not only have identical objective and subjective symptoms but who are also unaware of their diagnosis at the moment of psychometric assessment. Moreover, the examiner should also be unaware or at least uncertain of the patient's diagnosis to avoid uncontrolled-for influences on the experimental or control subjects. This double-blind design, analogous to that used in controlled pharmacological studies, is essential for a valid comparison of different disease groups. Naturally, should significant personality differences be found, they can only be considered limited to the particular situation explored, and cannot be used to construct specific typologies until confirmed by comparison with other control groups.

As noted above, the personality picture revealed by the MMPI is invariably confounded by the patients' reactions to illness and to other stressors accompanying it. From this perspective, the illness itself may be considered a situation of natural stress or as a relatively consistent stressor. This is particularly true for acute or especially serious diseases (for example, heart disease) that act as powerful anxiety-producing stimuli mobilizing the person's defenses and defense mechanisms. The emotional reaction to the stimulus "illness" may be considered an instance of a "sample" of the person's usual way of reacting to distressing situations. This conception of illness as stimulus permits the discrimination of stress-respondent and -nonrespondent subjects, each of whose characteristics then may be correlated with specific somatic symptoms or with course of illness.

This design was used in a recent MMPI study by Pancheri, Bellaterra, and colleagues (1978) on myocardial infarct patients, where the heart attack was viewed as a natural stressor capable of producing diverse emotional reactions in different people. The experimental group completed the MMPI and other tests on the third day after entrance into the coronary unit. After seven days of standard medical therapy, the subjects were divided into two subgroups: improved and not improved. Statistical comparison of mean group profiles found significant differences (p ≤ .05) for all scales except *Mf* and *Ma*, and demonstrated how different reactions to the stressor "infarct" influenced the recovery of the patient (Figure 3.3).

STUDIES OF CLINICAL METHODOLOGY

Personality assessment in psychosomatic research is complicated by many problems. In spite of the mass of publications in this field, only a handful are of value because the majority have not respected the minimum methodological requisites discussed above. To define better the issues involved, the Unit of Psychosomatic Medicine of the Psychiatric Institute of the University of Rome has dedicated the last four years to a series of basically methodological studies to explore the limits and usefulness of the MMPI in psychosomatic research. Of the four studies to be described here, the first three focus on refining the selection of control groups, while the fourth study is an example of a short-term prospective design conducted on a sample at high risk for a psychosomatic disturbance.

Breast Cancer versus Fibrocystic Disease

This study (Connolly and Pancheri 1976) was designed to detect personality features of patients with breast cancer. Existing literature on psychosomatic factors in human cancer suggests the presence of a strong tendency toward denial and repression, difficulty in overt expression of emotions, and mild depression. The methodological issue was the separation of those personality traits possibly correlated with development of cancer from those personality reactions consequent to awareness of having a serious, life-threatening disease.

The study was conducted on 92 patients admitted for diagnostic evaluation to a state hospital specializing in neoplastic diseases. All patients were suffering for the same length of time (one to three months) and from the same

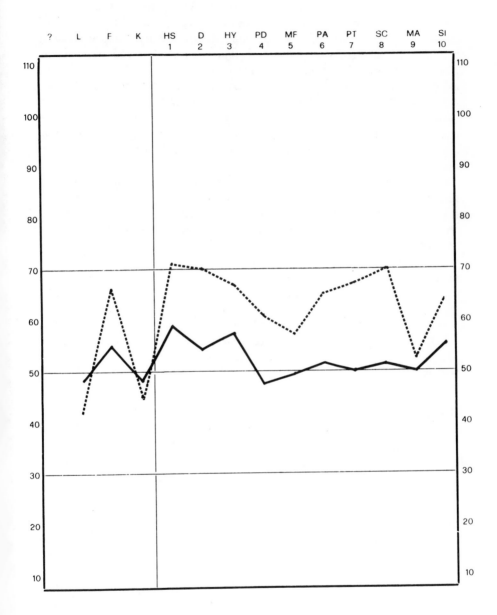

FIGURE 3.3: Initial mean MMPI profiles of improved (solid line) and not-improved (dotted line) infarct patients. From P. Pancheri, M. Bellaterra, S. Matteolo, M. Cristofari, C. Polizzi, and M. Puletti, "Infarct as a Stress Agent: Life History and Personality Characteristics in Improved versus Not-Improved Patients After Severe Heart Attack," *Journal of Human Stress* 4 (1978): 16. Copyright 1978 by *Journal of Human Stress*, Reprinted by permission.

symptoms: breast swelling, pain, and so on. The average age of the patients was 45.4 years (σ = 6.8), average number of years of education was 6.3 (σ = 3.1), and all were from the lower middle socioeconomic class. The first group included 41 breast cancer patients, while the second group was composed of 51 women with fibrocystic disease. For both groups, the means and standard deviations were calculated for each MMPI scale, and the between-group profiles were then compared (ANOVA, p $\leqslant$ .05) for significant differences. The mean MMPI profiles of the two groups were nearly overlapping in both their general configuration and T score values. the ANOVÁ analysis did not reveal any significant differences on any scale. The code type for both groups was 1-6-8, with scores in the normal range (Figure 3.4).

The results did not support the findings of earlier published investigations. That is, no real personality differences were found between cancer patients and patients suffering from other diseases with similar symptoms. However, the choice of the control group, although correct from a general methodological standpoint, is not adequate for the purpose of detecting personality patterns in neoplastic disease. Both breast cancer and fibrocystic disease can be considered neoplastic illnesses; both are thought to be partially dependent on endocrine dysfunctions, both are dependent on the same risk factors, and fibrocystic disease tends to be seen as a benign form of breast cancer. Thus one might assume that both diseases are interacting with the same personality factors. The only conclusion to be drawn from the data is that there are no differences in personality structure as evaluated by the MMPI between patients with benign and those with malignant breast tumors.

Rheumatoid Arthritis versus Osteoarthrosis

This research project (Pancheri, Teodori, and Aparo 1978) was intended to assess personality features in rheumatoid arthritis patients. According to the literature, these patients were expected to be more prone than controls to guilt and depression and to use denial and repression to defend against emotional conflict. Aside from exploration of this hypothesis, the study was important for its methodological implications. The task was to avoid the error inherent in the cancer control group discussed above by finding a control group characterized by similar symptoms but a substantially different pathology.

The study included 35 patients suffering from rheumatoid arthritis from five to seven years previous to evaluation. The average age of the subjects was 48 years (σ = 6.3), average number of years of education was 10 (σ = 3.4), and all were from the lower middle socioeconomic class. The control group was composed of 30 patients suffering for the same length of time from osteoarthrosis. Both diseases are chronic, affect the articular system, and have the same subjective symptomatology: articular pain, progressive motor invalidity, and deformation of articular joints. From a clinical standpoint, there are, of course, specific differences between these two diseases, but they are not relevant to the

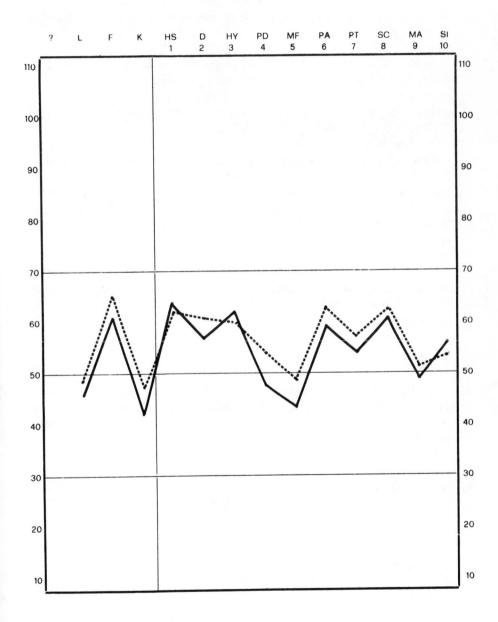

FIGURE 3.4: Mean MMPI profiles of breast cancer (solid line) and fibro-cystic disease (dotted line) patients. *Source:* Constructed by the authors.

patients' psychological reaction to the suffering and disability caused by these illnesses. The main point is that the pathogenesis of these diseases is different. Osteoarthrosis is considered a degenerative disease, while rheumatoid arthritis is an autoimmune disease caused by specific dysfunctions of the immunitary system.

The mean MMPI profiles of these groups are very similar in configuration, as both profiles seem to reflect the "general psychosomatic personality pattern" that has been interpreted as reactive to a state of worry, pain, and invalidity (Figure 3.5). However, when the two profiles were compared scale by scale (ANOVA), a statistically significant difference was found for the D scale (p < .05). While both profiles reflect characteristics common to patients with severe somatic pathology, such as somatic preoccupation, anxiety, search for emotional support, tendency to introversion, and depressive thoughts, there is nevertheless a pronounced difference in mood intensity, consistent with the initial hypothesis. The results do suggest that depressive traits, low emotional reactivity, and tendency to repress emotional conflict are in some way correlated with auto-aggressive immunitary mechanisms considered to be the etiological determinants of rheumatoid arthritis.

The importance of this study remains, however, methodological. The data obtained demonstrate that a careful selection of controls enables the separation of premorbid and postmorbid personality features, the former assumedly having pathogenic weight.

Psychogenic Amenorrhea

The studies described above exemplify some of the methodological difficulties faced by any psychosomatic researcher. As was shown in the study on enoplastic diseases, it is difficult to discriminate personality differences between patient groups having identical subjective symptoms and structurally similar pathologies, whereas groups having different pathologies may also have different subjective conditions and consequently different reactions. The study (Ermini et al. 1978) that follows is part of a broader research on personality patterns in secondary amenorrhea, and is reported here both for its methodological implications and for its empirical support of a general psychosomatic model.

The experimental group consisted of 24 patients with secondary amenorrhea six to twelve months prior to the study. The average age was 20 years (σ = 3.2) and the educational level varied between 8 and 12 years. All patients underwent a complete physical and gynecological examination prior to psychological assessment to exclude the possibility of physical illness etiologically related to the amenorrhea. Patients also underwent endocrinological tests to search for correlations between endocrine constellation and psychological variables. According to recent psychoendocrinological studies, hematic prolactin level can be used as an indicator of the functional condition of the hypothalamic centers responsible for the cyclic release of the gonadotropic hormones. On this basis,

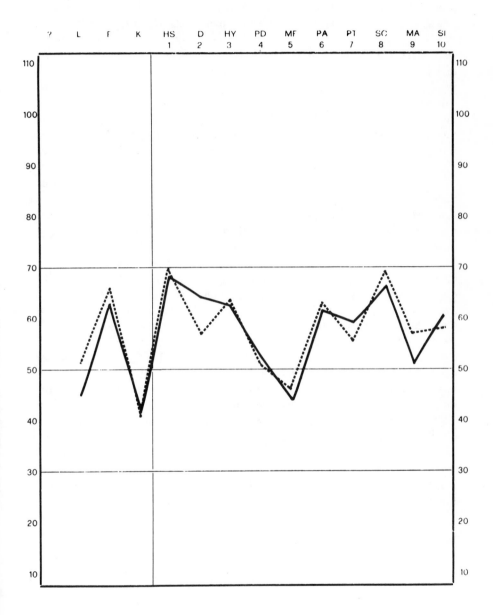

FIGURE 3.5: Mean MMPI profiles of rheumatoid arthritis (solid line) and osteoarthritis (dotted line) patients. From P. Pancheri, S. Teodori, and U. L. Aparo, "Psychological Aspects of Rheumatoid Arthritis vis-à-vis Osteoarthrosis," *Scandanavian Journal of Rheumatology* 7 (1978): 43. Copyright 1978 by the *Scandanavian Journal of Rheumatology*. Reprinted by permission.

the experimental group was split into two subgroups according to serum levels of prolactin found. Group A (13 patients) was characterized by normal prolactin levels, while group B (11 patients) showed high levels of prolactin. On the basis of these psychoendocrinological considerations, subgroups A and B can be considered as two stages of the same functional process, stage B being a more severe evolutive condition of stage A.

Due to the well-known functional and anatomical connections of the emotional brain to the hypothalamic centers, it was expected that some kind of difference in emotional status would be found. Methodologically, this study provided an ideal design because all patients were suffering from the same symptom for the same length of time and all had the same concerns and expectations. The only apparent difference was in the variable of hypothalamic functioning.

The mean profile of the composite experimental group did not provide relevant information about the personality characteristics of these patients. It is a normal range profile showing the usual dual elevations in the neurotic and psychotic areas. Comparison of the subgroup profiles, however, revealed significant differences. The normal prolactin group presented a high-ranging personality pattern (code type 2-8-4), while the high prolactin group showed a completely normal range profile (code type 1-8). Significant differences occurred on scales D ($p \leqslant .01$) and Pd ($p \leqslant .01$) only (Figure 3.6).

As expected on the basis of the proposed hypothesis, the two subgroups were clearly discriminated into a more "pathological and a more "normal" group. This finding is methodologically sound because the experimental design eliminated the possible influence of differing postmorbid reactions. On the other hand, the endocrinological examination evidenced a real intrinsic biological difference between the groups. More intriguing is the interpretation of the results showing greater psychopathological impairment of the patients characterized by less severe somatic dysfunction. The normal prolactin women showed a clinical picture of passive-aggressive personality (2-8-4), with a stronger tendency to express depressive and aggressive feelings behaviorally. These results support the hypothesis of a psychophysiological complementarity discussed in Pancheri and Benaissa's psychobiological model (1978), that is, stronger behavioral manifestations are associated with fewer biological disturbances and vice versa.

MMPI Scores Predictive of the Course of Labor

The three preceding studies focused on present personality of patients affected by various diseases and on the choice of adequate control groups. This study (Zichella et al. 1977) instead was designed as a short-term prospective research project conducted in controlled experimental conditions and using the labor of childbirth as a natural stressful situation at high psychosomatic risk. The scope of the study was to ascertain whether personality structure as assessed by the MMPI in the ninth month of pregnancy could have predictive value for the course of labor and the appearance of obstetrical complications. Literature on this subject suggests that the presence of anxiety during pregnancy can influence labor and favor obstetrical complications. The general aim of the research was to explore the capacity of the MMPI to predict the reaction of a

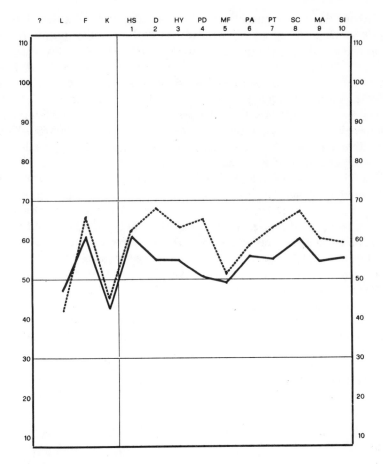

FIGURE 3.6: Mean MMPI profiles of high-prolactin (solid line) and low-pro-
lactin (dotted line) secondary amenorrhea patients. From M. Ermini, D. Man-
ziglo, L. Zichella, P. Pancheri, L. Pancheri, and M. Bellaterra, "Psychoneuroendocrine Aspects of Secondary Amenorrhea," in *Psychoneuroendocrinology
in Reproduction*, ed. C. Carenza, P. Pancheri, and L. Zichella, 1978. Copyright by Academic Press, Inc. (London) Limited, 1978. Reprinted with permission.

normal population sample without psychiatric problems to a standardized situation of natural stress.

The experimental design included an MMPI assessment of a group of normal women in their ninth month of pregnancy and a successive serial evaluation
at regular intervals during labor of three parameters: state anxiety, subjective
pain, and pain threshold. The subjects were 80 pregnant women who did not
display any signs of medical or somatic pathology at the interview and clinical
exam. None was suffering or had suffered from psychiatric disturbances. All
were at their first or second partum, their ages ranged between 20 and 30 years
(average 25.3, $\sigma = 4.8$), average number of years of education was 8.5 ($\sigma = 4.0$),
73.5 percent were housewives, 11.8 percent were white-collar workers, 9.7 percent were blue-collar workers, and all were married.

At the final prepartum obstetric control, subjects were explained the purpose of the research and administered the MMPI. The profiles then were classified in two groups: normal (n = 33) in which all clinical and validity scale scores were below 70 and others in which at least one clinical scale exceeded 70 T score points (n = 47). These deviant profiles then were separated into three groups on the basis of code types (group 1-3/3-1, group 8-6/6-8, and group 2-7/7-2). At dilation-dependent intervals during labor (0, 4, 7 cm., complete dilation), state anxiety was measured by the State Trait Anxiety Inventory (STAI) (Spielberger, Gorsuch, and Leshene 1970), subjective pain was measured by a simple metric scale, and pain threshold by a pressure method.

Mean state anxiety values during labor showed that subjects with deviant MMPI profiles obtained higher scores than subjects with normal profiles, especially during the terminal part of labor (Figure 3.7). For both groups subjective pain increased progressively during labor, but again, subjects with deviant MMPIs obtained higher scores, but the differences were not statistically significant (Figure 3.8). While pain threshold decreased continuously in both groups as labor progressed, pain tolerance was statistically lower (p ≤ .01) in the deviant MMPI group at all labor intervals (Figure 3.9).

State anxiety scores as a function of code types demonstrated that the MMPI profile in pregnancy can be a valid predictor of psychophysiological reactions during labor. Subjects obtaining normal MMPIs as well as subjects ob-

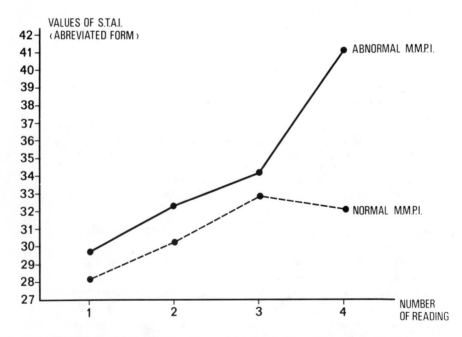

FIGURE 3.7: Changes in state anxiety during labor for patients obtaining normal or deviant MMPI profiles. *Source*: Constructed by the author.

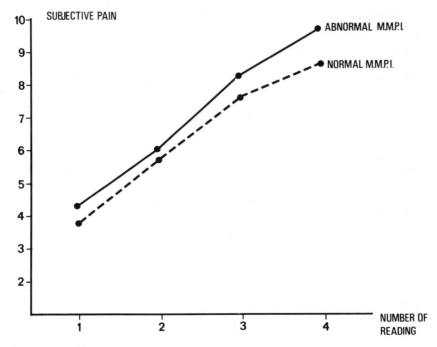

FIGURE 3.8: Changes in subjective pain during labor for patients obtaining normal or deviant MMPI profiles. *Source:* Constructed by the author.

taining normal MMPIs as well as subjects obtaining MMPI code type 1-3/3-1 showed significantly lower (p ≤ .01) state anxiety levels across the labor intervals than subjects obtaining either MMPI code type 2-7/7-2 or 8-6/6-8 (Figure 3.10).

Aside from the clinical and theoretical implications of the data, this study is important for its methodology because it is an example of a controlled short-term prospective study conducted in a situation of psychophysiological stress. In this experimental condition the MMPI may have predictive value on the course of the important psychosomatic phenomenon of labor.

CONCLUSIONS

There is practically no area of medicine in which the MMPI has not been used to explore personality patterns associated with disease or to explore patient reactions to being a patient. Dahlstrom, Welsh, and Dahlstrom (1975), in their review of the literature on the applications of the MMPI in medicine, listed over 200 bibliographical citations covering the most varied sectors of medical interest, from metabolic and endocrine disturbances (96 entries) to circulatory disorders (42 entries), otolaryngological disorders (36 entries), and surgical prob-

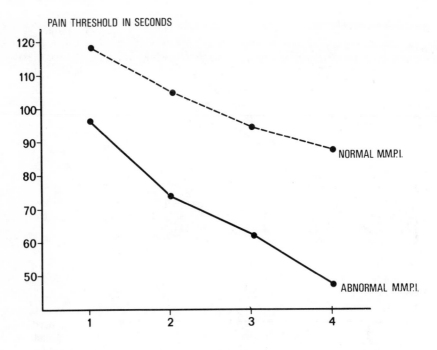

FIGURE 3.9: Changes in pain threshold at four readings during labor for patients obtaining normal or deviant MMPI profiles. *Source*: Constructed by the author.

lems (22 entries). In reality, the literature on the uses of the MMPI in medicine is much greater if one considers the publications in nonpsychiatric specialized medical reviews and the psychosomatic studies in which the MMPI has been used as an accessory assessment instrument in conjunction with other measures. A conservative estimate of the number of published works in which the MMPI is cited would raise the number of bibliographical entires to between 300 and 400, thereby making the MMPI by far the most frequently used assessment instrument in general and psychosomatic medicine.

A literary review is not among the aims of this chapter, which instead centers on methodological issues. Nonetheless, it is interesting to ask why the MMPI so often has been the instrument of choice in psychosomatic studies. Aside from its intrinsic characteristics and its demonstrated reliability and validity, the ease of administration and the wealth of information provided undoubtedly have played a role of primary importance. For example, in medical and surgical hospital wards where it is objectively difficult to conduct long psychological interviews or administer complex diagnostic batteries of tests, the MMPI allows the collection of a mass of data on personality features and emotional problems in a short period of time without the aid of specialized personnel. Moreover, the information provided is easily understandable and utilizable by the attending physician. For these attributes the MMPI is often requested or at least accepted by hospital staff for purposes other than just research.

Internationally, the MMPI is the most diffuse personality instrument with translations available in all the main languages, as normative and validity studies have been conducted on several different cultural groups (Butcher and Pancheri 1976). This permits the comparison of data and the control of experimental results on different cross-national samples. One of the principal problems in transcultural psychosomatic research is the incomparability of data collected in diverse contexts with diverse methods and instruments. While biological parameters do not change, or at least change less than psychological variables in different cultures, psychometric measures require a local standardization of the assessment instrument on each new population. No other instrument available today adapts itself to this requirement as well as the MMPI.

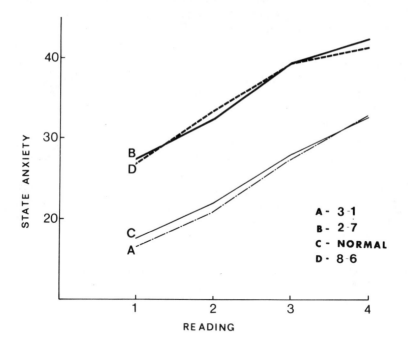

FIGURE 3.10: Changes in state anxiety during labor as a function of MMPI code types. *Source*: Constructed by the author.

Undoubtedly, the role and the limits of applicability of objective personality instruments in psychosomatics need to be redefined. It should be remembered that the MMPI was originally designed to detect easily and quickly psyciatric symptoms and disorders in a general medical population. The latter diffusion of the inventory into completely different areas should not allow one to forget that the sensitivity and efficiency of this measure increase in proportion to the evidence of an emotional or personality disturbance. In psychosomatics, the majority of profiles fall within the normal range, and the personality differences between groups with similar symptoms but different pathologies are often so subtle that they cannot be detected in the usual psychological interview. Even in accurately controlled studies, the between-group differences are very small and easily confounded in the range of experimental error. For this reason, very careful control of subject homogeneity, great precision in the experimental design, adequate control groups, and control of all the parasitic variables likely to influence the results are needed. Naturally, these are fundamental requisites of any research design. However, where differences are small, a rigid approach to reduce the margin of error is necessary.

In an attempt to increase the sensitivity of the MMPI and to adapt it to the needs of psychosomatic research, special scales for particular areas of somatic pathology were constructed, usually with the same empirical method used for the whole inventory. Special scales have been designed for allergies (Smith 1962), neurodermatitis (Allerhand, Gough, and Grais 1950), and ulcer personality (Scodel 1953). As is true for a majority of the special MMPI scales, these special somatic scales are characterized by rather poor or even nonexistent cross-validation studies. Frequently they have been derived from inadequate or insufficient samples, and in general their predictive power is low. At the present time, it does not seem that the items making up a psychosomatic "critical item" list or an organic pathology scale have provided satisfactory results. (See Chapter 14 regarding the development of special MMPI scales.)

On the other hand, the present development of psychosomatic research deemphasizes correlational studies of personality and illness. The illness itself should be considered only the last link in a psychobiological chain of events that have prepared and predisposed the organic substrate. As discussed, emotional stressors play an etiological role in preparing the biological terrain by inducing persistent and irreversible functional alterations finally leading up to the manifestation of the disease. Both in etiological and clinical investigations, research should focus on the precursors to somatic disease and their correlation with personality structure and life stress events.

Such an orientation naturally requires a preliminary knowledge of the biological modifications preceding disease (endocrine, hematochemical, and tissue alterations), followed by the study of "personality-precursors" and not "personality-disease" typologies. The difficulties associated with this approach are innumerable, if for no other reason than a multidisciplinary effort is required, but the advantages accruing to psychosomatic research are indisputable. Above all, the present problem of separating causal from reactive components would be resolved given that subjective suffering is minimal at the precursory stage. This approach still allows the simultaneous use of psychometric and biological variables, both expressed numerically, and permits the utilization of complex statistical methods (multiple correlation, complex factorial, discriminant and variance analyses). On a therapeutic and preventive level, identification of links between particular emotional patterns and biological alterations makes timely psychotherapeutic intervention possible. The most interesting applications of the MMPI to psychosomatics in the next few years will probably be in this area.

How much does the MMPI contribute to psychosomatic research? Generally speaking, if this type of research aims at clarifying the links between psychological and biological variables, then the present psychological measures are too imprecise and crude to be compared with the highly refined biological measures available today. In psychoneuroendocrinology, for example, the methods of hormonal dosing have reached a very high sensitivity, while in psychometrics the most sophisticated and complex tests hardly detect even notable variations in emotional state. In this respect, the MMPI retains its importance in psychosomatic research when it is associated with other data collection instruments. Even in studies investigating precursors and personality, every personality measure should be associated with a standardized life stress events measure. A recent study by Pancheri, De Martino et al. (1979) demonstrated that the association of psychometric instruments with a life stress events list noticeably increased the capacity to discriminate between groups of medical patients beyond that of any instrument considered separately.

The introduction of a new instrument specifically designed for psychosomatic research and clinical assessment is highly recommended and indispensable to the identification of the subtle changes in emotional state that accompany biological alterations in conditions of emotional state. In the meantime, adequate use can be made of the MMPI by perfecting the experimental design and using it in conjunction with other instruments, but always being aware of the present limits of psychometric personality assessment in a field as complex as psychosomatics.

REFERENCES

Alexander, F. 1950. *Psychosomatic Medicine*. New York: Norton.

Allerhand, M. E., H. Gough, and M. L. Grais. 1950. "Personality Factors in Neurodermatitis." *Psychosomatic Medicine* 12: 386–90.

Bakker, C. B., and R. M. Levenson. 1967. "Determinants of Angina Pectoris." *Psychosomatic Medicine* 29: 621–33.

Bahnson, C. B. 1969. "Psychophysiological Complementarity in Malignancies: Past Work and Future Vistas." *Annals New York Academy of Sciences* 164: 319–30.

——, and M. B. Bahnson. 1964. "Cancer as an Alternative to Psychosis: A Theoretical Model of Somatic and Psychological Regression." In *Psychosomatic Aspects of Neoplastic Disease*, edited by D. M. Kissen and L. LeShan, pp. 42–62. London: Pitman.

Brozek, J., A. Keys, and H. Blackburn. 1966. "Personality Differences Between Potential Coronary and Non-Coronary Subjects." *Annals New York Academy of Sciences* 134: 1057–64.

Bruhn, J. G., B. Chandler, and S. Wolf. 1969. "A Psychological Study of Survivors and Non-Survivors of Myocardial Infarction." *Psychosomatic Medicine* 31: 8–19.

Butcher, J. N., and P. Pancheri. 1976. *A Handbook of Cross-National MMPI Research*. Minneapolis: University of Minnesota Press.

Connolly, A., and P. Pancheri. 1976. "Personality Characteristics in Breast Cancer." Paper presented at the International Symposium on Personality Assessment, Rome, June.

Dahlstrom, W. G., G. S. Welsh, and L. E. Dahlstrom. 1975. *An MMPI Handbook*, vol 2. Minneapolis: University of Minnesota Press.

Ely, N. E., and M. H. Johnson. 1966. "Emotional Responses to Peptic Ulcer Management." *American Journal of Psychiatry* 122, 1362–71.

Ermini, M., D. Mangiglio, L. Zichella, P. Pancheri, L. Pancheri, and M. Bellaterra. 1978. "Psychoneuroendocrine Aspects of Secondary Amenorrhea." In *Psychoneuroendocrinology of Human Reproduction*, edited by C. Carenza, P. Pancheri, and L. Zichella, pp. 112–60. New York: Academic Press.

Frankenhaeuser, M. 1975. "Experimental Approaches to the Study of Catecholamines and Emotions." In *Emotions: Their Parameters and Measurement*, edited by L. Levi, pp. 209–34. New York: Raven Press.

Fullerton, D., E. Kollar, and A. Caldwell. 1962. "A Clinical Study of Ulcerative Colitis." *Journal of American Medical Association* 181: 463–70.

Heiskell, C. L., J. M. Rhodes, and K. H. Thayer. 1959. "Some Psychosomatic Aspects of Asthma." *Journal of American Medical Association* 170: 1764–67.

Ibrahim, M. A., C. D. Jenkins, J. C. Cassel, J. R. McDonough, and C. G. Hames. 1966. "Personality Traits and Coronary Heart Disease: Utilization of a Cross-Sectional Study Design to Test Whether a Selected Psychological Profile Precedes or Follows Manifest Coronary Heart Disease." *Journal of Chronic Diseases* 19: 255–71.

Jenkins, C. D. 1971. "Psychologic and Social Precursors of Coronary Disease." *New England Journal of Medicine* 284: 244–54.

Jones, N. F., R. Kinsman, R. Schum, and C. Resnikoff. 1976. "Personality Profiles in Asthma." *Journal of Clinical Psychology* 32: 285–97.

Lebovits, B. Z., R. B. Shekelle, A. M. Ostfeld, and P. Oglesby. 1967. "Prospective and Retrospective Psychological Studies of Coronary Heart Disease." *Psychosomatic Medicine* 29: 265–72.

Levi, L. 1974. "Psychological Stress and Disease: A Conceptual Model." In *Life Stress and Illness*, edited by E. K. E. Gunderson and H. R. Rahe, pp. 215–42. Springfield, Ill.: Charles C. Thomas.

——. 1972. "Stress and Distress in Response to Psychosocial Stimuli." *Acta Medica Scandinavica* supplement 191: 528.

Lewinsohn, P. M. 1956. "Personality Correlates of Duodenal Ulcer and Other Psychosomatic Reactions." *Journal of Clinical Psychology* 12: 296–98.

Lourens, P. J. D. 1973. "An Exploratory Psychological Study of Digestive Diseases." *Alabama Journal of Medical Science* 10: 308–17.

Mason, J. W. 1975a. "A Historical View of the Stress Field." *Journal of Human Stress* 1: 22–36.

——. 1975b. "Emotion as Reflected in Patterns of Endocrine Integration." In *Emotions: Their Parameters and Measurement*, edited by L. Levi, pp. 143–81. New York: Raven Press.

Moos, R. H., and G. F. Solomon. 1965. "Psychologic Comparisons Between Women with Rheumatoid Arthritis and Their Non-Arthritic Sisters. I. Personality Test and Interview Rating Data." *Psychosomatic Medicine* 27: 135–49.

Mordkoff, A. M., and M. A. Rand. 1968. "Personality and Adaptation to Coronary Artery Disease." *Journal of Consulting and Clinical Psychology* 32: 648–53.

Nalven, F. B., and J. F. O'Brien. 1968. "On the Use of the MMPI with Rheumatoid Arthritic Patients." *Journal of Clinical Psychology* 24: 70.

Ostfeld, A. M., B. Z. Lebovits, and R. B. Shekelle. 1964. "A Prospective Study of the Relationship Between Personality and Coronary Heart Disease." *Journal of Chronic Diseases* 17; 265–76.

Pancheri, P., M. Bellaterra, S. Matteoli, M. Cristofari, C. Polizzi, and M. Puletti. 1978. "Infarct as a Stress Agent: Life History and Personality Characteristics in Improved or Not-Improved Patients After Severe Heart Attack." *Journal of Human Stress* 4: 16.

Pancheri, P., and C. Benaissa. 1978. "Stress and Psychosomatic Illness." In *Stress and Anxiety*, edibed by C. D. Spielberger and I. G. Sarason, vol. 5, pp. 61–82. Washington, D.C.: Hemisphere.

Pancheri, P., V. De Martino, G. Spiombi, M. Biondi, and R. Mosticoni. 1979. "Life Stress Events and State and Trait Anxiety in Psychiatric and Psychosomatic Patients." In *Stress and Anxiety*, edited by C. D. Spielberger and I. G. Sarason, vol 6. Washington, D.C.: Hemisphere.

Pancheri, P., S. Teodori, U. L. Aparo.1978. "Psychological Aspects of Rheumatoid Arthritis vis-a-vis Osteoarthrosis." *Scandanavian Journal of Rheumatology* 7: 47.

Reda, G. C., N. Lalli, P. Pancheri, A. Torsolo, and R. Caprilli. 1968. "Contribution to the Study of Personality in Idiopathic Rectocolitis." *Rivista di Psichiatria* 3: 543–66.

Resh, M. G. 1970. "Asthma of Unknown Origin as a Psychological Group." *Journal of Consulting and Clinical Psychology* 35: 429.

Scodel, A. 1953. "Passivity in a Clan of Peptic Ulcer Patients." *Psychological Monographs* 67, no. 360.

Shekelle, R. B., B. Z. Ostfeld, B. Z. Lebovits, and O. Paul. 1970. "Personality Traits and Coronary Heart Disease: A Reexamination of Ibrahim's Hypothesis Using Longitudinal Data." *Journal of Chronic Diseases* 23: 33–38.

Smith, R. E. 1962. "An MMPI Profile of Allergy." *Psychosomatic Medicine* 24: 543–53.

Solomon, G. F., and R. H. Moos. 1965. "The Relationship of Personality to the Presence of Rheumatoid Factor in Asymptomatic Relatives of Patients with Rheumatoid Arthritis." *Psychosomatic Medicine* 27: 350–60.

Spielberger, C. D., R. L. Gorsuch, and R. E. Lushene. 1970. "Manual for the State-Trait Anxiety Inventory." Palo Alto, Calif.: Consulting Psychologist Press.

West, K. L. 1970. "MMPI Correlates of Ulcerative Colitis." *Journal of Clinical Psychology* 26: 214.

Wyatt, S. 1975. "Psychologic Factors in Arthritis." In *Arthritis and Physical Medicine*, edited by E. Licht, pp. 127–43. Philadelphia: Saunders. 1970.

Zichella, L., P. Pancheri, A. Connolly, and E. Calzolari. 1977. "The Measurement of Pain and Anxiety in Labor." In *Therapy in Psychosomatic Medicine*, edited by F. Antonelli, pp. 186–219. Rome, Italy: Luigi Pozzi.

4 / MMPI CHARACTERISTICS OF OPIATE ADDICTS, ALCOHOLICS, AND OTHER DRUG ABUSERS

Patricia B. Sutker
Robert P. Archer

Over the past three decades, **MMPI** researchers have attempted to describe common personality characteristics among individuals dependent upon drugs or alcohol and to examine the extent to which personality patterns can be differentiated from those of other groups categorized as socially deviant, psychiatrically disturbed, or blatantly criminal. Investigative efforts have reflected in varying degrees the assumption that there are certain "person" variables, conceptualized as enduring trait or fluctuating state characteristics, that are correlated with or causative of drug experimentation and dependence. Nevertheless, researchers exploring such questions have neither necessarily espoused addiction-prone hypotheses to explain drug dependence nor affirmed that addiction represents a unitary phenomenon explicable only in terms of a simplistic person model. Recently, the importance of assessing situation and drug-effect variables, in addition to testing the applicability of social learning principles, has been recognized as critical for understanding and predicting the complexities of drug abuse behavior. Some investigators have also acknowledged the role of person-situation interactions in influencing drug use and abuse.

The use of objective personality inventories to aid in clinical diagnosis and personality assessment has increased greatly in the past 40 years despite opposition and speculation that the methodology represented is incompatible with social learning approaches to personality. The **MMPI** has become a particularly popular medium for studying the personality correlates of addictive states, and Butcher and Owen (1978) reported that 96 publications addressing alcohol and drug abuse issues have appeared in scientific journals between 1972 and 1977 alone.

In addition to the **MMPI**, other instruments have been used to measure seemingly relevant person variables in attempts to identify shared traits or states among individuals who have become dependent upon drugs, alcohol, or drug combinations. For example, investigators have explored personality dimensions among addict samples using the Internal-External Locus of Control (Berzins and Ross 1973) and Sensation Seeking (Carrol and Zuckerman 1977) scales and such inventories as the Gough Adjective Check List (Platt 1975), the California Psychological Inventory (Kurtines, Hogan, and Weiss 1975), and the Edwards Personality Preference Schedule (Reith, Crockett, and Craig 1975). Uses of these and other paper-and-pencil measures of personality dimensions to investigate correlates of drug use and abuse have been reviewed elsewhere by Platt and Labate (1976) and Kilpatrick, Sutker, and Smith (1976).

It would be impossible to provide a detailed synopsis of the numbers of MMPI studies that have attempted to delineate the personality characteristics of addicts, alcoholics, and other abusers. Therefore this chapter will focus on important trends and recent issues in personality descriptions of addict groups, specifically opiate addicts, alcoholics, and abusers of other licit and illicit drugs. The emphasis for the chapter will be upon MMPI descriptions and differentiation of abuser samples; however, results of studies using other personality measures will be included where relevant. Special attention will be focused on issues related to assessment of situation variables that have been shown to exert important influences on MMPI responding, as well as controversies that have emerged in the literature, for example, addiction-prone hypotheses, voluntarism and MMPI responding, and addict-alcoholic comparisons.

OPIATE ADDICTS

It is undeniable that MMPI studies of addict samplers were initially based upon the assumption that certain personality characteristics, particularly enduring personal traits, were at least in part responsible for development of heroin or opiate dependence. Much of this reasoning derived from psychoanalytical formulations of basic personality defects that were hypothesized to result in reliance on chemicals to cope with daily stresses. This theme pervades a number of articles and research reports describing the personality characteristics associated with addiction (for example, Pittel 1972; Khantzian, Mack, and Schatzberg 1974; Wurmser 1974). However, deficit explanations need not necessarily be associated with personality studies of addictive phenomena. For example, Naditch (1975) defined three classes of motives for drug-taking behaviors among college drug users, which included use for therapeutic intent, use for curiosity or pleasure, and reluctant use from peer pressure. Thus, in addition to self-medication hypotheses, pleasure- or curiosity-seeking motives and explanations that rely heavily on principles derived from social learning and reinforcement theories have been emphasized. It is also apparent that certain numbers of relatively "normal" individuals can become addicted to opiates with subgroups of drug abuser samples of 6 percent (Sheppard, Fracchia et al. 1972), 12 percent (Sutker 1971), and 5.5 percent (Hill, Haertzen, and Glaser 1960) reported to produce normal MMPI profiles.

Composite MMPI Profiles

Having recognized these issues, it is possible to review relevant literature cast in a broader based perspective for personality assessment. As Platt and La- bate (1976) pointed out, most studies show that opiate addicts demonstrate signs of significant psychopathology, whether reflected by MMPI, clinical inter- view, or social history data. Of course, such findings must be interpreted in light of the fact that data are usually collected among samples of drug abusers apply- ing for treatment, incarcerated in prison systems, or undergoing psychiatric intervention in inpatient or outpatient settings. Indeed, there are few relevant data to describe personality or psychosocial characteristics of opiate users who have never come into contact with treatment or criminal justice systems (Zin- berg 1977). Most frequently, MMPI researchers have attempted to derive compo- site profile patterns to represent commonalities among samples of heroin addicts. Before discussion of the salient features of composite addict profiles, it is im- portant to emphasize that few contemporary investigators would seriously sug- gest that a single personality profile is common to all or most individuals chronic- ally abusing drugs, or that opiate addicts, for example, represent a homogeneous group with respect to a certain set of personality characteristics. Rather, identifi- cation of characteristic composite MMPI profiles for heroin addicts has been re- garded as one mechanism by which to understand the modal features of individ- uals categorized by drug abuse behavior and as a necessary preliminary step to examining potential subclasses of characteristics applicable to specific subtypes.

Probably the most uniform and striking finding of MMPI studies of heroin addicts is the predominance of sociopathic features among personality descrip- tors reflected by significant elevations on scale 4. As early as 1959, Astin re- marked on the frequency of marked scale 4 elevations among male heroin ad- dicts and indicated that approximately 60 percent of addicts in the Lexington U.S. Pulbic Health Service Hospital produced their highest score on this MMPI scale. Other personality descriptions of male narcotic addicts have yielded simi- lar findings, that is, addicts, often regardless of heterogeneity on other measures, tend to score high on scale 4 (Hill, Haertzen, and Glaser 1960; Hill, Haertzen, and Davis 1962; Gilbert and Lombardi 1967; Pugliese 1975; Sutker 1971; Sut- ker and Allain 1973; Zuckerman et al. 1975). Results of the Sutker and Allain (1973), Skolnick and Zuckerman (in press), and Zuckerman et al. (1975) in- vestigations suggest that elevations on scales 4 and 9 are relatively constant over varied assessment conditions. Similarly, MMPI profiles for narcotic addicts consistent with the above findings were obtained by Overall (1973) in which the composite prototypic code type for heroin addicts was 4-9. Results from Viet- nam veteran populations (Black 1975; Hampton and Vogel 1973; Jarvis, Simne- gar, and Traweek 1975), addict physicians (Hill, Haertzen, and Yamahiro 1968), and female heroin addicts (Olson 1964; Ross and Berzins 1974; Sutker and Moan 1972) are also consistent with these findings. Indeed, investigations designed to specify reliable behavioral correlates of sociopathy often are based upon heroin addict samples (Sutker, Archer, and Kilpatrick, in press).

Findings pointing to marked elevations on scale 4 as a high point among modal MMPI profiles should not be interpreted to suggest that heroin addiction is confined to groups of sociopaths alone. Emphasizing this point, Berzins, Ross, and Monroe (1971) found that profile patterns varied significantly, depending upon the situation in which addicts responded to the personality inventory. These investigators showed that addicts in four subgroups (representing different conditions of admission to the Lexington treatment facility) demonstrated considerable general personality maladjustment and produced a consistently tri-modal profile shape with peaks on scales 4, 2, and 8, indicating, in addition to social deviance, affective disturbance and cognitive idiosyncrasy. They also cautioned that hospitalized addicts may not necessarily show the hallmarks of sociopathy and that the pervasiveness of the sterotype might well bear examination in other treatment settings. Related to this issue is the report by Sheppard, Fracchia et al. (1973) that MMPI responding may vary significantly, depending upon the treatment applicant pool with volunteers for methadone maintenance demonstrating greater psychopathology than was observed to be descriptive of other treatment groups. Similarly, in a comparison of heroin-dependent and-nondependent servicemen, Kojak and Canby (1975) reported no significant differences in psychopathology on the MMPI.

Next in significance to the presence of symptomatology suggestive of antisocial personality or sociopathy is evidence indicating that neurotic personality patterns are associated with addiction to opiates. However, rarely are constellations of purely neurotic features observed. With the possible exception of scale 9, probably the second most frequently elevated scale in composite MMPI profiles of heroin addicts is scale 2, which reflects feelings and thoughts of pessimism, depression, and despondency. In fact, a number of studies that present the mean profile patterns of heroin addicts show the two highest scale elevations on 4 and 2 (Gilbert and Lombardi 1967; Ross and Berzins 1974; Sutker 1971). Considering the association of neurotic features, the pressures of the street environment, and opiate dependence, Sutker and Allain (1973) compared groups of unincarcerated street addicts with prisoners who had a history of heroin addiction and those who had never experimented with opium derivatives. Unincarcerated street addicts showed significantly more psychopathology than both prison groups on scales 1, 2, 3, 4, and 7, with the greatest degree of relationship between group membership and scales making up the neurotic triad. Studies by Hill, Haertzen, and Glaser (1960) and Sheppard, Fracchia et al. (1972) also showed that neurotics represented as much as 19 and 16 percent of their respective addict samples.

These and other MMPI reports emphasize the association of drug dependence and neurotic features; however, more recent findings suggest that neurotic symptomatology is most characteristic of protocols produced at entrance or on application to drug treatment programs. Looking at MMPI changes in heroin addicts following short- and long-term inpatient care, Sutker, Allain, and Cohen (1974) found that two samples of male addict clients at intake tended to produce pronounced elevations on scales 4 and 2, while after a period of treatment, the mean profile pattern was clearly 4–9 (see Figure 4.1). Similarly, as illustrated in Figure 4.2, Zuckerman et al. (1975) reported virtual disappearance of depressive and neurotic patterns among male residents with a history of hard drug use who completed the first phase of a therapeutic community program. Although not as exaggerated, changes in neurotic symptoms were also reported by Skolnick and Zuckerman (in press) among hard and soft drug users incarcerated for comparable periods of time. Interpreted as support for the hypothesis that neurotic features represent reactive complications in the course of drug dependence rather than causal forces, these results complement those of DeLeon, Skodol, and Rosenthal (1973), who found reductions in psychiatric disturbance, including depression, hostility, anxiety, and psychoticism, following approximately seven months in a therapeutic community program. Whether or not neurotic symptomatology can be attributed a causal role in the development of opiate dependence is another matter; nevertheless, clinicians and researchers alike have speculated that anxiety, depression, and hostility are important in contributing to initial and sustained drug use.

Results of a recent study (Sutker, Archer, and Allain 1978) suggest that there are interesting interrelationships among sociopathic and neurotic features measured by the MMPI, sensation-seeking, and drug use patterns among chronic users of illicit drugs. High scores on Zuckerman's (1972) Sensation Seeking Scale (SSS) were related to use of drugs from a greater number of pharmacological categories, earlier age at first drug use, and curiosity as a motive for initial alcohol use. Drug abusers classified as high sensation seekers scored higher than middle and low sensation seekers on MMPI scales, reflecting attitudinal deviance, sociopathy, and heightened activity (scales F, 4, and 9) and lower in social introversion (scale 0). As shown in Figure 4.3, low sensation seekers produced higher scores than other groups on scales L, 1, 3, and R, indicating greater neurotic involvement, repression, and denial. Similar relationships among SSS and MMPI variables have been reported in correlational studies with prisoners (Blackburn 1969) and alcoholics (Kish and Busse 1969) and are compatible with theoretical approaches associating chronic use of illicit drugs with two seemingly conflicting views of addiction proneness, for example, ego-deficit theories, career motivation, or lifestyle explanations.

That many addicts exhibit signs of psychopathology suggestive of psychotic or confused thinking states is clearly demonstrated in a study by Berzins et al. (1974), who found that approximately one third of subjects in their representative sample of male and female, black and white addicts showed highest elevations on scales 2, 4, and 8. Other investigators reported a high frequency of elevations on scale 8 among addict samples, suggesting considerable psychopathology of a possibly psychotic nature (Greaves 1971; Kwant, Rice, and Hays 1976). There is also evidence that changes in psychotic symptomatology are

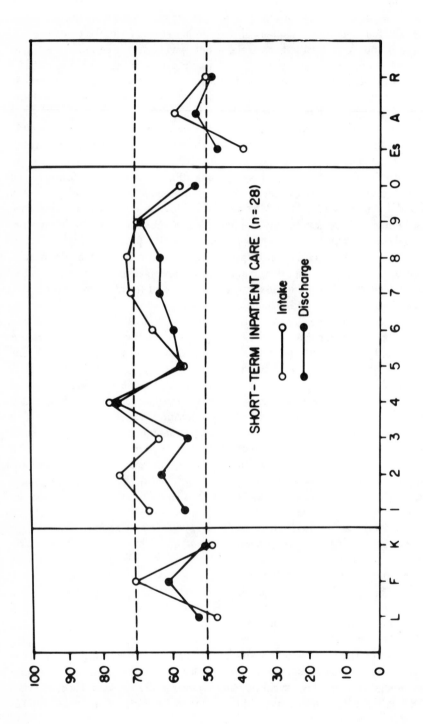

SHORT-TERM INPATIENT CARE (n=28)

○ Intake
● Discharge

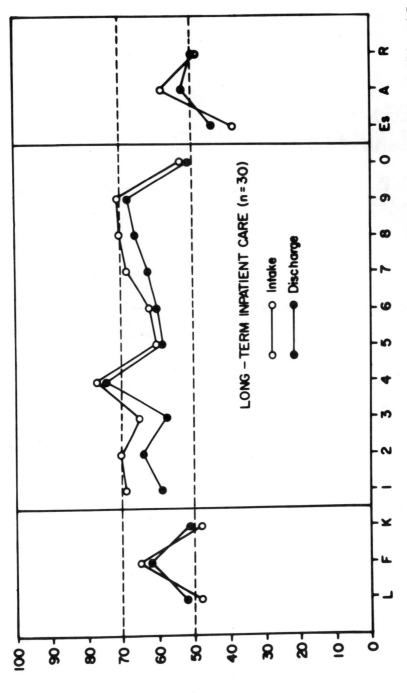

FIGURE 4.1: Changes in mean MMPI scales of addicts following short- and long-term hospitalization. From P. B. Sutker, A. N. Allain, and G. H. Cohen, "MMPI Indices of Personality Change Following Short- and Long-Term Hospitalization of Heroin Addicts," *Psychological Reports* 34, (1974): 495–500, Figures 1 and 2. Copyright 1974 by *Psychological Reports*. Reprinted by permission.

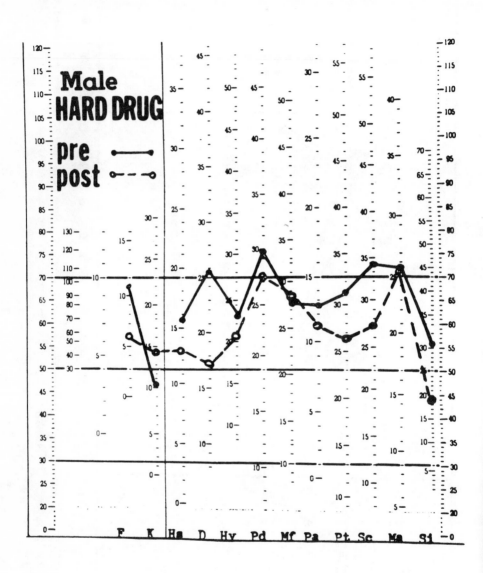

FIGURE 4.2: MMPI pre-postchange scores at male hard drug centers. From M. Zucker-man, S. Sola, J. Masterson, and J. V. Angelone, "MMPI Patterns in Drug Abusers Before and After Treatment in Therapeutic Communities," *Journal of Consulting and Clinical Psychology* 43 (1975): 286–96. Copyright 1975 by the American Psychological Association. Reprinted by permission. MMPI profile sheet copyrighted 1948 by the Psychological Corporation. Reproduced by permission granted in the test catalog.

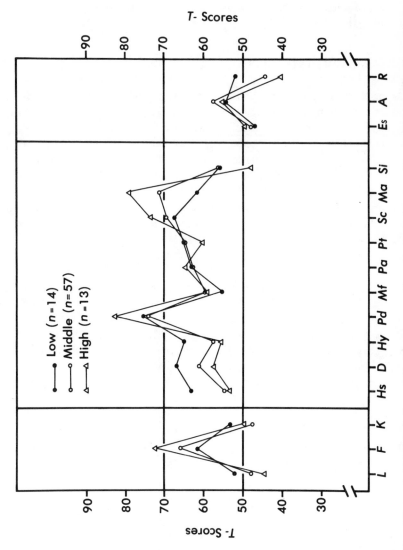

FIGURE 4.3: Mean Minnesota Multiphasic Personality Inventory profile patterns for low-, medium-, and high-sensation-seeking groups. From P. B. Sutker, R. P. Archer, and A. N. Allain, "Drug Abuse Patterns, Personality Characteristics, and Relationships with Sex, Race, and Sensation Seeking," *Journal of Consulting and Clinical Psychology* 46 (1978): 1374. Copyright 1978 by the American Psychological Association. Reprinted by permission.

slower than neurotic features to develop over the course of treatment, as well as more characteristic of treatment quitters than those who stay (Zuckerman et al. 1975). However, the extent to which elevations on psychotic scales are exhibited may also be dependent upon the situation in which MMPI responding occurs. For example, Sutker and Allain (1973) found greater psychopathology among applicants for methadone maintenance than has been typically reported for other addict groups.

MMPI-Based Profile Typologies

As noted from review of the literature above, MMPI composite profile types descriptive of heroin addicts have been characterized by marked elevations on scales 4, 2, 8, and 9. The most frequent two-point code types have been 2-4/4-2 and 4-9/9-4; however, code types including elevations on combinations of scales 2, 4, and 8 have been reported with frequency. A perhaps more sophisticated approach to identify homogeneous subgroups within addict samples has been the use of mulitvariate clustering techniques to describe commonalities in profile patterns. Although more research has applied these techniques to classify alcoholic profile patterns, one study in particular describes two relatively independent and highly replicable MMPI profile types for heroin addicts with applicability across race and sex groups. Attempting to delineate homogeneous MMPI profile subgroups through multivariate clustering procedures and to provide a basis by which addict groups could be compared with other groups, Berzins et al. (1974) identified two types of MMPI patterns using stringent criteria among treatment admissions to the Lexington Clinical Research Center. Type I individuals, representing roughly one third of addict samples, were characterized by high levels of subjective distresss, nonconformity, and confused thinking as reflected by pronounced elevations on scales 4, 8, and 2. These addicts attributed to themselves a wide range of psychopathology and tended to deprecate themselves as individuals. In contrast, type II individuals, characterized by striking elevations on scale 4 with secondary elevations on scale 9, were suggested to view their addiction as ego syntonic. It was also noted that the profile types bore striking similarity to the two larger replicable profile types delineated by Goldstein and Linden (1969) for male alcoholics.

MMPI Addiction Scales

Researchers have worked to devise separate MMPI scales to identify alcoholics and drug abusers and to differentiate them from other groups. One of the first attempts to identify heroin abusers was that of Cavior, Kurtzberg, and Lipton (1967), who constructed a 57-item scale (He) that accurately identified 80 percent of incarcerated male heroin addicts from incarcerated nonaddicts. Testing the validity of the He scale, Sutker (1971) found that street heroin addicts scored significantly higher than nonaddict prisoners, but considerable overlap in the ranges of scores hindered determination of a satisfactory cutoff for group classification. Other studies reported that the He scale successfully differentiated between samples of male heroin addicts in a state hospital and nonaddict inmates as well as between samples of heroin addicts and two samples of alcoholic patients (Sheppard, Ricca et al. 1972) and between methadone addict and nonaddict vocational rehabilitation clients (Kwant, Rice and Hays 1976). More recently, Burke and Marcus (1977) showed that the He scale successfully separated patients with a history of drug abuse from those with no history of drug or alcohol abuse, but that drug abusers were not differentiated from alcoholics. Haertzen, Hill, and Monroe (1968) also devised the 87-item AAF scale, which was designed to classify alcoholics, opiate addicts, and criminals into their respective groups. However, this measure has had limited usefulness, particularly for differentiating alcoholics from criminals.

Opitate-Alcohol Addict MMPI Differentiation

The question of whether or not alcoholics and opiate addicts display similar personality characteristics has sparked considerable investigative curiosity. In an early study, Hill, Haertzen, and Davis (1962) suggested that similarities in MMPI responding far exceeded the differences among groups of alcoholics, narcotic addicts, and criminals. These results are in agreement with reports that alcoholics and opiate addicts were similar in personal values (Toler 1975), mood fluctuations (Greenwald, Carter, and Stein 1973), and personality characteristics as measured by the Sixteen Personality Factor Questionnaire (Ciotola and Peterson 1976). In contrast, the work of other investigators indicated that, though addicts and alcoholics may share certain features, there are personality differences between the two groups. For example, Lorefice et al. (1976) reported that alcoholics were more neurotic than opiate addicts as measured by the Eysenck Personality Inventory. More recently, Holland (1977) found such dimensions as neurotic hypochondriacal and generalized psychopathic tendencies to be critical in distinguishing types of drug abusers who reported varying combinations and degrees of alcohol and drug use.

More successful than devising scales by which to characterize addict groups or mean profile group comparisons has been application of discriminant function analysis to determine weights to be accorded each MMPI variable for differentiation of alcohol and addict samples. Based upon the prototypic profiles of groups of alcoholics and narcotic addicts shown in Figure 4.4, Overall (1973) devised a discriminant function formula that resulted in 85 percent accuracy in separating alcoholic and addict groups. Results indicated substantial differences in the pattern of MMPI elevations between the two groups. Though alcoholics and addicts were characterized by an elevated scale 4 component, the profile for alcoholics showed greater elevations on scales 2, 3, 7, 6, and 8, while the addicts' profile had higher scales K and 9 components. The discriminant function contrast

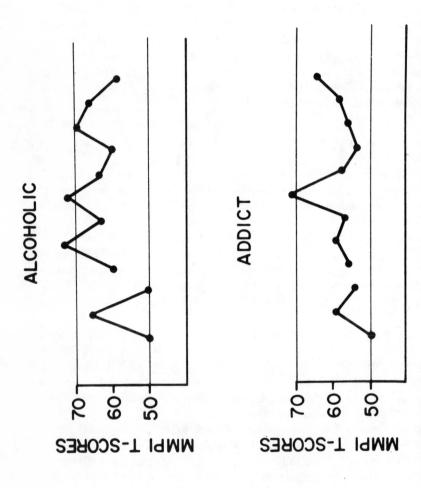

FIGURE 4.4: Composite MMPI profile prototypes of alcoholics and narcotic addicts. From, J. E. Overall, "MMPI Personality Patterns of Alcoholics and Narcotic Addicts," *Quarterly Journal of Studies on Alcohol* 34 (1973): 104–11. Copyright 1973 by the *Journal of Studies on Alcohol.* Reprinted by permission.

showed that profiles with primary elevations on scales 4 and 9 relative to scales 3 and 7 were more likely associated with drug addiction, whereas marked elevations on scales 3 and 7 in addition to scales 4 and 9 were suggestive of alcohol abuse. Hence, addict profiles were most often suggestive of sociopathy or antisocial cognitions and behavior with secondary elevations indicating impulsiveness, hostility, demandingness, and pessimism, whereas alcoholics tended to combine antisocial symptomatology and marked neurotic and passive-dependent features such as depression and anxiety. Adding support to this conclusion, McLachlan (1975a) applied Overall's discriminant function to MMPI profiles of 2,200 alcoholics and correctly classified 65 percent of sample subjects.

Controversial Issues in Drug Abuse Personality Research

The literature on personality characteristics of opiate addicts has been well summarized by Platt and Labate (1976), who noted that controversy has arisen regarding interpretation of personality differences found between or among various groups, as well as the role of potentially confounding variables that might influence study results. Disagreements focus on the question of whether addicts may be differentiated from other antisocial groups and whether demonstrated differences can be interpreted as evidence of predisposing personality characteristics or correlates of opiate dependence. A subordinate argument is whether or not a voluntarism factor confounds findings in personality investigations and reliably biases subject responding on objective inventories. Summarizing their review of related literature, Butcher and Owen (1978) indicated that there were significant between-group differences among alcoholics, drug abusers, and nonabusers, but that attempts to predict specific types of abuse from test data may lead to false interpretations.

Taking a more critical approach, Gendreau and Gendreau (1970, 1971, 1973) argued that many of the positive findings of personality differences between addict and nonaddict groups were artifacts of uncontrolled subject variables such as socioeconomic level, criminal background, age, and intelligence. They found that addict and nonaddict prisoners matched for age, socioeconomic level, and intelligence were essentially similar in MMPI profile productions (1970). In contrast, Sutker's (1971) comparison of unincarcerated or "street" addict and nonaddict prisoner groups equated for age, education, intelligence, months incarcerated, and criminal background showed addicts produced more deviant scores on MMPI scales 1, 2, 3, 4, 8, and 0. Gendreau and Gendreau (1973) subsequently proposed that these findings were confounded by the effects of volunteering, and suggested that volunteers may exaggerate their symptoms or exhibit greater maladjustment than nonvolunteers. These investigators (1973) collected data from 50 prisoners divided into four groups on the basis of whether they showed a history of drug addiction and were known to have volunteered recently for treatment within the correctional setting. Volunteers, whether addict or not, produced more elevated MMPI profiles. However,

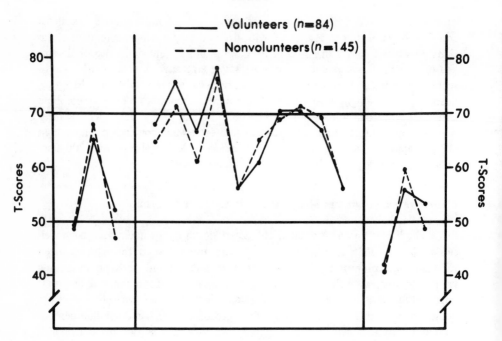

NARA

Volunteers (*n*=84)
Nonvolunteers(*n*=145)

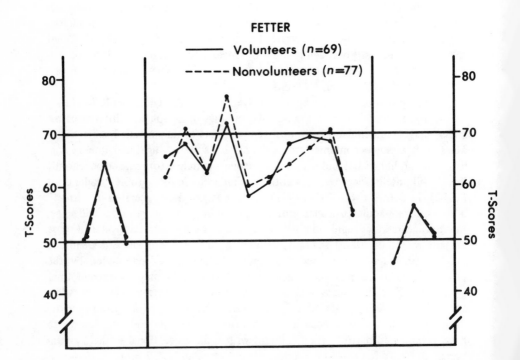

FETTER

Volunteers (*n*=69)
Nonvolunteers (*n*=77)

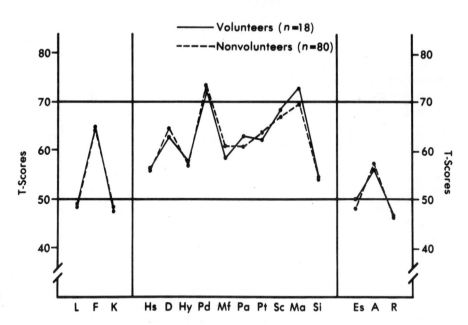

FIGURE 4.5: Mean MMPI profile patterns for volunteer and nonvolunteer subject groups within NARA, Fetter, and Odyssey drug treatment programs. From P. B. Sutker, R. P. Archer, and A. N. Allain, "Voluntarism and Self-Reported Psychopathology Among Opiate Addicts," *Journal of Abnormal Psychology* 88 (1979): 59–67. Copyright 1979 by American Psychological Association. Reprinted by permission.

statistical comparisons were not used to evaluate the significance of between-group differences. Futher, data were not presented regarding group comparability on those potentially confounding personal characteristic variables that Gendreau and Gendreau (1970, 1971) emphasized as critical in earlier reports.

Penk and Robinowitz (1976) also raised the possibility that voluntarism exerts a significant influence on addict MMPI responses and reported that treatment volunteers in a Veterans Administration hospital facility, whether opiate or other drug users, scored significantly higher on all MMPI clinical scales than drug abuse patients involuntarily placed in treatment by military authorities. Control of voluntarism minimized scale differences occurring between volunteer heroin users and nonheroin users, but not between nonvolunteer heroin users and nonheroin drug users, who differed significantly on four MMPI scales. Reexamining the voluntarism issues in three nonveteran drug abuse treatment programs, Sutker , Archer, and Allain (1979) found that opiate addicts differed significantly in MMPI scale elevations across program conditions, but that volunteer-nonvolunteer status had little consistent or pervasive influence on test responses (see Figure 4.5). Differences between volunteers and nonvolunteers were found for one treatment applicant sample, but the pattern of scale elevations failed to replicate Penk and Robinowitz's (1976) findings of generalized higher psychopathology across clinical dimensions. Examining results within the context of assessment conditions characteristic of each program setting, it appeared that higher levels of psychopathology were more likely found when personality testing occurred prior to treatment admission. When assessment occurred as part of routine acceptance or following several weeks of treatment, levels of reported psychopathology were substantially lower. Hence, if addict responses affected treatment admission decisions, both volunteer and nonvolunteer applicants produced more elevated profile patterns.

Examples of other variables that could potentially bias responding on personality measures are subject gender and ethnic characteristics. In personality comparisons of male and female drug abusers, women have been shown to demonstrate greater psychopathology than men across several indexes (DeLeon 1974; Gossop 1976; Olson 1964), and there is evidence that white drug abusers are more deviant than nonwhites (DeLeon 1974). Exploring interactions among drug use patterns, personality dimensions, sex, and race among chronic users of illicit drugs undergoing treatment in a therapeutic community, Sutker, Archer, and Allain (1978) found, consistent with the results of Kaestner, Rosen, and Appel (1977), that blacks showed less psychopathology on the MMPI, lower levels of sensation seeking, past use of fewer drug categories, and later drug use onset than white addicts. Thus, despite the possibility that MMPI norms may exaggerate T score estimates of psychopathology for some groups of blacks (Gynther 1972), urban black drug abusers appeared less socially deviant and psychologically aberrant than whites. Male-female comparisons also showed that female drug abusers were no more psychologically deviant than men in reference to their normative sex group. Results are supported by findings reported by Penk et al. (1978), who found that black veteran drug abusers admitted to a Veterans Administration methadone maintenance program produced lower scores on MMPI scales F, 2, 4, 7, 8, and 0 than did their white counterparts, whether or not the effects of age, intelligence, or socioeconomic status were controlled. Additionally, Sutker, Archer, and Allain (in press) showed that among nonveteran drug abusers applying to two geographically distant drug abuse treatment programs, men and women differed little in extent or type of psychopathology on the MMPI, but whites were more antisocial, behaviorally deviant, and neurotic than blacks.

ALCOHOLICS

Alcoholism represents an area of continued interest for biological and psychosocial researchers over the past several decades. Review of related literature reveals literally hundreds of studies attempting to identify the characteristics of alcohol abusing individuals. As is common for MMPI investigations among drug abusing populations, significant attention has been devoted to approaches that might unravel psychosocial and/or personality factors important to the etiology of maladpative drinking and alcoholism. Similarly, considerable work has been undertaken to discover personality characteristics diagnostic of alcohol abuse in its early stages as well as relevant to design or selection of appropriate treatment strategies and therapeutic outcome. Researchers have also used the MMPI to study the personality characteristics of alcoholics' spouses and to investigate the marital interaction and adjustment patterns among alcoholics (see Clopton 1978). Only recently, however, have investigators polished study design to consider the potentially confounding effects of important variables such as sex and race, the need to explore concomitantly person dimensions measured by other than MMPI indexes, and the role of environmental or situational factors in interacting with person variables to contribute to the maladaptive use of alcohol. For example, the work of Jones and Jones (1976a, 1976b) suggests the need to investigate potential sex-specific differences in drinking patterns and personality changes that might be related to the female sexual cycle.

Composite MMPI Profiles

In one of the earliest examinations of the MMPI characteristics of alcoholics, Hewitt (1943) identified the typical profile of male and female alcohol-dependent individuals as displaying peak elevations on scale 4, often with secondary elevations on the neurotic or psychotic scale. Numerous other studies have described composite MMPI features of alcohol samples as marked by primary elevations on scale 4 (Button 1956; Goss and Morosko 1969; Hill, Haertzen, and Davis 1962; Hoffman and Nelson 1971; Jansen and Hoffman 1973; Lanyon 1968; McWiliiams and Brown 1977; Overall 1973; Rohan 1972; Rosen 1960; Williams 1968). Overall (1973), for example, examined mean alcoholic MMPI profiles derived from Lanyon (1968), as well as 460 profiles from his own sample of inpatient alcoholics, and reported modal features characterized by high-point elevations on scales 4 and 2 with secondary peaks on scale 7. This configuration was described by Gilberstadt and Duker (1965), who associated heightened feelings of anxiety, inferiority, and guilt with chronic alcoholism. Graham (1977) also characterized the 2-4 profile type as common among habitual alcoholics whose histories included financial, legal, and social losses resulting from excessive drinking.

Reviewing the literature on female alcoholism, Curlee (1967) commented that investigators have typically assumed that alcoholism is manifested similarly in both sexes without providing empirical data to substantiate such conclusions. However, Mulford (1977) showed important differences in alcohol consumption histories and help-seeking behaviors between male and female alcoholics, and Goodwin et al. (1977) suggested that the etiology of alcoholism among women may be different than that for men. There is also evidence to suggest that mood state changes associated with the female sexual cycle may affect the female physiological response to alcohol and drinking patterns, per se (Jones and Jones 1976a, 1976b; Schuckit and Morrissey 1976).

Unfortunately, few MMPI studies have examined the issue of potential sex differences within alcoholic samples and no effort has been made to investigate the role of tension reduction or depressive mood states and female alcohol intake. Hewitt (1943) noted that female alcoholics tended to produce a different composite profile than male alcoholics with particularly elevated scores on scale 6 by comparison. The mean profile type for men in Hewitt's study was 4-2, whereas women produced peak elevations on scales 4 and 6. Graham (1978) indicated that while scale 4 elevations were most prominent for male and female alcoholics, men typically produced secondary elevations on scales 2, 7, and 9 as contrasted with scale 6 for women. Looking at the frequency of high-point pairs among alcoholic inpatients, McLachlan (1975b) found that a greater proportion of women than men showed peak elevations on scale 4, and Jansen and Hoffman (1973) reported higher scores on scales 3, 2, and 7 for male as opposed to female alcoholics. In contrast, studies by Curlee (1970) and Zelen et al. (1966) showed essentially no sex differences in profiles among alcoholics.

Research examining potentially confounding effects of age on MMPI responding, while equally sparse, tends to be more consistent. Results of cross-sectional studies by Hoffman, Jansen, and Wefring (1972), Hoffman and Nelson (1971), McGinnis and Ryan (1965), and Wilson et al. (1977) demonstrated that the MMPI profiles of alcoholics were characterized by lower scale elevations as the sample age increased. Both Hoffman and Nelson (1971) and McGinnis and Ryan (1965) noted lower scores on scale 4 among alcoholics in the fourth and fifth decades of life and suggested a "burning out" of antisocial tendencies accompanied by reduced legal and social conflicts. While age does seem to affect significantly the relative elevation of alcoholic profiles, the reasons for this phenomenon have not been established. Indeed, considerable evidence has been summarized against postulating a "burning out" process among groups of sociopaths, drug addicts, and alcoholics (Sutker, Archer, and Kilpatrick, in press).

Several longitudinal studies have attempted to identify the prealcoholic characteristics of individuals who later became alcohol dependent (Jones 1968; McCord and McCord 1962; Robins 1966; Robins, Bates, and O'Neal 1962), but only two investigations employed the MMPI as a data source. Kammeier, Hoffman, and Loper (1973) compared the MMPI profiles of 38 men hospitalized for alcoholism treatment with those produced during routine collegiate testing approximately 15 years before. The mean composite profile configuration for this group at the time of college evaluation was characterized by subclinical elevations on scales 5 and 9, whereas the treatment admission profile displayed the 4-2 profile pattern frequently characteristic of other composite profiles for alcoholic samples. The authors observed considerable response heterogeneity across assessment periods, but elevations on scales 2, 4, 7, and 8 occurred with high frequency at the time of both assessments. They concluded that scores on these particular scales could serve as possible signals of later alcohol dependence among prealcoholic individuals.

Extending this line of research, Loper, Kammeier, and Hoffman (1973) compared the MMPI profiles of 32 male college freshmen later hospitalized for alcoholism treatment with those of 148 male classmates who were not retrospectively identified as prealcoholic. Though showing few signs of gross maladjustment, prealcoholics scored significantly higher than their peer controls on scales 4 and 9, a pattern suggestive of greater gregariousness, more impulsiveness, and less social conformity than non-prealcoholics. Similar results were reported by Jones (1968), who identified more frequent undercontrolled, assertive, rebellious, impulsive, hostile, and limit-testing behaviors among prealcoholic adolescents than their peers. Results of other longitudinal studies that did not use MMPI data (McCord and McCord 1962; Robins, Bates, and O'Neal 1962) also pointed to socially deviant or sociopathic attitudes and behavior as potentially predictive of later alcoholism.

Attempting to describe personality correlates of alcohol addictive states and to assess treatment outcome, researchers have compared pre- and posttreatment composite MMPI profiles for alcoholic patients. Remarkably consistent across studies is evidence of significant reductions in scores on scales 2 and 7 over the course of treatment (Bean and Karasievich 1975; Ends and Page 1959; Huber and Danahy 1975; Rohan, Tatro, and Rotman 1969; Shaffer et al. 1962; Soskin 1970; Wilkinson et al. 1971). While most of these studies were conducted within the context of a residential or hospital setting, the particular therapeutic strategies varied widely; hence demonstrated reductions in anxiety and depression do not appear to be treatment specific. For example, Soskin (1970) compared MMPI treatment changes between alcoholics who received lysergide (LSD) inpatient therapy and alcoholics undergoing residential treatment with emphasis on interpersonal skills development. While greater personality changes for LSD-treated patients were reported, inspection of results shows essentially equivalent shifts in MMPI patterns for both patient groups. Further, in the four studies that found significant decreases in MMPI scale 4 scores following treatment (Bean and Karasievich 1975; Huber and Danahy 1975; Rohan, Tatro, and Rotman 1969; Wilkinson et al., 1971), the pattern of clinical scale reductions was such that elevations on scale 4 remained marked. Thus, while treatment intervention has been shown to be effective in reducing the subjective distress of anxiety and depression by alcoholics, the antisocial attitudes and behaviors measured by scale 4 remained the dominant feature of composite profiles at discharge.

MMPI researchers have also explored the possibility that there may be personality differences between alcoholics who terminate residential treatment prematurely and those who remain. Such studies have yielded inconsistent findings, and significant relationships for specific scales have not been uniform (Heilbrun 1971; Hoffman and Jansen 1973; Huber and Danahy 1975; Krasnoff 1976; Lin 1975; Mozdzierz et al. 1973; Wilkinson et al. 1971). Further, several studies failed to find evidence of significant differences on any MMPI scale between alcoholics who completed treatment and those who terminated prematurely (Hague, Donovan, and O'Leary 1976; Krasnoff 1976; McWilliams and Brown

1977). Similarly, negative findings have been shown in MMPI studies related to treatment outcome. Haertzen, Hill, and Monroe (1968) and Muzekari (1965) reported that MMPI scores were unrelated to whether alcoholics successfully abstained from alcohol or relapsed following completion of treatment. Thus, while MMPI studies suggest relatively consistent composite profile change patterns for alcoholics who complete residential treatment, the literature does not show established relationships between MMPI variables and treatment completion and/or success as defined in terms of alcohol abstinence.

MMPI-Based Profile Typologies

As previously noted, the 4-2 composite MMPI profile characteristic of large samples of alcoholics has not been considered representative of alcoholics, per se. As early as 1950, Brown suggested that no single MMPI profile could accurately classify chronic alcoholics and advocated subdivision of profiles into those showing primarily neurotic or sociopathic features. Hodo and Fowler (1976) and McLachlan (1975b) showed that in large samples of alcoholics where mean profiles were described by primary elevations on scales 4 and 2, frequency analyses of two-digit code types revealed only 13 to 21 percent of all alcoholics actually produced a 4-2 profile. Also noting liabilities in the use of composite profile types in alcohol research, Partington and Johnson (1969) indicated that composite profiles obscure identification of potentially more homogeneous personality subgroupings within alcoholic samples as well as reduce the sensitivity of statistical analyses based upon group data.

Following this line of reasoning, researchers have attempted to identify subcategories or personality clusters within samples of alcoholics using multivariate statistical analyses (Button 1956; Goldstein and Linden 1969; Skinner, Jackson, and Hoffman 1974; Whitelock, Overall, and Patrick 1971). The number of empirically derived profile types generated by cluster analysis ranges from two (Button 1956) to eight (Skinner, Jackson, and Hoffman 1974), with substantial similarity in basic profile characteristics across studies. Results have been essentially consistent with Brown's (1950) contention that alcoholics may be divided into psychopathic and neurotic profile types. Additionally, Whitelock et al. (1971) showed that more severe histories of alcohol abuse are significantly associated with neurotic profiles and lower levels of self-reported alcohol abuse with psychopathic tendencies.

Given that certain personality types may be reliably identified in future research within alcoholic samples, a crucial issue will involve the degree to which clusters of MMPI characteristics are relatively specific to individuals who abuse alcohol and are significantly different from profile types found representative of other populations. Selecting independent samples of male prison inmates, alcoholics, general psychiatric patients, and normal college students, Skinner, Reed, and Jackson (1976) studied the representativeness of eight profile types derived previously from the Differential Personality Inventory (DPI) on alcohol-depenent patients (Skinner, Jackson, and Hoffman 1974). The DPI is a 423-item objective personality measure yielding scores on one validity and 27 clinical scales.

The eight profile types applied to individuals in selected samples resulted in successful classification hit rates of 25 percent for one college student group, 34 and 47 percent for two samples of psychiatric patients, 35 percent for female alcoholics, 56 percent for male alcoholics, and 54 percent for male prison inmates. Hit rates for all samples in this study were significantly above that expected by chance, and classification efficiency attained for the original alcoholic and prisoner samples was essentially identical. DPI profile types showed marked generality when compared to alcoholic profile types derived from MMPI data in prior research. These results indicate that personality typologies based upon alcoholic responses also generalized to nonalcoholic samples and raise doubts that the extent to which alcoholics report unique clusters of symptomatology on this and other self-report objective personality measures. Clearly, the Skinner, Jackson, and Hoffman (1974) findings should be pursued in research involving MMPI-based personality clusters in diverse alcoholic and nonalcoholic samples (see Chapter 10).

MMPI-Derived Alcoholism Scales

As reviewed by Miller (1976), the development of MMPI-derived scales to identify alcoholics has rested upon assumptions that alcoholics and nonalcoholics differ reliably in endorsement of particular items, and that item analysis can be used to differentiate the responses of alcoholics from those of control group subjects and build a valid measure of alcoholism or prealcoholism. This approach may be contrasted with more direct techniques that select items with obvious alcohol-related content, that is, related to consumption patterns. Three alcoholism scales were developed in the 1950s that included items from the MMPI selected for their ability to discriminate alcoholics from normal respondents, and attempts were made to validate the instruments with various groups of normals and psychiatric patients. These measures consisted of a 125-item scale developed by Hampton (1953), Button's (1956) presentation of the Holmes 59-item scale, and Hoyt and Sedlacek's (1958) 68-item special alcoholic scale. Hampton (1953) indicated that his scale could have value in differentiating alcoholics from nonalcoholics and among categories of drinkers. Button (1956) concluded that the Holmes scale was successful in differentiating alcoholics from normal and from psychiatric patients in general. Hoyt and Sedlacek validated their measure by contrasting scores in two groups of alcoholics, four groups of psychiatric patients including neurotic and psychotic samples, and three groups of normals. While the special alcoholism scale did not successfully discriminate alcoholics from psychiatric samples, it did correctly identify 75 to 80 percent of alcoholic and normal respondents.

MacAndrew and Geertsma (1964), Rotman and Vestre (1964), and Uecker, Kish, and Ball (1969) further evaluated the relative effectiveness of these three alcoholism scales in discriminating male alcoholics from male psychiatric patients. In the first two studies, significant group separation was achieved for all scales, but Uecker, Kish, and Ball (1969) found significant group differences on the Hoyt and Sedlacek and Holmes scales, but not for the scale developed by Hampton. MacAndrew and Geertsma (1964) noted that while alcoholism scales purported to measure the same construct and contained questions selected from identical item pools, only seven items appeared on all three scales. Further, Korman (1960) reported a weak relationship (r = .26) between scores on the Hampton and Hoyt and Sedlacek scales. Thus MacAndrew and Geertsma (1964) concluded that these alcoholism measures were most likely indexes of general psychopathology or maladjustment rather than response tendencies or personality characteristics unique to alcoholics. This latter notion appears particularly applicable to the Hampton scale, which has been shown by Rosenberg (1972) to be significantly correlated (r = .89) with scores on the Welsh First Factor (A) scale.

Recognizing the weaknesses of prior alcoholism scales, MacAndrew (1965) devised his own measure, referred to in subsequent literature as the AMac, MAC, or Mac scale. This scale was developed by contrasting MMPI item endorsements of 300 male outpatient alcoholics with those of 300 male psychiatric outpatients and excluding items relating directly to alcohol consumption that might render the scale purpose transparent. The final 49 items correctly classified 81.5 percent of subjects in MacAndrew's cross-validation combined samples of male alcoholic and nonalcoholic psychiatric outpatients. Subsequent validity studies have shown the AMac to discriminate alcoholic from nonalcoholic psychiatric inpatients (Groot and Adamson 1973; Uecker 1970) and outpatients (Rhodes 1969). Additionally, the AMac scale has performed consistently well in comparison to earlier alcoholism scales (Apfeldorf and Hunley 1976; Rich and Davis 1969; Vega 1971). Suggesting that AMac may have application in identifying individuals at risk for the development of alcoholism, other studies showed that adult and collegiate heavy drinkers (Williams, McCourt, and Schneider 1971), as well as prealcoholic college students (Loper, Kammeier, and Hoffman 1973), tended to score in the higher ranges of the scale. Rohan, Tatro, and Rotman (1969) and Chang, Caldwell, and Moss (1973) also reported that AMac scores remained elevated in samples of alcoholics who had successfully completed treatment, indicating that the measure may reflect a history of alcohol problems even for individuals who no longer abuse alcohol.

As is true for other MMPI indexes that may predict future alcoholism, the AMac scale has been less successful in identifying alcoholics from among other respondents who are characterized by antisocial behaviors. For example, it has not been useful in differentiating alcoholics from drug abusers and addicts (Burke and Marcus 1977; Fowler 1975; Kranitz 1972; Lachar et al. 1976). Representative of these studies, Kranitz's (1972) examination of AMac scores among institutionalized addicts, alcoholics, and nonalcoholic psychiatric patients revealed no significant differences between addict and alcoholic samples.

These findings led Kranitz (1972) and later Lachar et al. (1976) to suggest that AMac may reflect a general tendency toward substance dependence, including alcohol and other drugs. Apfeldorf and Hunley's (1975) findings of equivalent AMac scores for disciplinary offenders and alcoholics in a domiciliary setting and Ruff, Ayers, and Templer's (1975) report of similar scores for both male alcoholics and male psychiatric patients under criminal charges further clouded the picture. Subsequently, Schwartz (1977) investigated the possibility that the AMac scale may actually measure tendencies toward antisocial behavior or general deviance. The results of his study, as reported by Butcher and Owen (1978), indicated that female alcoholics scored higher on the AMac scale than female psychiatric patients diagnosed antisocial personality; however, significant differences were not found for male comparisons. While controversy clearly surrounds the usefulness and validity of MacAndrew's measure, it remains the most promising of current MMPI-derived alcoholism scales. (See chapter 14 regarding the development of special MMPI scales).

OTHER DRUG ABUSERS

Despite trends toward increasing multiple drug use, there have been few personality studies of multidrug abusers or of individuals who use drugs regularly from a variety of categories, including illicit drugs, prescription medications, and alcohol in various combinations. An exception is the work of Cohen and associates (Cohen, White, and Schoolar 1971; Schoolar, White, and Cohen 1972), who compared samples of drug abuse patients composed predominantly of polydrug abusers with control psychiatric outpatients matched individually for age and sex. Reflecting greater psychopathology among drug abusers, significant between-group differences were found for scales F, 4, 6, 8, and 9 for the male samples and for scales 4 and 9 for female subgroups. Data derived from the Interpersonal Check List, in addition to MMPI findings, led these investigators to describe drug abusers as more actively deviant and critical, more likely to idealize behavior not valued by society, and less experienced with genuine parental closeness than psychiatric outpatients.

Testing the hypothesis derived from clinical experience that nonnarcotic polydrug abusers may be experiencing psychological disturbance rather than manifesting sociopathy or social nonconformity, Stauss, Ousley, and Carlin (1977) compared MMPI profiles produced by hospitalized polydrug abusers with three groups of traditional psychiatric patients, including inpatients, outpatients, and patients attending a behavioral/educational oriented program. Results showed that polydrug abusers, characterized by highest elevations on scales F, 2, 4, 7, 8, and 9 and most similar to psychiatric inpatients, represented a markedly disturbed group. Suggesting that most polydrug abusers could be classified as either recreational users or straight self-medicators, Stauss, Ousley, and Carlin (1977) postulated that psychopathology may be related to patient status parameters. Other investigators have described polydrug abusers as a highly disturbed group (Benvenuto and Bourne 1975; Burke and Eichberg 1972), although there is no conclusive evidence to indicate that their psychopathology predated drug use. Finally, comparing polydrug abusers with nonusers in a veteran population on dimensions other than those derived from the MMPI, Kilpatrick et al. (1976) found that polydrug abusers produced significantly higher scores on measures of neuroticism, anxiety, and sensation seeking than nondrug abusing medical patients.

The picture of personality features is indicative of considerable psychopathology among multiple drug users, but review of research reports suggests chronic users of amphetamines to be the most psychologically deviant substance abuse population. In 1967, Ellinwood described amphetamine addicts and amphetamine psychosis, thus tying together the symptoms of psychosis and chronic amphetamine abuse. He noted that stimulant addicts differed from other drug abusing groups in showing a higher incidence of antisocial, schizoid, and paranoid personalities, as well as proportionately more schizophrenic reactions. MMPI profile configurations were described by marked elevations on scales 8, 7, and 4. Brook, Kaplun, and Whitehead (1974) also found amphetamine users less variable in MMPI responding than a group of nonusers with particularly high scores on scale 8. Suggesting that amphetamine users were characterized by disorganized thinking, bizarre mentation, and inner conflicts, these investigators postulated that social, academic, family, and personal difficulties predated drug use. Brook, Szandorowska, and Whitehead (1976) also hypothesized that amphetamine abuse was one manifestation of underlying personality and social maladjustment as evidenced by extreme elevations on scales 8 and 7 with lesser scores on scales 2 and 4.

Investigating changes in psychopathology among nonnarcotic drug abusers hospitalized for inpatient treatment, Graf, Baer, and Comstock (1977) compared intake and discharge MMPI profiles defined on the basis of stimulant, barbiturate, other sedative-hypnotic, or multidrug use. At admission, the composite profile for all abuser categories was suggestive of psychosis with little variation between groups. At the time of discharge, which followed two weeks of hospitalization, MMPI profiles were interpreted to be consistent with a diagnosis of sociopathy. Examination of Figure 4.6, however, shows profiles at intake and discharge for groups of amphetamine and multidrug abusers reflected comparatively little therapeutic change as evidenced by MMPI indexes. Although the number of subjects represented by each mean profile is small, it is interesting to note that both amphetamine abusers and the multidrug group retained marked elevations on scale 8, suggesting greater psychopathology among these types of abusers.

Smart and Jones (1970) explored the personality correlates of illicit LSD users and found a high incidence of psychopathology with 96 percent of profiles classified as abnormal. Primary elevations occurred on scales 4, 9, 8, and 3, and profiles were classified predominantly into psychotic and conduct disorder categories. Interview information from this study, as well as data from other investi-

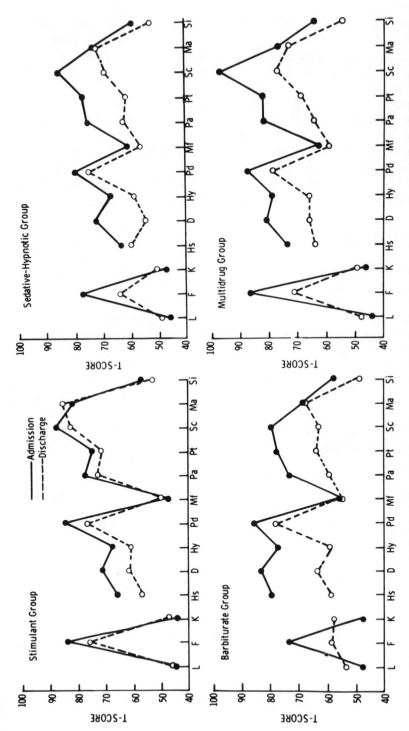

FIGURE 4.6: Group MMPI profiles at admission (solid line) and discharge (dashed line) for four drug groups. From K. Graf, P. E. Baer, and B. S. Comstock, "MMPI Changes in Briefly Hospitalized Non-Narcotic Drug Users," *Journal of Nervous and Mental Disease* 165 (1977): 126–33. Copyright 1977 by the Williams & Wilkins Company. Reprinted by permission.

gators (Welpton 1968), has been interpreted to suggest that psychological disturbances predated drug usage. Comparing LSD users and nonusers matched on social background, drug use, and personality variables, Smart and Fejer (1969) found LSD users were more likely diagnosed as psychotic and conduct disorder with 96 percent producing abnormal MMPI protocols. Toomey (1974) also compared hallucinogen users with opiate addicts and found that hallucinogen users scored significantly higher than the narcotic group on scales 5 and 8, but because LSD users were younger it was suggested that age may have biased study findings. In general, results of MMPI studies suggest that LSD users are less psychologically stable, less conforming, and more likely to display major types of psychopathology than groups of nonusers. However, as Keller and Redfering (1973) urged, no conclusions can be drawn regarding cause and effect.

CONCLUSIONS

There is no shortage of research studies that attempt to identify and describe the unique personality characteristics of drug-dependent individuals. Perusal of almost any scientific journal, including research on psychosocial issues and human behavior, will uncover at least one report pertinent to opiate addiction, alcohol abuse, or inappropriate use of prescription medications. Similarly, the MMPI continues to be a popular medium for describing the personality correlates of addictive phenomena. Recently, several reviews have addressed the major problems and issues related to research in personality and the addictions (Butcher and Tellegen 1978; Nathan and Lansky 1978; Reppucci and Clingempeel 1978). As Butcher and Tellegen (1978) noted, there are many advantages to using the MMPI to describe psychopathology among groups of individuals such as addicts and alcoholics. The instrument is easily administered and lends itself well to situations where addict-clients or alcoholics are found seeking treatment or other assistance. For these and other reasons, the MMPI may be used in poorly planned and casually conducted studies that yield data of minimal importance. Indeed, some of the research reviewed in this chapter is characterized by methodological problems, specious reasoning, and theoretical controversy.

Among the more critical design problems found commonly in the MMPI literature relevant to drug abuse are inadequate or nonexistent control groups. failure to use appropriate statistical techniques, artificial dichotomization of subjects into user and nonuser samples, and formation of subject comparison groups across such potentially confounding personal characteristic variables as sex, race, age, intelligence, socioeconomic class, and history of antisocial behavior. Although it might seem obvious that unequal distribution of sex or ethnic characteristics within groups could significantly bias results, many studies fail to take these factors into account. Additionally, data collected from small samples, often composed of drug abusers of varying ilk, have often formed the basis for considerable speculation regarding drug use predispositions, drug effects, motivations for use, and predictions for treatment outcome. Probably the most important variables influencing responding in any situation are those that are cognitive, including intellectual competence, expectancy sets, attitudes, and values. However, few studies have begun to address the problem of specifying relationships among cognitive variables, more traditionally conceived personality dimensions, and drug-related behaviors.

In addition to problems associated with use of the MMPI as a descriptor of psychopathology for drug abusers, more general issues have been raised regarding personality research. Many personality studies of drug abusers are born of a rationale that implicitly or explicitly assumes that targeted subjects will demonstrate deficits in psychological functioning reflected on chosen response measures. In fact, much of the research reviewed in this chapter has its origins in psychoanalytical and other trait-oriented explanations of drug or alcohol dependence that tend to postulate person deficits. Indeed, the very use of the MMPI presupposes some degree of psychopathology. Though deficit hypotheses have unnecessarily restricted research focus and design, drug abuse research shows evidence of trends to explore more positive parameters possibly related to drug use and abuse. Taking an approach that focuses on the sociocultural context in which drug use occurs, opiate addicts have been described as vigorously immersed in an active, career-oriented lifestyle that perpetually propels them to increasing involvement in antisocial activities and social nonconformity (Agra 1971; Preble and Casey 1969). Similarly, there are efforts to define environmenal or social stimuli associated with initial or sustained drug use (Sutker 1974), to specify motives for drug use that take into account social factors (Naditch 1975), and to devise descriptive and functional typologies for drug-dependent individuals specifying the conditions under which drug use occurs (Carlin and Stauss 1977). Other investigators have explored relationships among such relevant dimensions as sensation seeking, drug use preferences, and patterns of the drug abuse (Carrol and Zuckerman 1977; Harford 1978; Schwartz, Burkhart, and Green 1978; Sutker, Archer, and Allen 1978).

Another assumption too commonly reflected in personality research is that once certain characteristics are reliably identified as descriptive of a specific population type regardless of the setting, those characteristics may be counted upon to be consistent across situations. The issue of whether or not behavior may be conceived of as cross-situationally consistent is discussed at length by several psychologists who have attempted to influence and predict directions for personality measurement (Bem and Allen 1974; Bem and Funder 1978; Mischel 1973, 1977). Review of research with drug-dependent groups shows that opiate addicts, for example, differ significantly in terms of self-reported psychopathology as a function of the specific situation in which assessment occurs. Hence aspects of the general environmental context, conditions of assessment, as well as potential person-situation interactions, become critically important to consider before attempting to speculate about possible etiological and/or personality correlates of addictive states. Certainly, as investigators become more aware of these problems, there will be less tendency to elicit MMPI responses from particular drug abuse subgroups and to generalize regarding their personality characteristics or psychopathology from one assessment condition to another or from periods of drug involvement to those of pre- or no-drug involvement.

One of the consequences of attempting to identify associations between enduring person traits or negative affect states and drug dependence has been minimal attention to the multidetermined nature of behavior and assessment of environment or situation variables and their potential interactions. It has now become necessary for researchers to take a more sophisticated approach to identification and measurement of cognitions and behavior related to drug abuse by refining and/or defining relevant person, situation, or context variables and assessing their interactions. As Reppucci and Clingempeel (1978) chided, there is no substitute for discriminant and convergent construct validation or use of the multitrait-multimethod matrix early proposed by Campbell and Fiske (1959). Expressing this in practical terms, it will be important to expand MMPI investigations to make use of two or more measures of defined personality and situation dimensions, as well as to demonstrate that measures of one variable are not significantly correlated with measures purported to reflect distinctly different constructs. Not only should drug abuse personality research address itself to validation of familiar and well-worn constructs but also to specification of more relevant and precisely defined person and situation variables.

An example of research aimed at understanding drug abuse phenomena within a framework that incorporates environment and personality factors is that of Sadava and Forsyth (1977). These investigators conceived of social-psychological predictor variables in terms of a two-dimensional, four-system matrix where person and environment systems are defined within proximal and distal contexts. Although one might wish to modify the variables measured as representative of the four systems, there can be no quarrel that such a methodology is long overdue in drug abuse personality research. Using this multivariate framework to predict drug-using behavior among 374 undergraduate students in a longitudinal design, Sadava and Forsyth (1977) discovered a pattern of predictors that included variables classified in proximal environment and distal person (personality characteristic) systems. Their work showed the value of a nonlinear or genuinely interactive model suggesting that the environment does not merely supplement person variables in prediction or vice versa. Both person and environment variables contributed independently and significantly at proximal and distal levels to account for substantial variance in drug-using behavior. Summarizing, these investigators stated:

> Clearly, drug use patterns cannot be accounted for solely in terms of personal function (reasons, "motives") and/or perceived environment supportive of and tolerant toward drug use. Neither the data nor the theory strongly supports a conception of an "addictive" personality or demography. But distal personal and demographic

predispositional factors, in combination with proximal functions and environmental attributes directly pertaining to drug use, are useful in both prediction and explanation. (p. 237)

Notwithstanding the common methodological and theoretical problems described above, it should be possible to use the voluminous data collected to speculate on personality precursors, correlates, and antecedents of drug experimentation and dependence. Unfortunately, there is little concrete basis by which to differentiate predisposing and antecedent conditions given the current literature. For obvious reasons, a few longitudinal studies have been undertaken, and the various studies that sample drug or alcohol abusers across different situations or time periods provide a bare context in which to draw conclusions. However, at present it is impossible to cite certain person characteristics that have been identified reliably among groups of individuals who have become drug dependent. For example, opiate addicts tend to score high on measures that suggest social nonconformity, hostile dependence, aggressiveness, personal immaturity, high needs for sensation seeking, and behavioral acting out. Depending upon the situation and the individuals studied, neurotic or schizotypic symptomatology may also be exhibited. Elevations on measures of neurotic involvement tend to be more transitory than stable (Skolnick and Zuckerman, in press; Sutker and Allain 1973; Zuckerman et al. 1975), but psychotic manifestations are often relatively resistant to change (Graf, Baer, and Comstock 1977; Zuckerman et al. 1975). In contrast, there is almost unanimity of opinion that alcoholics score high on measures reflecting such neurotic symptomatology as depression and anxiety, as well as social nonconformity (Kurtines, Ball, and Wood 1978; Overall 1973; Skinner, Jackson, and Hoffman 1974), whereas amphetamine addicts, for example, often demonstrate marked and stable psychotic symptomatology (Graf, Baer, and Comstock 1977).

Although drug abusing groups may share common constellations of personality features, significant and reliable between-group differences have been demonstrated. For example, opiate addicts and alcoholics can be differentiated on the basis of single MMPI scale elevations, composite profile types, or constructs measured by other instruments. Alcoholics and addicts can also be separated using combinations of variables or by cluster analysis techniques. Summarizing results of such efforts, it is apparent that alcoholics, as abusers of a legal, socially sanctioned, and even encouraged drug, differ from illicit drug abusers and particularly opiate addicts on at least two important dimensions: neurotic symptomatology and social nonconformity or sociopathy. Similarly, it has been demonstrated that among other drug abusers, those who use amphetamines with regularity exhibit the greatest degree of psychopathology, particularly of a schizotypic nature. Indeed, treatment intervention among such groups does not always result in amelioration of psychotic symptomatology. These and other findings point to the presence of serious emotional disturbances among amphetamine addicts and chronic multidrug abusers that may have led to extended drug use as well as been exacerbated by its use.

Proponents of the hypothesis that certain personality characteristics pre-dispose one to drug abuse, if not specific addictions, per se, point to such evidence as the constancy of antisocial cognitions and behavior among groups of heroin addicts regardless of assessment conditions. Studies measuring personality variables over time have shown that a marked antisocial component is typical of most opiate addict groups regardless of other aspects of the personality profile composite. Life history data also suggest that in many cases antisocial activity predated drug experimentation and addiction and may be a good predictor of opiate experimentation and dependence (Robins, and O'Neal 1962). This evidence is consistent with reports of high needs for sensation-seeking, curiosity, and pleasure motives for drug use and low scores on measures of socialization and responsibility among opiate addicts. Symptom states of neurotic depression and anxiety are more likely to fluctuate over given assessment conditions, al-though there seems to be a subgroup of opiate addicts who combine chronic neurotic and sociopathic features. Conversely, purely neurotic and/or psychotic manifestations among opiate addicts are relatively rare. Studies have shown a somewhat different personality profile among alcoholics. Although there is evidence of characteristic antisocial cognitions and behavior, MMPI elevations on measures reflecting depression and anxiety seem to be more pronounced. Nevertheless, the longitudinal research of Kammeier and associates (1973) suggests that early clues of mild social deviance and perhaps sociopathy pre-cede alcoholism among college-educated men. Precursors of alcohol misuse among women, particularly those which may be sex-specific, are only now being explored.

The extent to which personality factors, in interaction with yet unspeci-fied other-person or environmental variables, influence the patterns of problem or excessive drinking or drug experimentation and dependence is unknown. Critical in exacerbating the symptoms of psychopathology seen on psychological measures such as the MMPI may be the psychosocial and physiological effects of extended alcohol and drug use. One might speculate that for some individuals a general disposition toward social deviance manifests itself under certain socio-cultural circumstances in antisocial activities, including experimentation with such illicit drugs as opiates or alcohol abuse. Continued involvement in drug-related behavior may be maintained subsequently by reinforcing stimuli in the sociocultural context and the physiological effects of the drug, which in turn influence psychological functioning. For another subset of individuals, pre-sumably those who share high levels of anxiety and personal discomfort, both initial and continued drug or alcohol use may serve primarily needs for self-medication or tension reduction. Unfortunately, these and other hypotheses can only be tested within a complex, longitudinal experimental protocol de-signed to assess the relative influences of critical person and environment vari-ables and their interaction. As discussed earlier in this chapter, a discriminant function formula has been devised by Overall to discriminate the characteristics of alcoholics from those of addicts, and indeed, it is possible to describe both drug-dependent groups reliably. Yet, there is little concrete basis upon which to predict addiction, per se, if not specific types, from personality variables alone.

It would be shortsighted if MMPI researchers interested in drug use and abuse did not attempt to expand study foci to incorporate measurement of person variables other than those derived from MMPI responses, situation-environment variables, as well as possible person-environment interactions. Investigators must also satisfy themselves regarding the convergent and divergent validity of those favorite constructs that they use to explain drug use phenomena. Certainly, the literature reviewed in this chapter provides sufficient basis upon which to generate a variety of hypotheses for experimentation. Much of the work in specifying motives for drug use, patterns and preferences of drug use, and predispositions toward sensation seeking or tension reduction, particularly when cast in a person-environment conceptual framework, is prototypic of future trends in addiction research. The role of naturalistic observation, most easily applied to carefully controlled situations but possible even in the street environment, is also worth greater exploration. Further, as Mischel (1977) emphasized, subjects themselves may represent the best possible source of explanatory information about their behavior. Often ignored, subject attitudes, cognitive sets, values, and competencies are undoubtedly extremely relevant to drug use preferences, drug use patterns, and potential for change in the treatment setting. It then falls to MMPI investigators to take special consideration of these areas reflecting progress and change and to devise innovative methodologies for future research.

REFERENCES

Agar, M. H. 1971. "Folklore of the Heroin Addict: Two Examples." *Journal of American Folklore* 84: 175–85.

Apfeldorf, M., and P. J. Hunley. 1976. "Exclusion of Subjects with *F* Scores at or Above 16 in MMPI Research on Alcoholism." *Journal of Clinical Psychology* 32: 498–500.

——. 1975. "Application of MMPI Alcoholism Scales to Older Alcoholics and Problem Drinkers." *Journal of Studies on Alcohol* 36: 645–53.

Astin, A. W. 1959. "A Factor Study of the MMPI Psychopathic Deviate Scale." *Journal of Consulting Psychology* 23: 550–54.

Bean, K. L., and G. O. Karasievich. 1975. "Psychological Test Results at Three Stages of Inpatient Alcoholism Treatment." *Journal of Studies on Alcohol* 36: 838–52.

Bem, D. J., and A. Allen. 1974. "On Predicting Some of the People Some of the Time: The Search for Cross-Situational Consistencies in Behavior." *Psychological Review* 81: 506–20.

Bem, D. J., and D. C. Funder. 1978. "Predicting More of the People More of the Time: Assessing the Personality of Situations." *Psychological Review* 85: 488–501.

Benvenuto, J., and P. G. Bourne. 1975. "Tne Federal Polydrug Abuse Project: Initial Report." *Journal of Psychedelic Drugs* 7: 115–20.

Berzins, J. I., and W. F. Ross. 1973. "Locus of Control Among Opiate Addicts." *Journal of Consulting and Clinical Psychology* 40: 84–91.

——, G. E. English, and J. V. Haley. 1974. "Subgroups Among Opiate Addicts: A Typological Investigation." *Journal of Abnormal Psychology* 83: 65–73.

Berzins, J. I., W. F. Ross, and J. J. Monroe. 1971. "A Multivariate Study of the Personality Characteristics of Hospitalized Narcotic Addicts on the MMPI." *Journal of Clinical Psychology* 27: 174–81.

Black, F. W. 1975. "Personality Characteristics of Viet Nam Veterans Identified as Heroin Abusers." *American Journal of Psychiatry* 132: 748–49.

Blackburn, R. 1969. "Sensation Seeking, Impulsivity, and Psychopathic Personality." *Journal of Consulting Psychology* 33: 571–74.

Brook, R., J. Kaplun, and P. C. Whitehead. 1974. "Personality Characteristics of Adolescent Amphetamine Users as Measured by the MMPI." *British Journal of Addiction* 69: 61–66.

Brook, R., B. Szandorowska, and P. C. Whitehead. 1976. "Psychosocial Dysfunctions as Precursors to Amphetamine Abuse Among Adolescents." *Addictive Diseases: An International Journal* 2: 465–78.

Brown, M. A. 1950. "Alcoholic Profiles on the Minnesota Multiphasic." *Journal of Clinical Psychology* 6: 266–69.

Burke, E. L., and R. H. Eichberg. 1972. "Personality Characteristics of Adolescent Users of Dangerous Drugs as Indicated by the Minnesota Multiphasic Personality Inventory." *Journal of Nervous and Mental Disease* 154: 291–98.

Burke, H., and R. Marcus. 1977. "MacAndrew MMPI Alcoholism Scale: Alcoholism and Drug Addictiveness." *Journal of Psychology* 96: 141–48.

Butcher, J. N., and P. L. Owen. 1978. "Objective Personality Inventories: Recent Research and Some Contemporary Issues." In *Clinical Diagnosis of*

Mental Disorders: A Handbook, edited by B. B. Wolman, pp. 475–545. New York: Plenum.

Butcher, J. N., and A. Tellegen. 1978. "Common Methodological Problems in MMPI Research." *Journal of Consulting and Clinical Psychology* 46: 620–28.

Button, A. D. 1956. "A Study of Alcoholics with the MMPI." *Quarterly Journal of Studies on Alcohol* 17: 263–81.

Campbell, D. T., and D. W. Fiske. 1959. "Convergent and Discriminant Validation by the Multitrait-Multimethod Matrix." *Psychological Bulletin* 56: 81–105.

Carlin, A. S., and F. F. Stauss. 1977. "Descriptive and Functional Classifications of Drug Abusers." *Journal of Consulting and Clinical Psychology* 45: 222–27.

Carrol, E. N., and M. Zuckerman. 1977. "Psychopathology and Sensation Seeking in 'Downers,' 'Speeders,' and 'Trippers': A Study of the Relationship Between Personality and Drug Choice." *International Journal of the Addictions* 12: 591–601.

Cavior, N., R. I. Kurtzberg, and D. S. Lipton. 1967. "The Development and Validation of a Heroin Addiction Scale with the MMPI." *International Journal of the Addictions* 2: 129–37.

Chang, A., A. B. Caldwell, and T. Moss. 1973. "Stability of Personality Traits in Alcoholics During and After Treatment as Measured by the MMPI: A One-Year Follow-up Study." *Proceedings of the 81st Convention of the American Psychological Association* 8: 387–88.

Ciotola, P. V., and J. F. Peterson. 1976. "Personality Characteristics of Alcoholics and Drug Addicts in a Merged Treatment Program." *Journal of Studies on Alcohol* 37: 1229–35.

Clopton, J. R. 1978. "Alcoholism and the MMPI. *Journal of Studies on Alcohol* 39: 1540–58.

Cohen, C. P., E. H. White, and J. C. Schoolar. 1971. "Interpersonal Patterns of Personality in Drug Abusers and Their Therapeutic Implications." *Archives of General Psychiatry* 24: 353–58.

Curlee, J. 1970. "A Comparison of Male and Female Patients at an Alcoholism Treatment Center." *Journal of Psychology* 74: 239–47.

——. 1967. "Alcoholic Women: Some Considerations for Further Research." *Bulletin of the Menninger Clinic* 31: 154–63.

DeLeon, G. 1974. "Phoenix House: Psychopathological Signs Among Male and Female Drug-Free Residents." *Addictive Diseases: An International Journal* 2: 135-51.

——, A. Skodol, and M. S. Rosenthal. 1973. "Phoenix House: Changes in Psychopathological Signs of Resident Drug Addicts." *Archives of General Psychiatry* 28: 131-35.

Ellinwood, E. H. 1967. "Amphetamine Psychosis. I. Description of the Individuals and Process." *Journal of Nervous and Mental Disease* 144: 173-83.

Ends, E. J., and C. N. Page. 1959. "Group Psychotherapy and Concomitant Psychological Change." *Psychology Monographs* 10: 1-31.

Fowler, R. 1975. "A Method for the Evaluation of the Abuse Prone Patient." *American Academy of Family Physicians*, Chicago.

Gendreau, P., and L. P. Gendreau. 1973. "A Theoretical Note on the Personality Characteristics of Heroin Addicts." *Journal of Abnormal Psychology* 82: 139-40.

——. 1971. "Research Design and Narcotic Addiction Proneness." *Canadian Psychiatric Association Journal* 16: 265-67.

——. 1970. "The 'Addiction-Prone' Personality: A Study of Canadian Heroin Addicts." *Canadian Journal of Behavioral Science* 2: 19-25.

Gilberstadt, H., and J. Duker. 1965. *A Handbook for Clinical and Actuarial MMPI Interpretation*. Philadelphia: Saunders.

Gilbert, J. G., and D. N. Lombardi. 1967. "Personality Characteristics of Young Male Narcotic Addicts." *Journal of Consulting Psychology* 31: 536-38.

Goldstein, S. G., and J. D. Linden. 1969. "Multivariate Classification of Alcoholics by Means of the MMPI." *Journal of Abnormal Psychology* 74: 661-69.

Goodwin, D. W., F. Schulsinger, J. Knop, S. Mednick, and S. B. Guze. 1977. "Alcoholism and Depression in Adopted-Out Daughters of Alcoholics." *Archives of General Psychiatry* 34: 751-55.

Goss, A., and T. E. Morosko. 1969. "Alcoholism and Clinical Symptoms." *Journal of Abnormal Psychology* 74: 682-84.

Gossop, M. 1976. "Drug Dependence and Self-Esteem." *International Journal of the Addictions* 11: 741-53.

Graf, K., P. E. Baer, and B. S. Comstock. 1977. "MMPI Changes in Briefly Hospitalized Non-Narcotic Drug Users." *Journal of Nervous and Mental Disease* 165: 126–33.

Graham, J. R. 1978. "MMPI Characteristics of Alcoholics, Drug Abusers, and Pathological Gamblers." Paper presented at the 13th annual MMPI Symposium, University of the Americas, Puebla, Mexico, March.

——. 1977. *The MMPI: A Practical Guide*. New York: Oxford University Press.

Greaves, G. 1971. "MMPI Correlates of Chronic Drug Abuse in Hospitalized Adolescents." *Psychological Reports* 29: 1222.

Greenwald, S. R., J. S. Carter, and E. M. Stein. 1973. "Differences Between the Background, Attitude, Functioning, and Mood of Drug Addicts, Alcoholics, and Orthopedic Patients." *International Journal of the Addictions* 8: 865–74.

Groot, W., and J. D. Adamson. 1973. "Responses of Psychiatric Inpatients to the MacAndrew Alcoholism Scale." *Quarterly Journal of Studies on Alcohol* 34: 1133–39.

Gynther, M. D. 1972. "White Norms and Black MMPIs: A Prescription for Discrimination?" *Psychological Bulletin* 78: 386–402.

Haertzen, C. A., H. E. Hill, and J. J. Monroe. 1968. "MMPI Scales for Differentiating and Predicting Relapse in Alcoholics, Opiate Addicts, and Criminals." *International Journal of the Addictions* 3: 91–106.

Hague, W. H., C. M. Donovan, and M. O'Leary. 1976. "Personality Characteristics Related to Treatment Decisions Among Inpatient Alcoholics: A Non-Relationship." *Journal of Clinical Psychology* 32: 476–79.

Hampton, P. J. 1953. "The Development of a Personality Questionnaire for Drinkers." *Genetic Psychology Monographs* 48: 44–115.

Hampton, P. T., and D. B. Vogel. 1973. "Personality Characteristics of Servicemen Returned from Viet Nam Identified as Heroin Abusers." *American Journal of Psychiatry* 130: 1031–32.

Harford, R. J. 1978. "Drug Preferences of Multiple Drug Abusers." *Journal of Consulting and Clinical Psychology* 46: 908–12.

Heilbrun, A. B. 1971. "Prediction of Rehabilitation Outcome in Chronic Court-Case Alcoholics." *Quarterly Journal of Studies on Alcohol* 32: 328–33.

Hewitt, C. C. 1943. "A Personality Study of Alcohol Addiction." *Quarterly Journal of Studies on Alcohol* 4: 368–86.

Hill, H. E., C. A. Haertzen, and H. Davis. 1962. "An MMPI Factor Analytic Study of Alcoholics, Narcotic Addicts, and Criminals." *Quarterly Journal of Studies on Alcohol* 23: 411-31.

Hill, H. E., C. A. Haertzen, and R. Glaser. 1960. "Personality Characteristics of Narcotic Addicts as Indicated by the MMPI." *Journal of General Psychology* 62: 127-39.

Hill, H. E., C. A. Haertzen, and R. S. Yamahiro. 1968. "The Addict Physician: A Minnesota Multiphasic Personality Inventory Study of the Interaction of Personality Characteristics and Availability of Narcotics." In *The Addictive States*, edited by A. Wikler, pp. 321-32. Baltimore: Williams & Wilkins.

Hodo, G. L., and R. D. Fowler. 1976. "Frequency of MMPI Two-Point Codes in a Large Alcoholic Sample." *Journal of Clinical Psychology* 32: 487-89.

Hoffman, H., and D. G. Jansen. 1973. "Relationships Among Discharge Variables and MMPI Scale Scores of Hospitalized Alcoholics." *Journal of Clinical Psychology* 34: 1133-39.

——, and L. R. Wefring. 1972. "Relationships Between Admission Variables and MMPI Scale Scores of Hospitalized Alcoholics." *Psychological Reports* 31: 659-62.

Hoffman, H., and P. C. Nelson. 1971. "Personality Characteristics of Alcoholics in Relation to Age and Intelligence." *Psychological Reports* 29: 143-46.

Holland, T. R. 1977. "Multivariate Analysis of Personality Correlates of Alcohol and Drug Abuse in a Prison Population." *Journal of Abnormal Psychology* 86: 644-50.

Hoyt, D. P., and G. M. Sedlacek. 1958. "Differentiating Alcoholics from Normals and Abnormals with the MMPI." *Journal of Clinical Psychology* 14: 69-74.

Huber, N. A., and S. Danahy. 1975. "Use of the MMPI in Predicting Completion and Evaluating Changes in a Long-Term Alcoholism Treatment Program." *Journal of Studies on Alcohol* 36: 1230-37.

Jansen, D. G., and H. Hoffman. 1973. "Demographic and MMPI Characteristics of Male and Female State Hospital Alcoholic Patients." *Psychological Reports* 33: 561-62.

Jarvis, L. G., R. R. Simnegar, and A. R. Traweek. 1975. "An MMPI Comparison of U.S.A.F. Groups Identified as Drug Users." *Psychological Reports* 37: 1339-45.

Jones, B. M., and M. K. Jones. 1976a. "Women and Alcohol: Intoxication, Metabolism, and the Menstrual Cycle. In *Alcoholism Problems in Women and Children*, edited by M. Greenblatt and M. A. Schuckit, pp. 103–32. New York: Grune & Stratton.

——. 1976b. "Male and Female Intoxication Levels for Three Alcohol Doses or Do Women Really Get Higher Than Men? A Brief Communication." *Alcohol Technical Reports* 5: 1–14.

Jones, M. C. 1968. "Personality Correlates and Antecedents of Drinking Patterns in Adult Males." *Journal of Consulting and Clinical Psychology* 32: 2–12.

Kaestner, E., L. Rosen, and P. Appel. 1977. "Patterns of Drug Abuse: Relationships with Ethnicity, Sensation Seeking, and Anxiety." *Journal of Consulting and Clinical Psychology* 45: 462–68.

Kammeier, M. L., H. Hoffman, and R. G. Loper. 1978. "Personality Characteristics of Alcoholics as College Freshmen and at Time of Treatment." *Quarterly Journal of Studies on Alcohol* 34: 390–99.

Keller, J., and D. L. Redfering. 1973. "Comparison Between the Personalities of LSD Users and Nonusers as Measured by the Minnesota Multiphasic Personality Inventory." *Journal of Nervous and Mental Disease* 156: 271–77.

Khantzian, E. J., J. E. Mack, and A. F. Schatzberg. 1974. "Heroin Use as an Attempt to Cope: Clinical Observations." *American Journal of Psychiatry* 131: 160–64.

Kilpatrick, D. G., P. B. Sutker, J. C. Roitzsch, and W. C. Miller. 1976. "Personality Correlates of Polydrug Use." *Psychological Reports* 38: 311–17.

Kilpatrick, D. G., P. B. Sutker, and A. D. Smith. 1976. "Deviant Drug and Alcohol Use: The Role of Anxiety, Sensation Seeking, and Other Personality Variables." In *Emotions and Anxiety: New Concepts, Methods and Applications*, edited by M. Zuckerman and C. D. Spielberger, pp. 247–78. Hillsdale, N.J.: Erlbaum Associates.

Kish, G. B., and W. Busse. 1969. "MMPI Correlates of Sensation-Seeking in Male Alcoholics: A Test of Quay's Hypothesis Applied to Alcoholism." *Journal of Clinical Psychology* 25: 60–63.

Kojak, G., and J. P. Canby. 1975. "Personality and Behavior Patterns of Heroin-Dependent American Servicemen in Thailand." *American Journal of Psychiatry* 132: 246–50.

Korman, M. 1960. "Two MMPI Scales for Alcoholism: What Do They Measure?" *Journal of Clinical Psychology* 16: 296–98.

Kranitz, L. 1972. "Alcoholics, Heroin Addicts and Nonaddicts: Comparisons on the MacAndrew Alcoholism Scale of the MMPI." *Quarterly Journal of Studies on Alcohol* 33: 807–09.

Krasnoff, A. 1976. "Differences Between Alcoholics Who Complete or Withdraw from Treatment." *Journal of Studies on Alcohol* 37: 1666–71.

Kurtines, W. M., L. R. Ball, and G. H. Wood. 1978. "Personality Characteristics of Long-Term Recovered Alcoholics: A Comparative Analysis." *Journal of Consulting and Clinical Psychology* 46: 971–77.

Kurtines, W. M., R. Hogan, and D. Weiss. 1975. "Personality Dynamics of Heroin Use." *Journal of Abrnormal Psychology* 84: 87–89.

Kwant, F., J. A. Rice, and J. R. Hays. 1976. "Use of Heroin Addiction Scale to Differentiate Addicts from Rehabilitation Clients." *Psychological Reports* 38: 547–53.

Lachar, D., W. Berman, J. L. Grisell, and K. Schoof. 1976. "The MacAndrew Alcoholism Scale as a General Measure of Substance Misuse." *Journal of Studies on Alcohol* 37: 1609–15.

Lanyon, R. 1968. *A Handbook of MMPI Group Profiles*. Minneapolis: University of Minnesota Press.

Lin, Tien-Teh. 1975. "Use of Demographic Variables, WRAT, and MMPI Scores to Predict Addicts' Types of Discharge from a Community-like Hospital Setting." *Journal of Clinical Psychology* 31: 148–51.

Loper, R. G., M. L. Kammeier, and H. Hoffman. 1973. "MMPI Characteristics of College Freshman Males Who Later Became Alcoholics." *Journal of Abnormal Psychology* 82: 159–62.

Lorefice, L., R. A. Steer, E. W. Fine, and J. Schut. 1976. "Personality Traits and Moods of Alcoholics and Heroin Addicts." *Journal of Studies on Alcohol* 37: 687–89.

MacAndrew, C. 1965. "The Differentiation of Male Alcoholic Outpatients from Nonalcoholic Psychiatric Outpatients by Means of the MMPI." *Quarterly Journal of Studies on Alcohol* 26: 238–46.

——, and R. H. Geertsma. 1964. "A Critique of Alcoholism Scales Derived from the MMPI." *Quarterly Journal of Studies on Alcohol* 25: 68–76.

McCord, W., and J. McCord. 1962. "A Longitudinal Study of the Personality of Alcoholics. In *Society, Culture and Drinking Patterns*, edited by D. J. Pittman and C. R. Snyder, pp. 413–30. New York: Wiley.

McGinnis, C. A., and C. W. Ryan. 1965. "The Influence of Age on MMPI Scores of Chronic Alcoholics." *Journal of Clinical Psychology* 21: 271–72.

McLachlan, J. F. C. 1975a. "An MMPI Discriminant Function to Distinguish Alcoholics from Narcotic Addicts: Effects of Age, Sex and Psychopathology." *Journal of Clinical Psychology* 31: 163–65.

———. 1975b. "Classification of Alcoholics by an MMPI Actuarial System." *Journal of Psychology* 31: 145–47.

McWilliams, J., and C. C. Brown. 1977. "Treatment Termination Variables, MMPI Scores and Frequencies of Relapse in Alcoholics." *Journal of Studies on Alcohol*, 38: 477–86.

Miller, P. M. 1976. *Behavioral Treatment of Alcoholism*. New York: Pergamon.

Mischel, W. 1977. "On the Future of Personality Measurement." *American Psychologist* 32: 246–54.

———. 1973. "Toward a Cognitive Social Learning Reconceptualization of Personality." *Psychological Review* 80: 252–53.

Mozdzierz, G. J., F. J. Macchitelli, J. A. Conway, and H. Krauss. 1973. "Personality Characteristic Differences Between Alcoholics Who Leave Treatment Against Medical Advice and Those Who Don't. II." *Journal of Clinical Psychology* 29: 78–82.

Mulford, H. A. 1977. "Women and Men Problem Drinkers: Sex Differences in Patients Served by Iowa's Community Alcoholism Centers." *Journal of Studies on Alcohol* 38: 1624–39.

Muzekari, L. H. 1965. "The MMPI in Predicting Treatment Outcome in Alcoholics." *Journal of Consulting Psychology* 29: 281.

Naditch, M. P. 1975. "Relation of Motives for Drug Use and Psychopathology in the Development of Acute Adverse Reactions to Psychoactive Drugs." *Journal of Abnormal Psychology* 84: 374–85.

Nathan, P. E., and D. Lansky. 1978. "Common Methodological Problems in Research on the Addictions." *Journal of Consulting and Clinical Psychology* 46: 713–26.

Olson, R. W. 1964. "MMPI Sex Differences in Narcotic Addicts." *Journal of General Psychology* 71: 257–66.

Overall, J. E. 1973. "MMPI Personality Patterns of Alcoholics and Narcotic Addicts." *Quarterly Journal of Studies on Alcohol* 34: 104–11.

Partington, J. T., and F. G. Johnson. 1969. "Personality Types Among Alcoholics." *Quarterly Journal of Studies on Alcohol* 30: 21–34.

Penk, W. E., and R. Robinowitz. 1976. "Personality Differences of Volunteer and Nonvolunteer Heroin and Nonheroin Drug Users." *Journal of Abnormal Psychology* 85: 91–100.

Penk, W. E., W. A. Woodward, R. Robinowitz, and J. L. Hess. 1978. "Differences in MMPI Scores of Black and White Compulsive Heroin Users." *Journal of Abnormal Psychology* 87: 505–13.

Pittel, S. M. 1972. "Psychological Aspects of Heroin and Other Drug Dependence." In *It's So Good, Don't Even Try It Once*, edited by D. E. Smith and G. R. Gay, pp. 137–43. Englewood Cliffs, N.J.: Prentice-Hall.

Platt, J. J. 1975. "'Addiction Proneness' and Personality in Heroin Addicts." *Journal of Abnormal Psychology* 84: 303–06.

———, and D. Labate. 1976. *Heroin Addiction: Theory, Research, and Treatment*. New York: Wiley.

Preble, E., and J. J. Casey. 1969. "Taking Care of Business: The Heroin Users' Life on the Street." *International Journal of the Addictions* 4: 1–24.

Pugliese, A. C. 1975. "A Study of Methadone Maintenance Patients with the Minnesota Multiphasic Personality Inventory." *British Journal of Addiction* 70: 198–204.

Reith, G., D. Crockett, and K. Craig. 1975. "Personality Characteristics in Heroin Addicts and Nonaddicted Prisoners Using the Edwards Personaltiy Preference Schedule." *International Journal of the Addictions* 10: 97–112.

Reppucci, N. D., and W. G. Clingempeel. 1978. "Methodological Issues in Research with Correctional Populations." *Journal of Consulting and Clinical Psychology* 46: 727–46.

Rhodes, R. F. 1969. "The MacAndrew Alcoholism Scale: A Replication." *Journal of Clinical Psychology* 25: 189–91.

Rich, C. C., and H. G. Davis. 1969. "Concurrent Validity of MMPI Alcoholism Scales." *Journal of Clinical Psychology* 25: 425–26.

Robins, L. N. 1966. *Deviant Children Grown Up*. Baltimore: Williams & Wilkins.

———, W. M. Bates, and P. O'Neal. 1962. "Adult Drinking Patterns of Former Problem Children." In *Society, Culture, and Drinking Patterns*, edited by D. J. Pittman and C. R. Synder, pp. 395–412. New York: Wiley.

Rohan, W. P. 1972. "MMPI Changes in Hospitalized Alcoholics—A Second Study." *Quarterly Journal of Studies on Alcohol* 33: 65–76.

——, R. L. Tatro, and S. R. Rotman. 1969. "MMPI Changes in Alcoholics During Hospitalization." *Quarterly Journal of Studies on Alcohol* 30: 389–400.

Rosen, A. C. 1960. "A Comparative Study of Alcoholic and Psychiatric Patients with the MMPI." *Quarterly Journal of Studies on Alcohol* 21: 253–66.

Rosenberg, N. 1972. "MMPI Alcoholism Scales. *Journal of Clinical Psychology* 28: 515–22.

Ross, W. F., and J. I. Berzins. 1974. "Personality Characteristics of Female Narcotic Addicts on the MMPI." *Psychological Reports* 35: 779–84.

Rotman, S. R., and N. D. Vestre. 1964. "The Use of the MMPI in Identifying Problem Drinkers Among Psychiatric Hospital Admissions." *Journal of Clinical Psychology* 20: 526–30.

Ruff, C. F., J. Ayers, and D. I. Templer. 1975. "Alcoholics' and Criminals' Similarity of Scores on the MacAndrew Alcoholism Scale." *Psychological Reports* 36: 921–22.

Sadava, S. W., and R. Forsyth. 1977. "Person-Environment Interaction and College Student Drug Use: A Multivariate Longitudinal Study." *Genetic Psychology Monographs* 96: 211–45.

Schoolar, J. C., E. H. White, and C. P. Cohen. 1972. "Drug Abusers and Their Clinic-Patient Counterparts: A Comparison of Personality Dimensions." *Journal of Consulting and Clinical Psychology* 39: 9–14.

Schuckit, M. A., and E. R. Morrissey. 1976. "Alcoholism in Women: Some Clinical and Social Perspectives with an Emphasis on Possible Subtypes." In *Alcoholism Problems in Women and Children*, edited by M. Greenblatt and M. A. Schuckit, pp. 5–36. New York: Grune & Stratton.

Schwartz, M. F. 1977. "The MacAndrew Alcoholism Scale: A Construct Validity Study." Ph.D. dissertation, Kent State University.

Schwartz, R. M., B. R. Burkhart, and S. B. Green. 1978. "Turning On or Turning Off: Sensation Seeking or Tension Reduction as Motivational Determinants of Alcohol Use." *Journal of Consulting and Clinical Psychology* 46: 1144–45.

Shaffer, J. W., T. E. Hanlon, S. Wolf, N. H. Foxwell, and A. A. Kurland. 1962. "Nialamide in the Treatment of Alcoholism." *Journal of Nervous and Mental Disease* 135: 222–32.

Sheppard, C., J. Fracchia, E. Ricca, and S. Merlis. 1973. "Indications of Psychopathology in Applicants to a County Methadone Maintenance Program." *Psychological Reports* 33: 535-40.

——. 1972. "Indications of Psychopathology in Male Narcotic Abusers, Their Effects and Relation to Treatment Effectiveness." *Journal of Psychology* 81: 351-60.

Sheppard, C., E. Ricca, J. Fracchia, N. Rosenberg, and S. Merlis. 1972. "Cross-Validation of a Heroin Addiction Scale from the Minnesota Multiphasic Personality Inventory." *Journal of Psychology* 81: 263-68.

Skinner, H. A., D. N. Jackson, and H. Hoffman. 1974. "Alcoholic Personality Types: Identification and Correlates." *Journal of Abnormal Psychology* 83: 658-66.

Skinner, H. A., P. L. Reed, and D. N. Jackson. 1976. "Toward the Objective Diagnosis of Psychopathology: Generalizability of Modal Personality Profiles." *Journal of Consulting and Clinical Psychology* 44: 111-17.

Skolnick, N. J., and M. Zuckerman. In Press. "Personality Changes in Drug Abusers: A Comparison of Treatment in a Therapeutic Community and Prison (No-Treatment)." *Journal of Consulting and Clinical Psychology.*

Smart, R., and D. Fejer. 1969. "Illicit LSD Users: Their Social Backgrounds, Drug Use and Psychopathology." *Journal of Health and Social Behavior* 10: 294-304.

Smart, R., and D. Jones. 1970. "Illicit LSD Users: Their Personality Characteristics and Psychopathology." *Journal of Abnormal Psychology* 75: 286-92.

Soskin, R. A. 1970. "Personality and Attitude Change After Two Alcoholism Treatment Programs." *Quarterly Journal of Studies on Alcohol* 31: 920-31.

Stauss, F. F., N. K. Ousley, and A. S. Carlin. 1977. "Psychopathology and Drug Abuse: An MMPI Comparison of Polydrug Abuse Patients with Psychiatric Inpatients and Outpatients." *Addictive Behaviors* 2: 75-78.

Sutker, P. B. 1974. "Field Observations of a Heroin Addict: A Case Study." *American Journal of Community Psychology* 2: 35-42.

——. 1971. "Personality Differences and Sociopathy in Heroin Addicts and Nonaddict Prisoners." *Journal of Abnormal Psychology* 78: 247-51.

——, and A. N. Allain. 1973. "Incarcerated and Street Heroin Addicts: A Personality Comparison." *Psychological Reports* 32: 243-46.

——, and G. H. Cohen. 1974. "MMPI Indices of Personality Change Following Short- and Long-Term Hospitalization of Heroin Addicts." *Psychological Reports* 34: 495–500.

Sutker, P. B., R. P. Archer, and A. N. Allain. In Press. "Psychopathology of Drug Abusers: Sex and Ethnic Considerations. *International Journal of the Addictions.*

——. 1979. "Voluntarism and Self-Reported Psychopathology Among Opiate Addicts." *Journal of Abnormal Psychology* 88: 59–67.

——. 1978. "Drug Abuse Patterns, Personality Characteristics, and Relationships with Sex, Race, and Sensation Seeking." *Journal of Consulting and Clinical Psychology* 46: 1374–78.

Sutker, P. B., R. P. Archer, and D. G. Kilpatrick. In Press. "Sociopathy and Antisocial Behavior: Theory and Treatment." In *Handbook of Clinical Behavior Therapy*, edited by S. M. Turner, K. S. Calhoun, and H. E. Adams. New York: Wiley.

Sutker, P. B., and C. E. Moan. 1972. "Personality Characteristics of Socially Deviant Women: Incarcerated Heroin Addicts, Street Addicts, and Non-Addicted Prisoners." In *Drug Addiction: Clinical and Socio-Legal Aspects*, edited by J. M. Singh, L. H. Miller, and H. Lal, vol. 2, pp. 107–14. Mt. Kisco, N.Y.: Futura.

Toler, C. 1975. "The Personal Values of Alcoholics and Addicts." *Journal of Clinical Psychology* 31: 554–57.

Toomey, T. C. 1974. "Personality and Demographic Characteristics of Two Sub-Types of Drug Abusers." *British Journal of Addiction* 69: 155–58.

Uecker, A. E. 1970. "Differentiating Male Alcoholic from Other Psychiatric Inpatients." *Quarterly Journal of Studies on Alcohol* 31: 379–83.

——, G. B. Kish, and M. E. Ball. 1969. "Differentiation of Alcoholism from General Psychopathology by Means of Two MMPI Scales." *Journal of Clinical Psychology* 25: 287–89.

Vega, A. 1971. "Cross-Validation of Four MMPI Scales for Alcoholism." *Quarterly Journal of Studies on Alcohol* 32: 791–97.

Welpton, D. 1968. "Psychodynamics of Chronic Lysergic Acid Diethylamide Use: A Clinical Study of 10 Voluntary Subjects." *Journal of Nervous and Mental Disease* 147: 377–85.

Whitelock, P. R., J. E. Overall, and J. H. Patrick. 1971. "Personality Patterns and Alcohol Abuse in a State Hospital Population." *Journal of Abnormal Psychology* 78: 9–16.

Wilkinson, A. E., W. M. Prado, W. O. Williams, and F. W. Schnadt, 1971. "Psychological Test Characteristics and Length of Stay in Alcoholism Treatment." *Quarterly Journal of Studies on Alcohol* 32: 60–65.

Williams, A. F., W. F. McCourt, and L. Schneider. 1971. "Personality Self-Descriptions of Alcoholics and Heavy Drinkers." *Quarterly Journal of Studies on Alcohol* 32: 310–17.

Williams, J. H. 1968. "Characterization and Follow-Up of Alcoholic Patients. In *Alcoholism, the Total Treatment Package*, edited by R. J. Cantanzaro, pp. 154–63. Springfield, Ill.: Charles C. Thomas.

Wilson, A., E. A. Mabry, K. A. Khavari, and D. Dalpes. 1977. "Discriminant Analysis of MMPI Profiles for Demographic Classificiations of Male Alcoholics." *Journal of Studies on Alcohol* 38: 47–57.

Wurmser, L. 1974. "Psychoanalytic Considerations of the Etiology of Compulsive Drug Use." *Journal of the American Psychoanalytic Association* 22: 820–43.

Zelen, S. L., J. Fox, F. Gould, and R. W. Olson. 1966. "Sex-Contingent Differences Between Male and Female Alcoholics." *Journal of Clinical Psychology* 22: 160–65.

Zinberg, N. E. 1977. "Patterns of Drug Abuse." Paper presented at Conference on Recent Development in Chemotherapy of Narcotic Addiction. Washington, D.C., November 3–4.

Zuckerman, M. 1972. *Manual and Research Report for the Sensation-Seeking Scale (SSS)*. Newark: University of Delaware.

——. 1970. "Drug Usage as One Manifestation of a Sensation Seeking Trait." In *Drug Abuse: Current Concepts and Research*, edited by W. Keup. Springfield, Ill.: Charles C. Thomas.

——, S. Sola, J. Masterson, and J. V. Angelone, 1975. "MMPI Patterns in Drug Abusers Before and After Treatment in Therapeutic Communities." *Journal of Consulting and Clinical Psychology* 43: 286–96.

5/ THE MMPI AND SUICIDE

James R. Clopton

Suicide is a vexing problem for the general public as well as for mental health professionals. Most individuals who kill themselves or make serious suicide attempts give warnings, but some people commit suicide without warning and without a clear motive. Psychologists have examined the relationship of suicidal behavior to environmental stress, to demographic variables, and to psychological test data. Theoretically, knowing the characteristics of suicidal individuals will assist in understanding what leads people to consider killing themselves and in predicting who will attempt suicide.

Because the MMPI is used routinely in many mental health facilities, psychiatric patients who commit suicide or attempt suicide will sometimes have completed the MMPI prior to their suicidal act. Also, some individuals are hospitalized following suicide threats or suicide attempts and may complete the MMPI as part of the routine admission procedures of the psychiatric hospital. Due to these circumstances, psychologists have gained clinical experience with psychological test records, including MMPI profiles, from suicidal patients and have been able to conduct research comparing the MMPI data of patients showing various suicidal behaviors (threats, attempts, actual suicides) with MMPI data obtained from nonsuicidal patients.

The purpose of this chapter is to review the MMPI research literature on suicide, after first briefly mentioning clinical impressions formed by psychologists who have examined the MMPI records of suicidal psychiatric patients. Methodological guidelines for future research will also be presented. A current review of the MMPI research literature on suicide is needed because several significant studies (for example, Leonard 1977) have been reported since the publication of earlier review articles (Brown and Sheran 1972; Clopton 1974, Devries 1968; Lester 1970a).

CLINICAL IMPRESSIONS

Extreme elevations on the D scale are usually present in the MMPIs of persons who have suicidal ideas. The Pt scale is frequently the second highest scale. This D-Pt high-point pair suggests a pattern of self-devaluation, internal distress, and intropunitiveness that could quite easily be associated with thoughts of suicide. However, the D-Pt high-point pair is also frequent among the profiles of psychiatric patients who do not attempt suicide, being the most common two-point code in psychiatric populations.

Other MMPI scales that have been linked with suicidal behavior are Pd, Sc, and Ma. Elevations on the Pd and Sc scales are indicative of impulsiveness and poor judgment. Therefore elevations on these two scales, together with high scores for the D and Pt scales, are considered to lead to an increased likelihood of suicide attempts (Carson 1969; Graham 1977). Graham (1977) suggests that if a person is extremely insecure and dissatisfied with life, as suggested by elevations on the D and Pt scales, thoughts of suicide may be expected, but if the Ma scale is low, then the person may lack the energy to make a suicide attempt. However, as the Ma scale becomes more elevated, a depressed and uncomfortable person is increasingly more likely to have sufficient energy to act on suicidal ideas.

The clinical literature reveals two other suggestions regarding the relationship of D scale scores and suicidal risk. Dahlstrom, Welsh, and Dahlstrom (1972) state that suicidal risk is greater when a person's MMPI profile has a significant elevation on the D scale but the person denies depressive thoughts and feelings, and shows no behavioral indications of depression, than when the depression indicated by the D scale elevation is clearly reflected in the person's behavior. Graham (1977) notes that there is clinical evidence that for some severely depressed individuals suicide attempts become more likely when there begins to be some improvement in the depression. If the MMPI has been periodically administered to a severely depressed person, significant decreases on the D scale might alert the clinician that suicide attempts could become more likely.

RESEARCH EVIDENCE

There are four basic ways in which differences in the MMPI profiles of suicidal and nonsuicidal patients can be examined. The first and most common approach is to compare the scores of suicidal and nonsuicidal patients on each of a number of MMPI scales. The second approach is to look for differences in the profile patterns of suicidal and nonsuicidal patients. This approach goes beyond the consideration of individual scales to investigate relationships among the various scales. A third approach is to examine whether there are individual MMPI items that can be used to identify suicidal patients. The final approach is to investigate the ability of clinicians to identify the MMPI records of suicidal patients.

Scale Differences

Studies that have compared suicidal psychiatric patients with nonsuicidal patients on individual MMPI scales have produced inconsistent results. For example, Clopton and Jones (1975) found that male psychiatric patients who committed suicide did not obtain scores on any of the standard MMPI scales that differed significantly from the scores of nonsuicidal patients, while in a similar study Foster (1975) found male suicides to score significantly higher than nonsuicidal males on seven MMPI scales (*F, Hs, D, Hy, Pa, Pt,* and *Sc*). Disparate findings also have occurred among studies that have compared suicide attempters and nonsuicidal patients (Clopton, Pallis, and Birtchnell 1979; Faberow 1956; Foster 1975; Kinsinger 1973; Marks and Haller 1977; Rosen, Hales, and Simon 1954; Tarter, Templer, and Perley 1975). Here again, some investigators (Farberow 1956; Tarter, Templer, and Perley 1975) have found no significant differences in MMPI scale scores, while others (for example, Clopton, Pallis, and Birtchnell 1979; Foster 1975) have found several scales on which suicide attempters score significantly higher than nonsuicidal patients. Table 5.1 presents the mean MMPI scale scores found for psychiatric patients who either threaten suicide, attempt suicide, or actually commit suicide.

A few research studies have attempted to relate the scores of MMPI scales with particular suicide methods or with the lethality of suicide attempts. Simon (1950) examined the MMPI scale scores of male suicide attempters and found that a peak on the *D* scale appeared to be particularly characteristic of patients who attempted suicide by hanging. However, two later studies (Lester 1970b; Simon and Gilberstadt 1958) found no relationship between MMPI scale scores and the method chosen by male psychiatric patients who committed suicide. Tarter, Templer, and Perley (1975) administered the MMPI and a lethality scale (Weisman and Worden 1972) to males and females who had attempted suicide and found the lethality scores were not related to the scores of any standard MMPI scales.

MMPI Profile Analysis

Some studies attempting to find a way to use the MMPI to assess suicidal risk have employed profile analysis. The relative elevation of the standard MMPI scales in profiles obtained from suicidal patients has been examined. More typically, suicidal and nonsuicidal groups have been compared using multivariate procedures, such as discriminant analysis and multivariate analysis of variance, which simultaneously consider scores from several MMPI scales.

Marks and Seeman (1963) identified 16 common profile code types among MMPI records obtained from psychiatric patients (inpatients and outpatients of both sexes). Each profile code type was defined by a set of explicit rules and was identified by the two or three highest scale scores for that profile type. For each

TABLE 5.1

Mean MMPI Scale Scores for Psychiatric Patients Who Threatened, Attempted, or Committed Suicide

Study	Sex	n	L	F	K	Hs	D	Hy	Pd	Mf	Pa	Pt	Sc	Ma	Si
								Suicide Threateners							
Farberow (1956)	M	32	51	68	51	77	86	75	80	66	73	85	88	68	—
Kinsinger (1973)	F	25	50	74	47	67	78	70	77	43	75	74	80	61	68
Foster (1975)	M	13	3*	11*	10*	17*	29*	26*	30*	27*	12*	33*	32*	24*	34*
								Suicide Attempters							
Rosen, Hales, and Simon (1954)	M	50	3*	9*	13*	11*	28*	27*	23*	26*	14*	23*	22*	20*	32*
Farberow (1956)	M	32	52	61	54	71	78	67	70	61	61	68	68	56	—
Kinsinger (1973)	F	60	48	68	49	60	69	66	78	46	67	67	74	63	62

MMPI Scales

Study	Sex	49	4*	13*	11*	18*	29*	25*	29*	29*	14*	35*	37*	22*	36*
Foster (1975)	M		–												
Tarter, Templer, and Perley (1975)	F	38	–	66	49	59	73	66	69	43	65	70	71	58	63
	M	12	–	80	45	73	85	73	75	65	74	76	86	70	63
Clopton, Pallis, and Birtchnell (1978)	F	43	55	63	50	72	78	64	74	48	64	88	87	62	65
	M	32	53	68	46	78	81	63	75	64	65	94	93	66	62
Suicides															
Holzberg, Cohen, and Wilk (1951)	M	1	50	57	54	49	62	51	50	51	53	56	65	40	–
Clopton and Jones (1975)	M	22	54	70	54	69	83	68	73	63	67	78	84	61	60
Foster (1975)	M	29	3*	11*	12*	28*	26*	28*	28*	14*	35*	36*	23*	34*	
Leonard (1977)	F	16	47	67	49	67	83	75	77	51	72	75	80	66	67
	M	20	47	71	52	68	86	74	77	75	70	83	86	62	63

Note: Scores marked with an asterisk are raw scores; other scores are T scores. Foster (1975) did not report whether the scores in her study had K corrections added. All other scores, however, are K corrected. Two studies did not report the mean L scale score. One study did not report the mean Si scale score.

Source: Compiled by the author.

profile type, Marks and Seeman (1963) reported the frequency of suicidal behavior (attempts, thoughts, and threats) among female patients. The base rates for suicide attempts, suicidal thinking, and suicide threats among this group of patients were 16.9, 23, and 4.7 percent, respectively.

Patients with either of two profile code types, *Pd–Sc–D* and *Pd–Pa–D*, were found to be higher than the base rate for all three suicidal behaviors. The highest incidence of suicidal behavior was found among patients with the *Pd–Sc–D* profile type. For example, 45 percent of the patients with this profile type had attempted suicide. Patients with profile types *D–Pt–Sc* and *D–Sc* had a high incidence, compared to base rates, of both suicidal thoughts and suicidal threats, but not of suicide attempts. Patients with profile type *Pd–Pa* had 39 percent suicide attempts but did not have a high incidence of suicidal thoughts or suicide threats. It is surprising to note that several of the profile types with elevations on the *D* scale had rates for the various suicidal behaviors that were lower than the base rates. This was most evident if, in addition to an elevation for the *D* scale, the profile was defined by elevations for the *Hs* and *Hy* scales or by an elevation for the *Pt* scale.

Devries and Farberos (1967) used discriminant analysis to differentiate four groups of psychiatric patients: nonsuicidal patients, patients who had threatened suicide, patients who had attempted suicide, and patients who had committed suicide. Instead of utilizing all thirteen standard MMPI scales, only the six clinical scales (*D, Pd, Pa, Pt, Sc,* and *Ma*) previously found (Farberow 1956) to show promise in differentiating suicidal and nonsuicidal groups were considered. The mean scores of the six scales differed significantly among the four groups. The discriminant analysis correctly classified 52 percent of the nonsuicidal patients, 17 percent of the patients who attempted suicide, 59 percent of the patients who threatened suicide, and 28 percent of patients who committed suicide. The overall efficiency (number of patients correctly identified divided by the total number of patients) was 41 percent. Using the six MMPI scales to separate patients who committed suicide from other psychiatric patients, 25 percent of the suicide patients were correctly identified and 15 percent of the patients in the other three groups were misclassified as being in the suicide group. In general, the Devries and Farberow (1967) results were consistent with other MMPI research (Farberow 1956; Rosen, Hales, and Simon 1954; Simon and Gilberstadt 1958) in indicating that patients who threaten suicide are the most easily identified suicidal group and that patients who commit suicide are the most difficult suicidal group to differentiate from other patient groups.

Ravensborg and Foss (1969) obtained the MMPI profiles of psychiatric patients who had committed suicide, patients who died of natural causes, and a random sample of other psychiatric patients from the same hospital. Group profiles were analyzed by profile analysis of variance (Block, Levine, and McNemar 1951), and the mean profiles of the three groups of patients did not differ significantly. In this study patients in the suicide group were significantly younger and better educated and had significantly higher intelligence scores than comparison patients. As Leonard (1978) observed, it is remarkable that despite these important group differences there were no significant differences in the MMPI profiles of the three groups.

Devries and Shneidman (1967) obtained the MMPI records from five suicidal patients (three males and two females; two patients had attempted suicide, two had suicidal thoughts, and one was described as being depressed and lonely) who received the MMPI monthly for a period of a year. Each patient also made monthly ratings of his or her suicidal intent on a nine-point lethality scale. A discriminant analysis correctly grouped together the MMPI profiles for each patient, and the profiles were sorted by two clinicians with 75 percent accuracy. Thus, even though the patients' ratings indicated important changes in their suicidal intent, there was a very high degree of consistency in their MMPI profiles over time. Of course, these results may have been highly dependent on the high degree of heterogeneity among the five patients in this study. Devries and Shneidman also correlated each patient's lethality ratings with the scores for 12 of the standard MMPI scales (the *Si* scale was not included). No MMPI scale correlated significantly with the lethality ratings of more than two patients, and *D* scale scores did not correlate significantly with lethality ratings for any patient. It appeared therefore that although each of the five patients had shown increases and decreases in suicidal intent, these changes were not consistently related to changes in MMPI scale scores. There was certainly no evidence that when suicidal patients are acutely suicidal their MMPI scale scores converge in a general suicidal profile.

Clopton and Jones (1975) compared the MMPI profiles of male psychiatric patients who committed suicide with nonsuicidal male psychiatric patients. The 13 scales of the standard profile were subjected to a discriminant analysis to find the combination of variables (MMPI scales) that would most correctly classify patients as suicidal or nonsuicidal. (The discriminant functions can be obtained from the authors.) Correct classification occurred for 73 and 59 percent of the suicidal and nonsuicidal patients, respectively. However, the nature of the profile differences was not clear. For example, the frequency of particular high-point pairs did not differ remarkably in the suicide and nonsuicidal groups. Few profiles in either group belonged to any of the Marks and Seeman (1963) profile code types.

Another investigation that employed discriminant analysis was the excellent study of Leonard (1977), who compared the MMPIs of three groups of psychiatric patients: suicides, highly suicidal patients (patients who had attempted and/or threatened suicide), and nonsuicidal patients. Patients in the three groups were matched by age and sex. Because of clear sex differences, the MMPI data for male and female patients were analyzed separately. The MMPI profiles of female suicides differed significantly from the profiles of both female comparison groups. The discriminant analysis for female suicides versus highly suicidal females indicated seven variables—*F, K, Hy, Mf, Si,* and special MMPI scales for authority conflict and familial discord (Lingoes 1960)—that correctly classified all female suicides and all but two highly suicidal females. Use of the discriminant function analysis revealed that the MMPI profiles of male suicides differed significantly from the profiles of the nonsuicidal males but not from the profiles of highly suicidal males. The results of this study suggested to Leonard (1977) that clinicians may be able to use the MMPI to predict which female psychiatric patients with suicide attempts or threats will eventually commit suicide, but that a similar determination for male psychiatric patients might not be possible.

Clopton, Pallis, and Birtchnell (1979) compared the MMPI profiles of psychiatric patients who had made suicide attempts with the profiles of non-suicidal psychiatric patients. Multivariate analysis of variance of the MMPI profiles resulted in a significant difference as a function of sex. Thus separate analyses were performed for males and females. While the profiles of suicidal and non-suicidal females differed significantly, there were no significant differences on the MMPI profiles of suicidal and nonsuicidal males.

A discriminant function analysis also was conducted in this study that provided frequences of correct and incorrect classification of suicidal and non-suicidal patients. In the original comparison of suicidal and nonsuicidal males, correct classification was obtained for all suicidal patients and for almost all (97 percent) of the nonsuicidal patients. However, when the discriminant function derived in this analysis was extended to a new sample of suicidal and nonsuicidal males, all suicidal patients were misclassified. For females, 36 percent of the suicidal patients were correctly classified in the original analysis, but on cross-validation a reduction to only 28 percent accuracy occurred.

Clopton, Pallis, and Birtchnell (1979) also used cluster analysis of MMPI profiles to identify subtypes of suicidal and nonsuicidal patients. To allow direct comparisons between groups and to avoid clusters of extremely small sizes resulted in the derivation of three clusters for each of the following four groups: suicidal males, suicidal females, nonsuicidal males, and nonsuicidal females. (The mean MMPI profiles for the 12 clusters can be found in the original article.) The mean MMPI profile for one cluster among the suicidal males was within normal limits. Eight clusters had mean MMPI profiles in which the *Pt* and *Sc* scales were the two scales with the highest scores. Among these eight clusters, the mean profiles for suicidal clusters all had the *D* scale as the third most elevated scale, while the mean profiles for nonsuicidal clusters all had the *Hs* scale as the third most elevated scale.

All individual MMPI profiles that had *Pt* and *Sc* as the two most elevated scales were examined. Inspection of these profiles revealed that for 64 percent of the suicidal patients the *D* scale score was greater than the *Hs* scale score, while the *Hs* scale score was greater than the *D* scale score for 60 percent of the nonsuicidal patients. Thus, among patients whose MMPI profiles had the *Pt* and *Sc* scales as the two most elevated scales, the relative elevation of the *D* and *Hs* scales was significantly associated with whether or not the patient had attempted suicide.

Research comparing the MMPI scale scores of suicidal and nonsuicidal patients is generally multivariate, regardless of whether or not multivariate statistics are actually used. There is a need, though, for increased use of multivariate techniques such as multivariate analysis of variance and discriminant analysis. Some studies (for example, Foster 1975; Kinsenger 1973) have included several patient groups and have examined all the standard MMPI scales, but the data analysis has been limited to a comparison for each scale of the mean scores of two groups at a time. Without overall statistical comparisons, such studies are of limited value. To perform 150 t-tests, as Foster (1975) did, without an overall test (preferably multivariate analysis of variance) for differences among the various patient groups, is indefensible statistically (Hays 1963, pp. 375–76). Furthermore, studies that employ nothing more than multiple t-tests cannot provide information about differences in the MMPI profile patterns of suicidal and nonsuicidal patients. Multivariate statistics must be used to examine profile patterns.

MMPI Item Analysis

The attempt to find MMPI items that identify suicidal patients is important for two reasons. First, there is a need to establish whether a patient's responses to items whose content is relevant to suicide, such as item 339 "Most of the time I wish I were dead,"* can be used to help assess the risk of a suicide attempt. Second, because of the success of other special MMPI scales (see Chapter 14), investigators have sought to explore the possibility of developing a special MMPI suicide scale.

Simon and Hales (1949) examined the MMPI responses of male psychiatric patients who were judged to be preoccupied with suicide. They reported finding only seven items from the *D* scale and ten items from the *Pt* scale that were answered in the scored direction by a majority of the suicidal patients. Item 88 "I usually feel that life is worthwhile"* was answered in the negative direction by less than one sixth of the suicidal patients.

Simon and Galberstadt (1958) contrasted the MMPI responses of patients who committed suicide with the responses of nonsuicidal patients in an attempt to derive a scale to predict suicide. An item analysis indicated that 23 MMPI items significantly differentiated the groups. However, these investigations concluded, perhaps erroneously (see Devries 1967), that this number of significant differences could be obtained strictly by chance. The item content of the 23 items did not appear to be relevant to suicide. Apparently the items did not

---

*Reproduced from the MMPI by permission. Copyright 1943, renewed 1970, by the University of Minnesota. Published by The Psychological Corporation. All rights reserved.

stand up under cross-validation, although the cross-validation data were not presented.

Farberow and Devries (1967) did an item analysis of the MMPI responses of suicidal and nonsuicidal male psychiatric patients. One group of patients had committed suicide while in a psychiatric hospital, while another group had been admitted to the hospital following suicide attempts and a third group had been admitted as a result of suicide threats. Each of the four patient groups (suicides, patients who attempted suicide, patients who threatened suicide, and non-suicidal patients) was divided to allow for two independent sets of item analyses. The MMPI responses of each group of patients were compared with the responses of every other group. Only when the number of significant items in a comparison of two groups exceeded the number estimated to be expected by chance (Devries 1966b) in both analyses was it assumed that there was a significant differentiation between the groups. Only the suicide threat group satisfied this criterion; none of the other groups was significantly differentiated from each other in both comparisons. The 52 MMPI items that significantly differentiated the suicide threat group from the nonsuicidal group in both item analyses were selected for an MMPI Suicide Threat scale. The items and direction for scoring can be found in Dahlstrom, Welsh, and Dahlstrom (1975, p. 326).

Ravensborg and Foss (1969) scored the suicide threat scale for the three groups of patients (suicides, natural deaths, and nonsuicidal patients) in their study and obtained mean scores of 21.7 for patients who committed suicide and 22.9 for the other two groups. An analysis of variance performed on suicide threat scale scores indicated that the scores of the suicide group did not differ significantly from the scores of the other two groups, and that the scores of male and female patients did not differ. The sex x patient group interaction, however, was significant. Inspection of means revealed that nonsuicidal female patients obtained the highest mean score on the Suicide Threat scale.

Devries (1966c), in a follow-up study to that of Farberow and Devries (1967),* included a group of patients who had attempted suicide, a group of patients who had threatened suicide, and a group of patients who had both threatened and attempted suicide, and compared these three groups with non-suicidal psychiatric patients. As in the Farberow and Devries (1967) study, the samples were divided to allow for two independent sets of item analyses. For both sets of comparisons the MMPI responses of each of the four patient groups were compared with those of every other group for all 373 short-form MMPI items. All comparisons of the various suicidal groups with each other were not significant. Devries (1966c) found that every comparison of one of the three

---

*Despite being published later, the Farberow and Devries (1967) study was the earlier of the two.

suicidal groups with the nonsuicidal group resulted in a greater number of differentiating items than would be expected by chance. However, few items significantly differentiated any of the suicidal groups from the nonsuicidal group on both of the independent item analyses.

Devries (1967) attempted to demonstrate that controlling appropriate variables increases the ability of the MMPI to differentiate suicidal and nonsuicidal patients. Unfortunately, the definition of "suicidal" used in this study was not specified. Beginning with suicidal male patients and nonsuicidal male patients, Devries sorted each population into categories for diagnosis, age, education, occupation, marital status, and number of hospital admissions. After first sorting both populations by diagnostic category, the subcategory with the most patients (psychosis) was selected for further sorting on the basis of the next variable, age. Again the subcategory with the most patients (younger than 40) was retained for further sorting.

Using this procedure the remaining patients were sorted in turn for subcategories of education, occupation, marital status, and number of hospital admissions. The two samples obtained in this manner consisted of 8 suicidal patients and 13 nonsuicidal patients. These were all psychotic patients who were not over 40 years old, had a high school education, were single, were unemployed service workers or laborers, and had one hospital admission. The response frequencies (number of true responses and the number of false responses) of the two groups were compared for each of the 373 short-form MMPI items. Sixteen items were found to make a significant differentiation, and this number of items was found to be greater than the number of items that would be expected by chance alone to differentiate the two groups. Devries, however, failed to report the item numbers and direction of scoring (response more frequent among suicidal patients) for the 16 items, and no cross-validation of his findings has been published.

In a related study Devries (1966s) identified characteristics of suicidal individuals found in his review of the suicide literature. Using these characteristics, 55 true-false items were written and administered to nonsuicidal male psychiatric patients and to male psychiatric patients who had made suicide attempts and/or threats. Using a cutoff score of 7 with the 13 items found to make a significant differentiation between the groups, 56 percent of the suicidal patients could be identified with 31 false positives occurring (nonsuicidal patients falsely identified as being suicidal).

Lester (1967) found the 13-item Devries (1966a) scale to differentiate significantly between nonsuicidal college students and college students who had attempted or threatened suicide. Furthermore, this differentiation was not merely a result of group differences in emotional disturbance (Lester 1968). Leonard (1977) mistakenly stated that the Devries (1966a) scale was developed from MMPIs of male suicidal veterans. Such mistakes are probably common because the 55 true-false items used in the Devries (1966a) study were quite similar to MMPI items and because Devries has been so active in MMPI research on suicide risk assessment.

In the Clopton and Jones (1975) study, an item analysis compared the response frequencies of patients who had committed suicide with the response frequencies of nonsuicidal patients. The 12 MMPI items that differentiated between the suicidal and nonsuicidal groups lacked face validity as suicide indicators.* One item (328) of the Suicide Threat scale (Farberow and Devries 1967) was found to differentiate suicidal and nonsuicidal patients, but the response (false) more frequent among suicidal patients in this study was opposite to the item's scoring direction in the Suicide Threat scale.

Koss, Butcher, and Hoffman (1976) studied male patients admitted to a psychiatric hospital while in a crisis involving "depressed-suicidal ideation." The authors did not specify whether all these patients had thoughts of suicide or whether other suicidal behaviors were present. The MMPI item responses of these patients were contrasted with the responses of noncrisis psychiatric patients, and 89 MMPI items were found to differentiate the two groups. The content of only 3 of the 89 items (88, 142, 339) had relevance to suicide.

Clinical Judgments

The only available study on the ability of clinicians to identify the MMPI profiles of suicidal persons is by Clopton and Daucom (1979). The MMPI profiles of male psychiatric patients who committed suicide and male nonsuicidal patients, which had been used in another study (Clopton and Jones 1975), were presented to six clinical psychologists with expertise in MMPI interpretation. Each profile was judged as likely or not likely to have come from a male psychiatric patient who later killed himself. For each profile, ratings were made for eight variables thought to be important in the assessment of suicide risk: impulse control, intropunitiveness versus extrapunitiveness, self-evaluation, social conformity, activity level, optimism versus pessimism, somatic symptoms of depression, and affective symptoms of depression. None of the judges identified suicidal and nonsuicidal patients with an accuracy that was significantly better than chance. Furthermore, the ratings of the eight suicide variables did not differ for suicidal and nonsuicidal patients.

METHODOLOGICAL GUIDELINES FOR FUTURE RESEARCH

Research on the MMPI and suicide has generally improved since early descriptive studies (for example, Simon and Hales 1949). Indeed, some recent studies show a high degree of sophistication. Nevertheless, investigators in this

---

*The 12 items and the responses obtained most frequently from suicidal patients were as follows: 38F, 39F, 59F, 75F, 117F, 127F, 143F, 174F, 224F, 328F, 426F, 456F.

area of research need to be reminded of some common errors in past research studies and of some general methodological issues.

Given the small amount of data that are usually available for an MMPI study of suicide, a common mistake has been to combine MMPI data from individuals showing different suicidal behaviors. Broida's (1954) suicidal groups consisted of patients who either attempted suicide or were rated by ward psychiatrists as having excessive suicidal thinking. The high-suicide group in Leonard's (1977) study contained patients with histories of prolonged threats and preoccupation. Combining patients who threaten suicide with those who attempt suicide is a questionable procedure. Previous MMPI research reveals that patients who threaten suicide have the most elevated MMPI profiles of any suicidal group and that there are differences in the MMPI profiles of patients who threaten suicide and those who attempt suicide (Farberow 1956; Farberow and Devries 1967; Rosen, Hales, and Simon 1954; Simon and Gilberstadt 1958). A related procedure that is also highly questionable is to regard patients who show various suicidal behaviors as varying along a unitary dimension of "suicidality" (for example, Leonard 1974; Poeldinger, Gehring, and Blaser 1973).

There is evidence that multivariate analysis can differentiate suicidal and nonsuicidal patients (Clopton and Jones 1975; Devries and Farberow 1967; Leonard 1977). However, multivariate procedures have rarely been cross-validated, nor have they been demonstrated to be of practical value to clinicians attempting to predict suicidal behavior (Clopton 1978). The combination of differentiating variables (for example, MMPI scales) needs to be derived in one comparison of suicidal and nonsuicidal individuals and then extended to new samples. The percentage of correct classifications may be considerably lower in the validation samples, as demonstrated by Clopton, Pallis, and Birtchnell (1979). Furthermore, it may be difficult to describe the exact nature of the profile differences when a discriminant analysis significantly differentiates suicidal and nonsuicidal patients (for example, Clopton and Jones 1975).

Early studies typically included data from male patients only, but recent studies have shown greater balance by including data from both sexes (for example, Leonard 1977). Two recent studies (Clopton, Pallis, and Birtchnell 1979; Leonard 1977) have found significant differences in the MMPI profile patterns obtained from male and female patients. Therefore, when MMPI data are available for both males and females, the data for the two sexes should be analyzed separately. In general, investigators would do well to follow Leonard's (1977) lead in reporting fully the personal characteristics of patients and in considering that differences in MMPI data obtained from suicidal and nonsuicidal patients may be directly related to such characteristics as sex, age, and voluntary versus involuntary psychiatric admission.

One limitation of many MMPI studies of suicide is the length of time between MMPI administration and suicidal act. This time interval has exceeded two years for some of the suicidal patients studied (for example, Clopton and Jones 1975; Leonard 1977). Such time intervals limit the usefulness of an assessment instrument, such as the MMPI, which measures not only enduring traits of a person but also changing states. If the time interval does not exceed one year and the median time interval is in the range of four to twelve months (for example, Clopton and Baucom 1979), then a study would appear to have the most clinical relevance. Such time intervals (four to twelve months) are representative of many inpatient settings where MMPI administration occurs at the time of admission and the greatest risk of suicide is during the first six months following discharge from the hospital (Temoche, Pugh, and MacMahon 1964).

Two related limitations of MMPI research on suicide are no doubt evident to clinicians faced with the task of predicting suicide risk among psychiatric patients. First, studies have examined conditional probabilities in suicide prediction, not posterior probabilities (MacKinnon and Farberow 1976). That is, studies investigate whether the MMPI records of psychiatric patients who have shown suicidal behavior could have been identified, not whether patients who have been predicted as likely to attempt suicide on the basis of their MMPI profiles do indeed later attempt suicide. Second, the differentiation of suicidal and nonsuicidal patients is most often made solely on the basis of MMPI data. In clinical practice, however, judgments regarding suicidal risk nearly always occur after a variety of information has been considered. Thus the research question of most clinical relevance is whether MMPI data are of assistance in the identification of individuals who will later attempt suicide, not whether MMPI data are sufficient for such identification.

Clinicians and research investigators interested in the use of the MMPI in suicidal assessment must remember that the statistical infrequency of suicide places a formidable burden on any procedure used to assess suicidal risk. Even a highly accurate test may predict no more accurately than always predicting the nonoccurrence of suicide. Given the low rate of suicide among psychiatric patients, even if the MMPI were found to identify correctly 80 percent of patients, both suicidal and nonsuicidal, it would be impractical, and ethically questionable, to treat as suicidal the large number of false positives (Rosen 1954). Any change in the criterion so as to reduce the number of false postiives would also automatically reduce the detection of patients who were truly suicidal.

SUMMARY AND CONCLUSIONS

To date, neither standard MMPI scales, MMPI profile analysis, nor specific MMPI items have been found to be reliable in predicting suicide at useful levels. The only standard MMPI scale that might be expected to differentiate suicidal and nonsuicidal groups is the D scale. However, several studies have found no differences in the D scale scores of suicidal and nonsuicidal patients (Clopton and Jones 1975; Farberow 1956; Rosen, Hales, and Simon 1954; Simon and Gilberstadt 1958). Suicidal and nonsuicidal patients do not differ consistently on any of the other standard MMPI scales, and MMPI scale scores have been found to be unrelated to the lethality of suicide attempts or to the particular methods used by suicidal individuals.

Attempts to develop a special MMPI suicide scale or to validate the accuracy of particular MMPI items as suicide predictors have generally been unsuccessful. Few MMPI items significantly differentiate suicidal and nonsuicidal patients. Furthermore, MMPI items whose content is related to suicide (for example, item 339) are often found not to be answered in the significant direction by suicidal patients (Clopton and Jones 1975; Simon and Hales 1949). A suicide threat scale has been developed (Farberow and Devries 1967), but is of questionable value because its scores cannot identify patients who will kill themselves or make suicide attempts (Clopton and Jones 1975; Farberow and Devries 1967; Ravensborg and Foss 1969).

Studies that have shown some differentiation of patients who either attempt or commit suicide and nonsuicidal patients (Clopton and Jones 1975; Clopton, Pallis, and Birtchnell 1979; Devries and Farberow 1967; Leonard 1977) have generally employed multivariate techniques to examine MMPI profile patterns. Suicidal psychiatric patients have sometimes been found to have MMPI profiles that are within normal limits (Clopton, Pallis, and Birtchnell 1979; Holzberg, Cohen, and Wilk 1951), and there is certainly no evidence of a general suicidal profile. Instead of attempting to find overall profile differences between suicidal and nonsuicidal psychiatric patients, future research should examine the extent to which certain MMPI profile patterns (for example, the relative elevation of the *D* and *Hs* scales) can be used among particular types of patients to help assess the risk of suicide.

REFERENCES

Block, J., L. Levine, and Q. McNemar. 1951. "Testing for the Existence of Psychometric Patterns." *Journal of Abnormal and Social Psychology* 46: 356–59.

Broida, D. C. 1954. "An Investigation of Certain Psychodiagnositc Indications of Suicidal Tendencies and Depression in Mental Hospital Patients." *Psychiatric Quarterly* 28: 453–64.

Brown, T. R., and T. J. Sheran. 1972. "Suicide Prediction: A Review." *Life-Threatening Behavior* 2: 67–98.

Carson, R. C. 1969. "Interpretative Manual to the MMPI." In *MMPI: Research Developments and Clinical Applications*, edited by J. N. Butcher, pp. 279–96. New York: McGraw-Hill.

Clopton, J. R. 1978. "A Note on the MMPI as a Suicide Predictor." *Journal of Consulting and Clinical Psychology* 46: 335–36.

——. 1974. "Suicidal Risk Assessment Via the Minnesota Multiphasic Personality Inventory (MMPI)." In *Psychological Assessment of Suicidal Risk*, edited by C. Neuringer, pp. 118–33. Springfield, Ill.: Charles C. Thomas.

——, and D. H. Baucom. 1979. "MMPI Ratings of Suicide Risk." *Journal of Personality Assessment* 43: 400–406.

Clopton, J. R., and W. C. Jones. 1975. "Use of the MMPI in the Prediction of Suicide." *Journal of Clinical Psychology* 31: 52–54.

Clopton, J. R., D. J. Pallis, and J. Birtchnell. 1979. "MMPI Profile Patterns of Suicide Attempters." *Journal of Consulting and Clinical Psychology* 47: 135–39.

Dahlstrom, W. G., G. S. Welsh, and L. E. Dahlstrom. 1975. *An MMPI Handbook: Research Applications*, vol. 2. Minneapolis: University of Minnesota Press.

——. 1972. *An MMPI Handbook: Clinical Interpretation*, vol 1, rev. ed. Minneapolis: University of Minnesota Press.

Devries, A. G. 1968. "Prediction of Suicide by Means of Psychological Tests." In *Proceedings of the Fourth International Conference for Suicide Prevention*, edited by N. L. Farberow. Los Angeles: Delmar.

——. 1967. "Control Variables in the Identification of Suicidal Behavior." *Psychological Reports* 20: 1131–35.

——. 1966a. "A Potential Suicide Personality Inventory." *Psychological Reports* 18: 731–38.

——. 1966b. "Chance Expectancy, Sample Size, Replacement and Nonreplacement Sampling." *Psychological Reports* 18: 843–50.

——. 1966c. "Identification of Suicidal Behavior by Means of the MMPI." *Psychological Reports* 19: 415–19.

——, and N. L. Farberow. 1967. "A Multivariate Profile Analysis of MMPIs of Suicidal and Nonsuicidal Neuropsychiatric Hospital Patients." *Journal of Projective Techniques and Personality Assessment* 31: 81–84.

Devries, A. G., and E. S. Shneidman. 1967. "Multiple MMPI Profiles of Suicidal Persons." *Psychological Reports* 21: 401–05.

Farberow, N. L. 1956. "Personality Patterns of Suicidal Mental Hospital Patients." In *Basic Readings on the MMPI in Psychology and Medicine*, edited by G. S. Welsh and W. G. Dahlstrom, pp. 427–32. Minneapolis: University of Minnesota Press.

——, and A. G. Devries. 1967. "An Item Differentiation Analysis of Suicidal Neuropsychiatric Hospital Patients." *Psychological Reports* 20: 607–17.

Foster, L. L. 1975. "MMPI Correlates of Suiciding Patients." *Newsletter for Research in Mental Health and Behavioral Sciences* 17: 9–10.

Graham, J. R. 1977. *The MMPI: A Practical Guide.* New York: Oxford University Press.

Hays, W. L. 1963. *Statistics.* New York: Holt, Rinehart and Winston.

Holzberg, J. D., E. R. Cohen, and E. K. Wilk. 1951. "Suicide: A Psychological Study of Self-Destruction." *Journal of Projective Techniques* 15: 339–54.

Kinsinger, J. R. 1973. "Women Who Threaten Suicide: Evidence for an Identifiable Personality Type." *Omega* 4: 73–84.

Koss, M. P., J. N. Butcher, and N. G. Hoffmann. 1976. "The MMPI Critical Items: How Well Do They Work?" *Journal of Consulting and Clinical Psychology* 44: 921–28.

Leonard, C. V. 1978. "Response to 'A Note on the MMPI as a Suicide Predictor.'" *Journal of Consulting and Clinical Psychology* 46: 337–38.

——. 1977. "The MMPI as a Suicide Predictor." *Journal of Consulting and Clinical Psychology* 45: 367–77.

——. 1974. "Depression and Suicidability." *Journal of Consulting and Clinical Psychology* 42: 98–104.

Lester, D. 1970a. "Attempts to Predict Suicidal Risk Using Psychological Tests." *Psychological Bulletin* 74: 1–17.

——. 1970b. "Personality Correlates Associated with Choice of Method of Committing Suicide." *Personality* 1: 261–64.

——. 1968. "Suicide as an Aggressive Act: A Replication with a Control for Neuroticism." *Journal of General Psychology* 79: 83–86.

——. 1967. "Suicide as an Aggressive Act. *Journal of Psychology* 66: 47–50.

Lingoes, J. C. 1960. "MMPI Factors of the Harris and Wiener Subscales." *Journal of Consulting Psychology* 24: 74–83.

MacKinnon, D. R., and N. L. Farberow. 1976. "An Assessment of the Utility of Suicide Prediction." *Suicide and Life-Threatening Behavior* 6: 86–91.

Marks, P. A. and D. L. Haller. 1977. "Now I Lay Me Down for Keeps: A Study of Adolescent Suicide Attempts." *Journal of Clinical Psychology* 33: 390–400.

Marks, P. A., and W. Seeman. 1963. *The Actuarial Description of Abnormal Personality*. Baltimore: Williams & Wilkins.

Poeldinger, W. J., A. Gehring, and P. Blaser. 1973. "Suicide Risk and MMPI Scores, Especially as Related to Anxiety and Depression." *Suicide and Life-Threatening Behavior* 3: 147–53.

Ravensborg, M. R., and A. Foss. 1969. "Suicide and Natural Death in a State Hospital Population: A Comparison of Admission Complaints, MMPI Profiles, and Social Competence Factors." *Journal of Consulting and Clinical Psychology* 33: 466–71.

Rosen, A. 1954. "Detection of Suicidal Patients." *Journal of Consulting Psychology* 18: 397–403.

——, W. M. Hales, and W. Simon. 1954. "Classification of 'Suicidal' Patients." *Journal of Consulting Psychology* 18: 359–62.

Simon, W. 1950. "Attempted Suicide Among Veterans." *Journal of Nervous and Mental Disease* 111: 451–68.

——, and H. Gilberstadt. 1958. "Analyses of the Personality Structure of 26 Actual Suicides." *Journal of Nervous and Mental Disease* 127: 555–57.

Simon, W., and W. H. Hales. 1949. "Note on a Suicide Key in the Minnesota Multiphasic Personality Inventory." *American Journal of Psychiatry* 106: 222–23.

Tarter, R. E., D. I. Templer, and R. L. Perley. 1975. "Social Role Orientation and Pathological Factors in Suicide Attempts of Varying Lethality." *Journal of Community Psychology* 3: 295–99.

Temoche, A., T. F. Pugh, and B. MacMahon. 1964. "Suicide Rates Among Current and Former Mental Institution Patients." *Journal of Nervous and Mental Disease* 136: 124–30.

Weisman, A., and J. Worden. 1972. "Risk-Rescue Rating in Suicide Assessment." *Archives of General Psychiatry* 26: 553–60.

6/ MMPI STUDIES OF EXTREME CRIMINAL VIOLENCE IN INCARCERATED WOMEN AND MEN

Patricia B. Sutker
Albert N. Allain

Few empirically based studies have attempted to describe or explain the phenomena surrounding extremely aggressive behavior among women. However, there is a sizable literature that offers armchair speculation to account for female criminality. One of the earliest criminologists to theorize about why women commit crimes was Lombrozo whose book, *The Female Offender*, was published in 1897. Klein (1973) quoted Lombrozo as stating:

> Women have many traits in combination with children: their moral sense is deficient, they are revengeful, jealous. . . . In ordinary cases these defects are neutralized by piety, maternity, want of passion, sexual coldness, weakness, and an undeveloped intelligence. . . . The criminal woman is a monster . . . when these counter influences fail, and a woman commits a crime, we may conclude that her wickedness must have been enormous before it could triumph over so many obstacles. (p. 152)

Many of these notions, some expressed more recently than the 1800s (for example, Gleuck and Gleuck 1934), reflect the extreme societal ambivalence, if

The authors wish to acknowledge the helpful assistance of C. L. Williams, C. D. Langford, S. W. Altman, S. C. Kilpatrick, P. D. Thompson, and W. Klimek, who aided in the collection and processing of data. Appreciation is expressed to W. O. Leeke, commissioner; J. L. Salisbury, director of division of treatment services; Wardens M. A. Taylor, L. D. Brown, and J. L. Harvey; and to R. E. Chapman, J. S. Shirley, and K. Earle, who facilitated this research project by allowing access to inmates in the South Carolina Department of Corrections. Additionally, the authors are grateful to officials of the Louisiana Department of Corrections for making this study possible in correctional centers at Angola and St. Gabriel. Special attention is expressed to Superintendent R. T. Hall and Warden C. M. Henderson.

This research was supported in part by GSR 22620–A800, A Biomedical State Research Award from the Medical University of South Carolina.

not utter disdain, directed toward women who deviate from expected role patterns. As representative of their gender, women are regarded as virtuous and pure; conversely, those who are atypical or become criminal are often viewed as significantly more maladjusted than men who exhibit similar behaviors. These ideas are echoed in the work of Eysenck and Eysenck (1973), who interpreted their personality comparison of male and female prisoners as evidence of greater instability in incarcerated women as opposed to men.

Simon (1975) contended that it was Otto Pollak's book, *The Criminality of Women* (1950), which first challenged basic assumptions concerning female involvement in criminal behavior. According to Pollak, the types of crimes women commit are less likely to be detected, reported when detected, or punished by arrest, conviction, or sentencing because of the double standard favorable to women. Pollak contended that women are not endowed with greater morality and decency then men, but that their roles in society assume goodness, charity, and morality and can serve as useful masks for criminal activities. Hypothesizing that female involvement in violence typically arises out of frustration, subservience, and dependence characteristic of the traditional feminine role, Simon (1975) predicted that female violence would not increase as women became liberated from the home environment. Others reasoned that the movement toward equality of the sexes would provide increasing opportunity for women to engage in violence (Rosenblatt and Greenland 1974). This position incorporates the assumption that women, being not very different from men in their repertoire of possible motivational states or personality characteristics, may express themselves in a manner heretofore typical of the male gender, or at least with more freedom as a function of fewer sociocultural restrictions.

Representing perhaps the antithesis to traditional feminity, female murderers would seem to hold great interest for potential investigators. Certainly, the public has been fascinated by accounts of murder by such famous women as Lizzie Borden. Nevertheless, criminologists have overlooked the area of female violence, often with the rationalization that few crimes are committed by women. Few studies have employed psychological test measures, systematic behavioral observations, or sociomedical history questionnaires to identify constellations of personality, cognitive, psychosocial, or physiological factors that might interact with important situational variables and differently characterize murdering women from nonmurdering female felons, murdering men, or nonviolent control groups. Perhaps reluctance to undertake such investigations can be attributed in part to such factors as general disinterest in female deviants, assessment of the amazingly few numbers of demonstrably violent women available for systematic study, doubts regarding the usefulness of psychosocial data to describe and/or predict aggressive behavior among men or women, and/or dismay at the complex interaction of person x situation variables requiring measurement or control in attempting to predict violence.

REVIEW OF RELEVANT STUDIES ON VIOLENCE

Violent Behavior Among Men

Among the behavioral scientists studying the nature of male criminal violence is Edwin Megargee, who has attempted to identify problems in defining assaultive behavior, methodological issues in conducting related research, motivational and situational factors leading to aggression, and uses of structured personality inventories to predict violence (see Megargee 1966, 1970, 1976, 1977). Following investigation of 12 MMPI scales designed to measure hostility and control (Megargee and Mendelsohn 1962), Megargee and his associates have repeatedly emphasized the heterogeneity of persons who engage in assaultive acts and the importance of instigating, inhibiting, and situational factors in understanding such behavior. In 1966, Megargee hypothesized that there are at least two types of personalities involved in antisocial aggression: the undercontrolled aggressive and chronically overcontrolled types. Although the undercontrolled type was reasoned to be relatively easy to identify by behavior or personality test indexes, overcontrolled individuals inclined toward violence seemed to require innovative detection techniques. Subsequently, Megargee, Cook, and Mendelsohn (1967) developed the overcontrolled-hostility scale (O-H) from MMPI items to identify chronically overcontrolled and yet potentially aggressive men. The proposed relationship between overcontrolled hostility and violence has stimulated a growing body of research with supportive (Haven 1973; Vanderbeck 1973; White 1975; White, McAdoo, and Megargee 1973), as well as contradictory (Hoppe and Singer 1976; Mallory and Walker 1972; Rawlings 1973), implications.

Considering the MMPI clinical scales and range of experimental scales that might discriminate aggression criterion groups, there is little consistent evidence that assaultive and nonassaultive male offenders differ significantly on clearly defined trait or type dimensions. Comparing four groups of male criminals varying by degree of violence, Deiker (1974) found differences between nonviolent criminal controls and individuals sentenced for criminal homicide on scales *F*, *K*, 4, 7, 8, and 9, with murders exhibiting the less deviant mean profile. However, he interpreted his findings in the light of a naysaying response style rather than by reference to the more obvious test dimensions. Similarly, attempts to identify particular MMPI code types more frequently characteristic of violent offenders have met with limited success. For example, the 4-3 type has been associated with poorly controlled hostility and temper outbursts in Veteran Administration patients (Gilberstadt and Duker 1965) and hostile-aggressive behavior in samples of state hospital, prison, and medical center subjects (Davis and Sines 1971). Persons and Marks (1971) also found that rates of current incarceration for violent crimes were significantly higher for 4-3 codes compared to the institutional base rate and other code-type groups among male inmates of a medium security prison. In contrast, results of other studies have not confirmed greater incidence of more assaultive behaviors among 4-3 code-type individuals.

Gynther, Altman, and Warbin (1973) found no more assaultive behaviors among 4-3/3-4 code types in state hospital patients than for four other code types. Attempting to remedy possible methodological issues that might confound results, Buck and Graham (1978) also failed to identify a relationship between the 4-3 code type and violent behavior among male penitentiary inmates. They concluded that the way in which the 4-3 profile was defined, the criteria used to specify aggressive behavior, and the relative age or race of subjects could not account completely for result discrepancies. Comparing assaultive and nonassaultive male misdemeanor offenders on MMPI scales and code types, McCreary (1976) found no evidence of personality differences between assaultive and nonassaultive offenders. Further, code-type analyses were not interpreted as consistent with the Davis and Sines (1971) notion that the 4-3 code type represents men who tend to be hostile consistently across settings.

To summarize, there is yet inconclusive support for existence of single, clearly defined sets of traits or profile types reliably associated with specific forms of criminal violence among men. However, it is reasonable to assume that important relationships exist between MMPI-measured person variables and a given crime. This line of speculation does not ignore the importance of social influences on learned behavior and its instigation but assumes that assessment of personality characteristics or cognitive styles may be useful in predicting how individuals will respond to various situational or reinforcement parameters. As an example, Megargee (1977), Megargee and Bohn (1977), and Megargee and Dorhout (1977) developed a complex MMPI-based personality classification system to identify homogeneous subgroups of offenders who might share common etiologies or respond similarly to particular treatment strategies. Results incicated that the MMPI profiles of youthful offenders fell into reliable, natural groupings and guidelines could be formulated to classify profiles into these types with reliability. Megargee and Dorhout (1977) presented a taxonomy of 10 types of profiles for antisocial individuals, and Megargee and Bohn (1977) described the demographic characteristics, propensities for types of antisocial behavior, interpersonal styles, and implications for treatment definitive of each type.

Violent Behavior Among Women

Concomitant with the women's movement has been increased interest in the extent and nature of female social deviance. Investigations have focused on the psychosocial characteristics of female drug abusers (Ross and Berzins 1974; Sutker and Moan 1972), relationships between drug abuse and crime (d'Orban 1973; Weissman and File 1976), comparisons between female felon groups defined by criteria relevant to violent behavior (Climent et al. 1973; Frederiksen 1975), or comparisons of men and women in investigations of violent or other criminal behavior (Rosenblatt and Greenland 1974; McCreary 1976). In studies where women were examined exclusively, categorization was based on degree of violence; however, groups were not composed exclusively of women incarcerated for the most extreme of violent crimes—murder or manslaughter. Only one exception is the study of Cole, Fisher, and Cole (1968), who used psychiatric interview data and a seemingly intuitive system of classification to describe common psychological and behavioral characteristics of women who murdered. Even among those studies that examined violence in male offenders, few attempts were made to separate men convicted for murder from those found guilty of forcible rape or other violent crimes (see Rader 1977).

Although plagued by several methodological problems, the Cole, Fisher, and Cole Study provided the first systematically gathered information on a large group of women who had killed. These investigators found that in 47 percent of the cases women murdered intimates, while 20 and 35 percent killed children and casual acquaintances, respectively. Approximately one third of the women had no record of prior conviction, and alcohol was associated with 50 percent and narcotics with 10 percent of the crimes. Murderers were characterized in terms of six personality classifications, including the masochistic, overtly hostile, covertly hostile, inadequate, psychotic, and amoral types. Categorization was based on interview and record data, and no classificatory rules were specified. No estimate was made of relative frequencies of personality types, and no control groups were included.

Frederiksen (1975) studied three groups of women (high, medium, and nonassault) to identify potential personality or background variables that might aid in their differentiation. Her high assault group, composed of a variety of violent offenders, was not directly comparable to the Cole, Fisher, and Cole murderers. Contrary to results often reported for men, Frederiksen found that MMPI elevation on scale 3 was not necessarily a significant factor in the personality makeup of assaultive women. However, high O-H women were shown to cause more severe physical injury to their victims, but they engaged in illegal behavior other than assaults as well. A high O-H score was also shown to result in substantially higher postdiction hit rates than would be achieved by using the available base rates for highly assaultive offenses. All offender groups in this study reported high frequencies of victimization by sexual assault, molestation, stabbing, and beating, and 56 percent of the high assault group were under the influence of alcohol or drugs at the time of the act.

Looking at a wider range of medical and psychiatric variables, Climent et al. (1973) found nine factors correlated with violence among female prisoners, including neurological disorders, familial medical disorders, easy access to weapons, the dyscontrol syndrome, loss of parental figure, homosexuality, and severe parental punishment. They found that the nonviolent group showed more evdience of psychiatric pathology (psychiatric hospitalization or outpatient contacts before first conviction, drug addiction, and alcoholism) but fewer nonneurological medical problems. No differences in MMPI scale scores were apparent between violent and nonviolent groups. However there was an almost significant tendency for nonviolent women to score higher on scales 4 and 9. This study was unique in that categorization of violent and nonviolent groups was based on a self-evaluation questionnaire designed to allow women to rate themselves on the basis of their previous experience with different types of violent behavior. Finally, McCreary (1976) reported significant differences between assaultive and nonassaultive female misdemeanors, with assaultive offenders showing less repression and more masculine self-concepts, reflected by elevations on scale 5.

DESCRIPTION OF STUDIES

General Purpose

The purpose of this series of three investigations was to attempt to identify MMPI trait characteristics and/or type patterns, as well as other psychosocial variables, that might shed light on the nature or prediction of extreme violence, with particular focus on women who murdered as compared with nonviolent female criminal offenders and male murderers. Extreme violence was defined as any set of circumstances that resulted in conviction and subsequent incarceration for manslaughter or murder, excluding women and men who failed to confirm that such a killing had taken place either through direct or indirect means. Nonviolence was defined for each subject as no record of conviction for a violent offense of any variety. Selection of subjects was conducted in two geographical locations to test for reliability of findings. Study 1 describes a comparison of extremely violent and nonviolent female offenders across two areas of the country. Studies 2 and 3, which also included samples of male felons from two geographical locations, were designed to compare male murderer and male nonviolent offenders as well as women and men who had committed manslaughter or murder.

The following questions guided data collection: Are there differences between groups of extremely violent and nonviolent female offenders that replicate across geographical regions? Are there specific MMPI traits, code type patterns, or psychosocial characteristics that are more frequently characteristic of women who murdered than of nonviolent female felons? Do combinations of MMPI variables classify female offender groups with acceptable levels of accuracy and have relevance for prediction of violence? Do men who have killed another individual differ from nonviolent criminal male offenders in the same manner that women who have murdered differ from similar control groups? Do women who have murdered differ from men who have murdered in MMPI traits, profile patterns, or psychosocial histories?

General Description of Subject Samples and Procedures

Samples of violent and nonviolent women and men were selected from penal institutions in two geographical locations: Louisiana Correctional Institutes for Women (LCIW) in St. Gabriel, Louisiana, and Men (Angola) in Angola, Louisiana, and Women's Correctional Center (WCC) and Kirkland Correctional Institute for Men (KCI) in Columbia, South Carolina. Women and men selected from the Louisiana prisons made up the original samples in studies 1 and 2, and South Carolina prisoners served as cross-validation samples to increase the limits of confidence in obtained results. All samples excluded newly inducted inmates (those imprisoned less than two months) to reduce potential effects of situational crises or inmate initial response to imprisonment on test performance. Hence, as much as possible, testing was timed to reflect dispositional differences between groups, rather than transitory mood or state changes.

Excluded from the extremely violent groups were individuals incarcerated for filicide, because of the assumption that this crime may represent an entirely different phenomenon than the killing of another adult (see Scott 1973). Felons convicted of previous violent crimes of any type were also excluded from the nonviolent samples of both men and women. Other exclusions from subject samples were imposed for individuals who were unable to read sufficiently well or did not produce a valid MMPI profile, using the criterion of $K > 90$ T scores, and/or potential subjects who, after informed of study purposes, were unwilling to participate.

Data collection procedures were highly similar in all prison settings. Potential subjects were assembled initially by a team including male and female experimenters in a large room, individually questioned regarding their willingness to participate in a psychological investigation, and requested to read and sign informed consent agreements. Small numbers of women and men declined in each setting and were allowed to return to their daily activities. Those who had difficulty in reading completed as much of the test battery as possible in addition to the individual interview unless they wished to be excused, but their protocols were excluded from statistical analyses. The Shipley Institute of Living scale, a background history questionnaire, and the MMPI were administered in random order to subjects in group situations. Private interviews were conducted to obtain additional background history information. Prison records for each subject were also examined carefully for evidence of previous crimes of violence. Sixteen MMPI scales were scored and converted to T score values: the ten standard clinical scales, the three validity scales, Welsh's A and R scales, and Barron's Es scale. Additionally, the experimental revised O–H scale (Megargee, Cook, and Mendelsohn 1967) was scored, but no T score transformation was applied. In addition to age, education, Shipley IQ, a total time incarcerated, and total number of convictions, 18 continuous variables and 24 variables defined in terms of categories were derived from clinical interview material (see Table 6.1).

TABLE 6.1

Social History Variables Derived from Personal Interview Data

Continuous Variables:	Age first arrest
	Age disruption of childhood home
	Age left childhood home
	Number siblings
	Age first marriage
	Number marriages
	Number divorces and separations
	Number children
	Number children born out of wedlock
	Total time employed
	Length longest employment
	Average monthly church attendance
	Age first alcohol use
	Age first drug use
	Number categories of drugs used
	Number months addicted to opiates
	Number juvenile convictions
	Number suicide attempts
Discrete Variables:	Hollingshead-Redlich Two Factor Index of Social Position
	Raised primarily by parents
	Adopted
	Disrupted childhood home
	Left childhood home prior to age 18
	Birth order
	Father criminal record
	Mother criminal record
	Marital status
	Spouse or cohort criminal record
	Military service
	Type military discharge
	Occupational level (Hollingshead-Redlich categories)
	Religious preference
	Frequency alcohol use
	First drug used
	Reason for first drug use
	Drug of choice
	Use of opiates
	Father use of drugs
	Mother use of drugs
	Sibling use of drugs
	Spouse or cohort use of drugs
	Previous psychiatric care

Source: Compiled by the author.

Study 1

Subjects

Subjects from LCIW (n = 32) consisted of female inmates incarcerated for crimes of extreme violence and property or drug offenses within a random sample of 51 women chosen from a roll of 150 felons prior to data collection. Pretest refinement of the sample was accomplished by exclusion of potential subjects who did not wish to participate (2 to 5 percent of those contacted) and women unable to read sufficiently well to complete test requirements (10 to 15 percent). Individuals in both categories were replaced by selections from a previously prepared alternative list. Following data collection, sample size was further reduced to exclude women sentenced for violent crimes other than murder or manslaughter, those convicted for drug or property crimes with a history of previous violent offenses, and women productive of MMPI profiles judged invalid. The final breakdown included 12 women convicted for murder or manslaughter and 20 women sentenced for property or drug offenses. Women from WCC (n = 30) were selected from a population of approximately 180 felons in the same manner, that is, application of random sampling techniques, systematic reduction and replacement of potential subjects unable to read (about 15 percent) or unwilling to participate (about 3 percent), and posttest exclusion of women convicted for violent crimes less extreme than homicide or who produced invalid profiles. The cross-validation sample included 10 violent and 20 nonviolent women. Distribution by race was equal for violent and nonviolent categories in both samples, and groups did not differ on personal or life history variables of age, education, Shipley IQ, total time incarcerated, and total number convictions.

Data Analyses

K-corrected T scores were subjected to one-way analyses of variance for each of the 16 MMPI scales to evaluate differences between violent and nonviolent groups in both samples. One-way analyses of variance were also performed to evaluate differences between prison samples within offender categories. Because violent and nonviolent groups collapsed across prison samples showed no significant differences on MMPI clinical scales, prison samples were subsequently combined for stepwise discriminant function analysis and principal components analysis (Dixon 1975) to identify common sources of independent variation or factor structures that might be descriptive of personality types. Resulting factor socres were subjected to univariate analyses of variance and stepwise discriminant function analysis to characterize the nature of differences and similarities in response patterns between criminal type groups. Using a more practical method of classification, profiles were categorized by high-point code types and by Meehl criteria (1956), which require rapid inspectional diagnosis, separating profiles first into normal and abnormal categories and further dividing those defined as abnormal into three classes: psychotic, neurotic, and conduct disorder. One-way analyses of variance were also performed on O-H raw score values to test for significant differences between combined samples of violent and nonviolent women. Groups of violent and nonviolent offenders were collapsed across prisons for comparisons on the 42 additional social history variables identified from personal history information. Chi-square analyses were performed for 24 discrete variables, and F-tests were used to compare groups on 18 continuous variables.

Results

Women incarcerated for extreme violence, regardless of prison source, responded to the MMPI in less deviant fashion than female nonviolent offenders. As can be seen in Figure 6.1, LCIW violent offenders produced a group mean profile that fell completely within the range commonly defined as "normal," while that generated by nonviolent offenders within the same prison was characterized by a pronounced and single spike on scale 4, $F(1,30) = 4.29$, p $<$ .05. Comparisons of violent and nonviolent criminal groups in the cross-validation sample at WCC yielded similar results (see Figure 6.1). Again, the composite profile for murderers was contained within normal limits, and between-group differences were found on scales 4, $F(1,28) = 6.10$, p $<$ .05, and 2, $F(1,28) = 5.29$, p $<$ .05. Comparisons between offender groups across prison samples showed the groups to be highly similar with only one exception. Murderers in WCC produced more elevated scores on scale L than did LCIW murderers, $F(1,20) = 6.75$, p $<$ .05. This was the only difference between groups within offender categories of a possible 32 to exceed the level required for statistical significance, and prison samples were combined for additional analyses.

Murderers in combined prison samples produced significantly lower scores on scales F and 4 and higher scores on scales K and 5 as evaluated by one-way analyses of variance summarized in Table 6.2. Eta correlation ratios calculated for each variable differentiating between violent and nonviolent groups ranged from .26 for scale F to .38 for scale 4, indicating the greatest degree of relationship between group membership and scale 4. Prediction of group identity using stepwise discriminant function analysis was moderately accurate with 82 percent of violent and 78 percent nonviolent offenders correctly classified. Categorization that arranged variables in order of effectiveness in accounting for between-group variation was heavily dependent upon scores on scales 4, 5, K, and A, in that order, with optimal classification observed after eight variables had been considered in combination (4, 5, K, A, 1, 2, 9, 7).

Principal components analysis with orthogonal rotation and Kaiser normalization identified five independent components, selected for rotation using the scree test (Cattell 1966), which accounted for 78 percent of the total variance after rotation (see Table 6.3). These factors are summarized below:

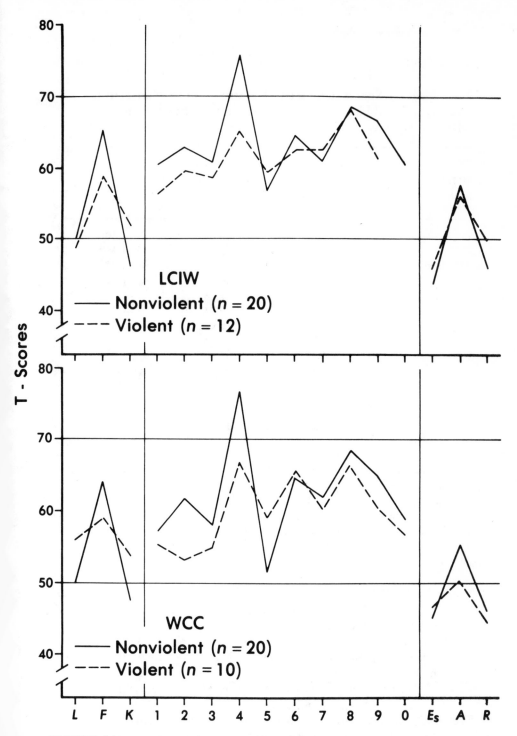

FIGURE 6.1: Mean MMPI profile patterns for nonviolent and violent female offender groups in Louisiana and South Carolina prison samples. *Source*: Constructed by the authors.

TABLE 6.2

Mean MMPI T Scores, Univariate F Ratios, and Eta Correlation Ratios for Combined Samples of Female Violent and Nonviolent Offender Groups

MMPI Scale	Violent (n = 22)	Nonviolent (n = 40)		
	M	M	F	n
L	51.91	50.00	.80	.11
F	58.77	64.65	4.45[a]	.26
K	52.59	46.80	6.07[a]	.30
1	55.91	58.77	1.01	.13
2	56.64	62.35	3.70	.24
3	56.95	59.45	1.04	.13
4	65.86	76.05	10.09[b]	.38
5	59.13	53.05	5.09[a]	.28
6	63.82	64.62	.08	.03
7	61.50	61.45	.00	.00
8	67.50	68.37	.06	.03
9	61.68	65.85	2.62	.20
0	59.41	59.72	.02	.02
Es	46.18	44.52	.32	.07
A	53.50	56.55	1.03	.13
R	47.36	46.30	.20	.06

[a] $p < .05$.
[b] $p > .01$.

Source: P. B. Sutker, A. N. Allain, and S. Geyer, "Female Criminal Violence and Differential MMPI Characteristics." *Journal of Consulting and Clinical Psychology* 46 (1978): 1141–43. Copyright 1978 by the American Psychological Association. Reprinted by permission.

Factor 1, labeled Anxiety Maladjustment, accounted for 29 percent of variance; characterized by high positive loadings for scales 2, 7, 0, and A and high negative loadings for K and Es.

Factor 2, labeled High Activity-Low Repression, accounted for 13 percent of variance; showed a single high positive loading for scale 9 and a high negative loading for scale R.

Factor 3, labeled Neurotic Conversion, accounted for 13 percent of variance; characterized by high positive loadings for scales 1 and 3.

Factor 4, labeled Masculinity-Feminity, accounted for 12 percent of variance; characterized by high negative loadings for scale 5 and moderately high negative loadings for scales 6 and 8.

Factor 5, labeled Sociopathy, accounted for 11 percent of variance; characterized by high positive loadings for scale 4 and a moderate negative loading for scale *L*.

Factor 5, labeled Sociopathy, was differentially related to offender classification, $F(1,60) = 9.44$, p $< .01$, but no differences were observed for factors 1, 2, 3, and 4. Discriminant function analysis showed group categorization was heavily dependent upon individual relationships to factor 5, with 95 percent of classification efficiency achieved after consideration of this single variable.

Analysis of profile patterns by code types revealed that among murderers the most prevalent high-point code type was 4-5/5-4, accounting for 23 percent of combined group profile patterns. Other high-point codes were 2-8/8-2, 1-6/6-1, and 6-8/8-6, each accounting for about 10 percent of profiles. Remaining

TABLE 6.3

Orthogonal Rotated Factor Pattern Matrix for 16 MMPI Scales for Combined Samples of Female Violent and Nonviolent Offender Groups

MMPI	Factor				
Scale	1	2	3	4	5
L	-.26	-.42	.01	-.08	-.59
F	.52	.12	.24	-.48	.43
K	-.76	-.46	-.11	-.06	-.19
1	.28	.02	.90	-.15	-.08
2	.76	-.35	.19	-.01	.32
3	-.03	-.01	.95	-.02	.12
4	.09	.02	.03	-.06	.88
5	-.19	-.15	-.09	-.72	-.21
6	.29	.21	.23	-.64	.14
7	.70	.05	.20	-.42	.23
8	.56	.03	.15	-.63	.27
9	.05	.75	.07	-.30	.34
0	.90	-.18	-.17	.05	.01
Es	-.77	-.24	-.23	16	.11
A	.85	.31	.07	-.12	.22
R	-.04	-.88	.03	-.12	.03

Source: P. B. Sutker, A. N. Allain, and S. Geyer, "Female Criminal Violence and Differential MMPI Characteristics." *Journal of Consulting and Clinical Psychology* 46 (1978): 1141–43. Copyright 1978 by the American Psychological Association. Reprinted by permission.

profile patterns were classified in more unique fashion, and no 4–9 code types were represented among murderers with only one 9–4. In contrast, 4–9/9–4 code types were most prevalent among nonviolent offenders and accounted for as many as 30 percent of group profile patterns, followed by 4–8/8–4, which characterized 20 percent. The 4–5/5–4 type, most common among the violent group, accounted for only 5 percent of the nonviolent offender group, and no other code type accounted for as many as 10 percent of profile types. Using the Meehl classification system, 50 percent of murderer profiles were categorized as normal as compared to 25 percent of nonviolent offenders X^2 (1) = 3.96, p < .05. Further breakdown of abnormal profile patterns into psychotic, neurotic, and conduct disorder categories by criminal offender groups showed no significant differences in distribution, with 42.5 percent of nonviolent offender profiles classified as conduct disorder, 20 percent as psychotic, and 2.5 percent as neurotic; 14 percent of murderer profiles were labeled conduct disorder, 36 percent psychotic, and 0 percent neurotic.

Combined groups of murderers and nonviolent offenders were also compared on the O–H scale and the 42 social history variables. There were no significant differences between murderer (M = 16.5, SD = 4.02) and nonviolent offender (M = 15.15, SD = 3.13) groups in O–H raw scores, $F(1,60)$ = .95, p > .05. Relative frequencies of high and low scores on the O–H scale, defined as numbers scoring above or below the mean score, showed no significant differences in distribution of low and high scorers across groups. Comparisons between violent and nonviolent offender groups on social history variables listed in Table 6.3 also revealed few significant differences. Violent and nonviolent groups were more similar than different with only three exceptions. Nonviolent offenders were significantly more likely to have used opiates, $X^2(1)$ = 12.24, p < .01, and to have siblings who used drugs, $X^2 91)$ = 24.07 p < .05, while women who had murdered were unlikely to have ever used illicit drugs, $X^2(1)$ = 13.28, p < .01, with 73 percent reporting no illicit drug use. In contrast, extremely violent women were as likely as nonviolent women to have used alcohol on a frequent basis with roughly 35 percent of each group reporting such. Additionally, F-test comparisons between groups showed that women who had killed reported use of fewer drug categories, $F(1,60)$ = 8.54, p < .01, than nonviolent women.

Study 2

Subjects

Selected in the same manner specified in study 1, subjects from Angola (n = 45) consisted of male inmates incarcerated for crimes of extreme violence and property or drug offenses within a random sample of 150 men chosen prior to data collection from a roll of 4,000 felons. Pretest sample refinement excluded potential subjects who did not wish to participate (2 to 5 percent) and men unable to read sufficiently well to complete test requirements (5 to 10 percent). Sample size was further reduced to exclude men sentenced for violent crimes other than murder or manslaughter, convicted for drug or property offenses with a history of previous violent offenses, and men who produced MMPI profiles judged invalid. The final sample included 10 violent and 35 nonviolent men. The cross-validation sample for KCI (n = 61) was selected similarly from a random sample of 193 men of a population of 1,000. Rates for exclusion at both pre- and posttest conditions were similar to those above. The final sample included 35 violent and 26 nonviolent offenders. Distribution by race across violent and nonviolent categories was relatively equal in both prison samples, and groups did not differ on such personal or life history variables as education, Shipley IQ, total time incarcerated, and total number convictions. However, within the KCI sample, violent offenders were significantly older than those classified as nonviolent, $F(1,59) = 11.02, p < .01$.

Data Analyses

Data analysis procedures paralleled those of study 1 with the following exception. Where significant between group differences were observed on age, this variable was examined as a covariate.

Results

As suggested by the mean profile patterns presented in Figure 6.2, elevations on scale 4 were prominent among groups of men convicted for criminal homicide and nonviolent offenses. Nonviolent offenders produced a profile configuration with only scale 4 exceeding a T score of 70, while for violent inmates, mean elevations exceeded normal limits on scales 4 and 8. Analyses of variance showed no significant differences in single scale elevations in either Angola or cross-validation samples. In the Angola sample, however, age was significantly related to scores on scale 4, and inclusion of age as a covariate in analysis of covariance indicated that violent offenders produced significantly higher adjusted scores on this scale than did nonviolent felons, $F(1,42) = 7.95$, p < .01. Comparisons between offender groups across prison samples also showed one significant difference, with violent offenders at Angola producing a higher elevation on scale 4, $F(1,43) = 8.06$, p < .01, than KCI murderers. Murderers and nonmurderers in combined prison samples did not differ on a single scale as indicated by analyses of variance summarized in Table 6.4. Stepwise discrimination function analysis yielded only fair prediction of group identity with 73 percent of violent and 72 percent of nonviolent offenders correctly classified. Maximum accuracy was achieved after nine variables had been entered, with classification dependent upon scores on scales Es, 7, 8, 1, 0, L, 6, F, and 9 in that order.

Using principal components analysis with application of the scree test, six independent components were identified that accounted for 81 percent of the total variance after rotation (see Table 6.5):

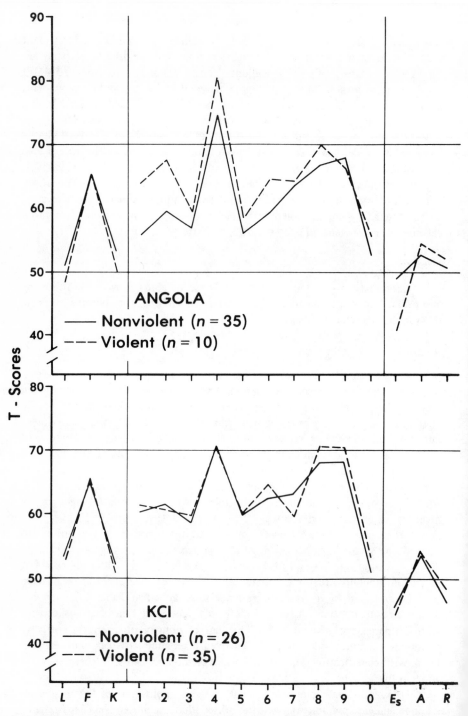

FIGURE 6.2: Mean MMPI profile patterns for nonviolent and violent male offender groups in Louisiana and South Carolina prison samples. *Source*: Constructed by the author.

TABLE 6.4

Mean MMPI T Scores, Univariate F Ratios, and Eta Correlation Ratios for Combined Samples of Male Violent and Nonviolent Offender Groups

MMPI Scale	Violent (n = 45)	Nonviolent (n = 61)	F	η
L	51.89	51.93	.00	.01
F	65.56	65.11	.03	.02
K	50.73	52.72	1.31	.11
1	62.00	57.82	2.16	.14
2	62.22	60.46	.48	.07
3	59.67	57.74	.86	09
4	72.78	72.87	.00	.00
5	59.82	57.64	1.31	.11
6	64.78	60.70	2.98	.17
7	60.76	63.57	1.11	.10
8	70.56	67.31	1.10	.10
9	69.27	68.00	.35	.06
0	53.91	51.93	1.00	.10
Es	43.58	47.51	3.58	.18
A	54.09	52.98	.22	.05
R	48.89	48.66	.02	.01

Source: Compiled by the author.

Factor 1, labeled Generàl Madadjustment, accounted for 31 percent of variance; characterized by high positive loadings for scales F, 6, 8, and A and high negative loadings for scales K and Es.

Factor 2, labeled Neurotic Conversion, accounted for 15 percent of variance; characterized by high positive loadings for scales 1 and 3.

Factor 3, labeled Low Activity-High Repression, accounted for 12 percent of variance; showed a high positive loading for scale R and a high negative loading for scale 9.

Factor 4, labeled Sociopathy, accounted for 9 percent of variance; characterized by a single high positive loading for scale 4.

Factor 5, labeled Defensiveness, accounted for 8 percent of variance; characterized by a single high positive loading for scale L.

Factor 6, labeled Masculinity-Feminity, accounted for 6 percent of variance; characterized by a single high positive loading for scale 5.

Mean factor scores did not differ for violent and nonviolent groups on any of the above factors as indicated by one-way analyses of variance, and stepwise dis-

TABLE 6.5

Orthogonal Rotated Factor Pattern Matrix for 16 MMPI Scales for
Combined Samples of Male Violent and Nonviolent Offender Groups

MMPI	Factor					
Scale	1	2	3	4	5	6
L	−.12	.06	.25	−.06	.89	−.03
F	.82	.11	−.17	.30	−.02	−.04
K	−.72	.22	.27	.27	.31	−.09
1	.21	.90	−.02	.02	−.01	−.05
2	.60	.44	.39	.20	−.09	.14
3	.08	.84	.11	.15	.14	.10
4	.08	.18	.01	.91	−.06	.12
5	.16	.05	−.10	.11	−.04	.96
6	.76	.12	−.14	.27	.21	.06
7	.64	.51	.03	.22	−.31	.03
8	.71	.51	−.09	.26	−.08	.03
9	.17	.07	−.79	.20	−.17	−.02
0	.72	.12	.49	−.09	−.20	−.01
Es	−.79	−.23	−.01	.13	−.05	−.20
A	.82	.11	−.20	−.13	−.28	.11
R	−.10	.14	.80	.24	.18	−.17

Source: Compiled by the author.

criminant function analysis showed poor accuracy in predicting group membership, with only 49 percent of violent and 62 percent of nonviolent offenders
correctly assigned.

In terms of two-point code types, 4–9/9–4 patterns were most common
and characterized 33 percent of nonviolent offender and 20 percent of violent
groups. Other frequently occurring code types among murderers were 8–9/9–8
(16 percent) and 6–8/8–6 (11 percent), and no remaining code type was represented by as much as 10 percent of this group. Code type 7–8/8–7 was found
among 11 percent of the nonviolent inmates, and no other code type accounted
for as much as 10 percent of profile patterns. Few differences emerged using the
Meehl classification system with no differences in distribution of normal/ab-
normal profile patterns, or for classes of abnormal profiles, among male nonviolent and violent offenders. Yet, 51 percent of nonviolent offenders were classified as conduct disorder as compared to 29 and 5 percent categorized psychotic and neurotic, respectively. Among murderers, 44 percent were labeled psychotic, 29 percent conduct disorder, and 7 percent neurotic.

Comparisons of violent (M = 15.22, SD = 3.45) and nonviolent (M = 15.52, SD = 3.00) male offenders showed no significant differences in raw O–H scores, and offender groups did not differ in distribution of high or low O–H scoring subjects. Murderers and nonviolent offenders also tended to be highly similar across personal and life history variables with three exceptions. Among offenders reporting use of illicit drugs, murderers and nonviolent felons differed in drug of choice, $X^2(6) = 14.92$, p < .05. More than half of nonviolent offenders listed opiates as their drug of preference compared to 11 percent of murderers. Marijuana (39 percent) was the preferred drug among drug-using murderers but ranked second (30 percent) among nonmurderers. Nonviolent offenders were more likely to have been arrested at an earlier age than murderers, $F(1,104) = 10,30$, p < .01, and had experienced more adult convictions, $F(1,104) = 5.62$, p < .05.

Study 3

Subjects

Subjects included all female and male violent and nonviolent offenders who comprised samples for studies 1 and 2 collapsed over prisons with a break-down as follows: 67 violent offenders (22 women and 45 men) and 101 non-violent offenders (40 women and 61 men). No differences were observed between offender or sex groups in age, education, Shipley IQ, or race. Potential differences on other variables such as age at first arrest, total time incarcerated, marital status, and social class status are considered under the section on results.

Data Analyses

Data analyses closely paralleled those employed in studies 1 and 2. However, two-way analyses of variance with factors of offense (violent versus non-violent) and sex (male versus female) were used. F-tests for simple effects were performed subsequent to analyses of variance to examine significant offense x sex interactions. Scale 5 was not entered in multivariate analyses, because both men and women were included in the subject samples.

Results

As may be seen in Figure 6.3, mean profile patterns were highly similar with the exception of women who murdered. Women convicted of extreme criminal violence produced a mean profile configuration that fell within the range defined as normal, while other offender groups tended to produce higher mean scale elevations. Offender groups differed on scale 4 (see Table 6.6), but the significant main effect on this scale was qualified by a significant offense x sex interaction. Female murderers produced lower scores on scale 4 than did male murderers and both female and male nonviolent offenders. A significant

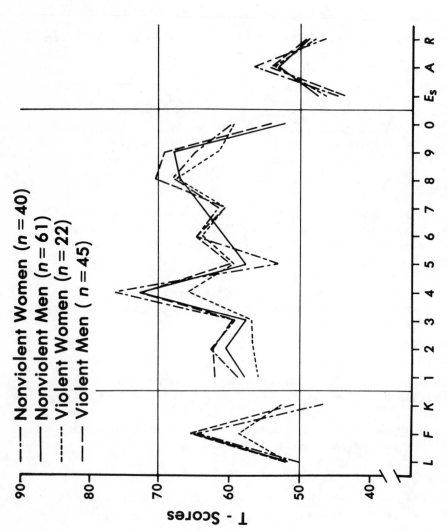

FIGURE 6.3: Mean MMPI profile patterns for male and female offender groups combined across prison samples. *Source:* Constructed by the author.

TABLE 6.6

Mean MMPI T Scores and Univariate *F* Ratios for Combined Samples of Female and Male Violent and Nonviolent Offender Groups

MMPI Scale	Violent		Nonviolent				
	Female (n = 22) M	Male (n = 45) M	Female (n = 40) M	Male n = 61) M	*F* (Offense)	*F* (Sex)	*F* (O X S)
L	51.91	51.89	50.00	51.93	.45	.48	.50
F	58.77	65.56	64.65	65.11	2.02	3.58	2.72
K	52.59	50.73	46.80	52.72	1.70	1.94	7.10*
1	55.91	62.00	58.77	57.82	.09	1.38	2.60
2	56.64	62.22	62.35	60.46	.94	.83	3.38
3	56.95	59.67	59.45	57.74	.03	.09	1.76
4	65.86	72.78	76.05	72.87	8.13*	1.07	7.84*
6	63.82	64.78	64.62	60.70	.74	.61	1.66
7	61.50	60.76	61.45	63.57	.47	.12	.50
8	67.50	70.56	68.37	67.31	.23	.16	.70
9	61.68	69.27	65.85	68.00	.70	7.87*	2.45
0	59.41	53.91	59.72	51.93	.26	16.71*	.50
Es	46.18	43.58	44.52	47.51	.41	.01	2.47
A	53.50	54.09	56.55	52.98	.25	.58	1.12
R	47.36	48.89	46.30	48.66	.18	1.58	.07

*p < .01.
Source: Compiled by the author.

offense x sex interaction was also observed for scale *K*, $F(1,164) = 6.86$, p < .01, with women convicted of nonviolent offenses scoring lower than female murderers, male nonmurderers, and male murderers. Main effects for sex were found on scales 9, $F(1,164) = 7.87$, p < .01, and 0, $F(1,164) = 16.71$, p < .01, with men scoring higher on scale 9 and lower on scale 0. Stepwise discriminant function analysis resulted in unimpressive group differentiation with 61 percent of subjects correctly classified, including 64 percent of violent women, 60 percent of nonviolent women, 58 percent of violent men, and 62 percent of nonviolent men. Maximum accuracy was accomplished after entry of 13 variables in the discriminant function.

Results of the principal components analysis were highly similar to those reported in studies 1 and 2. Five factors were selected for rotation based on the scree test, which accounted for 79 percent of the total variance after rotation as described below:

Factor 1, labeled General Maladjustment, accounted for 33 percent of variance; characterized by high positive loadings for scales F, 6, 8, and A and high negative loadings for K and Es.

Factor 2, labeled Neurotic Conversion, accounted for 15 percent of variance; characterized by high positive loadings for scales 1 and 3.

Factor 3, labeled Low Activity-High Repression, accounted for 12 percent of variance; defined by high positive loading for scale R and a high negative loading for 9.

Factor 4, labeled Defensiveness, accounted for 10 percent of variance; characterized by a single high positive loading for scale L.

Factor 5, labeled Sociopathy, accounted for 10 percent of variance; characterized by a single high positive loading for scale 4.

Univariate analyses of variance showed that sex or offender groups did not differ on scores on factors 1, 2, 3, or 4. However, significant main effects for offense, $F(1,164) = 5.90$, p $< .05$, and sex, $F(1.164) = 5.83$, p $< .05$, were found for factor 5. Nonviolent offenders were more sociopathic as defined by this factor than murderers, and men were more sociopathic than women. Nevertheless, discriminant function analysis using factor scores resulted in poor subject classification with only 41 percent of the sample correctly assigned (44 percent of male nonmurderers, 33 percent of male murderers, 43 percent of female nonmurderers, and 46 percent of female murderers).

In terms of two-point code-type patterns, only the 4-9/9-4 (25 percent) accounted for more than 10 percent of profile configurations. Distribution of profile types did not differ across offender or sex groups, but the 4-9/9-4 pattern was characteristic of 33 percent of male nonmurderers, 30 percent of female nonmurderers, 20 percent of male murderers, and only 5 percent of female murderers. Indeed, the occurrence of 4-9/9-4 profiles among nonmurderers was significantly more prevalent than among murderers, $X^2(1) = 4.52$, p $< .05$. There were, however, no differences in the relative distribution of 4-9/9-4 code types among men and women. Profiles defined as normal by Meehl criteria were disproportionately represented among female murderers (50 percent) as compared to female nonviolent offenders (25 percent), male murderers (20 percent), and male nonviolent offenders (15 percent) $X^2(3) = 11.62$, p $< .05$. No differences were found in the distribution of abnormal profile types across the four groups. However, when protocols for murderers and nonmurderers were examined without regard to sex, there were differences in frequency of abnormal profiles, $X^2(2) = 7.26$, p $< .05$. Conduct disorder (59 percent) was the most common abnormal classification among nonviolent offenders, followed by psychotic (36 percent) and neurotic (5 percent) profiles. For murderers, psychotic profiles (60 percent) were most frequent among abnormal profiles, while conduct disorder and neurotic labels were assigned to 34 and 6 percent, respectively. Men and women did not differ in the distribution of abnormal profiles among neurotic, psychotic, and conduct disorder classifications.

Scores on the experimental revised O-H scale did not vary significantly across sex and offender groups. Offender and sex groups were observed to differ, however, on several personal history variables. Men were more likely to be single than women, and female murderers were more often widowed than other groups (they killed their husbands), $X^2(18) = 46.90$, $p < .01$. Women married at earlier ages than men, $F(1,88) = 5.09$, $p < .05$, and reported more children, $F(1,164) = 9.68$, $p < .01$, and more children born out of wedlock, $F(1,64) = 5.63$, $p < .05$. Criminal records of spouses or cohorts were more prevalent among women than men, $X^2(3) = 22.40$, $p < .01$. Men were more likely to hold skilled manual employment, while women, particularly female murderers, were more often employed in unskilled occupations, $X^2(12) = 33.11$, $p < .01$. In terms of employment stability, murderers reported a longer period of uninterrupted employment than nonviolent offenders, $F(1,141) = 8.32$, $p < .01$. Men were far more likely to have had military experience, $X^2(3) = 22.42$, $p < .01$, as no women had served in the armed forces. Women had been convicted less frequently as juveniles than men, $F(1,164) = 7.57$, $p < .01$, and had served fewer total months in correctional institutions, $F(1,164) = 16.48$, $p < .01$. Nonmurderers had been convicted more frequently as adults than murderers, $F(1,164) = 6.70$, $p < .01$. Significant effects for sex, $F(1,164) = 16.48$, $p < .01$, and an offense x sex interaction, $F(1,164) = 4.71$, $p < .05$, indicated that male nonviolent offenders had also been arrested at earlier ages than remaining groups, while male murderers had been younger at first arrest than their female counterparts.

Men tended to drink alcohol at earlier ages than women, $F(1,105) = 16.35$, $p < .01$. With regard to drug use, female murderers were most likely to report no prior drug use, while female nonviolent offenders reported the highest frequency of opiates and stimulants as the first illicit drug used, $X^2(18) = 33.19$, $p < .05$. Significant effects for offense, $F(1,159) = 17.48$, $p < .01$, and an offense x sex interaction, $F(1,159) = 11.32$, $p < .01$, indicated that female murderers had experimented with fewer drug categories than had male murderers. Nonviolent offenders, both male and female, were more likely to prefer opiates; while marijuana was most frequently the drug of choice among female murderers, $X^2(21) = 32.78$, $p < .05$. More than half (53 percent) of nonviolent female offenders had used opiates, compared to 40 percent of nonviolent male offenders, 36 percent of male murderers, and 5 percent of female murderers, $X^2(3) = 14.32$, $p < .01$. Groups also differed in terms of history of emotional problems as suggested by previous psychiatric care, with such treatment most prevalent among nonviolent female offenders, $X^2(3) = 13.92$, $p < .05$. In a similar vein, significant effects for sex, $F(1,164) = 5.62$, $p < .05$, and an offense x sex interaction, $F(1,164) = 5.41$, $p < .05$, indicated that female nonviolent offenders reported more suicide attempts than any other group.

DISCUSSION

These investigations showed significant relationships between extreme criminal violence and MMPI trait dimensions among women sentenced for homicide or property and drug offenses, while no differences were observed for comparable groups of male offenders. Data were generated by independent samples of violent and nonviolent offenders of both sexes in two geographical locations, suggesting that findings are reliable for men and women. Results cannot easily be accounted for by such variables as age, education, incarceration, or intelligence, because groups were similar on these dimensions as well as racially balanced. Among female felons, murderers from both prison sources produced remarkably subdued group mean profiles, while nonviolent offenders were characterized by striking and significantly higher elevations on scale 4, indicating cognitive and behavior patterns of marked nonconformity or social deviance. Women convicted for criminal homicide were more defensive, less in touch with impulses to action, less socially nonconforming, and more removed from a stereotyped definition of their femininity than violent offenders, as indicated by lower scores on scales 4 and F and higher scores on K and 5. Results are consistent with reports by McCreary (1976) and Huesmann, Lefkowitz, and Eron (1978) that endorsement of MMPI items suggesting greater masculinity is associated with aggressive behavior in women.

Relationships have been described between the 4-3 high-point code type and extreme aggression among male criminals. However there was no tendency for this profile type to appear with significant frequency among male or female murderers. Among violent women, the most frequently occurring profile types were 4-5/5-4 and those in which scales 8, 2, and 6 were high points. For men who murdered, 4-9/9-4 types were observed most often and were followed closely in frequency by 8-9/9-8 and 6-8/8-6 profile patterns. Perhaps of more interest, however, was the distribution of Meehl classification labels within violent groups. Normal profiles occurred significantly more frequently among women who murdered, followed by psychotic profiles, whereas psychotic and character disorder profiles predominated among men convicted for homicide. Further, as noted in study 3, the pattern of abnormal profiles was differentially distributed over offense groups with conduct disorder labels most frequently assigned to nonviolent offenders and psychotic profiles most commonly descriptive of violent offenders.

Principal components analysis produced remarkably consistent results in identifying independent clusters of MMPI variables across the three studies, including dimensions interpreted as general maladjustment, high activity-low repression, neurotic conversion, masculinity-femininity, and soicopathy. Among female felons, scores on the sociopathy dimension were highly predictive of offender group status, with women who murdered scoring significantly lower. While similar components were identified among male offenders, classification into violence criterion groups was poor based upon scores on any identified component. From these results it might be suggested that sociopathic tendencies were strongly associated with convictions for nonviolent offenses among female felons, whereas sociopathic women were conspicuously absent from groups of women incarcerated for murder. In contrast, the sociopathy dimension was not useful in differentiating between groups of male felons, although sociopaths, defined by two-point code types or Meehl criteria, were found with greater frequency among male nonviolent offenders. One might speculate that sociopathy among women may represent a different phenomenon or be expressed differently than among men, or that unspecified person x situation interactions become critical in attempting to predict violent behaviors with sex-specific ramifications.

Contrary to findings supportive of the hypothesized relationship between overcontrolled hostility and extreme violence, no differences between crime category groups for either men or women were observed on the revised O-H scale. Overcontrolled individuals were as frequently represented as those classified as undercontrolled on the O-H measure among nonviolent and violent offender groups. Nevertheless, projected MMPI profile interpretations applicable to many of the female murderers seemed compatible with the Megargee, Cook, and Mendelsohn (1967) description of high O-H scorers, particularly when contrasted with the personality profile characteristics of nonviolent female offenders. It has been reasoned that high O-H scorers combine pronounced aggressive impulses and strong expressive inhibitions. Hence, for them the chance of enacting violence might be enhanced under conditions where high frustration and high situational provocation occurred simultaneously. Further, at least in the case of many of the women who murdered, Megargee's description of overcontrolled personality types was consistent with demonstrated tendencies toward rigidity, repression, social conformity, and reluctance to admit psychological problems. There was no evidence of a consistent or significant relationship between overcontrolled hostility and murder among male felons.

Looking across trait, type, or other personality classificatory dimensions, results suggest that women who murdered differed in important ways from men who performed similar supposedly nonrecurrent acts of extreme aggression. One may speculate about possible common or uncommon determinants of such acts and about sex-specific differences in the acquisition and expression of aggressive behaviors. It may be reasoned that among female children and women, aggressive behaviors are considered to be sex-inappropriate and therefore negatively sanctioned and infrequently encouraged. Men are more likely to have acquired, practiced, and been reinforced for behaviors with physically injurious potential. For example, Bandura (1965) showed that boys and girls differed in the performance of aggressive acts, but that social circumstances were important in influencing whether or not aggressive responses were performed. In this study, girls were found reticent to behave aggressively until they received direct assurance of its acceptability, whereas boys were more spontaneous in emitting aggressive responses, which were accelerated when well received.

In a recent investigation that spanned both sexes, Huesmann, Lefkowitz, and Eron (1978) examined the relationship between MMPI K-corrected T scores and concurrent and prior ratings of aggression for a sample of 426 19-year-old, middle-class adolescents. Peer ratings of aggressive behavior were obtained while subjects were in the third grade, and concurrent ratings were generated in grade

13 using peer and self-report indexes. Multiple regression analysis showed the best weighted composite of T scores for measuring aggression included scales 4 and F across sexes, scale 9 for males but not for females, and scale 5 with differential predictive direction depending upon sex. Comparing samples of male and female delinquents (n = 283) with those normal adolescents described above, Heusmann, Lefkowitz, and Eron (1978) found that the sum of scales F, 4, and 9 was an excellent discriminator between groups, even when IQ and social class were controlled. Hence they concluded that this unitary value served as a reliable and valid measure of aggression. Representing an innovative approach in research related to aggressive behavior, this investigation can serve as a model for future work. It integrates such features as longitudinal design and multiple criteria for specifying aggressive behavior within a framework that ties early and normal aggressive responses to delinquent behavior with implications for identifying the sex-specific aspects of aggression.

It seems reasonable to assume that whether or not aggressive behavior will occur is a complex function of the person, that is, cognitive styles and personality traits, past learning experiences, and the given situation in which the behavior is exhibited. Aggression is conceptualized simply as a learned phenomenon subject to instigational and reinforcement conditions. Nevertheless, it can be hypothesized that it takes a certain "kind" of person in a certain "kind" of situation to perform an act of extreme violence. For men, most of whom have practiced and been rewarded for aggressive responses more than women, an act of extreme violence or murder may be less dependent upon specific person or personality characteristics than for women. In the present study, men who had murdered, whether labeled psychotic or conduct disorder by Meehl criteria, undoubtedly shared more common experiences of reward for and greater acceptance of potentially violent behavior than their female counterparts. Consequently, the probability of their performing an act of aggression would be on the one hand more likely and yet dependent upon the specific situation in which they found themselves. However, among women incarcerated for murder, most extreme aggression did not seem as likely to represent one step further in a series of aggressive events or an act committed by antisocial and otherwise aggressive women as described by the Huesmann, Lefkowitz, and Eron $F + 4 + 9$ formula (1978).

It is suggested that in attempting to understand and predict specific types of criminal violence appropriately for both sexes, it will be important to employ a multitrait, multimethod matrix (Campbell and Fiske 1959) that takes into account relevant situation and person factors. For an example of the approach required, one could refer to the work of Sadava and Forsyth (1977), who developed a two-dimensional, four-system matrix to conceptualize and investigate person and environment variables and their interaction as useful in predicting drug use patterns. Obviously, for research related to drug abuse as well as criminal violence, many of the critical person and situation variables have yet to be identified. Hence one important focus for future research would be to explore the relationships among particular kinds of aggressive acts or offenses, the types of situations in which the behaviors occur, and the perceived functional value of specific aggressive acts. Such investigation, particularly if implemented longitudinally, would allow tests of the hypothesis that different types of individuals are provoked to violence by different kinds of situations. Another approach would be to explore the relationship between personality dimensions and the conditions under which individuals could imagine, and/or have committed, certain aggressive acts using incarcerated and normal samples of men and women. For example, it may be speculated that different situational factors or conditions of reinforcement prompt conduct disorder women to extreme violence than are significant for women or men diagnosed as psychotic or normal.

Social history variables were of little value in differentiating groups of violent and nonviolent offenders. In fact, questions regarding past drug and alcohol use represented the only area where significant differences were found with reliability. In part, it may be that failure to find important social history variable differentiation is a result of selection of poor potential predictors with insufficient emphasis on past learning experiences that would teach or reinforce aggressive responding, that is, severe punishment by parental figures, physical beatings from spouse, or minimized behavioral control such as alcohol use at time of act. It is suggested, then, that not only is it important to assess carefully the situation in which aggressive acts occur but also to specify the individual social learning experiences or conditions that might have facilitated its expression.

Present results showed that women who murdered differed significantly across MMPI trait, type, and classification variables from women incarcerated for nonviolent offenses, and MMPI variables differentiated groups with at least moderate levels of accuracy. In contrast, male violent felons could not be discriminated from men incarcerated for nonviolent offenses, and women who murdered shared few features in common with men who had behaved similarly. Findings are limited by their postdictive nature and neither generalize to more normal populations nor predict less extreme forms of aggression; however, they target areas for future research. For example, that higher scores on the masculinity-femininity dimension of the MMPI are predictive of extreme violence or aggressive behavior among women in this and other studies (Huesmann, Lefkowitz, and Eron 1978; McCreary 1976) underscores the need for research focusing on female attitudes toward self, men, and society and the relationships of sex-specific cognitive sets or assertive or violent behavior. Systematic study of instigating factors and background variables significant to expression of aggression among both sexes with particular reference to offender psychological types is also required. Research of this ilk could lead to important hypotheses regarding violent behavior in men and women and be extended in analog or psychophysiological experiments to explore relationships between hostile cognitions and less extreme aggressive responding. Such investigation could thereby provide one link to integrate the study of person variables with efforts to specify the stimulus conditions under which specific responses occur, that is, those studies designed to test the principles of social learning theory as related to aggression.

REFERENCES

Bandura, A. 1965. "Influence of Models' Reinforcement Contingencies on the Acquisition of Imitative Responses." *Journal of Personality and Social Psychology* 1: 589-95.

Buck, J. A., and J. R. Graham. 1978. "The 4-3 MMPI Profile Type: A Failure to Replicate." *Journal of Consulting and Clinical Psychology* 46: 344.

Campbell, D. T., and D. W. Fiske. 1959. "Convergent and Discriminant Validation by the Multitrait-Multimethod Matrix." *Psychological Bulletin* 56: 81-105.

Cattell, R. B. 1966. "The Scree Test for the Number of Factors." *Multivariate Behavioral Research* 1: 245-76.

Climent, C. E., A. Rollins, F. R. Ervin, and R. Plutchik. 1973. "Epidemiological Studies of Women Prisoners. I. Medical and Psychiatric Variables Related to Violent Behavior." *American Journal of Psychiatry* 130: 985-90.

Cole, K. E., G. Fisher, and S. S. Cole. 1968. "Women Who Kill: A Sociopsychological Study." *Archives of General Psychiatry* 19: 1-8.

Davis, K. R., and J. O. Sines. 1971. "An Antisocial Behavior Pattern Associated with a Specific MMPI Profile." *Journal of Consulting and Clinical Psychology* 36: 229-34.

Deiker, T. E. 1974. "A Cross-Validation of MMPI Scales of Aggression on Male Criminal Criterion Groups." *Journal of Consulting and Clinical Psychology* 42: 196-202.

Dixon, W. J., ed. 1975. *BMDP: Biomedical Computer Programs*. Berkeley: University of California Press.

d'Orban, P. T. 1973. "Female Narcotic Addicts: A Follow-Up Study of Criminal and Addiction Careers." *British Medical Journal* 4: 345-47.

Eysenck, S. B. G., and H. J. Eysenck. 1973. "The Personality of Female Prisoners." *British Journal of Psychiatry* 122: 693-98.

Frederiksen, S. J. 1975. "A Comparison of Selected Personality and History Variables in Highly Violent, Mildly Violent, and Nonviolent Female Offenders." Ph.D. dissertation, University of Minnesota. *Dissertation Abstracts International* 36 (1975), 3036B. University Microfilms no. 72-27, 151.

Gilberstadt, H., and J. Duker. 1965. *A Handbook for Clinical and Actuarial MMPI Interpretation*. Philadelphia: Saunders.

Gleuck, S., and E. Gleuck. 1934. *Five Hundred Delinquent Women*. New York: Knopf.

Gynther, M. D., H. Altman, and R. W. Warbin. 1973. "Behavioral Correlates for the Minnesota Multiphasic Personality Inventory 4–9/9–4 Code Types: A Case of the Emperor's New Clothes?" *Journal of Consulting and Clinical Psychology* 40: 259–63.

Haven, H. J. 1972. "Descriptive and Developmental Characteristics of Chronically Overcontrolled Hostile Prisoners." Ph.D. dissertation, Florida State University. *Dissertation Abstracts International* 33 (1973): 5515B. University Microfilms no. 72–31, 400.

Hoppe, C. M., and R. D. Singer. 1976. "Overcontrolled Hostility, Empathy, and Egocentric Balance in Violent and Nonviolent Psychiatric Offenders." *Psychological Reports* 39: 1303–08.

Huesmann, L. R., M. M. Lefkowtiz, and L. D. Eron. 1978. "Sum of MMPI Scales *F*, 4, and 9 as a Measure of Aggression." Journal of Consulting and Clinical Psychology 46: 1071–78.

Klein, D. 1973. "The Etiology of Female Crime: A Review of the Literature." *Issues in Criminology* 8: 3–29.

McCreary, C. P. 1976. "Trait and Type Differences Among Male and Female Assaultive and Nonassaultive Offenders." *Journal of Personality Assessment* 40: 617–21.

Mallory, C. H., and C. E. Walker. 1972. "MMPI O–H Scale Responses of Assaultive and Nonassaultive Prisoners and Associated Life History Variables." *Educational and Psychological Measurement* 32: 1125–28.

Meehl, P. E. 1956. "Profile Analysis of the MMPI in Differential Diagnosis." In *Basic Readings on the MMPI in Psychology and Medicine*, edited by G. S. Welsh and W. G. Dahlstrom, pp. 292–97. Minneapolis: University of Minnesota Press.

Megargee, E. I. 1977. "The Need for a New Classification System. I." *Criminal Justice and Behavior* 4: 107–14.

——. 1976. "The Prediction of Dangerous Behavior." *Criminal Justice and Behavior* 3: 3–22.

——. 1970. "The Prediction of Violence with Psychological Tests." In *Current Topics in Clinical and Community Psychology*, edited by C. D. Spielberger, vol. 2, pp. 97–156. New York: Academic Press.

——. 1966. "Undercontrolled and Overcontrolled Personality Types in Extreme Antisocial Aggression." *Psychological Monographs* 80, no. 611.

——, and M. J. Bohn, 1977. "Empirically Determined Characteristics of the Ten Types. IV." *Criminal Justice and Behavior* 4: 149–210.

Megargee, E. I., P. E. Cook, and G. A. Mendelsohn. 1967. "Development and Validation of an MMPI Scale of Assaultiveness in Overcontrolled Individuals." *Journal of Abnormal Psychology* 72: 519–28.

Megargee, E. I., and B. Dorhout. 1977. "Revision and Refinement of the Classificatory Rules. III." *Criminal Justice and Behavior* 4: 125–48.

Megargee, E. I., and G. A. Mendelsohn. 1962. "A Cross-Validation of Twelve MMPI Indices of Hostility and Control." *Journal of Abnormal and Social Psychology* 65: 431–38.

Persons, R. W., and P. A. Marks. 1971. "The Violent 4–3 MMPI Personality Type." *Journal of Consulting and Clinical Psychology* 36: 189–96.

Pollak, O. 1950. *The Criminality of Women.* Philadelphia: University of Pennsylvania Press.

Rader, C. M. 1977. "MMPI Profile Types of Exposers, Rapists, and Assaulters in a Court Services Population." *Journal of Consulting and Clinical Psychology* 45: 61–69.

Rawlings, M. L. 1973. "Self-Control and Interpersonal Violence: A Study of Scottish Adolescent Male Severe Offenders." *Criminology* 11: 23–48.

Rosenblatt, E., and C. Greenland. 1974. "Female Crimes of Violence." *Canadian Journal of Criminology and Corrections* 16: 173–80.

Ross, W. F., and J. I. Berzins. 1974. "Personality Characteristics of Female Narcotic Addicts on the MMPI." *Psychological Reports* 35: 779–84.

Sadava, S. W., and R. Forsyth. 1977. "Person-Environment Interaction and College Student Drug Use: A Multivariate Longitudinal Study." *Genetic Psychology Monographs* 96: 211–45.

Scott, P. D. 1973. "Parents Who Kill Their Children." *Medicine, Science, and the Law* 13: 120–26.

Simon, R. J. 1975. "The Contemporary Woman and Crime." In *Crime and Delinquency Issues.* Washington, D.C.: U.S. Government Printing Office.

Sutker, P. B., and C. E. Moan. 1972. "Personality Characteristics of Socially Deviant Women: Incarcerated Heroin Addicts, Street Addicts, and Non-

Addicted Prisoners." In *Drug Addiction: Clinical and Socio-Legal Aspects*, edited by J. M. Singh, L. H. Miller, and H. Lal, vol. 2, pp. 107–14. Mt. Kisco, N.Y.: Futura.

Vanderbeck, D. J. 1973. "A Construct Validity Study of the O–H (Overcontrolled Hostility) Scale of the MMPI, Using a Social Learning Approach to the Catharis Effect." *FCI Research Reports* 5: 1–18.

Weissman, J. C., and K. N. File. 1976. "Criminal Behavior Patterns of Female Addicts: A Comparison of Findings in Two Cities." *International Journal of the Addictions* 11: 1063–77.

White, W. C. 1975. "Validity of the Overcontrolled-Hostility (O–H) Scale: A Brief Report." *Journal of Personality Assessment* 39: 587–90.

——, W. G. McAdoo, and E. I. Megargee, 1973. "Personality Factors Associated with Over- and Undercontrolled Offenders." *Journal of Personality Assessment* 37: 473–78.

7 / MMPI PROFILES AND THE LONGITUDINAL PREDICTION OF ADULT SOCIAL OUTCOME

Cathy S. Widom

One could hardly dispute the usefulness of the MMPI and its numerous scales in assessing psychological adjustment in certain personal and social areas. This chapter is an attempt to explore the usefulness of the MMPI as a longitudinal predictor of later social outcomes. In psychological research, longitudinal prediction represents an attempt to discover signs, test scores, or any other indicators (Hathaway and Monachesi 1963) that precede the outcome of interest and can be used to reduce the base rate of error in the prediction of that outcome. The present work will limit discussion to research utilizing the MMPI and its scales in predicting social outcomes. Concern, therefore, is with aspects of social behavior and outcome that may result from particular MMPI personality profiles.

Because the MMPI was developed as a tool to aid in psychiatric diagnosis and hence the original scales were psychiatrically oriented, it is not surprising that most studies incorporating the MMPI involve the prediction of negative social outcomes thought to be a product of the particular psychiatric disorder. However, this chapter will not be limited to the adverse social consequences of MMPI personality profiles; rather, it will include research utilizing a wide range of outcomes. On the other hand, this review makes no attempt to be exhaustive, but attempts to illustrate and through these examples assess the usefulness of the MMPI. Studies correlating MMPI profiles and outcome measures concurrently (which do not include a follow-up) will not be included here. (For a review of such correlational research, see Dahlstrom, Welsh, and Dahlstrom 1975.)

The first section of this chapter discusses the concept and measurement of social coutcome, explores the stability of MMPI scale scores, and reviews a study involving the longitudinal prediction of normality. The next section argues for the importance of prospective longitudinal research in the development of psychopathology and provides examples of research using this approach, including a study by Robert Dworkin and Cathy Widom on undergraduate MMPI profiles and the longitudinal prediction of adult social outcome. The third section, presenting a diverse group of studies using the MMPI in predicting social outcome, is divided into studies concerned with the longitudinal prediction of treatment outcomes (drug treatment programs, affiliation with Alcoholics Anonymous, influence of wives on treatment outcome of alcoholics, and group psychotherapy with prisoners) and those concerned with the longitudinal prediction of vocational adaptation and occupational performance. In the concluding section, the author highlights some of the major themes in the research reviewed, speculates on areas where the MMPI might be most useful, and suggests the proverbial areas for future research.

SOCIAL OUTCOME

Typically when one thinks of social outcome studies in the context of the MMPI, it is with the assumption of psychopathology and some form of negative, adverse social consequences. In contrast, the present chapter will consider studies in which positive outcome variables have been included in addition to possible negative ones. For example, one might propose that given an encouraging and supportive environment, certain kinds of "schizotypic" or "psychopathic" predispositions might predict positive social outcomes such as creativity in the former and spontaneity in the latter. For the most part, however, researchers have focused on negative outcomes.

Regardless of whether one is predicting positive or negative social outcomes, there are three classes of variables generally included in investigations: IQ and academic achievement, social class and socioeconomic status, and interpersonal and personal adjustment. In most research, all three aspects appear to be included. However, there is an important principle guiding the selection of outcome variables that emphasizes that there is a different set of relevant outcome measures dependent on the population being studied. A researcher must choose outcome measures that are appropriate for the group on whom the predictors are made. For example, outcome variables will differ considerably if one is opposed to a group of long-term drug addicts. It would be meaningless to propose "decreased contact with known criminals and drug abusers" as a social outcome measure for college students, whereas it could be argued to be an important indicator of positive social outcome (improvement) for someone who had previously spent time in the company of cons and drug abusers.

Another important issue in regard to the selection of outcome measures, particularly in investigations attempting to evaluate the effectiveness of various treatment programs, is the tendency to select measures that reflect the conventional ethics of the American middle class. Consider, for example, criteria frequently selected to determine the success or failure of drug treatment programs. Success is often defined in terms of the client's obtaining legitimate employment, terminating illegal and criminal acts and behaviors, ending associations with known drug users and criminals, becoming family and community oriented, and so on (for example, Levine et al. 1972).

The social outcome measures included here represent a range of variables from success or failure in various treatment programs to reported delinquency to subtleties in level of educational achievement and interpersonal adjustment. Yet these represent only a fraction of social outcome studies, most of which have examined outcome variables concurrently with MMPI personality profiles.

STABILITY OF MMPI SCORES

One might propose that longitudinal studies investigating the relationship between early personality test profiles and later behavior cannot be expected to predict effectively for individuals whose personality may be in transition during the time interval investigated (Hathaway and Monachesi 1963). While this argument demands thoughtful response and might prove critical to certain approaches, it is argued here that if the predisposition is manifested at an earlier age and is reasonably stable at that time, that is, not changing from day to day, then the longitudinal stability of that predisposition is a separate issue and could be construed as an outcome measure itself.

Before proceeding any further, in consideration of the importance of this short-term stability issue, let us review research on the test-retest stability of MMPI scores. Table 7.1 and 7.2 present a compilation of test-retest reliability coefficients from studies of the MMPI over periods ranging from one day to three years with normal and psychiatric populations.

As can be seen from both tables, short-term test-retest reliability of the MMPI is quite high and shows a progressive decline as the amount of time between intervals increases. For example, over brief intervals of one or two days, there is fairly high test-retest reliability, whether the subjects are college students or psychiatric cases. In studies using various forms of the MMPI format (for example, Butcher and Dahlstrom 1974; Mauger 1972), data on retesting within a short interval also suggest that for most subjects there is little shifting in scores.

Test-retest coefficients based on longer intervals of eight months to several years reveal considerably less stability and raise more complicated issues, specifically the stability of personality attributes over time. However, venturing into such a debate in the context of the present chapter would seem to be a diversion and will be resisted. Nonetheless, it is assumed that test-retest reliability for the MMPI scales over a short time duration is sufficiently high to justify its usage in longitudinal studies predicting later social outcome. No assumptions are made as to the nature of MMPI profiles at follow-up.

LONGITUDINAL PREDICTION OF NORMALITY

In one of the rare studies attempting to predict "normals," Golden and his colleagues (1962) defined a sample of "normal" men from the original Hathaway and Monachesi (1963) study. Individuals were selected on the basis of their

TABLE 7.1

MMPI Test-Retest Coefficients Scale

Interval and Study	Subjects	L	F	K	1	2	3	4	5	6	7	8	9	0
One-day interval Faschingbauer 1973	Male college students (n = 28)	.73	.97	.89	.49	.88	.81	.95	.91	.89	.93	.95	.96	.94
	Female college students (n = 33)	.85	.82	.87	.92	.96	.85	.91	.77	.71	.93	.95	.85	.96
One week interval Windle 1955	Female college students (n = 55)	.79	.62	.92	.73	.84	.71	.84	—	.81	.92	.82	.79	—
One to two-week interval Butcher and Dahlstrom 1964	Male college students (n = 42)	.66	.84	.78	.65	.69	.63	.77	.72	.49	.74	.79	.63	.83
Eight month interval Mauger 1972	Male college students (n = 201)	.64	.61	.67	.50	.57	.54	.61	.63	.44	.55	.57	.59	.73
	Female college students (n = 289)	.58	.51	.64	.49	.56	.52	.53	.58	.42	.46	.51	.64	.76
Three year interval Hathaway and Monachesi 1963	Male adolescents (n = 1922)	.39	.45	.52	.34	.38	.37	.36	.45	.32	.37	.37	.47	.54
	Female adolescents (n = 2054)	.50	.49	.56	.41	.47	.44	.38	.43	.36	.50	.42	.45	.61

Source: Adapted from W. G. Dahlstrom, G. S. Welsh, and L. E. Dahlstrom, *An MMPI Handbook*, vol. 2, *Research Applications* (Minneapolis: University of Minnesota Press, 1975), p. 253–56.

TABLE 7.2

MMPI Test-Retest Coefficients for Psychiatric Samples

Interval and Study	Subjects	L	F	K	1	2	3	4	5	6	7	8	9	0
One-day interval Newmark 1973	Female psychiatric cases (n = 39)	.74	.81	.56	.80	.86	.82	.75	.79	.61	.73	.75	.81	.87
One- to two-day interval Newmark 1971	Male psychiatric cases (n = 35)	.78	.80	.46	.85	.72	.64	.69	.83	.71	.77	.82	.71	.80
One- to two-week interval Jurjevich 1966	Male psychiatric cases (n = 50)	.68	.87	.85	.86	.89	.80	.70	.79	.80	.83	.74	.71	.88
	Female psychiatric cases (N = 21)	.70	.86	.71	.79	.80	.66	.59	.76	.78	.86	.86	.74	.80
One-year interval Stone 1965	Male psychiatric cases (n = 55)	.61	.63	.72	.65	.49	.72	.58	.34	.59	.58	.64	.43	.64
Sines, Silver, and Lucero 1961	Female psychiatric cases (n = 49)	.35	.76	.42	.38	.50	.36	.49	.37	.65	.49	.56	.52	.63

Source: Adapted from W. G. Dahlstrom, G. S. Welsh, and L. E. Dahlstrom, *An MMPI Handbook*, vol. 2, *Research Applications* (Minneapolis: University of Minnesota Press, 1975), p. 257–59.

self-descriptions at approximately age 14, who reported the absence of psycho-pathology as measured by the MMPI. "Normality" was operationally defined as an MMPI profile with no T scores above 55.

Of the 1,953 male ninth-grade students tested originally, 73 (3.7 percent) met this criterion, reporting no indication of significant pathology. Of these 73 potential subjects, 23 were excluded for miscellaneous reasons (13 moved from the state, 7 were not able to be located, 1 was deceased, 1 could not come to the interview, and 1 refused to participate).

The reader is undoubtedly asking several questions at this point. How meaningful can a definition of "normality" be when less than 4 percent of this ninth-grade population was designated "normal"? Furthermore, can we reasonably generalize from this small sample (n = 73) when approximately one third of those defined as normal by this criterion were not included in the follow up?

The men were originally selected as being "at the norm" in their MMPI profiles, but it is almost this false normativeness (that is, less than 4 percent of the sample) that some might find hard to accept. It is akin to an example frequently used in research methods courses to discuss the statistical concept of the "mean" scores for a group but at the same time emphasizing that there may be no one individual whose score falls on that mean.

However, recognizing that it is not the purpose of this discussion to argue the validity of Golden et al.'s criteria for normality, but to assess the adequacy of the MMPI in predicting later social outcome, further skepticism and criticism of these criteria will be avoided. It is sufficient to make the reader question this definition of normality and perhaps be stimulated to offer alternative formulations.

The men at follow-up were approximately 25 to 26 years old and showed extensive similarity in demographic characterisitcs. These "normal" men showed some differences in occupational choices, although none reported working in unskilled, laboring, services, or domestic categories. Their incomes were fairly narrowly distributed with 96 percent of the 50 men earning between $3,000 and $10,000 and only one man earning more and one man earning less. Of the 40 married men, none had experienced separations or broken marriages and all were high school graduates. Therefore these overall findings reflect remarkable consistency and uniformity among this sample of 50 men.

The authors offer support for this encouraging "normal" picture by reporting that 23 percent showed no significant psychopathology. One wonders whether this result is considered a success (that is, as compared to other unselected normal populations that presumably would have had a higher degree of pathology) or a failure of prediction (that is, 23 percent is too high a rate of psychopathology for a "normal" group). Lacking a control group, one can only speculate and be aware that any further conclusion must be left for empirical testing.

The authors confess that a more creative, spontaneous type of personality organization may have been sacrificed in the selection for normality. The men were found to have little imagination and limited interests, activities, and educational and vocational aspirations for themselves and their children. Can we define an MMPI profile that would be useful in predicting creative, imaginative, and spontaneous individuals? What might it look like?

In assessing the contribution of the MMPI as a tool for longitudinal prediction, it is tempting to lose sight of the contribution of this study while making value judgments about the long-term outcome of these men. But regardless of any ambivalence concerning the outcome of this study, it does provide support for the usefulness of the MMPI in identifying subgroups with particular predispositions whose later behavior fulfills our expectations. These "normal" men developed into what might have been expected from people so defined.

DEVELOPMENT OF PSYCHOPATHOLOGY

For a number of reasons, longitudinal studies have become increasingly important tools in psychological research. As Hathaway, Monachesi, and Salasin (1970) have emphasized, there is a major flaw in studies that retrospectively identify the proportion of a particular clinical population showing a particular social outcome. What we want is a determination of the percentage of that clinical population who later develop particular social outcome characteristics.

Comparisons between abnormal and control populations confound the antecedents and consequents of the disorder under study and cannot adequately address etiological issues. Prospective longitudinal studies allow us to put the clinical, or subclinical, profile type before the social outcome, making it possible to determine what happens later to people with specific clinical predispositions. When this kind of prediction is possible, we might have a more rational basis for treatment and intervention.

Prospective studies provide test data before one is labeled delinquent or problematic and processed by legal and medical authorities or others. Examples are the recent longitudinal studies of the children of schizophrenic parents (Garmezy 1974a, 1974b) and follow-up studies of other samples with different high-risk characteristics (for example, Robins 1966). Studying high-risk persons who have parents with a particular form of psychopathology or biological relatives of those patients with some disorder is extremely worthwhile. However, the results of such investigations have limited generalizability, as most people who do develop schizophrenia, for example, do not have a schizophrenic parent or schizophrenic biological relative (Mosher and Gunderson 1973).

A basic assumption of this kind of longitudinal research is that there are "precursor psychological symptoms that foreshadow the more severe disorder" (Hathaway, Monachesi, and Salasin 1970, p. 174). However, even if assuming the existence of premorbid psychological symptoms, we are relatively ignorant about the relationship between these premorbid symptoms and the later development of adverse social outcomes.

Concentrating our attention and limiting our research to hospitalized, incarcerated, or otherwise institutionalized populations is misleading in the sense that any dysfunctions observed are confounded with the severity and deterioration of the disorder or the effects of institutionalization and are away from the essence of the disorder. Furthermore, researchers have become increasingly sensitive to the proposition that people are placed in institutions for a variety of reasons (that is, not necessarily because they are the most needy in terms of hospitalization or the only guilty parties).

Institutionalized populations therefore often represent biased and limited segments of the clinical population of interest. For this reason, epidemiological studies assessing the incidence and distribution of various clinical symptoms and syndromes have begun to provide a much needed extension of our understanding of psychopathology, as have recent attempts to study noninstitutionalized subclinical populations (for example Widom 1977).

Once we have defined a group of individuals who are characterized by distinctive premorbid predispositions, we may then follow them and record their behavior before they experience the effects of labeling and institutionalization. Finally, this form of prospective longitudinal research allows us to examine the possible effects of the environment, particularly as it acts as a "buffer" for certain individuals with certain predispositions.

PREDICTION OF DELINQUENCY

In 1947, over 4,000 Minneapolis ninth-grade students were administered the MMPI at the initiation of probably the largest longitudinal study involving the MMPI. This initial testing was followed in 1954 by a statewide sample of more than 11,000 ninth-graders (Hathaway and Monachesi 1963). The MMPI was not found to be as useful in predicting later delinquency as were teachers' predictions. These results are not surprising considering that an MMPI test profile emphasizes the role of individual personality organization and does not take into account school and socioeconomic data (to which the teacher has access), and particularly in light of recent research on teacher expectancy and labeling effects (for example, Rosenthal and Jacobson 1966). As Hathaway and Monachesi (1963) emphasized, children with personality patterns predisposing to delinquency are often protected by favorable environmental forces such as a good family or good organizational affiliations.

Although no single code class dramatically predicted delinquency, MMPI test data did identify certain subgroups of children who were considered "difficulty-prone," as well as some who would be considered relatively resistant to difficulties. For example, high MMPI scale *Pd* students had delinquency rates well above the general base rate, as did the schizoid (high scale *Sc* profile) children. Other personality profiles predicted no delinquency about as accurately as others predicted it (for example, no high-point profiles had greatly reduced delinquency rates).

A shortcoming of many MMPI studies, and even of this large-scale study, is the limitation placed on any conclusions drawn because of the small numbers of individuals in each of the subgroups. In addition, the frequent need to combine groups tends to minimize relationships between the particular profile types and social outcomes. Nevertheless, the original Minnesota study provided an exceptional source of MMPI data for use in longitudinal studies and suggested the importance of understanding the role of the environment in exaggerating or alleviating (buffering) what might be genetic predispositions or premorbid symptomatology.

Wirt and Briggs (1959) conducted a series of follow-up studies on the original Minneapolis sample, and in the three-year interval found a delinquency rate for boys of 21.1 percent. Those boys with elevated MMPI scale *Pd, Sc,* and *Ma* combinations were found to be three times as likely to become delinquent as those with more inhibitory high-point profiles. Briggs, Wirt, and Johnson (1961) carried their analysis further in documenting the interaction between personality variables on the MMPI and familial crises or disruptions. Boys with MMPI profiles with scales *Pd, Sc,* and *Ma* prominent who also had three major adverse familial circumstances (for example, paternal absence via abandonment or death, maternal illness, economic difficulties) were found to be known delinquents in almost 90 percent of the cases, whereas only 30 percent of the boys with the same MMPI profiles without the adverse familial circumstances were found to be delinquent.

The most successful efforts to identify predispositions to delinquency appear to involve the use of the MMPI in conjunction with other information (for example, Rempel 1958, 1960; Briggs, Wirt, and Johnson 1961). In these delinquency studies, the MMPI was useful as a sensitive index of possibly premorbid predispositions, but the determination of who developed into the more complete clinical manifestation appeared to be a function of the environment in interaction with predisposition.

Follow-up Study of MMPI High 8 Children

More recently, Hathaway, Monachesi, and Salasin (1970) hypothesized that the high *Sc* children from their earlier study, having test patterns similar to those seen in adult schizophrenic patients, would manifest symptoms in their later social behavior that would be related to the adult syndrome of schizophrenia. Incidence rates of high *Sc* profile types were 5.1 and 4.4 percent among the total sample of boys and girls, respectively. Ninth-graders with high *Sc* profiles were found to have lower high school ranks, completed less schooling, and were of lower socioeconomic status at age 25 than those who obtained normal MMPI profiles in the ninth grade. These differences disappeared only when those with high intelligence were examined. Therefore, a high *Sc* score predisposition alone did not forecast a disabling academic outcome, whereas the interaction of high *Sc* and low IQ seemed to place a double burden on the children, creating an unfavorable prognosis in social outcome terms.

Based on these findings, Hathaway, Monachesi, and Salasin suggested that the MMPI might prove useful in the selection of samples for experimental and longitudinal research on predisposing factors in the development of schizophrenia, research on the antecedents and consequents of the disorder might be facilitated.

UNDERGRADUATE MMPI PROFILES AND ADULT SOCIAL OUTCOME

In light of many of the issues raised previously Dworkin and Widom (1977) attempted to determine whether the usefulness of the MMPI in longitudinal prediction extends to groups of individuals of higher socioeconomic status with the many social advantages that accrue with that status.* They also sought to determine whether undergraduates with MMPI profiles indicative of two very different kinds of psychopathology, schizophrenia and psychopathy, would show differences in social outcome variables 10 years later.

Follow-up information on several social outcome variables was obtained for a sample of individuals who had taken the MMPI during their junior year in college. This sample differs in two important respects from samples in previous studies. First, these undergraduates generally represented the higher end of the socioeconomic distribution, were of high intelligence, and were in late adolescence when the data were collected. Second, the longitudinal investigation was extended to include a sample of individuals who during college had "psychopathic" MMPI profiles. Because psychopathy (for example, Robins 1966) and schizophrenia (for example, Kohn 1973) appear to have different social correlates, the comparison of these three groups—individuals with undergraduate MMPI profiles indicative of subclinical schizophrenia, subclinical psychopathy, and normality—allow consideration of whether the different profile types are associated with different social outcomes, with social class and educational level at the outset essentially held constant.

Method

Twenty-five percent random samples of two consecutive male classes at a select, private New England university were studied longitudinally from fresh-

---

*This research was supported in part by an NIMH Graduate Traineeship to Dr. Dworkin and a Biomedical Research Fund grant (Harvard University) to Widom. Thanks to S. H. King for making the MMPI data available, to B. Bee for help in the data analysis, and to I. L. Gottesman, A. L. Megela, and P. Segal for their suggestions and assistance.

man to senior years. By the junior year, 62.5 percent of the original participants remained in the study, and these students were administered the MMPI.

MMPI raw scores obtained from these 417 students were plotted, and individuals whose profiles met one of three sets of criteria were selected for inclusion in the groups. Profiles with raw *F* scores of 22 or greater (Hathaway and Monachesi 1963) were not included in the analysis. Selection criteria for the profile types were based on published code types (Gilberstadt and Duker 1965; Hathaway and Monachesi 1963; Marks, Seeman, and Haller 1974), sources on the MMPI and subclinical schizophrenia (Hathaway, Monachesi, and Salasin 1970; Koh and Peterson 1974), and MMPI profiles of psychopaths (Craddick 1962; Doctor and Craine 1971; Hare 1970). Final criteria were established after an examination of the distribution of profiles within the sample and with a consideration that roughly equivalent sample sizes across the three groups should be drawn. Scores on scales *Mf* and *Si* were not examined. Specific criteria for the three groups are as follows:

1. High *Sc* MMPI profiles: Scale *Sc* was most elevated and greater than or equal to T score of 75; or scale *Pa, Pt,* or *Ma* was most elevated and greater than or equal to T score of 75, and scale *Sc* was the second most elevated and greater than or equal to T score of 75.
2. High *Pd* MMPI profiles: Scale *Pd* was most elevated and greater than or equal to T score of 69, with the exception of scales *Hs, Hy, Pt,* and/or *Ma*; or scale *Ma* was most elevated and greater than or equal to T score of 70, and scale *Pd* was the second most elevated regardless of its level.
3. No high-point (control) MMPI profiles: All T scores were less than or equal to 60.

Applying these criteria to the sample of 417 MMPIs from the two classes yielded 42 high *Sc* profiles, 35 high *Pd* profiles, and 52 no high-point profiles. Ten-year follow-up information on social outcome was obtained for a total of 94 of the 129 individuals in the three groups: 30 high *Sc* individuals (71.4 percent), 27 high *Pd* individuals (77.1 percent), and 37 no high-point individuals (71.2 percent). This information was obtained from alumni questionnaires and class reports. From these sources, it was decided to limit the present analyses to the basic demographic data, that is, marital status, number of children, education, and an index of socioeconomic status based on occupation (Reiss 1961). The groups did not differ significantly with respect to the follow-up information.

For each of the three groups, t-tests were calculated to compare the mean validity and clinical MMPI scale scores of those individuals for whom follow-up information was available with those for whom follow-up information was not available. Of the 39 two-tailed t-tests calculated, only 1 was significant. Individuals with high *Sc* MMPI profiles in college without follow-up information were significantly more elevated on scale *Hs* than the similar group for which follow-up information was available, t(40) = 2.21, p < .05. This was also the only comparison of the 39 on which the groups differed by more than five T score points. With respect to their college MMPI profiles therefore, the groups for which follow-up information was available appear to be quite similar to the groups without follow-up information.

Mean MMPI profiles for the three subject groups with 10-year follow-up data available are presented in Figure 7.1.

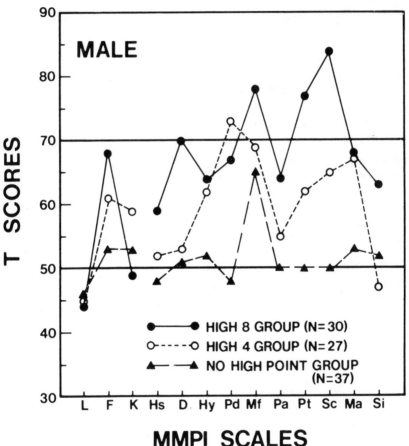

FIGURE 7.1: Mean MMPI profiles for high *Pd*, high *Sc*, and no high-point profile groups with 10-year follow-up data available. From R. H. Dworkin and C. S. Widom, "Undergraduate MMPI Profiles and the Longitudinal Prediction of Adult Social Outcome," *Journal of Consulting and Clinical Psychology* 45 (1977): 620–24. Copyright (1977) by the American Psychological Association. Reprinted with permission.

Results

Table 7.3 presents a summary of the 10-year follow-up data for these three groups. Of the variables at follow-up dealing with marriage and family, only the percentage of individuals ever married differed significantly among the three groups, $X^2(2) = 5.89$, p = .053. Fisher's exact tests were calculated, and the results indicated that the high Sc profile group had significantly more individuals who had ever been married (p ≤ .05) than either the high Pd profile or the control groups, which did not differ significantly from each other. (Two-tailed tests are reported.)

TABLE 7.3

Undergraduate MMPI Profiles and Adult Social Outcome

	Profile Type		
Adult Follow-up Variable	High Pd (n = 27)	High Sc (n = 30)	No High Point (n = 37)
Marital status (percent)			
Married	81.5	70.0	67.6
Remarried	3.7	.0	2.7
Divorced	7.4	.0	.0
Separated	3.7	3.3	5.4
Ever married	96.3	73.3	75.7
Single (never married)	3.7	26.7	24.3
Years married if still married to first wife			
M	6.77[a]	6.05[a]	6.56
SD	3.34[a]	3.48[a]	2.91
Number of children, if ever married			
M	1.19	1.00	.89
SD	1.11	1.00	.82
Education (percent)			
Schooling beyond college	85.2	86.7	97.3
Completed advanced degree	81.5	73.3	97.3
Occupational status (Reiss 1961)			
M	81.81	82.17	83.37[b]
SD	17.25	15.11	10.46[b]

[a]One individual did not respond.
[b]One student and one unemployed individual were excluded.
Source: R. H. Dworkin and C. S. Widom, "Undergraduate MMPI Profiles and the Longitudinal Prediction of Adult Social Outcome," *Journal of Consulting and Clinical Psychology* 45 (1977): 620–24. Copyright (1977) by the American Psychological Association. Reprinted with permission.

Although the groups did not differ significantly with respect to the percentage of individuals with some education beyond college, the percentage who completed an advanced degree did differentiate the three groups, $X^2(2) = 7.90$, $p \leqslant .01$. Both the high *Sc* and high *Pd* profile groups had significantly fewer individuals who had completed advanced degrees than the control groups (Fisher's exact test, $p \leqslant .01$, $p \leqslant .05$, respectively. The high *Sc* and high *Pd* profile groups did not differ significantly from each other. (For educational attainment, one-tailed tests are reported, as the direction of difference was predicted in advance.)

Although certain aspects of the marital status and educational variables did distinguish the three groups, Reiss's (1961) index of socioeconomic status based on occupation did not differ among the groups. (In examining the last line of Table 7.3, it is apparent that the variances for occupational status differ markedly among the groups. Although both the high *Pd* and high *Sc* profile groups have significantly greater variance than the control group, these differences are due to a single outlier of very low occupational status in each of these two groups. When the variances were recalculated with these two individuals removed, the differences disappeared.) Although there were no significant differences in occupational status, anecdotal evidence suggests that there were certain individuals who fulfilled expectations as to likely adult occupations of undergraduate high *Sc* and high *Pd* MMPI profile types.

Discussion

Dworkin and Widom (1977) found that undergraduate MMPI profiles indicative of subclinical schizophrenia and psychopathy predicted significant differences in adult social outcome when compared to normal control undergraduate MMPI profiles. Such differences were found in spite of the generally high intelligence level of the sample. In comparing Dworkin and Widom's findings with those of Hathaway, Monachesi, and Salasin (1970) (which suggest that ninth-grade high *Sc* profiles combined with high intelligence do not predict later social disadvantages), the difference may be due either to the grade levels at which the samples were administered the MMPI or to the different levels of educational attainment studied. In their study, Dworkin and Widom analyzed the percentage of individuals completing an advanced degree, whereas in the Hathaway, Monachesi, and Salasin study, schooling beyond high school was the only educational outcome variable examined.

Results suggest that undergraduate MMPI profile types indicative of subclinical psychopathy and schizophrenia are sensitive to some underlying predispositions even in this highly intelligent and college-educated sample. The high educational and occupational attainments of these two groups suggests that in the presence of moderating factors, such as intelligence and high social class, the MMPI does not predict severe social disability for most individuals.

Occupational status did not differentiate the three groups, although it is possible, given the differences found with respect to education, that more sensitive measures of occupational status would have been more discriminating.

An interesting aspect of these results is that the two profile types indicative of psychopathology were found to have both similar and different social outcomes. Both the high *Sc* and high *Pd* profile types predicted significantly lower percentages of educational attainment (that is, completing an advanced degree) when compared to the control profile type. However, with respect to marital status, the high *Pd* profile group differed significantly from the other two groups, as the former were more likely to have been married. One can only speculate about the reasons for this unanticipated result. However, the well-known characteristic of impulsiveness in psychopaths might lead to more (impulsive?) marriages, albeit not necessarily more stable or long-lasting relationships.

One can consider this research from either of two perspectives. First, it can be viewed as an attempt to assess the adequacy of the MMPI in longitudinal predictions of social outcome in privileged groups and to extend the generality of a research literature previously limited to longitudinal predictions of schizotypy and delinquency to include subclinical psychopathy. Second, one might consider the present research as an attempt to explore the role of the environment in interaction with MMPI-identified predispositions. In contrast to previous studies, where the role of the environment was generally a hostile one, the present research assumes the advantages of a favorable environment.

If one were primarily interested in the first perspective, then this research must be viewed as fairly successful. However, from the second perspective, one would want more convincing evidence that the two subclinical groups identified actually differed in behavioral terms during adolescence. Was there other evidence that these undergraduates were manifesting psychopathological symptomatology at the time? In other words, if it could be demonstrated that there was clinical and overt evidence of psychopathology among these young men, as juniors in college, then the positive effects of the environment would be more convincing. On the other hand, if the only indication of subclinical psychopathology was in their scores on the MMPI, then it is more difficult to argue an environmental buffer effect.

Finally, strenuous efforts must be made in the future to locate nonresponders in studies such as this. Particularly in an investigation that focuses on psychopathology, who but the most deviant members would be likely not to respond, be it for any number of reasons (death, psychiatric institutionalization, incarceration, no known address, and so on)?

PREDICTION OF TREATMENT OUTCOMES

Success in Drug Treatment Programs

Although the MMPI has been frequently employed to describe the personality characteristics of drug addicts (for example, Hill, Haertzen, and Glaser

1960; Hill, Haertzen, and Davis 1962; Gilbert and Lombardi 1967; Sutker 1971; Sutker and Allain 1973), few studies have utilized the MMPI in longitudinal investigations of drug addicts. The reason for this dearth of studies is understandable, considering the difficulty in obtaining participation from the subjects, let alone locating them for further follow-up. However, one follow-up study reports on the first group of men who had completed six months in aftercare after hospitalization at the National Institute of Mental Health Clinical Research Center in Lexington, Kentucky (Bowden and Langanauer 1972). These men were participating in the Narcotic Addict Rehabilitation Act treatment program and represented the first group completing the program. For this group of men, MMPI scores at admission failed to differentiate between the 14 successes and 49 failures. It is interesting to note, however, that the failures had somewhat higher T scores on scales *Pd* and *Sc*.

Unfortunately, this is the only study known to the author that met the criterion for inclusion in this review (that is, a longitudinal study using the MMPI at initiation of the project for predictive purposes), and it is not very encouraging in terms of the usefulness of applying the MMPI as a prognostic indicator of performance in a drug treatment program. However, there are enough methodological limitations to the Bowden and Langenauer (1972) study to preclude being completely persuaded of the uselessness of the MMPI. In addition, their results hinted at more MMPI-defined psychopathology in the failure group.

Prediction of Affiliation with Alcoholics Anonymous

Trice and Roman (1970) published their results of a longitudinal study of postdischarge Alcoholics Anonymous (AA) affiliation that followed 378 white males treated for alcoholism in a state hospital from 1960 to 1963. In contrast to previous studies, the authors emphasized that this was noa a "'skid row' population, with the patients being mainly of middle class origin and having occupational histories typical of middle and lower-middle social strata" (p. 55). Collected on admission from each of the men was information from a battery of 81 variables, 26 of which were sociodemographic and the remaining 55 psychological, including the MMPI. Using stepwise multiple regression, the authors hoped to provide actuarial information on the best predictors of success in a particular posthospital maintenance regimen, namely, affiliation with AA.

Contrary to the authors' expectations, psychological and physical characteristics were found to be the more accurate predictors of successful AA affiliation at 18 months following discharge from the hospital than sociological traits. That is, the 24 significant predictors were composed primarily of psychological variables, with only 7 sociological. Three of these 24 predictors were from the MMPI. Positive associations were found with scale A (anxiety) and with the Homes scale Am and a negative association with scale *D*.

Regarding their unexpected results, Trice and Roman concluded that although social experiences may be necessary for Alcoholics Anonymous affiliation, they do not appear to be sufficient in view of the importance of the psychological predictors. A clear implication of these results is that the determinants of success in sociotherapeutic regimens are not necessarily social but are in large part a function of personality predispositions. The design and evaluation of sociotherapeutic tactics in community psychiatry presently appear to be devoid of such considerations, with emphasis placed almost totally upon sociological factors, particularly social class. The inclusion of psychological factors in the design of such programs appears important in filling apparent blind spots in understanding the dynamics of therapeutic success and failure (Trice and Roman 1970).

Influence of Wives on Treatment Outcome of Alcoholics

On the basis of MMPI profiles, Rae and Forbes (1966) distinguished between two groups of alcoholics' wives, those who were supportive and realistic in their attitudes toward their husbands' illness and those whose attitudes appeared to be the reverse and who were characterized by having a high scale *Pd* as a prominent feature of their personality profiles.

In a related study, Rae (1972) assessed the influence of these 62 women on their alcoholic inpatient husbands' treatment outcome measured two years after hospital admission. The patients and their wives completed the card form of the MMPI during the early part of the patients' hospital stay, and 58 of these patients were successfully reevaluated two years after their discharge.

Rae divided husbands and wives into groups on the basis of their MMPI profiles. The *Pd* group represented those individuals whose scores on the *Pd* scale were among the highest three clinical scales, while the non-*Pd* group represented all others. Although previous studies with married male alcoholics using the MMPI have found that scores on scale *Pd* distinguished with a high degree of confidence between those whose marriages were rated as well and those judged only moderately or poorly adjusted (for example, Barry, Anderson, and Thomason 1967), these studies have primarily been concurrent with the administration of the MMPI and not longitudinal.

In the present study, Rae found that alcoholic patients with elevated *Pd* scores were more likely to have various kinds of social and marital instability, but this was related to prognosis only in the context of marital setting. Failing patients (as defined by those never abstinent, although improved, and no improvement in drinking behavior) had wives whose mean score on the *Pd* scale was significantly higher than that of wives with successful husbands. Failing patients also more often had wives with *Pd* type profiles who had a greater likelihood of "sociosexual disturbance" than non-*Pd* wives. Prognosis therefore appeared to be related to the profile type of the marital partners, with both partners showing elevated *Pd* as the worst prognostic indicator. Eight of the 10 *Pd* husbands with *Pd* wives were treatment failures, whereas the number dropped to only 5 of 12 for non-*Pd* husbands with *Pd* wives, to 3 of 13 when neither spouse was a *Pd* type, to 2 of 14 for non-*Pd* wives and *Pd* husbands.

Rae's study not only provides support for the usefulness of the MMPI as a predictor of social outcomes, in this case defined by treatment outcome of hospitalized alcoholics, but also provides concurrent validity for the *Pd* scale of the MMPI. As noted in several of the studies previously reviewed, apparently it is not the MMPI alone that is a useful indicator of later social outcome but the MMPI in conjunction with environmental information.

Group Psychotherapy Outcomes with Prisoners

Jacobson and Wirt (1969) reported on a study of 446 male volunteer inmates in the Minnesota State Prison who were seen in group therapy over a period of eight years. The follow-up involved an estimate of the inmate's adjustment at home and in the community following his parole or discharge from the prison. The first of the 40 groups was in therapy during 1957 and the last sessions were held in mid-June 1964. At the time of the follow-up (January 1965), some of the men were still in prison and others had been discharged and returned to prison for various reasons. A control group of inmates fitting varying selection criteria and matched with regard to demographic data was used.

Overall, the control groups appeared to show a better adjustment than the experimental groups, and Jacobson and Wirt reported that "the best predictors of success were our behavior-rating measures and the Kuder Preference Record, not the MMPI" (p. 200). However, the authors compared groups making acceptable and unacceptable adjustment in the community on approximately 240 MMPI scales and found that somewhat less than one quarter significantly differentiated postprison adjustment. The unacceptable group was higher on *Pd* and *Ma*, whereas the acceptable group was higher on *Hs* and *Si*. As a group, the inmates making acceptable adjustments in the community were more neurotic and inhibited. On the other hand, the poorly adjusted were deviant, more psychopathic, and more impulsive.

The authors emphasized that their results are totally consistent with previous therapeutic efforts, which have generally been found to be more successful with neurotic rather than character-disordered or psychotic individuals. The results also reinforce the usefulness of the MMPI in suggesting which prison groups might benefit from this type of group psychotherapy.

However, it is unfortunate that the data were not presented in such a way as to indicate which of the MMPI variables had the most predictive power. One would have liked some sense of the strength of a subset of the best MMPI scales and perhaps a discriminant function analysis predicting acceptable and unacceptable adjustment. With so many groups and such a large sample, these authors were in the unique position of being able to do multivariate statistical analyses without worrying about extremely small sample sizes in each group. Finally, it is regrettable that the report leaves numerous questions unanswered regarding the length of time of follow-up for the inmates, the percentage of acceptable and unacceptable groups back in prison, the percentage never released, and so on.

PREDICTION OF ADULT VOCATIONAL ADAPTATION

In addition to extensive information obtained from interviews, tests, and questionnaire data, the MMPI was used to predict vocational adaptation in a longitudinal study of 68 professional and managerial men (Heath 1976). As freshmen entering a highly selective men's college, an original group of 80 students was chosen to participate in the study, with roughly one third representing the most mature, one third the most immature, and a final third randomly selected for comparison purposes (Heath 1965).

When these men were in their early 30s (approximately 12 to 15 years later), they were followed up with 10 to 12 hours of additional tests, questionnaires, and interviews. Eighty-five percent of the original group completed the follow-up, and Heath reported that the 12 nonparticipants did not differ significantly from participants on adolescent measures of aptitude, grade level, personality, interest, or values. Degree of adult vocational adaptation was measured by a 28-item vocational adaptation scale (Heath 1976) completed by each man, his wife, closest friend, and colleague who knew his vocational adjustment most intimately.

Three MMPI scales showed significant correlations between adolescent personality and adult vocational adaptation, and seven significant correlations were found between adult personality and vocational adaptation. Table 7.4 presents correlations between adolescent and adult MMPI scores and adult vocational adaptation.

Heath's findings generally support the notion that maturity and psychological health as defined here predicted vocational adaptation 12 to 15 years later. However, it would be extremely interesting to know which of the diverse ways of measuring adolescent maturity, either Rorschach, Strong Vocational Interest Blank, or MMPI scale scores, were the strongest predictors and how much variance in adult vocational adaptation is explained by these predictors.

Again, the MMPI apparently has been useful in predicting social outcomes longitudinally. However, on inspection of Table 7.4 it is clear that the relationships between adolescent MMPI scores and adult vocational adaptation are relatively weak, albeit significant.

PREDICTION OF OCCUPATIONAL PERFORMANCE

People have often expressed the need for reliable and valid predictors of police performance (see Becker and Felkenes 1968, for a review) and attempts have been made to provide this information. For example, one study by Blum (1964) found significant correlations over seven years between predictors (including the MMPI) and outcome measures, such as supervisor ratings, misconduct, and commendations. Marsh (1962), describing a 10-year predictive study of sheriffs employed in Los Angeles County that utilized the MMPI, found that in addition to biographical information (for example, height, age, and so on),

TABLE 7.4

Correlations Between Adolescent and Adult MMPI Scores and
Adult Vocational Adaptation

MMPI Scale	Description	Correlation Coefficient
	Adolescent Predictors	
Sr	"Impression of enhanced healthiness that one gives to others"	.25
At	Physiological and behavioral signs of manifest anxiety	−.27
Dy	Dependency	−.26
	Adult Correlates	
To	Tolerance	.54
ReR	Social responsibility—revised	.34
Si	Social introversion	−.31
F	Inconsistency in response	−.32
D	Depressive character traits	−.38
Es	Ego strength	.33
Dy	Dependency	−.38

Source: Adapted from D. H. Heath, "Adolescent and Adult Predictors of Vocational Adaptation," *Journal of Vocational Behavior* 9 (1976): 1–19. Copyright (1976) by Academic Press. Reprinted with permission.

MMPI scales *Ma, HY,* and *D* were useful in predicting successful job performance.

More recently, Azen, Snibbe, and Montgomery (1973) reported on their 20-year follow-up of these same men who were originally appointed as deputy sheriffs in Los Angeles County between 1947 and 1950. They used six criterion measures of success and performance for the subjects, which included employment and rank status as of 1970, job type as of 1970 or termination date, average of all supervisors ratings, job-related accidents prior to 1958, and job-related accidents prior to 1970. Using a stepwise discriminant analysis, the authors found the MMPI scale *Ma* to be the best predictor of auto accidents both between 1947 and 1958 and for the entire time period. Scale *D* was also found to be modestly (p ≤ .10) associated with auto accidents during both periods, but was not among the "best" predictors. Other variables were found to predict employment and rank status, job type, and average supervisor ratings.

The findings of Azen and his colleagues directly support the earlier finding of Marsh regarding the strength of MMPI scales as predictors of auto accidents over this 20-year period. Both scales *Ma* and *D* were found to be inversely related to deputy sheriffs' auto accidents over the first and second 10-year periods. These findings are rather striking, and as the authors suggest, may have additional implications for nonpolice driving. Clearly, they support the usefulness of these particular MMPI scales in the longitudinal prediction of one form of social outcomes, auto accidents.

CONCLUSION

Using the MMPI, researchers have identified groups of people with particular predispositions or characteristics, have followed these individuals, and assessed later social outcomes. What is probably the most salient theme throughout these studies is the interactive nature of the MMPI's predictive power. MMPI scale *Sc*, for example, did not alone predict disabling academic outcome (Hathaway, Monachesi, and Sasasin 1970). MMPI profiles with scales *Pd, Sc,* and *Ma* prominent in conjunction with adverse familial circumstances predicted a high rate of delinquency (Briggs, Wirt, and Johnson 1961) and high *Pd* profiles in the wives of alcoholics in conjunction with the patients' characteristics affected the alcoholics' treatment outcome (Rae and Forbes 1966). That one can rely solely on MMPI-identified groups to predict later social outcomes is too simplistic and does not reflect research findings. To be at all effective, longitudinal predictions must represent more complex, multidimensional designs, including social demographic background variables as well as personality characteristics and predispositions as defined by the MMPI. In this respect, it is interesting that Trice and Roman (1970), coming from a decidedly sociopsychological perspective, have recognized the importance of including personality variables in their approach to alcoholism.

Our knowledge of developmental changes also reinforces the necessity of including environmental variables in longitudinal prediction. For example, the MMPI 4/9 profile is frequently found among adolescents, but, by age 21 much of the negative reactions and rebelliousness disappears and this profile is found less frequently in adults (Hathaway and Monachesi 1963).

We still must ask what the relationship is between adolescent or earlier MMPI profiles and later outcomes. What are the moderator variables? Does the environment provide a buffer by certain experiences for certain individuals? Unfortunately, the answers to these questions largely remain speculations.

There are indications that adverse family circumstances, for example, interact with particular predispositions to result in negative social outcomes, but what might be some of the key variables influencing the development of positive social outcomes? In addition, then, to studying individuals who have positive instances of various disorders (for example, schizophrenia), broader knowledge of predisposing causes requires that we study negative instances, those persons who may have the predisposition but do not develop the disorder fully. The study by Widom and Dworkin (1977) was an attempt to do this.

Many persons without obvious symptomatology have abnormal MMPI profiles. To the extent that similarity in MMPI profiles justifies our assuming a certain amount of identity between MMPI identified adolescents and adult persons, diagnosed as having a particular disorder, then research on various psychopathological disorders may be enhanced by studying subclinical populations.

An important advantage of utilizing the MMPI in the longitudinal prediction of later outcome is that there are numerous sets of data banks in existence from which significant research might be generated. These existing sources of archival data would permit researchers to bypass the expensive, tedious, and lengthy first steps involved in administering MMPIs to a large group of people and then waiting a number of years to study outcomes.

For a long time, prisons and mental hospitals routinely administered the MMPI on admission to their inmates, and in most cases such data exist relatively undisturbed in archives. Drug and alcoholism investigations, particularly those conducted pre-1970, frequently involved the administration of the MMPI, although very little follow-up work has been reported with these populations. In addition, there have been several large administrations of the MMPI to normal populations (for example, Gottesman 1965) that would provide opportunities for studying the development of other personality dispositions in addition to the obvious psychopathological ones. For example, what happens to people who as adolescents score high in ego strength (scale Es) when they mature? Are there differences between men and women? How do environmental factors influence the outcome?

Given that we are in an era of limited research money and that the usefulness of the MMPI in longitudinal prediction has been documented in a variety of domains, these archival resources are too important to ignore. Researchers would have to make a relatively small investment, both financial and temporal. At a minimum, defining certain groups and then following them in some way, ranging from checking group records to the more ambitious and expensive mail survey follow-ups to face-to-face interviews, would suffice.

Given the advantages of using the MMPI in longitudinal research, there is unfortunately a major drawback that severely limits its usefulness in this area. In the literature reviewed, administration of the MMPI has been limited to adolescents and older populations and has not been used with children younger than those in the original Hathaway and Monachesi sample (ninth-graders or approximately 15 years old).

A brief summary of the results of a computer search* identifying studies from the present back to 1967 concerned with the longitudinal prediction of adult social outcomes is relevant here. Of the 138 citations, only 4 reported

---

*The author wishes to thank A. Katz, research librarian, William James Hall, Harvard University, for her help with this computer search.

using the MMPI in their abstracts. Fifty-four (39.1 percent) had their first contact with the individuals studied before they were in ninth grade and 34 (24.6 percent of the entire group) were first tested at or before kindergarten. Obviously, researchers are currently attempting to assess developmental changes by studying individuals from as early an age as possible, with many of the studies beginning at birth or within the first few months of life. Thirteen longitudinal studies were initiated during the college years, while 31 (22.5 percent) were with adults (noncollege) predicting to later career choice, occupational performance, marital status, and so on. Only three studies represented longitudinal investigations of gerontological populations.

The purpose of reviewing the findings of this computer search is not to suggest that researchers should develop children's picture forms of the MMPI. Rather, the purpose is to make the reader aware that there is a serious limitation to the usefulness of the MMPI in longitudinal research that may be forgotten in one's general enthusiasm. Although attempts are frequently made to develop personality inventories for children (for example, Hampton 1970), the usefulness of these inventories has been generally limited to specific populations (for example, delinquency), and the age limitations remain a major drawback. However encouraging are the studies reviewed here with respect to the longitudinal prediction of adult social outcome, the scope of future investigations appears to be narrowed because of the restrictions inherent on the earliest age of administration of the MMPI.

One area of research that did not fare as well as some of the others involved longitudinal predictions from earlier normal MMPI test profiles. Golden et al.'s (1962) research was found to be problematic because of the difficulty in defining normal samples. However, this may be partly a function of using a test that was initially developed for psychiatric populations as an aid in psychiatric diagnosis. With the recent surge of interest in normal personality development and the development of nonclinical global personality inventories (for example Jackson's Personaltiy Research Form [Jackson 1967]), longitudinal studies of individuals with normal personality predispositions might be initiated. However, research reviewed here emphasizes the usefulness of the MMPI with a variety of groups applied to a broad range of social outcomes, and researchers should not feel constrained to use the MMPI with traditionally defined clinical populations.

REFERENCES

Azen, S. P., H. M. Snibbe, and H. R. Montgomery. 1973. "A Longitudinal Predictive Study of Successful Performance of Law Enforcement Officers." *Journal of Applied Psychology* 57: 190–92.

Barry, J. H., H. E. Anderson, and O. Bruce Thomason. 1967. "The MMPI Characteristics of Alcoholic Males Who Are Well and Poorly Adjusted in Marriage." *Journal of Clinical Psychology* 23: 355–60.

Becker, H. K., and G. T. Felkenes. 1968. *Law Enforcement: A Selected Bibliography*. Metuchen, N.J.: Scarecrow Press.

Blum, R. H. 1964. *Police Selection*. Springfield, Ill.: Charles C. Thomas.

Bowden, C. L., and B. J. Langenauer. 1972. "Success and Failure in the NARA Addiction Program." *American Journal of Psychiatry* 128: 853–56.

Briggs, P. F., R. D. Wirt, and R. Johnson. 1961. "An Application of Prediction Tables to the Study of Delinquency." *Journal of Consulting Psychology* 25: 46–50.

Butcher, J. N., and W. G. Dahlstrom. 1964. "Comparability of the Taped and Booklet Versions of the MMPI." Unpublished paper. University of North Carolina.

Craddick, R. A. 1962. "Selection of Psychopathic from Non-Psychopathic Prisoners Within a Canadian Prison." *Psychological Reports* 10: 495–99.

Dahlstrom, W. G., G. S. Welsh, and L. E. Dahlstrom. 1975. *An MMPI Handbook*, vol. 2, *Research Applications*. Minneapolis: University of Minnesota Press.

Doctor, R. M., and W. H. Craine. 1971. "Modification of Drug Language Usage of Primary and Neurotic Psychopaths." *Journal of Abnormal Psychology* 77: 174–80.

Dworkin, R. H., and C. S. Widom. 1977. "Undergraduate MMPI Profiles and the Longitudinal Prediction of Adult Social Outcome." *Journal of Consulting and Clinical Psychology* 45: 620–24.

Faschingbauer, T. R. 1972. "A Short Written Form of the Group MMPI." Ph.D. dissertation, University of North Carolina. *Dissertation Abstracts International* 34 (1973): 409B. University Microfilms no. 73-16, 469.

Fine, H. K. 1973. "Studying Schizophrenia Outside the Psychiatric Setting." *Journal of Youth and Adolescence* 2: 291–301.

Garmezy, N. 1974a. "Children at Risk: The Search for the Antecedents of Schizophrenia. I. Conceptual Models and Research Methods." *Schizophrenia Bulletin*, no. 8: 14–90.

——. 1974b. "Children at Risk: The Search for the Antecedents of Schizophrenia. II. Ongoing Reserach Programs, Issues and Intervention." *Schizophrenia Bulletin*, no. 9: 55–125.

Gilberstadt, H., and J. Duker. 1965. *A Handbook for Clinical and Actuarial MMPI Interpretation*. Philadelphia: Saunders.

Gilbert, J. G., and D. N. Lombardi. 1967. "Personality Characteristics of Young Male Narcotic Addicts." *Journal of Consulting Psychology* 31: 536–38.

Golden, J., N. Mandel, B. C. Glueck, and Z. Feder. 1962. "A Summary Description of Fifty 'Normal' White Males." *American Journal of Psychiatry* 119: 48–56.

Gottesman, I. I. 1965. "Personality and Natural Selection." In *Methods and Goals in Human Behavior Genetics*, edited by S. G. Vanderberg, pp. 63–80. New York: Academic Press.

Hampton, A. C. 1969. "Longitudinal Study of Personality of Children Who Became Delinquents Using the Personality Inventory for Children (PIC)." Ph.D. dissertation, University of Minnesota. *Dissertation Abstracts International* 30 (1970): 10B. University Microfilms no. 70-5565, 4792.

Hare, R. D. 1970. *Psychopathy: Theory and Research*. New York: Wiley.

Hathaway, S. R., and E. D. Monachesi. 1963. *Adolescent Personality and Behavior*. Minneapolis: University of Minnesota Press.

——, and S. Salasin. 1970. "A Follow-up Study of MMPI High 8, Schizoid, Children." In *Life History Research in Psychopathology*, edited by M. Roff and D. F. Ricks, pp. 171–88. Minneapolis: University of Minnesota Press.

Heath, D. H. 1976. "Adolescent and Adult Predictors of Vocational Adaptation." *Journal of Vocational Behavior* 9: 1–19.

——. 1965. *Explorations of Maturity*. New York: Appleton-Century-Croft.

Hill, H. E., C. A. Haertzen, and H. Davis. 1962. "An MMPI Factor Analytic Study of Alcoholics, Narcotic Addicts, and Criminals." *Quarterly Journal of Studies on Alcohol* 23: 411–31.

Hill, H. E., C. A. Haertzen, and R. Glaser. 1960. "Personality Characteristics of Narcotics Addicts as Indicated by the MMPI." *Journal of General Psychology* 62: 127–39.

Jackson, D. N. 1967. *Manual for the Personality Research Form*. Gishen, N.Y.: Research Psychologists Press.

Jacobson, J. L., and R. D. Wirt. 1969. "MMPI Profiles Associated with Outcomes of Group Psyhcotherapy with Prisoners." In *MMPI: Research Developments and Clinical Applications*, edited by J. N. Butcher, pp. 191–205. New York: McGraw-Hill.

Jurjevich, R. M. 1966. "Short Interval Test-Retest Stability of MMPI, CPI, Cornell Index, and Symptom Check List." *Journal of General Psychology* 74: 201–06.

Koh, S. D., and R. A. Peterson. 1974. "Perceptual Memory for Numerousness in Nonpsychotic Schizophrenics." *Journal of Abnormal Psychology* 83: 215–26.

Kohn, M. L. 1973. "Social Class and Schizophrenia: A Critical Review and a Reformulation." *Schizophrenia Bulletin* no. 7: 60–69.

Levine, D. G., D. B. Levin, I. H. Sloan, and J. N. Chappel. 1972. "Personality Correlates of Success in a Methadone Maintenance Program." *American Journal of Psychiatry* 129: 440–46.

Mahan, J. L., and G. A. Clum. 1971. "Longitudinal Prediction of Marine Combat Effectiveness." *Journal of Social Psychology* 83: 45–54.

Marks, P. A., W. Seeman, and D. L. Haller. 1974. *The Actuarial Use of the MMPI with Adolescents and Adults*. Baltimore: Williams & Wilkins.

Marsh, S. H. 1962. "Validating the Selection of Deputy Sheriffs." *Public Personnel Review* 23: 41–44.

Mauger, P. A. 1972. "The Test-Retest Reliability of Persons: An Empirical Investigation Utilizing the MMPI and the Personality Research Form." Ph.D. dissertation, University of Minnesota. *Dissertation Abstracts International* 33 (1972): 2816B.

Meehl, P. E. 1962. "Schizotaxia, Schizotypy, Schizophrenia." *American Psychologist* 17: 832–38.

Mosher, L. R., and J. G. Gunderson. 1973. "Special Report: Schizophrenia, 1972." *Schizophrenia Bulletin* 7: 12–52.

Newmark, C. S. 1973. "Brief Retest Stability with Female Psychiatric Cases." Unpublished materials, University of North Carolina.

——. 1971. "MMPI Comparison of the Oral Form Presented by a Live Examiner and the Booklet Form." *Psychological Reports* 29: 797–98.

Peskin, H. 1972. "Multiple Prediction of Adult Psychological Health from Preadolescent and Adolescent Behavior." *Journal of Consulting and Clinical Psychology* 38: 155–60.

Rae, J. B. 1972. "The Influence of the Wives on Treatment Outcome of Alcoholics: A Follow-up Study at Two Years." *British Journal of Psychiatry* 120: 601–13.

——, and A. R. Forbes. 1966. "Clinical and Psychometric Characteristics of Wives of Alcoholics." *British Journal of Psychiatry* 112: 197–200.

Reiss, A. J., Jr. 1961. *Occupations and Social Status.* New York: Free Press.

Rempel, P. B. 1960. "Analysis of MMPI Data for Classification Purposes by Multivariate Statistical Techniques." *Journal of Experimental Education* 28: 219–28.

——. 1958. "The Use of Multivariate Statistical Analysis of MMPI Scores in the Classification of Delinquent and Nondelinquent High School Boys." *Journal of Consulting Psychology* 22: 17–23.

Robins, L. N. 1966. *Deviant Children Grown Up.* Baltimore. Williams & Wilkins.

Rosenthal, R., and L. Jacobson. 1966. "Teachers' Expectancies: Determinants of Pupils' I.Q. Gains." *Psychological Reports* 19: 115–18.

Sines, L. K., R. J. Silver, and R. J. Lucero. 1961. "The Effect of Therapeutic Intervention by Untrained 'Therapists.'" *Journal of Clinical Psychology* 17: 394–96.

Stone, L. A. 1965. "Test-Retest Stability of the MMPI Scales." *Psychological Reports* 16: 619–20.

Sutker, P. B. 1971. "Personality Differences and Sociopathy in Heroin Addicts and Nonaddict Prisoners." *Journal of Abnormal Psychology* 78: 247–51.

——, and A. N. Allain. 1973. "Incarcerated and Street Heroin Addicts: A Personality Comparison." *Psychological Reports* 32: 243–46.

Trice, H. M., and P. M. Roman. 1970. "Sociopsychological Predictors of Affiliation with Alcoholics Anonymous: A Longitudinal Study of 'treatment success.'" *Social Psychiatry* 5: 51–59.

Widom, C. S. 1977. "A Methodology for Studying Non-Institutionalized Psychopaths." *Journal of Consulting and Clinical Psychology* 45: 674–83.

Windle, C. 1955. "Further Studies of Test-Retest Effect on Personality Questionnaires." *Educational and Psychological Measurement* 15: 246–53.

Wirt, R. D., and P. F. Briggs. 1959. "Personality and Environmental Factors in the Development of Delinquency." *Psychological Monographs* 73, no. 485.

8/ THE USE OF THE MMPI IN ASSESSING BEREAVEMENT OUTCOME

Catherine M. Sanders

To date, no one has looked at the effect of personality correlates in connection with bereavement patterns. Bereavement has primarily been examined as a single process with little latitude allowed for individual differences. Few would deny that most persons do exhibit characteristic idiosyncratic responses to stress and, interestingly, we allow this notion to prevail in a wide variety of situations but not, it seems, in the case of mourning. Rather, where bereavement is concerned, societal stereotypes prevail. For example, there is a tendency to think in such terms as "good grief," "bad grief," "pathological grief," even "sick grief." The use of these expressions suggests that bereavement itself is a malady, a psychological impairment, or weakness as it were, from which the bereaved person must be extricated or cured—and the sooner the better. This stereotypic notion of the way people experiencing grief should behave places unrealistic limitations on the need to cope in their own, characteristic ways. This notion also presupposes, quite erroneously, that all persons possess equal quantities of those elements that make up individual personalities—ego strength, optimism, frustration tolerance, emotionality. Based upon developmental theory, this appears to be an unreasonable assumption.

CONCEPTS OF PATHOLOGICAL MOURNING

The concept of pathological grief and its many correlates has done more to exploit the notion of stereotypes than it had done to help explain behavior. Theorists, for the most part, have used anecdotal incidents from which to generalize bereavement processes, thereby promoting subjectively derived opinions on what is pathological and what is normal. The continuum of grief ranges from "too much, too long" to "too little, too short." Thus the parameters for what has been considered acceptable grieving have become narrowly focused on the mean of an imagined population that shifts in degree from one theorist to another. Relatively few writers have taken into consideration premorbid characteristics of the bereaved when explaining their behavior.

Freud was one of the first theorists to attempt an explanation of the psychodynamics of grief (1917). Interestingly, he was also one of the few writers to speak to the predisposition of the bereaved as an explanation for pathological mourning. He felt that in cases where there was an inclination to obessional neurosis, the conflict of ambivalence exacerbated the grief response. In other words, the mourner, by previously desiring the demise of the dearly departed, became in fact responsible for the death itself. In these cases, self-reproaches take on the nature of flagellation, and self-recriminations become constant ruminations. According to Frued, however, it is through this destructive behavior that ambivalent conflict is finally brought under control. Each single incident of ambivalence disparages the object and deprecates it, thereby disengaging the fixation of the libido to it. Through this process, he theorized, pathological mourning could be brought under control. Implicit in Frued's thinking is the element of neuroticism, which shades the personality of the mourner and thereby colors the response to grief.

In his interpersonal theory of personality, Sullivan (1956) proposed that grief was an extremely valuable and protective device. Because we cloak most of our relationships in illusion, when death comes we are in danger of enlarging these illusions into wish-fulfilling fantasies. Grief, according to Sullivan, serves to erase the attachments to the deceased and free the bereaved from being fixed in an illusory life. If, however, the loss threatens our place in the community or our own self-respect, the erasing action of grief will not take place. In this case, grief is continued for the protection of security and is used as a secondary gain. Grief becomes a way of life as well as a barrier to life. To Sullivan, this nonadaptive response is analogous to "morbid grieving" and is considered a serious maladjustment, even a mental disorder. He did not attempt to identify those who were at risk for this condition or to offer suggestions for resolution.

Bowlby (1961), who advocates a bereavement theory based on an ethological perspective, describes pathological mourning as an inability to accept and express anger. When it is repressed and unconscious, anger is thus insulated from change. Consequently, it persists in the bereaved, causing disruption and continued yearning for the lost person. Bowlby feels that the mourning response commonly seen in infancy and early childhood bears many of the same features that are hallmarks of pathological mourning in adults. He also places considerable emphasis upon childhood loss of a parent as a contributing factor in pathological mourning. But ultimately, all grief intensities relate to expressed or unexpressed anger. The expectation that Bowlby has placed on the bereaved person, then, is that there must always be anger. When anger is not overtly manifested, it is nevertheless there but repressed and will cause considerable damage as long as it remains submerged.

Other writers are not in agreement with Bowlby on the issue of anger. According to Parkes (1972), there is great variation among individuals with regard to the expression of anger and hostility. There are some individuals who habitually express aggression, while others tend to be more submissive. Parkes feels that there are no discrete symptoms peculiar to pathological grief. He further adds, however, that extreme expression of guilt, identification symptoms, and delay of onset of grief of more than two weeks' duration could lead to pathological grieving. In spite of this disclaimer, Parkes assumes a nonjudgmental approach in allowing wide latitude in bereavement responses. He alludes to the notion of the "grief-prone person" when he stresses that the major determinants of the magnitude of grief can be expected to be personality factors deriving from the genetic givens and previous life experience of the individual. This is an important step in the recognition that grief itself is neither pathological nor normal, but instead a psychosocial event that, in most cases, produces enormous stress. What inner strength or psychological health an individual possesses will be a mitigating influence on the ability to cope.

STEREOTYPES OF BEREAVEMENT

One who did much to add to our knowledge of the symptoms of grief but also to establish a stereotype of grief as it related to temporal events was Erich Lindemann (1944). While Lindemann is correctly credited with focusing attention on the existence of the syndrome of grief, he nevertheless placed an unrealistic limitation on the duration of the process. He estimated a time frame of between four to six weeks in most cases, rather than several years, which has now emerged as a result of more recent studies. As a consequence, time limitations have been incorrectly placed on the bereaved, often causing withdrawal of social support and subsequent unnecessary anguish.

Stereotypes often occur as a result of poor research methodology. One of the major problems arising from bereavement studies derives from sampling techniques. Because bereavement reactions were initially studied within the confines of psychiatric institutions, the approach to grief was focused on psychopathology. Consequently, the emphasis on pathological bereavement took undue precedence in early investigations. However, even when this imbalance was recognized and rectified, researchers continued to make use of available hospital populations when attempting to define normal grief. For example, in one well-known study (Clayton, Desmarais, and Winokur 1968). subjects were relatives of patients who had died in hospitals. This can hardly be called a representative sample of death because the investigators excluded home deaths, accidents, or deaths that occurred in a place other than the hospital. They nevertheless concluded that the symptoms observed were representative of normal bereavement.

Similar sampling bias was seen in Parkes' study (1971) of 22 London widows. The participants were bereaved women who had been seen by their physicians in the interim since the deaths of their husbands. Subsequently they were referred to Parkes by the attending physicians. Again, a definition of normal bereavement may have been confounded by the excessive stress that these women were experiencing. The fact that the sample was composed of widows needing medical attention during bereavement would preclude their being classified in the category of "unselected widows," as Parkes had labeled them.

A second problem found in bereavement research and that further contributes to the notion of stereotypes is the lack of a standardized assessment instrument. Data have been gathered using a wide variety of approaches, including unstructured interviews, case notes, medical records, and symptom inventories that represent various aspects of the multivariate concept of the grief syndrome, that is, depression, somatization, and anxiety. Much of the information has been anecdotal. Without psychometrically sound methods of identifying key variables, or parceling out confounding or over lapping elements, results only could be applicable to the discrete sample represented. The lack of a suitable assessment instrument has placed severe limitations on any attempts to obtain generalizable data.

Further problems have been noted in bereavement studies because of the lack of control groups. It becomes impossible to determine what bereavement groups have experienced symptoms specific to the situation without a reliable comparison group. While studies such as those done by Lindemann (1944) and Marris (1958) are always important for their heuristic value, nevertheless one can never be sure if the symptomatology reported was conditional upon the event of the bereavement or if those symptoms could be expected to have occurred by chance alone. When no comparison group is used, it is difficult to ascertain the viable parameters of the grief syndrome.

The focus of the present study lies in the concept of typologies of bereavement. Heretofore, typologies have been represented in terms of response to grief—"chronic grief," "delayed grief," or "pathological grief"—rather than as a basic function of the predisposition of characteristics of the bereaved. Granted, the assumption of types of grief based upon the premorbid personality has been difficult to evaluate because questionnaire material utilized in bereavement studies has not attempted to assess basic personality characteristics. The present study is the first attempt at such an endeavor. By using a well-validated personality inventory such as the MMPI and pairing it with a newly developed standardized bereavement inventory, it was felt that the anecdotal problems could be eliminated and the way paved to investigate personality constructs as they related to bereavement intensities. While it is recognized that there are no pre-bereavement personality measures of the bereaved group, it nevertheless appears to be a reasonable assumption that the basic MMPI profile configurations are indicative of premorbid adjustment strategies that have been exacerbated by the stress of bereavement. Thus the same person who manifested disturbed reactions as a trait syndrome displayed the same disturbed reactions in an exaggerated form as a state syndrome. Similarly, those who used denial as a protective defense mechanism displayed those same characteristics to a greater degree when coping with a loss or inordinate stress.

By interviewing bereaved individuals shortly after the death of a significant family member and utilizing the MMPI and a validated bereavement inventory, it was felt that bereavement patterns could be discerned. By retesting these same individuals 18 months to 2 years after the death when grief intensities had subsided, personality baselines could be established that determined the effect of bereavement on various types of coping patterns. The purpose of the study therefore was to dispel the notion of a single stereotypic response to grief by showing that there are indeed many coping strategies utilized by individuals that are fairly predictable and based upon basic lifestyle adjustments.

The present study tests the hypothesis that there will be a positive relationship between participants' responses to the MMPI and the Grief Experience Inventory (GEI) in that respondents who show elevations on the scales representative of disturbed mentation will indicate more overt grief symptoms on the GEI. Those who show relatively normal adjustments on the MMPI will have fewer overt grief symptoms recorded. Those scales indicative of denial on the MMPI such as *K, Hs*, and *Hy* should be related to lowered scores on the GEI. Further, the types of personalities identified by the MMPI will be an indication of outcome of bereavement when respondents are retested with the same instruments 18 months to 2 years following the death. Thus the bereavement patterns expressed would be a function of the individual's coping style rather than a function of the bereavement situation itself.

METHODOLOGY

Subjects

Respondents were identified through the obituary section of a daily newspaper on the basis of having lost a spouse, parent, or child within the past three months. A letter was sent to the appropriate survivor approximately one and a half months following the death explaining the purpose of the study and inviting cooperation. The letters indicated that they would receive a call from the principal investigator within a few days. (The author was the principal investigator and conducted all the interviews except for two cases.) If the potential respondent indicated a willingness to participate, an appointment was arranged, Because it was realized that these individuals had already experienced a stressful event, there was no pressure to participate. The respondents were given the choice of either being visited in their home or at the university, with the majority choosing the former option.

Of the 165 contacted, 102 (62 percent) agreed to participate. This represents a slightly higher acceptance rate than obtained in the Harvard study (Glick, Weiss, and Parkes 1974) but lower than that reported by Vachon and her group (1976). Of the 102 respondents who agreed to be interviewed, 93 completed the MMPI. During the course of the following 18 months, 14 (14 percent) moved, 6 (6 percent) indicated that they did not wish to continue in the study, and 2 (2 percent) could not be scheduled because of continued ill health. This left 80 (78 percent) participants who cooperated in the entire study, but only 73 (78 percent) who had completed the MMPI at both the initial and final interviews. The analysis for this study therefore was based upon 73 respondents (55 female, 17 male) who had completed MMPIs at both interviews.

Respondents were white, had a mean age of 52 years, were predominantly Protestant (84 percent), and of American birth and ethnic background. They were interviewed by the author in their homes on an average of 2.2 months following the death, 5 months after the first interview, and a final interview 18 months after bereavement.

Materials

The MMPI, the GEI (Sanders, Mauger, and Strong 1977), and a demographic questionnaire were used. The GEI is a self-report inventory consisting of 135 true-false items and is designed to assess experiences, feelings, symptoms, and behaviors of individuals during the grief process. The inventory is composed of 11 scales that are seen to tap adequately the multidimensional quality of the bereavement syndrome. These scales include two validity scales, Denial (DEN) and Atypical Responses (AR), and nine clinical scales, Despair (DES), Anger/Hostility (AH), Guilt (GU), Social Isolation (SI), Loss of Emotional Control (LC), Rumination (RU), Depersonalization (DR), Somatization (SOM), and Death Anxiety (DA). In addition there are seven research scales, which, because of the small number of items, are included for exploratory purposes. The first four of these are subscales of the SOM scale—Sleep Disturbance (SSD), Appetite (SAP), Vigor (SVI), and Physical Symptoms (SP). The remaining research scales are Optimism versus Despair (OD), Dependency (DEP), and Social Desirability (SD). Internal consistency and test-retest reliability are reported elsewhere (Sanders 1977).

A factor analysis was conducted on the GEI and MMPI using responses of the newly bereaved group (GEI = 102, MMPI = 93). The high loadings of the GEI scales of Despair (.83), Somatization (.84), and Loss of Emotional Control (.75) agree with high loadings of F (.61), D (.70), Pt (.76), and Welsh's A (.75), along with negative loadings on K (-.54) and Barron's Ego Strength scale (-.62). This gives strong support to the relationship between the two inventories in that scales reflecting acute psychological disturbance have high positive loadings, while scales indicating emotional control have high negative loadings.

Controls

Controls received a separate form that incorporated demographic data and 93 true-false statements from the GEI, with the items referring to a specific death event removed. Sixty-four of the control subjects (44 female, 20 male) were willing to complete the MMPI. The criterion for control selection required that subjects had not experienced a bereavement during the past five years. Every attempt was made to include a highly heterogeneous sample. Controls were obtained from a variety of sources, including the retired teachers association, churches, university personnel, and a mobile home retirement community. As was the case of the bereaved participants, the controls were predominantly Protestant (83 percent) and of American birth and ethnic background. The average age, however, was somewhat younger (44 years). This discrepancy arose primarily from the difficulty in identifying older individuals who had not experienced a bereavement within the past five years. As one grows older, time periods between grief experiences become shorter. There were more housewives and retired persons in the bereaved group (bereaved = 56 percent, controls = 27 percent) and consequently the average income was less for the bereaved group. Despite these discrepancies, the range of ages was matched and it was felt that the controls represented an adequate comparison group.

Controls indicated significant differences from bereaved participants when t-tests were performed on the scales of the GEI. Of the 12 scales utilized (6 scales were deleted due to the 35 items pertaining to a specific death), only Denial ($t = 1.68$, $p < .095$) and SAP (research scale) ($t = 1.11$, $p < .267$) were not significant at the .05 level. These data add to the validity of the GEI as a unique instrument with which to assess bereavement reactions.

Procedure

Each participant was oriented to the purpose of the study. The principal investigator then administered the GEI, following which the participants were asked to complete the demographic questionnaire. Because the initial interview required an investment of much time and emotional effort on the part of the respondent, the MMPI was left with the participant with a self-addressed mailing envelope to be returned as soon as it was completed. It is understood that some control is forfeited by this procedure, but one must remember that individuals experiencing early bereavement do not have the stamina or patience to be involved in several hours of interview and questionnaires. It was the most efficient possible compromise.

In the final interview, which was conducted 18 months to 2 years following the initial interview, both the MMPI and GEI were readministered. In this case, the MMPI was completed during the course of the interview.

RESULTS AND DISCUSSION

In order to determine types of grief, MMPI profiles were blindly sorted by a skilled MMPI interpreter, using a combination of the Gilberstadt-Duker and

Marks-Seeman coding procedures (Dahlstrom, Welsh, and Dahlstrom 1972). Based upon profile configurations, four categories were identified: a disturbed reaction with psychotic overlay and low ego strength, a depressive-anxiety reaction with depletion of ego strength, denial with somatization, and normal reactions with little evidence of anxiety or depression and showing good ego strength. Table 8.1 shows distribution of categories by original sort of MMPI profile.

TABLE 8.1

Distribution of Categories by Original Sort of MMPI Profiles of Bereaved Sample

Type of Personality	Disturbed (n = 6)	Depressive (n = 14)	Denial (n = 14)	Normal (n = 38)
Spouse M	0	5	2	4
F	2	4	7	13
Parent M	0	0	1	3
F	4	1	1	13
Child M	0	2	3	0
F	0	2	0	5
Total	6	14	14	38

Source: Compiled by the author.

A composite profile for each category was then plotted using the mean of that group. While it is difficult to generate precisely modal MMPI profiles based on numerous individual responses, it still appears to be the most efficient method for examining basic differences among groups.

A similar analysis was made on profiles of the control group (Table 8.2 shows distribution of sample). The MMPI profiles again tended to group into four categories: disturbed, slight depression, denial, and normal. When composite profiles were plotted, there was remarkable similarity to the four bereavement composite plots, with the exception that the bereaved denial and disturbed groups showed higher but insignificant elevations on scales *D, Hs,* and *Hy.* The disturbed bereaved mean profile also showed higher but insignificant elevations on scales *Pa* and *Pt* than did the control group. Both the control and bereaved disturbed mean profiles, however, showed the same basic configuration: *F* greater than *K* and positive slope, both of which, in general, are indicative of disturbed mentation. Thus the use of a control group was important in showing that individuals who survive the death of a family member generate significant responses on the GEI, although their MMPI responses do not clearly differentiate

TABLE 8.2

Distribution of Categories by Original Sort of MMPI Profiles of Control Group

Type of Personality	Disturbed	Depressive	Denial	Normal
Controls M	3	2	4	11
F	2	3	5	34
Total	5	5	9	45
Total				64

Source: Compiled by the author.

the bereaved group from the controls. The GEI clearly taps a state component of bereavement that is separate and independent of the MMPI trait measurements.

Disturbed Group Initial Interview

The disturbed group obtained a profile that resembled that of a schizoid personality with depressive reactions. As shown in Figure 8.1 major elevations occur on scales *Sc, Pt, Pd*, and *D*, with *F* approaching 70. Both *K* and Ego Strength are low.

Halbower (1955) selected this code type as one of the four MMPI groups that he used as criterion cases in his actuarial comparison. His decision to use this code type was based, in part, upon the frequency with which it was seen in psychiatric practice. Halbower described these people as being worriers, nervous, introspective, ruminative, and overideational. Their personality difficulties appeared to be of a chronic nature and they were plagued with feelings of inadequacy, inferiority, and insecurity. They lacked rewarding socialization experiences in their past and seemed to have difficulty forming satisfactory interpersonal relationships. They had few defenses that could serve to provide relief or freedom from distress and rarely did they profit from their own experiences.

The disturbed group in the present sample consisted of two widows and four women who had lost a parent. The two widows had cared for their husbands through a long terminal illness but neither had acknowledged the possibility of impending death. When it came, they were shocked and totally unprepared. This is not necessarily unusual in the death of someone close, but in these two cases it was the degree of feelings of unreality that differentiated them from other bereaved persons. Of the four women whose parent had died, three admitted to having serious chronic problems with their spouses. In one case, it

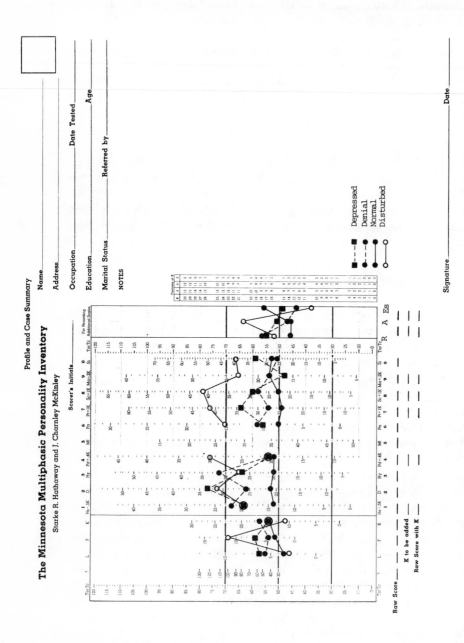

FIGURE 8.1: MMPI composite profiles for the four typologies when tested initially. MMPI Profile sheet copyrighted 1948 by the Psychological Corporation. Reproduced by permission granted in the test catalog.

was the father who had been the only stabilizing factor in her life. When he died, even with two children of her own, she felt that there was little of significance left in her life. Like Halbower's group, these women felt extremely inadequate, anxious, and alienated. Before the deaths occurred, their unhappy lifestyles kept them in a constant state of stress. They functioned on the periphery of good mental health and when faced with the added emotional burden of grief, these women had few resources on which to draw.

When a composite profile for the GEI was plotted for this group, there were comparable high levels of grief intensity evidenced (see Figure 8.2). The highest peaks are seen on the Despair (OD) and Depersonalization (DR) scales, indicating acute feelings of helplessness, as well as a sense of unreality. Second-ary peaks on Anger (AH), Guilt (GU), and Rumination (RU) all point to the degree of inner turmoil experienced. Loss of emotional control was evidenced by the elevation on that scale (LC). These individuals were in deep despair, indicat-ing a high level of death anxiety and a large number of physical complaints. When this personality type suffers a severe loss, the expression is one of deep desolation.

Depressed Group Initial Interview

The second type that was identified by the MMPI profile sort was that of a highly depressed, anxious, isolated individual. The mean MMPI profile is pre-sented in Figure 8.1 showing elevations occurring on scales *D, Pt, Hy,* and *Hs.* The presenting difficulties of the individuals making up this group approximate those shown in a group identified by Hathaway and Meehl (1951). They found numerous complaints of depression with tenseness and nervousness along with anxiety, insomnia, and inordinate sensitiveness. Guthrie (1949) found that when scale *D* was the only one above 70 and scale *Ma* was the low point of the pro-file (see Figure 8.1), depression tended to be mild, although there were indica-tions of fatigue and loss of energy. This same unipolar effect has been noted by Donnelly and Murphy (1976) when, in examining differences between bipolar (both *D* and *Ma* elevated) and unipolar subjects, they found significant differ-ences in affective symptomatology. They noted that the unipolar subjects may have preexisting or persistent obsessive, hysterical, or oral-dependent features. In a replication, Donnelly et al. (1976) suggested a relation between chronically anxious subjects and subjects susceptible to recurrent unipolar depression dis-orders. In the present study bereaved participants making up this group almost invariably had a history of multiple family losses. One had been orphaned at age three by the deaths of both parents. That early losses contribute to chronic anxiety and depression would be supported by bereavement literature (Klein 1940; Bowlby 1961; Freud 1965; Parkes 1972; Furman 1974).

Those individuals showing high grief reactions were distributed across the three categories of bereavement as well as across sex. These participants reacted with higher depression, anxiety, somatization, and alienation. This is much the

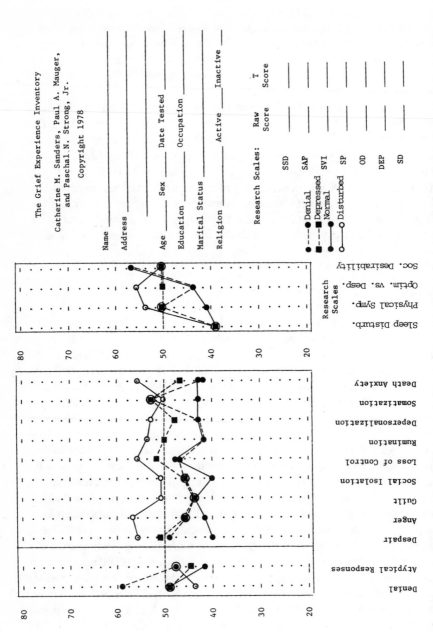

FIGURE 8.2: GEI composite profiles for the four typologies when tested initially. Copyright 1978. Catherine M. Sanders, Paul A. Mauger, and Paschal N. Strong, Jr.

same picture that Schmale and Iker (1971) presented in the predisposed character traits of predicted cancer patients. These investigators reported that patients' reactions to hopelessness, within six months prior to diagnosis of their cancer, provided evidence of psychological character traits that could be associated with a high predisposition for hopelessness. (The MMPI also was utilized in this study showing elevations on scales *D* and *Pt* that paralleled those obtained from the depressed typology in Figure 8.1.) Engel (1967) has referred to this syndrome as the "giving up-given up" complex in which the individual becomes more vulnerable to the pathogenic influences of his or her external environment while at the same time is predisposed to internal derangements. Engel feels that disease is more apt to appear at such times of disruption and increased vulnerability.

Looking at the GEI composite of the depressed group in Figure 8.2, it appears that these individuals respond in quite characteristic patterns. Loss of emotional control and despair are evident. However, the highest peak occurs on the Somatization scale. Their grief finds expression in lack of sleep, numerous physical complaints, fatigue, and anorexia. There are feelings of isolation, of being alone in their grief, that result from the extreme sensitiveness felt by these grieving persons. Yet, intensities of grief are not as strong as those evidenced by the disturbed group and, while there is pervasive sadness, it appears to be situational or temporary.

Denial Group Initial Interview

The third typology indicated, denial, identified individuals who needed to employ strong defense mechanisms in order to survive crises. This MMPI profile was characterized by a 31 code type (see Figure 8.1). These people use physical symptoms as a means of solving difficult conflicts or avoiding responsibilities. This characteristic tends to be a way of life and may be so ingrained that the person is not aware that such a defense mechanism is being utilized. According to Guthrie (1949), symptoms of the 31 code type range from headaches, backaches, pain in the chest, and abdominal discomfort to extreme fatigue that does not seem to match physical exertion. He observed, however, that conversion hysteria was not common, and that 31 individuals were rarely incapacitated by their symptoms. Carson (1969) noted that people showing a high scale *Hy* tend to deny that things are not going well. Duckworth and Duckworth (1975) noted that individuals with T scores above 70 on scale *Hy* are reluctant to see unpleasantness and "bad things," especially when this is the peak scale of the profile. In the present sample, widows were predominant in the denial typology, although there were three widowers included.

Examining the GEI composite in Figure 8.2, it can be seen that scales measuring denial and social desirability are the outstanding peaks. Both of these scales measure the individual's reluctance to admit to common human foibles.

In keeping with the admitted physical symptoms on the MMPI, the GEI scales of Somatization (SOM) and Physical Symptoms (SP) are the next two highest peaks on the profile. Because Death Anxiety and Sleep Disturbance (SSD) are the two lowest elevations, it is suggested that these are the areas of greatest denial. However, all other bereavement scales also are low. These people were adamant in their desire to maintain a "stiff upper lip." Many managed to survive their grief by a flight into activity reflected in personal work, community activity, or church interaction. The expression "determined optimists" appears to fit this typology best. This is not to say that there was no sadness manifested by these individuals, but rather there was an intensification of normal activity that prevailed in spite of their loss. Because denial is a pejorative term in American vocabulary, caution must be used in applying this label. Instead, for these persons denial was an apparently adaptive defense that served them well in crises. It was not the denial of the event of death, but rather a denial of their overt emotions surrounding the bereavement.

Normal Group Initial Interview

The normal group was composed of those individuals whose MMPI profiles were so categorized. They, for the most part, were seen as having medium to high ego strength, but low depression, somatization, and anxiety. Some tended toward acting out and some toward denial, but basically all showed normal profile configurations. These persons showed good emotional control, with relatively little preoccupation with the deceased or feelings of unreality.

The GEI composite indicates that loss of emotional control is evident, but also the need to maintain a high degree of socially desirable behavior. These were not unresponsive individuals devoid of feeling, for they felt their loss and expressed sadness, many weeping openly at times during the interview. Rather, these were individuals who recognized that losses occur during a lifetime and were attempting to deal with this loss straightforwardly and openly. The essence of their personalities was maintained in a crisis situation. Hence they were able in responding to questionnaires to separate a clearly temporary event from responses that typify their basic personality structure.

Thus the sorting of MMPI profiles first and then the matching the MMPI profile to the corresponding GEI profile provided a method to compare bereavement reactions to personality modes. Therefore it appeared safe to conclude tentatively that on the basis of the initial interview four distinct typologies of bereavement patterns emerged.

We turn now to examine retest responses when participants were seen 18 months to 2 years following the death.

Disturbed Group Follow-up

For the disturbed group, the mean retest MMPI profile configuration was closely related to their mean profile seen at initial testing (see Figure 8.3). Although there was a slight reduction on all scales, these shifts were not statistically significant. Only scale *D* remained above a T score of 70.

Figure 8.4 shows that the mean GEI profile remained that of an acutely bereaved person. Anger can be seen as the highest scale (there was no change in this elevation), with elevations also seen on Despair (OD), Loss of Control (LC), and Rumination (RU). The Death Anxiety (DA) scale is still high, which suggests that what appears to be deep concern for the deceased may in some cases become a personal death fear. This is not necessarily a selfish reaction. When the death of a loved one engenders feelings in the survivors that part of themselves has also died, then it can be concluded that egocentric pain is experienced. It is unusual, however, for a high death anxiety to persist for such a period and appears to be specific to the disturbed group.

One common denominator in this group was obviously their ongoing difficulty with living. When asked if life continued to be a struggle, they all agreed that it was even more of a struggle than usual. Asked if they felt that they had been taking things hard, the reply was again, "More than usual," and in some cases, "Much more than usual." In the case of one 49-year-old widow, it was necessary for her to receive psychological help at a day care mental health unit for nearly a year. This woman had nursed her husband through a long bout with cancer but was totally unprepared when death came. She said, "I felt extreme disbelief and horror that it [death] could happen even though I should have been prepared because of his long illness."

Now, 18 months later, she is still angry with her in-laws for their lack of concern for her. She feels she received far less help than she wanted or needed. Everything is perceived in terms of deprivation—loss of self-confidence, loss of religious faith, loss of financial security (although she admitted that finances had not been a problem), loss of support of any kind—and she is anxious and fearful about the future. Her MMPI profile shifted from an 8247"0' to 24780". Grief intensities have all increased. She is more depressed, anxious, angry, despairing, guilty, and isolated than she was at initial interview. This woman exhausts all who seek to help her, but without help prognosis is poor.

As a group, these disturbed individuals were grieving almost as deeply as they had indicated at the initial interview. Caregivers and families should become sensitive to the needs of individuals represented by this typology and provide even more service and support than would ordinarily be expected.

Depressed Group Follow-up

The depressed group showed the same basic MMPI configuration on retest as they had initially. As seen in Figure 8.3, there were increased elevations on

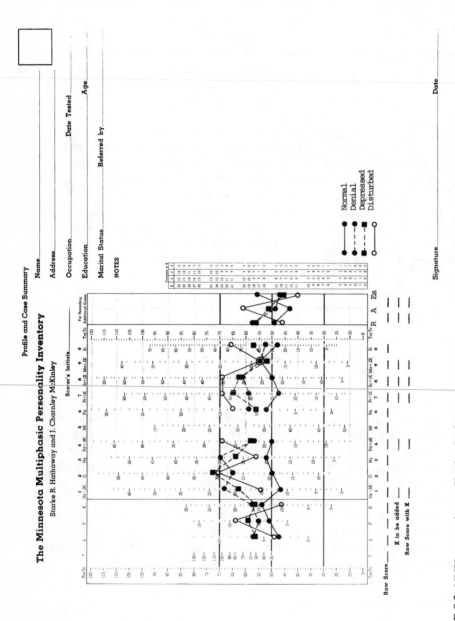

FIGURE 8.3: MMPI composite profiles for the four typologies when tested 18 months following bereavement. MMPI Profile sheet copyrighted 1948 by the Psychological Corporation. Reproduced by permission granted in the test catalog.

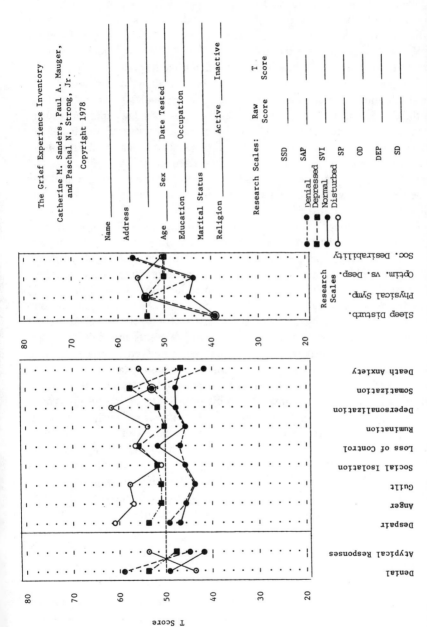

FIGURE 8.4: GEI composite profiles for the four typologies when tested 18 months following bereavement. Copyright 1978. Catherine M. Sanders, Paul A. Mauger, and Paschal N. Strong, Jr.

Pd, Pa, Sc, and *Ma,* as well as on all three validity scales, but none reached significance. In contrast, a nonsignificant decline occurred on scale *D.*

When the composite retest for the GEI was examined (see Figure 8.4), the grief intensities for this group decreased moderately, with changes seen on somatization (test $\overline{X}$ = 9.0, retest $\overline{X}$ = 6.5, t = 1.89, p < .07) and loss of control (test $\overline{X}$ = 6.29, retest $\overline{X}$ = 5.07, t = 1.96, p < .06). These differences are indicators that this group is still experiencing feelings of acute grief.

Too, almost without exception, these individuals were surrounded with unusual situations not conducive to healing. For example, a divorced mother, after the difficult and painful death of her daughter from leukemia and struggling to support three sons, had to write her doctoral dissertation or risk losing her position and financial security. In another case a widow experienced painful eye surgery two weeks following her husband's sudden death. And a professional dancer, whose wife had been his dance partner for many years, found her drowned in their swimming pool that he had recently purchased for her. The death occurred on her birthday.

"Working through" for most of these individuals was still in progress at 18 months. Because anxiety exists for these individuals as a trait phenomenon, when inordinate stress occurs they are subject to intense emotionality. This is further confounded by the multitude of previous losses experienced. It is suggested that these reactions can best be explained in terms of Seligman's (1975) learned helplessness model of depression. According to Seligman, a major component of reactive-affective disorder is seen as the degree one perceives himself or herself to be exerting control over significant life events and their outcomes. The model predicts a positive relationship between perceived control and degree of depression. Seligman viewed this as a result of developmental learning history. In other words, learned helplessness may be acquired if the individual has experienced a learning history characterized by an inability to control life events. Thus one may develop a relatively consistent, traitlike sense of helplessness that can be seen to generalize to any number of situations. This depressed group, with the many losses and situational crises experienced, can readily be seen as fitting Seligman's model. There is no question that when death occurs, the survivors are left with feelings of loss control over their universe and many times over their own emotions. While many of these participants indicated that they were feeling somewhat better than they had following the death, there still was much reparation to be done.

Denial Group Follow-up

The denial group is of particular interest, especially in view of the popular notion that if people do not talk about their grief or ventilate their emotions, there is real danger of subsequent breakdown. This does not appear to be the case in the present study. Follow-up at 18 months showed the mean MMPI profile (Figure 8.3), as well as the GEI profile (Figure 8.4), to be extremely similar to the initial profiles. There was no change in interpersonal responding and little change from the low level of grief evidenced at the first interview. What seems to be the common thread or denominator in this group was their determination to make the best of the situation. This was a resolute group of people. Caldwell (1974) has suggested that people of this MMPI code type suffer a profound fear of emotional pain. Because they evidence a high incidence of loss of love in childhood, to be rejected by or to lose a loved one is extremely painful. Another similarity within this group was the number of physical problems that seemed to occupy much of their thoughts and energies while not causing a great deal of concern. One widow, when asked if she were experiencing other crises at the time of death, listed a disability from a torn muscle, osteoarthritis, osteoporosis, and degeneration in spine, hips, and neck. While she needed a walker for ambulation, she still minimized her problems as well as her own grief. This "belle indifference" concerning physical symptoms was pervasive within the group.

As Dahlstrom, Welsh, and Dahlstrom (1972) have emphasized, the focus of attention for these individuals is on specific medical symptoms rather than on their life situation or emotional difficulties, but their response to treatment is indifferent. However, the coping mechanism appears to be facilitative. Eighteen months following the deaths they appeared to be as determined to survive their bereavement as they had at first interview. Parkes (Parkes and Brown 1972) used the term "compulsive self-reliance" to describe this quality. Whatever the label, these individuals are managing to survive their bereavement by using a characteristic coping device.

Normal Group Follow-up

The fourth group, the normals, as expected, indicated the best adjustment to bereavement of all the groups. The mean MMPI Profile configuration seen in Figure 8.3 changed only slightly and none of the scale differences was significant. The profile remains consistent for this typology. The most dramatic changes, however, occurred on the mean GEI profile (see Figure 8.4). There were consistent reductions of grief intensities on all scales. Table 8.3 describes the mean, standard deviation, and t-values for scales where scores reached significance.

It must be stressed that the bereavement situation was not the controlling variable in better outcome for this group. There were deaths involving children, spouses, and parents in all three categories. These people were deeply wounded by their losses. In the case of one widow, two sons had died prior to her husband, resulting in a death every year for three years. At the final follow-up, the interviewer learned of yet a third son who had died two months previously. Nevertheless, this woman was continuing to care for her grandchildren and find meaning in her life.

Among demographic characteristics, this group was better educated than the other groups (56 percent had some college) and earned higher incomes (49

TABLE 8.3

t-Tests on Scales of the GEI for Test-Retest of the Normal Bereaved Group

Scale Name	Means		Standard Deviation			Two-tailed
	Test	Restest	Test	Retest	t-Value	Probability
Despair	6.45	3.18	4.05	2.43	4.26	.000
Anger	3.32	2.39	2.41	1.60	1.96	.050
Somatization	4.63	2.97	3.04	2.11	2.76	.008
Sleep disturbance	0.97	0.50	0.86	0.60	2.73	.008
Physical symptoms	1.95	1.18	1.59	1.45	2.18	.032
Optimism versus despair	1.37	0.74	1.44	0.76	2.39	.02

Source: Compiled by the author.

percent had annual incomes over $10,000). These data support Parkes' (1975) finding that higher socioeconomic level is facilitative of good outcome in bereavement. Yet, in this case, these elements are seen only as contributing factors. Good outcome for this group was more a function of stable personalities, good ego strength, and personal resiliency.

SUMMARY

That four typologies of bereavement have emerged from this study is encouraging to the extent that the stereotype of grief can be examined. Elliot discussed this as early as 1930 when he said:

> People's stereotype responses to death are based in great part upon archaic patterns and are found to be very different from, and often conflict with their inner feelings. It seems that objective studies in the field of these conflicts would be a valuable contribution to knowledge. (p. 546)

The bereaved have not been given the latitude necessary to encompass the range of adaptive behavior appropriate to individual personality characteristics. There has been a tendency to call pathological those responses that appear inordinant, as well as a tendency in the other direction to accuse the bereaved of not caring enough when responses are limited or brief. On the basis of the identification of these premorbid characteristics, intervention of caregivers and family associates becomes a viable reality. But even more, broader latitude should now be allowed the grieving individual relevant to emotional responses. This study therefore suggests that there is no one intervention strategy that meets the needs of all bereaved individuals. It may well be that individuals of the normal, grief-contained group will not need the services of a community intervention group. Intervention with individuals of denial typology should focus on encouraging those behaviors that strengthen the basic denial mechanism and should avoid attempts to have the individuals abreact their grief. The disturbed and depressed types of individuals, on the other hand, may be most helped by those processes that encourage abreaction such that despair, anxiety, guilt, and hostility are discharged in a highly supportive situation.

The significance of the present study lies in the use of a sound methodological approach to investigate a problem area that heretofore has been dealt with either anecdotally or with inadequate research techniques. Stereotypes have prevailed in the absence of such research. By utilizing the MMPI along with a reliable questionnaire to ferret out bereavement symptoms, four distinct typologies of bereavement patterns have emerged: a disturbed group, a depressed, high grief group, a denial group, and a normal, grief-contained group. Each of these groups has been shown to have a high interrelationship with the basic underlying personality characteristics of the individuals involved. Further, it is suggested that these different responses to bereavement may be adaptive for that particular individual. These typologies offer a sound basis on which to dispute the stereotypic notion that it is bereavement, per se, that causes complications rather than the psychodynamics of the personality itself. Patterns of bereavement do exist, and it is the contention of the author that those patterns represent adaptive and facilitative differences as represented by the bereaved's basic lifestyle adjustments.

REFERENCES

Bowlby, J. 1961. "Process of Mourning." *International Journal of Psychoanalysis* 42: 317–40.

Caldwell, A. 1974. "Characteristics of MMPI Pattern Types." Paper presented at the Ninth Annual Symposium on the MMPI, Los Angeles.

Carson, R. C. 1969. "Interpretative Manual to the MMPI." In *MMPI: Research Developments and Clinical Applications*, edited by J. N. Butcher, pp. 279–96. New York: McGraw-Hill.

Clayton, P., L. Desmarais, and G. Winokur. 1968. "A Study of Normal Bereavement." *American Journal of Psychiatry* 125: 168–78.

Dahlstrom, W. G., G. S. Welsh, and L. E. Dahlstrom. 1972. "An MMPI Handbook," , vol. 1, rev. ed. Minneapolis: University of Minnesota Press.

Donnelly, E. F., and D. L. Murphy. 1976. "Primary Affective Disorders: MMPI Differences Between Unipolar and Bipolar Depressed Subjects." *Journal of Clinical Psychology* 32: 610–12.

——, Waldman, and Reynolds. 1976.

Duckworth, J., and E. Duckworth. 1975. *Interpretation Manual for Counselors and Clinicians.* Muncie, Ind.: Accelerated Development.

Elliot, T. D. 1930. "The Adjusted Behavior of Bereaved Families: A New Field of Research." *Social Forces* 9: 543–49.

Engel, G. L. 1967. "A Psychological Setting of Somatic Disease: The 'Giving Up-Given Up' Complex." *Proceedings of the Royal Society of Medicine* 60: 553–55.

Freud, A. 1965. *Normality and Pathology in Childhood.* New York: International Universities Press.

——. 1917. "Mourning and Melancholia," In *A General Selection from the Works of Sigmund Freud.* New York: Doubleday/Anchor Books.

Furman, E. 1974. *A Child's Parent Dies: Studies in Childhood Bereavement.* New Haven, Conn.: Yale University Press.

Glick, I., R. S. Weiss, and C. M. Parkes. *The First Year of Bereavement.* New York: Wiley.

Guthrie, G. M. 1949. "A Study of the Personality Characteristics Associated with the Disorders Encountered by an Internist." Ph.D. dissertation, University of Minnesota.

Halbower, C. C. 1955. "A Comparison of Actuarial Versus Clinical Prediction to Classes Discriminated by MMPI." Ph.D. dissertation, University of Minnesota. *Dissertation Abstracts International* 15 (1955): 1115. University Microfilms no. 55–149.

Hathaway, S. R., and P. E. Meehl. *An Atlas for the Clinical Use of the MMPI.* Minneapolis: The University of Minnesota Press, 1951.

Klein, M. 1940. "Mourning and Its Relationship to Manic Depressive States." *International Journal of Psychoanalysis* 21: 125–53.

Lindemann, E. 1944. "Symptomatology and Management of Acute Grief." *American Journal of Psychiatry* 101: 141–48.

Marris, P. 1958. *Widows and Their Families.* London: Routledge and Kegan Paul.

Parkes, C. M. 1972. *Bereavement: Studies of Grief in Adult Life*. New York: International Universities Press.

———. 1971. "The First Year of Bereavement: A Longitudinal Study of the Reaction of London Widows to the Death of Their Husbands." *Psychiatry* 33: 449-61.

———, and R. J. Brown. 1972. "Health After Bereavement: A Controlled Study of Young Boston Widows and Widowers." *Psychosomatic Medicine* 34: 449-61.

Sanders, C. M. 1977. "Typologies and Symptoms of Adult Bereavement." Ph.D. dissertation, University of South Florida. *Dissertation Abstracts International*, 38B. University Microfilms no. 3372-B.

———, P. A. Mauger, and P. N. Strong, Jr. 1977. "A Manual for the Grief Experient Inventory." Unpublished document, University of South Florida, Tampa.

Schmale, A. J., Jr., and H. Iker. 1971. "Hoplessness as a Predictor of Cervical Cancer." *Social Science and Medicine* 5: 95-100.

Seligman, M. E. P. 1975. *Helplessness*. San Francisco: Freeman.

Sullivan, H. S. 1956. *Clinical Studies in Psychiatry*. New York: Norton.

Vochon, M. L. S., A. Formo, K. Freedman, W. A. L. Lyall, J. Rogers, and S. J. J. Freeman. 1976. "Stress Reactions to Bereavement." *Essence* 1: 22-33.

9/ INTERPRETIVE ACCURACY AND EMPIRICAL VALIDITY OF ABBREVIATED FORMS OF THE MMPI WITH HOSPITALIZED ADOLESCENTS

Charles S. Newmark
John R. Thibodeau

The popularity of the MMPI has surpassed the expectations of its developers. Literally thousands of scholarly papers are published each year based in part or entirely on the MMPI. Between 1963 and 1972 a study on the MMPI was published nearly every day (Buros 1974). Consequently, an archive of empirical data now eixsts exceeding that for any other psychometric instrument. Nearly 500 scales provide for a variety of screening, assessment, selection, and prediction applications, while clinical code types provide an actuarial alternative to the traditional Kraepelinian classifications and computerized interpretations provide useful information to a variety of medical, counseling, educational, and industrial professionals.

However, there are numerous clinical situations where the extreme length of the MMPI prohibits its use. Nowhere is this more evident than with adolescents on a psychiatric inpatient ward. The approximately two-hour testing session tends to provoke and irritate restless adolescents, who then express their anger and defiance by seizing on the legitimate option of omitting items or failing to complete the test (Dahlstrom, Welsh, and Dahlstrom 1972). This submarginal compliance with routine procedures tends to vitiate the results. Occasionally, staff insistence will lead to a completed MMPI but only after the adolescent has grudgingly completed a few items at a time over a period of several days. Often, important changes in the patient's mood or behavior are noted to occur during this test-taking period.

In addition, the great expenditure of staff time needed to obtain such a profile may lead the assessor to abandon efforts to obtain an MMPI profile on

Appreciation is extended to R. Boren, K. Prillaman, D. Ziff, and M. Simpson, who assisted with these investigations.

adolescent patients. For those who have come to appreciate the usefulness of the MMPI in suggesting potentially fruitful areas for further interview inquiry, in correcting diagnostic biases, and in providing a single, briefly grasped, easily communicated, and stored record of several personality variables, such a situation is regrettable (Faschingbauer and Newmark 1978).

Despite the obvious need for an abbreviated form of the MMPI, only a few investigators, until recently, had undertaken such a task. Several investigators attempted to eliminate unsystematically items from the MMPI (Briggs and Tellegen 1967; Ferguson 1946; Grant 1946; Holzberg and Alessi 1949; Jorgenson 1958; MacDonald 1952a, 1952b; Olson 1954). The lack of success apparently was due to the large number of items retained (average of approximately 300 items for above studies), the aribtrary and unsystematic methods used to eliminate items (for example, Grant 1946; Jorgenson 1958), the use of pseudo-experimental procedures and concepts such as "clinical significance" (Holzberg and Alessi 1949), a failure to assess adequately reliability and validity, which often were unsatisfactory or unreported, low correlations with the standard MMPI, a lack of replication across samples, inproper assessment of contextual effects, and a failure to present the data in a form that could be readily compared to the extensive MMPI literature (Hugo 1971). In summary, attempts to abbreviate the MMPI by unsystematically eliminating items proved futile due to difficulties in rationale, design, and execution. The number of items were not reduced substantially, yet scale reliability and validity were reduced to a degree where confidence in the MMPI was eroded (Faschingbauer and Newmark 1978).

Impetus to developing an abbreviated form was rejuvenated by Kincannon (1968). Using cluster analysis and then proportionately selecting those items from each cluster with the greatest scale overlap, the test was reduced to 71 items and called the Mini-Mult. Scales *Mf* and *Si* were omitted completely. However, numerous investigations with a variety of normal and psychiatric samples as summarized by Faschingbauer and Newmark (1978) accent the marked limitations of this instrument.

In an attempt to remedy some of the difficulties inherent in the Mini-Mult, Dean (1972) revised the item pool for those scales, namely, *L, F,* and *Ma,* which consistently yielded the lowest correlations with standard MMPI scales. To derive these new scales, the standard MMPI was administered to a sample of 125 patients from a normal medical population. With Comrey's (1958a, 1958b) factor analysis results as a basis, varying combinations of items were utilized until revised abbreviated forms of *L, F,* and *Ma* correlated at least .80 with their comparable long forms. Regression equations were derived to convert these abbreviated scale scores into estimated standard form equivalents. This revision, which now contains 86 items, has been entitled Midi-Mult.

Hugo's (1971) 173-item abbreviated form was developed by administering the standard MMPI to 176 college subjects and having their responses to the 566 items punched onto IBM cards. Multiple linear regression analyses were performed for these data for each of the 13 clinical and validity scales by an IBM

360/50 computer using point-biserial and phi correlations. Those items whose regression weights divided by their standard errors yielded a significant t-value, including no less than one third and no more than one half of the original scale total were selected for inclusion. The final item total was 173 with scales ranging in size from 10 to 31 items. A set of conversion tables then was developed for use with either sex.

Faschingbauer's (1974) abbreviated MMPI (FAM) was developed in a manner similar to Kincannon's (1968) Mini-Mult. Furthermore, because Comrey omitted factor analyses of scales *Mf* and *Si*, Graham, Schroeder, and Lilly's (1971) factor analyses of these scales were used. All items loading $\geq$ .40 (absolute) on each factor were considered to constitute a cluster. This method proved useful and was used later when items were added to scales not clustered (*L, K, Hs, D, Hy*, and *Pt*). From that third of the items in each cluster with the greatest number of intercorrelations $\geq$ 0.30 (absolute) with other items in the cluster, equal numbers of items were selected from relatively unrelated subclusters. One third of these were chosen because they showed the greatest amount of scale overlap, one third because they showed the least amount of overlap, and one third because they showed the greatest number of intercorrelations with other cluster items $\geq$ 0.30. All unclustered items were given fractional consideration in the item selection process. The MMPI answer sheets of college males then were scored for both the MMPI and FAM scale items, and correlation coefficients were computed between the two scores for each scale. Only those FAM scales correlating $\geq$ 0.85 with the corresponding MMPI scales were retained. Other scales had items added or deleted until the criterion was met. The resultant scales required 166 items.

Overall and Gomez-Mont (1974) attempted to devise an abbreviated form of the MMPI that employed only the first 168 items of the standard MMPI. Their decision to use 168 items was made primarily because item 168 appears as the last item at the bottom of page 7 on standard Form R and thus provides a convenient stopping point. Least-squares regression equations were derived to estimate the conventional *K*-corrected raw scores from the raw scores obtained from the MMPI-168. In several cases it was necessary to estimate the conventional scale scores from a weighted combination of two or more MMPI-168 scores. The authors further documented that most of the reliable variance in the standard MMPI clinical scales is adequately represented in these first 168 items on standard Form R.

Two abbreviated MMPIs have been developed independently by McLachlan (1974) and Spera and Robertson (1974), both of which are entitled Maxi-Mult. McLachlan's Maxi-Mult was developed as a result of rather low two-year test-retest stability with chronic alcoholics of an abbreviated form consisting of the Mini-Mult and Midi-Mult scales as well as Graham and Schroeder's (1972) abbreviated scales *Mf* and *Si*. Items from the standard form scales were selected for content appropriateness and added one at a time until increased reliability resulted. No description of or rationale for the procedures used was presented.

The resultant 94-item Maxi-Mult was intended to be a research instrument that only could be given as a posttest so that outcomes of clinical treatment could be examined in relation to changes from embedded pretest scales scored from intake MMPIs. No attempt was made in the derivation of this Maxi-Mult to estimate means or T scores of the MMPI clinical scales because the Maxi-Mult scales were seen as ends in themselves to be used as indicators of group performance.

Spera and Robertson (1974) modified the Mini-Mult by adding Grayson's (1951) 38 Critical Items, and the resultant 104-item abbreviated form is entitled the Maxi-Mult. Grayson's items were selected for inclusion because of the valuable clinical information furnished and in order to increase the number of items for certain scales on the Mini-Mult shown to have limited predictive power. Regression equations for converting the Maxi-Mult raw scores into predicted MMPI raw scores with the accompanying conversion tables were developed.

In order to evaluate the relative efficacy of five of the previously discussed abbreviated forms with adults to the Midi-Mult, Spera and Robertson's Maxi-Mult, the Hugo, FAM, and MMPI-168—a series of investigations were conducted by Newmark and colleagues (Newmark, Newmark, and Faschingbauer 1974; Newmark et al. 1975; Faschingbauer and Newmark 1978). The Mini-Mult was omitted from this analysis because of its similarity to the Midi-Mult and because it has been evaluated sufficiently in approximately 25 investigations, resulting in minimal support for its continued use (Faschingbauer and Newmark 1978), while McLachlan's Maxi-Mult was intended for use only as a research instrument to assess posttest outcomes of clinical treatment.

Although the criteria for acceptability of an abbreviated MMPI vary with each prospective user, some conclusions can be drawn from the above comparative investigations: (1) The Midi-Mult has limited applicability with both psychiatric in- and outpatients because it appears insensitive to extreme psychopathology. However, this instrument seems appropriate for use with a normal college sample. (2) While the Maxi-Mult appears applicable with psychiatric inpatients, numerous weaknesses were strikingly evident when it was used with mildly pathological outpatients and a normal college sample. These deficits were consistently greater with females. (3) The Hugo appears extremely vulnerable when used with psychiatric inpatients, has potential usefulness with mildly pathological psychiatric outpatients, but appears most appropriate for use with normal college subjects. This likely reflects its use of linear regression conversion values based solely on a college student sample. The Hugo, with its high reliability and nonoverlapping scales, would seem to warrant the development of substitution (or multiple regression) based conversion values for other populations such as Faschingbauer (1976) did with the Mini-Mult. (4) Both the FAM and MMPI-168 are the most versatile of these abbreviated forms and are extremely useful with psychiatric inpatients and normal college students. Some deficiencies, however, are evident with mildly pathological psychiatric outpatients, especially with regard to high-point code correspondence.

One obvious criticism of the above investigations is that the methodology employed used abbreviated forms that were obtained in the context of the standard form MMPI administration. Any adverse effect may be less for the MMPI-168, as subjects receiving the MMPI-168 ordinarily do not know how far to proceed in the test booklet when they begin, or, if they do, the mere statement of a terminal item should not be expected to affect performance (Overall and Gomez-Mont 1974).

The majority of these studies focused solely on comparisons with the standard MMPI of group mean data and individual profile pairs concerning validity, high points, general elevations, code-type correspondence, configural analyses, and application of various MMPI-derived diagnostic rules. With few exceptions (Armentrout and Rouzer 1970; Mlott 1973; Newmark and Glenn 1974) these studies have used adults as subjects. The utility of an abbreviated MMPI in settings other than that used by the developer cannot be assumed (Armentrout and Rouzer 1970). A wealth of research evidence (Dahlstrom, Welsh, and Dahlstrom 1972) has shown that frequencies of item endorsement, and thus profile characteristics, vary with the subject's age, sex, psychiatric status, socioeconomic level, and intelligence. It is possible therefore that the items selected for inclusion on an abbreviated form are not equally predictive of the scale they represent for different populations. That is, items that satisfactorily predict the content of a given scale for adult psychiatric patients may be much less representative of that scale's content for a different population, such as adolescents.

However, previous investigations with adolescents have not dealt with two crucial issues. First, is the interpretation obtained from an abbreviated form comparable to that obtained from the standard MMPI? If not, regardless of whether or not individual and group mean data are comparable, the abbreviated form should not be used. Two recent investigations with adult psychiatric inpatients showed this to be a potentially fruitful area. Newmark, Conger, and Faschingbauer (1976) had psychiatric residents evaluate the accuracy of interpretations of both the FAM and standard MMPI on their patients. Although significantly higher mean ratings resulted for the standard MMPI, when data were collected across sexes, the quantity of loss was significantly lower than expected. That is, the FAM functioned as an instrument 80 percent as long as the standard MMPI, even though it contains only 30 percent of the items.

Newmark, Falk, and Finch (1976) also compared the interpretive accuracy of the standard MMPI and three abbreviated forms with a sample of psychiatric inpatients. Although significantly higher mean ratings resulted from the standard MMPI when compared with either the FAM or Hugo abbreviated form, comparable ratings by psychiatric teams were obtained when comparing the MMPI-168 and standard form MMPI interpretations. Two major limitations of these latter two studies include the failure to assess interrater reliability and to provide the rules and principles used in making the MMPI interpretations.

A second and more crucial issue concerns the empirical validity of the standard and abbreviated forms when compared with direct measures of psychopathology. In all but one (Newmark et al. 1978) of the 95 to 100 investigations (see Appendix A), the utility of the abbreviated form has been based on concurrent validity with the standard form MMPI. Thus, though one abbreviated form may predict the standard form MMPI more precisely than another abbreviated form does, the latter abbreviated form might predict psychopathology more accurately than either the former abbreviated form or standard form MMPI.

The initial investigation assessed the relative interpretive accuracy of five abbreviated MMPIs and the standard MMPI with a sample of psychiatric adolescent inpatients. The Mini-Mult was omitted from this analysis because of its similarlity to the Midi-Mult and because the significant deficiencies of this instrument have been documented thoroughly (for example, Armentrout and Rouzer 1970; Faschingbauer and Newmark 1978; Fillenbaum and Pfeiffer 1976). McLachlan's Maxi-Mult also was not evaluated because of its intended use only for posttest group mean data. These abbreviated forms showing comparable interpretive validity with the standard MMPI then were used in a subsequent investigation. The focus of this latter study was to compare the empirical validity of abbreviated forms and the standard form with direct measures of psychopathology.

These investigations seem necessary because there is no reason to use an alternative version of a psychometric instrument, whether longer or shorter, unless it possesses greater interpretive or empirical validity than the form it replaces or unless it is significantly less expensive to administer with no loss in interpretive and/or empirical validity. Rand (1976) and Overall, Higgins, and DeSchweinitz (1976) independently concluded that using external criteria is a vital prerequisite for evaluating abbreviated forms of the MMPI.

STUDY 1

Method

Subjects

The subjects were 239 consecutive adolescent admissions to either a private or university psychiatric inpatient facility. For numerous reasons, primarily lack of cooperation, confusion, limited intellectual ability, or cerebral dysfunction, MMPIs were not obtained from 53 patients. Forty-one patients obtained uninterpretable invalid MMPI profiles ($? \geqslant 60$, or $F \geqslant 90$, or $K \geqslant 70$). The remaining 76 females and 69 males who were between the ages of 13 and 16 (M = 14.6) served as subjects. There were no significant differences between the sexes as a function of age, intelligence (as measured by an abbreviated form of the Wechsler Intelligence Scale for Children), marital status, race, or frequency or length of previous hospitalizations. First admissions to a psychiatric hospital made up 87 percent of the sample. No attempt was made to control for a social class variable, because, as Meehl (1971) has emphasized, the tendency among social scientists to view correlations uncorrected for social class as automatically spurious is unjustified unless it can be demonstrated that a causal relationship exists between social class and the correlated variable.

Procedure

The subjects were tested approximately 48 to 72 hours following admission to the hospital as part of the routine screening procedure. All standard MMPIs were hand-scored in the traditional manner. All abbreviated form items were extracted from the standard MMPI protocols and converted to standard scale raw scores via the corresponding conversion tables or regression equations. The *Mf* and *Si* scales are not scored on the Midi-Mult, but were scored on the other four abbreviated forms. Conversion of raw score to T scores was accomplished using age-specific non-*K*-corrected adolescent norms (Dahlstrom, Welsh, and Dahlstrom 1972). The T score then was plotted in the body of the profile to correspond to those printed in the extreme left and right T score columns. The T scores obtained from raw score conversions should not be plotted on the raw scores that typically appear in the body of the standard adult profile. The general rationale for adoption of these new norms for the evaluation of adolescent inpatients is that the resulting profile provides the clinician an index of each patient's status in relation to his/her peer reference group, rather than the patient's status in relation to a reference group of pre-World War II Minnesota adults (Lachar, Kline, and Grissell 1976).

While the extracted method has been besieged by excessive criticism (Newmark, Galen, and Gold 1975), it would seem impossible to conduct the present study with independently administered forms due to the already discussed reluctance of adolescents to complete psychometric tests. Nevertheless, the extracted method possesses inherent flaws. Most notably a perfect reliability of scores is assumed because the same items scored were used on both the abbreviated and standard forms. Thus the optimal level of correlation between the forms results.

A programmed interpretation system developed by Lachar (1974b) that is capable of producing a general personality description in narrative form based entirely on MMPI data was used in a mechanical fashion. The procedure is described as mechanical or programmed because the relationship between the test characteristic and the descriptive statements is specified so that the statement is automatically assigned without the intervention of human judgment whenever the test characteristic occurs (Fowler 1969). Lachar's approach generates fairly comprehensive blind interpretations, with all of the limitations of other blind interpretations, as well as the positive features of a systematic approach and high reliability (Lachar 1974b). This system of interpretive statements and rules attempts to simulate the steps taken in clinical interpretation of MMPI profiles and is unique in that the organization of statements and specification of rules reflects Lachar's experience. That the narratives generated from adolescent norm profiles are significantly more accurate than narratives generated from adult norm profiles has been demonstrated with adolescent psychiatric patients using Lachar's system (Lachar, Klinge, and Grisell 1976). Information regarding the development, utility, and accuracy of this system is available elsewhere (Lachar 1974a, 1974b).

Both abbreviated and standard MMPI interpretations of approximately 250 to 300 words then were presented to the psychiatric team (psychiatrist, psychiatric resident, psychologist, psychiatric nurse) in charge of primary care for the patient. Approximately one week later, the psychiatric team was requested to evaluate for each patient the accuracy of each interpretation on a five-point scale as follows:

1 = The report is completely erroneous, inadequate, and contradicts what can be verified objectively.
2 = The report is generally incomplete and inaccurate, even though some minor statements are fairly descriptive.
3 = The report is accurate in some respects, but contains enough inaccurate material to render it of questionable usefulness.
4 = The report is generally complete and describes the patient accurately, even though there are some minor inconsistencies.
5 = The report is totally accurate, compatible with what can be verified objectively, and no inconsistencies exist.

Such a rating scale has been used elsewhere in the evaluation of the accuracy of automated MMPI interpretation systems (for example, Adams and Shore 1976; Lachar, Klinge, and Grisell 1976). The week time interval was necessary so that the psychiatric team would be more familiar with the patient. That such a procedure has merit in increasing rater reliability has been demonstrated by Newmark, Falk, and Finch (1976).

The same psychiatric team rated all 145 patients, with each member rating each patient. Raters were not aware as to which interpretation was generated by which MMPI form and ratings were made independently. The final rating given each interpretation was based on a consensus. This model has been shown to be an advantageous procedure by Overall, Hollister, and Dalah (1967) based on the theory that random errors tend to cancel when independent ratings are averaged. Both the abbreviated and standard form interpretations of each profile were evaluated together so that a direct comparison could be made in case of equal ratings. If equal ratings occurred, one interpretation was chosen as being more conclusive and helpful.

Results

Interpretation ratings for females on the standard MMPI (M = 4.19, σ = .47) were significantly higher than the ratings obtained from the Midi-Mult (M = 2.97, σ = .74), t (75) = 9.17, p ≤ .001; Hugo (M = 3.36, σ .79), t (75) = 6.24, p ≤ .001;

and Maxi-Mult (M = 3.32, σ = .70), t (75) = 6.44, p $\leqslant$ .001. In contrast, no significant differences occurred when comparing the interpretation ratings on the standard MMPI with ratings obtained from either the FAM (M = 4.09, σ = .55) or MMPI-168 (M = 4.11, σ = .59). Ratings on the FAM were significantly higher than ratings obtained from either the Midi-Mult, t (75) = 8.86, p $\leqslant$ .001; Hugo, t (75) = 5.95, p $\leqslant$ .001; or Maxi-Mult, t (75) = 6.07, p $\leqslant$ .001. Ratings on the MMPI-168 also were significantly higher than ratings obtained from either the Midi-Mult, t (75) = 8.13, p $\leqslant$ .001; Hugo, t (75) = 5.67, p $\leqslant$ .001; or Maxi-Mult, t (75) = 5.91, p $\leqslant$ .001.

For the standard MMPI, FAM, and MMPI-168, 72, 70 and 68 percent, respectively, of the interpretations were rated $\geqslant$4 $\leqslant$5, while 3, 5, and 7 percent, respectively, were rated <3. For the 76 profile pairs, the standard MMPI was rated higher in 41 cases as compared with 28 cases where the FAM was rated higher. Of the 7 cases where equal ratings occurred, the standard MMPI interpretation was rated as being more conclusive and useful in 5 cases. For the 76 profile pairs, the standard MMPI was rated higher in 39 cases as compared with 31 cases where the MMPI-168 was rated higher. Of the 6 cases where equal ratings occurred, the standard MMPI interpretation was rated as being more conclusive and useful in 4 cases. For the 76 profile pairs, the FAM was rated higher in 34 cases, while the MMPI-168 was rated higher in 38 cases. Of the 4 cases where equal ratings occurred, the interpretations from each abbreviated form were rated higher in 2 cases.

Interpretation ratings for males on the standard MMPI (M = 4.21, σ = .49) were significantly higher than the ratings obtained from the Midi-Mult (M = 2.98, σ = .76), t (68) = 8.65, p $\leqslant$ .001; Hugo (M = 3.40, σ = .73), t (68) = 5.98, p $\leqslant$ .001; and Maxi-Mult (M = 3.36, σ = .71), t (68) = 6.11, p $\leqslant$ .001. In contrast, no significant differences occurred when comparing the interpretation ratings on the standard MMPI with ratings obtained from either the FAM (M = 4.13, σ = .51) or MMPI-168 (M = 4.15, σ = .53). Ratings on the FAM were significantly higher than ratings obtained from either the Midi-Mult, t (75) = 8.21, p $\leqslant$ .001; Hugo, t (68) = 5.66, p $\leqslant$ .001; or Maxi-Mult, t (68) = 5.80, p $\leqslant$ .001. Ratings on the MMPI-168 also were significantly higher than ratings obtained from either the Midi-Mult, t (75) = 7.94, p $\leqslant$ .001; Hugo, t (68) = 5.49, p $\leqslant$ .001; or Maxi-Mult, t (75) = 5.77, p $\leqslant$ .001.

For the standard MMPI, FAM, and MMPI-168, 71, 68, and 71 percent, respectively, of the interpretations were rated $\geqslant$4 $\leqslant$5, while 3, 4, and 4 percent, respectively, were rated <3. For the 69 profile pairs, the standard MMPI was rated higher in 37 cases as compared with 28 cases where the FAM was rated higher. Of the 4 cases where equal ratings occurred, the standard MMPI interpretation was rated as being more conclusive and useful in 3 cases. For the 69 profile pairs, the standard MMPI was rated higher in 33 cases as compared with 29 cases where the MMPI-168 was rated higher. Of the 7 cases where equal ratings occurred, the standard MMPI interpretation was rated as being more conclusive and useful in 4 cases. For the 69 profile pairs, the FAM was rated higher in 30 cases, while the MMPI-168 was rated higher in 33 cases. Of the 6 cases where equal ratings occurred, the MMPI-168 was rated as being more conclusive and useful in 5 cases.

The interpretation ratings on the Midi-Mult were significantly lower than ratings obtained from either the Hugo, t (75) = 2.87, p ⩽ .01; or Maxi-Mult, t (75) = 2.70, p ⩽ .01, for females and from either the Hugo, t (68) = 2.95, p ⩽ .01, or Maxi-Mult, t (68) = 2.95, p ⩽ .01, for males. No significant differences occurred for either sex when comparing the interpretation ratings of the Hugo and Maxi-Mult.

Product-moment reliability coefficients across the four raters ranged from .77 to .84 (M = .81). There were no significant differences as a function of inter-rater reliability between the standard form or any abbreviated form.

Discussion

Interpretations obtained from the standard MMPI were rated generally accurate and significantly more accurate than interpretations obtained from either the Midi-Mult, Hugo, or Maxi-Mult. In contrast, standard form interpretations were rated comparable to the interpretations obtained from either the FAM or MMPI-168. There was no significant difference with regard to the interpretation ratings of either of these latter two abbreviated forms. However, when tie ratings occurred, the standard MMPI interpretation was selected as being more conclusive and useful than either the FAM or MMPI-168 interpretation in 70 percent of the cases.

While no significant differences occurred as a function of sex, ratings for males were consistently higher than those obtained for females on each of the abbreviated forms. This is not surprising because Lachar's system of interpretive statements and rules was developed using a sample containing 75 percent males. Nevertheless, use of such a programmed system is critical in order to increase reliability and facilitate replication.

The interpretations obtained from the Midi-Mult were significantly less accurate than interpretations obtained from any other abbreviated form or standard form MMPI, regardless of sex. One possible reason for the low interpretation ratings may be the exclusion of scales *Mf* and *Si* from the Midi-Mult. While neither is considered a basic clinical sacle, the interpretive information gleaned from each often is quite valuable (Graham, Schroeder, and Lilly 1971).

Compared with the results of similar studies using clinicians as interpreters (for example, Newmark, Conger, and Faschingbauer 1976; Newmark, Falk, and Finch 1976) with adult psychiatric inpatients, the present interpretations were consistently rated almost one-half category lower. It is doubtful if this reflects on the accuracy of Lachar's interpretive system, which is based on empirically validated decision rules and replicated scale correlates. Most likely, the lower interpretation ratings were due to the use of adolescent subjects in the present study. That difficulties are more pronounced in interpreting MMPI profiles obtained from adolescents as compared with adults is common knowledge. Also, there is some controversy regarding whether adult or adolescent norms should be used with adolescent psychiatric patients (for example, Berry and Marks 1972; Lachar, Klinge, and Grisell 1976).

While some limitations of this investigation are readily apparent, they nevertheless are consistent with procedures that occur regarding the use of the MMPI in many psychiatric adolescent inpatient settings. That is, interpretations are done by a clinician following a rather cookbook, programmed approach and usually are presented to the psychiatric team in charge of the patient. Feedback often is presented to the clinician regarding the accuracy of the interpretations. Nevertheless, use of the extracted abbreviated forms possesses inherent flaws because a perfect reliability of scores occurs. Also, the sample size may have been somewhat smaller than is sufficient for MMPI studies (Butcher and Tellegan 1978) and there was no attempt to control for medication effects, as has been strongly advocated by Garfield (1978). The latter limitation can be alleviated partially by administering the test as soon as possible following admission to the hospital. The use of mental health professionals as the final criterion of interpretation accuracy may be subject to criticism and more objective measures are needed. Finally, the five-point rating scale appears somewhat deficient because there was no substantiation that these five points were a true equal interval scale. Nevertheless, from a practical point of view there is evidence to suggest that the interpretations of both the MMPI-168 and the FAM were highly accurate and comparable to interpretations obtained from the standard MMPI with psychiatric adolescent inpatients.

STUDY 2

Method

Subjects

The subjects were 162 male and 167 female consecutive admissions to either a private or university psychiatric inpatient facility who received the MMPI as standard routine admission procedure. For numerous reasons, primarily invalid profiles ($? \geqslant 60$, or $F \geqslant 90$, or $K \geqslant 70$), lack of cooperation, confusion, limited intellectual ability, and a concomitant diagnosis of either acute or chronic organic brain syndrome, 54 males and 39 females were eliminated from this investigation. The resultant 108 males and 128 females, between the ages of 12 and 16.5 (M = 14.9), served as subjects. There were no significant differences between the sexes as a function of age, intelligence (as measured by an abbreviated form of the Wechsler Intelligence Scale for Children), marital status, race, or frequency or length of previous hospitalizations. First admissions to a psychiatric hospital made up 83 percent of the sample.

Apparatus

The Brief Psychiatric Rating Scale (Extended Version). The rating scale that was used to record clinical observations in this investigation was a 42-item instrument devised by Pokorny, in collaboration with Overall and others, for use in a survey of the Texas state hospital population (Pokorny and Overall 1970). It consists of the widely used 18-item Brief Psychiatric Rating Scale (BPRS) (Overall and Gorham 1962) plus 24 additional rating constructs from various syndrome scales chosen to span the range of lesser psychopathologies. Each symptom construct on the BPRS, and on the extended version used here, is rated on a seven-point scale of severity. Approximately half of the BPRS ratings are based on observations of the patients, their modes of communication, and the organization of their mental processes without regard to specific content. Information regarding the development, scoring procedure, reliability, and validity of this instrument can be found elsewhere (Overall and Gorham 1962; Overall and Klett 1972).

The BPRS was chosen as the criterion variable in this investigation because it has been used fruitfully for the isolation and identification of psychopathological syndromes and categories in numerous studies (Auerbach and Ewing 1964; Overall 1974; Overall et al. 1966; Overall, Hollister, and Pichot 1967; Pokorny and Overall 1970; Steer 1974) and because the practical utility of rating scales as objective measures of psychopathology has been extensively documented (Lorr 1954; Norton 1967; Schreier, Reznikoff, and Glueck 1962; Wittenborn 1972). Furthermore, the BPRS has symptom labels similar to those found on the MMPI scales. The development of rating scales in an attempt to standardize, fractionate, and objectify the process of clinical decision making has been among the most significant achievements in psychodiagnosis during the past decade (Goldberg 1974). That behavioral rating scales have largely supplanted psychological tests as criterion measures has been discussed recently by Cleveland (1976).

The Mental Status Schedule. To complete the BPRS, Overall and Gorham (1962) advocated the use of an 18-minute generally nondirective interview. However, this interview proved impractical in the present investigation because of its brevity and lack of structure and because the usefulness of rating scales has been shown to be limited when there is significant variability in the interview procedures on which the ratings are based (Spitzer et al. 1964). Therefore the Mental Status Schedule (MSS), which was developed by Spitzer, Burdock, and Hardesty (1964) to provide a standardized interview to assess the major dimensions of the mental status in which the content and order of questions are fixed, was used in this investigation.

The MSS contains an interview schedule and a matching inventory of 248 dichotomous items descriptive of small units of psychopathological behavior that the interviewer evaluates as true or false. The inventory was not used in this study. The interview schedule is a series of 82 questions arranged in a definite sequence to provide a natural progression of topics that cover a wide range of psychopathology that the interviewer uses to elicit information from the patient. Fifty-one supplementary questions were provided to clarify or probe the areas in which the patient's responses seemed incomplete. The schedule provided alternative phraseology for many questions so that the examiner could ask the question in the form and tense most appropriate to the circumstances. Thus, even though standardized, the procedure has enough flexibility so that when properly administered it seems like a typical clinical interview, allowing good rapport between interviewer and patient (Spitzer et al. 1965).

The items on the inventory were developed by surveying standard psychiatric texts and by interviewing several hundred psychiatric patients with preliminary forms of the MSS to obtain a comprehensive coverage of overt signs of psychopathology. Efforts were made to word the questions so that even inpatients with minimal education or psychological insight could comprehend them. The length of the interview varied from 20 to 60 minutes, depending on the patient's verbal productivity, amount of psychopathology present, and cooperation. A detailed description of the MSS as well as information bearing on the reliability, validity, and administration of this instrument can be found elsewhere (Spitzer, Endicott, and Cohen 1964; Spitzer et al. 1964; Spitzer et al. 1967).

The advantages of the MSS over other commonly used assessment procedures include the incorporation of a standardized interview schedule to reduce inconsistency and oversight due to variability in interviewing technique and coverage of psychopathology, awareness of what questions are asked to provide a framework within which the patient's responses can be understood by others not present at the interview, and the use of a score sheet that serves simultaneously as a permanent clinical record and as a form for automated data processing. The use of the same interview schedule for all patients also has the research advantage that differences observed among patients tend to reflect actual differences rather than artifacts caused by differences in areas of psychopathology explored or interviewing techniques used.

Procedure

Subjects were tested approximately 48 to 72 hours after admission as part of the routine screening procedure. While the extracted method of administration has been beseiged by excessive criticism (Newmark, Galen, and Gold 1975) it would seem impossible to conduct the present study with independently administered forms due to the already discussed reluctance of adolescents to complete psychometric tests. Nevertheless, the extracted method processes inherent flaws. Most notably a perfect reliability of scores is assumed because the same items scored were used on both the abbreviated and standard forms. Thus, the optimal level of correlation between the form results.

The standard form MMPI answer sheets were hand-scored in the traditional manner. The FAM was scored and converted into standard scale raw scores using Faschingbauer's (1973) tables of conversion for each sex. Conversion of prorated raw scores to T scores then was accomplished following the standard procedures. The MMPI-168 was scored and converted into standard scale K-corrected raw scores using regression equations for each scale as derived by Overall and Gomez-Mont (1974). K-corrected raw scores were used for statistical analysis as advocated by Butcher and Tellegen (1978), but K-corrected T scores are presented in the tables in order to be consistent with the literature and facilitate comparisons.

Four raters, consisting of two clinical psychologists, one psychiatrist, and one psychiatric nurse, were presented detailed operationally defined explanations of the symptoms on the BPRS as defined by Overall and Gorham (1962) and Porkorny and Overall (1970) in an attempt to reduce idiosyncratic biases. Although definitions can never be rigorous or complete except in mathematics, they nevertheless serve to demarcate a concept even though its boundaries remain somewhat blurred (Zubin 1967). All raters had at least five years of diagnostic experience. Such a procedure was necessary because it has been demonstrated (Kreitman 1961) that variables relating to nomenclature and degree of experience were the greatest impediments to reliability in psychiatric diagnoses. Clearly definable terms and equivalent diagnostic experience are essential.

Initially, in an attempt to maximize interrater reliability, filmed MSS interviews with three psychiatric adolescent inpatients with varied degrees and types of psychopathology were presented to the four raters. Following each filmed presentation a detailed discussion of the rating differences occurred. That such a procedure has merit in increasing rater reliability has been confirmed by Raskin, Schulterbrandt, and Reatig (1966).

Each patient then was interviewed using the MSS by one of the raters while another rater observed this initial diagnostic interview behind a one-way mirror. Neither rater was familiar with the patient's history or observed ward behavior. Reliability is definitely enhanced if two raters observe the same interview rather than each rater observing a separate interview (Wittenborn 1972). Thus each patient was rated on the BPRS by two raters so that interrater reliability was assessed. Immediately following the interview, each rater recorded his observations independent of his colleague's rating.

When two raters observe the same patient, two distinct strategies exist for combining data (Overall 1968). One approach has been to have both observers discuss each rating at the conclusion of the interview and to arrive at a consensus rating. The other more frequently used model has been to have raters complete ratings independently and then to average the ratings on the theory that random errors tend to cancel. This latter model has been shown to be an advantageous procedure by Overall, Hollister, and Dalal (1967). Consequently, the mean ratings for each BPRS symptom were used.

Because several MMPI scales contain more than one interpretive factor, these scales were correlated with the means of more than one BPRS symptom rating using multiple correlation coefficients (Bruning and Kintz 1968). Only for scale L, which was correlated with only one BPRS symptom, was a product-moment correlation used. The MMPI scales and the corresponding BPRS scales with which they were correlated are as follows: L, Denial; F, Unusual Thought Content, Conceptual Disorganization, Intellectual Subnormality; K, Denial, Guardedness; Hs, Conversion Somatization, Somatic Concern; D, Depressive Mood, Introjection of Blame; Hy, Conversion Somatization, Dramatization, Manipulativeness, Denial, Emotionally Labile; Pd, Antisocial Trends, Impulsiveness, Projection of Blame, Hostility, Manipulativeness; Mf, Sexual Crossed Identification, Passive Dependency; Pa, Suspiciousness, Projection of Blame, Hostility; Pt, Anxiety, Tension, Guilt Feelings, Phobias, Compulsive Acts, Obsessive Thoughts; Sc, Conceptual Disorganization, Unusual Thought Content, Sexual Inadequacy, Emotional Withdrawal, Blunted Affect, Feelings of Unreality; and Ma, Excitement, Elevated Mood, Grandiosity, Tension. The BPRS ratings selected for inclusion were based on item analyses content and interpretive data of the MMPI scales as presented by Dahlstrom, Welsh, and Dahlstrom (1972), Fowler (1966), and Lachar (1974b).

Results

The T score means, standard deviations, and Pearson product-moment correlations of the comparable validity, clinical, and Mf scales of both the MMPI and the FAM are presented as a function of sex in Table 9.1 Note that in 9 of 12 cases for male and 8 of 12 cases for females, the standard deviation was larger for the FAM than for the comparable standard MMPI scales. Statistical analysis showed this to be a significantly reliable trend ($p \leqslant .05$).

Paired t tests yielded significant mean differences on L, t (53) = 2.94, p $\leqslant .01$; Hs, t (53) = 2.79, p $\leqslant .01$; and Pa, t (53) = 4.28, p $\leqslant .001$, for males and on F, t (63) = 3.92, p $\leqslant .001$; Pd, t (63) = 3.49, p $\leqslant .001$; and on Pt, t (63) = 3.22, p $\leqslant .01$, for females. In all cases the FAM significantly overestimated the MMPI scale scores. This finding is consistent with previously published results with both adult (Faschingbauer and Newmark 1978) and adolescent (Newmark and Glenn 1974) psychiatric patients, demonstrating that the FAM seemed to overestimate slightly MMPI scale means.

For males, scale correlations ranged from .67 on Pa to .81 on D (M = .76, Mdn = .77). For females, correlations ranged from .69 on Pa to .83 on Hy (M = .75, Mdn = .76). All correlations were significantly different from zero (p $\leqslant .001$).

The T score means, standard deviations, and Pearson product-moment correlations of the comparable validity, clinical, and Ms scales of both the MMPI and the MMPI-168 are presented as a function of sex in Table 9.2. Note in 7 of 12 cases for males and 7 of 12 cases for females that the standard deviation was smaller for the MMPI-168 than for the comparable standard MMPI scales.

TABLE 9.1

Mean T Scores, Standard Deviations, and Pearson Product-Moment Correlations for the Standard MMPI and the Faschingbauer Abbreviated MMPI (FAM)

| | Males (n = 54) | | | | | Females (n = 64) | | | | |
| | MMPI | | FAM | | | MMPI | | FAM | | |
Scale	M	SD	M	SD	r	M	SD	M	SD	r
L	50.5	6.9	52.1[a]	7.2	.80	52.7	7.1	53.0	7.3	.80
F	67.9	11.4	68.5	11.6	.76	63.4	12.2	66.9[b]	12.4	.76
K	58.4	7.5	58.6	7.7	.77	58.2	7.6	58.3	7.8	.72
Hs	47.9	6.9	49.1[a]	7.0	.80	50.6	8.7	52.0	8.4	.83
D	67.6	12.3	66.8	12.0	.81	68.4	12.1	67.8	11.9	.78
Hy	50.6	8.5	52.2	8.8	.76	58.1	10.3	57.7	10.3	.79
Pd	76.0	10.5	76.9	10.6	.72	70.6	9.8	73.4[b]	10.1	.70
Mf	54.5	7.2	54.5	7.5	.75	48.9	7.9	49.2	7.7	.71
Pa	63.2	9.7	67.0[b]	9.8	.67	62.5	7.8	63.5	7.9	.69
Pt	63.8	10.0	63.1	9.9	.79	63.6	11.5	66.0[a]	11.8	.80
Sc	69.7	13.3	68.8	13.0	.75	68.4	10.1	67.1	10.2	.74
Ma	70.3	12.4	69.5	12.5	.78	64.3	8.7	63.9	9.0	.76

[a] p ≤ .01.
[b] p ≤ .001.

Source: Compiled by the author.

TABLE 9.2

Mean T Scores, Standard Deviations, and Pearson Product-Moment Correlations for the Standard MMPI and the MMPI-168

Scale	Males (n = 54)					Females (n = 64)				
	MMPI		MMPI-168			MMPI		MMPI-168		
	M	SD	M	SD	r	M	SD	M	SD	r
L	49.4	6.2	49.6	5.9	.75	52.8	6.9	53.2	6.5	.77
F	64.6	10.7	67.7[b]	10.5	.74	64.9	10.2	66.0	10.0	.76
K	59.3	7.3	58.7	7.0	.70	58.1	6.9	57.5	7.0	.66
Hs	45.5	7.2	46.0	7.9	.82	53.6	8.5	52.3	8.5	.79
D	67.0	10.4	65.8	10.2	.79	66.9	10.6	67.2	10.8	.77
Hy	53.1	8.4	53.6	8.0	.77	58.8	10.1	59.2	9.9	.81
Pd	74.7	9.9	77.2[a]	10.3	.70	70.0	8.8	71.4	8.4	.73
Mf	54.9	7.6	54.6	7.8	.71	47.9	7.7	49.0	7.7	.72
Pa	64.3	9.6	63.7	9.9	.69	66.9	8.3	66.4	71.	.68
Pt	64.6	10.1	64.0	9.3	.77	65.7	10.0	66.9	8.8	.81
Sc	65.9	11.5	64.9	11.7	.78	65.8	13.8	65.5[a]	13.9	.66
Ma	70.4	10.8	69.2	10.5	.80	65.3	9.7	64.5	9.4	.79

[a] p ≤ .01.
[b] p ≤ .001.

Source: Compiled by the author.

Paired t-tests yielded significant mean differences on *F*, t (53) = 3.65, p ⩽ .001; and on *Pd*, t (53) = 3.40, p ⩽ .01, for males and on *Sc*, t (63) = 2.81, p ⩽ .01, for females. In all cases, the MMPI-168 significantly overestimated the MMPI scales scores. The results for males are rather surprising in view of several previously published reports (Newmark, Newmark, and Cook 1975; Newmark and Raft 1976; Newmark et al. 1978) that found no significant differences for a sample of both male medical patients and male psychiatric patients. In contrast, the studies by Newmark et al. showed no consistent patterns with regard to a sample of either female medical or female psychiatric patients.

For males, scale correlations ranged from .69 on *Pa* to .82 on *Hs* (M = .75, Mdn = .76). For females, scale correlations ranged from .66 on both *K* and *Sc* to .81 on both *Hy* and *Pt* (M = .74, Mdn = .77). All correlations were significantly different from zero (p ⩽ .001).

Table 9.3 presents the multiple correlation coefficients between the BPRS ratings and the corresponding MMPI and abbreviated form scales. All of the correlations were significantly different from zero (p ⩽ .001). For males, correlations ranged from .59 for *L*, *F*, and *Sc* to .81 for *Hs* (M = .69, Mdn = .71) on the standard form and from .54 for *Pa* to .83 for *Hy* (M = .70, Mdn = .72) on the FAM. For females, correlations ranged from .55 for *L* to .83 for *D* (M = .69, Mdn = .71) on the standard form and from .51 for *F* to .84 for *Hs* (M = .69, Mdn = .69) on the FAM. With regard to the MMPI and the MMPI-168 for males, correlations ranged from .57 for *Sc* to .81 on both *Hy* and *Ma* (M = .70, Mdn = .72) on the standard form and from .57 for *F* to .82 for *D* (M = .69, Mdn = .69) on the MMPI-168. For females, correlations ranged from .52 for *L* to .83 for *Hs* (M = .69, Mdn = .73) on the standard form and from .49 for both *L* and *Sc* to .82 for *Hs* (M = .67, Mdn = .71) for the MMPI-168.

Comparison of the multiple correlation coefficients between the BPRS ratings and the corresponding MMPI and abbreviated form scales revealed three significant differences. For males, the MMPI correlation was significantly higher than the FAM on *Pa*, t (53) = 3.02, p ⩽ .01, while for females, the MMPI again was significantly higher than either the FAM on *F*, t (63) = 3.34, p ⩽ .01, or the MMPI-168 on *Sc*, t (63) = 2.70, p ⩽ .01. However, these significant differences could occur by chance, as 48 comparisons were made.

Paired t-tests between the multiple correlation coefficients from the BPRS ratings and each abbreviated form yielded significant differences for males on *K*, t (53) = 2.15, p ⩽ .05; *D*, t (53) = 2.27, p ⩽ .05; and on *Pa*, t (53) = 2.09, p ⩽ .05. For *K*, the BPRS-FAM correlations were higher, whereas for *D* and *Pa* the BPRS-MMPI-168 correlation coefficients were higher. For females, significant differences occurred on *L*, t (63) = 2.69, p ⩽ .01; *F*, t (63) = 2.25, p ⩽ .05; *Mf*, t (63) = 2.38, p ⩽ .05; and on *Sc*, t (63) = 3.34, p ⩽ .01. For *L* and *Sc*, the BPRS-FAM correlations were higher, whereas for *F* and *Mf* the MMPI-168 correlations were higher.

Product-moment reliability coefficients across the four raters ranged from .75 to .87 (M = .80). Mean interrater reliabilities between the BPRS scores and

TABLE 9.3

Correlations Between the BPRS Ratings and the Corresponding MMPI and Abbreviated Form Scale Scores

Scale	Males		Females		Males		Females	
	MMPI	FAM	MMPI	FAM	MMPI	MMPI-168	MMPI	MMPI-168
L	.59	.57	.55	.57	.58	.59	.52	.49
F	.59	.58	.62	.51*	.62	.57	.60	.56
K	.73	.75	.72	.74	.72	.70	.71	.71
Hs	.81	.79	.82	.84	.80	.81	.83	.82
D	.76	.76	.83	.80	.78	.82	.77	.77
Hy	.80	.83	.80	.83	.81	.80	.80	.81
Pd	.62	.64	.60	.64	.64	.66	.62	.61
Mf	.75	.78	.72	.72	.73	.76	.75	.78
Pa	.63	.54*	.62	.61	.59	.59	.63	.59
Pt	.68	.70	.70	.69	.71	.68	.74	.72
Sc	.59	.62	.57	.59	.57	.59	.57	.49*
Ma	.77	.80	.75	.78	.81	.77	.75	.77

Note: n = 54 and 64 for males and females, respectively, in each group.

*p ≤ .01.

Source: Compiled by the author.

the corresponding MMPI scale scores were as follows: $L = .75, F = .80, K = .83,$ $Hs = .87, D = .84, Hy = .85, Pd = .78, Mf = .76, Pa = .76, Pt = .81, Sc = .79,$ and $Ma = .82$. Each rater rated the same number of patients.

Discussion

Across both sexes, the FAM and MMPI-168 significantly overestimated several of the comparable standard MMPI scale means. However, the actual mean differences that occurred were rather small, ranging from 1.4 to 3.8 and possibly were not of any practical significance (Newmark et al. 1978). Hill (1976) presented compelling evidence suggesting that the concepts of statistical validity and clinical utility were by no means identical and that it does not necessarily follow that one is a prerequisite for the other. Furthermore, related t-tests are concerned with the magnitude of the correlation so that when large correlations, as were obtained in this study, are found, the differences between the means can be rather small and still be statistically significant.

The majority of abbreviated form investigations have demonstrated a tendency for these forms to underestimate MMPI T score standard deviations, leading Dean (1972) to suggest that this is somehow inherent in shorter tests. However, this may be due not to the shortness of various scales, but to the use of regression analysis in developing the conversion tables for obtaining standard MMPI scale scores. A loss of variance should be expected because of regression toward the mean in regression analysis. According to Hays (1963), a particular individual will likely fall closer to the group mean on the variable being predicted than on the known variable. Regression toward the mean is entirely a consequence of choosing to predict in a linear manner. Faschingbauer (1976) therefore concluded that his use of a substitution model rather than a regression model in developing conversion values for the FAM would overcome this persistent tendency. Equivocal support for this hypothesis was found in the present investigation, as the FAM had generally larger standard deviations than did the standard form MMPI, whereas the MMPI-168, which was developed using a regression model, had higher standard deviations for approximately half of the scales for each sex.

The correlations obtained between the standard MMPI and the BPRS ratings were somewhat higher than results obtained from other investigations (Endicott and Jortner 1966, 1967; Endicott, Jortner, and Abramoff 1969; Harris et al. 1970), which correlated other objective measures of psychopathology with various standard MMPI scales. The higher correlations may have occurred in the present investigation because of the use of multiple correlation coefficients, which combine several objective measures of each MMPI scale rather than using just one measure. For example, instead of correlating *Pd* with objective measures of psychopathic deviancy only, a multiple correlation coefficient was obtained from objective measures of antisocial trends, impulsiveness, projection of blame, hostility, and manipulativeness.

The correlations obtained between the abbreviated forms and the BPRS ratings were significantly high and comparable to the MMPI-BPRS rating correlations. However, scales *L, F,* and *Sc* correlations (M = .56, .58, .57, respectively) were consistently lower, regardless of sex or MMPI form, than other scale correlations, which ranged from M = .63 on *Pd* to M = .82 on *Hs*. Scale *L* correlations were lower possibly because only one objective measure of psychopathology was correlated with it. These results are consistent with previously published data obtained from adult psychiatric inpatients (Newmark et al. 1978). There are no obvious reasons why the correlations for scales *F* and *Sc* were consistently lower even though the scale overlapping to the greatest extent with *F* is *Sc*. One possible explanation is that it is extremely difficult to separate the bona fide protocol of the adolescent from the partially or completely distorted record due to confusion or lack of cooperation (Dahlstrom, Welsh, and Dahlstrom 1972). While an attempt was made in the procedure to eliminate subjects who exhibited a lack of cooperation, negativism, and/or confusion, this effort may have been only partially successful.

The standard MMPI-BPRS rating correlations were significantly different in 2 of the 24 comparisons with the FAM-BPRS rating correlations and in 1 of the 24 comparisons with the MMPI-168-BPRS rating correlations. While the MMPI-BPRS rating correlations were higher in each case, no consistent superiority was demonstrated. The rating correlations for the FAM-BPRS and the MMPI-168-BPRS were significantly different in 7 of the 24 comparisons made. However, neither abbreviated form demonstrated any superiority.

The interrater reliabilities obtained in this investigation were comparable to those obtained in the original developmental investigation of the BPRS by Overall and Gorham (1962). However, the present results were somewhat higher than those obtained in the majority of recent BPRS investigations (for example, Anderson, Kuehnle, and Catanzano 1976), possibly owing to the attempt to maximize interrater reliability through the use of practice procedures, as advocated by Raskin, Schulterbrandt, and Reatig (1966).

As an additional anlaysis, the mean BPRS symptoms rating scores were obtained for each comparable MMPI scale. Both abbreviated and standard form MMPIs in each sample as a function of sex then were subgrouped using the mean BPRS ratings as a moderator variable. Means between 0 and 2.5 were included in the low ratings group, and means between 3.5 and 6.0 were included in the high ratings group. Means from 2.6 to 3.4 were excluded to provide more well-defined groups. The mean MMPI scale scores for the low ratings group and high ratings group were not significantly different from the mean abbreviated form scales for the low ratings and high ratings groups, respectively, within both samples regardless of sex.

Hoffmann and Butcher (1975), after describing the clinical limitations of abbreviated forms of the MMPI, concluded that the degree to which such instruments provide relevant information, permit classification, or facilitate decisions appears to be the most germane test of their utility. However, no attempt was made to compare the profile codes in terms of consensual diagnosis because the excessive (39 percent) number of elevated F scales ($F \geqslant 70$) precludes such an analysis (Dahlstrom, Welsh, and Dahlstrom 1972; Newmark and Glenn 1974). Additionally, it is impossible using configural rules to diagnose "adjustment reaction of adolescence" from the MMPI, which is a primary diagnosis for many adolescents on inpatient units.

Endinger et al. (1976) emphasized that in the absence of independent validation, none of the abbreviated forms developed can be recommended for clinical use. However, there is evidence from the present investigations that both the FAM and MMPI-168 were comparable to the standard form MMPI when compared with direct measures of psychopathology. Because both abbreviated forms are slightly less expensive to administer and result in more completed profiles with no loss in empirical validity, they appear to be an adequate substitute when administration of the standard form MMPI is not feasible with psychiatric adolescent inpatients.

The MMPI-168, however, has one critical advantage over the FAM. Because the MMPI-168 items appear in context and customary sequence, the examiner initially may attempt to obtain the full scale standard form MMPI from a patient or subject. If for numerous reasons the patient or subject fails to complete the entire MMPI, but at least completes the first 168 items, this abbreviated MMPI still is a viable alternative. With the FAM, as well as the other abbreviated forms, it is an "either-or" proposition because the items are not in customary sequence.

REFERENCES

Adams, K. M., and D. L. Shore. 1976. "The Accuracy of an Automated MMPI Interpretation System in a Psychiatric Setting." *Journal of Clinical Psychology* 32: 80–82.

Anderson, W. H., J. C. Kuehnle, and D. N. Catanzano. 1976. "Rapid Treatment of Acute Psychosis." *American Journal of Psychiatry* 133: 1076–78.

Armentrout, J. A., and D. L. Rouzer. 1970. "Utility of the Mini-Mult with Delinquents." *Journal of Consulting and Clinical Psychology* 34: 450.

Auerbach, A. H., and J. H. Ewing. 1964. "Some Limitations of Psychiatric Rating Scales: The Clinician's Viewpoint." *Comprehensive Psychiatry* 5: 93–99.

Berry, D. F., and P. A. Marks. 1972. "Comparison of Multivariate Procedures for Grouping MMPI Data." *Proceedings of the 80th Annual Convention of the American Psychological Association* 7: 387–88.

Briggs, P. F., and A. Tellegen. 1967. "An Abbreviation of the Social Introversion Scale for 373-Item MMPI." *Journal of Clinical Psychology* 23: 189–91.

Bruning, J. L., and B. L. Kintz. 1968. *Computational Handbook of Statistics*. Glenview, Ill.: Scott, Foresman.

Buros, O. K. 1974. *Tests in Print II*. Highland Park, N.J.: Gryphon Press.

Butcher, J. N., and A. Tellegen. 1978. "Common Methodological Problems in MMPI Research." *Journal of Consulting and Clinical Psychology* 46: 620–28.

Cleveland, S. E. 1976. "Reflections on the Rise and Fall of Psychodiagnosis." *Professional Psychology* 7 : 309–18.

Comrey, A. L. 1958a. "A Factor Analysis of Items on the *F* Scale of the MMPI." *Educational and Psychological Measurement* 18: 621–32.

——. 1958b. "A Factor Analysis of Items on the MMPI Hypomania Scale." *Educational and Psychological Measurement* 18: 313–23.

Dahlstrom, W. G., G. S. Welsh, and L. E. Dahlstrom. 1972. *An MMPI Handbook*, vol. 1, *Clinical Interpretation*. Minneapolis: University of Minnesota Press.

Dean, E. F. 1972. "A Lengthened Mini: The Midi-Mult." *Journal of Clinical Psychology* 28: 68–71.

Endicott, N. A., and S. Jortner. 1967. "Correlates of Somatic Concern Derived from Psychological Tests." *Journal of Nervous and Mental Disease* 144: 133–38.

——. 1966. "Objective Measures of Depression." *Archives of General Psychiatry* 15: 249–55.

——, and E. Abramoff. 1969. "Objective Measures of Suspiciousness." *Journal of Abnormal Psychology* 74: 26–32.

Endinger, J. D., P. C. Kendall, J. F. Hooke, and J. B. Bogan. 1976. "The Predictive Efficacy of Three MMPI Short Forms." *Journal of Personality Assessment* 40: 259–65.

Faschingbauer, T. R. 1976. "Substitution and Regression Models, Base Rates and the Clinical Validity of the Mini-Mult." *Journal of Clinical Psychology* 32: 70–74.

——. 1974. "A 166-Item Short Form of the Group MMPI: The FAM." *Journal of Consulting and Clinical Psychology* 42: 645–55.

——, and C. S. Newmark. 1978. *Short Forms of the MMPI*. Lexington, Mass.: Heath.

Ferguson, R. G. 1946. "A Useful Adjunct to the MMPI Scoring and Analysis." *Journal of Clinical Psychology* 2: 248–53.

Fillenbaum, G. G., and E. Pfeiffer. 1976. "The Mini-Mult: A Cautionary Note." *Journal of Consulting and Clinical Psychology* 44: 698–703.

Fowler, R. D. 1969. "Automated Interpretation of Personality Test Data." In *MMPI: Research Developments and Clinical Applications*, edited by J. N. Butcher, pp. 105–26. New York: McGraw-Hill.

——. 1966. *The MMPI Notebook: A Guide to the Clinical Use of the Automated MMPI*. Nutley, N.J.: Roche Psychiatric Service Institute.

Garfield, S. L. 1978. "Research Problems in Clinical Diagnosis." *Journal of Consulting and Clinical Psychology* 46: 596–607.

Goldberg, L. R. 1974. "Objective Diagnostic Tests and Measures." *Annual Review of Psychology* 25: 343–66.

Graham, J. R., and H. E. Schroeder. 1972. "Abbreviated *Mf* and S Scales of the MMPI." *Journal of Personality Assessment* 36: 436–39.

——, and R. S. Lilly. 1971. "Factor Analysis of Items on the *Si* and *Mf* Scales of the MMPI." *Journal of Clinical Psychology* 27: 367–70.

Grant, H. 1946. "A Rapid Personality Evaluation Based on the MMPI and Cornell Selective Index." *American Journal of Psychiatry* 103: 33–41.

Grayson, H. M. 1951. *A Psychological Admissions Testing Program and Manual*. Los Angeles: Veterans Administration Center.

Harris, R. J., W. Wittner, B. Koppell, and F. D. Hilf. 1970. "MMPI Scales vs. Interviewer Ratings of Paranoia." *Psychological Reports* 27: 447–50.

Hays, W. 1963. *Statistics*. New York: Holt, Rinehart and Winston.

Hill, A. D. 1976. "Validity and Clinical Utility of the Grid Test of Schizophrenic Thought Disorder." *British Journal of Psychiatry* 126: 251–54.

Hoffmann, N. G., and J. N. Butcher. 1975. "Clinical Limitations of Three MMPI Short Forms." *Journal of Consulting and Clinical Psychology* 43: 32–39.

Holzberg, J., and S. Alessi. 1949. "Reliability of the Shortened Minnesota Multiphasic Personality Inventory." *Journal of Consulting Psychology* 13: 288–92.

Hugo, J. A. 1971. "Abbreviation of the MMPI Through Multiple Regression. Ph.D. dissertation, University of Alabama. *Dissertation Abstracts International* 32: 1213B. University Microfilms no. 71-20, 115.

Jorgenson, C. 1958. "A Short Form of the MMPI." *Australian Journal of Psychology* 10: 341–50.

Kincannon, J. C. 1968. "Prediction of the Standard MMPI Scale Scores from 71 Items: The Mini-Mult." *Journal of Consulting and Clinical Psychology* 32: 319–25.

Kreitman, N. 1961. "The Reliability of Psychiatric Diagnosis." *Journal of Mental Science* 107: 876–86.

Lachar, D. 1974a. "Accuracy and Generalizability of an Automated MMPI Interpretation System." *Journal of Consulting and Clinical Psychology* 42: 267–73.

——. 1974b. *The MMPI: Clinical Assessment and Automated Interpretation*. Los Angeles: Western Psychological Services.

——, V. Klinge, and J. L. Grisell. 1976. "Relative Accuracy of Automated MMPI Narratives Generated from Adult Norm and Adolescent Norm Profiles." *Journal of Consulting and Clinical Psychology* 44: 20–24.

Lorr, M. 1954. "Ratings Scales and Checklists for the Evaluation of Psychopathology." *Psychological Bulletin* 51: 119–27.

MacDonald, G. L. 1952a. "A Study of the Shortened Group and Individual Forms of the MMPI." *Journal of Clinical Psychology* 8: 309–11.

——. 1952b. "Effect of Test-Retest Interval and Item Arrangement on the Shortened Form of the MMPI." *Journal of Clinical Psychology* 8: 408–10.

McLachlan, J. F. C. 1974. "Test-Retest Stability of Long and Short Form MMPI Scales over Two Years." *Journal of Clinical Psychology* 30: 189–91.

Meehl, P. E. 1977. "High School Yearbooks: A Reply to Schwartz." *Journal of Abnormal Psychology* 77: 143–48.

Mlott, S. R. 1973. "The Mini-Mult and Its Use with Adolescents." *Journal of Clinical Psychology* 29: 376–77.

Newmark, C. S., A. J. Conger, and T. R. Faschingbauer. 1976. "The Interpretive Validity and Effective Test Length Functioning of an Abbreviated MMPI Relative to the Standard MMPI." *Journal of Clinical Psychology* 32: 27–32.

Newmark, C. S., R. Falk, and A. J. Finch. 1976. "Interpretive Accuracy of Abbreviated MMPIs." *Journal of Personality Assessment* 40: 266–68.

Newmark, C. S., R. Galen, and K. Gold. 1975. "Efficacy of an Abbreviated MMPI as a Function of Type of Administration." *Journal of Clinical Psychology* 31: 639–42.

Newmark, C. S., and L. Glenn. 1974. "Sensitivity of the Faschingbauer Abbreviated MMPI to Hospitalized Adolescents." *Journal of Abnormal Child Psychology* 2: 299–306.

Newmark, C. S., L. G. Newmark, and L. Cook. "The MMPI-168 with Psychiatric Patients." *Journal of Clinical Psychology* 31: 61–64.

Newmark, C. S., L. Newmark, and T. R. Faschingbuaer. 1974. "Utility of Three Abbreviated MMPIs with Psychiatric Outpatients." *Journal of Nervous and Mental Disease* 159: 438–43.

Newmark, C. S., M. Owen, L. Newmark, and T. R. Faschingbauer. 1975. "Comparison of Three Abbreviated MMPIs for Psychiatric Patients and Normals." *Journal of Personality Assessment* 39: 261–70.

Newmark, C. S., and D. Raft. 1976. "Using an Abbreviated MMPI as a Screening Device for Medical Patients." *Psychosomatics* 17: 45–48.

Newmark, C. S., D. R. Ziff, A. J. Finch, and P. C. Kendall. 1978. "Comparing the Empirical Validity of the Standard Form with Two Abbreviated MMPIs." *Journal of Consulting and Clinical Psychology* 46: 53–61.

Newton, J. R. 1971. "A Comparison of Studies of the Mini-Mult." *Journal of Clinical Psychology* 27: 489–90.

Norton, W. A. 1967. "A Review of Psychiatric Rating Scales." *Canadian Psychiatric Association Journal* 12: 563–74.

Olson, G. 1954. "The Hastings Short Form of the Group MMPI." *Journal of Clinical Psychology* 10: 386–88.

Overall, J. E. 1974. "The Brief Psychiatric Rating Scale in Psychopharmacology Research." *Modern Problems of Pharmacopsychiatry* 7: 67–68.

——. 1968. "Standard Psychiatric Symptom Description: The Factor Construct Rating Scale (FCRS)." *Triangle* 8: 178–84.

——, and F. Gomez-Mont. 1974. "The MMPI-168 for Psychiatric Screening." *Educational and Psychological Measurement* 34: 315–19.

Overall, J. E., and D. R. Gorham. 1962. "The Brief Psychiatric Rating Scale." *Psychological Reports* 10: 799–812.

Overall, J. E., W. Higgins, and A. DeSchweinitz. 1976. "Comparison of Differential Diagnostic Discrimination for Abbreviated and Standard MMPI." *Journal of Clinical Psychology* 32: 237–45.

Overall, J. E., L. E. Hollister, and S. N. Dalal. 1967. "Psychiatric Drug Research: Sample Size Requirements for One Versus Two Rates." *Archives of General Psychiatry* 16: 152–61.

Overall, J. E., L. E. Hollister, M. Johnson, and V. Pennington. 1966. "Nosology of Depression and Differential Response to Drugs." *Journal of the American Medical Association* 195: 946–48.

Overall, J. E., L. E. Hollister, and P. Pichot. 1967. "Major Psychiatric Disorders." *Archives of General Psychiatry* 16: 146–51.

Overall, J. E., and C. J. Klett. 1972. *Applied Multivariate Analysis*. New York: McGraw-Hill.

Porkorny, A. E., and J. E. Overall. 1970. "Relationship of Psychopathology to Age, Sex, Ethnicity, Education and Marital Status in State Hospital Patients." *Journal of Psychiatric Research* 7: 143–52.

Rand, S. 1976. "A Comprehensive Validation of the Expanded Mini-Mult." MS thesis, University of Miami.

Raskin, A., J. G. Schulterbrandt, and N. Reatig. 1966. "Rater and Patient Characteristics Associated with Rater Differences in Psychiatric Scale Ratings." *Journal of Clinical Psychology* 22: 417–23.

Schreier, A. J., M. Reznikoff, and B. C. Glueck. 1962. "Controlled Clinical Evaluation of Acute Schizophrenia: A Comparative Study of Rating Instruments and Judges." *Comprehensive Psychiatry* 3: 343–53.

Spera, J., and M. Robertson. "A 104-Item MMPI: The Maxi-Mult." Paper presented at the meeting of the American Psychological Association, New Orleans.

Spitzer, R. L., E. I. Burdock, and A. S. Hardesty. 1964. *Mental Status Schedule*. New York: Biometrics Research, New York State Department of Mental Hygiene.

Spitzer, R. L., J. Endicott, and G. M. Cohen. 1964. *Manual of Instruction for the Mental Status Schedule*. New York: Biometrics Research, New York State Department of Mental Hygiene.

Spitzer, R. L., J. L. Fleiss, E. I. Burdock, and A. S. Hardesty. 1964. "The Mental Status Schedule: Rational, Reliability and Validity." *Comprehensive Psychiatry* 5: 384–93.

Spitzer, R. L., J. L. Fleiss, J. Endicott, and J. Cohen. 1976. "Mental Status Schedule: Properties of Factor-Analytically Derived Scales." *Archives of General Psychiatry* 16: 479–92.

Spitzer, R. L., J. L. Fleiss, W. Kernohan, J. C. Lee, and I. T. Baldwin. 1965. "The Mental Status Schedule: Comparing Kentucky and New York Schizophrenics." *Archives of General Psychiatry* 12: 448–55.

Steer, R. A. 1974. "Relationship Between the Brief Psychiatric Rating Scale and the Multiple Affect Adjective Checklist for Schizophrenic Women." *Psychological Reports* 35: 79–82.

Windle, C. 1954. "Further Studies of Test-Retest Effect on Personality Questionnaires." *Educational and Psychological Measurement* 15: 246–53.

Wittenborn, J. R. 1972. "Reliability, Validity, and Objectivity of Symptom-Rating Scales." *Journal of Nervous and Mental Disease* 154: 79–87.

Zubin, J. 1967. "Classification of the Behavior Disorders." *Annual Review of Psychology* 18: 373–403.

10/A MODEL OF PSYCHOPATHOLOGY BASED ON THE MMPI

Harvey A. Skinner

In many respects the clinical scales of the MMPI are analogous to a vintage 1941 Chevrolet. Both were developed during the same era and reflect the thinking and methodology in use at that time. The 1941 Chevrolet was driven widely in its day, but has since undergone frequent overhauls and redesigns. Likewise, the MMPI has been extensively used and has been given numerous overhauls in the guise of new scales. Indeed, the proliferation of additional scales has led Butcher and Tellegen (1978) to quip that "there are presently more MMPI scales than there are items on the inventory" (p. 622). The Chevrolet has been driven almost everywhere, sometimes on terrain that it was not designed for. Similarly, the MMPI's popularity and ease of administration have encouraged some inappropriate excursions. Recall that the clinical scales were developed to assess psychopathology as reflected by Kraepelinian nosology. Despite the frequent use of the MMPI as a general personality inventory, the clinical scales were not designed to be sensitive to personality variables within the normal range.

Today, because of technological advances and a growing emphasis on conservation, the trend in automobiles is toward smaller, safer, and more efficient models. Correspondingly, there is need to upgrade the aging clinical scales of the MMPI. The psychometric problems with the clinical scales are well documented, including the issues of item overlap, factorial complexity of the scales, and influence of response styles such as social desirability and acquiescence (Wiggins 1973). The response style controversy, in particular, continues to fuel considerable debate in the literature (for example, Schweder 1977; Edwards 1977; Block

This research was supported by the Addiction Research Foundation of Ontario. I wish to acknowledge the important contributions of D. N. Jackson to the development of this model and would like to thank K. R. Shoffner for her valuable assistance in preparing the figures.

1977). Limitations of the clinical scales and of the underlying Kraepelinian classification system were recognized by the test authors. The hope in 1941 was that this new instrument would spearhead the development of a more dynamic and clinically useful classification of psychopathology. This pioneering spirit is exemplified by Hathaway (1960) in his comment on the MMPI: "I see it as a steppingstone that permits useful communication at its own level even though the stone is rather wobbly" (p. viii).

Notwithstanding the shortcomings of the MMPI clinical scales, this instrument has generated a rich storehouse of data. For example, Dahlstrom, Welsh, and Dahlstrom (1975) cite over 6,000 references. Although this steppingstone in Hathaway's terms is "rather wobbly," much can be learned from attempts such as Goldberg's (1972) to synthesize these data.

Thus the overriding aim of this chapter is to describe a model that may be used to integrate within a coherent, parsimonious framework the diverse studies that have used the MMPI clinical scales. In essence, this dimensional classification schema provides a theoretical model of psychopatholgoy (Skinner and Jackson 1978). It may be used as a convenient roadmap or descriptive summary of the far-ranging travels of the MMPI clinical scales. Also, the model should serve a heuristic function for stimulating new research. This chapter has three major sections. First, the background and basic components of the model are discussed. Then an application of the model is described in some detail using the 233 deviant and normal MMPI samples compiled by Lanyon (1968). Finally, the theoretical implications and requisite steps in validating the model are reviewed.

MODEL OF PSYCHOPATHOLOGY

Background

Kluckhohn and Murray (1949) have remarked that every man is "like all other men, like some other men, and like no other men" (p. 35). Implicit in this statement is a classification schema that encompasses the various commonalities and unique traits among individuals. Classification is a basic device man uses for seeking order in the universe. It is a means of organizing our experiences into a system to which new events or entities may be compared and integrated. Riese (1945) has argued that this economizing principle of the human intellect is essential for learning. In science, classification is a fundamental process in the description of facts, in the search for some pattern or structure. This descriptive phase is a natural precondition for the formulation of underlying causal mechanisms or scientific theories (Hempel 1965).

The history of psychiatric classifications is both extensive and turbulent. From primitive beginnings around 2600 B.C. in Sumeria and Egypt, the number of recognized disorders has expanded and then contracted through numerous eras (Menninger 1963). Traditional psychiatric nomenclature and diagnostic principles have been widely criticized. These shortcomings range from empirical studies of the low interrater reliability and lack of predictive validity to demonstrations of the potentially harmful effects of diagnostic labeling (Kendell 1975). The publication of the American Psychiatric Association's (1978) "Diagnostic and Statistical Manual" (DSM-III) has stimulated renewed debate among various disciplines (for example, Schacht and Nathan 1977).

As an alternative to traditional psychiatric classifications, there has been an increasing emphasis on empirical methods to define major behavioral disorders. These methods are an outgrowth of the explosive development during the past 20 years of quantitative techniques for classification research (Sneath and Sokal 1973). Because these quantitative procedures are empirically based, the hope is that they will facilitate a more objective, reliable, and valid classification of abnormal behavior. For example, Paykel (1971) has employed an empirical clustering strategy to identify relatively homogeneous subgroups among depressed patients. In a partial validation of this typology, Paykel (1972) found a significant patient type-by-treatment interaction with respect to chemotherapy using amitriptyline.

The present model of psychopathology is grounded in this quantitative approach to classification. The conceptual framework was stimulated, in part, by a vector model of disease states in clinical medicine proposed by Sneath (1975). Basically, the course of a disease is represented as the movement of a point or vector in a multidimensional space of quantitative variables. Sneath's (1975) model makes an important distinction between the type of disease and the severity of its clinical symptoms. Imagine a three-dimensional space or cube. The center of this space (origin) defines the "normal" or reference population. That is, normal states are represented by a swarm of points about the origin. As a person becomes ill, his point moves away from the origin. One can envisage this process as an arrow (vector) traveling away from the center of the cube. The length of this vector, or distance from the origin, provides a measure of the symptom severity as reflected by such clinical variables as pulse rate, temperature, and respiration rate. The direction of the vector, on the other hand, indicates the kind or type of disease. For example, in the three-dimensional cube each independent axis could represent one of the three classical fevers: influenza, pneumonia, or typhoid. A person with influenza would have a vector close to the influenza reference axis in this space. As the person recovers from the illness, his vector would move back toward the origin.

Three Clinical Types

Our model of psychopathology is composed of three clinical types or syndromes: neurotic, psychotic, and sociopathic. These types were derived by Skinner and Jackson (1978) from the 19 code types of the Gilberstadt and Duker (1965) and 16 code types of the Marks, Seeman, and Haller (1974) MMPI actuarial systems. Because of the care involved in developing each system, it was felt that they would provide good foundation blocks for the formulation of a general model. Briefly, relationships among the 35 code types from each system were evaluated using an empirical classification procedure (Skinner 1977). Three underlying types or "modal profiles" were found to explain 81.92 percent of the covariation among the 35 code types. Thus, with the three superordinate types, one is able to capture most of the common variance among the Gilberstadt and Duker (1965) and Marks, Seeman, and Haller (1974) systems. These three types provide a simple, yet powerful representation of the information contained in each actuarial system.

The modal MMPI profiles that define the superordinate types are presented in Table 10.1. The neurotic type has high points on *Hs, D,* and *Hy.* The purest examples of this type were the Gilberstadt and Duker (1965) codes 1-3-2 and 1-2-3-7 and the Marks, Seeman, and Halles (1974) code 2-3-1. In contrast, the psychotic type has high points on *Sc* and *Pt.* The code 8-6 from each system was the best exemplar of this second type. Finally, the sociopathic type has high points on *Pd* and *Ma*, and was best exemplified by the code 4-9 from each actuarial system.

Similar to Sneath's (1975) vector model, each superordinate type in the system defines an orthogonal axis as depicted in Figure 10.1. From the center or origin (0) of the shaded area, each axis projects in a positive (+1) and negative (-1) direction. The cube from the positive section (0 to +1 on each axis) is enlarged for emphasis, as most individuals will be located in this area. Given the MMPI clinical scales in T score format, one may compute the coordinates for individual profiles in this cube. For example, if a person has high points on *Hs, D,* and *Hy*, his vector would be located near the neurotic axis. Likewise, a person with elevations on *Sc* and *Pt* would project along the psychotic axis, whereas another individual with a *Pd* and *Ma* configuration would be located near the sociopathic reference axis. The cosine of the angle between a person's vector and one of the three reference axes provides a quantitative index of the extent to which the individual resembles that superordinate type. Computationally, this cosine is equivalent to the product-moment correlation between the person's MMPI profile and the respective modal profile of Table 10.1 (Green and Carroll 1976, Chapter 3).

In any particular sample it is expected that a certain number of individuals will resemble only one type. Consequently, there will be a swarm of vectors near each reference axis of Figure 10.1. However, some persons will resemble to some extent more than one type. Their vectors will span the space between axes. In addition, other persons may not resemble the neurotic, psychotic, or soicopathic type. For these cases the vectors will be clustered near the origin. This conceptualization is similar to linear typal analysis described by Overall and Klett (1972, p. 216). The empirical import of the model is contingent on the degree to which a reasonable number of cases have a predominant location near a single reference axis. For these cases, one may use the respective superordinate type to characterize the subgroup without great loss of information. Furthermore, one may observe loci of vectors at other locations in Figure 10.1. These cases would repre-

TABLE 10.1

MMPI Modal Profiles

Clinical Scale	Neurotic		Psychotic		Sociopathic	
	Z Scores	T Scores	Z Scores	T Scores	Z Scores	T Scores
L	-.670	43	-1.590	35	-.820	42
F	-1.060	39	.596	56	-.171	48
K	-.256	47	-1.832	32	.093	51
Hs	1.716	67	-.580	44	.053	51
D	1.612	66	.655	57	-.563	44
Hy	1.665	67	-.561	44	.747	57
Pd	.059	51	.493	55	2.043	70
Mf	-.561	44	-.683	43	-.467	45
Pa	-.732	43	.705	57	-.068	49
Pt	.396	54	1.153	61	-.757	42
Sc	-.311	47	1.832	68	-.305	47
Ma	-1.255	37	-.125	49	1.886	69
Si	-.603	44	-.145	69	-1.671	33

Note: With the Z scores, each modal profile has a mean = 0.0 and standard deviation = 1.0, whereas with the T scores, each profile has a mean = 50 and standard deviation = 10.

Source: H. A. Skinner and D. N. Jackson, "A Model of Psychopathology Based on an Integration of MMPI Actuarial Systems," *Journal of Consulting and Clinical Psychology* 46 (1978): 231–38. Copyright (1978) by the American Psychological Association. Reprinted with permission.

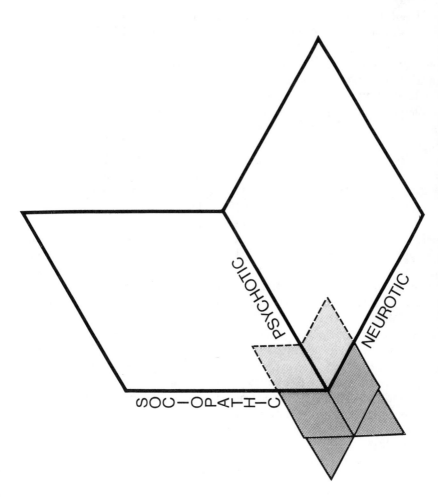

FIGURE 10.1: Three-dimensional representation of neurotic, psychotic, and sociopathic typal axes. *Source:* Constructed by the author.

sent mixed types. Of course, one may expect the proportion of cases that are salient on a given type to vary across different populations, such as prison inmates versus psychiatric patients.

Degree of Maladjustment

The neurotic, psychotic, and sociopathic types are hypothesized to reflect broad ways in which individuals can differ, with each type having certain biological and environmental determinants. Each type is defined empirically by a configuration of scores on the MMPI clinical scales (Table 10.1). In addition to examining the extent to which a person's MMPI profile resembles the pattern of scores for each type, it is important to consider the degree of symptom severity or maladjustment (see Sneath 1975).

In their classic paper on assessing similarity between profiles, Cronbach and Gleser (1953) made a distinction among shape, elevation, and scatter. Shape describes the actual pattern of "ups and downs" across variables in the profile. The neurotic type, for example, is marked by high points on *Hs, D,* and *Hy*, as well as low scores on *F* and *Ma*. Elevation is the mean score of the individual across all 13 MMPI clinical scales, whereas scatter denotes how dispersed scores are about the profile average. Skinner (1978a) has described the contribution of the three parameters to various indexes of profile similarity.

It is hypothesized that shape represents the clinical pattern or type of disorder. This is reflected in the common clinical practice of examining two-point code types (for example, Gynther et al. 1972). Indeed it is almost a reflex reaction when given a MMPI profile to look at the pattern of high points. Elevation, on the other hand, provides a quantitative index of symptom severity. For example, psychiatric and normal individuals may have the same profile shape on the MMPI, such as a code 1-2-3. However, the psychiatric patients should prove distinguishable from normals when profile elevation is examined, because the psychiatric patients' high points should exceed a T score of 70. Presumably, the psychiatric patients are experiencing a more severe array of symptoms. Finally, scatter is postulated to reflect the extent of personality differentiation or polarization. For example, two persons may have a similar syndrome of hypochondriasis. This tendency toward preoccupation with somatic complaints would be much more distinctive or pronounced for the profile with higher scatter. With the MMPI clinical scales, the elevation and scatter parameters tend to be highly correlated (see Figures 10.2, 10.3, and 10.4).

For illustrative purposes, the characteristic MMPI profiles for the neurotic, psychotic, and sociopathic types are given in Figures 10.2, 10.3, and 10.4, respectively. By standard convention for T scores, each modal MMPI profile is scaled to have a mean (elevation) equal to 50 and standard deviation (scatter) equal to 10. Also plotted in each figure is the average MMPI profile for a group taken from Lanyon (1968). These reference groups provide real-world exemplars of the three types. In Figure 10.2, the somatization reaction group (n = 39) pro-

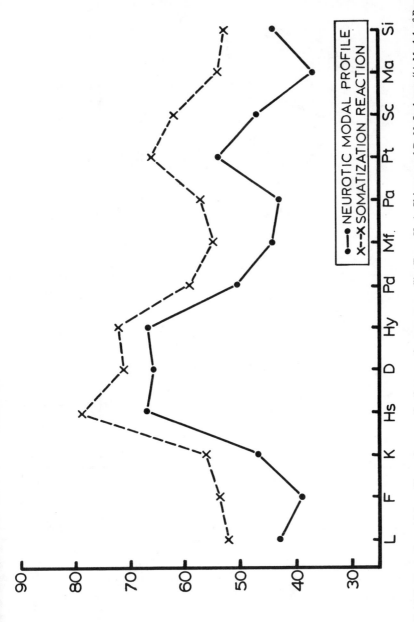

FIGURE 10.2: Neurotic modal profile and a somatization reaction group profile. From H. A. Skinner and D. N. Jackson, "A Model of Psychopathology Based on an Integration of MMPI Actuarial Systems." *Journal of Consulting and Clinical Psychology* 46 (1978): 231–38. Copyright 1978 by the American Psychological Association. Reprinted with permission.

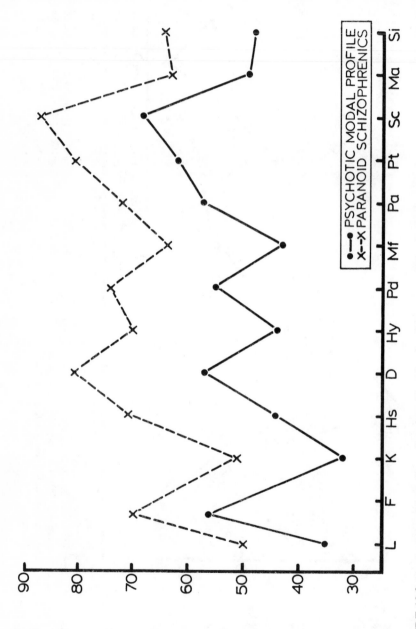

FIGURE 10.3: Psychotic modal profile and a paranoid schizophrenic group profile. From H. A. Skinner and D. N. Jackson, "A Model of Psychopathology Based on an Integration of MMPI Actuarial Systems," *Journal of Consulting and Clinical Psychology* 46 (1978): 231–38. Copyright 1978 by the American Psychological Association. Reprinted with permission.

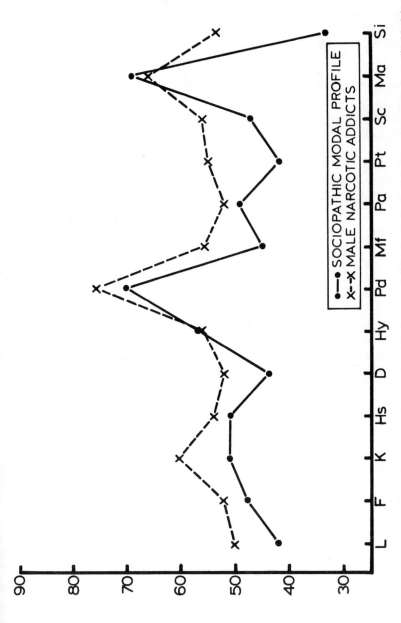

FIGURE 10.4: Sociopathic modal profile and a male narcotic addict's group profile. From H. A. Skinner and D. N. Jackson, "A Model of Psychopathology Based on an Integration of MMPI Actuarial Systems." *Journal of Consulting and Clinical Psychology* 46 (1978): 231–38. Copyright 1978 by the American Psychological Association. Reprinted with permission.

file has a marked similarity in shape (correlation = .93) to the neurotic modal profile, although the psychiatric profile is higher in elevation (60.92 compared with the modal profile reference standard of 50.00). A similar relationship holds between the psychotic modal profile and paranoid schizophrenic group (n = 100) in Figure 10.3 and between the sociopathic modal profile and male narcotic addicts (n = 60) in Figure 10.4.

Classification Model

Computationally, the modal MMPI profiles (Table 10.1) for the neurotic, psychotic, and sociopathic types were derived using least-squares estimates based on the singular value decomposition (Green and Carroll 1976, p. 230). Mathematical details are provided by Skinner (1977, 1978a, 1978b). The classification results may be summarized by a generalized principal components model. Let X_i represent a data matrix giving the scores of n individuals from sample $_i$ on the 13 MMPI clinical scales in T score format. The classification model can be depicted as

$$X_i = f \left\{ M_i, S_i, (A_i P' + E_i) \right\} \tag{1}$$

That is, relationships among MMPI profiles can be expressed as a function of (1) a column vector of profile elevation parameters M_i, (2) a column vector of profile scatter parameters S_i, and (3) a matrix of shape parameters A_i. The shape parameters describe the extent to which each individual's MMPI profile resembles the shape of the neurotic, psychotic, and sociopathic modal profiles (Figures 10.2, 10.3, and 10.4). Formally, the matrix A_i is a set of principal component loadings or weights, while the matrix P is a conformable set of component scores. Actually, the matrix P contains the modal MMPI profiles of Table 10.1 (Z score scaling). Finally, E_i is a residual matrix that provides a measure of how well the modal MMPI profiles "fit" the given sample X_i.

Several features of the classification model should be noted. First, the model provides a reduced rank solution. That is, the model attempts to partition systematic covariation among individuals from an error residual E_i. Because of this reduced rank approximation, one should expect the modal MMPI profiles P to be robust across different samples (see Gleason and Staelin 1973). Second, the model provides separate parameters for profile elevation, scatter, and shape. Following Skinner (1978a), the investigator may differentiate the independent contribution of each parameter in defining profile similarity. A logical strategy is to examine the shape parameters (A_i) and allocate individuals into relatively homogeneous subgroups according to their similarity to the neurotic, psychotic, or sociopathic type. Then, at a second stage, one may differentiate persons within each shape type with respect to profile elevation (M_i) and scatter (S_i). This strategy directly achieves the objectives of Guertin's (1966) two-stage analysis. Third, the parameters may be used as a set of predictor variables in multiple regression equations for predicting various criteria such as treatment outcome. In this way one may use all of the quantitative information contained in the interval metric of each parameter.

Finally, one may construct various graphic plots as a mechanism for summarizing the classification results. Examples of these plots are given by Skinner and Jackson (1978), as well as by the various figures presented in this chapter. The three shape parameters A_i provide the coordinates for plotting individual vectors in Figure 10.1. Another useful graph is to plot elevation by shape for a particular type (for example, Figure 4 in Skinner and Jackson 1978). This graph allows one to identify persons who have similar MMPI profile shapes, yet are different in the level of symptom severity (elevation parameter). For reference when constructing figures, the classification parameters for the Gilberstadt and Duker (1965) and Marks, Seeman, and Haller (1974) code types are given in Table 10.2. Following the example of Figure 4 in Skinner and Jackson (1978), one may plot the location of code types from the two actuarial systems to serve as reference points or marker variables.

Computational Summary

The steps for computing the parameters in Equation 1 are straightforward, and may be accomplished using a desk calculator or by employing a computer software package such as SPSS:

1. Score the 13 MMPI clinical scales and convert the raw scores to T scores.
2. Compute the average over the 13 MMPI clinical scales T scores to yield the elevation parameter (M_i).
3. Compute the standard deviation of the 13 clinical scales about this average to give the scatter paramter (S_i).
4. Compute the product-moment correlation of the MMPI profile with each of the three modal MMPI profiles (Table 10.1) to yield the three shape parameters (A_i).

Using SPSS Subprogram PEARSON CORR, input the three modal MMPI profiles (Z Scores of Table 10.1) as well as the MMPI profiles for all persons in the sample. (Note: Each MMPI profile is considered a variable, while the 13 clinical scale scores are the observations.) Then compute correlations between the sample profiles and the three modal profiles. The output for each person should include the profile mean (elevation parameter), standard deviation (scatter parameter), and correlations with the three modal profiles (shape parameters). An example of this output for the Gilberstadt and Duker (1965) and Marks, Seeman, and Haller (1974) code types is presented in Table 10.2.

TABLE 10.2

Classification Results for the MMPI Actuarial Systems

	Elevation	Scatter	N	Shape	
				P	S
Gilberstadt and Duker (1965)					
Code 1–2–3	62.61	13.22	.94	.00	-.01
Code 1–2–3–4	65.69	12.72	.90	.26	.27
Code 1–2–3–7	64.69	14.09	.96	.15	-.09
Code 1–3–2	59.31	12.09	.96	-.16	.07
Code 1–3–7	65.39	12.48	.74	.32	.07
Code 1–3–8	67.54	11.16	.73	.40	.10
Code 1–3–9	58.31	8.71	.54	.00	.66
Code 2–7	63.85	12.94	.80	.40	-.20
Code 2–7–4	66.92	12.26	.59	.66	.18
Code 2–7–8	74.00	16.37	.44	.82	-.26
Code 4	58.00	7.52	.16	.22	.79
Code 4–3	60.31	8.97	.61	.09	.63
Code 4–9	55.54	9.04	-.16	.06	.95
Code 7–8	70.23	13.36	.47	.83	-.07
Code 8–1–2–3	81.15	19.83	.67	.47	-.03
Code 8–2–4	68.15	12.50	.30	.86	.27
Code 8–6	70.61	14.26	-.08	.89	-.04
Code 8–9	63.31	11.28	-.34	.72	.43
Code 9	53.92	9.79	-.54	.21	.68

Marks, Seeman, and Haller (1974)

Code 2–3–1	63.54	12.07	.91	.30	-.10
Code 2–7	66.15	12.53	.78	.40	-.29
Code 2–7–4	67.54	12.35	.41	.73	-.03
Code 2–7–8	70.31	14.40	.55	.71	-.34
Code 2–8	72.39	13.65	.43	.87	-.10
Code 3–1	63.23	10.12	.85	-.17	.27
Code 3–2–1	67.31	13.25	.86	.40	.07
Code 4–6	64.23	11.25	.08	.66	.40
Code 4–6–2	67.54	14.73	.43	.73	.09
Code 4–8–2	69.61	11.91	.19	.88	.30
Code 4–9	61.08	8.37	-.04	.34	.90
Code 8–3	68.31	10.41	.62	.56	.27
Code 8–6	72.31	16.39	.03	.93	.04
Code 8–9	65.61	11.76	-.17	.83	.30
Code 9–6	57.79	9.20	-.50	.46	.56
Normal	54.31	3.85	.34	-.21	.60

Note: For the shape parameters, N = Neurotic, P = Psychotic, and S = Sociopathic.

Source: H. A. Skinner and D. N. Jackson, "A Model of Psychopathology Based on an Integration of MMPI Actuarial Systems." *Journal of Consulting and Clinical Psychology* 46 (1978): 231–38. Copyright (1978) by the American Psychological Association. Reprinted with permission.

EMPIRICAL EXAMPLE

Lanyon (1968) has compiled 112 research studies between 1940 and 1967 in which the average scores are given for the MMPI clinical scales. Complete data are available for 233 groups that represent the accumulated MMPI profiles of over 28,000 individuals. These MMPI data span a diverse range of samples, including psychotic patients (for example, paranoid schizophrenics), neurotic patients (for example, anxiety neurotics), sociopaths (for example, narcotic addicts), mixed psychiatric (for example, suicide attempt group), medical patients (for example, epilepsy), and normals (for example, college students). Using this data set, Goldberg (1972) compared the advantages of group MMPI data versus individual profiles in the construction of classification rules for psychiatric diagnoses. He concluded that "group data appear to contain such a high signal-noise ratio that they become extraordinarily efficient indicators of underlying processes—processes which are normally obscured by the unreliability inherent in individual profiles" (p. 121). Consequently, Lanyon's (1968) compendium provides a fertile ground for an empirical evaluation of the model of psychopathology. The 233 group average MMPI profiles were classified according to Equation 1, and the detailed results are presented in Appendix B. The number in brackets after each group name refers to the study number in Lanyon's (1968) book. A description of each study and appropriate reference are contained in Lanyon (1968).

Correlation Among Profile Parameters

The three modal MMPI profiles of Table 10.1 are statistically independent. Indeed, they provide a set of basis vectors (Green and Carroll 1976, p. 80) for constructing the model depicted in Figure 10.1. However, one should expect some correlation among the elevation, scatter, and shape parameters due to measurement properties of the clinical scales. That is, if the basic clinical scales are markedly elevated, the K validity scale is invariably low. The result is a high degree of profile scatter. Thus there is a built-in correlation between MMPI profile elevation and scatter. (Reversing the direction of scoring for the K scale would partially alleviate this correlation.)

Correlations among the five profile parameters are presented in Table 10.3. The values above the major diagonal are based on the 130 deviant groups (neurotic, psychotic, sociopathic, and mixed psychiatric). Here there is a substantial correlation (.81) between elevation and scatter, as expected. This result suggests that for deviant samples one should consider the elevation and scatter parameters synonymously as an index of symptom severity. Support for this construct interpretation is further evidenced by the positive correlation (.69) between elevation and the psychotic parameter. That is, behaviors related to the psychotic type generally would be rated as the severest form of maladjustment. An inverse relationship is evident between the three shape parameters. For ex-

TABLE 10.3

Correlations Among the Profile Parameters

	Elevation	Scatter	Neurotic	Psychotic	Sociopathic
Elevation	—	.81	.17	.69	−.46
Scatter	.59	—	.13	.50	−.33
Neurotic	.16	.11	—	−.33	−.62
Psychotic	.38	.35	−.39	—	−.07
Sociopathic	−.15	03	−.36	.16	—

Note: Data based on 130 deviant groups appear above the major diagonal, while data below the major diagonal are taken from the 78 normal groups.
Source: Compiled by the author.

ample, if an individual has a high similarity to one type, he will tend to have a low resemblance to the other two.

Data below the major diagonal in Table 10.3 are taken from the 78 normal groups. Observe that with normal MMPI profiles, the elevation and scatter parameters are less correlated (.59 compared with .81). Also, there is a lower degree of correlation between elevation and the three shape parameters. Thus the model parameters are more independent with normal MMPI profiles.

Differentiation of Psychiatric Classifications

Following Goldberg (1972), the Lanyon (1968) data may be partitioned into six major classes: psychotic samples (n = 22), neurotic samples (n = 19), sociopathic samples (n = 41), mixed psychiatric (n = 48), medical samples (n = 21), and normal samples (n = 78). Table 10.4 presents descriptive statistics for each class with respect to the five profile parameters. One can use these data as normative reference groups for computing standard scores (for example, T scores). For example, data for a given study could be compared to the mean and standard deviation for each parameter in the normal samples.

Several interesting trends are evident in Table 10.4. First, the elevation parameter is consistent in ranking the classes according to their expected degree of maladjustment—that is, (1) psychotic, (2) neurotic, (3) mixed psychiatric, (4) sociopathic, (5) medical, and (6) normal. Except for a reversal with the psychotic and neurotic samples, an identical ranking is observed with the scatter parameter. With respect to the shape parameters, the psychotic samples have a predominant similarity to the psychotic modal profile (Figure 10.3) and the neurotic samples have a marked similarity to the neurotic modal profile (Figure 10.2). However, the sociopathic samples have equal resemblance to the sociopathic (Figure 10.4) and psychotic types. This suggests the presence of two major types

TABLE 10.4

Descriptive Statistics for the Major Groups

		Profile Parameters			
	Elevation	Scatter	N	P	S
1. Psychotic samples (n = 22)					
Mean	63.11	7.07	.14	.73	.17
Standard deviation	(3.95)	(2.60)	(.38)	(.18)	(.16)
2. Neurotic samples (n = 19)					
Mean	61.69	8.40	.75	.42	.10
Standard deviation	(2.15)	(1.61)	(.16)	(.26)	(.14)
3. Sociopathic samples (n = 41)					
Mean	59.27	6.66	.04	.58	.55
Standard deviation	(2.12)	(1.47)	(.30)	(.19)	(.15)
4. Mixed psychiatric (n = 48)					
Mean	60.37	6.68	.54	.41	.23
Standard deviation	(5.04)	(2.82)	(.33)	(.34)	(.17)
5. Medical samples (n = 21)					
Mean	58.79	5.69	.49	.44	.24
Standard deviation	(2.87)	(1.89)	(.46)	(.27)	(.17)
6. Normal samples (n = 78)					
Mean	54.74	3.81	− .10	.31	.38
Standard deviation	(1.98)	(1.10)	(.26)	(.31)	(.29)

Note: N = neurotic, P = psychotic, and S = sociopathic.
Source: Compiled by the author.

among individuals who are generally grouped under a sociopathic rubric. Further empirical support for the prevalence of at least two types among "sociopathic" individuals is given by the classification hit rates for 314 prison inmates who were tested upon admission to a Canadian federal prison assessment center. Following the methodology of Skinner, Reed, and Jackson (1976), the classification rates for the three MMPI types were 9.2 percent neurotic, 34.7 percent psychotic, and 30.6 percent sociopathic, for an overall rate of 74.5 percent. The salience of the psychotic and sociopathic types may prove to have important implications regarding which prisoners would benefit from treatment or which prisoners are more likely to attempt to escape.

Not surprisingly, the mixed psychiatric samples have group profiles that resemble all three types. This mixture is evident among the medical samples, although their mean elevation parameter and scatter parameters are lower. Finally, the normal samples have only a modest shape resemblance to the psychotic and sociopathic modal MMPI profiles.

To provide a rigorous test of differences among the six classes, a multiple discriminant analysis was conducted using the five MMPI profile parameters as dependent measures (Cooley and Lohnes 1971). This multivariate technique derives linear combinations of the profile parameters that optimally differentiate the six classes. Significance tests (Wilk's lambda) are performed in a step-down fashion to identify the number of significant functions. The results are summarized in Table 10.5. Although all five potential functions were significant (p < .01), the first three captured almost 96 percent of the between-group dispersion. The standardized weights are analogous to beta weights in a multiple regression equation. They describe how each variable is weighted to form the composite score that optimally distinguishes the classes. Structure coefficients are simply the correlation between an original variable and the composite scores. Finally, the univariate F ratios allow one to evaluate the discriminatory power of each variable considered singly. Observe that all five profile parameters are significant discriminators.

Figure 10.5 presents the group centroids on the first three functions. The first function reflects symptom severity (elevation and scatter) with respect to neurotic tendencies (neurotic type). This linear combination accounts for nearly two thirds of the dispersion between groups. Essentially, function I contrasts the normal from the neurotic samples. The second function is characterized by symptom severity (elevation) in a psychotic and soicopathic orientation. This function serves to separate the psychotic and sociopathic samples from the other groups. Finally, the third function is defined by the presence of sociopathic tendencies. Note that the size of the dot in Figure 10.5 reflects the group's score on the third dimension. Thus function III distinguishes the sociopathic from psychotic samples.

In summary, the discriminant analysis of the six general classes provides considerable empirical support for the construct validity of the MMPI profile parameters. Either separately or in linear combination, the five parameters of the model are meaningful discriminators among the 233 MMPI group average profiles.

Selected Examples

A wealth of interesting comparisons can be made among selected MMPI groups in Appendix B. The largest elevation (72.42) and scatter (17.51) parameters are for fake bad tests by the normal group. This profile has a substantial correlation (.90) with the psychotic type, owing in part to item overlap between *Sc* and *F* scales. Two clinical groups achieve an elevation parameter score over 70, that is, a postpromazine test of schizophrenics (71.08) and a suicide threat group (70.90), whereas the lowest elevation score is for a group of nonpregnant

TABLE 10.5

Discriminant Analysis Summary

	Standardized Weights			Structure Coefficients			Univariate F Ratio
	1	2	3	1	2	3	
Elevation	.39	1.21	1.40	.60	.70	.39	39.53*
Scatter	.18	-.41	-1.30	.53	.46	-.13	29.53*
Neurotic	.66	-.50	-.49	.69	-.59	-.10	43.72*
Psychotic	.01	.07	-.18	.13	.72	.21	10.10*
Sociopathic	.06	.56	-.74	-.31	.47	-.70	19.20*
Percent dispersion	62.96	17.76	15.21				
Canonical correlation	.77*	.54*	.51*				

*p < .01.
Source: Compiled by the author.

294

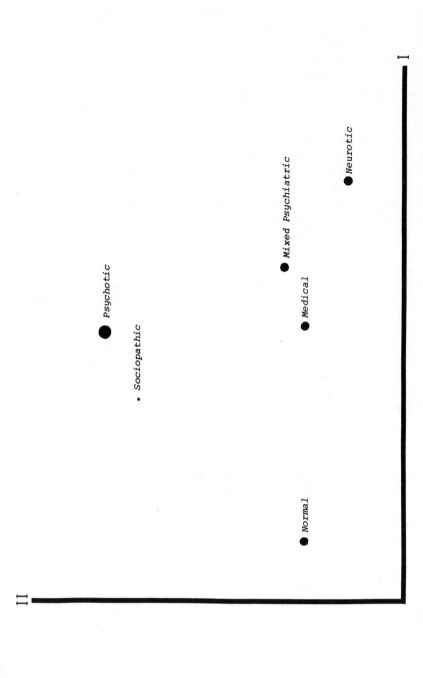

FIGURE 10.5: Group centroids plotted on the first two discriminant functions. The size of the dot for each group represents its projection on the third function. *Source:* Constructed by the author.

females (49.92) followed by a control group of mothers (52.05). Two of the groups with the highest elevation parameters (fake bad and suicide threat) also scored highest on Goldberg's (1972) predictor index ($Hs + 2Pd - Ma$) for differentiating deviant from normal samples.

The MMPI profiles for three schizophrenic groups at different ages are given in Figure 10.6. The subjects were clinically diagnosed schizophrenic patients at the Chicago State Hospital. The age 15 to 29 group (dashed line) has the highest elevation parameter (62.59), followed by the age 30 to 39 (solid line) score of 58.36 and the age 40 to 53 (dotted line) score of 56.89. An identical trend is evident for the scatter parameters (7.10, 3.51, and 2.43, respectively). These data suggest that the MMPI scores of schizophrenic patients tend to decrease with age. However, one should not necessarily conclude that the degree of maladjustment diminishes with age. Rather, this age trend may underscore the need to develop separate MMPI norms within major age groupings (see the Wechsler Adult Intelligence Scale). With respect to profile shape, the three age groups resemble the psychotic type in descending order of magnitude (.92 for age 15 to 29, .85 for age 30 to 39, .66 for age 40 to 53); that is, the youngest schizophrenic patients provide the clearest example of the psychotic modal MMPI profile (Figure 10.3). Of interest is the moderate correlation (.53) between the age 40 to 53 profile and the neurotic type, which suggests that neurotic tendencies among schizophrenics may increase with time. Again, this feature may only indicate the need for MMPI norms that are sensitive to the normal aging process.

There is evidence to support the utility of the elevation (and scatter) parameter as a predictor of treatment outcome. For example, in the psychotic samples, a recovery group (21) of schizophrenics has a lower profile elevation than an unimproved group (22) with respect to shock therapy (elevation = 63.67 versus 66.67). A similar trend under the mixed psychiatric samples is evident for shock therapy with affective disorder patients. The recovery group's (47) elevation of 61.89 is more than five points lower than the unimproved group's (48) value of 66.51. Likewise, with adult neurotic patients who underwent six months of psychotherapy in the outpatient service of a state hospital, the improved patients' (18) MMPI profile elevation of 60.13 is lower than the unimproved group's (19) score of 63.66. Finally, in the sociopathic samples, a successful threatment group (38) of female delinquents scored lower in elevation than the unsuccessful group (39) by a factor of six points (58.28 versus 64.28). In all cases, the MMPI was administered before the treatment began.

Support for the construct interpretation of profile elevation as a quantitative index of symptom severity is given by a study where patients were independently rated for the severity of psychopathology. A total morbidity score was derived as a composite of ratings by clinical psychologists and ward observations by nursing personnel. The high morbidity and low morbidity groups consisted of the top and bottom thirds of the distribution on the total morbidity scores (mixed psychiatric samples numbers 9, 10, 32, and 33). With both male

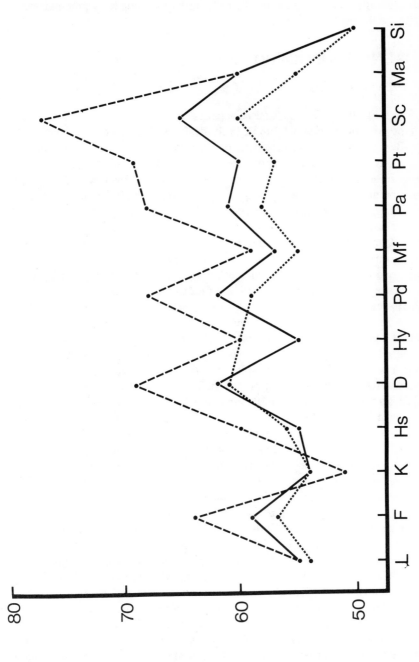

FIGURE 10.6: MMPI profiles for three groups of schizophrenic patients: age 15–29 (dashed line), age 30–39 (solid line), and age 40–53 (dotted line). *Source* Constructed by the author.

and female patients, the high morbidity groups' elevation parameter (male = 68.39, female = 67.54) exceeds the low morbidity groups' score (male = 63.69, female = 58.38). Also in both sexes the high morbidity group has a predominant similarity to the psychotic modal profile.

THEORETICAL IMPLICATIONS

Ideal Type Constructs

The neurotic, psychotic, and sociopathic types can be conceptualized as ideal type constructs (Hempel 1965). Each ideal type is defined as a hypothetical profile pattern that is characteristic of a subset of individuals in the population. Certain ideal types are hypothesized in a population with each member being more or less related to each type. For example, an individual's MMPI profile may be depicted as a weighted mixture of these three ideal types. Kretschmer (1925, p. 93) has termed this mixture the "constitutional alloy."

In discussing the role of ideal type constructs and scientific explanation, Hempel (1965) has argued that "this conception reflects an attempt to advance concept formation . . . from the stage of description and 'empirical generalization' . . . to the construction of theoretical systems or models" (p. 161). The ideal types as displayed in Figure 10.1 form a theoretical model of psychopathology. However, in order to subject this theoretical model to empirical evaluation, the constructs must be connected to observable data. The linking of hypothetical constructs to observable data is an essential requirement of a scientific theory. Thus corresponding to the neurotic, psychotic, and sociopathic ideal types is a set of MMPI profiles (Table 10.1) that were developed through empirical analyses (Skinner and Jackson 1978). The modal MMPI profiles of Table 10.1 provide an operational or epistemic definition of the three ideal type constructs. Each modal MMPI profile depicts the "center of gravity" of a subgroup of individuals who are salient on this dimension. The term "modal profile" is similar to Cliff's (1968) idealized individual concept in multidimensional scaling.

Rules of correspondence or constitutive links among the ideal type constructs may be formulated and evaluated to yield a deeper scientific understanding of the substantive domain. For example, one might hypothesize that the neurotic, psychotic, and sociopathic types reflect different genetic and environmental determinants (see Cattell 1970; Eysenck 1970). With a sample of depressed patients, one would expect individuals resembling the psychotic MMPI type to constitute a more severe form of depression (endogeneous) with characteristic features of mood fluctuations, guilt feelings, motor retardation, insomnia, and weight loss. There is evidence to suggest that endogeneous depression has a biological basis (Kendell 1976). In contrast, patients who resemble the neurotic MMPI type would be hypothesized to reflect a milder disorder (reactive depression) that fluctuates from day to day and is often preceded by stressful life events. The richness of the theoretical systematization parallels the degree to which the model of psychopathology evolves into a comprehensive theory having broad explanatory power. At present, work is needed to specify both the theoretical and empirical elements of the model.

In review, each ideal type may be viewed as a superordinate construct that implies a specified configuration on the MMPI clinical scales. The modal MMPI profiles of Table 10.1 provide an operational definition of the corresponding ideal type: neurotic psychotic or sociopathic. Thus the three ideal type constructs, with their conceptual and empirical relationships, form a typological theory of psychopathology that is open to empirical evaluation.

Categories Versus Dimensions

A substantial body of literature surrounds the controversy of whether psychiatric syndromes are best expressed as categorical, dimensional, or hierarchical schemata (Kendell 1975; Strauss 1973). Each approach represents a quite different conceptualization of what constitutes a "type." Categorical models emphasize qualitative differences between individuals assigned to discrete categories. The types are viewed as being internally cohesive and mutually distinct. In contrast, dimensional models are based on quantitative differences as reflected by the location of persons along axes in a multidimensional space. Hierarchical strategies, on the other hand, classify persons into subsets that are themselves successively classified into groups at different levels in the hierarchy. Although categorical systems traditionally have been most popular in psychiatric classifications, this popularity is not grounded in clinical validity or empirical studies. Rather, Strauss (1973) has argued that "dimensional models by their failure to define discrete types also fail to meet what seems to be an important psychological need to categorize with the feeling of mastery and knowledge that accompanies the bestowing of a name" (p. 448).

The present model of psychopathology is essentially a dimensional system. One major dimension orders persons according to the degree of symptom severity (elevation parameters), whereas the three dimensions of Figure 10.1 locate persons according to their quantitative resemblance to the three clinical types (shape parameters). A key advantage of the dimensional representation is that it stresses quantitative relationships and makes allowance for reliable individual differences. That is, individual characteristics are not distorted or ignored in order to fit predefined categories. Recently, considerable interest has grown in methods for fitting mixed or hybrid models (Carroll 1976). Given the dimensional representation exemplified by Figure 10.1, one may search for relatively distinct clusters within this space (Skinner 1978b). In this way, one may use the model of psychopathology to integrate the relative advantages of both dimensional and categorical systems.

Trait Versus Situational Distinction

By examining the independent contribution of elevation, scatter, and shape components of profile similarity, one may integrate aspects of the trait (core) and situational (social learning) theory approaches to the study of personality (Bowers 1973; Mischel 1973). That is, it is hypothesized that the shape parameters provide indexes of a person's more enduring personality disposition (Lorr 1966). In the present model, quantitative indexes are provided between the shape of an individual's MMPI profile and the three types: neurotic, psychotic, and sociopathic. For example, a person who resembles the psychotic type will have a higher probability of exhibiting certain behaviors such as blunted affect, unusual thought process, and hallucinations. This syndrome will be relatively enduring over time. However, the actual degree of maladjustment will vary according to situational factors and temporary stressors. It is hypothesized that elevation and scatter parameters are more sensitive to situational and temporal changes. Although a person may have a clear tendency to exhibit behaviors related to the psychotic type, the level of symptom severity can be expected to vary across situations as well as over time. Thus, if pre- and posttreatment data are available, it is hypothesized that the shape parameters will remain relatively invariant, whereas a decrease in the elevation parameter is predicted for persons who responded successfully to the treatment intervention.

The model has implications for a general taxonomy that integrates psychopathology and normalcy. Kaplan (1967) has argued the need to place more emphasis on the study of normal behavior and on the transition from normal to abnormal functioning. Longitudinal studies may show, for example, that college students classified on the basis of profile shape to the sociopathic type have a higher predisposition for problems with heroin addiction (see Chapter 4). As these individuals progress through the subclinical and clinical stages of addiction, one might observe a corresponding rise in the elevation parameter. This increase in elevation would reflect more severe symptoms related to antisocial attitudes, family and work problems, rebelliousness, and impulsiveness.

Empirical Validation

Blashfield and Draguns (1976) discuss four basic criteria for the evaluation of psychiatric classifications: reliability, coverage, descriptive validity, and predictive validity. First, reliability concerns the extent to which persons possessing similar attributes will be assigned to the same diagnostic category. A reliable classification should be consistent from user to user (interdiagnostician agreement) and within the same user over different occasions (intradiagnostician agreement). The variables used in the present model are objective and quantitative (that is, clinical scales of the MMPI). Also, the rules for ordering individuals along the dimensions of the model are mathematically defined. Thus the decision rules of the model are explicit and should be highly consistent across users. However, the reliability of the parameter estimates in Equation 1 is contingent on the reliability of the 13 MMPI clinical scales. That is, Conger and Lipshitz (1973) have demonstrated that the reliability of the Euclidean distance measures of profile similarity equals the average of the univariate reliability of each attribute measure. The median reliability of the 13 clinical scales is in the order of .80. Consequently, the model can be made more reliable by basing it on a new set of scales whose reliability estimates exceed values for the MMPI clinical scales.

The second criterion is coverage, which describes the domain of individuals encompassed by the classification system. Empirical studies with the Lanyon (1968) MMPI groups suggest that the current model has broad generalizability. Nevertheless, further research is needed, especially at the individual profile level, to document the prevalence of the neurotic, psychotic, and sociopathic types across diverse populations of deviant and normal groups.

Third, descriptive validity involves the degree to which the types are homogeneous on variables external to forming the taxonomy. For example, are individuals who resemble the same MMPI type similar on other relevant attributes such as demographic variables, treatment history, or alcohol use? Thus research is needed to establish external correlates of the neurotic, psychotic, and sociopathic types. A suggested starting point is to examine the various correlates that have been compiled for the Gilberstadt and Duker (1965) and Marks, Seeman, and Haller (1974) code types.

Last, predictive validity addresses the power of the classification system to predict criteria, such as treatment outcome and community follow-up variables. Predictive validity is a vital acid test of the model. That is, if the model of psychopathology is to have clinical usefulness, it must enhance decision making with respect to which intervention is most appropriate and effective for particular individuals. Therefore empirical studies of the predictive validity of the model parameters are needed across a number of clinical settings. An important example of this form of research is the finding of a patient type-by-treatment interaction in the area of depression (Paykel 1972).

CONCLUSION

The model of psychopathology provides a parsimonious framework for integrating research based on the MMPI clinical scales. Herein lies its strength and weakness. The strength of the model is evidenced by its ability to summarize a diverse array of studies within a convenient dimensional schema. Because the classification results may be represented by a series of graphs, this aspect should facilitate communication among researchers and clinicians. Following Sneath (1975), the model could serve an important teaching function for the training of health care professionals. By differentiating the contribution of profile elevation, scatter, and shape parameters, the model may be used to study the relative influences of trait and situational factors upon behavior (Bowers 1973). Although the clinical utility of the model needs to be established through various descriptive and predictive validity studies, this research can draw upon the wealth of empirical data that have accumulated on the MMPI.

The limitation of the present model, however, rests with the inherent psychometric problems of the aging clinical scales. The model is composed of three broad clinical types: neurotic, psychotic, and sociopathic. In order to move beyond this global taxonomy and make finer differentiations among individuals, one must base the classification system on a more diversified set of measures that ideally reflect alternative assessment modes. Preliminary steps in this direction have been taken with the Differential Personality Inventory (Jackson and Messick 1971). The 28 scales of the DPI were developed according to a construct validation paradigm (Jackson 1971). Using an identical classification strategy with the model, Skinner, Jackson, and Hoffman (1974) identified eight modal profiles (typal dimensions) that replicated across three samples of alcoholic patients. Evidence regarding the generalizability of the eight types to various deviant and normal samples was evaluated by Skinner, Reed, and Jackson (1976). Furthermore, Reed and Jackson (1975) have studied the conceptual or clinical validity of the DPI types in a clinical judgment experiment.

Ultimately, the value of this MMPI model of psychopathology rests empirically upon the predictive power of its parameters and theoretically upon the richness of constitutive links among the typal constructs.

REFERENCES

American Psychiatric Association. 1978. "Diagnostic and Statistical Manual of Mental Disorders," 3rd ed., DMS-III draft. Washington, D.C.

Blashfield, R. K., and J. G. Draguns. 1976. "Evaluative Criteria for Psychiatric Classification." *Journal of Abnormal Psychology* 85: 140–50.

Block, J. 1977. "An Illusory Interpretation of the First Factor of the MMPI: A Reply to Shweder." *Journal of Consulting and Clinical Psychology* 45: 930–35.

Bowers, K. S. 1973. "Situationism in Psychology: An Analysis and Critique." *Psychological Review* 80: 307–36.

Butcher, J. N., and A. Tellegen. 1978. "Common Methodological Problems in MMPI Research." *Journal of Consulting and Clinical Psychology* 46: 620–28.

Carroll, J. D. 1976. "Spatial, Non-Spatial and Hybrid Models for Scaling." *Psychometrika* 41: 439–63.

Cattell, R. B. 1970. "The Integration of Functional and Psychometric Requirements in a Quantitative and Computerized Diagnostic System." In *New Approaches to Personality Classification*, edited by A. R. Mahrer, pp. 9–52. New York: Columbia University Press.

Cliff, N. 1968. "The 'Idealized Individual' Interpretation of Individual Differences in Multidimensional Scaling." *Psychometrika* 33: 225–32.

Conger, A. J., and R. Lipshitz. 1973. "Measures of Reliability for Profile and Test Batteries." *Psychometrika* 38: 411–27.

Cooley, W. W., and P. R. Lohnes. 1971. *Multivariate Data Analysis*. New York: Wiley.

Cronbach, L. J., and G. C. Gleser. 1953. "Assessing Similarity Between Profiles." *Psychological Bulletin* 50: 456–73.

Dahlstrom, W. G., G. S. Welsh, and L. E. Dahlstrom. 1975. *An MMPI Handbook*, vol. 2. Minneapolis: University of Minnesota Press.

Edwards, A. L. 1977. "Comments on Shweder's 'Illusory Correlation and the MMPI Controversy.'" *Journal of Consulting and Clinical Psychology* 45: 925–29.

Eysenck, H. J. 1970. "A Dimensional System of Psychodiagnostics." In *New Approaches to Personality Classification*, edited by A. R. Mahrer, pp. 169–208. New York: Columbia University Press.

Gilberstadt, H., and J. A. Duker. 1965. *A Handbook for Clinical and Actuarial MMPI Interpretation*. Philadelphia: Saunders.

Gleason, T. C., and R. Staelin. 1973. "Improving the Metric Quality of Questionnaire Data." *Psychometrika* 38: 393–410.

Goldberg, L. R. 1972. "Man Versus Mean: The Exploitation of Group Profiles for the Construction of Diagnostic Classification Systems." *Journal of Abnormal Psychology* 79: 121–31.

Green, P. E., and J. D. Carroll. 1976. *Mathematical Tools for Applied Multivariate Analysis*. New York: Academic Press.

Guertin, W. H. 1966. "The Search for Recurring Patterns Among Individual Profiles." *Educational and Psychological Measurement* 26: 151–65.

Gynther, M. D., H. Altman, R. W. Warbin, and I. W. Sletten. 1972. "A New Actuarial System for MMPI Interpretation: Rationale and Methodology." *Journal of Clinical Psychology* 28: 173–79.

Hathaway, S. R. 1960. "Foreword." In *An MMPI Handbook*, by W. G. Dahlstrom and G. S. Welsh. Minneapolis: University of Minnesota Press.

Hempel, C. G. 1965. *Aspects of Scientific Explanation*. New York: Free Press.

Jackson, D. N. 1971. "The Dynamics of Structured Personality Tests: 1971." *Psychological Review* 78: 229–48.

——, and S. Messick. 1971. *The Differential Personality Inventory*. London, Canada: Authors.

Kaplan, A. 1967. "A Philosophical Discussion of Normalty." *Archives of General Psychiatry* 17: 325–30.

Kendell, R. E. 1976. "The Classification of Depressions: A Review of Contemporary Confusion." *British Journal of Psychiatry* 129: 15–28.

——. 1975. *The Role of Diagnosis in Psychiatry*. Oxford: Blackwell Scientific Publications.

Kluckhohn, C., and H. A. Murray. 1949. *Personality in Nature, Society and Culture*. New York: Knopf.

Kretschmer, E. 1925. *Psysique and Character*. Translated from second German edition by W. J. H. Spratt. New York: Harcourt, Brace.

Lanyon, R. I. 1968. *A Handbook of MMPI Group Profiles*. Minneapolis: University of Minnesota Press.

Lorr, M. 1966. *Explorations in Typing Psychotics*. Oxford: Pergamon Press.

Marks, P. A., W. Seeman, and D. L. Haller. 1974. *The Actuarial Use of the MMPI with Adolescents and Adults*. Baltimore: Williams & Wilkins.

Menninger, K. 1963. *The Vital Balance*. New York: Viking Press.

Mischel, W. 1973. "Toward a Cognitive Social Learning Reconceptualization of Personality." *Psychological Review* 80: 252–83.

Overall, J. E., and C. J. Klett. 1972. *Applied Multivariate Analysis*. New York: McGraw-Hill.

Paykel, E. S. 1972. "Depressive Typologies and Response to Amitriptyline." *British Journal of Psychiatry* 120: 147–56.

——. 1971. "Classification of Depressed Patients: A Cluster Analysis Derived Grouping." *British Journal of Psychiatry* 118: 275–88.

Reed, P. L., and D. N. Jackson. 1975. "Clinical Judgment of Psychopathology: A Model for Inferential Accuracy." *Journal of Abnormal Psychology* 84: 475–82.

Riese, W. 1945. "History and Principles of Classification of Nervous Diseases." *Bulletin of History of Medicine* 18: 465–512.

Schacht, T., and P. E. Nathan. 1977. "But Is It Good for the Psychologists? Appraisal and Status of DSM-III." *American Psychologist* 32: 1017–25.

Shweder, R. A. "Illusory Correlation and the MMPI Controversy." *Journal of Consulting and Clinical Psychology* 45: 917–24.

Skinner, H. A. 1978a. "Differentiating the Contribution of Elevation, Scatter, and Shape in Profile Similarity." *Educational and Psychological Measurement* 38: 297–308.

——. 1978b. "Dimensions and Clusters: A Hybrid Approach to Classification." Paper presented at the joint meeting of the Psychometric Society and Society for Mathematical Psychology, McMaster University, Hamilton, Canada, August 25–27.

——. 1977. "The Eyes That Fix You: A Model for Classification Research." *Canadian Psychological Review* 18: 142–51.

——, and D. N. Jackson. 1978. "A Model of Psychopathology Based on an Integration of MMPI Actuarial Systems." *Journal of Consulting and Clinical Psychology* 46: 231–38.

——, and H. Hoffmann. 1974. "Alcoholic Personality Types: Identification and Correlates." *Journal of Abnormal Psychology* 83: 658–66.

Skinner, H. A., P. L. Reed, and D. N. Jackson. 1976. "Toward the Objective Diagnosis of Psychopathology: Generalizability of Modal Personality Profiles." *Journal of Consulting and Clinical Psychology* 44: 111–17.

Sneath, P. H. E. 1975. "A Vector Model of Disease for Teaching and Diagnosis." *Medical Hypotheses*, March–April. 101–09.

——, and R. R. Sokal. 1973. *Numerical Taxonomy*. San Francisco: Freeman.

Strauss, J. S. 1973. "Diagnostic Models and the Nature of Psychiatric Disorder." *Archives of General Psychiatry* 29: 445–49.

Wiggins, J. S. 1973. *Personality and Prediction: Principles of Personality Assessment*. Reading, Mass.: Addison-Wesley.

11/MMPI SCORES AND ADAPTIVE BEHAVIORS

Joseph T. Kunce

MMPI interpretations typically focus on maladaptive aspects of human behavior. The corresponding personality descriptions too often reflect a "DSM-II mentality," wherein psychiatric symptoms become equivalent to personality definitions. Clinical practice perpetuates pathological MMPI interpretations because psychologists in this situation primarily are confronted with a client's behavioral problems. Furthermore, MMPI texts and handbooks encourage this type of interpretative bias by almost exclusively providing negative implications for elevated scale scores (Kunce and Anderson 1976). Positive and constructive aspects of a client's personality consequently are often overlooked.

It is the author's contention and experience that elevated MMPI scores can be suggestive of adaptive behavioral styles as well as descriptive of maladaptive behaviors. As far back as 1957, Diamond hypothesized that individual scales correspond to underlying dimensions of normal behavior. The *Hs* scale, for example, represented a self-pity facet and the *Sc* scale an intellectual escapism facet of coping with a basic social attachment need. Neither *Hs* nor *Sc* scores were considered to have positive behavioral implications. In contrast, Dahlstrom and Welsh (1960), in their classic MMPI text, made a token effort to mention the adjustive meaning of peak clinical scales for normal men and women. Normal males with peak scores on *Hs*, for example, were reportedly described by friends and acquaintances as " . . . kind, grateful, versatile, courageous, and having wide interest" and females as " . . . good tempered, responsive, modest, frank, verbal, and orderly." These adjectives contrast sharply to the "crabby, whiny, pessimistic, cynical, and defeatist" characteristics typically reported for persons in clinical settings similarly having peak *Hs* scores. Dahlstrom and Welsh speculated that such differences could be attributed in part to the fact that *Hs* "normals" had lower mean scores than *Hs* "patients." They failed, however, to link conceptually such terms as "kind" and "crabby" as adjustive-maladjustive points on a single underlying dimension of personality.

Existing methods to combat psychopathological implications of the MMPI are ineffective. Reference to an MMPI scale in terms of a numerical code unfortunately does not divorce a scale from its psychiatric connotations. Because this strategy does not work and has never gained universal application, the alphabetic scale codes are used in this chapter to ensure readability. Precautionary warnings issued by commerical MMPI computerized interpretative services regarding the psychiatric orientation of these reports are also ineffective. Psychologists using such interpretations as an assessment tool undoubtedly are influenced by a descriptive barrage of abnormal personality characteristics.

The psychopathological orientation pervades newer tests such as the Millon Multiaxial Clinical Inventory (Millon 1976). Although this test reportedly provides a description of "basic personality style," its eight basic personality dimensions are defined in negative terms such as asocial, narcissistic, and negativistic. Moreover, the supplemental scales deal only with pathological dimensions and symptoms and the extended personality descriptions center on maladaptive personality characteristics. In contrast, Graham, in his recent MMPI text (1977), included psychological resources as one of 17 topics discussed in an illustrative MMPI interpretation. In this category he used positive terms such as "reliable and conscientious" and "sensitive, kind, peace-loving, and generous" (pp. 175, 176). Thus a small but important spotlight is aimed at identifying psychological strengths.

In conclusion, the current usage of the MMPI reflects and perpetuates narrow formulations of personality functioning. Consequently, the potential implications of MMPI scores may not be fully realized. It is the thesis of this chapter that it is appropriate and possible to make positive personality inferences from elevated scale scores, for example, "kind" versus "crabby" for peak *Hs* scores. This conceptualization was first elaborated by Kunce and Anderson (1976). They hypothesized that each MMPI scale represents an underlying personality trait that could manifest itself in contrasting positive or negative ways according to situational pressures. From an extensive review of the literature they selected parallel positive and negative sets of descriptors for each of the MMPI clinical scales and placed them in juxtaposition. These descriptors are reprinted in Table 11.1. The magnitude of the peak scales, observational and historical data, and the relationship of the scales to each other are all necessary considerations in determination of the relevance of specific counterpart descriptors for any given person.

BASIC MMPI PERSONALITY DIMENSIONS

In order to demonstrate the applicability of a broader MMPI interpretative stance, several MMPI profiles representative of distinctly different personality types have been selected. To ensure diversity of examples, the three modal MMPI profiles identified and quantified by Skinner and Jackson (1978) (see Chapter 10) served as a guide for case selection. Their research showed that most

TABLE 11.1

MMPI Counterpart Behaviors

Scale	Underlying Dimensions	Counterpart Behaviors	
		Positive	Negative
Hs	Conservation	Conscientious, careful, considerate, sincere	Dependent, irritable, complaining, bodily preoccupations
D	Evaluation	Deliberate, objective, contemplative, realistic	Critical, anxious, depressed, pessimistic
Hy	Expression	Empathic, responsive, sensitive, optimistic	Denial, psychosomatic reactions, suggestible, overactive
Pd	Assertion	Energetic, enterprising, venturesome, social	Hostile, manipulative, impulsive, antisocial
Mf	Role flexibility	Colorful, dilettante, interesting	Self-recrimination, sex-role deviancy, identity confusion, unconventional
Pa	Inquiring	Investigative, curious, questioning, discriminatory	Grandiose, hypersensitive, suspicious, distrustful
Pt	Organization	Methodical, systematic, convergent thinker, organized	Rigid, compulsive, obsessive ritualistic
Sc	Imagination	Spontaneous, creative, imaginative, divergent thinker	Bizarre, irrational, confused, idiosyncratic
Ma	Zest	Enthusiastic, eager, wholehearted, exuberant	Hyper, ineffectual, disorganized, agitated
Si	Autonomy	Independent, self-reliant, free-lance	Reclusive, asocial, alienated

Source: J. T. Kunce and W. P. Anderson, "Normalizing the MMPI." *Journal of Clinical Psychology* 32 (1976): 776–80. Copyright 1976 by the Clinical Psychology Publishing Company. Reprinted with permission.

MMPI code types could be readily categorized according to their similarity to the following basic types: sociopathic (*Pd, Ma*), neurotic (*Hs, D, Hy*), and psychotic (*Sc, Pt*). The ubiquity of these profiles fits the author's own experience and research (for example, Anderson and Kunce, in press).

Consistent with the theme of encouraging a wide descriptive and conceptual framework for MMPI assessment, personality dimensions were formulated to encompass each of the three modal MMPI profiles for psychopathology identified by Skinner and Jackson (Talbe 11.2). First, an interpersonal activity dimension with "socially outgoing" and "socially reserved" was considered to encompass the sociopathic MMPI profile. The term "sociopathic" would be the negative counterpart for "socially outgoing," and a term such as "reclusive" could be the negative counterpart for "socially reserved." Socially outgoing behavior, whether it is manifested adaptively or maladaptively, is characterized by the Skinner and Jackson modal profile that has peaks on *Pd* and *Ma* and low *D, Si* scores. In contrast, socially reserved behavior would be indicated by the obverse of this profile, that is, peak *D* and *Si* scores and low *Pd, Ma* scores.

Second, a proclivity for emotional activity can be viewed as a personality dimension characterized by "internalization" and "externalization" of emotions. The respective negative counterpart terms would be neurotic and manic behaviors. *Hs, D,* and *Hy* peak scores with a low *Ma* represent Skinner and Jackson's neurotic modal type, whereas low *Hs, D, Hy,* and high *Ma* represent the polar opposite.

Finally, cognitive activity was formulated as a third dimension to represent "divergent" and "convergent" cognitive styles. The negative counterpart terms would be "psychotic" and "rigid ideation." Profile characteristics of the former are peaks on *F, D,* and *Sc*, while on the latter peaks occur on *L, K, Hs,* and *Hy*.

ILLUSTRATIVE CASE EXAMPLES

Literary license has been taken in describing the illustrative case examples to protect the identity of the persons involved. Six examples were selected from the author's case files to represent three pairs of polar opposites, one contrasting pair for each personality dimension. The relationships of each profile to the three modal MMPI profiles are presented in Table 11.3 (for example, profiles 11.1 and 11.2 correlate +.72 and −.44, respectively, with the sociopathic profile). Each person was experiencing considerable situational distress at the time of MMPI administration, but none required psychiatric care. Three required psychological help and three managed using their own personal and social resources. All were caucasian and had middle-class backgrounds, but varied considerably in age, educational level, and intelligence. A seventh case was also added to illustrate several other factors that can affect MMPI interpretations.

TABLE 11.2

Basic MMPI Types Extrapolated from Skinner and Jackson's Model of Psychopathology

Underlying Dimension	Personality Type	Peak MMPI Scales	Counterpart Behaviors	
			Positive	Negative
Interpersonal activity	Socially outgoing Socially reserved	*Pd, Ma* *D, Si*	Socially confident Self-reliant	Sociopathic Withdrawn
Emotional activity	Internalization Externalization	*Hs, D, Hy* *Ma*	Emphatic Adventurous	Neurotic Manic
Cognitive activity	Divergent Convergent	*F, D, Sc* *L, K, Hs, Hy*	Imaginative Focused	Psychotic Dogmatic

Source: Compiled by the author.

TABLE 11.3

Correlations of Profile Examples with Modal Personality Types

Example Profile	Skinner and Jackson Modal Types				
	Sociopathic	Neurotic	Psychotic	M	SD
Interpersonal					
Outgoing (Figure 11.1)	72	-12	-18	57.6	8.3
Reserved (Figure 11.2)	-44	16	27	51.2	9.1
Emotional					
Internalizer (Figure 11.3)	39	58	12	58.1	10.8
Externalizer (Figure 11.4)	15	-62	22	49.5	9.5
Cognitive					
Divergent (Figure 11.5)	-10	-06	81	62.5	13.7
Convergent (Figure 11.6)	28	30	-59	59.2	10.3
Psychotic reaction					
Acutely psychotic (Figure 11.7)	-16	20	80	69.4	14.1
Psychosis abated (Figure 11.8)	-46	14	65	61.1	7.8

Note: Q correlations based on the validity scales (*L, F, K*), the eight clinical scales, plus *Mf* and *Si*. Decimals omitted.
Source: Compiled by the author.

311

Interpersonal Examples

Socially Outgoing

Figure 11.1, an MMPI profile of an adult, married male, is characteristic of the modal sociopathic (*Pd, Ma*) type. He was functioning adequately in his general social-vocational-emotional environments at the time of testing, even though he was experiencing a marital crisis that subsequently culminated in divorce. Throughout the crisis, he held a responsible administrative position and performed in a highly ethical and efficient manner. Friends viewed him as energetic, socially assertive, and pragmatic. The negative descriptors for *Pd* and *Ma* in Table 11.1 fail to provide an accurate picture of this functioning, although the term "manipulative" might be considered to apply in a positive way to his administrative skills.

Socially Reserved

Figure 11.2 is distinctly different from the preceding profile. Specifically, Figure 11.2 has peaks on *D* and on *Si*, while both scales are low points of the typical sociopathic MMPI profile. The person having this *D, Si* profile was a young married woman. In contradistinction to the *Pd, Ma* "administrator," she had sought counseling and was reacting severely to a marital crisis. She was depressed and frustrated as a consequence of not receiving the intensity of affection and loyalty that she wanted from her spouse. In her case the negative descriptors for the *D, Si* scales in Table 11.1 had high concurrent validity.

Usually an adjusted person with peak *D, Si* scores tends to have the type of autonomy that Maslow sees in the actualized person—a person who dares to be "unpopular" and who has the "courage" to be highly independent of external social influences (Maslow 1971, p. 47). This type of actualization perhaps requires meaningful closeness to a spouse, family, or a small, close-knit group of friends. For the person in this example, adaptive behaviors in Table 11.1 for *D* and *Si* should emerge, given resolution of the marital conflict and reestablishment of an interpersonal "home base."

Persons having MMPI profiles like those in Figures 11.1 and 11.2 can be anticipated to have strong interpersonal needs. Disruption of need satisfaction can be especially distressing for these types. The case studies for these figures provide evidence that it is impractical, however, to predict the manifest problem (for example, divorce or loss of a close friend) from the MMPI. On the other hand, the MMPI could indicate the type of behavior to be expected as it relates to the problem and its resolution (for example, a socially reserved person might be expected to have more difficulties in handling marital stress, as persons of an introversive nature characteristically strive to avoid interpersonal confrontations. Other research findings similarly indicate that a specific problem cannot be predicted from the MMPI. A review of Duckworth and Duckworth's (1976) text showed, for example, over a dozen profile types associated with

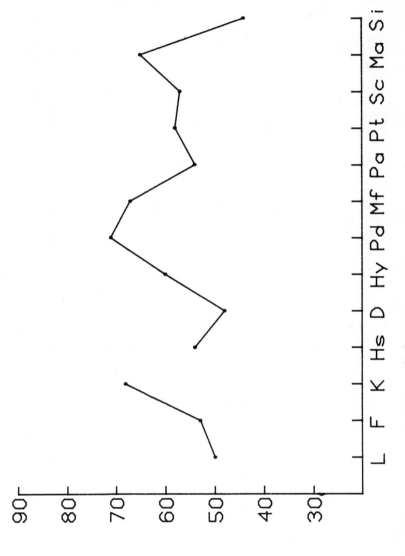

FIGURE 11.1: Socially outgoing profile. *Source:* Constructed by the author.

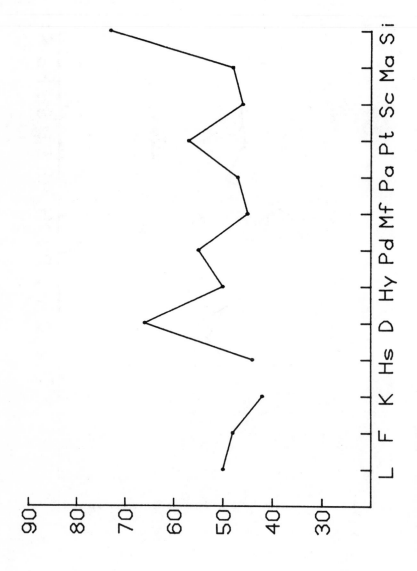

FIGURE 11.2: Socially reserved profile. *Source:* Constructed by the author.

alcoholism. Similarly, Anderson and Kunce (in press) could not identify any specific MMPI profile type singularly associated with sex offenders. Instead, the obtained profiles resembled the modal types found by Skinner and Jackson (1978).

Emotional Examples

Internalizer

Figure 11.3, a profile of an intelligent adult, married woman, is similar to persons in clinical situations readily categorized as neurotic. The T scores for *Hs* and *Hy* exceeded 70, and *Pa* was a tertiary peak. Use of the customary negative descriptors for her would have been distinctly misleading, whereas positive terms such as conscientious (*Hs*), emphatic (*Hy*), and questioning (*Pa*) would have been very characteristic and appropriate. Her marked scale elevations signified current distress stemming from an exacerbation of a chronic medical problem and from a midcareer change. Her high level of ego strength (*Es* = 70) apparently enabled her to maintain psychological equilibrium and the negative psychological characteristics expected from her MMPI profile simply did not become openly manifest. A retest six months later still had *Hs* and *Hy* as peak scores. All scales, however, had dropped below a T score of 70, which was consistent with her readjustment to a career change and a remission of her acute medical problem. Depending upon the point of view, the *Hs, Hy* configuration could be considered indicative of either a psychosomatic or somatopsychological reaction.

Externalizer

Figure 11.4 suggests a manic type of individual and contrasts sharply to Figure 11.3, as the slope of the scores on the clinical scales is positive and *Ma* is the peak score. At the time of testing, the *Ma* negative descriptors—hyperactive, ineffective, disorganized, and agitated—corresponded well with background information of the young man who took the test. This person, who had a mild seizure disorder and borderline intelligence, had recently graduated from special education classes. He had little interest in academic pursuits and had been a constant school discipline problem, partly because of inattentiveness and hyperactivity. The academic environment consequently constituted a stressful situation for him. Following supportive counseling and vocational placement as a trainee with a landscaping firm, his adjustment markedly improved. His employer, in contrast to his teachers, saw him as enthusiastic, energetic, willing, and motivated, all apt descriptors for an elevated *Ma*.

The changes in this young man over a period of three months illustrate the importance of environmental conditions as they interact with individual personal characteristics to influence adaptive or madadaptive behavior. When confronted by a situation incompatible with his abilities, this person exhibited the maladaptive behavior expected from his MMPI profile. Given an environment more

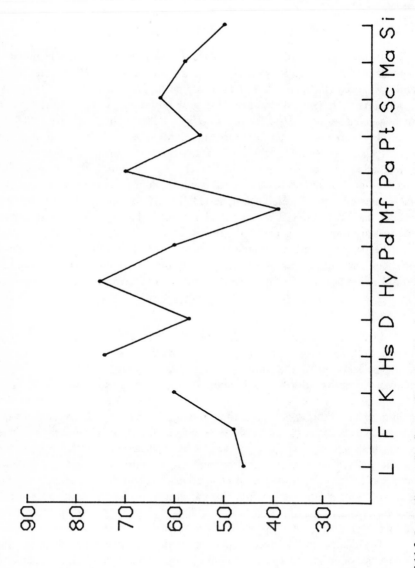

FIGURE 11.3: Internalizer proflie. *Source:* Constructed by the author.

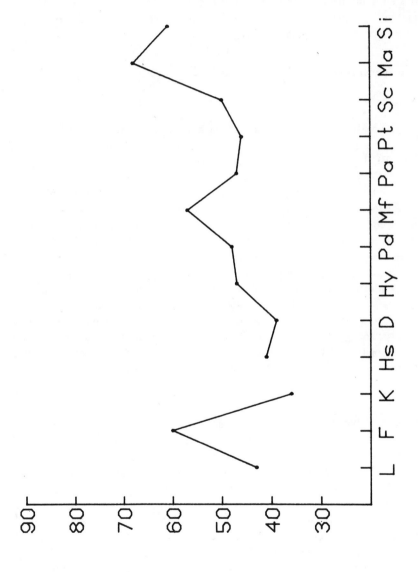

FIGURE 11.4: Externalizer profile. *Source:* Constructed by the author.

compatible with his capabilities, he exhibited the kind of positive behaviors expected from his personality type.

The internalizer and externalizer showed quite different behavioral reactions to stressful situations. The differences observed here support the conclusion that behaviors traditionally viewed as neurotic and as manic fall on opposite ends of the behavioral dimension termed as emotional activity. The internal and external components indicate whether reactions to pressure are internalized or released outward via hyperactivity.

Cognitive Styles

Divergent

The MMPI profile in Figure 11.5 closely resembles the modal profile type for psychosis identified by Skinner and Jackson (1978). Note that the T scores for the *Pa, Pt, Sc,* and *Si* all exceeded 70 and the *F* scale approached 70. The traditional psychiatric description once again inadequately describes the adult, highly intelligent, married female represented by this profile. The elevated scores reflected for her, as they did for the person in Figure 11.3, a stressful situation. Dohrenwend and Dohrenwend's (1974) concept of stress created by "life change events" is particularly applicable to her situation. This person and her husband had just relocated because of a change in his employment. This change required her to make different arrangements to complete her postgraduate work in science. In addition, she had to readjust to a new interpersonal network, a difficult task for a reserved and quiet person. She consequently experienced considerable stress, although she did not require psychological help. The dominant personality trait suggested by the *Pa, Pt,* and *Sc* scores is an investigative, ruminative, and creative cognitive style. Coupled with her own high level of intelligence, this cognitive style could be an asset for employment in a theoretical scientific field.

Convergent

The profile shape of Figure 11.6 is the inverse of the psychotic profile. It is somewhat a rarity in psychiatric settings but it is not uncommon in medical settings. Both *L* and *K* are markedly elevated in relationship to *F*, while both *Hs* and *Hy* are above *D* and the remaining scales fall within the 40 to 60 bracket. The middle-aged divorced woman of average intelligence having this profile apparently had avoided a difficult stress situation a year earlier as a consequence of a paralysis of her dominant hand and arm. She had received a neurological diagnosis for this condition and was treated on a medical ward for several months. It was later decided that her condition was psychologically, not neurologically, based. The negative scale descriptors for *Hs* (dependent, bodily preoccupations) and *Hy* (denial, psychosomatic, and suggestible) were characteristic of her hospitalized behavior.

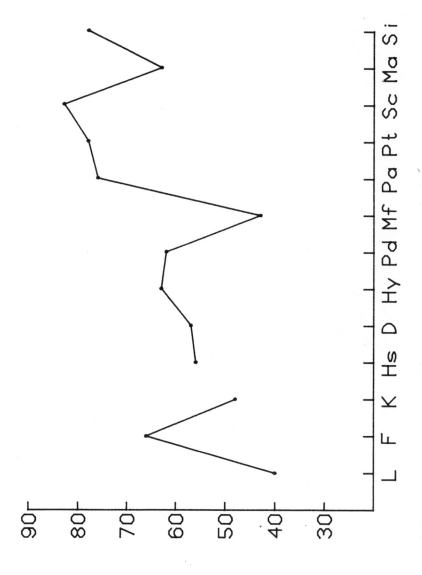

FIGURE 11.5: Divergent profile. *Source:* Constructed by the author.

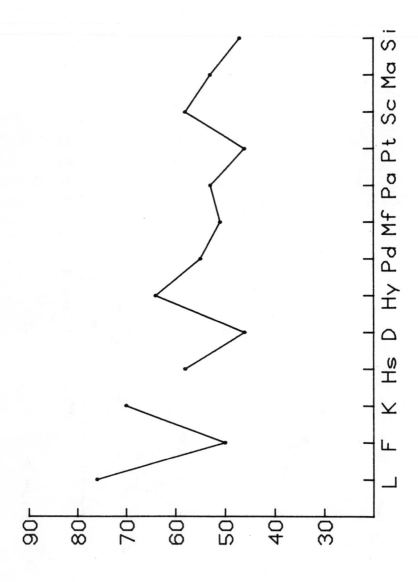

FIGURE 11.6: Convergent profile. *Source:* Constructed by the author.

The *Hy* suggestible characteristic proved to be a therapeutic asset. Mild posthypnotic suggestions about possible benefits of increased participation in physical therapy resulted in a "miraculous" return of physical function within two weeks. Subsequent counseling focused on helping her recognize and cope with a pollyannish perspective of people that predisposed her to suppress emotionally tinged situations. A repeat of the MMPI following successful counseling yielded an essentially identical profile, except the *L, K, Hs,* and *Hy* peaks were less pronounced. Parenthetically, Table 11.1 failed to provide sets of descriptors for *L, F,* and *K.* A positive descriptor for the V shape for these three scales could be "focused"; a negative descriptor "rigid." Counterpart terms for the inverted V could be "individualistic" and "bizarre."

Markedly different cognitive styles are suggested by Figures 11.5 and 11.6. The divergent person had an abstract, intellectual, scholastic, and imaginative style. In contrast, the person with a convergent style reflected an orientation to the practical and pragmatic. The convergent person's paralysis could be viewed as a psychological reaction where a problem was solved in a physical, concrete, and focused manner.

Special Considerations

Each person in the preceding six examples had an adaptive behavioral repertoire adequately predicted by peak MMPI scaled scores. A psychopathological interpretative stance would have missed identifying these behavioral potentialities and would have provided misleading personality descriptions. It cannot be arbitrarily assumed, however, that peak scores will invariably signify the person's more basic nature in terms of either positive or negative behaviors. The addition of another case study will help to illustrate this. Subsequently several important considerations in trying to predict or "postdict" behavior from the MMPI will be delineated: validity of the profile, selection of scale descriptors, personality change, and stress overlay.

Figure 11.7 shows the profile of a teenage female who was acutely delusional, hallucinatory, and depressed at the time of evaluation. This profile is congruent with Skinner and Jackson's psychotic profile type. It also strongly resembles the profile in Figure 11.5. In Figure 11.7, however, the *D* and *Pa* T scores are about 20 points higher. Shortly after testing, this person spontaneously recovered and was released from an inpatient psychiatric service to return to high school. She required rehospitalization two months later when she became acutely psychotic a second time. The *D, Si* profile high scores were consistent with her premorbid adjustment where she was seen as a shy and serious (contemplative) but self-reliant person. The *Pa, Sc* correlates were manifestly obvious in her distressed state but not obvious in her premorbid behavior.

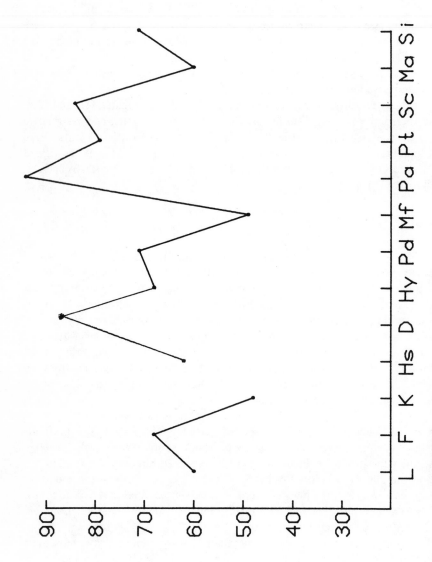

FIGURE 11.7: Acutely psychotic profile. *Source:* Constructed by the author.

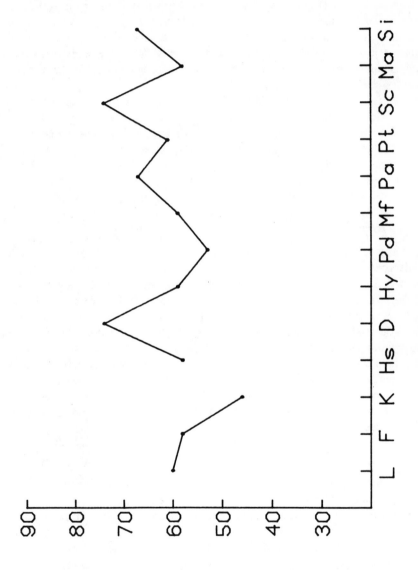

FIGURE 11.8: Postpsychotic profile. *Source:* Constructed by the author.

A search for sources of psychological stress led to the following observations. Her intellectual functioning was dull normal, but because she had been such a "nice" person, she had been essentially "socially" promoted each year in school. Now that she was in senior high school she studied past midnight each night striving to keep up with the increased educational demands. Yet she could only make C and D grades to her own and her parents' disappointment. She firmly believed that she had to succeed academically and graduate from high school. Through counseling it developed that she would prefer to quit school, obtain a job, eventually marry, and have a family. When she realized that her parents would not be angry if she quit school, the counselor helped her acquire an entry-level job in food service work.

Figure 11.8 shows the MMPI profile obtained three months after her second breakdown and after she had held employment for a month. The *D, Si* features were still present and were consistent with her pleasant, nonassertive but self-reliant and dependable behavior. Although lower in height, the *F, Pa, Pt,* and *Sc* were still prominent profile characteristics. Neither the positive nor negative behaviors expected from these scales were apparent in her current behavior or in her subsequent long-term stable psychological adjustment.

Test Validity

The characteristics of the individual represented by Figure 11.7 pose a challenge to the concept that peak scores invariably have positive behavioral counterparts. The *Pa* and *Sc* scores had clear-cut validity for behavior only when this person was reacting negatively to stress. The inability to infer accurately the previous or subsequent behavioral style of this person from her hospitalized profile could relate to its congruence ($r = .50$) with an "all random" MMPI profile (Duckworth and Duckworth 1975, p. 20). A random response tendency therefore could simply reflect a high degree of mental confusion at the time of testing. Thus peak scores influenced by random responses should not be expected to signify a person's distinguishing personality traits. Other response sets similarly influence profile configurations. An all "false" or an all "true" response set, for example, respectively approximates "neurotic" and "psychotic" profile types.

Selection of Descriptors

In the preceding example the young woman's retest profile (Figure 11.8) could not be considered random, yet *Sc* remained a prominent profile characteristic. A wider range of positive counterpart descriptors could help resolve this problem. Inclusion of words like idealistic in conjunction with related words such as imaginative for *Sc* in Table 11.1 would have provided appropriate positive descriptors for this person's observable cognitive sytle. Further revision, refinement, and elaboration of positive and negative descriptors for each MMPI scale are therefore needed. The expanded list of adjectives should be as specific as possible to the individual scales to avoid the "barnum" effect (Meehl 1956) where a description is perceived as universally applicable to most people. Additionally, adjectives selected for the various scales should be matched on levels of social desirability.

Personality Change

Given that the individual MMPI profiles can be "typed" (see Table 11.3), it becomes important to know whether or not subsequent testing would give equivalent profile configurations. Retest MMPI correlations were available for four of the basic types. The convergent person had the highest retest profile similarity, r = .88 after four months. The mean T score scale elevation of *L* through *Si* was three points lower. The externalizer's retest correlation after four months was .76, but the mean T score elevated five points. The internalizer and the socially outgoing persons had less stable MMPI configurations, but the retest intervals (6 to 12 months) were longer. The correlation for the internalizer was .50 and the mean T scale score declined six points; the major scale change was a drop of 26 T score points on the *Pa*. The correlation for the extroverted person was .48 with no change in mean scale scores. However, the *Pd* declined 27 points and the *Mf* increased 14 points. The changes in profiles for these two persons coincided with changes in lifestyles. These findings underscore the likelihood that an MMPI profile may be no more representative of a person over a time span than a photograph would be a permanent representation of one's changing physical appearance.

Stress Overlay

Although stress may enhance the likelihood of a person exhibiting the maladaptive features expected from the MMPI profile, a number of conditions impose features upon a MMPI profile that mask basic personality traits. The highly elevated scores in Figure 11.7 could be attributed in part to mental confusion contributing to a random response style. The *D* and *Si* scores that appeared most representative of her basic style were relatively submerged. In subsequent testing (Figure 11.8) these scores became more prominent and in Table 11.3 the profile shows a relationship to an introversive style (r = .44 with the sociopathic modal type). Other conditions that can impose transitional MMPI characteristics are traumatic losses (for example, loss of a loved one, or amputation of a body part), yielding an elevated *D*, and spinal cord injuries (for example, paraplegia), yielding an elevated *Hs*. Adebimpe (1978) also argued that an array of bodily malfunctions (for example, excess thyroid, brain tumor, heart disease) can create psychological reactions. If true, these conditions could be expected also to impose certain peak scores on MMPI profiles, thereby masking earlier personality traits.

The effects of various conditions upon MMPI performance underscore the need to utilize background information in MMPI interpretations to help separate state from trait personality characteristics.

CONCLUSIONS AND RECOMMENDATIONS

The basic question addressed in this chapter is whether the MMPI should be restricted in usage to codifying psychopathological symptomatology of psychiatric patients or should be used as a broader measure of personality. In answer to this question, it has been argued that MMPI scores can be used with a wide range of people to identify adaptive personality resources in addition to maladaptive behavior. Psychologists attuned to using MMPI profiles only for symptom identification may find the idea of using peak scores to predict adaptive personality characteristics remote. Regardless of how controversial the MMPI interpretative stance advocated in this chapter might be (see Dahlstrom 1972; Meehl 1972), it is the author's opinion that psychologists should place as much importance upon assessing client resources as they do upon assessing client symptoms.

The use of such terms as "sociopathic," "neurotic," and "psychotic" for major dimensions of personality ought to be replaced with broader categories having more neutral connotations. Interpersonal activity, for example, was presented as a better dimensional label for personality than sociopathy with the terms "socially outgoing" and "socially reserved" representing opposite ends of this continuum. Counterpart descriptors for the maladaptive behaviors, respectively, were "sociopathic" and "reclusive." The other two dimensions were emotional activity having "internalized" (neurotic) and "externalized" (manic) emotionality and cognitive activity having "divergent" (psychotic) and "convergent" (rigid) ideation. Case study data for persons with MMPI profiles statistically identified as representative of these three personality dimensions and their respective polar subtypes illustrate the kind of broader MMPI interpretative stance that appears feasible.

A number of conditions influence the accuracy of predictive behavioral inferences from MMPI profiles. Response style and specific stressors affect scale scores in a way that mask basic traits. Furthermore, actual changes in personality over a period of time make it somewhat hazardous to type-cast people on the basis of one test profile. The examples presented in this chapter nevertheless show sufficient personality continuity (retest correlations of .48 to .88) to warrant speculations about traits as well as states.

It is the author's conviction and experience that the MMPI can be used to measure personality in its broadest sense. Empirical research is needed to refine, expand, and establish the validity of MMPI scale counterpart descriptors. Sets of counterpart descriptors for MMPI validity and supplemental scales also need to be developed. If it is found that the MMPI cannot be used in the proposed manner, it is also the author's conviction that psychologists have an obligation to include other assessment strategies to ensure that their personality descriptions will address psychological resources in addition to psychopathology.

REFERENCES

Adebimpe, V. 1978. "A Rational for DSM-III'S Medical Model." *American Psychologist* 33: 853–54.

Anderson, W. P., and J. T. Kunce. "Sex Offenders: Three Personality Types." *Journal of Clinical Psychology*, in press.

Dahlstrom, W. G. 1972. "Whither the MMPI?" *Objective Personality Assessment*, edited by J. N. Butcher, pp. 85–115. New York: Academic Press.

——, and G. S. Welsh. 1960. *An MMPI Handbook: A Guide to Use in Clinical Practice and Research*. Minneapolis: University of Minnesota Press.

Diamond, S. 1957. *Personality and Temperament*. New York: Harper.

Dohrenwend, B. S., and B. F. Dohrenwend. 1974. *Stressful Life Events: Their Nature and Effects*. New York: Wiley.

Duckworth, J. C., and E. Duckworth. 1975. *MMPI Interpretation Manual for Counselors and Clinicians*. Muncie, Ind.: Accelerated Development.

Grahma, J. R. 1977. *The MMPI: A Practical Guide*. New York: Oxford University Press.

Kunce, J. T., and W. P. Anderson. 1976. "Normalizing the MMPI." *Journal of Clinical Psychology* 32: 776–80.

Maslow, A. H. 1971. *The Farther Reaches of Human Nature*. New York: Viking Press.

Meehl, P. E. 1972. "Reactions, Reflections, Projections." *Objective Personality Assessment*, edited by J. N. Butcher, pp. 131–89. New York: Academic Press.

——. 1956. "Wanted—A Good Cookbook." *American Psychologist* 8: 262–72.

Millon, T. 1976. *Million Multiaxial Clinical Inventory*. Minneapolis: National Computer Systems.

Skinner, H. A., and D. N. Jackson. 1978. "A Model of Psychopathology Based on an Integration of MMPI Actuarial Systems." *Journal of Consulting and Clinical Psychology* 46: 231–38.

12/ A SYSTEMATIC APPROACH TO PROVIDING FEEDBACK FROM THE MMPI

Philip Erdberg

INTRODUCTION

Although hundreds of thousands of individuals have plowed their way through the MMPI and psychologists have written millions of words to describe the results for other professionals, we are just now beginning to focus on that intersection of person and data that may well have the greatest utility of all: the presentation of findings to those who take the test in ways that have meaning for their past, present, and future. In traditional clinical practice, a client is tested on referral and a written report is returned to the referring professional. There is little survey information about what happens from there, but we do know that most mental health workers view the psychological report as a communication between professionals, not to be shown to the client. Indeed, two current books on psychological report writing (Hollis and Donn 1973; Tallent 1976) devote almost no attention to the writing of reports that are intended to be shared with the client. Dahlstrom, Welsh, and Dahlstrom (1972, pp. 338–39), in their comprehensive review of the MMPI clinical literature, cite only one example of a report for the client, expressing hope that more work will be done in the area.

The MMPI came of age during a period when this clinical practice of isolating clients from their test data was strong. At present, for a number of reasons, we are seeing a change. Increasingly, articles are appearing in the literature suggesting that not allowing a client to have access to his or her test findings is a holdover from an inappropriate scientism, antithetical to a humanistic stance in which client and professional work cooperatively and in mutual trust (Fischer 1972; Jourard 1972; Craddick 1975; Dana and Graham 1976; Sugerman 1978). Consumer activism and judicial decisions also have been potent forces in bringing people and their data together.

In addition to these philosophical and sociolegal trends, there is another extremely important reason to focus on the process of talking with people about their test findings. That reason comes from clinical experience, which suggests that simultaneous feedback of test data to client and referring professional can be of substantial value in facilitating their therapeutic work together (Erdberg 1977). With this joint feedback format, the assessing psychologist serves as a treatment consultant to therapist and client in a meeting that allows for immediate and very active integration of test data into the treatment process. Therapist and client react to the data, ask for elaboration of new material they find useful, and question whether the findings bear on other issues of importance to their work. Appropriately, there is a real combining of "assessment" and "therapy" data as client and therapist utilize the consultant in thinking about their current work and planning future directions.

Providing this sort of consultation to a wide variety of clients is a new skill for most psychologists, although their training in assessment, descriptive and developmental dynamics, and treatment modalities provides them with a unique set of building blocks for doing it. The purpose of this chapter is to provide a model of how results from one test, the MMPI, can be formulated for presentation to client and therapist in the context of the joint feedback meeting.

THE JOINT FEEDBACK TECHNIQUE

There are two sets of skills that the assessment psychologist must have in order to provide joint feedback treatment consultation. The first involves teaching the professionals who make testing referrals about this new format and the second involves formulating test data in ways that clients can integrate into their understanding of themselves and the treatment process.

The Referral

As noted above, most mental health professionals were trained in an era in which psychological reports were not shared with their clients. The format of the joint feedback session is unfamiliar to them, and a frequent question raised is whether some test findings may not be overwhelming, particularly for the "fragile" client. Although this issue has not been studied in all the settings in which the MMPI is used, clinical experience in universityvocational rehabilitation, and outpatient psychiatric situations suggests that it is possible to discuss issues that have included thought disorder, sexual identification, and suicidality (Craddick 1975; Erdberg, Walsh, and Dana 1978). Clients who have experienced the joint feedback process describe as anxiety-alleviating the experience of hearing this material verbalized, learning that others whom they see as concerned and supportive have some understanding of their subjective reality.

A useful procedure seems to be for the referring professional to contact the psychologist and briefly discuss the appropriateness of the referral. Ongoing consulting relationships can teach these referring professionals a good deal about what assessment can and cannot offer, promoting strong interdisciplinary co-operation in the process. If the situation seems to be one in which assessment can be of value, the referring professional then explains the process to the client, a task that generally turns out to be quite easy. The format makes intuitive sense to nearly all clients, and they tend to find it less threatening than the situation in which they are uncertain about what will happen with their test results. The assessment is then done and therapist and client meet with the assessing psychologist to discuss the results.

Presentation of MMPI Data

The joint feedback format demands that the psychologist formulate MMPI findings in ways that are useful for the client. A review of most clinical reports produced from MMPI data suggests that the pathology-oriented, diagnostic style in which psychologists typically present their findings would not be very helpful for the client's self-understanding. Instead, what is needed is a way to formulate the material so that clients can utilize it for a validation of their present experience, a conceptualization of their past, and an aid in thinking about ways to make their future more satisfying. Several workers have made contributions that help in producing this sort of formulation, and a brief review of their ideas and findings will be helpful.

Caldwell (1976, 1978) has noted that persons with elevations of specific MMPI scales are strikingly homogeneous in their style of psychological operation and demonstrably different from individuals with elevations on other scales. In trying to understand these clusters of psychological styles that seem so well bounded by various MMPI scale elevations, Caldwell hypothesizes that there may be a fairly specific conditioning event for each of them.

As an example, he suggests that the conditioning event for the MMPI depression scale may be an irretrievable, tremendously important loss. Some variety of this event has occurred in the lives of many of that subgroup of clients who have elevations in D, conditioning a specific and fairly homogeneous style of psychological operation that can be understood in terms of its ability to prevent repetitions of the traumatic occurrence. In the case of D, this psychological style involves a limiting of engagement with the present and future so as to guard against more loss. Although this response may be maladaptive in terms of the client's total life function, it makes sense in its ability to help avoid a repetition of the conditioning event. Caldwell further notes that this conditioning process may well extend to a neurophysiological, biochemical substrate, as in the lowered efficiency of neurotransmitters in depression.

An understanding of MMPI scale elevations in terms of these conditioning events has implications for treatment, which can be seen as the extinction of conditioned responses. In the case of D, for example, treatment involves confronting the loss directly so as to desensitize the client to its ability to evoke avoidance responses when present and future-oriented activities occur. The client then is able to expend psychological energy on the present and future, the opposite of depression.

The work of Kunce and Anderson (1976) (see Chapter 11) has been helpful in noting that there are adaptive aspects for moderate elevations of each of the MMPI clinical scales. Jackson (1978) has shown that the experience of taking a test places the client in a more accepting position of hear feedback. Leenaars, Bringmann, and Balance (1978) have suggested that, in terms of the wording of feedback, cleints find it easier to conceptualize psychological descriptions when they are phrased positively than when they are phrased negatively.

A synthesis of these ideas and findings allows an approach to formulating MMPI data for client feedback that can be summarized in this way:

Provide a description of the client's current behavior and experience. As it becomes available through the research literature, material about accompanying central nervous system states can be of value here.

Provide some hypotheses about the possible kinds of conditioning events that may have brought about this style of operating.

Facilitate client-therapist discussion of intervention approaches if it appears that a particular style of operating is consuming inordinate amounts of the client's energy output.

This kind of formulation serves the following functions:

Validates some of the experience the clients are currently having by allowing them to know that this is something with which others can have empathy. The clients may now be able to categorize a variety of previously disparate experiences under a single, more understandable heading. Frequently, this part of the joint feedback has allowed clients to tell their therapists about other experiences they were having, and much of this material has been new.

Allows the clients to conceptualize current experience in terms of the past. The concept of conditioning events is extremely helpful in its ability to evoke relevant associations, and the clients' identification of critical past events allows highly effective connection of historical material with present experience.

Allows the client and therapist to begin planning their future work together as the therapist moves into the role of expert on treatment modalities. As MMPI scale elevations increase, the amount of psychological energy consumed by a particular psychological style increases, frequently at the expense of other important parts of the client's life. The therapist can discuss ways of modifying the style so that it requires less energy, allowing more for other areas. The outcome of the meeting is that therapist and client have additional understanding of the client's present experience and the kinds of past events that may have conditioned the current style of psychological operation. They also have some thoughts about focus and directions for their work together. Client and therapist typically report a strengthening of their therapeutic bond, perhaps because of the additional important data that they now have in common.

The presentation of these formulations for some commonly seen MMPI scale elevations follows in the next sections of this chapter.

ANXIETY

The scale on the MMPI that is associated with that constellation of experiences characterized as anxiety is *Pt*. Cleints with *Pt* elevations spend an excessive amount of time worrying and often are concerned that something unexpected may happen. They tend to devote a great deal of time to making contingency plans that allow for all possible outcomes.

Caldwell (1976) suggests that *Pt* is conditioned by some disruptive event or events that have occurred unpredictably. This conditioning experience produces a state of constant apprehensiveness so as to ensure that nothing unanticipated will be able to occur again. As *K* increases with *Pt*, the fear becomes more focused. If *D* is also elevated, the conditioning event may have been an irretrievable loss that occurred unpredictably. As *K* decreases, the fear of unpredictable events becomes more diffuse. Kunce and Anderson (1976) comment on the adaptive aspects of the very methodical, systematic style that can characterize moderate elevations on *Pt*. Caldwell views counterconditioning for *Pt* as relaxation of what he calls the "all systems busy" style so as to allow new material to come in effortlessly.

A synthesis of these ideas would allow for the following sort of feedback to a client and therapist about the finding of an elevated *Pt*:

> I have a hunch that right now the world is a pretty frightening place for you. As you go through the day, you're concerned that something unpredictable can happen that will have a disastrous effect on you, and it leaves you needing to be in a constant state of alertness. But it's hard to stay that alert all the time, and you may be having some problems with sleep and a nagging sense that all hell is about to break loose. It's hard for you to relax enough to take much pleasure in the nice things that happen, because in the back of your mind there's always the fear that something bad could spring up. All told, it's an exhausting way to live.

Clients typically respond to this sort of description with substantial relief, much head-nodding, and verbalizations that it is good to have other people understand the sort of mine field they have to navigate each day.

The next part of the feedback involves some discussion of the conditioning event:

> There are some interesting ideas about what produces the sort of state you're in now. One thing that a lot of people who have these kinds of feelings have in common is that they've experienced some very upsetting things happening to them unpredictably. It might have been teasing from brothers or sisters which always took you by surprise, or possibly a single extremely upsetting event which came at you out of the blue. Whatever it was, it left you very concerned about the possibility of danger which can occur unpredictably, and there's a good possibility that your nervous system tries to keep constantly alert and active in order to guard against this sort of unpredictability.

Clinical experience suggests that this sort of conceptualization can be extremely useful for clients. One man made the association to an early childhood event that he had not mentioned previously in therapy: coming home from school one afternoon to find that his father had abandoned the family with no warning.

After client and therapist have had a chance to react, the final part of the feedback involves some discussion of possible interventions. This allows them to begin the process of integrating the new material into a treatment approach.

> This style of being extremely alert makes a lot of sense in terms of what we've said, and being very thorough and careful can be a tremendously useful approach in a lot of situations. But right now it may be using up too much of your energy, not allowing you to do some other things that would be satisfying for you. There may be some ways to help you relax this overly alert style, and I'd like to talk with the two of you about your thoughts on this.

The therapist now has the opportunity to provide specific information about treatment modalities, perhaps describing some techniques that allow desensitization or bringing up the issue of antianxiety medication.

DEPRESSION

Elevations on D are among the most common in outpatient mental health practice. Caldwell (1978) suggests viewing the client's elevation on K as an indicator of whether the tendency is toward depressive episodes that clear (low K) or toward sustained depression over lengthy periods of time (high K). K tends to modulate the intensity of emotional arousal, and as K increases, the client is unable to "let things out" in ways that would provide at least temporary relief.

Caldwell (1976, 1978) hypothesizes that the conditioning event for D is an irretrievable object loss of major emotional significance. This loss conditions an avoidance response that involves limiting connectedness with the present and future as a way of ensuring that no more losses will occur. The person spends a great deal of time focusing on the past, frequently with an "if only" quality about these ruminations. Whatever focus there is on the future tends to be diffuse and pessimistic. There may well be a slowing of central nervous system function as a way of blunting the sense of catastrophic loss. Depressives frequently report that time seems "stretched out" and that events occur more slowly than they previously did. Kunce and Anderson (1976) describe the evaluative, contemplative style that is involved in D as a sort of reflective thinking through of events. Caldwell suggests that treatment must engage the loss, defusing it of its ability to produce the avoidance responses. The person is then able to begin taking in new objects and finding satisfaction in the present and the future.

Feedback for a client with an elevation on D might be as follows:

I have the feeling that this is a difficult time for you. You're quite possibly having problems with sleeping, particularly with waking up during the night or very early in the morning. And your appetite may not be what it was, either. But more important is the way you must be feeling lately. It's hard for you to take much pleasure in what's happening in the present, and I'll bet it's even harder for you to get very excited about the future. You're thinking a lot about the past, and some of that thinking may be hooked up with wishing that things had turned out differently in some way. And all of these things that are going on with your emotions take up energy, and you may be feeling just plain fatigued some of the time. You may feel that you're not as alert as you used to be and that it takes longer for you to get a handle on things.

We're starting to know a little more about people who are going through this kind of experience, and one thing a lot of them have in common is that they've experienced a very specific kind of loss. What I'm talking about is the sort of loss that just can't be replaced and that's very important for you. And when that happens, it's such a painful experience that you can't help but dwell on it a lot, going over and over it in your mind to think how it might have come out differently. About the last thing you want is to leave yourself open for another loss, and that makes it hard to get very involved in the future. It's as if your whole nervous system is running slower to cushion you against the pain you're feeling.

We're also starting to know a little more about what helps get people moving again in this sort of situation, and I'd like to talk with you and your therapist about some ideas that may be useful for you. It seems important to think about some losses you may have experienced to see if we're on target in wondering if they're associated with the feelings you're having now. If they are, I think it may be useful for the two of you to talk them through in a lot of detail, even if you felt you had them pretty well squared away. And although I know it's the last thing you want to do right now, I think it might be of value to start thinking about your getting involved in some activities, so that you can talk about the feelings you're having as you try new things.

The description of depressive symptomatology seems a helpful way to initiate the feedback, communicating an understanding of the client's current experience. The client often responds by amplifying the description, and it seems a useful way to place a variety of seemingly spearate experiences under the same general category. The description of the conditioning event for depression has been of substantial value in clinical practice. Presented with feedback suggesting that they may still be concerned about a loss that has occurred in their lives, a number of clients have responded in cathartic ways that allowed therapy to continue with little need for additional feedback. As an example, one client spend the rest of the hour describing the events surrounding the death of a sister. Although this material had been brought up many times previously in therapy, the therapist felt that this discussion was qualitatively different in that the client, for the first time, attached his own emotions to the description.

SOMATIC CONCERN

Individuals who are overly concerned with health problems are probably a relatively high percentage of the patients seen in many general medical practices and in consultation with nonpsychiatric physicians. Psychological assessments can be of value to such patients and their physicians. These individuals obtain MMPIs with elevations on *Hs*, frequently with secondary elevations on *Hy*. They typically spend much time worrying about their health and seeking assistance from numerous physicians.

Caldwell (1976) has suggested that the conditioning event for *Hs* is the experience of an event or series of events so catastrophic that the person fears death is imminent. This experience conditions a maximum self-protective response, namely, the slowing down of motor output so as not to put the body in risky situations. *Hy*, he hypothesizes, may be conditioned by the experience of unbearable pain that seems to have no end. If that pain is physical, the client may shut down sensory function in order to block an experience that is viewed as never-ending and increasingly intense. Kunce and Anderson (1976) note that positive aspects of these styles include an appropriate concern about health and emotional sensitivity. Caldwell suggests a sort of desensitizing approach, in which a retelling of the experience many times diffuses some of the emotional charge, robbing it of its ability to create the avoidance response of continual monitoring of somatic function.

Feedback of these test findings, perhaps with a patient and internist, might be like this:

> It would seem that one area that is taking a lot of your psychological energy involves concern about your health. You spend a lot of time keeping tabs on how things are going with your body, and you often have the feeling that everything isn't going as it should. Even when you consult physicians, it's sometimes difficult for you to feel comfortable for very long with what they tell you. And sometimes, when you get sick or maybe have some sort of pain, you worry that it's just not going to end but instead is going to get worse and worse.

This sort of feedback is useful in its ability to emphasize with the experience involved in *Hs* elevations. One man responded by describing a concern he had during episodes of fatigue, namely, that he would become increasingly tired and never be able to get up from bed again.

> We have some ideas about the kinds of experiences that produce these concerns. A lot of people who have these feelings have had the experience of an extremely serious event at some time in their past which made them think their body was in serious physical danger to the extent that they were afraid they might die. It may have been a matter of illness or hunger when you were a child and didn't have the perspective to know that things would get better. Or perhaps a very serious accident or injury or period of illness in your life, maybe associated with a lot of pain that you weren't sure would get better. At any rate, the experience left you with real concerns that you could die or be in a lot of pain, and you may have responded by doing many of the very watchful things you do in order to keep your body out of situations that could be even potentially risky.

One man's association to this feedback was to remember a childhood event in which he had scarlet fever and was being carried into the doctor's office by his father while two siblings were saying that they thought he might be dying. In general, this sort of feedback can allow the patient to talk with the physician about the subjective experience associated with the medical problems under evaluation.

After both patient and physician have had a chance to think about these ideas and present some of their reactions, the feedback might continue in order to talk about possible interventions:

> This style certainly makes sense in light of the experiences you've had, and it's important to be concerned about good health. But thinking about your health may be taking up more than its share of your energy now, not leaving enough for other areas. What seems to be helpful is for you to have the chance to think back about these

experiences in a lot of detail, talk them over several times. Also, it might be helpful for the two of you to discuss ways you could learn more about positive physical function and begin enjoying physical activity.

This allows the physician to move into an expanded role that can include teaching and helping the patient plan less pathology-oriented programs, perhaps involving exercise or diet.

SOCIOPATHY

Sociopathic personality function, often associated with elevations on *Pd*, is a particularly entrenched style of psychological operation. These individuals typically do not initiate requests for intervention, and even when they do find themselves in mental health channels, often are not able to utilize treatment very productively. Their lives tend to be characterized by shallow interpersonal connections, and they are frequently deficient in family ties, long-term goals, and loyalty to groups. Although *Pd* was not normed on a criminal sample, some individuals with this elevation have the capacity for acting in coldly antisocial ways.

Cadlwell (1976) hypothesizes that this style of operation is conditioned by the childhood experience of not being wanted by parents. This creates an overload of stress for the child, and the response is to become emotionally numb so as not to experience the stress. Because attempts at interpersonal closeness were not rewarded, the client inhibits the anticipatory emotional arousal that characterizes interpersonal contact for most people. This shutting down results in a very low resting state of emotional readiness. Therapy is difficult because the client is not able to attach an emotional charge to the material being discussed. Elevated *Pd* tends to be associated with treatment difficulties in a wide variety of treatment settings. As an example, Campbell, Clarkson, and Sinsabaugh (1977) found that *Pd* was significant in its ability to discriminate between successful and unsuccessful clients in a Veterans administeration vocational rehabilitation program.

Although certainly no panacea for dealing with this frequently refractory syndrome, the joint feedback technique has been of some value in talking with clients and their therapists about elevated *Pd* findings:

Even when you're with a lot of people, it's hard for you to feel much connection with them. And things that many people get excited about—like whether their school football team wins or not—don't matter much for you. It's hard for you to get very excited at all by things that people do or say or the rules that they go by. Sometimes the only way for you to feel much sense of excitement is to do something like driving very fast. But even that doesn't last very long, and a lot of the time you just feel numb.

We're starting to have some ideas about how people get that sense of being emotionally numb. They may have been in a family situation where they just weren't wanted and where their parents were mostly concerned about themselves. That's a pretty stressful situation to be in, and after a while, a person just closes down his emotional reactions. That leaves you not having had much emotional experience, not having had much opportunity to care about other people and to feel their concern about you. When you did have those kinds of emotions in the past, they just sort of got cut off, and it left you feeling that it wasn't worth the effort to get emotional about other people.

It makes sense that with experiences like that you would have had those feelings about interactions with others, but your style may be cutting you off from some experiences of closeness with other people that would be satisfying for you. I think it might be helpful for the two of you to talk over some of those past experiences and how they fit into the way you feel about people now.

When this technique works successfully, it begins with the client's describing much anger and blame about parents or other authority figures, typically in a hostile but rather unemotional fashion. The progression is then to the feelings that were associated with those quite stressful interactions, resulting, in the case of one client, in his crying for the first time in his adult life. This ability to experience emotion in the context of an interpersonal event is the opposite of sociopathy.

PARANOIA

Another syndrome in which intervention is often difficult is paranoia. The client with an elevation on *Pa* is often abrasive, constantly concerned about the actions of others. Cues that would allow for increased relaxation in interpersonal situations are frequently misread.

Caldwell (1976) suggests that the conditioning event for *Pa* is the experience of having attempts made on the person's intactness or autonomy. This produces a constant vigilance in order to ensure that this overwhelming event cannot recur. He suggests that the projection so frequently seen in the paranoid style may be an extreme sensitization to the hostile motives of others.

Talking about this conditioning history can serve to align therapist and client in a mutual understanding of the person's history. When this alignment does occur, therapy can continue, and one important function that the therapist can serve is as a role model for the evaluation of interpersonal data. An important goal of therapy seems to involve the client's acquiring the skills to monitor interpersonal events in ways that require less vigilance. The client can then devote more energy to personal experiences instead of being locked into a totally outward focus that excludes any sort of internal awareness.

THOUGHT DISORDER

The joint feedback technique has been of substantial value in the area of thought disorder, mostly in its ability to communicate an understanding of the client's personal experience. Although Caldwell's formulation of conditioning events (1976, 1978) is of value in understanding schizophrenia, what seems more useful for the client experiencing cognitive disorganization is the opportunity for someone to talk with regarding what the experience must be like, particularly if it is new and ego-alien. An analysis of elevations on *Sc*, elevations on the *Sc* subscales developed by Harris and Lingoes (1955, 1968), and the presence of critical items (Grayson 1951) can be of value in formulating these descriptions. Here is one example of how talking with a client about thought disorder might sound.

> I have the feeling that the world can be a pretty confusing place for you. Sometimes things that people do or say don't make sense to you, and things may happen that leave you surprised or that you didn't expect. And there may be times when you miss something important and then later think to yourself that you should have noticed it. Examples might be running out of gas and then realizing that you should have looked at the gauge, or maybe saying something very cheerful and getting a bad response because you hadn't noticed that the person was looking unhappy. All these things add up to your feeling that it's awfully hard to handle the demands that the world makes on you, and frequently you feel uncertain about being able to do it.

Caldwell (1976) hypothesizes that the conditioning event for *Sc* is being intensely disliked by one's mother. The child is seen by the mother as being different and impossible to please, and the child invalidates the mother in a pathological dyadic interaction. The child feels in constant jeopardy in the situation of being disliked intensely by a person on whom survival depends, withdrawing massively as a protective response. This shutting down of information processing has a protective function, but the person misses some of the information necessary for crucial developmental tasks that would teach better coping ability. The continuing loss of important data ultimately produces reality distortion as well.

Clinical experience has suggested that feedback about these conditioning events may be appropriate later in the therapeutic process, after client and therapist have dealt with the issues of cognitive disorganization that were discussed in the initial session. The use of serial evaluations with ongoing feedback of results has been of substantial value in a number of the syndromes, and it seems of special use as a way of assessing how treatment is progressing in schizophrenia.

HYPOMANIC FUNCTION

In this psychological style, frequently associated with elevations on *Ma*, response output is accelerated and the individual operates at a rate of speed that does not allow concern for immediate detail. There is an intense focus on the future, often to the exclusion of attention for the present. Although the person can be expansive in the endorsement of the ideas of others, this emotion can quickly change to anger if others do not provide support and reward. Tolerance for any sort of frustration is poor.

Caldwell (1978) has suggested that the conditioning event for *Ma* is a sort of partial deprivation schedule in which the child is reinforced as a function of the parents' needs. This conditioning schedule results in a significant increase in response output in order to avoid deprivation. The client with *Ma* elevation is focused on the future, overanticipating the rewards that may come as a result of even more activity.

Talking with clients about their overaccelerated response style and the possibility of this sort of conditioning history has been quite valuable. The goal of treatment is helping the client take more pleasure in the present. Such feedback allows a contrasting of the client's future focus with the sense of discomfort experienced about slowing down enough to experience the present. The psychiatric therapist or consultant is able to talk with the client about the function of lithium carbonate in helping to facilitate this treatment approach.

FUTURE DIRECTIONS

The formulations described above are basic examples for providing MMPI data in ways that can be of value to client and therapist. Combining some of this material in a configural approach—as in the sense of hopelessness that occurs in the client who has elevations on both *D* and *Sc* and who has had conditioning experiences both of intense dislike from significant others and the loss of an important object—can be of substantial value.

It would seem that findings from a variety of other objective and projective personality instruments could also be formulated in terms of descriptive experience, hypotheses about conditioning events, and future treatment planning. The combination of the MMPI with these other instruments provides a way to conduct very comprehensive treatment consultation.

A new direction in the literature is exemplified by the study done by Donnelly et al. (1978), in which the MMPI was used to identify individuals who would respond well to antidepressant medication. It may become increasingly possible to tell clients and their therapists about their similarities to individuals who benefit from particular types of medications or treatment approaches.

REFERENCES

Caldwell, A. B. 1978. "MMPI Profile Interpretation." Paper presented at the annual MMPI Workshop, Mexico City, March.

——. 1976. "MMPI Profile Types." Paper presented at the annual MMPI Workshop, Minneapolis, January.

Campbell, H. G., Q. D. Clarkson, and L. L. Sinsabaugh. 1977. "MMPI Identification of Nonrehabilitants Among Disabled Veterans." *Journal of Personality Assessment* 41: 266-69.

Craddick, R. A. 1975. "Sharing Oneself in the Assessment Procedure." *Professional Psychology* 6: 27-282.

Dahlstrom, W. G., G. S. Welsh, and L. E. Dahlstrom. 1972. *An MMPI Handbook*, vol. 1; *Clinical Interpretation*. Minneapolis: University of Minnesota Press.

Dana, R. H., and E. D. Graham. 1976. "Feedback of Client-Relevant Information and Clinical Practice." *Journal of Personality Assessment* 40: 464-69.

Donnelly, E. F., F. K. Goodwin, I. N. Waldman, and D. L. Murphy. 1978. "Prediction of Antidepressant Responses to Lithium." *American Journal of Psychiatry* 135: 552-56.

Erdberg, P. 1977. "Assessment in Private Practice: Clinical Applications." Paper presented at the meeting of the Society for Personality Assessment, San Diego, March.

——, P. J. Walsh, and R. H. Dana. 1978. "The Joint Feedback Technique: A New Model for the Integration of Assessment Findings into the Treatment Process." Workshop presented at the meeting of the Society for Personality Assessment, Tampa, March.

Fischer, C. T. 1972. "Paradigm Changes Which Allow Sharing of Results." *Professional Psychology* 3: 364-69.

Grayson, H. M. 1951. *A Psychological Admissions Testing Program and Manual*. Los Angeles: Veterans Administration Center, Neuropsychiatric Hospital.

Harris, R. E., and J. C. Lingoes. 1955, 1968. "Subscales for the MMPI: An Aid to Profile Interpretation." San Francisco: Department of Psychiatry, University of California. Mimeographed.

Hollis, J. W., and P. A. Donn. 1973. *Psychological Report Writing Theory and Practice*. Muncie, Ind.: Accelerated Development.

Jackson, D. E. 1978. "The Effect of Test Taking on Acceptance of Bogus Personality Statements." *Journal of Clinical Psychology* 34: 66–68.

Jourard, S. M. 1972. "Some Reflections on a Quiet Revolution." *Professional Psychology* 3: 380–81.

Kunce, J. T., and W. P. Anderson. 1976. "Normalizing the MMPI." *Journal of Clinical Psychology* 32: 776–80.

Leenaars, A. A., W. G. Bringmann, and W. D. G. Balance. 1978. "The Effects of Positive vs. Negative Wording on Subjects' Validity Ratings of 'True' and 'False' Feedback Statements." *Journal of Clinical Psychology* 34: 369–70.

Sugerman, A. 1978. "Is Psychodiagnostic Assessment Humanistic?" *Journal of Personality Assessment* 42: 11–21.

Tallent, N. 1976. *Psychological Report Writing*. Englewood Cliffs, N.J.: Prentice-Hall.

13/ THE AUTOMATED MMPI

Raymond D. Fowler

The remarkable increase in testing in the fields of education, industry, and health has necessitated the development of increasingly efficient methods of processing the data. There has been a progression from hand-scoring stencils through electromagnetic scoring machines to optical scanner-computer combinations. Unfortunately, increased efficiency in scoring provides no relief to the test interpreter, and in many cases, test scores have not been used because interpreters are not available.

Interpretation is the assignment of meaning to observations. It is possible to program a computer, or for that matter, a clerk, to inspect test data according to a set of specified rules and to select from a store of previously compiled material the descriptive statements that are applicable. This "assignment of meaning" is the basis of automated interpretation.

Although it is possible, in theory, to develop an automated interpretation system for any psychological test, the Minnesota Multiphasic Personality Inventory has received the most attention, both because it is a widely used test and because the binary character of the responses makes it admirably suited for computer processing.

With its vast memory capacity, the computer can store great volumes of material about clinical groups and rapidly relate this information to new case data. This procedure offers a high level of accuracy and objectivity, as the computer can be programmed to utilize not only the body of published research literature relating to the MMPI but also a summation of the interpretive skills of a number of expert clinicians.

Also published in J. B. Sidowski, ed., *Technology in Mental Health Care Delivery Systems* (Norwood, N.J.: Ablex Publishers, 1979).

THE MMPI

The MMPI was developed in the late 1930s by Stark R. Hathaway and J. C. McKinley at the University of Minnesota. Since its publication in 1943 by the Psychological Corporation, the MMPI has become the most widely used instrument for objective personality assessment, and its use as a research instrument has increased each year.

The MMPI consists of 550 statements (or items) that concern attitudes, experiences, and behavior. For each item, the subjects respond true or false as it pertains to them. The scales were developed by comparing the responses of "normal" subjects with the responses of individuals with certain known characteristics or symptoms. Over the years, several hundred scales have been developed from the MMPI items, but most of the research and clinical use centers on the 14 "standard scales": 4 validity and 10 clinical scales. The current focus in the clinical utilization of the MMPI is upon the configural relationships among the scales and upon the use of the test data for personality description as opposed to diagnostic labeling.

Although computers have been used extensively in the standardization of psychological tests and the analysis of the data derived from such tests, using computers to interpret the meaning of test patterns and to generate psychological test reports is a fairly recent development.

Because the computer requires a structured input, it is not surprising that most of the progress in computer interpretation of personality tests has been with the objective personality inventories. Much of this work has been with the MMPI because it is widely used and thus familiar to most test users, there is a large research literature, and the traditions of the MMPI have emphasized an empirical approach to interpretation.

The rationale for computer interpretation of the MMPI was well stated by Hathaway (1976), who noted that the high rate of MMPI research has resulted in an accumulation of interpretational data too voluminous for even an experienced clinician to remember. Eichman (1972), in a review of computerized scoring and interpretation systems for *The Seventh Mental Measurements Yearbook* (Buros 1972), noted that the computer program, to the extent that the literature is adequate, can reflect the skills of many clinicians.

MMPI INTERPRETATION SYSTEMS

At least seven computerized MMPI interpretation systems are currently available. Others have been developed for use in specific mental health agencies, and several computerized MMPI systems are operational in other countries.

The Psychological Corporation/National Computer Systems Reporting System

The first computerized MMPI interpretation system was developed at the Mayo Clinic (Rome et al. 1965) to deal with the familiar pattern of large intake and small psychology staff. The Mayo group developed a method by which the MMPI could be scored and analyzed and a series of descriptive phrases and sentences printed out for use by the medical staff as part of a general medical evaluation.

This provided an efficient means of screening large numbers of medical patients who otherwise might have had no psychological or psychiatric screening, and it was well accepted by the medical staff and patients (Rome et al. 1962). The Mayo system was modified by Glueck and Reznikoff (1965) to produce a somewhat longer and more detailed report for use with a psychiatric population (the Institute of Living system), while Hedlund and associates (Bidus 1971) in the Army Medical Department adapted the Institute of Living system as part of a large-scale mental health computer applications study (COMPSY-Computer Support Military Psychiatry).

Permission was given by the Mayo group to the Psychological Corporation to make the interpretation system commerically available through National Computer Systems (NCS) at Minneapolis. The MMPI interpretation now in use at Mayo has gone through several revisions, but the system available through the Psychological Corporation has not been updated. Those reports consist, as did the original Mayo reports, of simple phrases based primarily on the absolute elevation of each standard MMPI scale with little concern for relative elevations or configurations of scales. In a reveiw of the Psychological Corporation-NCS reporting system prepared for *The Eighth Mental Measurements Yearbook* (Buros 1978), Butcher (1978) stated, "It is a rudimentary computerized system that simply lists out problem areas or hypotheses based on MMPI scale and some configural elements. The system's primary value is as a scoring service."

The Roche Psychiatric Service Institute System

The Roche Psychiatric Service Institute (RPSI) uses an interpretation system developed in the early 1960s by Fowler (1964, 1967) at the University of Alabama. The same system also underlies the reports provided by Psychological Assessment Services and the Hans Huber MMPI Service in Switzerland. A detailed description of the development of the Fowler system appears later in this chapter.

The Caldwell Report

The Caldwell Report is a division of Clinical Psychological Services, Inc. This interpretive system was developed by Alex B. Caldwell, then a faculty member in the Division of Psychology of the UCLA Medical School. The system has been under development since the early 1960s and became nationally available in 1970. The printout includes a lengthy and detailed narrative report, a profile sheet, and a listing of items from an extended critical item list (Caldwell 1969). The Caldwell report is perhaps the most ambitious effort to date to replicate the interpretive skills of an expert MMPI interpreter. The format, which is similar to the standard psychological report, is two to three pages long. The report highlights family dynamics and early experiences of the test subject as well as describing current behavior, symptoms, and diagnosis. A lengthy section on treatment considerations is a unique feature of the Caldwell report.

The Institute for Clinical Analysis

The Institute for Clinical Analysis (ICA) system initiated its services around 1966. No information is available on whether or not the system had been previously used on an experimental or pilot basis. Unlike the other MMPI interpretation systems, which are closely identified with the names of their developers, the ICA system appears to have been a corporate endeavor. Neither the manual nor the ICA descriptive literature identifies the developer or developers of the interpretation system.

The ICA printout includes a general personality report divided into such topics as validity, personality description, special coping problems, and symptom review. The responses to a set of critical items are shown, and the scores on a number of special scales are provided without interpretive statements. The report begins with two global severity of pathology indexes: the multiphasic index and the probability of significant disturbance. The MMPI components upon which these measures are based are nowhere specified.

The ICA system was criticized by Eichman (1972) and even more strongly criticized by Butcher (1978), who noted that the glaring inadequacies of the initial systems had not been altered. Butcher concluded that the ICA MMPI system offered a somewhat superficial MMPI interpretation based, to a large extent, on single-scale interpretations and two global indexes that have not been subjected to empirical scrutiny.

Behaviordyne Psychodiagnostic Laboratory Service

The Behaviordyne system, one of the earliest, was developed by Joseph Finney of the University of Kentucky (Finney 1965). Using a variety of scales and special norms, the Behaviordyne system produces seven types of reports for different settings and purposes, including one type of report for the subject's own information. The reports are long and somewhat psychoanalytically oriented.

DEVELOPMENT OF A COMPUTERIZED INTERPRETATION SYSTEM

The Fowler MMPI Interpretation system is currently in use by the Roche Psychiatric Service Institute (psychiatric patients), the Hans Huber MMPI Service of Switzerland (psychiatric and medical patients), and Psychological Assessment Services (law offenders, students, and employees). The development of the system began in 1961. The initial purpose was to produce a report similar in content and style to one written by a skilled MMPI interpreter, and the computer was programmed to follow the steps typically followed by a clinician in analyzing an MMPI protocol. The interpretation program utilized the same data available to a clinician.

Simulating the interpretive skills of a clinician does not rule out utilizing empirical actuarial data. In fact, few clinicians interpret an MMPI profile without taking into account the actuarial data of Marks, Seeman, and Haller (1974), Gilberstadt and Duker (1965), and various empirical studies. One advantage to the automated system is that the decision rules can be written to bring in relevant data, without the necessity of continuous reference to published material. Another advantage is the perfectibility of the system; interpretations may be "fine-tuned" by adjusting cutoff points. It may also be made more discriminating by including demographic data. For example, a prediction of violent behavior based on the MMPI might apply only to males and only within a specific age range.

During the four-year developmental period, the system was continuously revised on the basis of experience with several thousand patients of psychiatrists, psychologists, mental health centers, and alcoholism clinics. Feedback from clinicians and the case records of the patients were used in refining the decision rules and the language of the reports.

Because the purpose of the program was to simulate the clinician's decision making, the computer was programmed to follow the steps that might be followed by a clinician when analyzing an MMPI profile. The various configurations of the validity scales were specified and appropriate interpretive statements prepared to permit the reader of the report to determine the degree to which the test results could be considered valid. Also, the pattern of clinical scales was examined. Most interpreters use a configural approach rather than an interpretation of single-scale elevations. Because most of the interpretive literature focuses on the two-point code (the two most elevated clinical scales), this configuration was selected as the basis of the interpretive system. Several interpretive paragraphs were written for each two-point code, depending upon the elevation of the two scales and the relationship to other scale elevations. The computer was programmed to identify the two-point code and to select the statement library. Additional statements were prepared for other scale elevations and for several special scales that are used in the interpretive system.

Over a period of two years, interpretive statements for a large number of profile configurations were prepared along with decision rules to determine when they were applicable. These rules were designed so that all MMPIs were classifiable and interpretable. The statements were prepared so that all aspects of the profile would be covered for each individual. Statements were written in the form of paragraphs and organized so that the paragraphs that fit the decision rules were printed out in a standard order to produce a narrative report.

The early version of the interpretation system was designed for use by a secretary who followed a precise set of rules in order to select the paragraphs, which then were typed manually. The resulting reports were first compared with independently written clinical reports and then were included in the case evaluation conferences at various alcoholism and mental health clinics in Alabama. The resulting feedback from various professional staff members led to changes in the paragraphs. During the developmental period, the original paragraphs were polished and rewritten to make them more closely match the available clinical data. At the conclusion of the clinical evaluation phase, the rules were programmed for computer, thus making fully automated and computerized reports available.

The Roche Psychiatric Service Institute was established in 1966 by Roche Laboratories, a pharmaceutical firm, to make the Fowler MMPI system available to psychiatrists, psychologists, and mental health agencies. The RPSI service is currently the most extensively used automated MMPI service. Several thousand psychiatrists and psychologists and over 1,000 mental health agencies use the service on a regular basis.

Two other MMPI services, the Hans Huber Institut für Psychodiagnostic and Psychological Assessment Services, Inc., are based upon variations of the Fowler interpretation system. Both services use the same general decision rules, but print out reports based on statements modified for their special purposes.

COMPUTER INTERPRETATION OF THE MMPI IN EUROPE

Automated MMPI interpretation systems were introduced in Europe several years later than in the United States, partly because of the relative lack of high-capacity computers and partly because the MMPI has only recently become popular as a clinical instrument. At present, three automated interpretation systems are available and operational in Europe (Butcher and Pancheri 1976). The first European MMPI service, which was established in 1971 by F. Hoffmann La Roche Company in Basel, Switzerland (now distributed through Hans Huber of Berne, Switzerland), is based on the original Fowler system and closely resembles RPSI. Translations into several European languages exist, but the principal use is in the German-speaking countries.

Two other systems are also operational in Europe. The Brussels Automated MMPI (BAMMPI), developed by J. P. De Waele, D. De Schamphleire, and G. Van de Mosselaer of the University of Brussels, produces a narrative report in English from MMPIs administered in French and Dutch. Its use is primarily in Belgium.

The Institute of Psychiatry of the University of Rome system (IPUR), developed by Paolo Pancheri, prints a narrative report based on code-type interpretations and a probability estimate of the three most likely clinical diagnoses. It can be used through a CRT self-administered format in which items are computer administered. It has been translated into English and Spanish. Its primary use is in Italy, but it has been used to some extent in the United States and Canada.

PSYCHOLOGICAL ASSESSMENT SERVICES

The decision rules and interpretive statements used in the Roche Psychiatric Service Institute (RPSI) system were specifically designed for mental health patients and all potential users are informed that the system is not suitable for routine screening of presumably normal-range individuals. They are further informed that the service is not available for educational counseling or selection, vocational screening, occupational selection, correctional or law enforcement evaluation, and other non health-related activities. Psychological Assessment Services was organized in 1971 to provide reports based on modifications of the Fowler system for various nonpsychiatric populations.

Student Version

This version was designed for use in counseling and guidance services in various educational agencies and institutions. The statements in the RPSI system and in the other psychiatrically oriented automated systems tend to overinterpret the profiles of students. The student version contains statements that are adjusted to this phenomenon and take into account the special scales and research data on students. A complete description of the system has been published (Fowler 1968).

Personnel Version

This version was developed for use in business, industry, and government for special-purpose assessment of relatively normally functioning people. The statements emphasize the unique characteristics of the subject as opposed to psychopathology. It is not appropriate for "screening out" employees, but may be used to place an individual appropriately within an organization as a part of a larger personnel classification process.

Law Offender Version

This version of the Fowler program was developed in 1970 for use in the criminal justice system, and has been used in jails, prisons, juvenile facilities, probation and parole departments, and as a part of presentence investigation. Development of the system was encouraged by a study (Fowler 1972) in which RPSI reports on all prisoners admitted to one state prison for a one-year period were rated for accuracy by the psychology staff. The results of the rating scale study compared favorably with previous studies using psychiatric populations, but suggested some necessary statement modifications. The statement library was rewritten in collaboration with experienced correctional psychologists, and a follow-up rating scale evaluation indicated that the reports were considerably improved.

The law offender interpretation system was used as a part of a systemwide reclassification of all prisoners in one state prison system in 1976. Currently, it is being used to evaluate all individuals who enter the criminal justice system in another state. Convicted persons are tested as a part of the presentence investigation and are retested as necessary at various decision points, such as prison classification, parole evaluation, and community release.

THE REPORT

The reports based on the Fowler interpretation system follow the same format. Each report consists of several sections that provide different kinds of information.

The Narrative Report

The narrative report, one to two pages long, is a compilation of the paragraphs selected by the computer on the basis of the decision rules. It contains statements about the validity of the test, predicted behavior of the subject, and descriptions of current behavior, symptoms, and psychological functioning.

The Critical Item List

The critical item list is a subset of 55 MMPI items that sometimes suggest special problems that should be directly investigated by the clinician. For each patient, only those items answered in the deviant direction are printed. The items are grouped into content categories: suspicion and ideas of reference; unusual thoughts and ideas; depression, guilt, and self-destructive feelings; health and bodily concerns; sexual concerns and problems; alcohol and drug use.

The Content Scale Statements

The content scales (Wiggins 1969) are made up of items that are clearly and obviously related to the characteristic being measured. The content scale statements are brief paragraphs based on the subject's content scale scores. These statements are often closely related to the patient's self-perceptions rather than the statements in the narrative report.

The Profile

The MMPI scale scores are presented in graphic form permitting visual inspection of the scale patterns.

The Technical Section

A final page is printed to facilitate the use of the data for research. This page includes scores on 14 special scales, a numerical code to classify the profile, the score on the MacAndrews scale (addiction proneness) (see Chapter 4), along with a statement interpreting the scale, and a matrix of true-false responses by which the subject's answer to any item can be determined.

ISSUES RAISED BY AUTOMATED PSYCHOLOGICAL REPORTS

The ethical questions raised by automated test interpretation have been studied by the American Psychological Association (APA), and guidelines have been prepared to ensure their appropriate use. In 1966, the APA Council of Representatives adopted a set of principles entitled "Automated Test Interpretation Practices: An Interim Standard for Members of the APA and for Organizations by Whom Members Are Employed." The standards have received general recognition and acceptance by members of the profession, and no serious violations have been reported.

For better or worse, computer interpretation services are apparently here to stay. Each year they account for an increasingly large percentage of the MMPI reports produced. In the final analysis, computerized MMPI reporting systems have deeper significance than the practical considerations of speed, economy, and wide availability. They offer an alternative to the endless cycle of training new personnel, generation after generation, to do approximately the same thing with test data as their predecessors did. The prediction of behavior and the description of personality are far too complex to be subject to half-remembered norms and subjective extrapolation. Even a simple actuarial formula can usually exceed clinicians' accuracy in the prediction of phenotypic and genotypic descriptors. The economics involved in training clinical psychology students to accomplish what computers can already do is questionable; to train them to do what computers can potentially do is impossible. The computer can be a powerful tool to free the psychologists from tasks that they do not do well, while releasing them for responsibilities for which they are uniquely qualified.

REFERENCES

Bidus, D. 1971. "Computers in Mental Health and Behavioral Science." *Newsletter for Research in Psychology* 13 (2): 24–25.

Buros, O. K. Ed. 1978. *The Eighth Mental Measurements Yearbook*, pp. 947–48. Highland Park, N.J.: Gryphon Press, 1978.

——. 1972. *The Seventh Mental Measurements Yearbook*. Highland Park, N.J.: Gryphon Press.

Butcher, J. N. 1978. "Automated Psychological Assessment." In *The Eighth Mental Measurements Yearbook*, edited by O. K. Buros. Highland Park, N.J.: Gryphon Press.

——, and P. Pancheri. 1976. *Handbook of Cross-National MMPI Research*. Minneapolis: University of Minnesota Press.

Caldwell, A. B. 1969. "MMPI Critical Items." Available from Caldwell Reports, 3122 Santa Monica Blvd., Penthouse West, Los Angeles, Calif. Mimeograph.

Eichman, W. J. 1972. "(MMPI) Computerized Scoring and Interpretating Services." *The Seventh Mental Measurements Yearbook*, edited by O. K. Buros, pp. 250–66. Highland Park, N.J.: Gryphon Press.

Finney, J. C. 1965. "Purposes and Usefulness of the Kentucky Program for the Automatic Interpretation of the MMPI." Paper presented at the annual meeting of the American Psychological Association, Chicago.

Fowler, R. D. 1972. "The Use of Computer-Produced MMPI Reports with a Prison Population." Unpublished manuscript.

——. 1968. "MMPI Computer Interpretation for College Counseling." *Journal of Psychology* 69: 201–07.

——. 1967. "Computer Interpretation of Personality Tests: The Automated Psychologist." *Comprehensive Psychiatry* 8: 455–67.

——. 1964. "Computer Processing and Reporting of Personality Test Data." Paper presented at the meeting of the American Psychological Association, Los Angeles.

Gilberstadt, H., and J. Duker. 1965. *A Handbook for Clinical and Actuarial MMPI Interpretation*. Philadelphia: Saunders.

Glueck, B. C., Jr., and M. Reznikoff. 1965. "Comparison of Computer-Derived Personality Profile and Projective Psychological Test Findings." *American Journal of Psychiatry* 121: 1156–61.

Hathaway, S. R. 1976. "Foreword." In *The Clinical Use of the Automated MMPI*, by R. D. Fowler. Nutley, N.J.: Hoffmann-La Roche.

Marks, P. A., W. Seeman, and D. L. Haller. 1974. *The Actuarial Use of the MMPI with Adolescents and Adults*. Baltimore: Williams & Wilkins.

Rome, H. P., P. Mataya, J. S. Pearson, and T. L. Brannick. 1965. "Automatic Personality Assessment." In *Computers in Biomedical Research*, edited by R. W. Stacey and B. D. Waxman, vol. 1, pp. 505–24. New York: Academic Press.

Rome, H. P., W. M. Swenson, P. Mataya, C. E. McCarthy, J. S. Pearson, F. R. Keating, Jr., and S. R. Hathaway. 1962. "Symposium on Automation Techniques in Personality Assessment." *Proceedings of the Mayo Clinic* 37: 81–82.

Wiggins, J. S. 1969. "Content Dimensions in the MMPI." In *MMPI: Research Developments and Clinical Applications*, edited by J. N. Butcher. New York: McGraw-Hill.

14/DEVELOPMENT OF SPECIAL MMPI SCALES

James R. Clopton

The MMPI originally included three validity scales, which assess test-taking attitudes, and eight clinical scales, which identify common patterns of psychopathology. Two other scales (Masculinity-feminity, *Mf*, and Social introversion, *Si*)were developed later, and together with the original scales have formed the standard MMPI profile since 1950. From the time of the MMPI's first use, a multitide of special MMPI scales have been constructed. MMPI scale development continues unabated, and the subsequent number of currently available scales exceeds the number of MMPI items (Butcher and Tellegen 1978). As psychologists gained clinical experience with the MMPI they began to recognize that, despite the psychodiagnostic labels of the standard clinical scales, the MMPI could be used for general personality assessment and lead to meaningful inferences about normal individuals. Scales were therefore developed to measure dependency (Navran 1954), prejudice (Gough 1951), and a variety of other personality dimensions. Special scales have also been developed to detect types of psychopathology that are not assessed directly by the standard MMPI scales. For example, several investigators have constructed MMPI alcoholism scales (Atsaides, Neuringer, and Davis 1977; Hampton 1953; Holmes 1953; Hoyt and Sedlacek 1958; MacAndres 1965).

This chapter will review some special MMPI scales in frequent use and will then discuss in detail the logic and methodology for empirically derived special scales. Listings of special scales can be found in the two volumes of the *MMPI Handbook* (Dahlstrom, Welsh, and Dahlstrom 1972, 1975). Graham (1977, 1978) has provided detailed information about several special MMPI scales in frequent use.

FREQUENTLY USED SPECIAL SCALES

Special MMPI scales have been developed by intuitive procedures, by cluster and factor analyses, and by empirical scale construction. Many of the special scales, such as the success in Baseball (*Ba*) scale (LaPlace 1954), are too limited for widespread use. However, some special scales are frequently used both in clinical and research settings.

Intuitive Procedures

The standard clinical scales of the MMPI were developed empirically without consideration given to scale content. As a result, the item content of the standard clinical scales is quite heterogeneous. The same raw score on a clinical scale can be obtained by individuals endorsing very different sets of items. For this reason, some investigators have suggested that consideration of the subgroups of items within each clinical scale would add precision to interpretation of MMPI profiles. Harris and Lingoes (1955) developed subscales for six of the ten clinical scales by examining the items of each scale and grouping those items they judged either to be similar in content or to reflect the same attitude or trait. Each subscale was then given a name to indicate its presumed content.

Although it might be assumed that the resulting subscales are homogeneous, the internal-consistency reliability values for a few of the subscales are remarkably low (Gocka 1965). The Harris and Lingoes scales are widely used to help determine what kinds of items have been endorsed by a subject who obtains a high score on one of the clinical scales. One study (Calvin 1975) that attempted to identify behavioral correlates for the Harris and Lingoes subscales found that for psychiatric patients the subscales generally did not add significantly to analyses based on the standard clinical scales. Despite their popularity, surprisingly little research has been done to evaluate the Harris and Lingoes subscales.

The MMPI items in each Harris and Lingoes subscale and the direction of scoring for each item can be found in MMPI source books (Dahlstrom, Welsh, and Dahlstrom 1972; Graham 1977). The subscales for each of the six standard clinical scales are as follows (reprinted with permission of the authors):

Scale 2: Depression (*D*)
        Subjective depression (*D* 1)
        Psychomotor retardation (*D* 2)
        Physical malfunctioning (*D* 3)
        Mental dullness (*D* 4)
        Brooding (*D* 5)

Scale 3: Hysteria (*Hy*)
        Denial of social anxiety (*Hy* 1)
        Need for affection (*Hy* 2)
        Lassitude-malaise (*Hy* 3)
        Somatic complaints (*Hy* 4)
        Inhibition of aggression (*Hy* 5)

Scale 4: Psychopathic deviate (*Pd*)
        Familial discord (*Pd* 1)
        Authority problems (*Pd* 2)
        Social imperturbability (*Pd* 3)
        Social alienation (*Pd* 4A)
        Self-alienation (*Pd* 4B)

Scale 6: Paranoia (*Pa*)
        Persecutory ideas (*Pa* 1)
        Poignancy (*Pa* 2)
        Naivete (*Pa* 3)

Scale 8: Schizophrenia (*Sc*)
        Social alienation (*Sc* 1A)
        Emotional alienation (*Sc* 1B)
        Lack of ego mastery, cognitive (*Sc* 2A)
        Lack of ego mastery, conative (*Sc* 2B)
        Lack of ego mastery, defective inhibition (*Sc* 2C)
        Bizarre sensory experiences (*Sc* 3)

Scale 9: Hypomania (*Ma*)
        Amorality (*Ma* 1)
        Psychomotor acceleration (*Ma* 2)
        Imperturbability (*Ma* 3)
        Ego inflation (*Ma* 4)

Another example of a special MMPI scale that was rationally or intuitively constructed is Taylor's (1953) Manifest Anxiety scale (MAS). Five clinical psychologists were asked to select MMPI items that indicated manifest anxiety. There was 80 percent agreement among the psychologists on 65 items. These preliminary items were administered to a college student sample. The 50 items that were most highly correlated with the total score of the preliminary scale were selected for the final MAS and were interspersed among 175 MMPI items that were not scored. Taylor's (1953) caution against scoring the MAS from the standard MMPI protocol because of differences in buffer items has generally been ignored by clinicians and researchers alike.

The MAS was originally constructed to assess emotional responsiveness (one of the determinants of general drive level) so that predictions about the relationship between drive level and learning could be studied. The Hull-Spence learning theory predicted that subjects with high drive level (high MAS scores) would do better than low drive level subjects (low MAS scorers) on simple learning tasks but worse on complex tasks. Most of the empirical data support this hypothesis (Byrne 1974). High MAS scorers have also been found to obtain high scores on other anxiety scales, to show greater physiological responsiveness under stress, and to be rated by observers as high on anxiety. The MAS has a high degree of internal consistency (Gocka 1965) and temporal stability (Taylor 1953). MAS scores do not change in response to situational changes such as training in relaxation or stress introduced in a psychological experiment (Clopton 1974b). Despite Taylor's original intent in constructing the scale, the MAS is now regarded as an excellent measure of trait anxiety, that is, the general predisposition to respond with anxiety in stressful situations.

Cluster Analysis

The Tryon, Stein, and Chu (TSC) cluster scales represent an effort to use cluster analysis in constructing special scales to assess the main dimensions of the MMPI item pool (Chu 1966; Stein 1968; Tryon 1966). Cluster analysis procedures were applied to the MMPI item responses of psychiatric outpatients and normal military officers. Seven clusters of items were identified. Each cluster was judged to be homogeneous both statistically and with regard to item content. A scale was developed for each cluster by selecting the MMPI items that had the highest loadings for that cluster. Each scale then was named by examining the item content of the scale. The seven TSC scales are as follows:

I. Social introversion
II. Body symptoms
III. Suspicion and mistrust
IV. Depression and apathy
V. Resentment and aggression
VI. Autism and disruptive thoughts
VII. Anxiety, worry, and fears (tension)

Data regarding the temporal stability (test-retest reliability) of the TSC scales are lacking, but the procedures used in developing the scales ensured that the scales would have a high degree of internal consistency. Scores of the TSC cluster scales have been correlated with the scores of standard MMPI scales (Chu 1966). Some of the TSC scales were so highly correlated with standard scales that they appear to provide little information not already available from standard scales. For example, the correlation of scores on the Social introversion cluster scale and scores on the standard *Si* scale was .92. On the other hand, scores on the Suspicion and Mistrust cluster scale did not correlate highly with scores on any of the standard scales. The correlation of the Suspicion and Mistrust scale and the *Pa* scale was a mere .16. Therefore a few of the cluster scales, such as Suspicion and Mistrust, apparently assess characteristics not reflected in the standard MMPI scales.

Cluster analysis and factor analysis may also be used to identify the underlying dimensions of a particular MMPI scale. Comrey (1957a, 1957b, 1957c, 1958a, 1958b, 1958c, 1958d; Comrey and Marggraff 1958) factor-analyzed the intercorrelations of items within each of the eight original clinical scales. Comrey's research clearly demonstrated the lack of homogeneity within MMPI clinical scales. The factors produced for each scale were remarkably similar to the Harris and Lingoes subscales.

Little and Fisher (1958) administered the MMPI to hospitalized medical and psychiatric patients, and then applied cluster analysis to the intercorrelations among *Hy* scale items. Nine clusters were obtained. Five of these clusters were significantly correlated with each other and relatively independent of the remaining four clusters. The latter set of clusters had moderate to high positive correlations with each other. Inspection of the items in the five clusters, together with a consideration of their direction of scoring in the *Hy* scale, indicated that the items consisted mainly of bodily sumptoms to which the subject admitted. This group of items was labeled the Admission (*Ad*) scale. The other four clusters consisted mostly of items that were scored if subjects denied that they had poor interpersonal relations or any feelings of hostility and suspicion. The items in these four clusters, together with other items that were highly correlated with this set of items, became the Denial (*Dn*) scale.

Research studies reveal that the *Dn* scale measures both the verbal denial of anxiety and the cognitive coping strategy (that is, defense mechanism) of denial. The negative correlations obtained between *Dn* scale scores and anxiety scale scores (Houston 1971; Little and Fisher 1958) indicate that the *Dn* scale measures the general tendency not to report the presence of anxiety. That *Dn* also measures the predisposition to employ anxiety-reducing maneuvers is indicated by the finding that high *Dn* scores are associated with reduced affective response to stress (Houston 1973; Weinstein et al. 1968) and better memory performance in stressful situations (Houston 1971, 1973). Houston (1973) has suggested that adjusting *Dn* scores for anxiety predisposition (MAS scores) will result in a more sensitive measure of the tendency to use denial as a defensive coping strategy.

Empirical Scale Construction

The method of empirical scale construction has been used in the development of many special MMPI scales. Using this approach, an item analysis is performed comparing the response frequencies (number of "true" answers and number of "false" answers) of a criterion group with the response frequencies of a suitable comparison group. The MacAndres (1965) Alcoholism scale (AMac) and the Ego-strength scale (Barron 1953) are two commonly used special scales that were developed empirically.

MacAndrew (1965) developed an alcoholism scale consisting of those MMPI items that significantly differentiated outpatient alcoholics from nonalcoholic psychiatric outpatients. After removing two MMPI items (215 and 460) that refer directly to alcohol use, the final scale consisted of 49 items. Using a cutting score of 24 to identify alcoholism (for example, patients with scale scores of 24 or higher would be classified as alcoholic), the AMac scale correctly classified 81.5 percent of the cross-validation sample of outpatient alcoholics and nonalcoholic psychiatric outpatients. High scorers on the AMac scale have been found to be uninhibited, sociable individuals who appear to use repression and religion in attempting to control rebellious, delinquent impulses (Finney et al. 1971).

Validation research has shown that this scale can differentiate alcoholic and nonalcoholic patients in a variety of treatment settings (Clopton 1978). The percentage of correct classification of patients by the AMac scale has generally varied between 60 and 80 percent. AMac scale scores tend to remain stable over extended periods of time (Hoffman, Loper, and Kammeier 1974) and generally do not change as a result of treatment programs (Chang, Caldwell, and Moss 1973; Huber and Danahy 1975; Lanyon et al. 1972; Rohan et al. 1969; Vega 1971). Two studies (Dranitz 1972; Lachar et al. 1976) have found the AMac scale unable to differentiate alcoholics and heroin addicts, and thus suggest that this scale may be identifying a general propensity toward substance misuse.

The Ego-stength (*Es*) scale consists of 68 items found by Barron (1953) to differentiate between neurotic patients who were judged to be either improved or unimproved after six months of individual psychotherapy. To cross-validate the *Es* scale, Barron (1953) correlated pretherapy *Es* scores with ratings of improvement following psychotherapy for three different neurotic samples. The correlations (.38, .42, .54) were positive and statistically significant. Subsequent validity studies by other investigators (reviewed by Graham 1977; Meltzoff and Kornreich 1970) have often failed to confirm the usefulness of the *Es* scale in predicting change during psychotherapy. For example, Getter and Sundland (1962) found no relationship between pretherapy *Es* scores and ratings of improvement following therapy. However, some validation research does support the usefulness of the *Es* scale (for example, Holmes 1967; Wirt 1955), while some "failures" to replicate (for example, Distler, May, and Tuma 1964) have studied response to hospitalization, not change following psychotherapy.

Two explanations have been offered regarding this lack of consistency. Dahlstrom, Welsh, and Dahlstrom (1975) suggest that high *Es* scores will be predictive of improvement in psychotherapy only for persons who admit that they have problems in living. For therapy candidates who deny obvious conflicts or difficulties, high *Es* scores would probably not indicate a favorable response to therapy. Graham (1978) suggests that validation studies demonstrate that *Es* scores predict the response of neurotic patients to individual, psychoanalytically oriented therapy, and that predictions for other types of patients or for other types of treatment are not accurate.

Scores on the *Es* scale are positively correlated with intelligence and with amount of formal education (Tamkin and Klett 1957). Males consistently obtain higher *Es* scale scores than females, but Holmes (1967) performed an item analysis that indicated these sex differences were due to eight *Es* items. Most of these eight items were related to masculine role identification. In the Holmes study, male-female differences in *Es* scores were eliminated when the tests were rescored without the eight discriminating items, but the significant positive relationship between *Es* scores and response to psychotherapy found was not affected.

METHODOLOGY FOR EMPIRICAL CONSTRUCTION OF SPECIAL MMPI SCALES

To develop a new MMPI scale empirically, the responses of a criterion group to each MMPI item (number of "true" answers and number of "false" answers) are compared with the responses of a suitable comparison group. An item analysis is performed by using the 2 x 2 contingency table shown in Figure 14.1 for each of the 566 items. The letters in the cells of the contingency table indicate the observed frequencies. Thus A represents the number of "true" responses from subjects in the criterion group. A test of statistical association, such as the chi-square test, is used to determine whether the response frequencies of the two groups differ significantly. The traditional rule has been that the chi-square test may be used only if the expected frequency for each cell in the contingency table is at least five (Hays 1963; Wike 1971). The expected frequency for each cell in the contingency table is determined by multiplying the row total (either A + B or C + D) by the column to total (either A + C or B + D) and then dividing by n, the total number of subject responses. For example, the expected cell frequency for the upper left cell in the contingency table shown in Figure 14.1 would be obtained by multiplying A + B (the row total) by A + C (the row total) by A + C (the column total) and then dividing by n.

Even with a large number of test subjects, an expected cell frequency for a particular MMPI item may easily be less than five. Some MMPI items, such as item 85 "Sometimes I am strongly attracted by the personal articles of others such as shoes, gloves, etc., so that I want to handle or steal them though I have no use for them,"* are not scored for any of the clinical scales and are rarely endorsed by test subjects (Hathaway and McKinley 1940). For such items the two cells in the contingency table representing 'true' responses will often have expected cell frequencies less than five even with a large number of subjects in both criterion and comparison groups. When the chi-square test is not appropriate for determining whether or not criterion and comparison groups respond differently to an MMPI item, Fisher's exact probability test should be used. If only a few MMPI items are of interest and Fisher's exact test is to be used, then the investigator should consult tables of critical values for Fisher's test (Finney

---

*Reproduced from the MMPI by permission. Copyright 1943, renewed 1970, by the University of Minnesota. Published by The Psychological Corporation. All rights reserved.

	Number of True Answers	Number of False Answers
Criterion Group	A	B
Control Group	C	D

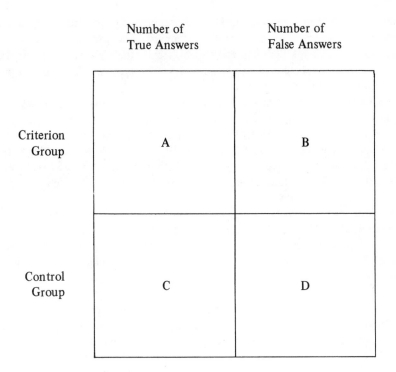

FIGURE 14.1: Contingency table for response frequencies to a particular MMPI item. *Source*: Constructed by the author.

et al. 1963; Pearson and Hartley 1964; Siegel 1956). There are limitations to these tables (Gregory 1973), one being that critical values are not listed for a total n greater than 60.

Recent research has questioned two traditional recommendations regarding 2 x 2 contingency tables. Two studies (Camilli and Hopkins 1978; Roscoe and Byars 1971) indicate that the chi-square test may be employed for 2 x 2 contingency tables even if an expected cell frequency falls considerably below five. Camilli and Hopkins (1978) found that the chi-square test provided accurate probability statements even when the expected frequencies in one or two cells are as low as one, provided that n is at least 20. Nearly all statistics textbooks (for example, Hays 1963) advise that use of the Yates correction for continuity will increase the accuracy of probability statements when using the chi-square test with 2 x 2 contingency tables. However, recent research (Camilli and Hopkins 1978; Grizzle 1967; Plackett 1964) has not supported this advice. Use of the chi-square test without the Yates correction has been found to yield accurate probability statements. In contrast, use of the Yates correction leads to significance tests that are far more conservative than indicated by the nominal value of statistical significance. The Yates correction for continuity actually reduces the accuracy of probability statements. Thus, in performing an item analysis to select MMPI items for a special scale, the chi-square test should be used unless an expected cell frequency is less than one, and Yates correction for continuity should not be used.

Neither the chi-square test nor Fisher's exact test is appropriate when subjects in the criterion group are matched with subjects in the comparison group. When the two groups consist of pairs of subjects and the members of each pair have been selected because they are alike in terms of some matching variable (age, educational attainment, and so forth), then McNemar's test for correlated proportions (Siegel 1956) should be used to determine which items should be selected for the special scale.

Whenever a statistically significant difference is found between the performance of two groups, there is an associated probability, which is indicated by the level of statistical significance, that the obtained difference could have occurred because of chance fluctuations. With a large number of statistical comparisons, the probability is increased that significant findings will be obtained that are due to chance alone. Therefore, after an MMPI item analysis has been performed, the investigator must consider whether the number of items found to differentiate significantly between the criterion and comparison groups exceeds the number of items that might be expected to reach statistical significance purely by chance. A commonsense solution to this problem has been to multiply the total number of items that were analyzed by the level of statistical significance used for the test of association. This solution would suggest that approximately 28 items could reach significance by chance if the .05 level of significance were used in testing the 566 MMPI items. A related solution is to use the binomial expansion to calculate the probability of any given number of items reaching significance by chance. Both of these solutions would be appropriate only if MMPI items were independent, or at least relatively independent. However, MMPI items are correlated with each other (Stein 1968), and the covariation of MMPI items can either increase or decrease the number of items to be expected to reach significance by chance.

Because of MMPI item intercorrelations, and because sample size has been found to affect the number of items found to be significant in an item analysis (Devries 1966), two other procedures are recommended. Block (1960) proposed an empirical solution to the problem of how many items to expect to be significant due to chance. He suggested that two samples of the same size as the criterion and comparison groups be selected on a purely random basis from the combined criterion and comparison groups and that an item analysis then be performed with these two random samples. If random samples are repeatedly selected and analyzed, a sampling distribution of items significant by chance alone can be obtained. This sampling distribution will be appropriate for the sample size and for the pattern of MMPI item intercorrelations in the particular set of data being considered. The sampling distribution of chance findings then can be used to evaluate the probability that the number of items found to be significant in the item analysis of the criterion and comparison groups is due to chance alone.

Another solution to the problem of items reaching significance by chance is to ensure that items selected for a special scale can reliably differentiate the criterion and comparison groups. With a sufficiently large number of subjects, the criterion and comparison groups can each be divided, and two separate item analyses can be performed. An item would become a member of the new scale only if it significantly differentiated between the criterion and comparison groups in both item analyses. The probability of an item reaching statistical significance by chance alone in the two independent analyses would be quite low. Also, roughly half of any items that reached significance by chance in both analyses would have an opposite direction of scoring in the two analyses. The procedure of using two item analyses in selecting MMPI items for a special scale is sometimes referred to as validation generalization. Neither of the two sets of samples, however, provides a cross-validation of the items selected for a new scale. If an investigator decided to use validation generalization in selecting scale items, and also wished to cross-validate the new scale (for example, Atsaides, Neuringer, and Davis 1977), three sets of data from criterion and comparison subjects would be required.

After the MMPI items for the new scale have been selected and the scoring direction for each item (the response that is more frequent in the criterion group than in the comparison group) has been determined, several additional tasks are performed to evaluate the new scale. The MMPI records of all criterion and comparison subjects are scored on the scale. Using these scale scores, the difference between the mean scale scores of criterion and comparison subjects is tested with the t-test. The internal structure of the new scale should be reported (internal consistency and possibly factor structure), along with its relation to other MMPI scales, especially the 13 standard scales. For special scales that will be used to classify subjects into dichotomous groups (for example, alcoholic and nonalcoholic), it is important to derive a single scale score to use as a cutting point at or above which subjects are said to exhibit the trait or behavior pattern shown by criterion subjects. The percentage of correct classifications with various possible cutting scores provides information about the accuracy with which the new scale identifies criterion and comparison subjects. As mentioned earlier, a demonstration of the classification accuracy of a new scale should be done with criterion and comparison subjects other than those used in developing the scale.

A table for the conversion of raw scale scores to T scores is frequently provided for a new MMPI scale. Criticisms of the T score format of the original MMPI scales (Rodgers 1972) are often equally relevant to the T scores provided for special MMPI scales. One such criticism is that the T score format is not consistent with dichotomous discrimination of criterion and comparison groups. A cutting score is important for this dichotomous discrimination, not a scaled distribution. Furthermore, as a result of empirical scale construction, most MMPI scales are multidimensional. Such multidimensionality adds to the power of dichotomous discriminations, but it cannot be linearly scaled in a meaningful way. This is especially true if the standard deviation unit for the scaling is derived from a comparison group that is designed to lack the characteristic being assessed by the new scale.

Clopton (1974a) presented a computer program that performs the item analysis needed to select MMPI items for a new scale. A set of computer programs (Clopton and Neuringer 1977) is available that also provides the following: (1) the raw scale scores for all subjects, (2) a t-test of the difference between mean scale scores of the criterion and comparison groups, (3) a table of correct classifications using various cutting scores, and (4) a T score conversion table. A limitation in using this set of computer programs is that the input for the programs consists of subjects' responses to all 566 MMPI items. Fortunately, automated keypunching can be used to avoid the laborious task of keypunching each subject's responses. However, few optical scanners can accommodate standard MMPI answer sheets. Therefore an investigator who wants automated punching of subjects' responses should use an alternate MMPI answer sheet that is suitable for optical scanning and automated keypunching.

ISSUES IN MMPI SCALE DEVELOPMENT

The K scale of the MMPI was developed to correct MMPI clinical scale scores for the influence of defensive test-taking attitudes. Five of the standard clinical scales made a better differentiation between criterion and comparison groups when K scale corrections were added to the clinical scale scores (McKinley, Hathaway, and Meehl 1956). The possibility that K scale corrections could improve the differentiation of criterion and comparison groups has been ignored in the development of special MMPI scales. Caldwell (1970) reported that K scale corrections were essential with several special scales, but his data have not been published and other data regarding the need for K corrections of special MMPI scale scores are lacking. To assess the need for K scale corrections, an investigator could use a trial-and-error method of adding a fractional value (.1, .2, .3, . . . , 1.0) of each subject's K scale score to his special scale score. For each fractional value, a cutting score analysis could be used to evaluate the overlap in the distribution of K corrected scores obtained from criterion and comparison subjects.

Despite the attractiveness of developing new MMPI scales for specialized tasks and the popularity of some of the special MMPI scales, there is a serious question regarding the possible redundancy or superfluity of special MMPI scales. Many special scales are probably redundant versions of existing scales (Butcher and Tellegen 1978). The continued development of special MMPI scales is certainly of doubtful value if the information they provide can be readily obtained from standard MMPI scales. Caldwell (1970) discovered that special MMPI scale scores could be predicted so well from standard scale scores that special scales did not appear to provide any new information. Here again, however, Caldwell's data have not been published. A recent study (Clopton and Klein 1978) indicated that scores of three special MMPI scales (the Prejudice scale, the Es scale, and the AMac scale) were highly correlated with the scores of the standard MMPI scales, but that individual scores of these special scales could not be accurately predicted from the standard scales. Thus these three special scales appear to provide information not available from the standard MMPI scales. Further research regarding the redundancy of special MMPI scales is needed.

When developing a special MMPI scale, an investigator should routinely determine whether scores for the special scale are more closely related than standard scale scores to external criteria (independent measures of relevant personality variables or patterns of abnormal behavior). Even if a special scale provides information not available from the standard scales, predictions made from standard scale scores may still be more accurate than predictions based on special scale scores. For example, in the Clopton and Klein (1978) study, alcoholic and nonalcoholic psychiatric patients were more accurately identified by the 13 standard scales than by the AMac scale.

The development and validation of special MMPI scales have often demonstrated a lack of conceptual clarity. This applies to the naming of newly developed scales, the selection of criterion and comparison groups, and the intended use of the new scale. Some new scales have been named on the basis of the difference between criterion and comparison groups used to develop the scale (for example, AMac scale). Another approach has been to name the scale for the hypothetical construct presumably underlying the scale (for example, Es scale, Overcontrolled Hostility scale [Megargee, Cook, and Mendelsohn 1967]). In either case, the name given to a scale can be misleading. Continued validation research can confirm a scale's name, or indicate that the name needs revision. Spence, Farber, and McFann (1956) stated that the name given to the MAS was unfortunate because it was intended to provide an index of drive, as the term is used in learning theory, not a measure of trait anxiety. Of course, numerous validation studies have justified use of the MAS as a measure of anxiety. In contrast, the name of the AMac scale may eventually be found to be too limited if research continues to suggest that it measures a general propensity toward addiction or substance misuse.

As Butcher and Tellegen (1978) emphasized, the development and evaluation of new MMPI scales have often consisted of contrasts between "samples of convenience," with important subject characteristics unknown. For example, validation research with MMPI alcoholism scales sometimes provides inadequate demographic information for alcoholics, and few investigators have indicated whether or not criterion and comparison groups include individuals who misuse drugs other than alcohol (Clopton 1978). In using samples of convenience, investigators have sometimes provided illogical comparisons. Ruff, Ayers, and Templer (1975) found the AMac scale unable to differentiate alcoholics and

and criminals. It would have been much more informative if the authors had attempted to use this scale to differentiate alcoholic and nonalcoholic criminals, not alcoholics and criminals. Farberow and Devries (1967) performed several item analyses to contrast the MMPI responses of four groups of male psychiatric patients (suicides, suicide attempters, patients who threatened suicide, and non-suicidal patients). As reported in Chapter 5, the only contrast that produced more significant items than would be expected by chance (Devries 1966) was the contrast of the suicide threat group and the nonsuicidal group. This led to the development of an MMPI Suicide Threat scale. An MMPI scale that can identify patients who threaten to commit suicide but who make no suicide attempts is of questionable value, especially when that scale has been found to be unable to identify patients who kill themselves or make suicide attempts (Clopton and Jones 1975; Farberow and Devries 1967; Ravensborg and Foss 1969).

The logical relationship between the development of a new MMPI scale and its intended use is not always made clear. In developing his alcoholism scale, MacAndrew (1965) used alcoholics who had voluntarily sought treatment as his criterion subjects. However, an alcoholism scale would seem to be of most clinical value if it could be used as a screening instrument to detect alcoholism in individuals who might not be honest about their difficulties. Without comment MacAndrew (1965) reported that he removed two items (215 and 460) from his scale because they refer directly to alcohol use. Although these two items differentiated between the alcoholic and nonalcoholic groups used to develop the scale, they would be of little help in identifying individuals who wish to conceal, or at least to minimize, their misuse of alcohol.

SUMMARY AND CONCLUSIONS

Many special MMPI scales have been constructed since the introduction of the MMPI. Special scales have been developed by intuitive procedures, by cluster and factor analyses, and by empirical scale construction. The MAS, the Dn scale, and the AMac scale illustrate these three general approaches. Furthermore, these three scales are good examples of special scales whose utility has been confirmed by validation research.

Empirically derived special scales have often been developed without sufficient attention to the methodology of empirical scale construction. To develop a new MMPI scale empirically, an item analysis is performed to find MMPI items that differentiate between criterion and comparison subjects. In this item analysis, the chi-square test can be used for most items, but Fisher's exact probability test must be used when an expected cell frequency in the contingency table for an item is extremely small. Levitt (1978) has stated that there is no mathematically sound way to determine whether the number of items that significantly differentiate criterion and comparison groups exceeds the number of items that could reach significance by chance. Actually, either of two procedures may be used. The number of items likely to be found significant by chance can be determined empirically.

Alternatively, criterion and comparison groups can be divided, and items can be selected for the new scale only if they significantly differentiate between the groups in two independent item analyses. If a special scale is designed to make dichotomous classification (for example, alcoholic versus nonalcoholic), then information should be presented about the percentage of correct classification achieved with the optimal cutting score. When a special scale is designed to assess a personality dimension, such as dependency, then a T score conversion table is more appropriate. An investigator should consider the need for *K* corrections of special scale scores and should routinely evaluate whether predictions made on the basis of the special scale are more accurate than predictions made from the standard MMPI scales. The logical relationship between the procedures used in developing the special scale and its intended use should be made clear. Finally, the name given to a newly developed special scale should be treated as provisional until there is sufficient research available to evaluate the properties of the scale.

REFERENCES

Atsaides, J. P., C. Neuringer, and K. L. Davis. 1977. "Development of an Institutionalized Chronic Alcoholic Scale." *Journal of Consulting and Clinical Psychology* 45: 609–11.

Barron, F. 1953. "An Ego-Strength Scale Which Predicts Response to Psychotherapy." *Journal of Consulting Psychology* 17: 327–33.

Block, J. 1960. "On the Number of Significant Findings to Be Expected by Chance." *Psychometrika* 25: 369–80.

Butcher, J. N., and A. Tellegen. 1978. "Common Methodological Problems in MMPI Research." *Journal of Consulting and Clinical Psychology* 46: 620–28.

Byrne, D. 1974. *An Introduction to Personality: Research, Theory, and Applications*. Englewood Cliffs, N.J.: Prentice-Hall.

Caldwell, A. B. 1970. "Recent Advances in Automated Interpretation of the MMPI." Paper presented at the Fifth Annual Symposium on Recent Developments in the Use of the MMPI, Mexico City, February.

Calvin, J. 1975. "A Replicated Study of the Concurrent Validity of the Harris Subscales for the MMPI." Ph.D. dissertation, Kent State University.

Camilli, G., and K. D. Hopkins. 1978. "Applicability of Chi-Square to 2 x 2 Contingency Tables with Small Expected Cell Frequencies." *Psychological Bulletin* 85: 163–67.

Chang, A. F., A. B. Caldwell, and T. Moss. 1973. "Stability of Personality Traits in Alcoholics During and After Treatment as Measured by the MMPI." *Proceedings of the 81st Annual Convention of the American Psychological Association* 8: 387–88.

Chu, C. 1966. "Object Cluster Analysis of the MMPI." Ph.D. dissertation, University of California, Berkeley.

Clopton, J. R. 1978. "Alcoholism and the MMPI: A Review." *Journal of Studies on Alcohol* 39: 1540–58.

——. 1974a. "A Computer Program for MMPI Scale Development with Contrasted Groups." *Educational and Psychological Measurement* 34: 161–63.

——. 1974b. "The Influence of Type of Ego Threat and Denial on Public and Private Compensatory Behavior." Ph.D. dissertation, University of Kansas.

——, and W. C. Jones. 1975. "Use of the MMPI in the Prediction of Suicide." *Journal of Clinical Psychology* 31: 52–54.

Clopton, J. R., and G. L. Klein. 1978. "An Initial Look at the Redundancy of Specialized MMPI Scales." *Journal of Consulting and Clinical Psychology* 46: 1436–38.

Clopton, J. R., and C. Neuringer. 1977. "Fortran Computer Programs for the Development of New MMPI Scales." *Educational and Psychological Measurement* 37: 783–86.

Comrey, A. L. 1958a. "A Factor Analysis of Items on the MMPI Hypomania Scale." *Educational and Psychological Measurement* 18: 313–23.

——. 1958b. "A Factor Analysis of Items on the MMPI Paranoia Scale." *Educational and Psychological Measurement* 18: 99–107.

——. 1958c. "A Factor Analysis of Items on the MMPI Psychasthenia Scale." *Educational and Psychological Measurement* 18: 293–300.

——. 1958d. "A Factor Analysis of Items on the MMPI Psychopathic Deviate Scale." *Educational and Psychological Measurement* 18: 91–98.

——. 1957a. "A Factor Analysis of Items on the MMPI Depression Scale." *Educational and Psychological Measurement* 17: 578–85.

——. 1957B. "A Factor Analysis of Items on the MMPI Hypochondriasis Scale." *Educational and Psychological Measurement* 17: 566–77.

——. 1957c. "A Factor Analysis of Items on the MMPI Hysteria Scale." *Educational and Psychological Measurement* 17: 586–92.

——, and W. Margraff. 1958. "A Factor Analysis of Items on the MMPI Schizophrenia Scale." *Educational and Psychological Measurement* 18: 301–11.

Dahlstrom, W. G., G. S. Welsh, and L. E. Dahlstrom. 1975. *An MMPI Handbook: Research Applications*, rev. ed., vol. 2. Minneapolis: University of Minnesota Press.

——. 1972. *An MMPI Handbook: Clinical Interpretation*, rev. ed., vol. 1. Minneapolis: University of Minnesota Press.

Devries, A. G. 1966. "Chance Expectancy, Sample Size, Replacement and Non-Replacement Sampling." *Psychological Reports* 18: 843–50.

Distler, L. S., P. R. May, and A. H. Tuma. 1964. "Anxiety and Ego Strength as Predictors of Response to Treatment in Schizophrenic Patients." *Journal of Consulting Psychology* 28: 170–77.

Farberow, N. L., and A. G. Devries. 1967. "An Item Differentiation Analysis of Suicidal Neuropsychiatric Hospital Patients." *Psychological Reports* 20: 607–17.

Finney, D. J., R. Latscha, B. Bennet, and P. Hsu. 1963. *Tables for Testing Significance in a 2 x 2 Contingency Table*. London: Cambridge University Press.

Finney, J. C., D. F. Smith, D. E. Skeeters, and C. D. Auvenshine. 1971. "MMPI Alcoholism Scales: Factor Structure and Content Analysis." *Quarterly Journal of Studies on Alcohol* 32: 1055–60.

Getter, H., and D. M. Sundland. 1962. "The Barron Ego Strength Scale and Psychotherapy Outcome." *Journal of Consulting Psychology* 26: 195.

Gocka, E. 1965. "American Lake Norms for 200 MMPI Scales." Unpublished manuscript. American Lake, Wash.: Veterans Administration Hospital.

Gough, H. G. 1951. "Studies of Social Intolerance. II. A Personality Scale for Anti-Semitism." *Journal of Social Psychology* 33: 247–55.

Graham, J. R. 1978. "Review of Minnesota Multiphasic Personality Inventory Special Scales." In *Advances in Psychological Assessment*, edited by P. McReynolds, vol. 4, pp. 11–55. San Francisco: Jossey-Bass.

——. 1977. *The MMPI: A Practical Guide*. New York: Oxford University Press.

Gregory, R. J. 1973. "A Fortran Computer Program for the Fisher Exact Probability Test." *Educational and Psychological Measurement* 33: 697–700.

Grizzle, J. E. 1967. "Continuity Correction in the Chi-Square Test for 2 x 2 Tables." *American Statistician* 21: 28–32.

Hampton, P. J. 1953. "The Development of a Personality Questionnaire for Drinkers." *Genetic Psychology Monograph* 48: 55–115.

Harris, R., and J. Lingoes. 1955. "Subscales for the Minnesota Multiphasic Personality Inventory." Langley Porter Clinic. Mimeographed.

Hathaway, S. R., and J. C. McKinley. 1940. "A Multiphasic Personality Schedule (Minnesota). I. Construction of the Schedule." *Journal of Psychology* 10: 249–54.

Hays, W. L. 1963. *Statistics.* New York: Holt, Rinehart and Winston.

Hoffman, H., R. G. Loper, and M. L. Kammeier. 1974. "Identifying Future Alcoholics with MMPI Alcoholism Scales." *Quarterly Journal of Studies on Alcohol* 35: 490–98.

Holmes, D. S. 1967. "Male-Female Differences in MMPI Ego Strength: An Artifact." *Journal of Consulting Psychology* 31: 408–10.

Holmes, W. O. 1953. "The Development of an Empirical MMPI Scale for Alcoholism." M.S. thesis. San Jose State College.

Houston, B. K. 1973. "Viability of Coping Strategies, Denial and Response to Stress." *Journal of Personality* 41: 50–58.

——. 1972. "Trait and Situational Denial and Performance Under Stress." *Journal of Personality and Social Psychology* 18: 289–93.

Hoyt, D. P., and G. M. Sedlacek. 1958. "Differentiating Alcoholics from Normals and Abnormals with the MMPI." *Journal of Clinical Psychology* 14: 69–74.

Huber, N. A., and S. Danahy. 1975. "Use of the MMPI in Predicting Completion and Evaluating Changes in a Long-Term Alcoholism Treatment Program." *Journal of Studies on Alcohol* 36: 1230–37.

Kranitz, L. 1972. "Alcoholics, Heroin Addicts and Nonaddicts: Comparison on the MacAndrew Alcoholism Scale of the MMPI." *Quarterly Journal of Studies on Alcohol* 33: 807–09.

Lachar, D., W. Berman, J. L. Grisell, and K. Schooff. 1976. "The MacAndrew Alcoholism Scale as a General Measure of Substance Misuse." *Journal of Studies on Alcohol* 37: 1609–15.

LaPlace, J. P. 1954. "An Exploratory Study of Personality and Its Relationship to Success in Professional Baseball." *Research Quarterly* 25: 313–19.

Lanyon, R. I., R. V. Primo, F. Terrell, and A. Wener. 1972. "An Aversion-Desensitization Treatment for Alcoholism." *Journal of Consulting and Clinical Psychology* 38: 394–98.

Levitt, E. E. 1978. "A Note on 'MMPI Scale Development Methodology.'" *Journal of Personality Assessment* 42: 503–04.

Little, K. B., and J. Fisher. 1958. "Two New Experimental Scales of the MMPI." *Journal of Consulting Psychology* 22: 305–06.

MacAndrew,C. 1965. "The Differentiation of Male Alcoholic Out-Patients from Nonalcoholic Psychiatric Patients by Means of the MMPI." *Quarterly Journal of Studies on Alcohol* 26: 238–46.

McKinley, J. C., S. R. Hathaway, and P. E. Meehl. 1956. "The *K* Scale." In *Basic Readings on the MMPI in Psychology and Medicine*, edited by G. S. Welsh and W. G. Dahlstrom, pp. 112–25. Minneapolis: University of Minnesota Press.

Megargee, E. I., P. E. Cook, and G. A. Mendelsohn. 1967. "Development and Validation of an MMPI Scale of Assaultiveness in Overcontrolled Individuals." *Journal of Abnormal Psychology* 72: 519–28.

Meltzoff, J., and M. Kornreich. 1970. *Research in Psychotherapy*. New York: Atherton.

Navran, L. A. 1954. "A Rationally Derived MMPI Scale to Measure Dependence." *Journal of Consulting Psychology* 18: 192.

Pearson, E. S., and H. O. Hartley. eds. 1964. *Biometrika Tables for Statisticians*, vol. 1. London: Cambridge University Press.

Plackett, R. L. 1964. "The Continuity Correction in 2 X 2 Tables." *Biometrika* 51: 327–38.

Ravensborg, M. R., and A. Foss. 1969. "Suicide and Natural Death in a State Hospital Population: A Comparison of Admissions Complaints, MMPI Profiles, and Social Competence Factors." *Journal of Consulting and Clinical Psychology* 33: 466–71.

Rodgers, D. A. 1972. "Review of the MMPI." In *The Seventh Mental Measurements Yearbook*, edited by O. K. Buros, vol. 1, pp. 243–50. Highland Park, N.J.: Gryphon Press.

Rohan, W. P., R. L. Tatro, and S. R. Rotman. 1969. "MMPI Changes in Alcoholics During Hospitalization." *Quarterly Journal of Studies on Alcohol* 30: 389–400.

Roscoe, J. T., and J. A. Byars. 1971. "An Investigation of the Restraints with Respect to Sample Size Commonly Imposed on the Use of the Chi-Square Statistic." *Journal of the American Statistical Association* 66: 755–59.

Ruff, C. F., J. Ayers, and D. I. Templer. 1975. "Alcoholics' and Criminals' Similarity of Scores on the MacAndrew Alcoholism Scale." *Psychological Reports* 36: 921–22.

Siegel, S. 1956. *Nonparametric Statistics for the Behavioral Sciences*. New York: McGraw-Hill.

Spence, K. W., I. E. Farber, and H. H. McFann. 1956. "The Relation of Anxiety (Drive) Level to Performance in Competitional and Noncompetitional Paired-Associates Learning." *Journal of Experimental Psychology* 52: 296–305.

Stein, K. B. 1968. "The TSC Scales: The Outcome of a Cluster Analysis of the 550 MMPI Items." In *Advances in Psychological Assessment*, edited by P. McReynolds, vol. 1, pp. 80–104. Palo Alto, Calif.: Science and Behavior Books.

Tamkin, A. S., and C. J. Klett. 1975. "Barron's Ego-Strength Scale: A Replication of an Evaluation of its Construct Validity." *Journal of Consulting Psychology* 21: 412.

Taylor, J. A. 1953. "A Personality Scale of Manifest Anxiety." *Journal of Abnormal and Social Psychology* 48: 285–90.

Tryon, R. C. 1966. "Unrestricted Cluster and Factor Analysis with Application to the MMPI and Holzinger-Harman Problems." *Multivariate Behavioral Research* 1: 229–44.

Vega, A. 1971. "Cross-Validation of Four MMPI Scales for Alcoholism." *Quarterly Journal of Studies on Alcohol* 32: 791–97.

Weinstein, J., J. R. Averill, E. M. Opton, Jr., and R. S. Lazarus. 1968. "Defensive Style and Discrepancy Between Self-Report and Psysiological Indexes of Stress." *Journal of Personality and Social Psychology* 10: 406–13.

Wike, E. L. 1971. *Data Analysis: A Statistical Primer for Psychology Students*. Chicago: Aldine-Atherton.

Wirt, R. D. 1955. "Further Validation of the Ego Strength Scale." *Journal of Consulting Psychology* 20: 123–24.

15/ THE FUTURE OF THE MMPI

Thomas R. Faschingbauer

I have been asked on many occasions to predict a person's future behavior from the MMPI. This is the first time, however, that anyone has asked me to predict the future of the MMPI itself. Actually, the two tasks are not really that different. In both cases one first must look for a sufficient level of integrity (or soundness) to ensure a future of any kind. With a patient this usually involves a global evaluation of mental and physical health to determine whether active or passive destruction is imminent. Once it seems reasonable that some future does exist for a patient, the next step is to determine the direction of future growth. Depending on a patient's present state and past behavior, one might predict growth in either a positive or negative direction. Positive growth usually involves overcoming shortcomings and expanding opportunities, while decline involves a failure to do so.

I see no reason to abandon this approach in attempting to predict the future of the MMPI. This chapter, then, will begin with an evaluation of the MMPI's psychometric health. The behavior of those working with the MMPI in the past will be used as a predictor of what can be expected in the future. Next, an attempt will be made to designate special areas where opportunities exist for the MMPI's shortcomings to be overcome. Finally, the pluses and minuses of this instrument will be tallied to arrive at an overall prognostication.

DOES THE MMPI HAVE A FUTURE?

Not everyone would agree that the MMPI has a future. There are those, of course, who have never held much hope for any objective personality test. More

Portions of this chapter have been extracted from *Short Forms of the MMPI* by T. R. Faschingbauer and C. S. Newmark, Lexington Books, D. C. Heath and Co., Copyright 1978. Reprinted by permission of the publisher.

importantly, there are several experts in the area of objective testing who have questioned the psychometric soundness of the MMPI.

Norman (1972),* for example, has described the MMPI as a diagnostic "mess." Its scales are heterogeneous, redundant, and overlapping. At times, subsets of items that are known to be inversely correlated are summed in what can only be a cancellation approach to a scale score. Over 100 items are not even scored. How much potentially useful information never enters the code type as a result is still unknown.

Additionally, the MMPI scales were based on Kraepelinian nosology, which is considered by many MMPI users to be somewhat anachronistic. Furthermore, Kraepelin's system was used to develop clinical scales that differentiate "normals" from groups with known types of psychopathology. Yet users of the MMPI are usually asked to differentiate among diagnoses, something the MMPI scales were never developed to do.

True, the shifts to numbered scales, code types, and actuarial rules have lessened the MMPI's dependency on Kraepelinian nosology while presenting ways of differentiating among abnormal groups. But this has increased the complexity (and likely reduced the accuracy) of interpretation enormously. As Loevinger (1972) noted, there clearly are less complex ways of classification than scoring 13 correlated scales, plotting a profile, calculating a code type, and then interpreting the result.

From a theoretical perspective, traits seem to be mixed with states in the MMPI code type in a haphazard manner. Does an elevation on D, for example, mean that a patient has a trait of depression or is situationally depressed? While this may be an answerable question when asked clinically in the context of several scale scores, there is nothing about the D scale, per se, that separates trait and state depression. (The two-type depressive scale [Wilson et al. 1970; see Volume 2 of Dahlstrom, Welsh, and Dahlstrom 1975, p. 284] does make a similar distinction, but only 7 of its 24 items are also scored on D.)

There is also evidence that state anxiety loads across many scales to further confound matters. Newmark et al. (1975) cofactor-analyzed the MMPI and the state-trait anxiety inventory (STAI) (Spielberger, Gorsuch, and Lushene 1970). Both state and trait anxiety significantly ($p \leqslant .001$) correlated with all of the clinical scales except Mf and Ma. Following an orthogonal rotation, state anxiety loaded -.71 on Factor 1, Adjustment. Other scales loading highly on Factor 1 were K and Es (+) and F and Si (-). Trait anxiety, on the other hand, loaded +.53 on Factor 4, Anxiety Proneness. The other scales loading highly on Factor 4 were Pt, Sc, D (+), and L (-). This factor seems to be similar to Welsh's A, one of the two major variables found to be measured by the MMPI in several factor analyses (Eithman 1961; Kassebaum, Couch, and Slater 195; Mees 1960; Welsh 1956; Wheeler, Little, and Lehner 1951).

---

*The author is indebted to Warren Norman, whose similar chapter nearly a decade ago served as a stimulus and a resource for much of this section.

These results suggest that anxiety induced during the administration of the MMPI may grossly distort a patient's responses to many items, further blurring the already slight distinctiveness among the usual clinical scales. Similar confusion exists in regard to the uni- or bipolarity of particular scales, which at times seems to bear little relationship to theory or clinical reality. For example, depression and hypomania have separate MMPI scales, while masculinity and feminity do not. It is not relevant here to argue whether particular traits (for example, masculinity, feminity) are bipolar or unipolar. Indeed, recent works (for example, Bem 1974; Russell and Sines 1978) suggest that such a conclusion is premature. The point is that, given the present state of theoretical debate on polarity, the MMPI has mixed bipolar and unipolar traits in an apparently thoughtless manner. (Donnelly et al. [1976] did find significant MMPI profile differences between unipolar and bipolar depressives, but scale *D* does not reflect those differences by itself.)

Clinically, there are further shortcomings. More specifically, the MMPI is too broad a test to be used for screening and differential diagnosis. If one merely requires a screening instrument, why use so many items? As many party-goers know, one can identify nearly anything with only 20 questions. If, on the other hand, it is important to distinguish between similar diagnostic categories (for example, paranoid versus nonparanoid schizophrenia), why ask about unrelated symptoms (for example, somatic concerns)?

Some MMPI items are anachronisms of the 1930s, using words with which many patients are not familiar. What does being a good mixer mean to the pot-smoking individualist of the 1980s? Who among the readers of this chapter has ever played "drop-the-handkerchief?" Other items are worded so complexly ("I have often wished I were a girl . . .") that they are often answered in error. Still other items seem unduly personal in their requests for sexual and religious information. They may offend the sensitive client and needlessly complicate both administration and interpretation.

But even when we can convince our clients to tolerate the items, how can we justify the norms? The Minnesota norm group is representative of the U.S. population in the 1930s. But the past four decades have brought tremendous demographic changes. Those most apparent include one in five families moving each year, three fourths of the population now living in urban megalopolises (many with large or even predominant "minority group" communities), the post-World War II "baby boom" and later "zero population growth," increased longevity and educational opportunities; large numbers of non-English-speaking immigrants, and a rising divorce rate. How can we therefore justify the common use of norms developed on white, rural, married persons with an elementary education in the 1930s?.

At this point the reader may be wondering how a test with so many shortcomings still has a present, much less a future. The answer, of course, is that the MMPI has been, and continues to be, useful. At present, the MMPI is the most widely used objective personality test in the world. Its major use is in the screening, diagnosis, and clinical description of psychopathology. Rarely a week passes when I and my colleagues are not awed by the power of the MMPI in this area. I believe that most other clinical psychologists and psychiatrists also consider the MMPI superior to other tests for this purpose.

But the usefulness of the MMPI has expanded beyond the original intentions of its developers. Nearly 500 scales provide for a variety of screening, assessment, selection, and prediction applications; clinical code types provide an actuarial alternative to traditional classification systems; and computerized interpretation provides timely information to a variety of medical, counseling, educational, and industrial professionals.

The research utility of the MMPI seems to equal or even surpass its clinical worth. Thousands of scholarly papers appear each year based in part or entirely on the MMPI. Buros' *Tests in Print II* (1974) shows that between 1963 and 1971 a study on the MMPI was published nearly every day. And an entire book has been written on cross-national research with the MMPI (Butcher and Pancheri 1976). Consequently, an archive of empirical data now exists for the MMPI that exceeds that for any other test.

With so much invested in the MMPI's clinical and scholarly applications, it seems unreasonable to expect its demise in spite of its shortcomings. This chapter, then, will attempt to project forward from present work with the MMPI in an effort to see what the future does hold. In doing so, it is assumed that the cost of redoing the MMPI, both in man-hours and dollars, is greater than the value to be obtained from a reworded, rescaled, and restandardized MMPI. This assumption is based on my experience and that of others (multiple personal communications since 1974) who have considered redoing the MMPI. Others may disagree with this, and they may be right. But for the purposes of this chapter the present MMPI will be assumed to be with us for a while to come, psychometric warts and all. The future of the MMPI appears to lie in expanding its use while overcoming its faults. The bulk of this chapter, then, suggests ways of overcoming many of these deficiencies and presents examples of how others have attempted to do so.

OTHER FORMS OF THE MMPI

Even though this chapter assumes that the MMPI will survive in its present form, it bears mentioning that there are many forms of the present MMPI. One of these is the original card form, which I have never seen. I am told, however, that a deck of cards, each with a different MMPI item, is shuffled and presented to the person being tested. The person is instructed to place each card in one of three piles: true, false, and cannot say. Each of the true and false piles is then sorted according to whether the lower right or lower left corner of each card has been cut off. One of these new piles consists of those true or false responses that are rarely given by normal adults. These are then entered on a record form, which in turn, is scored.

In spite of the greater ease of administering the card form to a bedridden patient, there are several problems that have led to its reduced use. Among these are its lengthy scoring procedure, confusion by testees about which pile is true and which false, the likelihood of patients losing, hoarding, or destroying cards, and the general unsuitability for computer scoring and interpretation services.

There is one advantage that the card form has over the other forms, however, that suggests it may enjoy wider use in the future. Namely, it can be split into component parts easier than the other forms. It is time consuming to extract individual scales, short forms of scales, subscales, or items from the booklet versions of the MMPI. Furthermore, the retyping and/or photocopying almost always involved in such an endeavor is often illegal. A panel consisting of several people associated with the MMPI met at the 1975 MMPI symposium to discuss this issue. There seemed to be general agreement among panelists of both the legal and psychological professions that reproduction of a large number of MMPI items without written permission of the University of Minnesota could constitute a breach of its copyright. Incidently, that copyright belongs to the university for the remainder of this century.

The reader may be shocked at the suggestion that anyone would dare to "cut up" the MMPI. To do so is to flaunt the warnings of such distinguished psychometric authorities as Gough (1946) and Guilford (1954). For one thing, the shortening of the MMPI that would result from omitting items would be expected to result in a reduction in its reliability and consequently in its validity. (This derives from Spearman's correction for attenuation. The maximum possible validity of a particular test is the square root of its reliability [Helmstadter 1964, p. 84]). Guilford (1954) put forth the notion that, all other variables held constant (fatigue, practice, and so on), the longer a test, the more reliable it should be because nonsystematic errors should cancel each other more completely. The Spearman-Brown formula permits one to determine the loss of reliability expected from a reduction of the MMPI item pool. Were the MMPI length to be significantly reduced by item elimination, one would expect sufficient declines in reliability and validity to impair its usefulness.

But these expected losses just do not seem to materialize in the usual testing situation. For example, Kincannon (1968) reduced the F scale from its usual 64 items to only 14. The Spearman-Brown formula predicted the F scale usual split-half reliability of from .73 to .92 (Dahlstrom and Welsh 1960, p. 474) would drop to .17. Instead, Kincannon found that the shorter scale had a slightly higher reliability over a one- to two-day interval than did the whole scale (.63 versus .62).

This does not mean that Brown, Guilford, and Spearman were wrong. Rather, those theoreticians assumed situations that may not hold for the administration of the MMPI. All other variables, as we have seen in the matter of state anxiety, are not held constant during the MMPI administration. Nor is there reason to assume, as the Spearman-Brown formula does, that all items in the test are equivalent and all item deletions are made at random.

The author's experience with several short forms of the MMPI suggests that shorter MMPI scales usually suffer far less loss of reliability than the theorists would have us fear. Indeed, as with Kincann's F scale, they sometimes have higher reliability. However slight the loss, though, the effect on validity would be even slighter, as the square root of the reliability coefficient would be involved. Hence, had Kincannon (1968) actually incurred the expected decline in test-retest reliability from .62 to .17 (a loss of .45), the maximum possible validity of F would have declined from .79 to .41 (a loss of .38). His actual increase in reliability, in fact, left the maximum possible validity unchanged.

The reader may still complain that taking items out of context will surely distort their meanings. It is one thing to inquire about headaches in the context of queries about aching of the feet or the back. It is quite another to ask that question along with others about blurred vision, nausea, and blows to the head. At least this is what Gough (1946) feared. The American Psychological Association included the following caution in its *Technical Recommendations for Psychological Tests and Diagnostic Techniques* (1954):

> When a short form of a test is prepared by reducing the number of items or organizing a portion of the test into a separate form, new evidence should be obtained and reported for that new form of the test. . . . This is especially important for inventories where, placing items in a new context might alter the person's responses. For example, the MMPI properly retains some items which were not scored on any key, because removing those items might alter the discriminating power of the items which were scored.

While the content of each item on the card form of the MMPI changes with each shuffle, Wiener (1947) and Rosen, Hales, and Peek (1958) found that the card and booklet forms of the MMPI yielded comparable results. Several studies (Charen 1954; Dana and Condry 1963; Ferguson 1946; Holzberg and Alessi 1949; MacDonald 1952, Machover and Anderson 1953; Olson 1961; Siegal and Feldman 1958) also have shown that removal of the unscored items has minimal effect on scale scores.

Perhaps most convincing, though, are the results of a study by Lieberman and Walters (1968). They expected that the preponderance of false answers usually given to F scale items by normal subjects might induce a set to respond "false" more often to Si scale items, which have approximately equal numbers of true and false scorable responses. They therefore alternated items from F and Si. Subjects receiving the Si items mixed in with the F items had the same mean scores as those receiving only the Si items. More importantly, the mean numbers of true responses were essentially equal for the two groups.

In a subsequent study, Lieberman (1968) found that even when F items were massed at the beginning of the test, there was no discernible effect on the responses to the Si items that followed. Again, neither Si mean scores nor the number of true responses to *Si* items differed from those of control subjects receiving only the *Si* items.

It seems reasonable to conclude that while particular alterations in context have produced marked effects for other inventories (Ellis 1947), such alterations have negligible effects on MMPI response patterns or scale scores. Gough's (1946) warning of unknown effects seems to be as inapplicable to real-life MMPI testing situations as Guilford's (1954) warning regarding test length.

There seems little reason, other than loss of information, for researchers or clinicians not to use only one or two scales or shorter versions of scales (see Faschingbauer and Newmark 1978) for answering limited questions. And for these purposes, the card form of the MMPI seems preferable to the various booklet forms.

Although we could eliminate all of the overlapping items in the MMPI using the card form, we would likely need to revalidate the remaining scales. Fortunately, Hugo's short form (see Chapter 9) provides an alternative. Hugo (1971) used multiple linear regression analysis in selecting his 173-item subset. Only those items with sufficient predictive power in the regression equations of two or more scales would have been multiply scored; none was. Hugo's short form scales correlate better with themselves over time than do those of the full MMPI. They also correlate about .70 with independent MMPI scale scores administered two weeks before or after them. Because it estimates MMPI scale scores via regression analysis, Hugo's short form underestimates MMPI standard deviations, which could reduce its accuracy with psychiatric patients. In this regard this short form seems to perform poorly in estimating pathological configural classifications. By overestimating K scale scores, it often leads to inaccurate decisions regarding validity in more severely disturbed psychiatric patients (Faschingbauer and Newmark 1978, p. 137). These same patients' MMPI highpoint codes were correctly detected by the Hugo short form only 32 percent or less of the time.

The Hugo short form performs much better with less severely disturbed or normal persons. It may eventually prove useful with psychiatric patients if estimation equations are developed using substitution or multiple regression procedures. Further information on the Hugo short form can be found in Faschingbauer and Newmark (1978, Chapters 4 and 8).

Other short forms of the MMPI, developed separately by John Overall (MMPI-168) and the author (FAM) seem to have better general utility than Hugo's. They do not, however, have the advantage of nonoverlapping scales that the Hugo does. Both the MMPI-168 and the FAM show consistently high ability to estimate clinically relevant material, however. In one recent study, similar to the investigation presented in Chapter 9, Newmark et al. (1978) compared the full MMPI, the MMPI-168, and the FAM with direct measures of psychopathology obtained from the brief psychiatric rating scale (BPRS) (Pokorny and Overall 1970) using psychiatric inpatients. The BPRS ratings were made in the context of structured interviews (Spitzer, Burdock, and Hardesty 1964) by experienced clinicians. Multiple correlations then were computed between the MMPI or short MMPI scales and those BPRS symptom scales that were most appropriate (for example, *Hy* with Conversion Somatization, Dramatization, Manipulativeness, Denial, and Emotionally Labile). Table 15.1 shows the ranges of those multiple correlation coefficients for each of the MMPI forms. No difference appears to exist among the three MMPI forms in their ability to identify psychiatric symptoms. Indeed, 50 percent of the multiple correlations computed for the FAM scales exceeded their MMPI counterparts. For the MMPI-168, 63 percent of the multiple correlations were higher than their counterparts.

TABLE 15.1

Ranges of Multiple Correlation Coefficients Between BPRS Sumptom Scales and Three Forms of the MMPI for Consecutive Psychiatric Admissions

	Subjects	
	Males	Females
MMPI	.64 to .84	.61 to .86
MMPI-168	.63 to .84	.64 to .86
MMPI	.61 to .86	.57 to .84
FAM	.63 to .85	.54 to .86

Source: C. S. Newmark, D. R. Ziff, A. J. Finch, Jr., and P. C. Kendall, "Comparing the Empirical Validity of the Standard Form with Two Abbreviated MMPIs," *Journal of Consulting and Clinical Psychology* 46 (1978): 53–61. Copyright (1978) by the American Psychological Association. Reprinted with permission.

Newmark et al. (1978, p. 60) concluded that both of these shorter MMPIs "are slightly less expensive to administer and result in more completed profiles with no loss in empirical validity. They appear to be an adequate substitute when administration of the standard form MMPI is not feasible." I expect that use of either of these short forms also would help to reduce the state anxiety that seems to result when some patients are confronted with the longer MMPI. This, however, has not yet been demonstrated.

Because more than 50 percent of the FAM items do not appear on the MMPI-168, it appears that these two otherwise comparable tests can be considered alternate forms of the MMPI. This should be especially advantageous to researchers observing relatively rapid changes in personality as a result of changes in some particular variable. Clinically, one can now repeat an invalid MMPI or repeatedly assess therapeutic change without wondering too much about boredom, practice effects, or patient rebellion from answering the same questions over.

Especially in the case of the MMPI-168, one now has an option to the present all-or-none approach to MMPI assessment. That is, until the development of short MMPIs, one either obtained a complete MMPI on a patient or had no data whatsoever. The patient or subject who, for one reason or another, completed only 200 or 300 MMPI items simply had not taken the MMPI. It is amazing how many uncooperative patients can be induced to "just finish the next two pages" so that the MMPI-168 items can be scored, which constitute the first seven pages of Form R.

To increase this benefit further, it would be useful to have validity information and conversion equations with which to obtain clinically relevant data regardless of where a testee decides to stop. We presently do use data from subsets of other tests like the TAT. Why not be able to use whatever data a patient gives on the MMPI? What seems to be required is a study like that of Newmark et al. (1978), with the only difference being the substitution of a number of arbitrary stopping points (after page 1, page 2, and so on) for the short forms. Multiple regression or substitution-based conversion equations could then be used to estimate full scale MMPI scores. These estimates could then be correlated both individually and multiply with the BPRS symptoms. The differential effectiveness of each subset of items, as well as full scale score estimation tables, could be easily computed.

Rather than letting the subject select a stopping point, Butcher and his colleagues have developed an on-line computer administration of the MMPI that selects a different short MMPI for each patient. Noting how the standard MMPI has a fixed set of items, whereas a clinical interview follows a patient's responses from one area to another, Butcher, Clavelle, and Hoffmann (1974) suggested that the prediction of code types be done by an on-line computer. The aim of each successive level of inquiry in this approach is to increase the degree of precision of the diagnostic formulation. The computer begins by obtaining some general idea of the patient's problem. It then uses this broad evaluation to select subsequent questions. For example, the patient who from the beginning shows a classic neurotic picture does not need to be asked the same questions as the individual whose responses are more similar to those of psychotics.

In a preliminary study, Butcher, Clavelle, and Hoffmann (1974) investigated whether it is possible to obtain reliable differentiation among profile categories using a small number of items and to narrow progressively the range of potential MMPI code types that an individual might closely resemble. Because 53.5 percent of all sample MMPIs were accounted for by only eight code types (13-31, 23-32, 24-42, 49-94, 68-86, 89-98, 248, and 278), plus a normal type (all scales less than 70 T), only those eight types were used in the study. In the developmental phase 100 samples of each code type were selected. Endorsement percentages were compared for every group against each other group and only those 69 items that displayed the greatest level of statistical difference between two or more code-type groups were retained. Those 69 items then served as predictors in a stepwise multiple discriminant function analysis with code-type group membership as the criterion. A case was considered to be classified into that group for which it obtained the highest probability. After the simulated administration of each of 10 items, hit-miss tables were constructed. With only 10 items, 48 percent accuracy was possible. This increased by a declining percentage as additional sets of 10 items were added, so that 20 items produced 59 percent accuracy but 40 items were required to produce 70 percent accuracy. At 60 items the maximum accuracy of 78 percent was reached.

When the criterion types were collapsed from the original 9 to only 5, accuracy increased, with 10 items yielding 62 percent accuracy, 30 items yielding 77 percent accuracy, and 60 items yielding 85 percent accuracy. Cross-validation studies on 50 samples of each code type produced slightly lower results. Accuracy ranged from 50 to 69 percent for the 9 original groups and from 65 to 81 percent for the collapsed group analysis.

To determine if it was possible to reduce the range of code types early in the testing process, Butcher, Clavelle, and Hoffmann (1974) tabulated the percentage of cases where the correct full form MMPI code type fell among the one, two, three, or four groups with the highest generated probabilities. Fifty-nine percent of the cases had their code type identified after the first 20 items and 95 percent had their code type in the four highest choices. After 30 items these increased to 65 and 97 percent, respectively, and after 69 items to 78 and 90 percent, respectively. Cross-validation results again were similar, though lower.

A number of more detailed decision rules then were added. For example, "after 30 items, eliminate all groups whose probability is less than .03 and whose rank order among the groups is more than 3." This particular rule led to the valid exclusion of six groups, five groups, and four groups, 73, 90, and 96 percent of the time, respectively. Cross-validation results were similar (70, 86, 95 percent). Hence, for approximately 7 out of 10 patients, the number of possible full form MMPI code types was reduced from 9 to 3 after the first 30 items, while for 86 out of every 100 patients, the number decreased by more than half, from 9 to 4.

Additionally, certain code types tended to be maintained or rejected as a group. For example, among the 13-31 patients, "psychotic" and "schizoid" or "borderline" code types all were eliminated in 90 percent of the cases after 30 items. Hence, there was usually a clinically meaningful pattern among those code types that fell above or below the cutoff points.

The approach of Butcher, Clavelle, and Hoffmann appears promising. Because there is little to be gained by administering an initial subset of more than 30 items, a branching procedure, in which the computer selects additional items on the basis of the patient's response to the first 30 items, seems to be a good starting point. This approach, however, has been criticized by Overall (1974), who questioned the use of code types as clinical classifications, as one first classifies the patients into groups on the basis of the standard MMPI and then counts as errors different classifications based on the short form. At least theoretically, there are errors in both. The results of Butcher, Clavelle, and Hoffmann (1974) would likely be more appealing if they had incorporated an external criterion like the BPRS. Nevertheless, their approach seems to be compatible with the goals of shortening the MMPI, reducing its inappropriateness for certain people, and reducing the complexity of interpretation while avoiding the cost of restandardization. It appears to be a very promising approach for the future.

This approach would be even more promising if other test results could be incorporated with the MMPI items in the computer presentation. For code types where CNS impairment should be ruled out, the most differentiating of neuropsychological test items could be presented. Figure drawings using an electric stylus or other projective techniques might be of value in other cases. Such an approach would likely add depth to an assessment. In responding to the MMPI, a person reports conscious self-perceptions. By including other tests this information base can be expanded to include objective assessments of abilities as well as more subjective assessments. In this way both the dynamic source of a person's symptoms and their effect on day-to-day performance can be seen.

To summarize: We have seen the expansion of the MMPI from the original card form to booklet forms, short forms, and on-line computer forms. Given the prohibitiveness of restandardizing the MMPI, one of the best ways to overcome many of the MMPI shortcomings is to develop alternate forms for special situations and applications. Studies to date suggest that concerns about reliability losses and changes in item meaning have been exaggerated for the MMPI. Caution must be paid, however, to the clinical validity of such alternate forms as well as to the copyright of the MMPI publisher. Because of its flexibility, the card form will enjoy greater use in the future. The most promising course, however, likely lies in computer administrations tailored to each person tested.

THE NEED FOR NEW NORMS

The MMPI was standardized on samples that differ in many ways from those groups to whom it is administered today. These differences can only be anticipated to increase in the future. In a similar chapter in a similar book of readings, Norman (1972, p. 79) stressed "the importance of establishing appropriate frames of reference in diagnostic testing." One must always preface, at least mentally, descriptions of persons with "compared to ———." When we give an interpretation based on the standard MMPI, we usually assume that our readers will know we mean "compared to the Minnesota norm group." I suspect that we may be assuming too much at times. I also suspect that the Minnesota norm group should not always be the comparison group. Increasingly, researchers have been developing alternate norms that consider such important demographic variables as age and ethnicity. Hopefully, this trend will continue to include other variables in the person's life situation.

Most of us learned in our introduction to mental measurement theory that every test score is the sum of a "true score" that the person being tested would have obtained had all things been ideal, plus an error variable that exists because things never are ideal. Helmstadter (1964, p. 60) gives the example of measuring several tables. When the tables are all of the same exact length, we can use the differences in repeated measurements as an index of the amount of error present in our measuring instrument.

> But, what if all the tables are not of the same length? . . . In this circumstance, the total variation in observed table lengths is partly due to true differences in the table size and partly due to errors which vary from one measuring to the next. Thus, the total variation in the reported table lengths can no longer be used as an index of error. However, . . . it is possible to conceive of the total variance as involving an error component and a true component.

This conception of total variance as the sum of true variance and error variance can be expressed algebraically as:

$$\sigma_x^2 = \sigma_t^2 + \sigma_e^2$$

where

σ_x^2 = the variances of the observed measures, σ_t^2 = the true measures, and σ_e^2 = the errors, respectively.

The reliability of a measuring device can then be defined as the ratio of true measurement variance to observed measurement variance. In theory, if a measuring device has perfect reliability, there is no variable error at all. Conversely, as variable is reduced, error measuring devices become progressively more reliable.

But people are not tables, not even tables of different sizes. People change as a function of the situation they are in to a much greater extent than do tables. We know, for example, that the MMPI can provide false information when the usual mental health testing environment is altered. Hence, we were taught as students to be concerned about the settings in which tests are administered. Some of us had this point personally accentuated when we sneaked off to take the MMPI in our offices only to be startled by the unusually high elevations this private setting produced. To be reliable and valid any test should be administered in a setting close to that employed in the normative studies.

Another way to increase the reliability of any test is to conceive of the error variance as the sum of situational variance plus other error variance:

$$\sigma_x^2 = \sigma_t^2 + \sigma_s^2 + \sigma_e^2$$

where σ_s^2 = situational variance. There is no reason to believe that personality research will increasingly focus on situational variables in the future. Roger

Barker discussed the why and how of this a decade ago. Rather than repeat his arguments, let me note that Barker and Wright (1955) found that they "could predict many aspects of children's behavior more adequately from knowledge of the behavior characteristics of the drugstores, arithmetic classes, and basketball games that they inhabited than from knowledge of the behavior tendencies of the particular children" (Barker 1969, p. 35).

We now attempt to measure some of this situational variance through the MMPI validity scales. There clearly seems to be a need to develop and use more diverse and specific scales of this sort in the future. Norman (1972, p. 75) wrote:

> There is already ample evidence to indicate that a very much larger number of more specific detection, control, or "validity" keys will be needed . . . and that they will have to be specifically calibrated for diverse subgroups and conditions of administration.

A perusal of Volume 2 of *An MMPI Handbook* (Dahlstrom, Welsh, and Dahlstrom 1975) shows that there are already about 65 "test response measures" for the MMPI. Unfortunately, there seems to be so much overlap that they have grouped them into just two categories: those dealing with acquiescence and those dealing with social favorability. So there still seems to be room for more moderator or control scales for the MMPI.

But scales like *L, F, K,* Acquiescence, and Social Desirability merely tell how the persons being tested react to the testing situations. We infer that this is representative of how they react to life situations in general. The question of growing concern is, as Barker (1969, p. 31) stated: "What are the consequences for human behavior [and its measurement, the present author might add] of such environmental conditions as poverty, . . . congested cities, transient populations, . . . large schools, 'bedroom' communities?" The effects of life situation variables such as these on test responses likely will not be assessable with moderator scales. Instead, I believe that we need to develop norms specific to many diverse life situations. This idea has roots as far back as 1954 when Aumach suggested the use of "smaller and more homogeneous standardization groupings" (p. 81) to avoid misinterpreting normative deviation, per se, as pathology. Norman (1972) felt that the whole idea of moderated relationships might be handled better this way.

The original Minnesota norm group, though it corresponded well to the 1930 census, seems to be an inappropriate reference group for the 1980s. The median individual in that group had an eighth-grade education, was married, lived in a small town or on a farm, and was employed as a lower level clerk or skilled tradesman. None was under 16 or over 65 years of age, and all were white. As a clinician I find it difficult to justify comparing anyone to such a dated group. When the person is 14 years old, Chicano, and lives in Houston's poor fifth ward, use of the original norms seems sinful.

In the future it will likely be possible to assess life situations directly. Recently, Kurtines (1978) presented a paper reporting his use of a semantic differential for this purpose. But until then, perhaps we should indirectly assess each person's life situation by considering age, sex, socioeconomic status, education, intelligence, occupation, geographic region, and the reason for referral, as well as the response to the testing setting. Perhaps, for example, we should have separate norms for 13-year-old, unemployed, urban, black females who have a seventh-grade education and are being tested by a juvenile court.

Clearly, there needs to be a limit to the proliferation of such specific norms, or their value for approximating zero points in scaling and for permitting comparison across large numbers of people will decline. Eventually, even the clerical errors involved in converting a raw score to a T score could exceed the original errors that such norms were developed to correct. What is needed is additional evidence about what life situation variables lead to important systematic MMPI errors. It seems safe at present to say that sex differences are important. Lushene (1967) found very different factors underlying male and female MMPI item responses, while Dahlstrom, Welsh, and Dahlstrom (1975) found that code types shifted drastically when the MMPIs of Hathaway and Briggs' (1957) refined Minnesota normal sample were scored using norms of the other sex. Similarly, small but stable age deviations have been reported. Marks and Briggs (1967) and Swenson (1961) therefore have developed special norms for adolescents and the elderly. There seem to be few changes in MMPI protocols or item endorsements as a function of religion, but ethnicity, socioeconomic status, and urban versus rural residence all appear to have some effect and need further study (Dahlstrom, Welsh, and Dahlstrom 1975).

The importance of group-specific norms becomes even greater when the MMPI item pool is reduced. This has become clear to me through my work with short MMPIs and their conversion tables, so I will use Kincannon's (1968) 71-item Mini-Mult to illustrate the problem. The Mini-Mult is generally considered not to be an effective alternative to the full MMPI. Among the reasons for this is its tendency to miss an unacceptably high percentage of invalid MMPI profiles. For example, across 13 samples of normal and psychiatric groups from around the country, the mean percentage of invalid MMPI profiles correctly identified by the Mini-Mult was only 34.3. By comparison, a 24-hour retest MMPI administered to a similarly mixed sample correctly detected invalidity in 83 percent of the cases (Faschingbauer and Newmark 1978, pp. 40–41). Quite a decline in an important clinical area!

Recently (Faschingbauer 1976) compared Kincannon's (1968) original sample parameters to those for a group of Roche Psychiatric Service patients. A random sample of 200 MMPIs was drawn by computer from the records of 472 male psychiatric patients furnished by Roche Psychiatric Service. The subjects ranged in age from 13 to 75 and in education from 1 to 20 years. They were predominantly white, married, and were nearly equally selected from psychiatric inpatients, clinic outpatients, and private practice patients. The MMPI and Mini-

Mult means and standard deviations, as well as correlations between the two forms, from this random sample and from Kincannon's (1968) original sample were used to construct separate sets of regression equations. These equations were then used to estimate MMPI scores from the Mini-Mult scores of the remaining 272 patients. The equations based on Kincannon's original sample parameters produced estimated T scores for *L, F,* and *K* such that only 53 percent of the 93 invalid MMPI profiles were so identified by the Mini-Mult. When the sample-specific equations were used, this figure rose to 68 percent accuracy. And the Roche norm group was still demographically quite diverse!

Finally, I suspect that we could greatly increase the diagnostic accuracy of the MMPI if we replaced our usual "normal" normative groups with psychiatric normative groups. What sense is there, once we have identified a person as a psychiatric patient, comparing this patient to nonpsychiatric patients? There is reason to believe that the predictive validity of the MMPI might be increased significantly, if once we have separated a person from the "normal" group we also interpreted the MMPI compared to psychiatric patients in general.

Kriedt (1949), for example, was able to differentiate successfully among subgroups of psychologists on the Strong Vocational Interest Blank only by comparing them to an "undifferentiated psychologist" group rather than the usual reference group. Rosen (1962) attempted to develop new scales for the MMPI that were more independent of each other than the current clinical scales "using psychiatric patients-in-general rather than normals as the basic reference group for the selection of items" (Rosen 1962, p. 1). The criterion groups for his scales were five homogeneous groups of patients diagnosed via Veterans Administration nomenclature as having symptoms of the following: anxiety reaction; conversion reaction; depressive reaction; somatization reaction; and schizophrenic reaction, paranoid type. The patients-in-general group consisted of every third case from an alphabetical list of discharged psychiatric patients over a two-year period (n = 250). Diagnoses ranged widely in this group from neuroses and psychoses to drug abuse and organic problems.

In selecting the items for each new scale, Rosen removed those patients-in-general who had ever received a primary diagnosis identical to patients in the diagnostic group under consideration. Although Rosen's resultant scales (Ar, Cr, Dr, Sn, and Pz) suffered from similarities among some of his criterion groups and were based on a homogeneous sample of only white, male, Veterans Administration patients, the idea of using psychiatric patients-in-general group norms in a secondary interpretation once psychopathology has been established may hold promise.

In summary, the MMPI norms most commonly used in clinical practice seem outdated. By including demographic variables found to affect performance on the MMPI, we may be able to control indirectly that portion of error variance accounted for by the lief situations of our subjects. This approach may even prove more valuable than current validity scales as a way of moderating interpretations. Finally, it may prove useful to develop norms for psychiatric patients-in-general to be used secondary to present norms in situations where psycho-pathology has been found and differential diagnosis or description is the primary goal.

GROUP- AND SITUATION-SPECIFIC INTERPRETATIONS

Not only do norms need revision but so too do interpretations. The "cookbook" actuarial interpretations of Gilberstadt and Duker (1965) or Marks and Seeman (1963) have gained wide use in the last decade. These and other systematic interpretative programs will likely continue to enjoy popularity in the 1980s. What is needed, however, is the same attention to demographic and situational specifics as was noted above regarding norms. Demographically homogeneous samples (for example, elderly males) need to be studied to determine what situation- (for example, medical patient) specific interpretations can be validly associated with a given code type.

Efforts in this direction have already been made by Marks, Seeman, and Haller (1974), who provided interpretive statements specific to adolescents. Their 61 code-type-based samples (including high versus low scoring subsamples) were small (mean n = 13.4). Nevertheless, important and useful interpretive differences from adult samples are evident. For example, although 68/86 adolescents are often described as paranoid and exhibit bizarre thoughts and behavior, they seem to differ from their adult counterparts in that they frequently are below average in intelligence, have histories of head trauma, and exhibit such somatic symptoms of anxiety and depression as dry mouth, fatigue, and sweating. They also have trouble getting out of bed in the morning, cheat at school, and bite their nails. Somewhat limited experience with the aged has led me to believe that similar age-specific code-type descriptions are needed for them. Other areas that come to mind include specific medical populations (for example, surgery patients) and applicants for certain occupations (for example, policemen).

Drake and Oetting's (1959) *An MMPI Codebook for Counselors* of college students is another example of such group-specific interpretative descriptions. It further extends MMPI interpretation to "normal" and lower ranging profiles. Drake and Oetting (1959) employ a coding approach that codes both high and low scales:

> No scale is coded high unless it has a T-score of 55 or above and no scale is coded low unless it has a T-score of 45 or less. Only the three highest scales are selected to represent the high coding of the profile. . . . In the case of the low scales only the two lowest with T-scores below 46 are coded. After the 3 highest and the two lowest scales are selected, the numbers of the scales are arranged in numerical order regardless of the relative size of the T-scores; a dash (–) separates the numbers for the high scales from the numbers for the low scales. (p. 37)

Kelley and King (1978) recently looked at the behavioral correlates of within-normal-limit MMPI profiles in a university counseling center. They described several groups of students with all of the MMPI clinical scales within normal limits who, nevertheless, exhibited psychopathology. One group of males and females had transient situational problems relating to marriage, sex, and dependency. Another group of males clearly exhibited severe psychopathology in the past but were now in remission.

Males with all of the clinical scales within normal limits, but with K between 65 and 70 T, were only children who were married, complained of sexual difficulties and seemed inhibited. Where K exceeded a T score of 70 and other scales were all within normal limits, dramatic differences emerged between the sexes:

> These males (had) . . . complaints of anxiety. Their cognitive processes were disrupted. . . . They interpreted proverbs in a concrete and often personalized manner. . . . Delusions and hallucinations were found to be characteristic of these men, who tended to come from families in which parents were divorced. Although the base rate for manic depressive psychosis-manic type was very low in our population (.7%), $K+$ men received this label significantly more often than other males in the clinic population. . . .
>
> Such severe pathology was not characteristic of women with the same $K+$ profile type. More often married or separated . . . they reported the unusual fact of having . . . a relative with an emotional disorder . . . interviewers saw them as immature . . . specific phobias, such as fear of injections, or height, were among the most common presenting complaint for this group. (pp. 698–99)

These or other approaches to "normal" and abnormally low scale scores would seem to deserve wider application. Low points are, theoretically, just as abnormal as high points, and some of them, such as *Hs, D, Mf, Ma,* and *Si* are routinely given clinical interpretations. Yet, to my knowledge, no one has ever studied low-point pairs or triads. The unexpected amount of psychopathology found by Kelley and King (1978) reminds us that even "normal" profiles are not always indicative of "normal" people. There is even less reason to consider abnormally low scores as "normal."

More importantly, as with the incomplete profile, there is often little to be said about the patient with an MMPI profile within or below normal limits. While the work of both Drake and Oetting and Kelley and King was limited to college students, their attempts to find meaning in this too long neglected area must be applauded. (See Chapter 11 for a discussion of this neglected area.)

SHIFTING THEORETICAL ORIENTATIONS

Most readers have probably been told that the MMPI is an atheoretical test. This is true in the sense that the MMPI items were drawn from several sources, including various other scales, case histories, and the clinical experiences of its developers. Surely, no one theoretical orientation was shared by the many authors of the several scales and case histories used. The authors of the MMPI, however, did seem to subscribe to a trait theory of personality. They selected criterion groups of patients (types) each with relatively homogenous characteristics (traits), and developed their scales so as to differentiate those groups from "normals." It is not surprising therefore that the resultant scales generally measure traits that combine into code types.

Although the standard MMPI scales reflect trait theory, the content of its item pool is relatively atheoretical or multitheoretical. As such, it presents a unique meeting place for many different theories of human behavior. Theorists of diverse orientations have worked with the MMPI over the years. At times, this has resulted in the synthesis of originally unrelated topics. For example, Taylor (1954) conducted her studies of manifest anxiety from a Hullian learning theory perspective. Haan (1965) seems to have used a Freudian view of man to develop MMPI scales for such defense mechanisms as repression and intellectualization, while a cognitive perspective seems to underlie the work of Altocchi (1961) and Byrne (1961, 1964) on repression-sensitization (R-S). Yet these scales have shown surprising overlap within the MMPI (see Dahlstrom, Welsh, and Dahlstrom 1975, p. 104, for a summary).

Psychology as a science seems to be badly in need of unifying concepts at present. This implies a need for common measures applicable to many theories (see, for example, Griffith and Byrne 1970; Kuhn 1962). The MMPI items may be one such common measure that future researchers of varied theoretical orientations will continue to employ. Most will likely do so out of ignorance or sloth, but some, as always, will carefully plan multitheoretical experiments incorporating MMPI items in a multimethod design. To the extent that the MMPI items are found useful (apart from method variance) in linking disparate theories, the MMPI will be retained in such research.

In some cases, by forcing the researcher to restate hypotheses in the MMPI's language, new insights will likely emerge within a theory. For example, Haan's use of the MMPI led her to propose that denial is a more modulated form of repression, displacement a more appropriate form of projection, and doubt a mild form of intellectualization (Dahlstrom, Welsh, and Dahlstrom 1975).

The MMPI will likely continue to be used more and more in interdisciplinary studies, too. A model of this application is the work of Roessler and his associates (Alexander, Roessler, and Greenfield 1963; Greenfield, Alexander, and Roessler 1963; McCollum, Burch, and Roessler 1969; Phaehler and Roessler 1965; Roessler, Alexander, and Greenfield 1963; Roessler, Burch, and Childers 1966; Roessler and Collins 1970; Roessler, Greenfield, and Alexander 1964; Strausbaugh and Roessler 1970.) Ego strength (Es), autonomic nervous system reactivity (psychogalvanistic reflex), and resistance to physical disease were carefully related. Among other findings, high scorers on Es (psychologically healthy subjects), in contrast to low scorers (neurotic subjects), "were able to respond promptly, appropriately and effectively to new demands made upon their adaptational defenses arising from the external situation or from invasions of the body by foreign organisms" (Dahlstrom, Welsh, and Dahlstrom 1975, p. 92).

CONCLUSIONS

Let me now try to tally the pluses and minuses reviewed above. To begin, the items of the MMPI are at times offensive, complexly worded, or outdated. Overall, however, they provide a more than adequate set of relatively atheoretical wordings covering a wide range of content. Furthermore, the various short forms provide for diverse item sets, one of which should be acceptable to all but the pickiest user. The evidence suggests that items not scored, or scored on no scale of interest, may be omitted without unduly disrupting the item matrix and the subsequent reliability of the MMPI.

For those still not satisfied, there is always the option of slightly rewording MMPI items. Of course, technically, one does not then consider the result the MMPI, but a separate test requiring validation. The work of Kincannon (1968) seems to represent the only instance where a rewording is considered a form of the MMPI. His Mini-Mult items were all reworded to an interrogative, verbal, interview format. Studies comparing interrogative and standard Mini-Mult items (Gayton, Ozman, and Wilson 1972; Percell and Delk 1973) suggest that there is little loss in the utility of the MMPI as a function of such minor rewordings. However, the Mini-Mult does not reproduce the MMPI sufficiently well to permit generalization to the larger test. Therefore it must be assumed that essentially nothing is known about slightly reworded MMPI items.

The MMPI clinical scales were faulted because of their lack of homogeneity and distinctness. One way to avoid scoring the same item on several scales is to use the Hugo short form where each item is scored on one and only one scale. Rosen's (1962) scales are similarly nonoverlapping but are different from the usual clinical scales. Finally, the card form of the MMPI can be used with the overlapping items omitted. This latter approach, like the rewording of items, leaves one using a test that is technically not the MMPI and would require revalidation.

Finally, there has been some promising work in providing alternatives to the generally outdated MMPI norms and interpretations. Marks and Briggs (1967), Drake and Oetting (1959), Kelley and King (1978), Marks, Seeman, and Haller (1974), and Swenson (1961) have all been active in this area. However, much more work needs to be done here. Other areas requiring more work include the development of multiple stopping points, separation of unipolar from bipolar traits, and greater testing of diverse theories using the MMPI.

In spite of all its shortcomings, the MMPI continues to be a robust test enjoying wide popularity. As noted at the end of another book (Faschingbauer and Newmark 1978), the MMPI is the "jackknife" of personality tests. I suspect that other, finer tests will be published in the next decade. But I also feel that there will still be room for the MMPI. What matters in the years ahead is how flexibly we can use this psychometric jackknife without breaking it. Here, as with most everything in life, we must try to change what we can, accept what cannot be changed, and learn to know the difference.

There are many things about the MMPI that likely cannot be changed. For example, several factor analyses (see those listed earlier in the disucssion of the state-trait anxiety plus item factor analyses by Barker, Fowler, and Peterson 1971; Hunter, Overall, and Butcher 1974; Tryon 1966) have reported from two to seven factors underlying performance on the MMPI. As long as the MMPI items are retained, it is unreasonable to expect them to measure anything, except as a function of those few factors. On the other hand, much of the research reviewed above suggests that there is much about the MMPI that might be changed. Whether or not they actually can be changed or will be changed will eventually determine the future of the MMPI.

REFERENCES

Alexander, A. A., R. Roessler, and N. S. Greenfield. 1963. "Ego Strength and Physiological Responsivity. III. The Relationship of the Barron Ego Strength Scale to Spontaneous Periodic Activity in Skin Resistance, Finger Blood Volume, Heart Rate and Muscle Potential." *Archives of General Psychiatry* 9: 58–61.

Altrocchi, J. 1961. "Interpersonal Perceptions of Repressors and Sensitizers and Component Analysis of Assumed Dissimilarity Scores." *Journal of Abnormal and Social Psychology* 62: 528–34.

American Psychological Association. 1954. *Technical Recommendations for Psychological Tests and Diagnostic Techniques*. Supplement to *Psychological Bulletin* 51.

Aumack, L. 1954. "Misconceptions Concerning the Interpretation of Sub-Group Variations Within Normative Data." *Journal of Psychology* 38: 79–82.

Barker, H. R., R. D. Fowler, and L. P. Peterson. 1971. "Factor Analytic Structure of the Short Form MMPI Items." *Journal of Clinical Psychology* 27: 228–33.

Barker, R. G. 1969. "Wanted: An Eco-Behavioral Science." In *Naturalistic Viewpoints in Psychological Research*, edited by E. Willems and H. L. Raush, pp. 31–43. New York: Holt, Rinehart and Winston.

——, and H. F. Wright. *Midwest and Its Children*. New York: Harper & Row.

Bem, S. Z. 1974. "The Measurement of Psychological Androgyny." *Journal of Consulting and Clinical Psychology* 42: 155–62.

Butcher, J. N., P. Clavelle, and N. Hoffmann. 1974. "Clinical Limitations of MMPI Short Forms and a Strategy for Developing Tailor-made MMPI Short Form." Paper presented at the annual meeting of the American Psychological Association, New Orleans, September.

Butcher, J. N., and P. Pancheri. 1976. *A Handbook of Crossnational MMPI Research*. Minneapolis: University of Minnesota Press.

Byrne, D. 1964. "Repression-Sensitization as a Dimension of Personality." *Progress in Experimental Personality Research*, edited by B. A. Maher, vol. 1. New York: Academic Press.

———. 1961. "The Repression-Sensitization Scale: Rationale, Reliability and Validity." *Journal of Personality* 29: 334–49.

Charen, S. 1954. "A Note on the Use of a Paper-and-Pencil Form of the MMPI *Hs* Scale for Hospital Use." *Journal of Consulting Psychology* 18: 344.

Dahlstrom, W. G., and G. S. Welsh. 1960. *An MMPI Handbook*. Minneapolis: University of Minnesota Press.

———, and L. E. Dahlstrom. 1972. *An MMPI Handbook*, vol. 1, *Clinical Interpretation*. Minneapolis: University of Minnesota Press.

———. 1975. *An MMPI Handbook*, vol. 2, *Research and Applications*. Minneapolis: University of Minnesota Press.

Dana, R. H., and J. C. Condry. 1963. "MMPI Retest Results: Context, Order, Practice and Test-Taking Anxiety." *Psychological Reports* 12: 147–52.

Donnelly, E. F., D. L. Murphy, I. N. Waldman, and T. D. Reynolds. 1976. "MMPI Differences Between Unipolar and Bipolar Depressed Subjects: A Replication." *Journal of Clinical Psychology* 32: 610–12.

Drake, L. E., and E. R. Oetting. 1959. *An MMPI Codebook for Counselors*. Minneapolis: University of Minnesota Press.

Eichman, W. J. 1962. "Factored Scales for the MMPI." *Journal of Clinical Psychology* 18: 363–95.

Ellis, A. 1974. "A Comparison of the Use of Direct and Indirect Phrasing in Personality Questionnaires." *Psychological Monographs* 61, no. 284.

Faschingbauer, T. R. 1976. "Substitution and Regression Models, Base Rates, and the Clinical Validity of the Mini-Mult." *Journal of Clinical Psychology* 32: 70–74.

———, and C. S. Newmark. 1978. *Short Forms of the MMPI*. Lexington, Mass.: D.C. Heath.

Ferguson, R. G. 1946. "A Useful Adjunct to the MMPI Scoring and Analysis." *Journal of Clinical Psychology* 2: 248–53.

Gayton, W. F., K. L. Ozman, and W. T. Wilson. 1972. "Investigation of a Written Form of the Mini-Mult." *Psychological Reports* 30: 275–78.

Gilberstadt, H., and J. Duker. 1965. *A Handbook for Clinical and Actuarial MMPI Interpretation.* Philadelphia: Saunders.

Gough, H. 1946. "Diagnostic Patterns on the MMPI." *Journal of Clinical Psychology* 2: 23–37.

Greenfield, N. S., A. A. Alexander, and R. Roessler. 1963. "Ego Strength and Physiological Responsivity. II. The Relationship of the Barron Ego Strength Scale to the Temporal and Recovery Characteristics of Skin Resistance, Finger Blood Volume, Heart Rate and Muscle Potential Responses to Sound." *Archives of General Psychiatry* 9: 129–41.

Griffith, W., and D. Byrne. 1970. "Procedures in the Paradigmatic Study of Attitude Similarity and Attraction." *Representative Research in Social Psychology* 1: 33–48.

Guilford, J. P. 1954. *Psychometric Methods.* New York: McGraw-Hill.

Haan, N. 1965. "Coping and Defense Mechanisms Related to Personality Inventories." *Journal of Consulting Psychology* 29: 373–78.

Hathaway, S. R., and P. F. Briggs. 1957. "Some Normative Data on New MMPI Scales." *Journal of Clinical Psychology* 13: 364–68.

Helmstadter, G. C. 1964. *Principles of Psychological Measurement.* New York: Appleton-Century-Crofts.

Holzberg, J., and S. Alessi. 1949. "Reliability of the Shortened Minnesota Multiphasic Personality Inventory." *Journal of Consulting Psychology* 13: 288–92.

Hugo, J. 1971. "Abbreviation of the Minnesota Multiphasic Personality Inventory Through Multiple Regression." Ph.D. dissertation. University of Alabama.

Hunter, S., J. E. Overall, and J. N. Butcher. 1974. "Factor Structure of the MMPI in a Psychiatric Population." *Multivariant Behavioral Research* 9: 283–302.

Kassebaum, G. C., A. S. Couch, and P. E. Slater. 1959. "The Factorial Dimensions of the MMPI." *Journal of Consulting Psychology* 23: 226–36.

Kelley, C. K., and G. D. King. 1978. "Behavioral Correlates for Within-Normal-Limit MMPI Profiles with and Without Elevated *K* in Students at a University Mental Health Center." *Journal of Clinical Psychology* 34: 695–99.

Kincannon, J. C. 1968. "Prediction of the Standard MMPI Scale Scores from 71 Items: The Mini-Mult." *Journal of Consulting and Clinical Psychology* 32: 319–25.

Kreidt, P. H. 1949. "Vocational Interests of Psychologists." *Journal of Applied Psychology* 33: 482–88.

Kuhn, T. 1962. *The Structure of Scientific Revolutions*. Chicago: University of Chicago Press.

Kurtines, W. M. 1978. "Situation or Person? Toward a Psychosocial Role-Theoretical Approach to Personality." Paper presented at the annual meeting of the Southeastern Psychological Association, Atlanta, March.

Lieberman, L. 1968. "Further Efforts to Find Context Effects in Personality Inventories." *Perceptual and Motor Skills* 26: 1277–78.

———, and W. Walters, Jr. 1968. "Effect of 'Background Items' on Responses to Personality Inventory Items." *Journal of Consulting and Clinical Psychology* 32: 230–32.

Loevinger, J. 1972. "Some Limitations of Objective Personality Tests." In *Objective Personality Assessment*, edited by J. N. Butcher. New York: Academic Press.

Lushene, R. E. 1967. "Factor Structure of the MMPI Item Pool." M.S. thesis, Florida State University. See Dahlstrom, Welsh, and Dahlstrom 1975, pp. 126–127, for a summary.

McCollum, M., N. R. Burch, and R. Roessler. 1969. "Personality and Respiratory Responses to Sound and Light." *Psychophysiology* 6: 291–300.

MacDonald, G. L. 1952. "Effect of Test-Retest Interval and Item Arrangement on the Shortened Forms of the MMPI." *Journal of Clinical Psychology* 8: 408–10.

Machover, S., and H. Anderson. 1953. "Validity of a Pencil-and-Paper Form of the MMPI Psychopathic Deviate Scale." *Journal of Consulting Psychology* 17: 459–61.

Marks, P. A., and P. F. Briggs. 1967. "Adolescent Norm Tables for the MMPI." Unpublished materials. See Dahlstrom, Welsh, and Dahlstrom, 1972, pp. 388–99, for norms.

Marks, P. A., and W. Seeman. 1963. *The Actuarial Description of Personality: An Atlas for Use with the MMPI*. Baltimore: Williams & Wilkins.

——, and D. L. Haller. 1974. *The Actuarial Use of the MMPI with Adolescents and Adults*. Baltimore: Williams & Wilkins.

Mees, H. L. 1960. "Preliminary Steps in the Construction of Factor Scales for the MMPI." Ph.D. dissertation, University of Washington.

Newmark, C. S., T. R. Faschingbauer, A. J. Finch, and P. C. Kendall. 1975. "Factor Analysis of the MMPI-STAI." *Journal of Clinical Psychology* 31: 449-452.

Newmark, C. S., D. R. Ziff, A. J. Finch, Jr., and P. C. Kendall. 1978. "Comparing the Empirical Validity of the Standard Form with Two Abbreviated MMPIs." *Journal of Consulting and Clinical Psychology* 46: 53-61.

Norman, W. T. 1972. "Psychometric Considerations for a Revision of the MMPI." In *Objective Personality Assessment*, edited by J. N. Butcher, pp. 59-83. New York: Academic Press.

Olson, G. 1961. "The Influence of Context on the Depression Scale of the MMPI in a Psychotic Population." *Journal of Consulting Psychology* 25: 178-79.

Overall, J. E. 1974. *Symposium on Short Forms of the MMPI*. Discussant at the annual meeting of the American Psychological Association, New Orleans, September.

——, and F. Gomez-Mont. 1974. "The MMPI-168 for Psychiatric Screening." *Educational and Psychological Measurement* 34: 315-19.

Percell, L. P., and J. L. Delk, 1973. "Relative Usefulness of Three Forms of the Mini-Mult with College Students." *Journal of Consulting and Clinical Psychology* 40: 487.

Phaehler, G. T., and R. Roessler. 1965. "Ego Strength and Intravenous Glucose Tolerance." *Journal of Psychosomatic Research* 8: 431-39.

Pokorny, A. E., and J. E. Overall. 1970. "Relationships of Psychopathology to Age, Sex, Ethnicity, Education and Marital Status in State Hospital Patients." *Journal of Psychiatric Research* 7: 143-52.

Roessler, R., A. A. Alexander, and N. S. Greenfield. 1963. "Ego Strength and Psysiological Responsivity. I. The Relationship of the Barron *Es* Scale to Skin Resistance, Finger Blood Volume, Heart Rate, and Muscle Potential Responses to Sound." *Archives of General Psychiatry* 8: 142-54.

Roessler, R., N. R. Burch, and H. E. Childers. 1966. "Personality and Arousal Correlates of Specific Galvanic Skin Responses." *Psychophysiology* 3: 115-30.

Roessler, R., and F. Collins. 1970. "Personality Correlates of Physiological Response to Motion Pictures." *Psychophysiology* 6: 732-39.

Roessler, R., N. S. Greenfield, and A. A. Alexander. 1964. "Ego Strength and Response Stereotype." *Phychophysiology* 1: 142-50.

Rosen, A. 1962. "Development of the MMPI Scales Based on a Reference Group of Psychiatric Patients." *Phychological Monographs* 76, no. 527.

——, W. M. Hales, and R. M. Peek. 1958. "Comparability of MMPI Card and Booklet Forms for Phychiatric Patients." *Journal of Clinical Psychology* 14: 387-88.

Russell, M. A., and J. O. Sines. 1978. "Further Evidence That M-F is Bipolar and Multidimensional." *Journal of Clinical Psychology* 34: 643-49.

Siegal, S. M., and M. J. Feldman. 1958. "A Note on the Effect on Self Description of Combining Anxiety and Hostility Items on a Single Scale." *Journal of Clinical Psychology* 14: 389-90.

Spielberger, C. D., R. L. Gorsuch, and R. E. Lushene. 1970. *Manual for the State-Trait Anxiety Inventory (Self-Evaluation Questionnaire).* Palo Alto, Calif.: Consulting Psychologists Press.

Spitzer, R. L., E. I. Burdock, and A. S. Hardesty. 1964. *Mental Status Schedule.* New York: Biometrics Research, New York State Department of Mental Hygiene.

Strausbaugh, L. J., and R. Roessler. 1970. "Ego Strength, Skin Conductance, Sleep Deprivation and Performance." *Perceptual and Motor Skills* 31: 671-77.

Swenson, W. M. 1961. "Structured Personality Testing in the Aged: An MMPI Study of the Gerontic Population." *Journal of Clinical Psychology* 17: 302-04. See Dahlstrom, Welsh, and Dahlstrom, 1972, pp. 384-85, for norms.

Taylor, J. A. 1953. "A Personality Scale of Manifest Anxiety." *Journal of Abnormal and Social Psychology* 48: 285-90.

Tryon, R. C. 1966. "Unrestricted Cluster and Factor Analysis with Applications to the MMPI and Holzinger-Harmon Problems." *Multivariate Behavioral Research* 1: 229-44.

Welsh, G. S. 1956. "Factor Dimensions A and R." In *Basic Readings on the MMPI in Psychology and Medicine*, edited by G. S. Welsh and W. G. Dahlstrom. Minneapolis: University of Minnesota Press.

Wheeler, W. M., K. B. Little, and G. F. J. Lehner. 1951. "The Internal Structure of the MMPI." *Journal of Consulting Psychology* 15: 134–41.

Wiener, D. 1947. "Differences Between the Individual and Group Forms of the Minnesota Multiphasic Personality Inventory." *Journal of Consulting Psychology* 11: 104–06.

Wilson, I. C., R. G. Carson, A. M. Rabon, and L. B. Alltop. 1970. "An MMPI Two-Type Depressive Scale." Unpublished paper. North Carolina Department of Mental Health, Raleigh. See Dahlstrom, Welsh, and Dahlstrom, 1975, pp. 21 and 284, for summary and items.

APPENDIX A/Bibliography on Abbreviated Forms of the MMPI

Compiled by Charles S. Newmark

JOURNAL ARTICLES

Armentrout, J. A. 1970, "Correspondence of the MMPI and Mini-Mult in a College Population." *Journal of Clinical Psychology* 26: 493–95.

Armentrout, J. A., and D. L. Rouzer. 1970. "Utility of the Mini-Mult with Delinquents." *Journal of Consulting and Clinical Psychology* 34: 450.

Bassett, J. E., G. C. Schellman, W. F. Gayton, and J. Tavormina. 1977. "Efficacy of the Mini-Mult Validity Scales with Prisoners." *Journal of Clinical Psychology* 33: 729–31.

Bolton, B. 1976. "Homogeneous Subscales for the Mini-Mult." *Journal of Consulting and Clinical Psychology* 44: 684.

Calsyn, D. A., D. N. Spengler, and C. W. Freeman. 1977. "Application of the Somatization Factor of the MMPI-168 with Low Back Pain Patients." *Journal of Clinical Psychology* 33: 1017–20.

Castro, G. A., and H. A. Quesada. 1971. "Mini-Mult: An Abbreviated form of the Minnesota Multiphasic Personality Inventory." *Acta Psiquiatrica y Psicologica Americana Latina* 17: 12–18.

Dean, E. F. 1972. "A Lengthened Mini: The Midi-Mult." *Journal of Clinical Psychology* 28: 68–71.

Edinger, J. D., P. C. Kendall, J. F. Hooke, and J. B. Brogan. 1976. "The Predictive Efficacy of Three MMPI Short Forms." *Journal of Personality Assessment* 40: 259–65.

Elsie, R. D., and J. F. C. McLachlan. 1976. "Reliability of the Maxi-Mult and Scale Equivalence with the MMPI. *Journal of Clinical Psychology* 32: 67–70.

Erickson, R. C., and C. Freeman. 1976. "Using the MMPI-168 with Medical Patients." *Journal of Clinical Psychology* 32: 803–05.

Erickson, R. C., and N. O'Leary. 1977. "Use of the MMPI-168 with Alcoholics. *Journal of Clinical Psychology* 33: 133–35.

Faschingbauer, T. R. 1976a. "Some Clinical Considerations in Selecting a Short Form of the MMPI." *Professional Psychology* 7: 167–76.

——. 1976b. "Substitution and Regression Models, Base Rates and the Clinical Validity of the Mini-Mult." *Journal of Clinical Psychology* 32: 70–74.

——. 1974. "A 166-Item Short Form of the Group MMPI: The FAM." *Journal of Consulting and Clinical Psychology* 42: 645–55.

——, D. T. Johnson, and C. S. Newmark. 1978. "Interpretative Validity of the FAM: Long-Term Psychotherapists' Ratings of Psychiatric Inpatients." *Journal of Personality Assessment* 42: 74–76.

Finch, A. J., Jr., G. L. Edwards, and J. L. Griffin Jr. 1975. "Utility of the Mini-Mult with Parents of Emotionally Disturbed Children." *Journal of Personality Assessment* 39: 146–50.

——, Jr., P. D. Kendall, W. M. Nelson, and C. S. Newmark. 1975. "Application of Faschingbauer's Abbreviated MMPI to Parents of Emotionally Disturbed Children." *Psychological Reports* 37: 571–74.

Freeman, C., D. Calsyn, and M. O'Leary. 1977. "Application of Faschingbauer's Abbreviated MMPI with Medical Patients. *Journal of Consulting and Clinical Psychology* 45: 706–07.

——, M. O'Leary, and D. Calsyn. 1977. "Application of the Faschingbauer Abbreviated MMPI with Alcoholic Patients." *Journal of Clinical Psychology* 33: 303–06.

Gaines, L. S., M. H. Abrams, P. Toel, and L. M. Miller. 1974. "Comparison of the MMPI and the Mini-Mult with Alcoholics." *Journal of Consulting and Clinical Psychology* 42: 619.

Gayton, W. F., M. E. Fogg, J. Tavormina, J. S. Bishop, M. M. Citrin, and J. S. Bassett. 1976. "Comparison of the MMPI and Mini-Mult with Women Who Request Abortion." *Journal of Clinical Psychology* 32: 648–50.

——, J. S. Bishop, M. M. Citrin, and J. S. Bassett. 1975. "An Investigation of the Mini-Mult Validity Scales." *Journal of Personality Assessment* 39: 511–13.

——, K. L. Ozmon, and W. T. Wilson. 1972. "Investigation of a Written Form of the Mini-Mult." *Psychological Reports* 30: 275–78.

——, and W. T. Wilson. 1971. "Utility of the Mini-Mult in a Child Guidance Clinic Setting." *Journal of Personality Assessment* 35: 569–75.

Gilroy, F. D., and R. Steinbacher. 1973. "Extension of the Midi-Mult to a College Population." *Journal of Personality Assessment* 37: 263–66.

Griffin, J. L., A. L. Finch, D. L. Edwards, and P. C. Kendall. 1976. "MMPI/Midi-Mult Correspondence with Parents of Emotionally Disturbed Children." *Journal of Clinical Psychology* 32: 54–56.

Hartford, T., B. Lubetkin, and G. Alpert. 1972. "Comparison of the Standard MMPI and the Mini-Mult in a Psychiatric Outpatient Clinic." *Journal of Consulting and Clinical Psychology* 39: 243–45.

Hedberg, A. G., L. M. Campbell, S. R. Weeks, and J. A. Powell. 1975. "The Use of the MMPI (Mini-Mult) to Predict Alcoholics' Response to a Behavioral Treatment Program." *Journal of Clinical Psychology* 31: 271–74.

Hedlund, J. L., D. Won Cho, and J. D. Wood. 1977a. "Comparative Validity of the MMPI-168 Factors and Clinical Scales." *Multivariate Behavioral Research* 12: 327–30.

——. 1977b. "MMPI-168 Factor Structure: A Replication with Public Mental Health Patients." *Journal of Consulting and Clinical Psychology* 45: 711–12.

Hedlund, J. L., D. Won Cho, and B. J. Powell. 1975. "Use of the MMPI Short Forms with Psychiatric Patients." *Journal of Consulting and Clinical Psychology* 43: 924.

Hobbs, T. R. 1974. "Scale Equivalence and Profile Similarity of the Mini-Mult and MMPI in an Outpatient Clinic." *Journal of Clinical Psychology* 30: 349–50.

Hobbs, T. R., and R. D. Fowler. 1974. "Reliability and Scale Equivalence of the Mini-Mult and MMPI." *Journal of Consulting and Clinical Psychology* 42: 89–92.

Hoffman, N. G., and J. N. Butcher. 1975. "Clinical Limitations of Three Minnesota Multiphasic Personality Inventory Short Forms." *Journal of Consulting and Clinical Psychology* 43: 32–39.

Hunter, S., J. E. Overall, and J. N. Butcher. 1974. "Factor Structure of the MMPI-168 in a Psychiatric Population." *Multivariate Behavioral Research* 9: 283–302.

Huisman, R. E. 1974. "Correspondence Between Mini-Mult and Standard MMPI Scale Scores in Patients with Neurologic Disease." *Journal of Consulting and Clinical Psychology* 42: 149.

Jabara, R. F., and S. F. Curran. 1974. "Comparison of the Minnesota Multiphasic Personality Inventory and Mini-Mult with Drug Users." *Journal of Consulting and Clinical Psychology* 42: 739–40.

Kincannon, J. C. 1968. "Prediction of the Standard MMPI Scale Scores from 71 Items: The Mini-Mult." *Journal of Consulting and Clinical Psychology* 32: 319–25.

King, G. D., D. A. Gideon, C. D. Haynes, R. L. Dempsey, and C. W. Jenkins. 1977. "Intellectual and Personality Changes Associated with Carotid Endarterectomy, *Journal of Clinical Psychology* 33: 215–20.

Lacks, P. B. 1970. "Further Investigation of the Mini-Mult." *Journal of Consulting and Clinical Psychology* 35: 126–27.

——, and B. J. Powell. 1970. "The Mini-Mult as a Personal Screening Technique: A Preliminary Report." *Psychological Reports* 27: 909–10.

McLachlan, J. F. C. 1977. "A Scale for the Evaluation of Psychological Distress." *Journal of Clinical Psychology* 33: 159–61.

——. 1974. "Test-Restest Stability of Long and Short Form MMPI Scales Over Two Years." *Journal of Clinical Psychology* 30: 189–91.

Mlott, S. R. 1973. "The Mini-Mult and Its Use with Adolescents." *Journal of Clinical Psychology* 29: 376–77.

Mlott, S. R., and R. L. Mason. 1975. "The Practicality of Using an Abbreviated Form of the MMPI with Chronic Renal Dialysis Patients." *Journal of Clinical Psychology* 31: 65–68.

Newmark, C. S., B. Boas, and T. Messerry. 1974. "An Abbreviated MMPI for Use with College Students." *Psychological Reports* 34: 631–34.

Newmark, C. S., A. J. Conger, and T. R. Faschingbauer. 1976. "The Interpretive Validity and Effective Test Length Functioning of an Abbreviated MMPI Relative to the Standard MMPI." *Journal of Clinical Psychology* 32: 27–32.

Newmark, C. S., L. Cook, M. Clarke, and T. Faschingbauer. 1973. "Application of Faschingbauer's Abbreviated MMPI to Psychiatric Inpatients." *Journal of Consulting and Clinical Psychology* 41: 416–21.

Newmark, C. S., L. Cook, and W. Greer. 1973. "Application of the Midi-Mult to Psychiatric Inpatients." *Journal of Clinical Psychology* 29: 481–84.

Newmark, C. S., R. Falk, and A. J. Finch. 1976. "Interpretive Accuracy of Abbreviated MMPIs." *Journal of Personality Assessment* 40: 266–68.

Newmark, C. S., and A. J. Finch. 1976. "Comparing the Diagnostic Validity of an Abbreviated and Standard MMPI." *Journal of Personality Assessment* 40: 10–12.

Newmark, C. S., R. Galen, and K. Gold. 1975. "Efficacy of an Abbreviated MMPI as a Function of Type Administration." *Journal of Clinical Psychology* 31: 639–42.

Newmark, C. S., and L. Glenn. 1974. "Sensitivity of the Faschingbauer Abbreviated MMPI to Hospitalized Adolescents." *Journal of Abnormal Child Psychology* 2: 299–306.

Newmark, C. S., L. G. Newmark, and L. Cook. 1975. "The MMPI-168 with Psychiatric Patients." *Journal of Clinical Psychology* 31: 61–64.

Newmark, C. S., L. Newmark, and T. R. Faschingbauer. 1974. "Utility of Three Abbreviated MMPIs with Psychiatric Outpatients." *Journal of Nervous and Mental Disease*, 159: 438–43.

Newmark, C. S., M. Owen, L. Newmark, and T. R. Faschingbauer. 1975. "Comparison of Three Abbreviated MMPIs for Psychiatric Patients and Normals." *Journal of Personality Assessment* 39: 261–70.

Newmark, C. S., and D. Raft. 1976. "Using an Abbreviated MMPI as a Screening Device for Medical Patients." *Psychosomatics* 17: 45–48.

Newmark, C. S., D. R. Ziff, A. J. Finch, and P. C. Kendall. 1978. "Comparing the Empirical Validity of the Standard Form with Two Abbreviated MMPIs. *Journal of Consulting and Clinical Psychology* 46: 53–61.

Newton, J. R. 1971. "A Comparison of Studies of the Mini-Mult." *Journal of Clinical Psychology* 27: 489–90.

Ogilvie, L. P., J. Kotin, and D. H. Stanley. 1976. "Comparison of the MMPI and the Mini-Mult in a Psychiatric Outpatient Clinic." *Journal of Consulting and Clinical Psychology* 44: 497–98.

Overall, J. E., J. N. Butcher, and S. Hunter. 1975. "Validity of the MMPI-168 for Psychiatric Screening." *Educational and Psychological Measurement* 35: 516–28.

Overall, J. E., and F. Gomez-Mont. 1974. "The MMPI-168 for Psychiatric Screening." *Educational and Psychological Measurement* 34: 315–19.

Overall, J. E., W. Higgins, and A. DeSchweinitz. 1976. "Comparison of Differential Diagnostic Discrimination for Abbreviated and Standard MMPI." *Journal of Clinical Psychology* 32: 237–45.

Overall, J. E., S. Hunter, and J. N. Butcher. 1973. "Factor Structure of the MMPI-168 in a Psychiatric Population." *Journal of Consulting and Clinical Psychology*, 41: 284–86.

Palmer, A. B. 1973. "A Comparison of the MMPI and Mini-Mult in a Sample of State Mental Hospital Patients." *Journal of Clinical Psychology* 29: 484–85.

Pantano, L. T., and N. L. Schwartz. 1978. "Differentiation of Neurologic and Pseudo-Neurologic Patients with Combined MMPI Mini-Mult and Pseudo-Neurologic Scale." *Journal of Clinical Psychology* 34: 56–60.

Percell, L. P., and J. L. Delk. 1973. "Relative Usefulness of Three Forms of the Mini-Mult with College Students." *Journal of Consulting and Clinical Psychology* 40: 487.

Platt, J. J., and W. C. Scura. 1972. "Validity of the Mini-Mult with Male Reformatory Inmates." *Journal of Clinical Psychology* 28: 528–29.

Poythress, N. G. 1978. "Selecting a Short Form of the MMPI: Addendum to Faschingbauer." *Journal of Consulting and Clinical Psychology* 46: 331–34.

Poythress, N. G., and P. H. Blaney. 1978. "The Validity of MMPI Interpretations Based on the Mini-Mult and the FAM." *Journal of Personality Assessment* 42: 143–47.

Pulvermacher, G. D., and W. G. Bringmann. 1971. "The Mini-Mult Used with French-Canadian College Students." *Psychological Reports* 29: 134.

Rusk, R., B. Hyerstay, D. Calsyn, and C. Freeman. 1979. "Comparison of the Utility of Two Abbreviated Forms of the MMPI for Psychiatric Screening of the Elderly." *Journal of Clinical Psychology* 35: 104–07.

Rybolt, G. A., and J. A. Lambert. 1975. "Correspondence of the MMPI and Mini-Mult with Psychiatric Inpatients." *Journal of Clinical Psychology* 31: 279–81.

Scott, N. A., M. K. Mount, and S. A. Costers. 1976. "Correspondence of the MMPI and Mini-Mult Among Female Reformatory Inmates." *Journal of Clinical Psychology* 32: 795–97.

Simono, R. B. 1975. "Comparison of the Standard MMPI and the Mini-Mult in a University Counseling Center." *Education and Psychological Measurement* 35: 401–04.

Streiner, D. L., C. W. Woodward, J. T. Goodman, and A. McLean. 1973. "Comparisons of the MMPI and Mini-Mult." *Canadian Journal of Behavioral Science* 5: 76–82.

Taulbee, E. S., and J. Samelson. 1974. "Mini-Mult vs. MMPI." *Journal of Personality Assessment* 38: 479.

Taulbee, E. S., and H. W. Wright. 1972. "Mini-Mult vs. MMPI." *Journal of Personality Assessment* 36: 590.

Thornton, L. S., A. J. Finch, and J. L. Griffin. 1975. "The Mini-Mult with Criminal and Psychiatric Patients." *Journal of Personality Assessment* 39: 394–96.

Trybus, R. J., and C. W. Hewitt. 1972. "The Mini-Mult in a Nonpsychiatric Population." *Journal of Clinical Psychology* 28: 371.

Tsushima, W. T. 1975. "Relationship between the Mini-Mult and the MMPI with Medical Patients." *Journal of Clinical Psychology* 31: 673–75.

Turner, J., and C. McCreary. 1978. "Short Forms of the MMPI with Back Pain Patients." *Journal of Consulting and Clinical Psychology* 46: 354–55.

Vincent, K. R. 1978. "Validity of the MMPI-168 on Private Clinic Subpopulation." *Journal of Clinical Psychology* 34: 61–62.

Walls, R., S. D. McGlynn, and D. H. Tingstrom. 1977. "An Evaluation of Three Short Forms Extracted from the Group Form MMPI Responses of Incarcerated Offenders." *Journal of Clinical Psychology* 33: 431–35.

UNPUBLISHED MANUSCRIPTS, THESES AND DISSERTATIONS

Bolton, B. 1975. "A Brief Instrument for Assessing Psychopathology in Rehabilitation Clients." University of Arkansas: Arkansas Rehabilitation Research and Training Center Report.

Faschingbauer, T. R. 1972. "A Short Written Form of the Group MMPI." Ph.D. dissertation, University of North Carolina. *Dissertation Abstracts International*, 1973, 34, 409B. (University Microfilms No. 73–16, 469).

Hugo, J. A. 1971. "Abbreviation of the MMPI Through Multiple Regression." Ph.D. dissertation, University of Alabama. *Dissertation Abstracts International*, 1971, 32, 1213B. (University Microfilms No. 71–20, 115).

Kincannon, J. C. 1967. "An Investigation of the Feasibility of Adopting a Personality Inventory for Use in the Mental Status Exam." Ph.D. dissertation, University of Minnesota. *Dissertation Abstracts International*, 1967, 28, 2625B. (University Microfilms No. 67–16, 250).

Rand, S. W. 1976. "A Comprehensive Validation of the Expanded Mini-Mult." Unpublished Master's Thesis, University of Miami.

Umansky, D. S. 1972. "Another Look at the Mini-Mult." Unpublished Master's Thesis, Eastern Michigan University.

PRESENTATIONS, WORKSHOPS AND SYMPOSIA

Bolton, B. 1975. "Development of Homogeneous Subscales for the Mini-Mult." Paper presented at the meeting of the Southwestern Psychological Association, Houston.

Butcher, J., P. Clavell, and N. Hoffman. 1974. "Clinical Limitations of MMPI Short Forms and a Strategy for Developing a Tailor-Made MMPI Short Form." Paper presented at the meeting of the American Psychological Association, New Orleans.

Faschingbauer, T. R. 1976. "The Psychometric Worth of Short Form MMPIs." Discussion Group Conducted at the meeting of the American Psychological Association, Washington, D.C. (Participants: W. T. Norman, J. H. Ricks, M. Robertson).

Faschingbauer, T. R., A. Conger, D. Johnson, and C. Neville. 1974. "New Conversion Values for the Mini-Mult." Paper presented at the meeting of the Southeastern Psychological Association, Hollywood, Florida.

Hartman, G., and M. Robertson. 1972. "Comparison of the Mini-Mult and the MMPI in a Community Mental Health Agency." Paper presented at the meeting of the American Psychological Association, Honolulu, September, 1972.

Hedlund, J. L., B. J. Powell, and D. Won Cho. 1974, "The Use of MMPI Short Forms With Psychiatric Patients." Paper presented at the meeting of the American Psychological Association, New Orleans.

Newmark, C. S. 1977a. "An Introduction to MMPI Interpretation and Short Forms of the MMPI." Workshop conducted at the meeting of the Society for Personality Assessment, Inc., San Diego, March, 1977.

——. 1977b. "Clinical Use of the MMPI Short Forms." Paper presented at the 12th annual MMPI Workshop, St. Petersburg, Florida, February, 1977.

——. 1974. "Comparing Abbreviated MMPIs within a Psychiatric Population." Paper presented at the American Psychological Association Meeting, New Orleans, September, 1974.

Newmark, C. S., T. R. Faschingbauer, and S. Mlott. 1975. "Present Status and Practical Applications of Abbreviated MMPIs." Discussion group conducted at the meeting of the Southeastern Psychological Association, Atlanta, March, 1975.

Spera, J., and M. Robertson. 1974. "A 104-item MMPI: The Maxi-Mult." Paper presented at the meeting of the American Psychological Association, New Orleans.

"Symposium on Short Forms of the MMPI." Presented at the meeting of the American Psychological Association, New Orleans, September, 1974.

(Participants: J. Butcher, P. Clavell, D. W. Cho, T. R. Faschingbauer, J. L. Hedlund, N. Hoffmann, C. S. Newmark, B. J. Powell, M. Robertson, J. Spera).

"Who Owns Test Items? Present Confusion and Anxieties about 1984." Discussion group conducted at the 10th Symposium on recent developments in the use of the MMPI. St. Petersburg, Florida, February, 1975. (Participants: J. N. Butcher, W. G. Dahlstrom, T. R. Faschingbauer, R. D. Fowler, S. R. Hathaway, S. H. Hunter, C. S. Newmark, A. H. Ricks).

BOOK

Faschingbauer, T. R., and C. S. Newmark. 1978. *Short Forms of the MMPI.* Lexington, Mass.: D. C. Heath & Co.

APPENDIX B/Classification Results for the Lanyon (1968) MMPI Groups

Compiled by Harvey A. Skinner

Note: In the following table, the number in parentheses following the group name corresponds to the study and figure number in Lanyon's (1968) book. For the shape parameters, N = Neurotic, P = Psychotic, and S = Sociopathic.

TABLE B.1

Classification Results for the 233 Lanyon (1968) MMPI Groups

Lanyon Group (Study #)	Elevation	Scatter	Shape		
			N	P	S
Psychotic Samples					
1 Acute schizophrenics (1A)	64.15	6.26	.27	.86	.19
2 Chronic schizophrenics (1B)	65.39	8.36	-.08	.78	.06
3 Acute affective psychotics (1C)	64.23	8.41	.86	.44	-.12
4 Chronic affective psychotics (1C)	62.69	4.78	.33	.48	.19
5 Paranoid schizophrenics (2)	69.08	10.46	.38	.92	.02
6 Schizophrenics male (5)	60.13	5.11	.19	.88	.33
7 Subclinical schizophrenics (7)	67.13	10.87	.53	.77	.09
8 Post-promazine tests male (24)	71.08	10.00	.06	.79	.17
9 Post-placebo tests male (24)	69.23	10.01	.02	.83	.08
10 Schizophrenia group male (35)	61.90	6.11	.53	.75	.30
11 Acute schizophrenics (1B)	61.15	4.97	-.11	.87	.10
12 Chronic schizophrenics (1B)	63.92	6.73	-.36	.65	.15
13 Acute affective phychotics (1D)	63.46	5.56	.52	.78	.00
14 Chronic affective psychotics (1D)	60.77	3.96	-.46	.71	.01
15 Schizophrenics female (4)	58.28	4.17	.08	.45	.51
16 Paranoid schizophrenics (3)	61.42	8.35	-.13	.87	.26
17 Manics male female (3)	56.35	8.21	-.73	.26	.55
18 Schizos age 15–29 (6A)	62.59	7.10	.14	.92	.13
19 Schizos age 30–39 (6A)	58.36	3.51	-.10	.85	.29
20 Schizos age 40–53 (6B)	56.90	2.44	.52	.66	.25
21 Shock ther on schizo-recovery (28A)	63.66	8.37	.49	.74	.05
22 Shock ther on schiz-unimproved (28A)	66.66	11.70	.20	.91	.22

Neurotic Samples

1 Anxiety state group (8)	64.28	10.08	.58	.66	.06
2 Inadequate personality (8)	61.05	7.86	.86	.04	.24
3 Outpatient neurotics male (11)	63.36	9.16	.65	.60	-.04
4 Inpatient neurotics male (11)	60.90	7.02	.70	.59	.06
5 Male neurotics (12A)	62.69	8.65	.74	.60	-.09
6 Neurotic outpatients male (13)	61.74	9.44	.87	.36	.11
7 Neurotic inpatients male (13)	59.43	7.75	.88	.40	.05
8 Dissociative-conversion (14A)	57.28	6.27	.84	-.22	.28
9 Somatization reaction male (14A)	58.51	6.78	.92	.02	.18
10 Anxiety reaction male (14B)	65.97	11.32	.77	.56	.08
11 Anxiety reaction (15A)	63.23	9.59	.80	.55	-.08
12 Depressive reaction (15A)	63.92	10.73	.76	.57	-.13
13 Conversion reaction (15B)	59.62	8.13	.91	.16	.24
14 Somatization reaction (15B)	60.92	8.18	.93	.17	.10
15 Outpatient neurotics female (10)	62.05	9.34	.80	.51	.09
16 Inpatient neurotics female (10)	61.66	9.93	.78	.46	.17
17 Female neurotics (12B)	61.69	6.26	.74	.49	-.01
18 Psychother prognosis-improved (27)	60.13	5.46	.39	.60	.41
19 Psychother progn-unimproved (27)	63.66	7.54	.34	.81	.20

(continued)

Table B.1, continued

Lanyon Group (Study #)	Elevation	Scatter	Shape		
			N	P	S
Sociopathic Samples					
1 Alcohol triment-success (18)	60.69	6.78	.50	.68	.22
2 Alcohol triment-unsuccess (18)	59.62	6.77	.46	.59	.50
3 Aged antisoc behvr-offenders (19)	55.77	4.19	.61	.31	.40
4 Adult negro narcotic addicts (20A)	57.05	5.73	-.15	.45	.72
5 Adult white narcotic addicts (20A)	57.59	5.62	.23	.43	.64
6 Teenage narcotic addicts (20B)	57.43	5.04	.05	.39	.73
7 Male narcotic addicts (21)	56.82	6.80	-.11	.03	.82
8 Personality disorder (22A)	59.23	5.01	.38	.56	.44
9 Psychopathic personality (23)	58.20	6.38	-.00	.56	.72
10 Male delinquents (43A)	57.62	5.76	-.21	.62	.66
11 Male Delinquents (46)	58.66	5.62	-.19	.72	.51
12 Male social delinquents (48)	59.54	8.26	-.23	.83	.44
13 Male solitary delinquent (48)	65.69	10.42	-.00	.90	.35
14 Delinquency prone males (50)	55.85	4.57	-.34	.63	.45
15 Army prisoners (59)	59.05	4.61	.15	.68	.68
16 Sex offender-pre-therapy (61)	58.66	4.79	.15	.32	.58
17 Sex offender-post-therapy (61)	58.13	6.32	-.06	.08	.66
18 Habitual criminal (62)	60.69	7.39	.64	.43	.47
19 Nonhabitual criminal (62)	60.46	6.76	.84	.38	.14
20 Homosexual prisoners (63)	58.23	7.86	-.38	.65	.49
21 Heterosexual prisoners (63)	61.46	7.90	-.01	.69	.54

22	Oral-literate prisoners (64)	58.38	6.39	-.12	.64	.71
23	Oral-semiliterate prisoners (64)	61.62	7.59	-.09	.82	.47
24	Self-mutilation prisoner (65A)	63.46	8.17	.12	.73	.64
25	Matched control group prisoners (65A)	59.15	6.26	.22	.47	.76
26	Model prisoners control (65B)	59.15	5.39	.50	.46	.61
27	Sex offenders-prisoners (66)	58.92	5.47	.44	.39	.38
28	Sex offender prisoners (67)	60.05	6.77	.27	.74	.53
29	Booklet test-literate prisoners (103B)	58.46	6.43	-.13	.62	.70
30	Oral test-literate prisoners (103B)	58.38	6.39	-.12	.64	.71
31	Booklet-semiliterate prisoners (103C)	62.23	7.50	-.09	.88	.38
42	Oral-semiliterate prisoners (103C)	61.62	7.59	-.09	.82	.47
33	Female narcotic addicts (21)	56.05	6.64	-.21	.53	.72
34	Personality disorder (22B)	59.62	6.22	.11	.54	.52
35	Female delinquents (43B)	58.00	9.95	-.39	.62	.66
36	Female delinquents (45)	59.38	6.15	-.28	.66	.50
37	Female delinquents (47)	59.31	7.69	-.16	.66	.66
38	Success treat delinq group (49)	58.28	8.07	-.35	.60	.54
39	Treat delinq girls-failures (49)	64.28	10.45	-.10	.76	.48
40	Admission tests females (110)	58.69	5.65	.02	.60	.55
41	Retests females (110)	58.46	5.57	-.12	.55	.58

(continued)

Table B.1, continued

Lanyon Group (Study #)	Elevation	Scatter	N	Shape	
				P	S
Mixed Psychiatric Samples					
1 Mixed psychiatrics male (7)	60.13	6.74	.87	.37	.06
2 Ages non-offenders male (19)	58.31	6.07	.90	.06	.14
3 Hospitalized male (25)	65.36	9.20	.59	.75	.11
4 Nonhospitalized male (25)	60.97	7.68	.85	.44	.07
5 Stay GRP in psychotherapy (26A)	64.59	10.22	.78	.54	.10
6 Nonstay GRP in psychotherapy (26A)	63.97	9.76	.76	.58	.12
7 Improved GRP after therapy (26B)	62.36	8.54	.84	.44	.07
8 Unimproved GRP after therapy (26B)	66.20	11.45	.74	.60	.10
9 Low morbidity group male (29A)	63.69	6.12	.51	.68	.42
10 High morbidity group male (29A)	68.39	8.52	.18	.91	.22
11 Suicide threat group male (30)	70.90	12.38	.49	.80	.24
12 Suicide attempt group male (30)	63.13	7.62	.75	.56	.16
13 Emotionally disturbed male (46)	61.36	5.85	.10	.84	.49
14 Functnl GRP adlesct som (57A)	58.85	5.70	.93	.22	.13
15 Fathers disturbed children (52A)	54.90	2.93	.68	-.28	.24
16 Fathers disturbed children (53)	52.31	2.94	.13	-.24	.48
17 Fathers disturbed children (54A)	56.20	3.53	.88	-.09	.22
18 Fathers disturbed children (55)	55.00	3.90	.83	.16	.22
19 Fathers disturbed children (56)	54.54	2.44	.76	.06	.30
20 Problem boys (57A)	60.00	7.39	-.05	.82	.51
21 Fathers problem boys (57B)	54.31	4.16	.42	-.31	.60
22 Negro psychiatric patients (85)	65.13	10.08	.77	.52	.17
23 White psychiatric patients (85)	63.82	9.55	.75	.56	.14

24	Male homosexuals (96)	59.23	8.22	-.07	.34	.22
25	Booklet tests male (102)	63.90	8.16	.68	.67	.20
26	Card tests male (102)	64.59	9.42	.72	.65	.14
27	Post stress tests-male (105)	51.31	2.70	-.45	-.10	.68
28	PSY patient original test (109)	65.38	8.97	.68	.71	.01
29	PSY patient restests (109)	64.92	8.27	.71	.67	.04
30	Real self tests male (111)	67.66	10.34	.54	.79	.13
31	Regular tests-males (112)	65.66	8.97	.25	.86	.37
32	High morbidity female (29B)	67.54	9.01	.11	.89	.16
33	Low morbidity female (29B)	58.38	4.67	-.14	.51	.45
34	Obesity-simple group female (34)	60.85	6.20	.55	.41	.37
35	Obesity-metabolic GRP female (34)	55.77	2.64	.89	.02	.20
36	Emotionally disturbed female (47)	59.62	5.09	.08	.78	.50
37	Functnl GRP-adolesc soma (51B)	59.54	4.75	.67	.39	.37
38	Mothers disturbed children (52B)	54.43	3.21	.60	.06	-.02
39	Mothers disturbed children (53)	51.23	2.39	-.15	-.00	.12
40	Mothers disturbed children (54B)	54.82	3.96	.58	.38	.18
41	Mothers disturbed children (55)	54.77	3.85	.66	.09	.17
42	Mothers disturbed children (56)	54.23	2.78	.64	.15	.12
43	Mothers problem boys (57B)	51.85	4.28	.54	-.23	.44
44	Booklet test-male and female (104)	60.36	5.97	.78	.43	.27
45	Oral test-male female (104)	59.66	6.22	.66	.49	.34
46	Non-schizophrenics female (4)	59.43	6.66	.57	.38	.47
47	Shock on affect disodr-recovery (28B)	61.90	9.02	.72	.51	-.01
48	Shock on aff disodr-unim (28B)	66.51	12.08	.61	.71	.04

(continued)

Table B.1, continued

Lanyon Group (Study #)	Elevation	Scatter	N	Shape	
				P	S
Normal Samples					
1 Male nondelinquents (43A)	54.92	4.08	-.29	.73	.48
2 Nondelinquency prone males (50)	53.46	2.65	-.33	.57	.44
3 Control group fathers (52A)	52.97	2.93	.20	-.37	.18
4 Control group fathers (54A)	53.51	2.17	.12	-.34	.34
5 Army nonprisoners (59)	54.43	2.68	-.08	.10	.78
6 Male actors (68A)	58.46	6.81	.06	.41	.21
7 Male students (68A)	55.54	3.50	.27	-.01	.44
8 Psych-socio majors male (70A)	55.66	5.13	-.01	.07	.58
9 Anthropology majors-male (70A)	55.28	4.00	-.03	.07	.24
10 Math-chem-physics majors (70B)	55.05	3.14	.32	-.01	.17
11 Engineering majors-male (70B)	53.97	3.38	.12	.26	.23
12 Business adminis majors (70C)	55.74	4.20	-.05	.09	.56
13 Art and music majors (70C)	58.66	5.60	-.07	.02	.34
14 Gifted adolescents-boy (71)	56.92	3.97	.29	.11	.04
15 Pre-training-Luthern ministers (73)	56.62	5.08	.13	.28	.32
16 Post-training-Luthern ministers (73)	54.62	5.78	-.02	.09	.39
17 Medical students as freshmen (74)	53.20	4.17	-.20	-.17	.37
18 Medical students as juniors (74)	53.28	5.15	-.02	-.09	.37
19 Ninth-grade boys (75)	54.62	3.81	-.39	.76	.37
20 Australian college students (78A)	55.43	3.29	-.04	.15	.35
21 German college students (79A)	62.15	6.50	.00	.78	.40
22 US college students male (79A)	54.31	2.33	-.28	.15	.54
23 Italian southern male (80A)	60.92	4.83	.41	.60	-.12
24 Italian central male (80A)	57.46	4.11	.08	.62	-.17

25	Italian northern male (80B)	57.23	2.94	.18	.27	-.15
26	Negro male students (82A)	56.54	4.18	-.12	.74	.45
27	White male students (82A)	54.69	4.14	-.33	.70	.49
28	Negro male students (83A)	54.46	4.58	.00	.35	.56
29	White male students (19–21) (83A)	53.38	4.65	-.29	.45	.44
30	Neg males matched se (83C)	54.69	4.87	-.06	.25	.68
31	Whi males matched se (83C)	54.62	5.08	.12	.57	.09
32	Negro high status group (86A)	56.69	4.16	-.09	.55	.54
33	Negro low status male (86A)	57.08	4.58	-.17	.42	.60
34	White high status male (86C)	54.62	4.03	-.02	.62	.66
35	White low status male (86C)	53.85	3.66	.01	.53	.72
36	Higher socio-econ group (87A)	55.43	2.72	-.43	.46	.46
37	Lower socio-econ group (87A)	56.13	3.76	-.46	.68	.42
38	Male drivers-poor (94)	54.77	4.73	-.07	.56	.70
39	Male drivers-good (94)	54.92	4.31	-.01	.54	.42
40	Male heterosexuals (96)	56.38	5.84	.06	.14	-.03
41	Pre-stress tests-male (105)	52.77	3.12	-.08	.40	.65
42	Original tests male (108A)	54.85	3.57	-.40	.78	.29
43	Retests males (108A)	53.62	3.56	-.10	.48	.68
44	Female nondelinquents (43B)	54.69	3.85	-.41	.68	.54
45	Control group mothers (52B)	52.90	3.02	.37	-.05	-.03
46	Control group mothers (54B)	52.05	3.08	.36	-.19	.03
47	Female actors (68B)	55.38	3.91	.15	.53	.48
48	Female Students (68B)	52.54	2.87	-.22	.08	.38
49	Gifted girl adolescents (71)	53.08	3.77	-.27	-.22	.18
50	Ninth-grade girls (75)	54.08	3.47	-.56	.59	.33
51	Australian college students (78B)	52.82	2.40	-.20	.32	.30
52	German college students (79B)	59.15	5.20	-.22	.79	.36
53	Italian college students (81)	57.92	4.78	-.00	.80	-.27

(continued)

417

Table B.1, continued

Lanyon Group (Study #)	Elevation	Scatter	Shape		
			N	P	S
54 Negro female students (82B)	55.38	6.79	-.48	.81	.08
55 White female students (82B)	54.62	3.65	-.37	.61	.63
56 Negro female students (83B)	53.23	2.97	-.20	.02	.78
57 White female students (83B)	52.23	3.42	-.19	.40	.58
58 Neg feml matched se (83D)	54.23	3.09	.21	.11	.72
59 Whi feml matched se (83D)	53.62	4.41	-.16	.64	.39
60 Negro high status female (86B)	55.08	3.10	-.28	.09	.63
61 Negro low status female (86B)	55.31	3.10	-.46	.58	.59
62 White high status female (86D)	53.77	3.92	-.02	.34	.67
63 White low status female (86D)	54.77	3.49	-.20	.65	.54
64 Higher socio-econ group (87B)	54.36	2.34	-.62	-.00	.35
65 Lower socio-econ group (87B)	53.97	2.72	-.63	.41	.36
66 Pregnant group female (99)	53.31	2.76	.48	.02	.44
67 Non-pregnant group female (99)	49.92	.62	-.04	.07	-.63
68 Hi susceptible hypnosis (100)	52.31	3.87	-.19	.12	.75
69 Unsusceptible hypnosis (100)	52.46	4.07	-.00	.26	.67
70 Booklet tests for nurses (103A)	53.08	3.65	-.19	.25	.75
71 Oral tests for nurses (103A)	53.08	3.63	-.20	.33	.73
72 Original tests females (108B)	53.46	3.03	-.62	.57	.28
73 Retests females (108B)	52.77	2.75	-.22	.40	.49
74 Male female graduates (72)	53.74	2.04	-.48	-.08	.25
75 Male female nongraduates (72)	55.13	2.58	-.19	-.06	.61
76 Old age group (90)	54.31	3.20	.57	-.32	-.66
77 Honest tests by normals (106)	53.04	3.96	-.24	.20	.35
78 Honest tests by normals (107)	53.89	4.14	-.28	.34	.48

Medical Samples

1 Physical injury male (35)	58.97	4.67	.76	.14	.56
2 Male aphasics (36)	61.97	6.05	.36	.83	.17
3 Male nonaphasics (36)	57.66	4.57	.89	.37	.08
4 Frontal brain lesion male (37)	55.08	4.14	.58	-.13	.30
5 Parietal lesion male (37)	58.69	6.89	.76	.47	.07
6 Multiple sclerosis male (39)	62.05	9.54	.95	.09	.04
7 Multiple sclerosis male (40)	60.00	6.60	.90	.20	.13
8 Traumatic brain injury (40)	57.54	5.61	.84	.10	.31
9 Organic GRP-adolescents (51A)	56.23	3.81	-.28	.83	.23
10 Male negro medical (84)	59.69	5.28	.53	.58	.46
11 Male white medical (84)	56.85	6.50	.64	.34	.55
12 Male TB age 20-29 (88)	56.38	3.73	.54	.49	.54
13 Male TB age 50-59 (88)	58.31	6.22	.82	.33	.16
14 Deaf college students-male (93)	66.69	10.03	-.19	.90	.02
15 Organic GRP adolescents (51B)	55.38	2.37	-.33	.58	.34
16 Deaf college student-female (93)	62.38	8.07	-.54	.75	.11
17 Lesion w/epilepsy group (38A)	58.66	4.49	.70	.58	.28
18 Lesion w/o epilepsy group (38A)	57.82	5.40	.84	.43	.07
19 Epilepsy without lesion (38B)	61.13	6.01	.63	.64	.25
20 Medical patients M + F (38B)	58.05	5.82	.88	.26	.16
21 Cerebral palsy-male female (91)	54.97	3.71	.02	.40	.32

Response Style Samples

1 Ideal self tests males (111)	58.97	4.09	-.38	-.47	.36
2 Simulated normal test-male (112)	55.74	3.61	-.50	-.04	.76
3 Fake good test by normal (106)	53.04	4.75	-.40	-.43	.29
4 Fake bad tests by normal (107)	72.42	17.51	.04	.90	.24

NAME INDEX

SUBJECT INDEX

ABOUT THE EDITOR AND CONTRIBUTORS

CHARLES S. NEWMARK, Ph.D., is associate professor and director of clinical psychology training in the Department of Psychiatry at the University of North Carolina School of Medicine. He has a Diplomate in Clinical Psychology from the American Board of Professional Psychology, has conducted numerous MMPI workshops, contributed over 60 articles to various professional journals, and has co-authored a book entitled *Short Forms of the MMPI*.

ALBERT N. ALLAIN is a research associate, Department of Psychiatry and Behavioral Sciences, Medical University of South Carolina, Charleston, South Carolina.

ROBERT P. ARCHER, Ph.D., is the director, Early Intervention Project, Florida Mental Health Institute, Tampa, Florida.

JAMES R. CLOPTON, Ph.D., is assistant professor, Department of Psychology, Texas Tech University, Lubbock, Texas.

PHILLIP ERDBERG, Ph.D., is in private practice in Greenbrae, California, and has a Diplomate in Clinical Psychology from the American Board of Professional Psychology.

THOMAS R. FASCHINGBAUER, Ph.D., is assistant professor, Department of Psychiatry and Behavioral Sciences, the University of Texas Medical School, Houston, Texas.

RAYMOND D. FOWLER, Ph.D., is professor and chairman, Department of Psychology, University of Alabama, University, Alabama.

JOSEPH T. KUNCE, Ph.D., is professor, Department of Counseling and Personnel Services, University of Missouri, Columbia, Missouri.

JAMES L. MACK, Ph.D., is assistant professor, Department of Psychiatry, Case Western Reserve University School of Medicine, Cleveland, Ohio.

KATHLEEN M. MCNAMARA, Ph.D., is assistant professor, School of Professional Psychology, Wright State University, Dayton, Ohio.

PAOLO PANCHERI, M.D., is professor, Institute of Psychiatry, School of Medicine, University of Rome, Italy.

HARVEY A. SKINNER, Ph.D., is director of Assessment Research, Addiction Research Foundation, Toronto, Canada.

CATHERINE M. SANDERS, Ph.D., is coordinator of the Loss & Bereavement Resource Center, Center for Applied Gerontology, University of South Florida, Tampa, Florida.

PATRICIA B. SUTKER, Ph.D., is professor and associate dean, Department of Psychiatry and Behavioral Sciences, Medical University of South Carolina, Charleston, South Carolina.

JOHN R. THIBODEAU, Ph.D., is a postdoctoral fellow in child psychology, Department of Psychiatry, University of North Carolina School of Medicine, Chapel Hill, North Carolina.

JAMES T. WEBB, Ph.D., is professor and assistant dean, School of Professional Psychology, Wright State University, Dayton, Ohio.

CATHY S. WIDOM, Ph.D., is associate professor, Department of Forensic Studies, Indiana University, Bloomington, Indiana.